·ore

]4

This book is dedicated to the late Dr. John O'Brien of the Department of History, UCC, who died in 1999 but is not forgotten.

The Irish Diaspora

edited by
ANDY BIELENBERG

Longman

an imprint of **Pearson Education**

Harlow, England · London · New York · Reading, Massachusetts · San Francisco
Toronto · Don Mills, Ontario · Sydney · Tokyo · Singapore · Hong Kong · Seoul
Taipei · Cape Town · Madrid · Mexico City · Amsterdam · Munich · Paris · Milan

Pearson Education Limited
Edinburgh Gate
Harlow
Essex CM20 2JE
England

and Associated Companies throughout the World.

Visit us on the World Wide Web at:
www.pearsoneduc.com

First published 2000

ISBN 0 582 36997 5 (Limp)
    0 582 36998 3 (Cased)

British Library Cataloguing-in-Publication Data
A catalogue record for this book can be obtained from the British Library

Library of Congress Cataloguing-in-Publication Data
The Irish diaspora / edited by Andy Bielenberg.
    p. cm.
    Includes bibliographical references and index.
    ISBN 0-582-36998-3 (alk. paper) — ISBN 0-582-36997-5 (pbk. : alk. paper)
    1. Irish—Great Britain—History. 2. Irish—Commonwealth countries—History. 3.
Ireland—Emigration and immigration. 4. Irish Americans—History. I. Bielenberg, Andy,
1959–

DA125.I7 I72 2000
941'.0049162—dc21   99–053717

10 9 8 7 6 5 4 3 2 1
05 04 03 02 01 00

Typeset by 35 in 10/12pt Sabon
Produced by Pearson Education Asia Pte Ltd.
Printed in Singapore

Contents

Acknowledgements

The genesis of this book emerged from a conference on the Irish Diaspora held in UCC in the autumn of 1997. It is therefore necessary to thank those who contributed to the conference, other than those who appear in this book. These include (in alphabetical order): Verdi Ahern, Pat Coughlan, Jim Devere (the founding patron of the Irish Centre for Migration Studies at UCC), Marian Elders, Siobhan Finn, Paddy Fitzgerald, Marita Foster, Prof. D. Keogh, J.J. Kett, Prof. J.J. Lee, John Lynch, Ruth McDonnell, Mel Mercier, Vic Merriman, Lucette Murray, Alph O'Brien, Prof. W. Smyth. On the production side I would like to acknowledge the assistance of Hilary Shaw and Magda Robson of Pearson. Thank-you one and all.

Andy Bielenberg
November 1999

Introduction

PIARAS MAC ÉINRÍ

(Irish Centre for Migration Studies, University College, Cork)

Migration studies: a rapidly changing field

Migration studies is a catch-all term encompassing a multidisciplinary field. It includes emigration (often the sole focus in Ireland and other 'exporting' countries), immigration, internal and return migration.[1] It embraces voluntarist and structuralist perspectives, labour migration and refugees, assimilation and expulsion. More recently the increasing use of the term *diaspora*[2] denotes a de-centred approach in which migration, migrants and their multi-generational societies and cultures are seen as phenomena in themselves and not simply in relation to the countries of origin and reception.

For most of its relatively short life, migration studies has focused disproportionately on immigration. This is not surprising. The immigrant is a real presence in the receiving society; the question of how natives and newcomers are to relate to one another is not an abstract one. If one adds to this sheer numbers and an ideology of openness towards the immigrant, characteristic of historical attitudes in the United States (especially if the subject in question is white and European), it is hardly surprising that American scholarship has long been dominant in migration studies. Even if Ravenstein[3] may be regarded as its parent, many of its best exponents have worked in the field of American historical scholarship and many of its paradigms, from the Chicago School[4] to the melting pot and beyond,[5] from multiculturalism[6] and world systems theories[7] to postmodernist questioning of identity politics,[8] have been American-inspired or have at least begun on American campuses.

By contrast, it would have been easy, at least until relatively recently, and especially in the Anglophone world, to underestimate the role of migration in European society. Yet France, for instance, has attracted large numbers of immigrants for centuries.[9] The postwar period saw an upsurge in mass migratory movements, characterized by south–north flows, the impact of decolonization and a tendency to see migrants as economic units but not as full members of society.[10] Unlike the USA, the European nation-state remained for the most part an ethno-national entity. This has created an ever-growing conflict between universalist Enlightenment ideals and state ideology, a conflict which has frequently centred on the place of minorities or immigrants, especially those of non-European origins,[11] within the state. In late twentieth-century Europe the upsurge in global forced migration, as opposed to economic migration, and the challenge posed by a potentially transnational European Union (EU) citizenship, are helping to define a new agenda. The shape of this new agenda is far from clear as yet and must regrettably be characterized for now as driven more by a desire to contain than to embrace.

The entire question of migration, the migrant identity and the place of migrants in society is the subject of global consideration from within many disciplines. Issues of multiculturalism, multi-ethnicity and hybridity are being explored; in the process the supremacy of a unitary, place-based ethnic identity is being called into question.[12] With globalization and the increasing integration of the world economic, cultural and information infrastructure, there is an increased danger of the emergence of a migrant elite on the one hand and a disempowered community of transients, serving the needs of an implacable globalized economy, on the other.

Previous assumptions of a discrete Ravensteinian, push–pull universe, divided between place of origin, intervening variables and place of arrival, reflected in a one-way assimilationist path, are being challenged by new realities. Migrancy, to use Chambers's[13] term, is increasingly seen as *process*, a state of being in itself, and not as a temporary transitional phase before the subject is absorbed by the new society. There are many alternatives to assimilation, from multiculturalism to outright expulsion. Host societies are themselves profoundly challenged and changed by the presence of migrants, and the process of integration is no longer seen as a one-way path in which the migrant becomes a member of an unchanged host society through the suppression of his/her own cultural values. It is no longer a matter of 'them' *becoming* 'us'.[14] Diasporic identities, transnational and subversive in character, challenge the security of identities defined, but also limited, by national boundaries.

There has been a major shift in the terms of the debate and the nature of the enquiry, hence the new emphasis on life history approaches, discourse analysis and feminist perspectives.[15] The comparative context of migration studies is receiving increasing emphasis. The specificities of migration, in terms of region, gender, class, ethnic and other factors, are receiving attention, as is the global and interlinked nature of migration. The impact of migration on the person at the heart of the process is also beginning to be studied. While the role of historical enquiry continues to be central, social science, legal, literary and behavioural approaches, as well as neo-Marxist and other structuralist perspectives, are all being brought to bear.

The result has been a remarkable flowering and diversity of research, teaching and publications in the field, accompanying the ever-greater significance being attached to it at political and social level. That said, and as the present volume bears out, historical enquiry is still central. The increasing emphasis on complexity and specificity confers a growing importance and value on local and regional studies as well as those, for instance, which emphasize longitudinal, sectoral and gender-based approaches, using a variety of new methodologies.

The background to the increasing interest in Irish migration studies

Alan O'Day[16] is probably correct when he suggests that the study of Irish migration is characterized by a strong emphasis on American sources (US and Canadian) and when he notes that, apart from certain prominent exceptions (singling out Doyle[17] and Fitzpatrick[18]), it is mainly the product of scholarship from outside Ireland – indeed, in a sense, this is fitting. In his stimulating overview *Revising the Diaspora* he is nonetheless critical of the field as a whole, suggesting that there is no conceptual/theoretical framework to link the Irish to international perspectives. He also notes that there is no standard interpretation of the diaspora (which is probably no bad thing). He pleads for a greater recognition of the complexity and specificity of Irish migration patterns, while recognizing the obvious gaps in statistical data, such as the non-availability of US data on religious affiliation. He notes that 'despite differences of origin, the chronology and methodology bears a remarkable resemblance to other areas of Irish history'. He also notes that, in spite of the American dominance, 'recent work on Australia, Britain and Canada suggests that this pre-eminence is under threat'.

Within post-independence Ireland, emigration was a silent haemorrhage, treated by denial, and about which only the historians had much to say. The palpable public silence persisted, with occasional exceptions such as the monumental *Report of the Commission on Emigration and Other Population Problems*[19] of the 1950s. The problem 'disappeared', or so people thought, in the 1960s and 1970s, only to reappear with renewed vigour in the 1980s. Largely due to a downturn in the Irish economy and the effect of the baby boom of the 1960s, the ghost of emigration, forgotten since the 1950s, returned to haunt the Irish body politic. One upshot of the change was the publication of only the second extensive official study on the impact of emigration, the National Economic and Social Council (NESC) report, in 1991.[20] Much public and political attention was paid to Irish undocumented aliens in the USA at this time, proof of the persistence of traditional choices, the enduring fascination of America (after all most emigrants were in fact still going to the UK but they received far less attention) and the new-found political strength of the emigrant lobby.[21] This possibly had partly to do with their more middle-class background in some cases, but partly to do with the opening up of Irish society and the fact that with the information revolution and the relative ease of return it was increasingly impossible to ignore the new generation of migrants. They would not remain silent and would not disappear.

Partly as a result of the above changes, the study of the Irish diaspora, in parallel with migration studies in general, has blossomed in recent years and decades. The context for these changes is multi-faceted and a number of public and/or political events played a significant role. Apart from the return of large-scale Irish migration in the late 1980s already mentioned, these included the bicentennial of the American Revolution in 1976 and the equivalent Australian celebration in 1988, both of which generated significant new scholarship in their respective fields.[22]

In the 1990s, the 150th anniversary of the Great Famine led to a new outpouring of interest and much new research into nineteenth-century migration. As the Famine Museum in Strokestown demonstrates, connections also began to be made between nineteenth-century Irish famine and forced migration and the experience of other peoples in other parts of the world in the present day.

Ireland has always denied its migrant children the most fundamental expression of their political rights – the right to vote – and continues to do so. Nonetheless, the 1980s and 1990s saw a new and remarkable emphasis on the ties between the Irish at home and those around the world. In part this was cultural – the new wave of Irish singers, musicians and cultural artists, from within the country but also from within the diaspora, who put Irish identity on the map and even made it cool. In part it was the attention paid by newly elected President Mary Robinson to the global Irish diaspora.

The word *diaspora* entered public discourse for the first time and, while not all were comfortable with it, it signified a new willingness to embrace a more inclusive and less territorially bounded notion of Irishness than heretofore. The Robinson years (1990–97) were marked by a new stress on the broader Irish community in the world. Moreover, she sought explicitly to acknowledge this new reality in her many visits to Irish communities around the world. At the same time she staked a claim to a broader Irishness by paying equal attention to the 'new Irish' – those immigrants, asylum-seekers and refugees who were beginning to arrive in some numbers, for the first time in modern history, in Ireland.

President Mary McAleese, who succeeded President Robinson in 1997, has continued in the same tradition. Both presidents, although differing in many ways, have been spectacularly successful in their mission to the diaspora and have opened a significant dialogue between the Irish at home and those of Irish descent around the world. There has been an increasing if initially grudging acceptance that the Irish identity of those within the diaspora is not simply a pale shadow of 'authentic' Irish identity in Ireland, but has something distinctive to contribute. Where once the Irish in Ireland laughed at the outlandishness of Irish-American culture, as they saw it, or claimed that Irish culture could only exist in bastardized form outside the Motherland, the Irish diaspora increasingly claimed its own place and denied that its culture was inferior. Such forwardness from the diaspora did not always go down well in Ireland – the brashness of *Riverdance* may have offended some who disagreed with its aesthetic values but it must have offended others because the proponents came from within the mainstream of Irish culture, but an Irish culture nurtured outside Ireland.

One must also pay tribute to the remarkable success of Irish political lobbying in Washington. This lobbying was successful, not only in placing Irish immigration high on the agenda in the Congressional debates on new migrants, but also in promoting Irish interests in the growing debate concerning the US role in Anglo-Irish affairs. The extraordinary success of Irish diplomats, lobbyists and politicians was tribute to a new confidence and maturity.

Finally, the much-spoken-of Celtic Tiger economy has not benefited all in Irish society, but it has had a dramatic effect on migration in and out of Ireland. Many former migrants have returned, while the country is also experiencing, for the first time, significant inflows of migrants with no Irish background, including EU citizens and forced migrants from many different countries.[23] As a country of significant net migration Ireland is faced with new challenges.[24] So far it is not dealing very successfully with these challenges, but it may be that a greater historical understanding of the difficulties faced by Irish migrants in other places may result in a more tolerant and welcoming policy towards immigrants.

New scholarship in Irish migration and diaspora studies

Well before the 1980s and 1990s, there were signs of a developing interest in the field. The pioneering work of such scholars as William Forbes Adams,[25] Arnold Schrier[26] and Damian Hannan[27] was followed by an upsurge of research from the 1970s onwards. Donald Akenson,[28] David Noel Doyle,[29] David Fitzpatrick,[30] Kerby Miller,[31] Cormac Ó Gráda,[32] Brendan Walsh[33] and Patrick O'Farrell[34] are among the dominant figures.

At the same time the general emphasis on cultural relativism character-istic of the post-1960s period and the 'roots' phenomenon associated with African-American self-awareness engendered a new interest in questions of ethnicity, identity and difference. The sometimes celebratory, sometimes crit-ical tone of earlier work (Glazer and Moynihan[35]) was carried out within an integrationist framework even while being critical of the limits of that frame-work, but this gave way to a new interest in the subject's point of view (for example Handlin[36]). A good example of the new approach is Miller's monumental *Emigrants and Exiles*,[37] a controversial hypothesis attempting to reconstruct the pre-modern world-view of the Irish 'exile', based on an exhaustive analysis of emigrant letters, folksong and other sources.

Many other scholars entered the field, from many disciplines and many coun-tries, using new methodologies. Thus, in more recent times, women migrants have been considered by a range of scholars, including Hasia Diner[38] and Janet Nolan.[39] Perspectives in geography, ethnic studies and sociology have been employed by such scholars as Mary Hickman,[40] Bronwen Walter[41] and Breda Gray.[42] Local immigration studies are exemplified by the fine *New York Irish*,[43] edited by Ronald Bayor and Timothy Meagher, with a significant input by Marion Casey. Theoretical areas concerning the representation of the migrant experience are being explored.[44] Longitudinal studies, among the most difficult of approaches, have been pioneered by Bruce Elliott,[45] while David Fitzpatrick has broken new ground in his use of discourse analysis and spatially based approaches to reconstruct kinship networks in *Oceans of Consolation*.[46] The new interest in Irish migration has also led to research in previously under-valued areas of Irish migration, such as the role of the Irish religious diaspora[47] (Edmund Hogan) and the Irish in Argentina (Eduardo Coghlan,[48] Patrick McKenna[49] and others). Sectoral, local and other specific studies have also been pioneered in recent years, notably in Patrick O'Sullivan's monumental six-volume collection on the Irish world-wide.[50] Recent scholarship has also embraced new critical perspectives, as exemplified by Jim Mac Laughlin's[51] use of world systems theory to explain the role of Irish emigration and postcolonial perspectives such as those offered by David Lloyd.[52] The shortcomings of past statistics are being addressed through the work of demographers such as Damian Courtney.[53] Return migration is beginning to be examined for the first time by scholars such as Elizabeth Malcolm[54] and Mary Corcoran,[55] while there have been as yet only a small number of studies into the 'new' Irish migrants of the 1980s.[56] Finally, Irish migration is increasingly being presented in a comparative European (for instance Delaney's work in this volume) and world context or through long-term enquiry, enabling the old chestnut of Irish 'exceptionalism', to use Akenson's phrase, to be measured against the experience of other groups.[57]

The noticeable increase in research in this field has been encouraged by the existence of active academic associations for the promotion of Irish Studies, including ACIS (American Committee for Irish Studies), BAIS (British Association for Irish Studies), CAIS (Canadian Association for Irish Studies), EFACIS (European Federation of Associations and Centres for Irish Studies), SOFEIR (Societé Française d'Études Irlandaises) and IASIL (International Association for the Study of Irish Literatures). It is noticeable that the number of papers on migration-related topics has grown steadily in recent years. New technologies are also playing a role, exemplified by the quiet but very effective work of Patrick O'Sullivan's Irish diaspora discussion forum.

Other recent innovative institutional responses include the establishment in 1993 of the Centre for Migration Studies (CMS) by the Ulster-American Folk Park in Omagh, Northern Ireland, while at the other end of the island the Cobh Emigration Museum was established about the same time to promote knowledge of Irish emigration through a dedicated museum located in the railway station from which so many had left.

The Irish Centre for Migration Studies (ICMS) was established at the National University of Ireland, Cork, in 1996. The first centre of its kind in the state, it aims to draw upon a broad range of interdisciplinary perspectives to explore the Irish experience of migration, past and present, through innovative programmes of teaching, research, publications, conferences and on-line databases. The Centre's first major event was 'The Scattering' conference in September 1997, a global, comparative overview of Irish migration and the Irish diaspora. This book reflects some of the major themes and some of the most innovative papers presented at the conference.

The present volume

The Irish Diaspora illustrates some of the themes and changes which have been outlined above. The contributions of a number of well-known and less well-known historians are complemented by sociological, geographical, political science and demographic perspectives, from several parts of the world as well as from Ireland. The volume consciously seeks to adopt a comparative world approach to Irish migration, considering the Irish migrant experience at different periods in Britain, the Americas and the British Empire as well as offering fresh perspectives on statistical, theoretical and comparative issues. This serves effectively to explore those aspects which might be supposed to be common to the Irish migrant experience in different times and places, while questioning a number of myths about such themes as the religious character and confessional relations between host community and Irish migrants and among Irish migrants themselves, the extent or lack of socio-economic advancement among Irish migrants compared to other migrant communities, and the underlying question of whether Irish migration may indeed be characterized as 'unique' or may be compared to other migration movements from other countries.

If there is one point which emerges more clearly than any other, it is the sheer diversity and complexity of Irish migration. The stereotypical image of Irish migrants as poorly educated, rural, poor and Catholic, settling in large numbers in east coast American cities and making their way only slowly in the host society, is countered by a fascinating range of alternatives. Patrick McKenna's synthesis of the Irish experience in Argentina is one of the most startling. Here is a group of midlands farmers and skilled and semi-skilled tradespeople who 'were without doubt the most financially successful group of Irish emigrants in the world at that time, and certainly the most successful ethnic group, by a wide margin, in Argentina'. The picture is rendered even more complex by the origins of this movement, with the arrival as far back as the sixteenth century of Irish colonists in the service of Spain. McKenna further makes the point that the Argentine case represents an alternative model to the individualist 'Anglo-American' migration experience, with a strong community-based ethos driving the process of migration and a consciously separatist culture maintaining, for better or for worse, a sense of diasporic identity.

Graham Davis examines pre- and post-Famine Irish migration to Britain. A nuanced discussion of the specific experiences of different Irish communities explores the extent to which the Irish were the victims of specific forms of negative stereotyping and whether they, in turn, developed a general 'oppression history' to explain their situation. Davis stresses the diversity of migrant streams, destinations and experiences. Stereotyping and scapegoating in some areas are contrasted with an absence of such representations, and an absence of negative relations, in other areas of significant Irish settlement. Davis's essay rejects any easy generalizations about the Irish experience in Britain.

The Irish in Scotland constituted the most numerically significant element of the Irish community in Britain for a long period. Richard McCready examines this experience, pointing to the patchiness of research in the area. The Irish in eastern Scotland, for instance, are largely ignored, yet almost 20 per cent of the population of Dundee in 1851 were Irish-born. Moreover, the Irish in Scotland had a range of socio-economic backgrounds and many were skilled labourers. McReady identifies the period of the Irish independence struggle and particularly the subsequent civil war as a key moment in the separation of the Irish in Scotland from Ireland.

Tracey Connolly's exploration of wartime migration to Britain identifies this often neglected period as more of a watershed than is often realized. The arrival of significant numbers of Irish workers and their integration into British society through their presence in the armed forces and industry foreshadowed the massive Irish labour migration of the 1950s. Connolly's chapter also highlights other lesser-known aspects of this period, such as the significant migration which took place to Northern Ireland.

The 'new Irish' of the 1980s are the subject of Breda Gray's chapter. She points to the mediatization of the image of the 'high-flying' emigrant, by inference a very different kind of migrant from those who had gone before. She discusses the new Irish in the light of their conscious positioning as an 'ethnic' group in 'multicultural' London and looks in particular at the role of women. Gray examines the extent to which the term 'diaspora' may now be a more useful way of evoking the experiences and representations of modern Irish migrants in Britain, as they negotiate double identities in a contingent, shifting universe.

Brendan Halpin analyses the current Irish population of Britain in detail, using the results of the Labour Force Survey and other statistical sources. His overall conclusion confirms the different characteristics of the 'new Irish' of the 1980s compared to those of the 1950s, but, as Halpin warns, 'the simple dichotomy between low-skill 1950s emigration and high-skill 1980s emigration does not hold entirely: even among more recent migrants, the poorly educated are well represented'.

Donald Akenson's chapter attacks the entire concept of Irish 'exceptionalism' in the field of migration. He disagrees sharply with Kerby Miller's vision, set out in *Emigrants and Exiles*, of a premodern Irish culture unable to cope with migration and change and falling back upon a nostalgic, passive vision of the past.

Kerby Miller's contribution to this volume is a fascinating examination of the multiple strands and considerable impact of Irish migration to the 'Old South' – US states south of the Mason–Dixon line. The eighteenth century is shown as a period when religious conversion was not uncommon and when many 'Scotch-Irish' – a contested term – were actually converts from Anglicanism or even Roman Catholicism and many came from the south, not the north, of Ireland. Yet subsequently they were all labelled as 'Scotch-Irish'. In more recent times, in a kind of ironic twist, Miller shows that a third of those who describe themselves as 'Irish' in the 1990 census are from the south – more than triple the figure in the 1860s – even though the designation 'Scotch-Irish' was an option. As Miller points out, 'ultimately of course the question of ethnicity is not one of ancestral birthplace or religious affiliation but one of individual and collective identification, which in turn is subjective and variable, shaped by a multitude of shifting social, political, and psychological circumstances'. Miller's contribution focuses on the lived experiences of a number of well-documented individual lives but also successfully invokes the shifting identity politics of multicultural America, suggesting that these may actually have been more flexible and more inclusive in the earlier, colonial period than subsequently.

Ruth-Ann Harris summarizes her extensive work on the *Boston Pilot*'s Missing Friends column (more than 30,000 persons between 1831 and 1863). Her approach shows how the social network of *Pilot* readers functioned as a virtual network for Irish migrants – well over a century before the Internet. She also analyses the changing class structure of migration, especially after the replacement of sail by steam. Diversity again emerges as a theme.

Malcolm Campbell's comparative exploration of Irish migrants in Minnesota and New South Wales shatters a number of myths. He stresses the value of cross-cultural analysis at regional level and compares and contrasts the fortunes of the migrant Irish in rural Minnesota and rural New South Wales. He points to the clear success of the Irish in New South Wales as proof that the Irish as migrants were not irredeemably urban – in the Australian case they were just as likely to be involved in farming as anyone else. In Minnesota, the ill-thought-out scheme to translate impoverished unskilled migrants from Connemara into an environment for which they did not have the skills needed to survive overshadowed other quite successful group migration schemes in which Archbishop John Ireland played a major role. Campbell suggests that the key factor in explaining the differential patterns of Irish experience in New South Wales and Minnesota is not the migrants themselves but the host society. Moreover, there were considerable similarities between the two groups.

A whole section of the book is rightly devoted to Irish participation in the building of the British Empire. Comparatively little research has been done on this area until the recent past. Apart from the dominance of American scholarship in Irish migration studies, this may reflect a certain reluctance in Irish circles to address the role of the Irish, not as the colonized, but as participants in the colonizing process. Akenson's trenchant views are well-known and may have raised hackles in the past, but he has also helped to open valuable new fields of enquiry.

Andy Bielenberg's point of departure is Akenson's *The Irish Diaspora*[58] because it is, as he points out, the only comprehensive survey of the topic of Irish migration and settlement in the British Empire (although not limited to it). Bielenberg uses Akenson to frame the debate about Irish 'exceptionalism' and examines the available evidence from a range of sources. He sees Irish migration as part of a broad European movement and says it has to be appreciated that the real victims of this movement were not Irish, but native Americans who lost their land and Africans whose labour was barbarically exploited. He also discusses the significance of the 'Second British Empire' as a destination for Irish migration, suggesting that up to 20 per cent of Irish migrants went there – comparable at the time with the numbers going to Britain itself. In general there was a 'skills bias' in favour of the colonies, compared to the United States, as well as a bias towards migrants from economically developed parts of Ireland; there were also more Protestants. In discussing relative performances of Catholic and Protestant migrants in rural and urban contexts, Bielenberg argues that Akenson is right in saying that Catholic social origin does not explain the over-representation of Irish Catholics at the lower end of the social urban scale and suggests that the really significant factors were social status, skills and literacy on departure from Ireland. 'Neither Irishness nor Catholicity were handicaps for Irish migrants moving to New Zealand, Australia, South Africa or Canada.' Overall, opportunities for Irish migrants in the British Empire were better than in the USA or Great Britain.

Michael Holmes explores the dual nature of the Irish role in India and paints a less than flattering picture. The Irish role in the military forces was extremely prominent and not even confined to the British army; he points out that in the eighteenth century they were also prominent in the French Indian forces. The Irish were 'particularly known for brutality'. Holmes points to the strong Irish presence in the Civil Service and the Medical Service and says their belief in their own racial superiority was no less than that of their British counterparts. He is scornful about Irish pretensions to a bridge-building role between the developed world and post-independence India and other former colonies: 'for a time the Irish Government had vague ideas of leading the decolonised world, but they were rapidly disabused of these notions'. In short, the Irish role in the European imperialist project was little different from that of their British mentors. Moreover, little is now left to connect Ireland and India and the two countries have pursued increasingly divergent strategic paths.

Donal McCracken's discussion of the Irish experience in South Africa highlights a relatively unknown strand. Irish migrants to South Africa were disproportionately skilled and disproportionately Protestant, compared to Irish migrants to other places. Although their numbers were never very significant, they made a strong contribution to administrative life and were prominent in the professions. Over time they became largely assimilated into the white minority and little trace of an Irish identity remains in South Africa today.

Angela McCarthy's examination of the Irish in New Zealand also addresses a subject which has received insufficient attention. There was a strong Irish presence in the 1860s–1880s, both Catholic and Protestant. McCarthy uses letters to and from Ireland and demonstrates the role of kinship and local networks in migration to New Zealand. In an interesting parallel with seventeenth-century British policy in Ireland, she points to the practice of granting land to settlers on condition that they would remain in occupation for a minimum period (most did not, like their seventeenth-century counterparts). A minority sympathized with the displaced Maoris and saw parallels with the Land War in Ireland.

The fourth part of the book address a series of topics of a more general nature. Damian Courtney discusses the statistical difficulties inherent in estimates of contemporary migration and the inadequacy of the old 'residual' method of calculating migration flows. He highlights the role of the new Quarterly National Household Survey in providing new and more accurate data and discusses a number of other new data sources such as child benefit statistics, the register of electors and school enrolments.

Jim Mac Laughlin's discussion of voluntarist and structuralist approaches to recent Irish migration highlights the extent to which a false construction of recent Irish migration overemphasizes an unrepresentative highly educated minority. This overlooks a fundamental continuity in migration patterns, in which largely disadvantaged migrants with limited opportunities in the 'Celtic Tiger' economy continue to perform low-skilled tasks in other economies. Mac Laughlin uses world systems theory, empirical data and comparisons with other 'emigrant nurseries' to analyse underlying structural and behavioural syndromes, stressing at the same time that recent changes in Irish society have been so radical 'that they constitute a . . . discontinuity with more traditional views of Ireland as a self-governing and identifiable territorial community'. Pessimistically, he sees the tendency of young people to look outside the country, even if the migration choice is now more likely to be Europe, as a reflection of a deterioration in national politics and of the emergence of a culture of dependency.

Enda Delaney places the Irish migration experience of the second half of the twentieth century in a comparative European perspective, pointing out that rural depopulation and mass migration are not unique to Ireland in this period. He identifies strong parallels with southern Europe, especially Italy, and sees these movements as classic periphery–core flows – 'clearly this is a movement out of the underdeveloped agricultural economy in to the advanced capitalist one, albeit across national boundaries'. He also points to the need for more comparative regional and local studies.

Delaney speculates in an interesting way about outward and return migration, suggesting that whereas the former is more likely to be for economic reasons, the latter is often for social and familial motives. This question should certainly be on the agenda of emerging research issues.

Conclusions

It is hoped that the present volume will constitute a modest addition to the growing scholarship in the field of Irish migration studies. Much remains to be done, however, and there are neglected areas of study. Gender has belatedly begun to receive a degree of attention but more work needs to be done in this field. The impact of class on migration is still under-theorized and understudied. The changing nature of Irish society itself, and the impact of return migration and of new immigration in Ireland, has only begun to be studied. There is a need to attend to marginalized and disadvantaged groups within the diaspora, such as the elderly Irish in Britain. More comparative and longitudinal studies are needed. Much can be gleaned from non-social science perspectives, including creative, literary critical and ethnomusicological viewpoints.

The comparative statistics set out in Baines[59] (and by Bielenberg in this volume) suggest that the Irish experience of migration, in terms of volume and persistence, may fairly be described as unique, at least for the period between the Great Famine and the mid-twentieth century. While this may give some comfort to defenders of the 'exceptionalist' viewpoint, Irish migration is nonetheless clearly part of a European pattern. Moreover, the diversity of reasons for leaving, the destinations chosen and the experience of integration into the new host society point to the dangers of any generalizations in this most complex field.

Notes

1. See, for example, J.A. Jackson, *Migration* (London and New York, 1986); S. Douglas, D.S. Massey, J. Arango, G. Hugo, A. Kouaouci, A. Pellegrino and J.E. Taylor, 'Theories of International Migration: A Review and Appraisal', *Population and Development Review*, 19, 3 (1993), pp. 431–66.
2. For an early Irish usage, see J.A. O'Brien, *The Vanishing Irish: The Enigma of the Modern World* (London, 1954), p. 8. See also Stuart Hall, 'Cultural Identity and Diaspora', in Jonathan Rutherford (ed.), *Identity: Community, Culture, Difference* (London, 1990); James Clifford, 'Travelling Cultures', in Cary Nelson, Paula A. Treichler and Lawrence Grossberg (eds), *Cultural Studies* (New York and London, 1992); Rey Chow, *Writing Diaspora. Tactics of Intervention in Contemporary Cultural Studies* (Bloomington and Indianapolis, 1993); Matthew Frye Jacobson, *Special Sorrows: The Diasporic Imagination of Irish, Polish, and Jewish Immigrants in the United States* (Cambridge, Mass., 1995); Avtar Brah, *Cartographies of Diaspora: Contesting Identities* (London and New York, 1996); Robin Cohen, *Global Diasporas: An Introduction* (London, 1997); P. Gilroy, 'Diaspora and the Detours of Identity', in K. Woodward (ed.), *Identity and Difference* (London, 1997); S. Lavie and T. Swedenburg (eds), *Displacement, Diaspora and Geographies of Identity* (Durham, N.C., 1998).
3. E.G. Ravenstein, 'The Laws of Migration', *Journal of the Royal Statistical Society*, 48, 2 (1885), pp. 167–227; 52, 2 (1889), pp. 241–301.
4. R.E. Park *et al.*, *The City* (Chicago, 1967).
5. N. Glazer and D.P. Moynihan, *Beyond the Melting Pot: The Negroes, Puerto Ricans, Jews, Italians, and Irish of New York City* (Cambridge, Mass., 1970).
6. D.T. Goldberg, *Multiculturalism: A Critical Reader* (Oxford and Cambridge Mass., 1994).
7. I. Wallerstein, *The Modern World-System* (New York, 1974).
8. See, for example, Jon Bird, Barry Curtis, Melinda Mash, Tim Putnam, George Robertson and Lisa Tickner (eds), *Travellers' Tales: Narratives of Home and Displacement* (London, 1994); Caren Kaplan, *Questions of Travel. Postmodern Discourses of Displacements* (London, 1996). Lavie and Swedenburg (eds), *Displacement*.
9. Y. Lequin, *La Mosaïque France: Histoire des Étrangers et de l'immigration en France* (Paris, 1988). S. Castles *et al.*, *Here for Good: Western Europe's New Ethnic Minorities* (London, 1984).
10. S. Castles and J.M. Miller, *The Age of Migration: International Population Movements in the Modern World* (London, 1993); S. Collinson, *Europe and International Migration* (London, 1993); R. King (ed.), *Mass Migration in Europe: The Legacy and the Future* (Chichester, 1995).
11. Karmela Liebkind (ed.), *New Identities in Europe: Immigrant Ancestry and the Ethnic Identity of Youth* (Aldershot, 1989); Keebet Von Benda-Beckmann and Maykel Verkuyten (eds), *Nationalism, Ethnicity and Cultural Identity in Europe* (Utrecht, 1995); P.C. Emmer and M. Morner (eds), *European Expansion and Migration: Essays on the International Migration from Africa, Asia and Europe* (Oxford, 1992); Sarah Collinson, *Migration, Visa and Asylum Policies in Europe* (London, 1995); S. Spencer, *Strangers and Citizens: A Positive Approach to Migrants and Refugees* (London, 1994); King (ed.), *Mass Migration*; David Cesarani and Mary Fulbrook (eds), *Citizenship, Nationality, and Migration in Europe* (London, 1996); Daniele Joly, *Haven or Hell? Asylum Policies and Refugees in Europe* (Basingstoke, 1996);

Adrian Favell, *Philosophies of Integration: Immigration and the Idea of Citizenship in France and Britain* (New York, 1998).

12. P. Jackson and J. Penrose (eds), *Constructions of Race, Place and Nation* (London, 1993).

13. I. Chambers, *Migrancy, Culture, Identity* (London and New York, 1994).

14. A. Zolberg *et al.*, *The Challenge of Diversity: Integration and Pluralism in Societies of Immigration* (Aldershot, 1996).

15. For an example, see Kaplan, *Questions of Travel.*

16. Alan O'Day, 'Revising the Diaspora', in *The Making of Modern Irish History: Revisionism and the Revisionist Controversy* (London, 1996).

17. For example, see D.N. Doyle and O.D. Edwards, *America and Ireland 1776–1976* (Westport Conn., 1980); D.N. Doyle, *Ireland, Irishmen and Revolutionary America 1769–1820* (Dublin, 1981).

18. See, for example, D. Fitzpatrick, *Irish Emigration 1801–1921* (Dublin, 1984); D. Fitzpatrick, *Oceans of Consolation: Personal Accounts of Irish Migration to Australia* (Cork, 1995).

19. Government of Ireland, *Report of the Commission for Emigration and Other Population Problems* (Dublin, 1956).

20. NESC, *The Economic and Social Implications of Emigration* (Dublin, 1991).

21. R. O'Hanlon, *The New Irish-Americans* (Niwot, Colo., 1998).

22. Doyle and Edwards, *America and Ireland*; Doyle, *Ireland*; P.J. Drudy (ed.), *The Irish in America: Emigration, Assimilation and Impact* (Cambridge, 1985); Patrick O'Farrell, *Letters from Irish Australia 1825–1929* (Sydney, 1990). Patrick O'Farrell, *The Irish in Australia* (Kensington NSW, 1986). Patrick O'Farrell, *The Irish in Australia* (Sydney, 1987). Patrick O'Farrell, *The Irish in Australia and New Zealand 1891–1879* (Oxford, 1989). Patrick O'Farrell, *Vanished Kingdoms: The Irish in Australia and New Zealand, A Personal Excursion* (Kensington NSW, 1990).

23. See D. Courtney, present volume; also P. Mac Éinrí, 'Some Recent Demographic Developments in Ireland', *Études Irlandaises* (Spring, 1997), 22–1, pp. 145–164.

24. Mac Éinrí, 'Some Recent Demographic Developments'.

25. W.F. Adams, *Ireland and the Irish Emigration to the New World from 1815 to the Famine* (Baltimore Md., 1980).

26. A. Schrier, *Ireland and the American Emigration, 1850–1900* (Minneapolis, 1958).

27. D. Hannan, *Rural Exodus: A Study of the Forces Influencing the Large-Scale Migration of Irish Rural Youth* (London, 1970).

28. See, for example, D.H. Akenson, *Being Had: Historians, Evidence and the Irish in North America* (Ontario, 1985); D.H. Akenson, *Small Differences: Irish Catholics and Irish Protestants, 1815–1922, An International Perspective* (Montreal, 1988); D.H. Akenson, *Half the World from Home, Perspectives on the Irish in New Zealand* (Wellington N.Z., 1990); D.H. Akenson, *Reading the Texts of Rural Immigrants: Letters from the Irish in Australia, New Zealand and North America* (Gananoque, 1990); D.H. Akenson, *Occasional Papers on the Irish in South Africa* (Grahamstown, 1991); D.H. Akenson, *The Irish Diaspora: A Primer* (Belfast, 1996).

29. See, for example, Doyle and Edwards, *Ireland and America*; D.N. Doyle, 'The Irish as Urban Pioneers in the United States 1850–1870', *Journal of Ethnic History* (Fall 1990-Winter 1991).

30. See, for example, Fitzpatrick, *Irish Emigration 1801–1921*; D. Fitzpatrick, 'A Share of the Honeycomb: Education, Emigration and Irishwomen', *Continuity*

and Change, 1, 2 (1986), pp. 217–34. Fitzpatrick, *Oceans of Consolation*; R. Fitzpatrick, *God's Frontiersmen: The Scots-Irish Epic* (London, 1989).

31. See, for example, K. Miller, 'Emigrants and Exiles: Irish Cultures and Irish Emigration to North America 1790–1922', *Irish Historical Studies*, 22 (1980), pp. 203–89; K. Miller, *Emigrants and Exiles: Ireland and the Irish Exodus to North America* (New York, 1985); K. Miller and B. Boling, 'Golden Streets, Bitter Tears: The Irish Image of America during the Era of Mass Migration', *Journal of Ethnic History*, 10 (1990); Kerby Miller, in R. Kearney (ed.), *Emigration, Capitalism and Ideology in Post-Famine Ireland* (Dublin, 1990); Kerby Miller, in V. Yans-McLaughlin (ed.), *Class, Culture and Immigrant Group Indentity in the United States: The Case of Irish-American ethnicity* (Oxford, 1990).

32. See, for example, C. Ó Gráda, 'Seasonal Migration and Post-Famine Adjustment in the West of Ireland', *Studia Hiberica*, 13 (1973), pp. 48–76; K. O'Rourke and C. Ó Gráda, *Migration As Disaster Relief: Lessons From The Great Irish Famine* (Dublin, 1996).

33. See, for instance, C. Ó Gráda and B.M. Walsh, 'The Economic Effects of Emigration: Ireland', in B. Asch (ed.), *Emigration and its Effects on the Sending Country* (Santa Monica, 1994).

34. O'Farrell, *Letters from Irish Australia 1825–1929*; O'Farrell, *The Irish in Australia*; O'Farrell, *The Irish in Australia and New Zealand 1891–1879*; O'Farrell, *Vanished Kingdoms*.

35. Glazer and Moynihan, *Beyond the Melting Pot*.

36. O. Handlin, *Boston's Immigrants: A Study in Acculturation* (New York, 1968); O. Handlin, *The Uprooted* (Boston, 1973).

37. Miller, *Emigrants and Exiles*.

38. H.A. Diner, *Erin's Daughters in America: Irish Immigrant Women in the Nineteenth Century* (Baltimore Md., 1992).

39. Janet Nolan, *Ourselves Alone: Women's Emigration from Ireland 1885–1920* (Lexington, 1989).

40. M. Hickman, *Religion, class and identity: the State, the Catholic Church and the Education of the Irish in Britain* (Aldershot, 1995).

41. Bronwyn Walter, *Gender and Irish Migration to Britain* (Cambridge, 1988); Bronwyn Walter, *Gender and Recent Irish Migration to Britain* (Dublin, 1991).

42. B. Gray, '(Dis)locating Irishness in the 1990s: The Views of Irish Women at Home and Abroad', in Jim Mac Laughlin (ed.), *Location and Dislocation in Irish Society: Multidisciplinary Essays on Emigration and Irish Identities* (Cork, 1997).

43. R. Bayor and T. Meagher, *The New York Irish* (Baltimore Md., 1996).

44. See, for instance, A. Feldman, ' "Gaelic Gotham": Decontextualising the Diaspora', *Eire-Ireland*, Spring/Summer 1996, XXXI, 1, pp. 189–201.

45. B.S. Elliott, *Irish Migrants in the Canadas: A New Approach* (Kingston, 1988).

46. Fitzpatrick, *Oceans of Consolation*.

47. E. Hogan, *The Irish Missionary Movement: A Historic Survey 1830–1980* (Dublin, 1990).

48. E.A. Coghlan, *Las Irlandeses en la Argentina – su actuacion y descendiencia* (Buenos Aires, 1987).

49. See McKenna's article in the present volume.

50. P. O'Sullivan (ed.), *The Irish World Wide: Irish Women and Irish Migration* (Leicester, 1992); P. O'Sullivan (ed.), *The Irish World Wide: Patterns of Migration* (Leicester, 1992); P. O'Sullivan (ed.), *The Irish World Wide: Religion and Identity* (Leicester, 1992); P. O'Sullivan (ed.), *The Irish World Wide: The Creative Migrant*

(Leicester, 1992); P. O'Sullivan (ed.), *The Irish World Wide: The Irish in the New Communities* (Leicester, 1992); P. O'Sullivan (ed.), *The Irish World Wide: The Meaning of the Famine* (Leicester, 1992).

51. See, for example, J. Mac Laughlin, 'Social Characteristics and Destinations of Recent Emigrants from Selected Regions in the West of Ireland, *Geoforum*, 22, 3 (1991), p. 323; J. Mac Laughlin, *Historical and Recent Irish Emigration: A Critique of Core and Periphery and Behavioural Models* (London, 1993); J. Mac Laughlin, 'Ireland: An "Emigrant Nursery" in the World Economy', *International Migration*, 31, 1 (1993), pp. 149–70; J. Mac Laughlin, 'Defending the Frontiers: The Political Geography of Race and Racism in the European Community', in C.H. Williams (ed.), *The Political Geography of the New World Order* (London, 1993); J. Mac Laughlin, *Ireland: The Emigrant Nursery and the World Economy* (Cork, 1995).

52. D. Lloyd 'Making Sense of the Dispersal' pp. 3–4. *The Irish Reporter* Issue. 13, First Quarter 1994.

53. D.A. Courtney, 'Recent Trends in Emigration from Ireland', paper given to Development Studies Association Annual Conference, QUB Belfast, 1989; also chapter on demography and migration in P. Clancy, *et al.*, *Irish Society: Sociological Perspectives* (Dublin, 1995); also chapter in present volume.

54. E. Malcolm, *Elderly Return Migration from Britain to Ireland: A Preliminary Study* (Dublin, 1996).

55. M.P. Corcoran, 'Informalization of Metropolitan Labour Forces: The Case of Irish Immigrants in the New York Construction Industry', *Irish Journal of Sociology*, 1, 1 (1991), pp. 31–51; M. Corcoran, *Irish Illegals: Transients Between Two Societies* (Westport Conn., 1993).

56. P. Mac Éinrí, 'The New Europeans: The Irish in Paris today', in J. Mulholland and D. Keogh (eds), *Emigration, Employment and Enterprise* (Cork, 1989), pp. 58–80; P. Mac Éinrí, The Irish in Paris: an Aberrant Community?' in R. King (ed.), *Contemporary Irish Migration* (Maynooth, 1991). 'La migration contemporaine irlandaise: quelques perspectives', *L'Irlande Politique et Sociale*, 4 (1992), pp. 105–15, Corcoran, 'Informalization of Metropolitan Labour Forces'.

57. See, for instance, D. Baines (1995); W.J. Smyth 'Irish Emigration, 1700–1920', in P.C. Emmer and M. Moren (eds), *European Expansion and Migration* (Oxford, 1992).

58. Akenson, *Irish Diaspora*.

59. D. Baines, *Emigration from Europe, 1815–1930* (Cambridge, 1995).

Part One
Great Britain

CHAPTER 1

The Irish in Britain, 1815–1939

GRAHAM DAVIS
(Irish Studies Centre, Bath)

Leaving Ireland

The *Liverpool Times* in reporting emigration from Ireland in 1846 made a distinction between what it chose to call 'the emigrants of hope' and 'the emigrants of despair'. The former consisted principally of small farmers with some capital 'who go to seek means of improving their condition in Canada and the States';.while the latter were the poorest of the poor who cannot afford the trip to America but 'who beg or borrow the trifle which is necessary to bring them over to this country'. Reporting a very great increase of pauper emigration in recent months from Ireland to Lancashire, the paper noted that the Irish tramping the roads from Liverpool to Manchester were of all ages and from every part of Ireland. When interviewed, 'they all say they cannot get a living of any sort in Ireland, and that they are coming over to England to see if they can find work for their children in the factories, and for themselves in any other way. Many of these poor people are most decent and respectable in their manners and language.' While the tone of the piece was clearly sympathetic to the plight of 'these poor creatures', there was no mistaking the 'fear that they will long produce a considerable effect on wages and poor rates in the country'.[1]

Here we have the classic British perspective throughout the nineteenth and most of the twentieth century which continued to associate Irish migrants with a whole host of problems: social, religious, economic and political. The story of the Irish in Britain is dominated by details of strikebreakers and slum conditions, sectarian riots, 'poor Paddy' on the railway, and sporadic incidents of political violence. It is argued in this chapter that what is at work here is a cultural filter that mirrors the values of the host nation without fully reflecting the variety of Irish migrant experience.

The migration and settlement of the Irish in Britain between the end of the Napoleonic Wars in 1815 and the outbreak of the Second World War in 1939 forms part of a wider movement throughout the Irish diaspora, and can be best understood in its relation to a global network. Before 1841, when mass migration had already seen an annual exodus of 50,000 from Ireland, Britain was the major destination ahead of Canada and the United States. From the

1840s until the 1920s the United States received about 75 per cent of the 5 million total of Irish migrants, while from 1851 to 1921 the proportion who settled in Britain was around one-fifth of that total world-wide. Finally, from 1921 to 1939 Britain resumed its role as the major destination for Irish migrants and this pattern has continued through to the end of the twentieth century.[2]

More significantly, the British experience remains unique within the Irish diaspora, firstly because it was 'the nearest place to home', and geographical proximity induced a sense of temporary presence among all Irish migrants with the ease of an anticipated return to Ireland. Secondly, Britain received an annual influx of thousands of seasonal workers, and facilitated the departure of several million Irish migrants from British ports to Canada, the United States, Australia and New Zealand. So, as Donald Akenson has argued, Irish migration to Britain represents 'a very large, very special case' because it was involved in Irish migration throughout the English-speaking world.[3]

Donald Akenson has also pointed to the inadequate statistical basis available to study the Irish in Britain. Following the Act of Union between Britain and Ireland in 1801, no adequate figures were kept before 1852 and it was only from 1876 that a tally was made of Irish migrants to Britain. With the partition of Ireland in 1920, separate figures were no longer recorded, so paradoxically the information is least reliable for the periods of highest migration to Britain. Reliance on census totals of the Irish-born, with all the limitations of not recording second and subsequent generations, provides the main guide to the scale of the Irish presence. The common identification of the Irish with the Catholic population of Britain has also tended to marginalize the estimated 20 per cent of the total who were, nominally, Irish Protestants. In 1841, the first census to include the Irish-born in Britain recorded a figure of 415,000. By 1861, the peak figure of 806,000 was reached and from then on the numbers declined so that by 1901 the total of Irish-born was down to 632,000. While the middle decades of the century saw the bulk of mass migration to Britain, the presence of the second and third generations born of Irish parents meant that a full definition of the Irish in Britain would place the numbers at over a million by the end of the century.[4]

Contrary to the exclusion of emigrants of hope and the restriction to emigrants of despair, there is every reason, because of the special relationship with the rest of the Irish diaspora, to include the Irish in Britain within a broad analysis of the explanations for all migrants leaving Ireland. These changed over time subject to changing conditions in Ireland and to new opportunities abroad.

Traditionally, pre-Famine emigration has been explained in terms of increasing population pressure and the system of land utilization that left some 3 million poor cotters and labourers, out of a population of 8.2 million in 1841, vulnerable to a series of poor harvests and food shortages. A chronic lack of employment in rural Ireland (available for less than half the year in western counties) was compounded by what proved to be a fatal dependence on a subsistence agriculture based (especially in the south and west of Ireland) on the monoculture of the potato.[5] Structural change within Irish agriculture involving a move away from labour-intensive arable farming towards pastoral farming, in response to good prices available for cattle and dairy products exported to Britain, provided less employment for the large class of landless labourers in Ireland.

At the same time, increasingly from the 1820s, peripheral Ireland was losing ground in its textile industry (with the notable exception of linen manufacture in the Belfast region) to the core centres of cotton and woollen cloth manufacture in the industrial belts of Scotland, Lancashire and Yorkshire. The increasing difficulty of combining domestic textile work with agricultural husbandry in Ireland led textile workers in the north midlands to migrate to Scottish cities and drew others from Queen's County (Laois) and towns like Bandon, County Cork, to Bradford in Yorkshire.[6] Distressed weavers found themselves heading for Lowell, Massachusetts, or the cotton towns of Lancashire.[7] Ireland's geographical situation as a relatively underdeveloped and over-populated economy located between two, dynamic societies in Britain and the United States created the conditions for the country to become an emigrant nursery, supplying labour to support the growth of industry and infrastructure on both sides of the Atlantic. Even before the famine years (1845–52), emigration became established as a permanent feature of Irish life, with children reared in Ireland but destined to settle abroad.

The evidence of an extensive enquiry of 1,500 witnesses in 1835 provides firm evidence of the reasons for emigration.[8] Local landlords, magistrates and clergy throughout Ireland identified a number of key, explanatory factors. What was pushing the main body of small farmers towards the contemplation of emigration was the pincer effect of high rents and low prices on income levels. The decline in textiles limited the possibilities of diversification, and improvements to farmholdings were not compensated by landlords at the expiration of leases when their renewal inevitably meant still higher rents. So emigration was considered as a viable alternative to be financed by the sale of leases and all the farm stock. In the long run, there was a genuine belief in the prospect of families bettering their condition and securing a future for the next generation. The most persuasive pressure came in the form of emigrant letters conveying news of relatives and neighbours abroad with very precise details of the cost of land, the wages of labourers and servants. Even before the famine years, successful migrants were sending back remittances to Ireland, a system that later developed into a huge traffic in pre-paid passage tickets that was to finance the great majority of voluntary migration. Emigration formed part of a family strategy of economic betterment, especially for the benefit of the next generation.[9]

A climate that fostered emigration was in place in Ireland during the 1830s when mass movement spread from the north-east and south-east of Ireland to affect all classes and both Catholics and Protestants throughout all parts of Ireland.[10] Cheaper steam navigation and the greater dissemination of appropriate knowledge from shipping agents facilitated travel to Britain. Employers were sending agents to Ireland to recruit labour for the Lancashire cotton mills and the evidence of the Commission into the State of the Irish Poor in Britain in 1836 points to higher expectations among labourers through emigration. Samuel Holme, a Liverpool builder, provided one such example:

> I had a conversation last week with an Irish labourer, named Christopher Shields: he said that the reason of his leaving Ireland was, that in the county of Wexford, his own county, he could only get 6d. a-day and his own meat: that at one time he rented a small cabin with a potato patch, and worked for the landlord. He then got 1s. a-day but the landlord charged him £3 for his holding. He told me that there was a general impression among his countrymen that if they came to England their fortunes would be made, wages are so much higher here. He told me that he could get his clothing as cheap here as at home, and generally all the things he wanted. He now gets 16s. a-week. He stated likewise that it was a great inducement to them to come here that they can get situations for their children, which they could not get at home. He told me likewise that he could more easily get his children educated here than in Ireland. This man lives in a cellar. He will never return to Ireland: he has no wish to go back.[11]

Taking into account the additional earnings of his children, Christopher Shields would have probably received at least three times the household income available to his family in Ireland. More pertinently, we should consider such labour migration not merely in terms of impersonal economic forces but accept there was also a process of self-selection among would-be migrants who made a rational decision about their own economic prospects.

This chapter explores some ideas for moving beyond the cultural filter that viewed the Irish presence in Britain as a problem. This perspective has been reinforced with the parallel tradition of 'oppression history', concerned to demonstrate that Irish migrants were outcast victims and were continually subject to racial discrimination. It is offered as a complement to other recently published surveys of the Irish in Britain which contain valuable historiographical summaries.[12]

Settlement patterns

An important starting place contests the idea that there was a uniform Irish migrant experience in Britain, or indeed elsewhere throughout the Irish diaspora. As David Fitzpatrick has succinctly put it: 'Irish society was not homogeneous, and neither was its emigration'.[13] In shaping the experience of the Irish in Britain, it mattered *where* migrants had come from in Ireland, *where* they chose to settle, and the *timing and subsequent persistence* of their settlement. In its place there is some merit in exploring the diversity of experience which depended on the interaction between the levels of Irish influx, the density of settlement, and the specific economic, political and religious circumstances found in particular localities.

While economic considerations remained the prime drivers of Irish migration to Britain, geography and existing coastal shipping lines provided the determinants of emigrant routes. The northern route linked Ulster and North Connacht to

Scotland, the midland route connected Connacht and Leinster to the north of England and the midlands, and the southern route went from South Leinster and Munster, often via South Wales or Bristol, to London. In broad terms, the Famine Irish, made destitute by the destruction of the potato crop in the west, mostly took passage to North America. The Irish in Britain tended to come from the more advanced parts of Ireland, especially from the industrialized north-east. That regional bias, with its higher preponderance of skills in eastern Ireland, would tend to qualify or even reverse the distinction made between the 'emigrants of hope' to America and the 'emigrants of despair' to Britain.

The distinction becomes even less meaningful with the recognition that the great majority of the Irish who came to Britain entered on a short-stay basis as a first step towards emigration to the United States, Canada or to Australia. While many of those who sailed overseas from Liverpool, Bristol or Plymouth spent little time in Britain, we know that innocent rural migrants from Ireland were easily duped by their fellow countrymen, the notorious 'emigrant trappers' who infested the docksides and relieved passengers of their money and belongings, so ensuring that instead of reaching America, they ended up in a Liverpool slum.[14]

Others continued the old pattern of entering and leaving on a seasonal basis, working as harvesters in agriculture or recruited on short-term contracts as railway navvies or as factory operatives. The fluidity of Irish migration included within the pattern of seasonal migration the cottiers of western Ireland who sustained their plots from harvest earnings in Scotland and England, the internal migrants who moved from the south-west of Ireland to the arable south-east and then further migrated to England, and from the 1860s the out-migration of the Irish from Leeds, Manchester and Glasgow into the surrounding harvest fields. Ruth-Ann Harris has argued that the transient nature of Irish labour migration to Britain before 1845 was often the prelude to emigration to the United States. Industrial skills and knowledge of political and trades union organization, plus the value of acquiring the English language, brought genuine dividends to Irish migrants who had spent time in Britain, thrust into a modern world, before settling in America.[15]

Transience also applied to those who settled permanently in Britain. While there was a concentration in three main areas in the west of Scotland, the north-western counties of England, and in London, there was also an increasing dispersal and mobility among the Irish in Britain. The big four centres, Liverpool, Manchester, Glasgow and London, took 48.5 per cent of the Irish recorded in the census of 1841.[16] The concentrations continued, albeit with decreasing proportions of the total. In both 1851 and 1861 at least 31 towns in England and Wales had an Irish-born population of over 1,000. Migration to Scotland occurred later than to England and concentrations persisted, so that by 1871 four of the 'top five Irish' towns were to be found in Strathclyde (Dumbarton, Greenock, Glasgow and Airdrie) and the high levels of Irish settlement helped to shape the character of the region.[17] Indeed, Irish settlers formed a higher proportion of the total population in Scotland (6.7 per cent) than in England and Wales (3.1 per cent) in 1861.

Although the great majority of Irish were unskilled and were largely drawn by employment prospects to settle in the greater industrial centres, experiences varied between cities with an Irish presence. It mattered *what skills* the Irish brought with them, and *where they came from* determined their familiarity with the English language and *the nature of their religious faith*. Further variations occurred in the *rate of influx* and in the *density of settlement* in what were dubbed Irish 'colonies' or 'ghettos'. In turn, the response of the host community varied not only in the scale of in-migration but in local conditions of employment and was shaped by local, religious and political allegiances.

To investigate this diversity of experience one first has to penetrate through the layers of hostile comment written by contemporaries, among whom the most influential were J.P. Kay, Friedrich Engels and Thomas Carlyle.[18] Their disparaging of the poor Irish owed much to the fears of an urban crisis that threatened to engulf municipal authorities, ill-equipped to cope with the pressing problems of rapid population growth, poverty, crime and epidemic disease. Kay's infamous depiction of 'Little Ireland', Manchester, became the symbol of the condition of the Irish in Britain during the nineteenth century:

> Ireland has poured forth the most destitute of her hordes to supply the constantly increased demand for labour. This immigration has been, in one important respect, a serious evil. The Irish have taught the labouring classes of this country a pernicious lesson. . . . Debased alike by ignorance and pauperism they have discovered, with the savage, what is the minimum of the means of life, upon which existence may be prolonged . . . As competition and the restriction and burdens of trade diminished the profits of capital, and consequently reduced the price of labour, the contagious example of ignorance and a barbarous disregard of forethought and economy exhibited by the Irish, spread.[19]

Kay's pamphlet was written during the panic induced by the cholera epidemic of 1832 and the Irish became the scapegoat for all the evils associated with early Victorian slums. The very notion of the urban slum was, in reality, a Victorian invention to provide a physical representation of the dangerous moral contagion of the under-class at the base of Victorian society.[20] Within the mental landscape of the educated middle classes, the 'savage and barbaric Irish' added human form to their worst fears that civilization itself was threatened by the contagion of numbers of the labouring poor. Engels, borrowing from Kay, in a strange, fantasy passage, likened the Irish to the animal condition of the pigs with whom they lived, ate, played and slept. The Irish fondness for potatoes, regarded as animal food by the English, confirmed the sub-human condition of poor, Irish migrants. Carlyle weighed in with his exaggerated prose style, deriding the wild, Milesian features of Irish vagrants, observed on the roadside.

Today, these accounts read as a hysterical response to what was seen as an invasion of destitute Irish who, allegedly, would take the jobs and lower the standards of the decent English and Scottish working class. Yet, for a long time, this body of writing was taken at face value as accurate descriptions of the condition of the Irish in early Victorian Britain. Both English and Irish historians agreed on the Irish in the Victorian ghetto.[21] The framework of the Irish as 'a problem' complemented the notion of the Irish in Britain continuing the long history of British oppression of Ireland. Recent research, carried out primarily by geographers, has undermined confidence in the moral certainties of Victorian commentators and severely qualified the notion of the Irish in the ghetto.

Lynn Lees, in a study of the Irish in mid-Victorian London, found that although the Irish were commonly identified with some of the vilest slums, they were not locked into ghettos but were mostly relegated to the back alleys or courts of their neighbourhoods. They lived close to English and European migrants, many lived in ordinary working-class districts, and clerks, teachers and a few middle-class professionals lived in predominantly English areas. Lees found that the Irish were present in every census district in London.[22] High concentrations of Irish, forming over 50 per cent of the population of a district, were comparatively rare, but these were just the areas of squalid housing that attracted the attention of sanitary reformers. The Irish who lived quietly in equal numbers and in lower concentrations in mixed centres of population went unnoticed. The London Irish were also a highly mobile population, moving from the riverside districts to the south and returning to traditional Irish quarters of central London wherever there was a demand for unskilled labour. Clearly, social class and employment opportunities were more important than ethnicity in determining the pattern of Irish settlement in London.[23]

John Papworth found similar results in studying the Irish in seven wards in 1841, located principally in the north and west of the city of Liverpool. After 1851, a shift in population occurred in the outlying districts of St Anne's and Scotland wards. Two discernible patterns were identified: a concentration and dispersal of Irish settlers. Only 50 per cent of the Irish-born lived in enumeration districts with a high concentration of Irish and these rarely contained more than half Irish. Papworth concluded that the terms 'ghetto' and 'colony' were not applicable to the Irish in Liverpool.[24] Geographers have identified the crucial importance of scale for an understanding of the condition of the Irish in Britain. At the street level, the perception of the Irish presence may have been alarming to the host community. At the level of the enumeration district, parish, township or county, in the way official figures were represented in recording only the Irish-born, there appeared less cause for concern.

More recently, the myth of 'Little Ireland', Manchester, has been laid to rest in the work of Mervyn Busteed.[25] A spacial analysis of the district in the 1851 census identified a degree of segregation between streets, with a predominance of Irish-born household heads physically separated from non-Irish households. J.P. Kay's lurid descriptions of the conditions in which the 'debased' Irish lived proved to be unsubstantiated and overthrown. All the available evidence pointed to conditions in the Irish part of the district as superior to the other part. Similar results were found in my own analysis of the notorious slum, Avon Street, in Bath. Negative press reporting of the Irish in the *Bath Chronicle*, particularly in the years of famine migration from County Cork, formed part of an atmosphere of scapegoating the Irish for the catalogue of poverty, overcrowding and epidemic disease that was associated with the 'plague spot' of Victorian Bath.[26] Lord Ashley, the future Lord Shaftesbury, philanthropist and champion of the oppressed, as one of the two city MPs, caught the mood of public anxiety in a speech in the Assembly Rooms in 1848, in proclaiming: 'Was it not found that where the Irish appeared wages were lowered, respectability disappeared, and slovenliness and filth prevailed?'[27] The 1851 census revealed a more sober picture. Firstly, the Irish presence was significant but not overwhelming. The 230 Irish-born inhabitants formed only 17.9 per cent of Avon Street's population. While concentrated at one end of the street in close proximity to one another and including an extreme case of 38 Irish out of 58 people in one lodging-house, they were virtually indistinguishable in terms of measurable indices from the rest of the working-class population of the street. Irish children attended school as commonly as their English neighbours, Irish adults had a high level of specified occupations and given the plight of famine migrants, remarkably few Irish were resident in the Bath Union Workhouse in 1851.[28]

However, it is as well to recognize that there is much that we do not know of the Irish in Britain, especially the internal evidence of personal experience. Apart from the broad surveys by J.E. Handley in Scotland, J.A. Jackson and K. O'Connor in England, most of what is known is built on the studies of individual towns and cities in England, Scotland and Wales.[29] Two very useful collections (with a third on its way) have been edited by Roger Swift and Sheridan Gilley which bring together many of the key articles.[30] What is interesting is the shift in emphasis between the first and second Swift and Gilley volumes on the Irish in Britain. The first was introduced with the notion of the outcast Irish, oppressed, alienated, suspected and discriminated against on account of their poverty, religion and politics. The second, by contrast, explored other themes and found a more varied picture of the Irish experience, thus casting doubt on uniform descriptions.

Diversity of the migrant experience

This shift in emphasis can be further developed in the recognition of diversity as a key concept in describing and explaining the Irish emigrant experience in Britain. Compare the two provincial cities of York and Bristol for the scale and character of Irish migration during the famine years. Whereas York experienced a very sharp rise in the numbers of Irish migrants and a concentration in poor quarters, Bristol experienced only a gradual increase in its Irish population, who were to be found in every part of the city. Most of the new migrants to York were from the decaying textile counties of Mayo and Sligo, while the Bristol Irish represented a wide variety of trades easily absorbed into the city's variegated labour market and were predominantly from County Cork, Dublin, Waterford and Limerick. Not surprisingly, Frances Finnegan found evidence of famine migrants facing a hostile reception in York in contrast with a more relaxed atmosphere before 1845.[31] The evidence of the Bristol papers suggests a contrasting and compassionate attitude to the Irish continued into the Famine years.[32]

Irish disorder can also be explained in terms of religious and cultural differences between Irish migrants and their place of settlement. The Irish in Bradford, Leeds and Manchester established a reputation for drunken violent behaviour, engaging in sectarian conflicts and Irish disputes over loyalty to different Irish counties. This included a fierce resistance by Irish women in the form of systematic stone throwing, to prevent the arrest of their menfolk by the local police. Concentrations of poor Irish, mixed settlement of Catholic and Protestant, east–west rivalries and the traditional distillation of spirits were contributing factors in the scale of Saturday night brawling. Yet, as Roger Swift has demonstrated in his study of the Irish in Wolverhampton, the concentration of Irish in Caribbee Island, a squalid and insanitary district, and the practice of illegal distillation and the sale of liquor in 'wabble shops', attracted police attention. The shops were singled out for special treatment with an aggressive form of policing aimed at suppressing the Irish population. The military style of policing was prompted by a proposal to reduce the numbers of police in Wolverhampton. In this case, and one wonders in how many others, the Irish population was deliberately picked on to provoke scenes of disorder and an increased level of convictions as a means of justifying and defending the size of the existing force.[33] The appointment of chief constables with experience of military-style policing in Ireland was also associated with Chartist activity in Lancashire towns, so reminding us that fear and alarm amongst the authorities could have the effect of making the Irish a target as scapegoats for disorder.[34] We should certainly beware of seeing the Irish experience only through the prism of Victorian middle-class assumptions.

What has attracted less attention than it deserves is the *absence* of serious disorder and conflict in places of Irish settlement. The reverse side of the coin to the pattern of violence observed in Bradford, Leeds, Manchester and Wolverhampton may be found in the relative tranquillity of Dundee, Hull and Bristol. Dundee experienced a rapid increase in Irish migration in the middle decades of the century and possessed at 18.9 per cent in 1851 as high a proportion of Irish settlement as any other Scottish city. The Irish in Dundee were predominantly Catholic and female and worked successfully in the expanding jute mills in the city. There was an absence of a distinctive Irish ghetto and of the sectarian divisions that occurred in Glasgow. Dundee was a staunchly Liberal town with a proud belief in religious toleration.[35] In Hull, the Irish-born represented only 3 per cent of its population in 1851. Appalling housing conditions, a death toll of 1,860 in the cholera epidemic in 1849, together with the Irish living in the poorest areas and prominent in local disorder, offered ripe conditions for trouble with the host community. The principal reason for the lack of serious conflict was the presence of a few key individuals in Hull who occupied positions of influence and authority. E.F. Collins, the editor of the *Hull Advertiser*, championed the cause of good housing, attacked religious bigotry and ended the deportation of Irish paupers. For 20 years he provided outstanding public leadership. In the field of public health reform he was supported by another Irishman, the local surgeon, Edward Owen Daly. Thirdly, the crucial post of Chief Constable of the Hull Police was held from 1836 to

1866 by Andrew McManners, who was drafted in from the Metropolitan Police. Between them, three Irishmen were able to exercise a sensitive handling of opinion and policy and ensure that the Irish in Hull were not made the subject of scapegoat abuse as in some other cities.[36]

Part of the fear of the host community lay with the advent of major cholera and typhoid epidemics in the 1830s and 1840s, which provoked a fervent hostility to Irish migrants as disseminators of killer diseases. Hard-pressed officials were tempted to use the Irish as a scapegoat in the face of epidemics that were beyond their control. The medical officer for the Cardiff Union identified the main cause of the increase in disease as the 'immense invasion of Irish destitute labourers, navigators and others, who had been brought over to this town by public works', and the majority of cases of fever 'may be said to have been imported direct from Skibbereen and Clonakilty'.[37] Faced with the same coincidence of epidemic disease and an Irish presence in the Sandgate area of Newcaste upon Tyne, Dr Robinson, in making a thorough investigation of the causes of the epidemic in 1846–47 did not even mention the Irish. The pattern was again repeated when cholera raged in 1853 and 350 lives were lost in a single parish. The Irish were not singled out for attack. The only body of people who tried to implicate the Irish were the outside commissioners for the Board of Health.[38] A different place evoked a different response.

Religious bigotry was a further cause of hostility to the Catholic Irish in Britain and sectarian conflict between Protestants and Catholics appeared to reinforce the Irish reputation for disorderly behaviour. Dramatic incidents such as the Stockport Riots in 1852, the Murphy Riots in 1867 and the repeated sectarian violence in Liverpool from the 1830s have tended to dominate our understanding of religious ill-treatment of Irish migrants. This has been explained in terms of a wider phenomenon of an endemic anti-Irish racism in Britain.[39] It has an obvious appeal to authorities who are attracted to a brand of oppression history that depicts Irish migrants as hapless victims forever condemned to a hopeless struggle against cruel adversity. While a blanket explanation has a particular ideological appeal, it tends to ignore the specific circumstances that can be found in each of the incidents and glosses over the fitful character of sporadic violence. It is also problematic in the suggestion of a uniform continuity of anti-Irish attitudes, suggested over a period of more than 150 years, based on the occurrence of single incidents at different times and in different places.

The Stockport Riots of 28–30 June 1852 coincided with the height of the Famine influx when the Irish were widely represented as a threat to the indigenous working population. Stockport was a one-industry cotton town facing a 10 per cent wage cut at a time of a trade depression. Nationally, the restoration of the Catholic hierarchy in England roused ancient Protestant fears of 'popery' on the march. Local Protestant leaders in Stockport whipped up anti-Catholic feeling and attacked the Irish community, who, when they retaliated, found themselves hauled before the magistrates for riot and disorder.[40] The Irish in Wolverhampton were associated with disease, crime and disorder, and the presence of militant Protestant preachers; Baron de Camin in 1859 and the notorious William Murphy in 1867, was accompanied by disturbances and rioting, as Irish Catholics protested against public attacks on their faith. The correspondence in the local press featured a debate over the issue of free speech versus public order. Moderate Protestants in Wolverhampton condemned the emotive Catholic baiting of the militants. It was the same with the Murphy Riots in Birmingham. The scurrilous methods employed to rouse anti-Catholic feeling served only to bring out the Catholic Irish in strength to demonstrate their disapproval of Murphy. In fact, moderate English opinion was appalled by the disorder that accompanied Murphy wherever he went. In truth, the Murphy Riots were anti-Murphy riots with a wish to preserve property and order, alongside a rejection of bigotry and prejudice.[41]

The Liverpool experience represented an extreme case where sectarian violence was encouraged by militant Protestants for political ends.[42] The legitimacy accorded to racial and religious bigotry by council officials, clergymen, and in newspaper editorials served to endorse street violence and indiscriminate attacks on Irish Catholics. By playing on fears of unemployment and in targeting the Irish presence as an explanation of social problems, like housing and crime, the authorities relieved themselves of the responsibility to find practical solutions. Even in Liverpool, which suffered from acute urban problems, militant Protestantism had an uncertain hold over the electorate or even within the Conservative party. Most Anglicans were neither Evangelical nor Tractarian in outlook, but believed in a broad Church and a degree of religious toleration. The leader of militant Protestantism in Liverpool, an Irish Anglican priest, Hugh McNeile, was a brilliant, pugnacious orator who revelled in the theatrical rough-and-tumble of democratic politics. His aggressive anti-Catholicism won over the crucial votes of Protestant dissenters, away from a Liberal allegiance, to the Tory side. With the very narrow majorities required with a limited franchise, it was possible to secure the control of the council through party organization targeting a small number of votes. So the Liberal triumph in 1835 based on 58 per cent of the votes cast was replaced by its disastrous defeat with 47 per cent in 1841. While the Tories remained the dominant force on Liverpool Council, McNeile's demagoguery was regarded as bitterly controversial and dangerous to social order, and ultimately as a threat to property. Humane voices were also raised in support of the plight of the Irish migrants in Liverpool. The warring factions in Liverpool politics probably represented a minority of opinion, and the Tory majority was secured as much by good organization as by an overwhelming hostility to the Catholic Irish.

In Edinburgh, a few instances of sectarian conflicts occurred in the 1850s and 1860s but rather less than in some other Scottish cities. Aspinwall and McCaffrey offer a structural explanation.[43] Edinburgh's social composition, with its rentier and professional classes living and working in a metropolitan city, attracted a higher number of English than Irish. The city prided itself on an enlightened Whiggish tradition, which incorporated religious toleration. Also Irish workers posed a real threat only to the employment of migrant Highlanders rather than to local labour in Edinburgh. In the longer term, the Catholic Irish achieved a social advance, assisted by self-help and better education. The Catholic Church, through the encouragement of thrift and self-improvement, cultivated a form of lace-curtain respectability. Bishop Gillis, its flamboyant leader, used his links with the local gentry to foster a concern for the Irish poor through the agencies of savings clubs, reading societies and boys' brigades. All these worthy activities recommended themselves to the Presbyterian Scots and eased the way for better relations between Protestants and Catholics.

In fact, the Victorian reformation of manners, normally seen as a Protestant phenomenon, was matched by a parallel Catholic mission to Irish migrants in Britain. In London, Lynn Lees found that Fr Mathew's crusade had broken the links between drinking and mass recreation in the 1830s and 1840s. His work paved the way for Cardinal Manning in the 1870s and 1880s, to develop a moral reformation, by borrowing the forms and tactics of the Salvation Army. The League of the Cross, temperance soldiers and brass bands were employed among the London dockers to ameliorate their condition. By the end of the century, the Catholic Church was no longer feared as a potentially subversive threat; rather it was recognized by its track record with poor Irish migrants as an important force for doing good.[44]

Irish labour

The theme of a duality of perception and a diversity of experience extends to the world of work. Modern economic historians have argued about the related questions of the Irish presence and the contentious issue of the standard of living question in the first half of the nineteenth century. Traditionally, the contemporary belief that Irish labour lowered real wages was endorsed by twentieth-century authorities such as Redford, Clapham and Pollard.[45] An allied assumption was that Irish migrants, a highly mobile, adaptable and above all cheap labour force, made a significant contribution to the progress of the British industrial revolution. The views of J.A. Jackson, J.E. Handley and E.P. Thompson may be grouped together, for convenience, as representing the *indispensability of Irish labour* to industrial growth in Britain.[46] Readers will detect a shift in emphasis and approach from a form of oppression history (Irish workers exploited with low wages) to a form of contribution history (Irish workers building the infrastructure of the nation).

A lack of reliable data on wages leaves the issue of lowering wages dependent on the views of contemporary witnesses such as the employers interviewed before the Commission on the State of the Irish Poor in 1836, but E.H. Hunt has questioned a reliance on what he describes as 'literary evidence' in place of quantitative assessments.[47] An attempt to fill the gap has been made by the Harvard economist Jeffrey Williamson, with a statistical measurement of the impact of the Irish on British labour markets during the period 1820–60. Williamson calculated that the proportion of Irish migrants into non-agricultural employment had the effect of crowding out native labour. He agreed with a comment in the 1836 report that if the Irish had not come to Britain, 'the demand for labour in the manufacturing districts of the North of England would, in part, have been satisfied by a migration from the south'.[48] He recognized that a predominantly adult Irish-born population had a higher labour participation rate than the rest of the British population, so reducing the social cost to the host community. Consequently, the Irish share of the British labour force rose from 3.4 to 8.8 per cent between 1821 and 1861, thus making its greatest impact during a period of rapid industrialization. For instance, during the 'Hungry Forties' almost a quarter of the increase in the British labour force was recruited from Ireland. Yet, despite these *contribution* features of Irish migrants, Williamson challenged the long-established view that Irish labour was critical in holding back a rise in living standards and in boosting industrialization in Britain.

If, as Williamson has argued, the level of Irish migration was 'simply too small to matter much, given the impressive absorptive capacity of the British economy', then other consequences would have followed. Without the Irish agriculture as a labour-intensive industry would have suffered from out-migration and wages in the rural south would have risen through a labour shortage. However, the speculation that agricultural labourers from the south of England would have moved north in search of industrial employment, if the Irish had not crowded them out, ignores the deep cultural conservatism and parochialism of rural communities. It begs the question why they failed to move to industrial towns doubling their wages at any time in the century. When Canon Girdlestone in 1866 began to organize the migration of labouring families from north Devon to northern industrial towns, he found some had never been more than a few miles from the parish and believed that Manchester was located somewhere overseas. To ensure that they arrived at the right destination, they had to be consigned to the railway company and labelled like so many evacuee children of a later generation.[49]

What is striking about Irish migrant labour is its marked diversity of experience. Different conditions affected seasonal harvesters, street traders, railway navvies, textile workers, dock workers and domestic servants. Not only the occupation but the place of settlement were vital in determining wages and conditions. So a general model that identified Irish migrants as a uniform, unskilled body is limited in terms of reconstructing the experience of the Irish in Britain.

Contemporary surveys of Irish labour provide examples of the degraded state of the Irish in Britain but also points to an improvement in their condition. In studying the street folk of mid-Victorian London, Henry Mayhew observed how Irish boys undersold the Jewish youths and were prepared to live harder, thus displacing them as competitors in the street orange trade.[50] In 1872, Hugh Heinrick contrasted the exploited Irish servant girls with the monopoly of Irish stevedores in the London docks.[51] Twenty years later, John Denvir reported how the Irish were spreading out into better districts and were increasingly found employed in the Civil Service as customs officials and in the Government Ordnance Survey. It was also observed how the Irish had risen from the ranks of costermongers at mid-century, to become substantial shopkeepers or wholesale traders and were represented in every profession.[52] In the prosperous north-east, the Irish earned good wages as artisans in shipbuilding, ironworks and chemicals. In the midlands, Heinrich found low wages and a depressed condition among the Irish in Burton-on-Trent, Kidderminster and Nottingham.[53] Yet among the Irish in Birmingham more progressive improvement was found in the building trades and in metal manufactures. There was also a greater degree of intermarriage and assimilation than in northern industrial towns, especially among the second generation.[54]

Local structures and conditions were a reflection of the regional economies that remained a vital part of Victorian Britain before the age of large-scale organizations and national wage negotiations. By avoiding low-wage employment in agriculture, except on a seasonal basis and settling in the major industrial centres, Irish migrants went where there was a demand for labour and continued to move from place to place as opportunities arose. Even as humble street traders, they were able to develop entrepreneurial skills that raised them to the marine store, to become respectable shopkeepers and property-owners. Irish lodging-house keepers and publicans thrived on the needs of their own communities.

By the end of the century, the descendants of mass migrants from the 1830s and 1840s were beginning to assert themselves as community leaders among the biggest ethnic minority in Britain. They had gained collectively along with the British working classes from a wider franchise, compulsory education, and the growth of trades unions. Irishmen had served with distinction in their thousands in the British army abroad, from the Crimea to South Africa, so it was not surprising that 150,000 fought in the Great War and specifically Irish batallions were raised in Glasgow, Edinburgh, London and Tyneside.[55]

The establishment of the Irish Free State in 1921 failed to mark the return home of the Irish in Britain. In fact, the old pattern of Irish emigration to Britain continued at a substantial rate during the 1920s. Most were still labourers or domestic servants, but 'a better class of emigrant' became more visible with an influx of graduates, mostly doctors and dentists. To serve the interests of these professional classes, the National University of Ireland Club was founded in London.[56] In terms of education, social status and cultural interests, members had little in common with their fellow countrymen among the working classes. The severe class divide of the interwar period was a reflection of British and Irish society. Arguably, women were less subject to the worst forms of anti-Irish prejudice that were still common in male labouring jobs and they were better able to make careers in nursing and teaching, or adjust to working conditions as office workers or domestic servants. Inevitably, assimilation through intermarriage with British partners was to have the effect of making the Irish in Britain at least partly British in outlook and identity.

A further change occurred in the emigrant flow from Ireland largely as the result of political change with the creation of the border between a Protestant Northern Ireland and a Catholic Irish Free State. The border reinforced the sectarian divide. From 1911 to 1926, the Protestants living in the 26 counties were reduced by a third, whereas the Catholic population fell by around 2 per cent. Between 1926 and 1946, the Protestant population dropped by almost a quarter at a time when the Catholic population increased.[57] Protestants, facing discrimination and hostility in a Catholic nation-state, were more likely to leave Ireland for Britain. The same process, in reverse, took place in Northern Ireland. Catholics, facing discrimination in housing and employment, were more prone to leave the province for Britain than their Protestant neighbours.

Whereas in Ireland, religious allegiance remained intense, it was eroded through the process of migration. Just as Catholic priests had feared, in counselling their flock against emigration at the risk of losing their faith, so it proved to be. Britain, increasingly secular after the First World War, had its influence on the Irish population, among whom half were seemingly untouched by organized religion, and were, in reality, non-practising.[58]

Cultural filters still apply as barriers to recognition of the complexity and diversity of the Irish migrant experience. In an independent Ireland, emigration was an embarrassment best ignored. Perhaps it was difficult for the leaders of the Irish Free State to recognize or identify with thousands of young, able and energetic people who continued to leave home and settle in the land of the conqueror. They enjoyed no voting rights in Ireland and little was done, except through voluntary agencies, to assist them in emigrating. The outbreak of the Second World War in 1939 and the reconstruction of postwar Britain were to throw up many new employment opportunities and the persistence of some old prejudices fuelled by the violence of 'the Troubles' that spilled over into Britain from Northern Ireland. Following the influx in the 1950s of Commonwealth immigrants, Britain's largest ethnic minority became incorporated into the politics of race relations and harnessed to the fashion for postcolonial theory which was retrospectively applied to the last century. The exposure of anti-Irish racism was lent credence by miscarriages of justice and discrimination amongst sections of the Irish in Britain while others shared in the growth of 'the affluent society'.

Throughout the period 1815–1939 and beyond, the chief characteristic of Irish migration to Britain and overseas was a positive movement of people in search of better economic opportunities that transcended the negative warnings of ministers of religion, ignored the condemnation of political leaders and broke free from the emotional ties of birthplace and family. Success was not guaranteed but the aspiration for a new life, cherished by the millions who left Ireland, forms a heroic, albeit uncomfortable part of the nation's history.

Notes

1. 'Emigration of the Irish Poor', *Liverpool Times*, reported in *The Nation*, 14 November 1846.
2. Jim MacLaughlin, *Ireland: The Emigrant Nursery and the World Economy* (Cork, 1994), pp. 23–30.
3. Donald H. Akenson, *The Irish Diaspora: A Primer* (Belfast, 1993), p. 192.
4. Cormac Ó Gráda has estimated that between 1852 and 1910 some 5 million people left Ireland, 1 million more than the official figures, and that most of the missing migrants went to Britain. Cormac Ó Gráda, 'A Note on Nineteenth-Century Irish Emigration Statistics', *Population Studies*, 29 (1973), pp. 143–9.

5. 'In terms of population, it has been calculated that 3.3 million people lived exclusively on the potato, that for 4.7 million it was the predominant item of diet, and that less than 0.7 million, on 25 per cent or less of a potato diet, could be said to be independent of the foodstuff.' Austin Bourke, *'The Visitation of God'?: The Potato and the Great Irish Famine*, ed. Jacqeuline Hill and Cormac Ó Gráda (Dublin, 1993), p. 52.

6. Brenda Collins, 'The Irish in Britain 1780–1921', in B.J. Graham and L.J. Proudfoot (eds), *An Historical Geography of Ireland* (London, 1993), pp. 375–6.

7. A few unlucky textile workers migrated from Ireland to Somerset and Wiltshire in the west of England only to find employment scarce when mills closed under the pressure of competition from the Yorkshire woollen cloth industry.

8. James H. Johnston, 'The Distribution of Irish Emigration in the Decade Before the Great Famine', *Irish Geography*, 21 (1988), pp. 78–87.

9. Bruce S. Elliot, *Irish Migrants in the Canadas: A New Approach* (Kingston, 1988).

10. Cecil J. Houston and W.J. Smyth, 'The Irish Diaspora: Emigration to the New World, 1720–1920', in Graham and Proudfoot (eds), *An Historical Geography of Ireland*, pp. 343–48.

11. Report on the State of the Irish Poor in Great Britain, Parliamentary Papers (1836) (40) XXX, iv, p. 432.

12. Roger Swift, 'The Historiography of the Irish in Nineteenth-Century Britain', in Patrick O'Sullivan (ed.), *The Irish World Wide, Vol. 2, The Irish in the New Communities* (Leicester, 1992), pp. 52–81.

13. David Fitzpatrick, 'Irish Emigration in the Late Nineteenth-Century', *Irish Historical Studies*, 22 (1980), p. 134.

14. Graham Davis, *The Irish in Britain, 1815–1914* (Dublin, 1991), pp. 75–6.

15. Ruth-Ann Harris, *The Nearest Place That Wasn't Ireland: Early Nineteenth-Century Irish Labor Migration* (Ames, 1994), p. 195.

16. Collins, 'The Irish in Britain 1780–1921', p. 372.

17. Ibid., p. 373.

18. J.P. Kay, *The Moral and Physical Condition of the Working Classes Employed in the Cotton Manufacture in Manchester* (1832), Friederich Engels, *The Condition of the Working Class in England* (1845) and Thomas Carlyle, *Chartism* (1839).

19. Kay, *The Moral and Physical Condition of the Working Classes*, pp. 21–2.

20. Graham Davis, 'Beyond the Georgian Facade: The Avon Street District of Bath', in S.M. Gaskell (ed.), *Slums* (Leicester, 1988), pp. 144–85.

21. See J.M. Werly, 'The Irish in Manchester, 1832–49', *Irish Historical Studies*, 18 (1972–73), pp. 345–58, and M.A.G. O'Tuathaigh, 'The Irish in Nineteenth-Century Britain: Problems of Integration', *Transactions of the Royal Historical Society*, 5th series, 31 (1981), pp. 149–74.

22. Lynn H. Lees, *Exiles of Erin: Irish Migrants in Victorian London* (Manchester, 1979), p. 63.

23. David Large also found the Irish were settled in every parish in Bristol, see D. Large, 'The Irish in Bristol in 1851', in R. Swift and S. Gilley (eds), *The Irish in the Victorian City* (London, 1985), pp. 37–58.

24. J. Papworth, 'The Irish in Liverpool, 1853–71: Family Structure and Residential Mobility', unpublished Ph.D. thesis (University of Liverpool, 1982).

25. Mervyn A. Busteed, Robert I. Hodgson and Thomas F. Kennedy, The Myth and Reality of Irish Migrants in Mid-Nineteenth-Century Manchester: A Preliminary Study', in O'Sullivan (ed.), *The Irish World Wide*, pp. 26–51.

26. Graham Davis, 'Social Decline and Slum Conditions: Irish Scapegoats in Bath's History', *Bath History*, 8 (forthcoming).
27. *Bath Chronicle*, 27 January 1848.
28. Graham Davis, 'Social Decline and Slum Conditions'.
29. J.E. Handley, *The Irish in Scotland, 1789–1845* (Cork, 1943), J.A. Jackson, *The Irish in Britain* (London, 1963), K. O'Connor, *The Irish in Britain* (London, 1972).
30. Swift and Gilley (eds) *The Irish in the Victorian City*; Roger Swift and Sheridan Gilley, *The Irish in Britain, 1815–1939* (London, 1989).
31. Frances Finnegan, 'The Irish in York', in Swift and Gilley (eds), *The Irish in the Victorian City*, p. 69.
32. Graham Davis, 'Little Irelands', in Swift and Gilley (eds), *The Irish in Britain, 1815–1939*, pp. 119–124.
33. Roger Swift, 'Another Stafford Street Row: Law and Order and the Irish Presence in mid-Victorian Wolverhampton', in Swift and Gilley (eds), *The Irish in the Victorian City*, pp. 179–206.
34. Stanley H. Palmer, *Police and Protest in England and Ireland, 1780–1850* (Cambridge, 1988), pp. 435–57.
35. W.A. Walker, *Juteopolis: Dundee and its Textile Workers, 1885–1923* (Edinburgh, 1979), pp. 113–47.
36. Edward Gillet and Kenneth A. MacMahon, *A History of Hull* (Oxford, 1980). I am also indebted to Jim Young of Hull WEA for his paper, 'The Irish in Hull', at the History Workshop Conference, Leeds, 1986.
37. H.J. Paine, *Report to the General Board of Health on the Town of Cardiff* (London, 1850), p. 44 in V.J. Hickey, 'The Origin and Growth of the Irish Community in Cardiff', unpublished M.A. thesis (University of Wales, 1959).
38. R.J. Cooter, 'The Irish in County Durham and Newcastle, c. 1840–1880', unpublished M.A. thesis (University of Durham, 1972), p. 57.
39. M. Hickman, *Religion, Class and Identity* (Aldershot, 1995).
40. P. Milward, 'The Stockport Riots of 1852: A Study of Anti-Catholic and Anti-Irish Sentiment', in Swift and Gilley (eds), *The Irish in the Victorian City*, p. 210.
41. Swift, 'Another Stafford Street Row', pp. 189–94; W.L. Arnstein, 'The Murphy Riots: A Victorian Dilemma', *Victorian Studies*, 19 (1975), pp. 51–71.
42. Frank Neale, *Sectarian Violence: The Liverpool Experience, 1819–1914* (Manchester, 1988), pp. 37–79.
43. Bernard Aspinwall and John McCaffrey, 'A Comparative View of of the Irish in Edinburgh in the Nineteenth-Century', in Swift and Gilley (eds), *The Irish in the Victorian City*, pp. 130–57.
44. For a fuller discussion of Irish Catholics and Protestants in a good regional study, see Donald M. MacRaild, *Culture, Conflict and Migration: The Irish in Victorian Cumbria* (Liverpool, 1998).
45. Arthur Redford, *Labour Migration in England* (London, 1926); J.H. Clapham, *An Economic History of Modern Britain* (Cambridge, 1930); Sydney Pollard, 'Labour in Great Britain', in P. Mathias and M.M. Postan (eds), *The Cambridge Economic History of Europe*, Vol. VII (Cambridge, 1978).
46. Jackson, *The Irish in Britain*; Handley, *The Irish in Scotland, 1789–1945*; E.P. Thompson, *The Making of the English Working Class* (London, 1963).
47. E.H. Hunt, *Regional Wage Variations in Britain, 1815–1914* (Oxford, 1973), p. 299.

48. Jeffrey Williamson, 'The Impact of the Irish on British Labour Markets during the Industrial Revolution', *Journal of Economic History*, XL, 3 (Sept. 1986), pp. 693–721; Report on the State of the Irish Poor, p. xxvi.
49. G.E. Mingay, *Rural Life in Victorian England* (London, 1979), p. 111.
50. Henry Mayhew, *London Labour and the London Poor* (London, 1864), Vol. II, p. 130.
51. Alan O'Day, *The Irish in England in 1872* (London, 1989), pp. 35, 69.
52. J. Denvir, *The Irish in Britain from the Earliest Times to the Fall and Death of Parnell* (London, 1892), pp. 437, 454.
53. O'Day, *The Irish in England in 1872*, pp. 49–55.
54. Denvir, *The Irish in Britain*, p. 415.
55. O'Connor, *The Irish in Britain*, p. 40.
56. Ibid., p. 44.
57. Akenson, *The Irish Diaspora*, pp. 208–9.
58. Gerard Connolly, 'Irish and Catholic: Myth and Reality? Another Sort of Irish and the Renewal of the Clerical Profession among Catholics in England 1791–1918', in Swift and Gilley (eds), *The Irish in the Victorian City*, pp. 225–54.

CHAPTER 2

Revising the Irish in Scotland: The Irish in Nineteenth- and Early Twentieth-Century Scotland

RICHARD B. MCCREADY

(Department of History, Dundee)

Introduction

This chapter seeks to set out an agenda to examine the role of the Irish in Scotland, in order to reassess currently held views of the part which they played in the recent history of Scotland. It will address the historiography of the Irish in Scotland, sectarianism, religion, politics, employment and assimilation, and finally will seek to place the Irish in Scotland in the context of the global Irish diaspora.

Historiography

The classic texts on the history of the Irish in Scotland are now 50 years old and are the work of James Edmund Handley.[1] There can be few other aspects of history where the definitive works are as old as in this case. Handley's works are an excellent source, having been extensively and thoroughly researched. His own background, as with that of all historians, may have somewhat coloured his view of the Irish in Scotland. He was Irish by birth and, probably more importantly, he was a religious brother in the Catholic Marist order. Indeed, Handley was famous in Catholic circles as Brother Clare, headmaster of the Marist order's then prestigious St Mungo's Academy in Glasgow. A recent important contribution to the discussion of the Irish in Scotland has been a volume of essays edited by Professor T.M. Devine.[2] This work contains essays from many of the leading scholars on the Irish in Scotland, although it is not a comprehensive history. More recently Devine has made a further contribution in his edited history of St Mary's Catholic Parish in Hamilton.[3] This type of localized study is very important, although it is obviously limited in this case to Catholic immigrants.

Over the past 20 years much has been added to our knowledge of the Irish in Scotland as many historians have published in this area. Tom Gallagher has given us detailed coverage of Glasgow and to a lesser extent Edinburgh.[4]

John McCaffrey and Bernard Aspinwall have published a range of work on Glasgow and the west of Scotland.[5] The many Protestants who migrated to Scotland from Ireland have been somewhat neglected in the past, although this position is presently being rectified by important contributions from a number of scholars.[6] In order to have a complete picture of the Irish in Scotland it is essential to remember that the immigrants were not only Roman Catholics.

Much of the above work is based on the experience of the Irish in Glasgow and the west of Scotland, as is the case with much of modern Scottish history. The Irish immigrant experience in Dundee or the east of Scotland has been largely ignored, although notable exceptions have been the work of Brenda Collins and the late W.M. Walker.[7] The historical analysis of the Irish in Britain has focused heavily on the west coast ports of Glasgow and Liverpool and their hinterlands. However, it is becoming increasingly clear that these cities may well be atypical of the Irish immigrant experience in Britain.[8] This experience must be looked at in areas other than Glasgow and Liverpool in order to get a broader picture of the Irish and their contribution to British society.

It is important to note that the Irish in Scotland were, as Roger Swift has noted of the Irish in Britain, 'by no means an homogeneous group, for their ranks contained both rich and poor, skilled and unskilled, Catholics and Protestants (and unbelievers), Nationalists and Loyalists, and men and women from a variety of distinctive provincial cultures in Ireland'.[9] Until historical writing takes account of this diversity then a definitive history of the Irish in Scotland is impossible. It is also useful to look further afield and compare the experience of the Irish in Scotland with the experience of the Irish diaspora in the USA, Canada, Australia, New Zealand and Argentina. Comparison should also be attempted between the experience of the Irish in Scotland and the experience of other immigrant groups arriving in Scotland, for example Italians, Germans, Poles, Russians, and even the English.[10] It may also be useful to compare the Irish with more modern migrants such as Asians in post Second World War Scotland.[11]

The Irish in Scotland

Professor T.M. Devine, perhaps the foremost Scottish historian of our day, has stated that, 'The immigration of the Irish into Scotland from the later eighteenth century forms one of the most significant themes of Scottish history'.[12] The influence of the Irish in Scotland was considerable, as can be seen when the percentage of Irish-born residents in Scotland is examined. In 1841 4.8 per cent of Scotland's population had been born in Ireland, but by 1851 this figure had risen to its peak at 7.2 per cent.[13] As Table 2.1 demonstrates, the Irish population in Scotland was proportionately higher than in England and Wales. The figures in Table 2.1 relate only to those born in Ireland and do not reflect the numbers of descendants of the Irish born in Scotland. The descendants of Irish immigrants saw themselves as Irish for several generations after their families had left Ireland and the indigenous community perhaps saw the descendants of immigrants as aliens for a longer period than they did themselves.[14]

Table 2.1: Irish-born in Britain

Year	England and Wales		Scotland	
	Number	% of population	Number	% of population
1841	289,404	1.8	126,321	4.8
1851	519,959	2.9	207,367	7.2
1861	601,634	3.0	204,083	6.7
1871	566,540	2.5	207,770	6.2
1881	562,374	2.2	218,745	5.9
1891	458,315	1.6	194,807	4.8

Adapted from: Roger Swift, *The Irish in Britain 1815–1914: Perspectives and Sources* (London, 1990), p. 12.

Another factor worth noting is that the national figures disguise important local and regional variations in the proportion of Irish-born: for example, in 1851, 18.9 per cent of Dundee's population had been born in Ireland as compared with a national figure of 7.2 per cent. More work is required on the Irish in small towns and villages in order to provide valid statistics: the east Dunbartonshire mining village of Croy, for example, was said locally to be entirely Irish and Catholic in its population, although this has not been substantiated.[15] In addition, although in general terms more Irish males came to Scotland than females, local studies would show that Dundee had a majority of female immigrants.

The traditional view of the Irish in Scotland has been dominated by concerns with Glasgow and the west of Scotland, and this is also true of Scottish historiography, especially on the period from the nineteenth century. Recently, however, historians have questioned the usefulness of the construct 'west of Scotland'.[16] This focus gives us a view of the Irish immigrant as male, a factory or engineering worker, a Celtic supporter, and frequently involved in sectarian violence. The reality of the Irish in Scotland is more complex than this picture allows. The Glasgow Irish were the largest element in the Irish community in Scotland but the Irish were prevalent in other areas. Ideas about the west of Scotland are also problematic as it is not always entirely clear which geographical areas are covered by the term. Often it refers only to Glasgow and the industrial areas of Lanarkshire but not necessarily areas such as Dunbartonshire, Ayrshire, Renfrewshire or west Stirlingshire. For example, the Dunbartonshire town of Kirkintilloch was the scene of one of the most important events in the history of the Irish in Scotland. This was the fire in a bothy in 1937 that resulted in the death of ten seasonal potato harvesters.[17] This tragedy led the Irish government to pay some attention to the plight of seasonal migrants.[18] This event has largely been ignored by historians of the Irish in Scotland; Tom Gallagher, for example, has described the event as having taken place in a 'remote agricultural district',[19] yet the fire took place no more than ten miles from Glasgow's city centre.

The experience of James Connolly in his early life can cast light on the lives of the Irish on the east coast of Scotland. Connolly was born in Edinburgh, he lived for the best part of a year in Dundee and was married in Perth. Indeed Connolly's thoughts on the Irish in Dundee can be seen as informative and he described Dundee thus: 'You could hear at once . . . the brogue of every county in Ireland, for there is not a county in the Emerald Isle but what sent its representatives here. I should think Dundee has, in proportion a stronger Irish population than any other town in Great Britain.'[20] It was in Dundee that Connolly began to be actively involved in politics and there is no doubt that his political career was hugely influential in modern Irish history.

There is scope for much more work on the many Irish communities in Scotland. A comparative analysis of Irish communities in areas with different geographical or industrial settings, with varying gender balances, and differing proportions of the different religious denominations, would be extremely useful.

Sectarianism

The history of the Irish in Scotland often appears to be a history of sectarian violence and the title of the most important work on communal relations in Glasgow, Gallagher's *Glasgow: The Uneasy Peace*, demonstrates this perception. Sectarianism is assumed to be the experience of the Irish in Scotland, but as Gallagher has stated there are difficulties in looking at the history of sectarianism in Scotland, since reliable information is difficult to find.[21] Sectarianism is accepted as a fact of life in Scotland but close examination of its origin and scope has been discouraged by many in the establishment.

Sectarianism was a complex issue in the nineteenth century, and took many forms in industrial Scotland.[22] It was more than a knee-jerk hatred; it was attractive to people because it offered individuals a positive identity as superior to some other group, which was becoming more important in an increasingly industrialized society.[23] There is a long history of sectarianism in Scotland dating back to the Reformation. Many of the laws of the state legitimized anti-Catholicism[24] and even as late as the twentieth century laws survived which limited the civil rights of Catholics.[25] Some of the worst sectarian violence in Scotland's history occurred in response to attempts to repeal anti-Catholic legislation in 1778–79 despite the fact that the size of the Catholic population in Scotland at this time was insignificant.[26]

Sectarianism in Scotland is often thought to have been imported from Ulster, where communal violence was fairly common and from where many Irish immigrants in Scotland originated. Communal violence led to many deaths in Ulster in the nineteenth century; this has never been the case in Scotland.[27] Despite this, some Scottish commentators believed that it was impossible for the Scots and the Irish to live in peace together. There was no doubt in their minds that the Irish were to blame for this: 'Donnybrook [fighting] is an institution that the Irish take about with them as the Jews did the Ark of the Covenant'.[28] Despite this claim there can be no doubt that sectarian violence was more prevalent in Ulster than in Scotland.

The entrepreneurial instincts of the Scots, and indeed the Irish, recognized that sectarianism was good for business. The best example of this is the 'Old

Firm' football rivalry between Celtic and Rangers.[29] Sectarian rivalry also helped to maintain high attendance levels at both Catholic and Protestant churches. Brown has suggested that the number of Catholics *per capita* could be used to predict the level of religious participation of all denominations in British cities.[30]

Sectarianism does not necessarily require violence; it can exist without physical conflict. In an analysis of the Irish in the north-east of England, Frank Neal has commented upon the lack of violence despite the fact that the remnants of sectarianism were still there.[31] In the context of Great Britain, Liverpool was the main focus of sectarianism; Scotland is said to represent the 'middle ground'.[32]

Many historians have focused their attention on incidents of sectarian violence and have therefore found it to be the experience of the Irish in Scotland. It is certainly the case that many historians have chosen to highlight hotspots of sectarian violence and tension rather than highlight the relatively peaceful experience which was the experience of the Irish in Scotland for the majority of the time. History is to a certain extent the study of things that have happened and not the study of things that did not, but it may be the case that for most of the time sectarian violence and tension were the 'dog that did not bark'. It is important to note that the lack of sectarian tension does not mean that communal relations were idyllic. The Irish were set apart from the host community and the Catholic Irish, at least, were culturally different from the indigenous Scottish population.

The prevalence of sectarianism may not be as great as has often been believed but there is no doubt that it was significant. For example, it is credited with having retarded the development of trade unionism in Scotland.[33] However, there are instances which contradict this general theory. In Dundee the Irish played a leading role in the establishment of the trade union in the jute industry, with the first secretary of the Jute and Flaxworkers' Union being also an official of the United Irish League in Dundee. Kenefick has also noted high levels of Irish involvement in dock unionism in Glasgow.[34]

The main commentator on the Irish in Dundee, W.M. Walker, has portrayed the situation in Dundee as different from the rest of Scotland. Walker has stated that communal relations were 'nothing like so black as . . . for the country in general'.[35] Gallagher has described Dundee as a 'city usually free of sectarian tension'.[36] This is true, but Dundee was not an idyllic city on the banks of the Tay where everyone lived in harmony. It experienced tension and, indeed, even violence.

Perhaps one of the most famous examples of sectarianism was found in the report of the 1923 General Assembly of the Church of Scotland entitled *The Menace of the Irish Race to our Scottish Nationality*. This report has had a huge impact on the historiography of the Irish in Scotland. The highpoint for sectarian tension in Scotland was the economically depressed years of the 1920s and 1930s. Many of the historians who have given us their view of sectarianism in Scotland lived through this period or were very influenced by it, and there is a tendency to extrapolate these experiences backwards into the nineteenth century.

Religion

Religion has also played a large part in the history of the Irish in Scotland. It often appears to be the case that the terms Irish and Catholic are interchangeable. Those modern-day Scots with an Irish identity tend to be Roman Catholics and this can obscure the fact that as many as one-third of the Irish immigrants to Scotland in the nineteenth century were Protestants.[37] There are several problems in studying the Protestant Irish in Scotland. The British government never collected data on religious denomination and place of birth, so the Protestant Irish are difficult to track. Many of the Protestant migrants came from Ulster, their forebears had emigrated from Scotland in the seventeenth and eighteenth centuries, so their names and customs resembled the indigenous population and allowed fairly rapid assimilation back into Scottish society.

Briefly, to set out the close association between Catholicism and the Irish, it was in many respects a product of the growth of Irish nationalism in the nineteenth century. Despite some famous examples of Protestant leaders of Irish nationalism, the Home Rule movement was largely a Catholic movement. It has been argued that in the nineteenth century the Irish were losing elements of their identity. For example, the Irish language was in decline, whereas the use of the Irish language had previously set the Irish apart from the rest of the United Kingdom. The nationalist Irish felt the need to emphasize the differences between themselves and the British. With reductions in the cultural distinctiveness of the Irish, many looked for alternative marks of distinction and Catholicism served this purpose. The dominance of the Catholic Irish in the history of the Irish in Scotland also reflects the personal background of many of the historians who have studied the subject.[38] It also reflects the fact that the present-day Catholic Church in Scotland represents an easily identifiable minority. Unfortunately there are few similar reminders of the immigration of the Protestant Irish.

In the nineteenth century the Protestant Irish certainly made their presence felt in Scotland. Perhaps the most obvious contribution of the Protestant Irish to Scottish society was the Orange Order, formed in September 1795 near Loughgall in County Armagh. It was established as a defensive society after attacks on Protestants by the Catholic Defender organization.[39] The Orange Order was to be found in Scotland as early as 1799 or 1800 and it is likely that the first Scottish Orangemen were in fact Irish immigrants.[40] It has often been stated that for the Orange Order to be vibrant in a specific area there needs to be a strong Irish Protestant immigrant community.[41]

The Orange Order was to be found all over industrial Scotland, including Dundee, despite Dundee having been described as peaceful in terms of sectarianism. Many of Dundee's Orangemen were members of the Church of Ireland before emigrating to Dundee, and there is evidence of high levels of Orange membership in the Scottish Episcopalian Church (the local branch of the Anglican Communion) in Dundee. The city of Dundee was the centre of ritualism in the Scottish Episcopalian Church.[42] The Episcopal mission of St Mary Magdalene in Dundee had a largely Orange Irish congregation. The incumbent of this mission was William Humphrey, a ritualist, who eventually became a Jesuit priest and was mentioned as a possible Roman Catholic bishop at the restoration of the hierarchy. In 1867 he irritated his Protestant congregation when on Sunday 12 July he followed Catholic liturgical practice for 'ordinary Sundays' and dressed the altar in green frontals.[43] Many members of this congregation eventually formed their own congregation of St John's Church of England in Dundee. This was an evangelical low church congregation more suited to the ecclesiastical tastes of Irish Protestant immigrants.

Clearly the history of the Irish in Scotland has to take account of the religious diversity of the immigrants including the Irish Protestant immigrants to be found throughout the country.

Politics

The Irish had a huge impact on Scottish politics in the nineteenth and twentieth centuries. To a large extent this was due to the important place of the Irish Question in late nineteenth- and early twentieth-century Britain.

The nationalist Irish found their political expression in the various Home Rule movements which existed at different times. However, despite what may be implied from much of what has been written, involvement in Irish nationalist politics was a minority pursuit amongst the immigrant community.[44] This having been said, Irish nationalist organizations were believed to exert considerable influence. To take the example of Dundee, in the famous 1908 by-election Churchill felt it necessary to visit meetings of the United Irish League and he went on to declare that his victory was 'a victory for Ireland!'.[45] The Irish vote was believed to be strong in some areas and many prominent politicians felt the need to placate their Irish constituents.

The nationalist Irish in Scotland had, for the most part, a very close relationship with the Liberals. Only in the famous case of the Parnell manifesto of 1885 did they generally vote Conservative. The instruction to vote against the Liberals on Parnell's orders created some anomalies and the Irish nationalists in the Blackfriars division of Glasgow were instructed to vote for the leader of Glasgow's Orangemen.[46] The Dundee Irish were instructed to vote for Edward Jenkins, formerly a Liberal MP for the town who had written what many considered to be an anti-Irish satirical book.[47]

Scotland was mainly represented by Liberals from the passing of the 1832 Reform Act until the beginning of the twentieth century. The Conservatives did badly in this period in Scotland, and nationalist Irish did not support them apart from one instance in 1885. Protestant or Unionist Irish immigrants had a close association with the Conservatives, as did the Orange Order. Working-class Protestants, many of whom had an Ulster background, helped to establish the Tories as a strong party in twentieth-century Scotland. The impact of Ireland upon Scottish politics is demonstrated by the fact that the Conservatives called themselves the Unionist Party in Scotland from 1912 until 1964[40] and under this title in 1955 they achieved the greatest share of the popular vote ever achieved by any party in Scotland.

In the twentieth century the Irish Catholic community in Scotland has become closely associated with the Labour Party.[49] Initially the Catholic Irish were believed to be holding back the advance of Labour in Scotland. However, Labour has never achieved majority support in Scotland and this singling out of the Irish for condemnation is surprising. Labour supported state-funding for Catholic schools and the granting of Home Rule to Ireland and this led the Irish to support Labour in the period after 1918. To this day Catholics are more likely to vote Labour than their counterparts in every socio-economic group in Scotland.

The Irish, both Catholic and Protestant, have played a major role in Scottish politics. In many respects this has been portrayed in simplistic terms and more detailed analysis is required. In terms of elected office it is only in the period since the 1960s that the descendants of Irish immigrants have really made an impact in Scottish politics. This contrasts somewhat with the experience in the USA.

Employment

The traditional romanticized image of the Irish migrant is that of a starving peasant being forced from his home by a rapacious landlord or the British government (or both). Irish emigrants left Ireland in search of work and in Scotland they have traditionally been viewed as having taken jobs in the lowest occupational groups.[50] They found these jobs because they were illiterate or unskilled. Swift suggests that they occupied the lower end of the occupational scale as a result of their 'lack of skill, capital and education; their low expectations and high leisure preferences, including a propensity to drink; the perceived impermanence of their residence in Britain, coupled with their contempt for authority, especially British authority; and the discrimination they faced from British employers and workers'.[51] It is also claimed that the fact that passage to Britain was the cheapest emigrant route from Ireland meant that those who did come to Britain were amongst the poorest emigrants. This is held to demonstrate their lack of skill, because it suggests that they earned either poor wages or no wages.[52]

The Catholic Irish are alleged to have shown little regard for 'getting on'; indeed 'getting on' was viewed within their communities as dangerous, leading as it often did to a loss of Catholicism or Irishness.[53] Another indicator of the attitude of the Irish towards 'getting on' can be seen in the fact that the occupational patterns established by the original migrants were likely to be followed for several generations by their descendants.[54] Whilst not achieving social or economic mobility, the Irish in Scotland were held to have been happy to work for lower wages and for longer hours. Even Keir Hardie, the Labour leader, could say that Irish coalminers in Lanarkshire had 'a big shovel, a strong back and a weak brain' and that they produced 'coal enough for a man and a half'.[55] It is often assumed that Irish immigrants caused a general reduction in wages and as Williamson has pointed out this would be true *ceteris paribus* but where the Irish were concerned *ceteris paribus* may not always have operated. It may be the case in a number of situations that the Irish took lower wages than the indigenous population without lowering the indigenous population's wage rates.[56]

There is often an image of the Irish gathered in one industry employed only in menial tasks, but this neglects the one asset the Irish did have which was their adaptability. In his assessment of the town of Greenock, Lobban has demonstrated that the Irish migrants were to be found in all the industries in the town, whilst Highland migrants were concentrated in one industry.[57] Many Irish emigrants left Ireland without marketable skills, indeed left in search of their first paid employment.[58] Their adaptability was the major feature that the Irish had to offer employers.

There were those amongst the emigrants, who were successful mostly through serving their own community. Small groups of businessmen, such as publicans and shopkeepers, and professionals, such as lawyers and doctors, came from the Irish immigrant stock and served the needs of their own community.[59] Writing in 1892, John Denvir had noted that a feature of Scottish towns with Irish communities was the number of Irish publicans and pawnbrokers.[60]

Irish emigration was largely a movement of families as the Irish tended to move to places where they had family or friends already established. The Dundee Irish, as we shall see, exemplified this. It was mainly young women who moved to Dundee because they knew of the job opportunities in the town specifically for women and also that there were many people who had already settled there from their own areas, southern Ulster and northern Leinster.[61]

Domestic service was a major employer of female members of the Irish diaspora, especially in the USA.[62] In Britain this appears not to have been the case. In York a few Irish women were employed in domestic service,[63] yet in Dundee Irish servants seem virtually non-existent.[64] In spite of their reputation for lawlessness and disloyalty, large numbers of Irishmen were found in the British army. Indeed the proportion of Irishmen in the British army exceeded the proportion of Irish people in the population of the United Kingdom.[65] James Connolly and his family were descendants of Irish immigrants and served in the British army. In Scotland the Irish were less likely to join the police than the Irish in other areas. Cinema and television give us a picture of the police force in the USA being staffed by Irish immigrants and their descendants and in New South Wales in 1872 the police force was dominated by the Irish, with over half of the force having been born in Ireland.[66]

As we have noted elsewhere, Dundee had a majority of female immigrants whilst the majority of Irish immigrants in other areas of Scotland were male. The main exceptions to the male dominance of Irish immigration into Britain was in textile towns, such as Dundee and Bradford.[67] In Dundee the Irish were said to have influenced the social and industrial structure of the town.[68] Similar claims are made about the city of Butte in Montana which was a steel-producing town.[69] The Irish came to Dundee knowing that they had useful skills which were in need in the city. Dundee's jute and flax industry grew at an opportune time for them, just as the textile industry in Cavan and Monaghan was in decline. Indeed, Dundee provided a place for people from these areas to continue to use their old skills.

The Irish who migrated from Ireland in the nineteenth century were, on the whole, economic migrants; they left their homes in order to find a more secure economic future. For most of those who left, and certainly for most who came to Scotland, emigration represented a rational decision to go to an area where the migrant knew that there were jobs and/or family and friends.

Assimilation

Many studies of the Irish world-wide have focused upon the assimilation or integration of the Irish within their host community. Assimilation is the process through which the immigrant comes to be accepted by the host community, either by adapting to or learning the customs and practices of the hosts.[70] This process is said to have been slow in Scotland. Scotland as a nation without a state expressed its national identity in non-political forms defining itself through its legal system, its education system, and most importantly in the nineteenth century through its religion. The majority of Scots belonged to Presbyterian churches and many saw Presbyterianism as a defining quality of the Scottish nation.[71] This may have made it harder for the Irish in Scotland to assimilate than it was in other countries, for example in the 'melting pot' of the USA. In the USA there were far more immigrant groups and so it was possible to assimilate more quickly, if not easily, than in Scotland. There was a constant stream of large-scale immigration into the USA from all parts of Europe. In Scotland it would take almost one hundred years for there to be any further large-scale immigration; this was the immigration of Asians in the period after 1945.[72]

Many of those who found themselves in Scotland intended to emigrate onwards elsewhere, with many expecting to earn some money and then leave for America. For those who intended eventually to move further afield there was no need initially to attempt to assimilate into Scottish society, even though many of them never made it to the USA.[73]

The popular view of the Irish in Scotland is that they lived in isolation from the rest of society. In social terms this was largely true in that it would have been possible for Irish Catholic migrants in Scotland to have led an entirely separate social life, with their own churches, schools, public houses, political societies, football teams and other forms of entertainment. However, in terms of housing, the Irish did not live separately in 'ghettos'.

As has been noted already, the Irish are said to have influenced the social make-up of Dundee, and so to a certain extent the Scots also had to assimilate. In cases such as this the similarity to the Irish way of life may have influenced the choice of destination by the migrant.[74] Another example of this may be the choice by many Ulster Protestants of Scotland as their destination. The Protestant culture of many migrants into Scotland facilitated their assimilation into Scotland's Protestant culture.

The Catholicism of the majority of the Irish who came to Scotland is often held to have slowed their assimilation into Scottish society. However, the Catholic Church in Scotland played an important role in integrating the migrants into

Scottish society. The leaders of Scottish Catholicism well into the twentieth century came from impeccable Caledonian stock and had no real wish for their flocks to remain Irish unless as a means of retaining their Catholicism. The Catholic Church worked hard to encourage its members to accept their place in Scottish society.[75] There was, however, one way in which the Catholic Church retarded this integration into Scottish society: through opposition to inter-marriage, that is marriage to non-Catholics. The Catholic Church in Scotland always discouraged marriage between Catholics and Protestants, fearing that it would lead to a diminution of the membership of the Catholic Church, and sometimes stressing publicly that it would weaken ethnic allegiances.[76]

War was the greatest factor in the assimilation of the Irish in Scotland. It was by playing a full part in the British and Scottish efforts during the First World War that the Irish came to be regarded as truly part of Scottish society. The internecine conflict in Ireland in the Civil War also persuaded many of the Irish in Scotland to break their mental links with Ireland.[77] In Dundee, in the aftermath of the assassination of Michael Collins, an Irish priest, Father Fahy of St Patrick's parish, said he would 'never mention Ireland again in his church'. By this point in time, few of the Irish in Scotland had personal experience of Ireland and they realized, as the future Labour Minister John Wheatley did, that they would not be 'returning to Ireland'.[78]

Conclusion

There is a wealth of literature on the Irish diaspora world-wide but the experience of the Irish in Scotland has rarely been compared and contrasted with the experience elsewhere. If it had been it would be easier to identify those characteristics which were common to the Irish experience world-wide and those which were common only to the Irish in Scotland. It is also clear that to understand fully the Irish in Britain we must take a closer look at the Irish in Scotland. The Irish in Scotland formed a proportionately larger part of the population than the Irish in England did, and were, in this sense, more significant in Scotland. It is clear that the experience of the Irish in Scotland is more complex than popular perceptions of it allow. There is a genuine need to examine the Irish in Scotland in greater detail to get a fuller picture of the reality of this experience. In so doing we will be able to revise the 'Irish in Scotland'.

Notes

1. James Edmund Handley, *The Irish in Scotland 1798–1845* (Cork, 1945); James Edmund Handley, *The Irish in Modern Scotland* (Cork, 1947). A somewhat edited version of these two volumes was published as James E. Handley, *The Irish in Scotland* (Glasgow, 1964).
2. T.M. Devine (ed.), *Irish Immigrants and Scottish Society in the Nineteenth and Twentieth Centuries* (Edinburgh, 1991).
3. Thomas M. Devine (ed.), *St. Mary's Hamilton: A Social History 1846–1996* (Edinburgh, 1995).

4. Tom Gallagher, *Glasgow: The Uneasy Peace. Religious Tension in Modern Scotland* (Manchester, 1987); Tom Gallagher, *Edinburgh Divided: John Cormack and No Popery in the 1930s* (Edinburgh, 1987).

5. For example, John F. McCaffrey, 'The Irish vote in Glasgow in the Later Nineteenth Century: A Preliminary Survey', *Innes Review*, 21 (1970) pp. 30–1; Bernard Aspinwall, 'Popery in Scotland: Image and Reality, 1820–1920', *Records of the Scottish Church History Society*, 21 (1986) pp. 235–57.

6. Elaine McFarland, *Protestants First: Orangeism in Nineteenth-Century Scotland* (Edinburgh, 1990); Graham Walker and Tom Gallagher (eds), *Sermons and Battle Hymns: Protestant Popular Culture in Modern Scotland* (Edinburgh, 1991); Graham Walker, *Intimate Strangers: Political and Cultural Interaction Between Scotland and Ulster in Modern Times* (Edinburgh, 1995); William S. Marshall, *The Billy Boys: A Concise History of Orangeism in Scotland* (Edinburgh, 1996); Steve Bruce, *No Pope of Rome: Anti-Catholicism in Modern Scotland* (Edinburgh, 1985).

7. Brenda E.A. Collins, 'Aspects of Irish Immigration Into Two Scottish Towns (Dundee and Paisley) During the Mid-Nineteenth Century', unpublished M. Phil. thesis (University of Edinburgh, 1978); W.M. Walker, 'Irish Immigrants in Scotland: Their Priests, Politics, and Parochial Life', *Historical Journal*, 15 (1972) pp. 649–67.

8. See Roger Swift, 'The Irish in Nineteenth Century Britain: Towards a Definitive History?', *Labour History Review*, 57, 3 (1992) pp. 8–12.

9. Roger Swift, *The Irish in Britain 1815–1914: Perspectives and Sources* (London, 1990), p. 4.

10. See, for example, David Stockdale, 'Dundee and European Migrants: 1860–1930', in C.A. Whatley (ed.), *The Remaking of Juteopolis: Dundee c. 1891–1991* (Dundee, 1991).

11. See Bashir Maan, *The New Scots: The Story of Asians in Scotland* (Edinburgh, 1992).

12. T.M. Devine, 'Introduction', in Devine (ed.), *Irish Immigrants and Scottish Society*, p. v.

13. Callum G. Brown, *The Social History of Religion in Scotland since 1730* (London, 1987), p. 46.

14. M.A.G. Ó Tuathaigh, 'The Irish in Nineteenth-Century Britain: Problems of Integration', in Roger Swift and Sheridan Gilley (eds), *The Irish in the Victorian City* (London, 1985), p. 15.

15. Olive and Sydney Checkland, *Industry and Ethos: Scotland 1832–1914* (Edinburgh, 1984), p. 94. In administrative terms Croy is now in North Lanarkshire.

16. Catriona MacDonald, 'Deconstructing the "West of Scotland": or, a Challenge to a Historiographical Expedient, Paisley Politics, 1885–1910', *The Association for Postgraduate Scottish Historical Research* (Glasgow, 1994).

17. Heather Holmes, 'The Kirkintilloch Bothy Fire Tragedy of September 16, 1937: An Examination of the Incident and the Resulting Legislation', *Review of Scottish Culture*, 9 (1995–96) pp. 57–75; National Archives of Ireland [hereafter NAI], Department An Taoiseach S10278, S10186, S10191A.

18. NAI, Department An Taoiseach, S10191A.

19. Gallagher, *Glasgow: The Uneasy Peace*, p. 123.

20. James Connolly in Dundee to Lillie Reynolds in Perth, 17 April 1888, James Connolly papers, National Library of Ireland, Ms. 13911.

21. Gallagher, *Glasgow: The Uneasy Peace*, p. 3.

22. Tom Gallagher, 'A Tale of Two Cities: Communal Strife in Glasgow and Liverpool Before 1914', in Swift and Gilley (eds), *The Irish in the Victorian City*, p. 106.

23. John Belchem, 'Britain, United States and Australia: Some Comparative Reflections', *Labour History Review*, 57, 3 (1992), p. 5.

24. Robert Kent Donovan, 'Voices of Distrust: The Expression of Anti-Catholic Feeling in Scotland, 1778–1781', *Innes Review*, 30 (1979), p. 64.

25. Brown, *The Social History of Religion in Scotland*, pp. 235–6.

26. Ibid., p. 164.

27. Sean Connolly, *Religion and Society in Nineteenth-Century Ireland* (Dublin, 1994), p. 22.

28. George Malcolm Thomson, *Caledonia or the Future of the Scots* (London, c. 1927), p. 14.

29. Bill Murray, *The Old Firm: Sectarianism, Sport and Society in Scotland* (Edinburgh, 1984).

30. Callum G. Brown, 'The Mechanism of Religious Growth in Urban Societies: British Cities since the Eighteenth Century', in Hugh McLeod (ed.), *European Religion in the Age of Great Cities* (London, 1995), p. 253.

31. Frank Neal, 'Ethnic Conflict in the North East of England: The Case of the Irish Immigrants', *Labour History Review*, 57, 3 (1992), p. 13.

32. John Wolffe, *The Protestant Crusade in Great Britain, 1829–1860* (Oxford, 1991), pp. 192, 195, 196.

33. Alan B. Campbell, *The Lanarkshire Miners: A Social History of their Trade Unions* (Edinburgh, 1979), p. 157.

34. William Kenefick, 'Irish Dockers and Trade Unionism on Clydeside', *Irish Studies Review*, 19 (1997), pp. 22–9.

35. W.M. Walker, *Juteopolis: Dundee and its Textile Workers 1885–1923* (Edinburgh, 1979), pp. 120–1.

36. Gallagher, *Glasgow: The Uneasy Peace*, pp. 150–1.

37. Brown, *A Social History of Religion in Scotland* pp. 45–6; Donald Harman Akenson, *The Irish Diaspora: A Primer* (Toronto and Belfast, 1993), p. 191.

38. For example, James Edmund Handley was a Marist Brother.

39. Connolly, *Religion and Society in Nineteenth-Century Ireland*, p. 20.

40. McFarland, *Protestants First*, p. 49.

41. Ibid., p. 103.

42. See Rowan Strong, *Alexander Forbes of Brechin: The First Tractarian Bishop* (Oxford, 1995).

43. Ibid., p. 86.

44. See John F. McCaffrey, 'Irish Issues in the Nineteenth and Twentieth Century: Radicalism in a Scottish Context?', in Devine (ed.), *Irish Immigrants and Scottish Society*, pp. 116–37.

45. *Dundee Catholic Herald,* 16 May 1908.

46. Catriona Burness Levy, 'Conservatism and Liberal Unionism in Glasgow, 1874–1912', unpublished Ph.D. thesis (University of Dundee, 1983), p. 122.

47. *Dundee Advertiser*, 25 November 1885.

48. Levy, 'Conservatism and Liberal Unionism in Glasgow', p. 460. Officially, in Scotland, they are now called the Scottish Conservative and Unionist Party.

49. Tom Gallagher, 'Catholics and Scottish Politics', *Bulletin of Scottish Politics*, 2 (1981), p. 23.

50. R.D. Lobban, 'The Irish Community in Greenock in the Nineteenth Century', *Irish Geography*, 6, 3 (1971), p. 275; Bernard Aspinwall and John F. McCaffrey, 'A

Comparative View of the Irish in Edinburgh in the Nineteenth Century', in Swift and Gilley (eds), *The Irish in the Victorian City*, p. 145.

51. Swift, *The Irish in Britain 1815–1914*, p. 17.
52. Jeffrey G. Williamson, 'The Impact of the Irish on British Labor Markets during the Industrial Revolution', in Roger Swift and Sheridan Gilley (eds), *The Irish in Britain 1815–1939* (London, 1989), p. 139.
53. Frances Finnegan, *Poverty and Prejudice: A Study of Irish Immigrants in York 1840–1875* (Cork, 1982), p. 119.
54. Gallagher, 'A Tale of Two Cities', p. 109.
55. Ibid., p. 110.
56. Williamson, 'The Impact of the Irish on British Labor Markets', p. 135.
57. Lobban, 'The Irish Community in Greenock', p. 271.
58. Fitzpatrick, *Irish Emigration 1801–1921*, p. 8.
59. John Archer Jackson, *The Irish in Britain* (London, 1963), p. 113; Martin J. Mitchell, 'The Catholic Community in Hamilton, *c.* 1800–1914', in Devine (ed.), *St. Mary's Hamilton*, p. 36.
60. John Denvir, *The Irish in Britain from the Earliest Times to the Fall and Death of Parnell* (London, 1892), p. 447.
61. David Fitzpatrick, 'Emigration, 1801–70', in W.E. Vaughan (ed.), *Ireland Under the Union I, 1801–1870: A New History of Ireland Vol. 5* (Oxford, 1989), p. 603; Collins, 'Aspects of Irish Immigration', *passim.*
62. John B. Duff, *The Irish in the United States* (Belmont, Ca., 1971), p. 18.
63. Finnegan, *Poverty and Prejudice*, pp. 5–6.
64. I am grateful to Dr Jan Merchant for this information. Dr Merchant's thesis was on domestic servants in Dundee.
65. David Large, 'The Irish in Bristol in 1851: A Census Enumeration', in Swift and Gilley (eds), *The Irish in the Victorian City*, p. 45.
66. Patrick J. O'Farrell, 'The Irish in Australia and New Zealand, 1791–1870', in Vaughan (ed.), *Ireland under the Union*, I, p. 674.
67. Colin G. Pooley, 'Segregation or Integration? The Residential Experience of the Irish in Mid-Victorian Britain', in Swift and Gilley (eds), *The Irish in Britain*, p. 66.
68. Collins, 'Aspects of Irish Immigration', pp. 237–8.
69. David M. Emmons, 'Faction Fights: The Irish Worlds of Butte, Montana, 1875–1917', in Patrick O'Sullivan (ed.), *The Irish in the New Communities* (Leicester, 1992), pp. 82–98.
70. J.A. Jackson, *Migration* (London, 1986), p. 7.
71. Tom Gallagher, 'The Catholic Irish in Scotland: In Search of Identity?', in Devine (ed.), *Irish Immigrants and Scottish Society*, p. 34.
72. Ibid., p. 31.
73. David Fitzpatrick, 'A Curious Middle Place: The Irish in Britain, 1871–1921', in Swift and Gilley (eds.), *The Irish in Britain*, p. 10.
74. Brenda Collins, 'Irish Emigration to Dundee and Paisley during the First Half of the Nineteenth Century', in J.M. Goldstrom and L.A. Clarkson (eds), *Irish Population, Economy, and Society* (Oxford, 1981), p. 195.
75. Bernard Aspinwall, 'The Catholic Irish and Wealth in Glasgow', in Devine (ed.), *Irish Immigrants and Scottish Society*, p. 91.
76. Collins, 'Aspects of Irish Immigration', pp. 85–6.
77. Gallagher, 'The Catholic Irish in Scotland', pp. 29–30.
78. Ibid., p. 34.

CHAPTER 3

Emigration from Ireland to Britain during the Second World War

TRACEY CONNOLLY

(Department of History, University College, Cork)

We had people and we exported them faster than cattle and like cattle . . .[1]

Emigration from Ireland during the Second World War marked a watershed in Irish emigration history. The aim of this chapter is to examine the main reasons for emigration to Britain, and to establish the profile of the typical wartime emigrant. In addition it assesses the impact of wartime emigration on Ireland.

From the early 1930s Britain replaced the United States of America as the destination favoured by Irish emigrants. The extent of Irish emigration to Britain during the 1930s and 1940s is revealed in the 1951 census where 627,021 Irish-born persons were enumerated as living in England and Wales, compared with 381,089 in the 1931 census.[2] In the same years the number of Irish-born living in Scotland actually declined. It is apparent that the depression significantly reduced Irish emigration to the United States, during which time the majority of Irish emigrants went to Britain, which became firmly established as the most popular destination for Irish emigrants. Disruptions in transatlantic travel during the war further curtailed emigration to the United States and other countries. Demand for labour in Britain was intense throughout the war years. Irish emigration to Britain therefore surged during the Second World War.

Much controversy surrounds the net emigration figure for the period. The 1946 Irish census put the total net emigration figure for the period 1936–46 at 189,942, an increase of 13.9 per cent since the 1926–36 census.[3] Emigration figures during the war were not dealt with in the 1946 census, but it can be assumed that the increase in emigration took place at the latter end of the census period, namely during the war years, as emigration during the 1930s was slight. The figure generally accepted for the war years is 26,000,[4] although this is questionable. Permits were required for Irish persons travelling to Britain and according to a Department of External Affairs memorandum on emigration a total of 172,574 permits were issued for persons travelling to Britain and Northern Ireland from 1941 to 1945, an annual average of

Table 3.1: Number of Eire-born serving in the British forces, September 1939 to February 1945

Men			Women		
Army	Royal Air Force	Total	Auxiliary Territorial Service	Women's Auxiliary Air Force	Total
27,840	9,600	37,440	3,060	1,450	4,510

Source: Public Records Office London (PROL) DO.35/1230, WX132/1/124.

34,514.[5] For 1940 the figure was 25,964, making a total figure of 198,538 for the years 1940–45.[6] This suggests that 26,000 per annum is too low. Delaney claims that at least 100,000 travelled to Britain from the Irish Free State during the war.[7] According to the Home Office statistics there were about 100,000 Irish labourers (from north and south) in Britain in July 1943,[8] but this appears to include emigrants who arrived in Britain before the war. In addition, many proceeded to Britain as visitors but took up employment and did not return. It is probable that there was much overlap between those who claimed to be going as visitors and those going as workers. Some were seasonal workers, who cannot be properly classified as 'emigrants' as the duration of their stay was brief. It was possible for the same person to hold more than one travel permit, which inflated statistics. In addition, it is impossible to know how many actually utilized their travel permits. As the war drew to a close the inward and outward movement increased, which again makes it impossible to calculate a definitive figure on emigration to Britain.

When the war broke out, Britain turned to Ireland for recruits and workers to supplement its labour force, which was being seriously drained by the war effort. Recruitment posters in Irish labour exchanges sought to entice volunteers. The exact figure of Irish men and women who served in the British forces during the war is also unknown, as records are hazy. However, it is believed that the number exceeded 50,000.[9] A number of obstacles hindered the compilation of statistics. Addresses given by Irish people enlisting were frequently those of accommodation in Britain, which consequently distorted their nationality. Those who were too young to enlist often gave fictitious names and addresses, as did those who deserted the Irish forces to join the British. An Irish Department of Defence memorandum in 1945 claimed that almost 5,000 non-commissioned officers and men of the Defence Forces were in a state of desertion. According to the memorandum, 'there is little doubt that the majority of them are or have been serving in the British Forces or in civilian employment in Great Britain and Northern Ireland'.[10] This substantial number of deserters indicates that greater pecuniary gains were to be made by joining the British forces or working in Britain than remaining in Ireland. There were 165,000 Irish next of kin addresses on record in the British army,[11] which suggests that the overall number of Irish or persons of Irish decent who contributed to the war must have been extensive. In February 1945 the British War office supplied the statistics shown in Table 3.1. Navy figures were not included, but were estimated at 5,000. If this data is to believed, 46,950 Eire-born persons served in the forces up to February 1945. However, contradictory totals were calculated. Figures estimated by the Service Departments claimed a smaller total of 38,000 of Eire volunteers and 42,000 from Northern Ireland.[12] The publication of such figures was considered but the British government came to the conclusion that 'the disadvantages of this course out weight the advantages' because they wanted to 'promote the restoration of friendly relations between the two Islands' and 'avoid controversial issues'. In addition, it was felt that 'for various reasons our figures are incomplete and not water-tight'.[13] A document entitled 'How Many Irish Volunteers Served in His Majesty's Armed Forces in the War 1939–1946' prepared by the British government in 1946 accounted for 43,249 (inclusive of 4,695 women) from Eire who served in the forces between 3 September 1939 and 31 August 1945. Of this figure 517 were in the Royal Navy and Royal Marines, 32,778 served in the army and 9,954 were in the Royal Air Force (RAF).[14] The document noted that 'the non-inclusion of enlistments in Great Britain of men and women of Eire origin as to which no figures are available spells the exclusion of many tens of thousands of Irish volunteers from the total Eire contribution to HM Forces'.[15] Bearing in mind the unknown numbers who were excluded, the document suggested that the total number of Irish volunteers who served in the forces might have exceeded 165,000. Taking all of these totals into account it can be concluded that the generally accepted figure of upwards of 50,000 is plausible.

Thousands from the Republic travelled to Britain to join the army, but it was more common to enlist in Belfast. Those joining the navy had to sign up in Liverpool. The majority of Irish men and women who were involved in the war served in the British forces, but hundreds fought with the American, Canadian, and Australian and New Zealand Army Corps (ANZAC) forces. Many of these recruits had emigrated to those countries before the war. It was estimated that 202 men born in Eire were killed or wounded while serving with the Royal Navy; no information was available on the number injured. The figures for those who served in the British army were 1,550 killed or missing and 2,550 wounded.[16] No satisfactory estimates were available in the case of the RAF. The Secretary of State for War claimed that up to 31 March 1946 the total number of awards made to persons born in Eire was in the region of 780, including eight Victoria Crosses and one George Cross.[17] Four of the Victoria Crosses were awarded to Co. Tipperary servicemen, which was the highest number won by any individual county serving in the British forces.

From 1940 to 1945 Irish workers going to Britain were classified as 'conditionally landed'. Under these terms they were exempt from conscription if they returned to Ireland after two years. Anyone who chose to remain in Britain after two years was liable to conscription. There were some cases of immigrants not knowing their rights who were enlisted. It appears that the majority of Irish recruits were propelled by economic necessity; being mostly young and unskilled, they were the group most affected by unemployment. One account recalled that the southern Irish recruits who joined the Royal Ulster Rifles did so largely out of economic need. As 'some of them' were 'literally, in their bare feet, because at that time there was very little work in the South and they came to join up for two shillings per day'.[18] The war presented the opportunity of employment and adventure. A wing commander of the RAF claimed that most of the 'youngsters' who enlist in the RAF 'have found a living difficult in Eire'. Whereas 'in the RAF they realise they have a rare chance to see what is going on over here and elsewhere, and as one of them said to me, they want to have a crack at Hitler'.[19] This statement summed up the main reasons for becoming a recruit. Other motives included the military tradition within families, particularly for the 'sons of men who fought in the last war' who did not 'want to be left out of this struggle'.[20] In Blake's words, 'the Irish, North and South, had a tradition of fighting other people's wars and took the King's shilling without betraying Ireland'.[21] However, he claimed economic reasons were their main motive in signing up: 'they enlisted because they has nothing better to do'.[22] It is also likely that new recruits influenced their peers at home to follow them. This was argued in the *Daily Telegraph*: 'They [RAF recruits from Eire] write home telling their parents and friends of their new life, and these letters are bringing forward more and more recruits among youths faced with difficulty of finding work in their own country'.[23]

Much negotiating took place between the British and Irish governments over the transfer of Irish workers. Throughout the war the British government was suspicious that some Irish migrants would spy in Britain. For security purposes newly arrived migrants were required to register with the police. In order to control migration, all passengers to Britain needed travel permits and those intending to work were required to arrange employment prior to their departure. Only persons over 22 years of age and who were unemployed were eligible to apply for a work permit, which was obtained through their local unemployment exchange. In 1940 the British Manpower Commissioner, Lord Beveridge, examined the labour situation and concluded that there would be 'a famine' of men if something was not done to help the labour shortage.[24] Employment agencies were established throughout Ireland for the purpose of replenishing the British labour force. According to the British Ministry of Labour and National Service, 'workers engaged by [British] employers' representatives in Ireland . . . constitute the large majority of the workers who travel' to Britain.[25] Labour was needed in all sectors but particularly in the manufacturing and construction industries. Thousands of Irish emigrants became employed in aerodrome construction, the manufacturing of armaments and other equipment necessary for the war. The setting up of British employment agencies in Ireland was an effective and swift method of securing workers. Many British employers advanced travel fares making emigration widely accessible. Wartime Irish emigration to Britain peaked from 1941 to 1943. A letter from the Ministry of Labour and National Service in London on 4 August 1943 highlighted the continuous congestion of immigrants at Holyhead: 'the processes of immigration are of necessity complex in time of war, rail transport is limited and bound to a strict timetable. We are therefore proposing to set up a Reception Hostel from which workers can be distributed to their destinations at leisure'.[26] At the hostel emigrants were examined by doctors for diseases such as typhus, which had broken out in Ireland in 1942. While the state carefully monitored the process, in some cases voluntary bodies and the Catholic Church took up the role of looking after emigrants. In 1942 the Archbishop of Dublin, John McQuaid, established the Emigrant Section of the Catholic Social Welfare Bureau (later called Emigrant Advice). Its main function was 'the care of emigrants, especially women and girls',[27] who were more vulnerable as they tended to be young and often emigrated alone.

Suspicion of British employment agents was evident in a telegraph to the Minister of External Affairs from the Fianna Fáil leader in Westport: 'British agents are recruiting Irish Labour all over West Mayo for work in England. Thousands of men are affected . . . [the] type of work and conditions of employment are not clearly set out. We suggest this is conscription in disguise . . . '.[28] The idea of 'conscription in disguise' was extreme and highlights a strong sense of distrust and a hint of Anglophobia. Concern over the 'type of work and conditions of employment . . . not clearly set out' was however understandable. The Bishop of Galway was also amongst those who opposed emigration. He argued that 'the country is being invaded by agents of foreign firms who are trying to get strong young Irishmen to leave the country to work abroad'.[29] It is clear that the bishop advocated a greater degree of social control of migration by the state. On the other hand many took the view that it alleviated unemployment in Ireland. Emigration was a necessary evil, as O'Donnell pointed out: 'Suppose our migrants had no outlet but the home market, and that the thousands who pour into the Lothians alone overflowed on to the Irish midlands, what a hobo camp it would become . . . if we are corralled in back here we shall have no option but to ask the sugar smugglers to open their routes to provide an escape . . . '.[30] While the immediate benefits of emigration (remittances) were clearly welcomed by the public at home, there appears to have been an obscure opposition to emigration at the same time.

There is evidence to suggest that Irish emigrants were better accepted in Britain than in Northern Ireland. A Department of Industry and Commerce memorandum stated that in Britain they were seen as valuable assets: 'In Britain our workers are taken as they come. In British official circles, far from there being any tendency to resent them, their presence is more or less frankly welcomed as a contribution to the war effort.'[31] The memorandum went on to compare the recruitment of Irish labour in Britain and in Northern Ireland: 'The Belfast Ministry of Labour has been hardly less assiduous than the British Ministry in its efforts to recruit labour here'.[32] According to the memorandum: 'Far from acknowledging their help . . . the attitude of the Belfast politicians is to represent our people as a lot of undesirable interlopers who have swarmed into the Six Counties to snatch the jobs of men in the British Forces. They invariably refer to our workers in the Six Counties in terms of contumely and insult.'[33] Between October 1942 and September 1946, Stormont (the Northern Irish government) granted 36,447 residence permits to citizens of the Republic.[34] In Dublin the Department of Industry and Commerce recommended that given the ill-feeling towards southerners in Northern Ireland 'it would be preferable that such emigration from this country as must continue should be directed to Great Britain rather than the Six Counties'.[35] In addition to generating greater

Table 3.2: Number of Irish males and females going to Britain and Northern Ireland, 1941–1945

Year	Males	Females
1941	31,860	3,272
1942	37,263	14,448
1943	29,321	19,003
1944	7,723	5,890
1945	13,185	10,609

Source: National Archives S11582, Department of External Affairs Memorandum, 30 August 1947.

competition for employment, Wolf argues that the presence of southerners (the majority were Catholic) in Northern Ireland threatened the communal balance.[36]

The emigrants who went to Britain during the Second World War were predominantly male. Men dominated net Irish emigration in 1801–1901, 1911–26 and 1936–46. All were periods of major wars involving Britain. Irish men immigrated to Britain either as recruits or as supplementary labour during these wars. Controls were placed on the number of female immigrants to Britain throughout the war, which further explains the fall in female emigration. Table 3.2 gives an idea of the proportion of male to female emigration. These figures do not reflect the actual total as an unknown number of Irish men and women claimed that they were going to Britain for personal reasons and took up employment there. On the basis of these statistics it is evident that the flow of Irish emigrants was very high from 1941 to the end of 1943. During these years the war effort was heightened and recruitment intensified. This in turn created a gap in the labour supply in Britain, which was largely filled by Irish immigrants. The sizeable decrease in emigration in 1944 can in part be attributed to the end of the war being in sight (especially after the invasion of Normandy) and the subsequent easing off of recruitment. British recruits were beginning to return home and take up employment. The massive rebuilding programme after the war is probably the reason for the 1945 hike in Irish emigration to Britain. The influx continued to expand for the first six months of 1946, when 7,226 Irish males and 6,832 Irish females went to Britain for employment.[37] After 1946 female emigration reoccupied the position held before the war, outnumbering its male counterpart. This growth was made possible by the removal of employment controls for females in Britain on 30 June 1946, followed by the Irish government's decision to remove emigration restrictions on females effective from 27 July 1946.

Traditionally the majority of Irish emigrants have been young in age. This was certainly the case during the war, as most were within the 16–34 year age group. Youth emigration was part of a tradition most likely propelled by a combination of unemployment, the quest for self-advancement and a sense of adventure. Table 3.3 gives an insight into the age structure of those who received travel permits from 1943 to 1945. What is most striking about these figures is the greater preponderance of females under 25 years of age who emigrated than males. Female emigrants have always been predominantly young and

Table 3.3: Percentage of age groups issued with travel permits 1943–1945

	Year	16–19	20–24	25–29	30–34	35 and over
Males	1943	6.9	26.4	20.9	14.5	31.3
	1944	12.3	28.8	18.1	13.1	27.7
	1945	12.8	33.8	17.9	12.5	23.0
Females	1943	20.3	39.3	18.5	9.1	12.8
	1944	22.2	38.8	18.1	8.9	12.0
	1945	29.2	40.7	14.7	6.9	8.5

Adapted from: *Report of the Commission on Emigration and Other Population Problems* (1956).

single. This table reveals that in 1943 59.6 per cent of all female emigrants were aged 16–24 years, rising to 61 per cent in 1944 and a staggering 69.9 per cent in 1945. The percentages for male emigrants in this cohort were 33.3, 41.1 and 46.6 per cent respectively, revealing that they were on average older. Bearing in mind the restrictions placed on female emigration, the female to male ratio in the younger age groups is remarkable. There were various reasons why emigration attracted younger females. Older married women were less inclined to emigrate unless as a family unit, and few families emigrated during the war. Much of the work available in Britain demanded young single females. British recruitment in Ireland allowed Irish women to join the forces, which gave many a chance to change their occupation. The menial place of women in the 1937 Constitution has been seen as an influence in the decision to emigrate in some cases.[38] For some farmers' daughters, emigration presented the opportunity to gain money as at home they were typically non-earning labourers, many having poor marriage prospects. Women were aware of better marriage prospects and greater autonomy elsewhere, which in most cases would result in greater social mobility.[39] Reporting to the Land Commission in 1944, R.M. Duncan wrote of rural girls' unwillingness to remain in their localities and marry. For those whose families were poor, girls generally wanted to escape the drudgery, while better-off girls who had 'been sent to good schools . . . will not contemplate becoming farmers' wives even when an adequate staff of servants is available'.[40] This suggests that social advancement and the desire to escape the boredom of rural life were important factors in female migration.

The number of males over 30 years of age was noticeably higher than that of females in the same age group. In 1943 45.8 per cent of males were 30 years and older, compared with 21.9 per cent of females. In 1944 a decline was apparent for both sexes as the percentages were 40.8 per cent for males and 20.9 per cent for females and by 1945 the percentages had fallen to 35.5 per cent for males and 15.4 per cent for females. There was a discernible increase in the number of older males emigrating during the war. This growth had waned by the early 1950s, and according to Table 3.3 had begun to fall as early as 1944. The rise in older males emigrating was typical of large scale male emigration during wartime. The 1946 census showed that the number of females per 1,000 men emigrating was 671 in 1936–46 compared with 1,285 in 1926–36.[41]

Table 3.4: Numbers of Irish female emigrants employed in different areas of work in Britain and Northern Ireland, September 1939 to December 1945

	Agriculture	Nursing	Domestic	Other (including factory work)
1939	57	3,132	5,396	1,350
1940	492	1,634	5,285	1,125
1941	176	785	1,343	789
1942	657	2,233	6,037	5,060
1943	422	2,838	9,125	6,255
1944	307	1,125	2,760	1,591
1945	466	3,523	4,719	1,694

Source: Trinity College Dublin, March Papers 8300/1–31.

Irish emigrants tended to settle in urban areas. During the war the majority of migrants went to urban centres in Britain, such as London, Birmingham, Manchester and Liverpool, where work was most available. The 1951 British census showed that one-third of Irish immigrants living in England and Wales were in Greater London and two-fifths of the Irish in Scotland were living in Glasgow.[42] It is probable that a sizeable proportion of the Irish enumerated in the 1951 census immigrated to Britain during the war and remained on.

The search for better jobs or escaping unemployment appears to have been an important reason for emigration. The *Report of the Commission on Emigration and Other Population Problems* (1956) revealed that most Irish emigrants during the war 'came from agricultural occupations or else were unemployed and unskilled'.[43] This highlights the importance of employment opportunities in the decision to emigrate. Much male employment was created in Ireland as a result of the war in areas such as agriculture, turf-cutting and the defence forces. During the war male unemployment showed signs of decline largely due to the creation of these new jobs and emigration. Female unemployment rose, and by December 1943 female unemployment in Dublin was double the level in 1939, whereas male unemployment had dropped by 36 per cent.[44] Much female unemployment can be attributed to the restrictions placed on female emigration. Wages in Britain were considerably higher than in Ireland during the war, which must have been an incentive for many emigrants. Ó Gráda suggests that by comparing industry-wide levels in 1938 and 1946, the difference between Irish and British wages rose from 16 to 32 per cent, while that in women's wages rose from 8 to 31 per cent.[45] Emergency orders in Ireland restricted wages. The fact that pre-war wages were not achieved again until 1949[46] reflects the rather depressed economic climate at the time in Ireland. Wages and the standard of living fell, while the cost of living rose during the war. Therefore unemployment may not necessarily have been the main economic cause of wartime emigration.

Female emigrants were largely employed in nursing, domestic, factory and agricultural work. Table 3.4 shows the work which Irish female emigrants engaged in from September 1939 and December 1945 in Britain and Northern Ireland. Irish women were most represented in domestic work, with a total

Table 3.5: Numbers of Irish male emigrants employed in different areas of work in Britain and Northern Ireland, September 1939 to December 1945

	Agriculture	Building construction	Clerks and skilled workers	Unskilled workers
1939	843	956	2,266	3,251
1940	5,408	1,180	2,278	5,901
1941	1,773	2,655	3,156	21,035
1942	4,767	1,172	3,873	23,830
1943	3,584	1,473	3,468	18,310
1944	1,361	226	1,414	4,340
1945	3,148	632	2,085	6,244

Source: Trinity College Dublin, March Papers 8300/1–31.

of 34,665 employed for these years. Nursing and other employment (which included factory work) were the next biggest sectors, and engaged 15,270 and 17,864 respectively. Only 2,577 were engaged in agriculture. Females frequently emigrated alone; this was normally the case with those going as domestics, whereas men usually emigrated in a group. For females loneliness was often a repercussion of the type of employment they were engaged in. Table 3.5 deals with the sectors males were employed in during the same years.

The Commission on Emigration and Other Population Problems found that females who emigrated during the war were more likely to be skilled than men were. This is quite probable considering that such a high number of nurses alone were employed. Table 3.5 verifies that more Irish male emigrants were employed as unskilled than as skilled workers during the war. Both tables display an obvious hike in the numbers employed from 1941 and 1943, which were the highest years of Irish emigration during the war.

Remittances from emigrants greatly increased during the war. Money sent home was seen as a compensation for the separation of a family member. Healy notes that 'while fathers, sons and daughters cried all the way to the train and the bus and ship, the flow back of emigrant cheques and money orders evaporated the maternal and wifely tears so that on the threshold of the Post Office or Hibernian Bank below in Main Street you could smile a little more with every passing week'.[47] In 1939 a little over £1 million of postal orders and money orders were received from Britain and Northern Ireland.[48] By 1941 this figure had doubled. These sums applied only to postal orders, money orders and Bank of England notes. Obviously no information was available as to remittances by cheque or coin, and so the real total was likely to be much larger. Wages must have been high given that emigrants had money to spare to send home. This was probably a major factor in the decision to emigrate. There were certainly large financial gains to be made by enlisting as between 1939 and 1942 the number of British army pensions and allowances paid in Ireland increased from 28,700 to 69,509.[49] These figures not only show the extent of emigration but also indicate that migrants reaped some pecuniary rewards, which benefited both them and their family at home.

It appears that the Irish government neither endorsed nor opposed emigration. As a neutral country it didn't want to appear to be helping the Allies by permitting recruits and war workers to move freely to Britain. Travel restrictions prevented this problem. The halting of emigration was irrational, as it reduced unemployment and maintained some degree of social and economic stability. But the government sought to disguise the high level of emigration as it could have reflected badly on its inability to create employment with satisfactory wages and conditions for the population.[50] T.J. Coyne, the controller of censorship during the period, was fearful that the publication of the facts that surrounded emigration would weaken morale at home. He claimed that 'picturing thousands of starving Irish workers flocking across to the bombed areas of England or to join the British forces, or maybe to throw themselves into the sea, have simply got to be stopped if public morale is not to be hopelessly compromised'.[51]

Emigration was of course practical as it allowed Irish unemployment figures to drop from 15 per cent in 1939 to 10 per cent in 1945.[52] According to an article in the *Irish Press*, this decrease was 'due – apart from the increase in the Defence Forces together with the numbers employed in turf-cutting and other emergency schemes – to a resumption of emigration on a very substantial scale'.[53] A memorandum from the Department of Finance emphasized that 'from both moral and economic points of view it is preferable that workers should be allowed to obtain employment outside the country' rather than 'remain in idleness at home'.[54] The advantages of remittances were acknowledged: 'the worker employed at good wages in Great Britain is in a position to send substantial contributions to his dependants at home, and thereby break for them the monotony of continuous poverty'.[55] The Department of Industry and Commerce in a 1941 memorandum felt confident that the 'placing of Irish unemployed workers in employment in Great Britain would provide a very welcome mitigation of the difficulties at home'.[56] In *The Bell*, Peadar O'Donnell argued 'that the Government should co-operate with seasonal workers listing vacancies at the labour exchanges and even advancing the fares'.[57] His project was ignored as in his opinion 'The government could not appear to encourage migration!'.[58]

The government, however, was quietly assisting Irish emigration, though it insisted that Irish labour requirement should not be undermined. In 1941 when arrangements were being made for the establishment of a British Liaison Officer for Labour in Dublin, the Irish government stressed 'the necessity for the retention of adequate labour in the national interests, especially insofar as the production of food and fuel was concerned'.[59] The function of the Liaison Officer was to ensure that Irish workers were entering an employment approved by the British Ministry of Labour and National Service. Arrangements were also made with the Irish Department of External Affairs that travel permits were to be granted only to persons who had offer of employment in Britain certified by an Employment Exchange Officer in Ireland. Throughout the war restrictions on male workers applied mostly in the western counties, to all men experienced in agriculture and turf production. Some viewed these restrictions negatively because 'they would debar many families from enjoying a decent livelihood' as their wages from these schemes 'would not be sufficient to allow these workers to allocate a certain sum out of their wages to help their parent and families at home'.[60] The problem of agricultural and turf workers being unemployed during the winter months was raised in the Dáil Debates.[61] In response to this issue the Minister for Industry and Commerce, Lemass, pointed out that the granting of seasonal permits for work in Britan to these workers alleviated this situation. Thus, it is clear that the government saw emigration as a solution to unemployment but maintained the right to restrict it if the people were needed at home. The Irish government was anxious to secure agreement with Britain not to conscript Irish migrants, and arrangements were made in 1941 whereby only those who remained in Britain longer than two years were liable. In addition, any Irish persons injured while in the British forces would be paid compensation.

Another threat emigration presented for the government was the fear of a mass return of emigrants after the war. The Assistant Secretary of External Affairs, F. Boland, warned that the 'British authorities [desire] to rush all these workers . . . who have no doubt imbibed a good deal of "leftism" in Britain . . . back to this country as quickly as they can' produced the 'danger of social revolution'.[62] Such a view was quite extreme but the notion that unemployment would soar was very real for the government, especially if emigrants returned 'all at once, or over a short period' as the Department of Industry and Commerce pointed out.[63] In 1942 the government expressed the hope 'that it would later be possible to agree on an arrangement [with Britain] for spreading out this return in such a way as to facilitate this country in coping with the problem of their re-employment and re-settlement'.[64] Although numerous communications were made between the Irish and British governments in connection with the heavy burden of returning migrants on the Irish exchequer, no official reciprocity agreement was made. Funds paid by Irish emigrants were not transferred to Ireland. The British argued that the threatened flow of Irish emigrants back to Ireland did not occur and so there was no need to transfer funds to Ireland. Postwar reconstruction kept emigrants in Britain and coaxed more people to emigrate. In Britain any unemployment insurance due to Irish emigrants was granted, and Wolf has argued that this may be the reason why many Irish stayed on in Britain after the war.[65]

In many ways the Second World War was a turning point in Irish emigration, as the numbers emigrating to Britain increased and continued to do so after the war. The opportunities that the war presented were attractive, especially the fact that employment was greater and wages were higher in Britain than in Ireland. The fact that some employers advanced fares enabled many to emigrate who otherwise may not have done so. The postwar development of the welfare state in Britain benefited the Irish living there, particularly Irish women as employment expanded in areas such as nursing and teaching. Some emigrants returned to Ireland after the war but thousands did not, rendering the following apocalyptic prediction of the Assistant Secretary of External Affairs void:

immediately the 'cease-fire' order is given, the whole aim and purpose of the British authorities will be to rush all these workers back to this country as quickly as they can . . . Therefore, no problem that we are likely to have to face during the war is likely to be so serious as the problem we will have when up to as many as a hundred thousand or more unemployed men . . . are dumped back here . . . To have piled on top of them in the course of a short time afterwards all the Irish citizens demobilised from British armed forces.[66]

Those who had emigrated during the war stayed on in Britain primarily because postwar Britain provided more employment than Ireland could offer. The massive rebuilding programme in particular required much labour, which could be filled by Irish emigrants already in Britain and additional supplies from Ireland. British industry demanded workers and Irish females continued to be highly represented in domestic work and nursing. The British Ministry of Labour affirmed that Irish labour would be vital for postwar reconstruction and that it would not be necessary 'to require any substantial numbers of Eire workers transferred to this country during the war to return to Eire because of unemployment in this country'.[67] Various schemes and grants for ex-service men were inducements for Irish recruits to stay on in Britain. Many started up their own business, often with friends they had made in the forces. In 1944 the British Legion in Dublin recommended that 'everything possible should be done to dissuade men from coming to their homes in Eire pending release from the services' owing to 'practically no work to be found for ex-servicemen in Eire'.[68] Once Irish emigrants established themselves in a job and accommodation the path was paved for chain migration, which became possible once wartime restrictions ceased. By the end of the war numerous Irish communities had been established throughout Britain, and these were to be important contact points for the large numbers of Irish who migrated there in the postwar era.

Notes

1. John Healy, *No One Shouted Stop!* (Achill, 1988), p. 16.
2. J.A. Jackson, *The Irish in Britain* (London, 1963), p. 15.
3. *Census of Population 1946 Preliminary Report*, p. 13.
4. Kieran Kennedy, Thomas Giblin and Deirdre Mc Hugh, *The Economic Development of Ireland in the Twentieth Century* (London, 1988), p. 51.
5. National Archives S11582, Department of External Affairs Memorandum, 30 August 1947.
6. *Report of the Commission on Emigration and Other Population Problems* (Dublin, 1956), p. 128.
7. Enda Delaney, 'State, Politics and Demography; The Case of Irish Emigration, 1921–71', *Irish Political Studies*, 13 (1998), p. 31.
8. Public Record Office London (PROL) DO.35/1230, WX.132/1/124.
9. Nicholas Mansergh, *Nationalism and Independence: Selected Irish Papers* (Cork, 1997), p. 160.
10. National Archives, Department of Foreign Affairs, Department of Defence Memorandum, 20 June 1945, p. 81.
11. Mansergh, *Nationalism and Independence*, p. 92.

12. PROL, DO.35/1230, WX132/1/124.
13. Ibid.
14. Ibid.
15. Ibid.
16. National Archives, Department of Foreign Affairs, extract from official report House of Commons debates, 8 April 1946, col. 272, Questions for the Secretary of State for War, p. 81.
17. Ibid.
18. Myles Duggan, *Distant Drums: Irish Soldiers in Foreign Armies* (Belfast, 1993), p. 146.
19. *Belfast News Letter*, 24 September 1943.
20. *Daily Telegraph*, 24 September 1943.
21. W. Blake, *Northern Ireland and the Second World War* (Belfast, 1956), p. 199.
22. Ibid., p. 199.
23. Ibid.
24. James Wolf, 'Witholding their Due: The Dispute between Ireland and Great Britain over Unemployment Insurance Payments to Conditionally Landed Wartime Volunteer Workers', *Saothar*, 21 (1996), p. 39.
25. National Archives S11582, R.P. Winnington-Ingram, Ministry of Labour and National Service, London to R.C. Ferguson, Department of Industry and Commerce, Dublin Castle, 4 August 1943.
26. Ibid.
27. National Archives S11582, Memorandum on the growth of emigration control by the Department of Social Welfare.
28. National Archives S11582, Telegraph to De Valera, Minister for External Affairs, from the Fianna Fáil Leader, Westport, 24 March 1941.
29. Bishop of Galway's address at Ardrahan, 'First Loyalty is to Land and People of Ireland: Peril of Emigration', in *The Standard*, 2 August 1941.
30. Peadar O'Donnell, 'Migration is a Way of Keeping Grip', *The Bell*, November 1941.
31. National Archives S11582, Department of Industry and Commerce Memorandum, 18 November 1942.
32. Ibid.
33. Ibid.
34. Wolf, 'Withholding their Due', p. 39.
35. National Archives S11582, Department of Industry and Commerce Memorandum, 18 November 1942.
36. Wolf, 'Withholding their Due', p. 41.
37. National Archives S11582, Department of External Affairs Memorandum on emigration for the government, 30 August 1947.
38. Kate Kelly and Triona Nic Giolla Choille, *Emigration Matters for Women* (Dublin, 1990), p. 12.
39. National Archives S9636.
40. National Archives S13413/1.
41. *Census of Population 1964 Preliminary Report*, p. 14.
42. Robert E. Kennedy, *The Irish: Emigration, Marriage and Fertility* (Berkeley, Ca., 1973), p. 75.
43. *Report of the Commission on Emigration and Other Population Problems* (Dublin, 1956), paragraph 272.
44. Mary E. Daly, 'Women in the Irish Free State, 1922–1939: The Interaction between Economics and Ideology', in John Hoff and Morueen Coulter (eds), *Irish*

Women's Voices Past and Present. Journal of Women's History (Winter/Spring 1995), p. 111.

45. Cormac Ó Gráda, *A Rocky Road: The Irish Economy since the 1920s* (Manchester, 1997), p. 21.

46. Ibid., p. 17.

47. Healy, *No One Shouted Stop!*, p. 16.

48. National Archives S12865, Remittances from emigrants, Department of Industry and Commerce Memorandum, June 1942.

49. Ibid., Letter from the Department of Post and Telegraphs, 28 May 1942.

50. Donal Ó Drisceoil, *Censorship in Ireland, 1939–1945 Neutrality, Politics and Society* (Cork, 1996), p. 256.

51. Ibid., p. 257.

52. Ellen Hazelkorn, 'We All Can't Live on a Small Island: The Political Economy of Irish Migration', in Patrick O'Sullivan (ed.), *The Irish World Wide, Vol. 2, The Irish in the New Communities* (Leicester, 1992), p. 189.

53. 'The Problem of Emigration', *The Irish Press*, 6 October 1944.

54. National Archives S11582, Memorandum for the Government from the Department of Finance, 19 September 1941.

55. Ibid.

56. Ibid., Memorandum for the Government from the Department of Industry and Commerce, 13 March 1941.

57. O'Donnell, 'Migration is a Way of Keeping Grip'.

58. Ibid.

59. National Archives S11582, Memorandum for the Government from the Department of Industry and Commerce 1942.

60. Dáil Debates, Vol. 92 Cols 1783–1784, 29 February 1944.

61. Dáil Debates, Vol. 98, Cols 192–193, 11 October 1945.

62. National Archives S11582, May 1942.

63. Ibid., Memorandum from the Department of Industry and Commerce, 12 November 1942.

64. Ibid.

65. Wolf, 'Withholding their Due', p. 44.

66. National Archives S12882, F.H. Boland on the postwar period.

67. PROL, DO35/1230/WX132/62.

68. PROL, DO35/1229/WX132/39.

CHAPTER 4

From 'Ethnicity' to 'Diaspora': 1980s Emigration and 'Multicultural' London

BREDA GRAY

(Irish Centre for Migration Studies, University College, Cork)

Introduction

The 1980s generation of Irish emigrants has been variously described by academics and the Irish media as 'the Ryan Air generation', an 'emigrant aristocracy' and 'new wave' emigrants in order to distinguish it from previous generations of emigrants. The media in the Republic of Ireland appropriated the high-flying emigrant as a symbol of a new and confident country, implying that these emigrants were leaving a 'new' Ireland.[1] If Ireland was being constituted as 'modern' through a discourse of Irish emigration as a young and educated phenomenon in the 1980s, then many of the cities in which these Irish emigrants settled were being characterized as 'global cities' and were making claims to progressiveness through discourses of 'multiculturalism'.

The destinations of 1980s emigrants included cities in Britain, North America, Australia and continental Europe, with Britain accounting for about 70 per cent of those leaving at the end of the decade.[2] The British destinations of Irish emigrants were mainly London and the south-east of England, the headquarters of high technology industries, financial and information services sectors of the late twentieth century.[3] By the early 1990s the media in both Britain and Ireland were suggesting that for many young Irish adults, 'London, not Dublin, [was] becoming their capital city'.[4]

This chapter offers an overview of debates surrounding 1980s emigration from the Republic of Ireland and the shifting positions of the Irish in London in this decade. In doing so, it investigates the gendering of emigration and immigration and how these processes might be understood in relation to discourses of 'multiculturalism' and 'diaspora'. The chapter is structured in four sections, the first of which focuses on the profile of 1980s emigration as well as official and academic responses to it. The second section addresses the encounter between the 1980s generation of Irish immigrants and a London that was celebrating its cultural diversity through official discourses and policies of 'multiculturalism'.[5] The third and fourth sections pay closer attention to gendered experiences of immigration to London by considering key themes identified in research with Irish women immigrants to London. The chapter concludes with a brief discussion of discourses of 'multiculturalism' and 'diaspora' and how these discourses frame the gendered Irish emigrant/immigrant experience at the end of the twentieth century.

Background to 1980s emigration

Following a history of net emigration since the establishment of the state, the 1970s was the first decade in which net immigration to the Republic of Ireland was recorded. However, by the 1980s, the outflow of migrants began to overtake immigration again. Table 4.1 points to the dramatic increase in emigration between the first and second half of the 1980s. When we take the large numbers of Irish 'illegals' in the United States into account, the figures in Table 4.1 are likely to be an underestimate. The United States Irish Immigration Reform Movement calculated that the number of Irish 'illegals' in the United States was approximately 135,000 in the early 1990s.[6]

Table 4.2 outlines the figures for out-migration to various destinations and the total figures for in-migration between 1988 and 1997. It shows the high rates of emigration at the end of the 1980s and how these have tailed off in the 1990s. It is clear from Table 4.2 that about two-thirds of all emigrants in the late 1980s chose the UK as their country of destination.[7] By 1992, the proportion of emigrants going to the UK fell to about half of all those leaving, reflecting a significant fall. Figures for 1991, referred to by Hickman and Walter, point to the significance of the south-east of England and more specifically London as a destination, particularly for those from the Republic of Ireland. These figures record 73 per cent of women arrivals to England from the Republic, 45.1 per cent of women from Northern Ireland, 68.5 per cent of men from the Republic, and 41.7 per cent of men from Northern Ireland settling in the south-east of the country.[8] Another notable feature of the new arrivals was their age, with more than 70 per cent under 30 years old.[9]

The description of 1980s emigration as different from previous periods of emigration is justified by Russell King and Ian Shuttleworth because, first, out-migration seemed to affect all geographical areas in Ireland,[10] second, more emigrants were in professional or managerial work than in the past, and third, highly educated people were leaving in large numbers – a phenomenon

Table 4.1: Estimated net migration in the intercensal periods 1981–1986 and 1986–1991

Intercensal period	Estimated net migration (outward less inward)
1981–1986	71,883
1986–1991	134,170

Adapted from: Central Statistics Office, Census 1991 Volume 1 (June 1993), p. 24.

Table 4.2: Estimated migration classified by country of destination, 1988–1997 ('000s)

Year	Out-migration				Immigration	Net migration
	UK	EU	USA	Rest		
1988	40.2	2.8	7.9	10.2	19.2	−41.9
1989	48.4	3.9	8.2	10.0	26.7	−43.8
1990	35.8	5.1	7.7	7.6	33.3	−22.9
1991*	23.0	3.1	4.8	4.4	33.3	−2.0
1992*	16.9	7.5	3.5	5.5	40.7	+7.3
1993*	16.4	7.3	5.6	5.8	34.7	−0.4
1994*	14.8	5.5	9.6	4.9	30.1	−4.7
1995*	13.3	5.1	8.2	6.6	31.2	−2.0
1996*	14.1	5.1	5.2	6.8	39.2	+8.0
1997	12.9	4.1	4.1	7.9	44.0	+15.0

* Revised based on 1996 Census of Population
Adapted from: Central Statistical Bulletin (March 1996) and Population and Migration Estimates (April 1997)[11]

referred to as the 'brain drain'.[12] The latter points are supported by Hickman and Walter's research, which found that the 1980s emigrants from Ireland to Britain were more strongly represented in managerial and professional occupations requiring higher qualifications, compared with earlier generations of Irish immigrants.[13] Those Irish immigrants between the ages of 18 and 29, i.e. most 1980s immigrants, were more highly represented in employment requiring high levels of qualifications than those in other age groups of the Irish-born in Britain. Both women and men in this younger age category were over-represented in managerial and professional categories when compared to the total British population.[14] Nearly half (45.4 per cent) of all Irish-born women between 18 and 29 years were in the managerial and professional categories compared with 26.5 per cent for the total population.[15] The proportion of Irish-born men between 18 and 29 years in these categories of work was 39 per cent compared with 26.5 per cent for the total population. These figures support King and Shuttleworth's characterization of 1980s emigrants as constituting a 'brain drain'.

The profile of 1980s immigrants is, however, more nuanced than the discussion so far suggests. For example, young Irish-born men were over-represented in low skilled and casual work, mainly in personal services.[16] This was a significant finding given that men accounted for a higher proportion of Irish migrants in the 1980s. Further, these figures may be an underestimate of Irish men in this category because young male migrants in casual work are often not registered in the census or in household surveys.[17] For all the rhetoric of a changing profile of Irish emigration in the 1980s, this group of men reflects the continuing significance of this category of male migrant and reinforces the stereotype of the Irish emigrant linked with previous generations of emigration.

The profile of Irish women's emigration in the 1980s suggests some discontinuities with previous decades. As already noted, the labour market profile of Irish women immigrating to Britain changed in the 1980s with more of them occupying managerial and professional categories. Also, Irish women's levels of emigration fell to 75 per cent of men's levels. This contrasts with previous decades when women's emigration levels were often higher than those of men.[18] Lee puts the drop in women's emigration down to the changing sex-ratio of the labour force in Ireland. Between 1971 and 1988, there was a 27 per cent rise in female employment in the Republic of Ireland. This rise was mainly in the insurance and professional services sectors.[19] Changing labour market conditions in Ireland and Britain, as well as Irish women's increased levels of education by the 1980s,[20] meant that some members of this generation of Irish women were more career mobile at home and abroad. Although these labour market factors impacted on women's decisions about emigration, it is important to recognize that the 1980s also represented a time when women's rights were being publicly eroded north and south of the border. O'Carroll argues that for many Irish women, emigration was a response to social attitudes and the implementation of repressive social legislation in Ireland.[21] The socio-political climate of Ireland, north and south, has also been a factor in gay and lesbian emigration.[22]

Although fewer young Irish women were entering low-paid, unskilled casual work in Britain than in the past,[23] Irish women's visibility as emigrants remained low and their changing profile as immigrants to Britain tended to go unnoticed. This may be partly accounted for by the relative absence of a stereotype of the Irish woman immigrant to Britain,[24] higher levels of out-marriage among Irish women,[25] women's locations in less ghettoized labour market niches,[26] and the ongoing tendency to overlook women's experiences in accounts of Irish migration.[27] King and Shuttleworth's characterization of the ways in which 1980s emigration is different from previous generations is nuanced by the above discussion of complex continuities and changes in the locations of 1980s Irish immigrants within the British labour market. This discussion suggests that the 'brain drain' from Ireland to Britain in the 1980s was a gendered one and challenges the idea that 1980s emigrants can be represented as an 'emigrant aristocracy'.[28]

The 1991 National Economic and Social Council (NESC) report on emigration (the most recent governmental synthesis of information on emigration) located 1980s emigration in a context of (un)employment in the Republic of Ireland and implied that the Irish government was in a position to reduce emigration by rectifying the unemployment problem.[29] This analysis is limited by its failure to attend to the wider socio-cultural and gender factors involved. It also takes a nation-state based approach which ignores the effects of changes in the global labour market on emigration patterns.[30] A small number of 'global' cities emerged in the 1980s which became 'the control points in the world economy', gaining economic dominance and attracting large numbers of migrant workers.[31] Cities like London and New York had, by the 1980s, become key sites for the production of specialized services for complex and spatially dispersed transnational companies and the global financial industry.[32]

The centralization of financial and corporate headquarters in a few cities necessitated the development of an international 'elite' labour market because career prospects for the ambitious professional were only available in 'global cities'. These cities also developed an informal, low-skilled, service labour economy to support the lifestyle needs of the 'elite' workforce. London, as a 'global city' experiencing a boom in the late 1980s, attracted Irish workers at both the top and bottom ends of the market.[33] Hanlon concludes that some middle-class professionals, i.e. those in demand by the multinational corporations of these cities, leave Ireland because their career paths and personal aspirations require international experience.[34] These professionals emigrate whatever the economic climate in Ireland, whereas the working classes emigrate out of necessity in times of economic hardship.[35] This formulation is nuanced somewhat by Sexton's findings which suggest that those with higher qualifications who did not find work in Ireland emigrated, while those with second-level qualifications tended to endure longer periods of unemployment before leaving.[36] For many in Britain and Ireland in the 1980s, geographical mobility was an important aspect of attaining and maintaining class position. The statistics in Britain show that 'entry into middle-class occupations was often accompanied by movement from one region to another'.[37] Movement involves 'different geographies of power' because 'global migration is far easier for highly-skilled workers and those with capital than it is for those without training and resources'.[38]

The findings of the NESC report suggest that emigration from the Republic of Ireland in the 1980s was most concentrated among those at the top and those at the bottom class-wise. These 'geographies of power' are explained by the report in relation to push/pull factors, with push factors being most evident in the emigration of the poorly educated and pull factors influencing the decisions of educated middle-class emigrants. The solutions offered in the report include: first, the development of a stable economy, second, a programme of structural reforms leading to increased investment and an increase in employment opportunities, and third, policies directed at long-term unemployment. These proposals arise out of an analysis based on modernization theory, 'which assumes that Ireland's problems are simply attributable to [Ireland's] relative lack of development in the industrialisation process'.[39] The report does not engage with theories of the changing formations of capitalism, its increasingly global nature including the development of 'global cities' and reliance on a mobile labour force.

Although the global, national and regional structures of the labour market and changing formations of capitalism impact greatly on patterns of migration, analyses focusing on only these often miss the social, cultural, political and religious factors that influence migration. Shuttleworth's survey of Irish graduates between 1983 and 1986 suggests that cultural, personal and familial motives, unrelated to the labour market, were highly significant factors in the decision to emigrate. The leading factor was 'lifestyle', referring, in this case, to adventure and the chance to escape the restrictions of life in Ireland.[40] He also noted the significance of a national and family history of emigration which meant that Irish graduates were acculturized to emigration.[41] The political factors affecting emigration are also significant and may partly account for the different rates of emigration from Northern Ireland and the Republic. Emigration from the North was much higher in the 1970s and 1980s than in previous decades.[42] These figures suggest that any investigation of emigration from the North needs to address the political as well as the economic factors affecting rates of emigration.[43]

I have argued elsewhere that the often romanticized and uncritical sense of Irish collective self-identity leaves little discursive space for the articulation of non-economic reasons for high levels of emigration. The incredible silence that marks the Irish experience of emigration at both public and private levels makes it impossible to fully account for this phenomenon in the 1980s or in any other decade.[44] By the 1990s, public attention was focusing on immigration to a 'Celtic Tiger' Ireland as an indication of national 'success', or a source of 'social problems', while ongoing high levels of emigration continue to be publicly ignored.[45] Emigration, however, represents only one aspect of the Irish diasporic experience. Once emigrants find themselves in another country, they have to find ways of negotiating their relationships with both their country of origin and their country of destination. In the following sections of this chapter, I turn my attention away from emigration and focus on the related processes of immigration and settlement in London in the 1980s.

'Multiculturalism' and Irish identity in 1980s London

There was a shift towards a 'multicultural' based model of society in 1980s Britain whereby a rhetoric of cultural diversity was fostered by city councils in particular. London, through the left-wing Greater London Council (GLC) elected in 1981, led the way in developing 'multicultural' policy and service provision and in fostering 'ethnic' cultural activities. Rattansi argues that both 'multiculturalism' and anti-racist initiatives in the 1980s set about challenging the structural and cultural marginalization of black minority communities in Britain.[46] Debates between 'multicultural' approaches and anti-racist approaches to politics and policy located 'multiculturalism' within a broadly liberal framework and anti-racism within a left radical context. However, in practice, these approaches shared many assumptions.[47] Alongside the more politicized debates regarding ethnic identity and anti-racism, the broad and fluid rhetoric of 'multiculturalism' fostered a celebration of 'ethnic' cultural activities. Both of these strands of a loosely defined 'multiculturalism' partly structured the formation of Irishness in London in the 1980s.

Irish identity and the political context of 'multiculturalism'

In order to set the context for a discussion of Irish immigration to London in the 1980s, it is important to recognize the complex mix of increased confidence alongside vulnerability that marked Irish communities in Britain in the previous decade. In the 1970s, a number of Irish activist and cultural groups were set up which produced the beginnings of a more self-conscious and coordinated Irish identity in Britain. The Federation of Irish Societies[48] was established by Irish activists in 1973 to promote the interests of the Irish community in Britain through community care, education, culture, arts, youth welfare and information provision. With the establishment of the *Irish Post* newspaper in the 1970s, its editor Mac Lau asserted that the concept of being Irish in Britain had been further developed among a diverse range of Irish groups, not least the *Irish Post* newspaper itself. He noted the many movements that had started in the 1970s and the increasing emphasis amongst the Irish on cultural activities and Irish history.[49] As well as carrying out the usual functions of a newspaper, the *Irish Post* saw itself as 'a rallying point for a sense of community among the Irish in Britain'.[50] These developments suggest an expansion of points of reference for the Irish in London and a de-centring of the Catholic Church as the main focus for the Irish community.[51]

The 1970s also saw an upsurge in anti-Irish prejudice in the aftermath of the IRA bombings in England and the introduction of the Prevention of Terrorism Act.[52] Holohan suggests that the 'fear of being "innocent until proven Irish" meant that many feel this to be a dark chapter in the lives of Irish people in Britain'.[53] The St Patrick's Day Parade in Birmingham was cancelled following the bombings in Birmingham in 1974 and was not held again until 1996, even if then in the shadow of the Canary Wharf bombing marking the breakdown of the IRA cease-fire.[54] The hunger strikes[55] began in 1980 and drew some Irish in Britain together in solidarity, while others played down their Irishness in public. Although issues of visibility and a public Irish voice have been a source of contention in relation to the Irish presence in Britain since the nineteenth century at least,[56] these issues were re-figured by the changed political and social context of the 1970s and 1980s.

The GLC provided a significant impetus for the increased activism of the Irish in London by recognizing the Irish as an 'ethnic minority', thereby legitimating the funding of specifically Irish welfare and cultural projects. Ken Livingstone, then leader of the GLC, contributed to the visibility of Irishness in England, and more specifically in London, by his strong and public support for Irish groups.[57] The first local government Irish Liaison Officer was appointed by the GLC in 1983 and a consultation conference was held to shape policies for the Irish community in London. By the end of 1985, there were about 30 specifically Irish welfare and cultural services established in London.[58] The GLC's Strategic Policy Unit produced a *Policy Report on the Irish Community* in 1984 which highlighted widespread discrimination against Irish people in the areas of housing, employment, education and media stereotyping. A key recommendation of the report was to make provisions for the preservation of Irish culture and identity in Britain.[59]

The overall picture of London's Irish community in this report indicates a community poorly housed, and suffering from a disproportionately high incidence of mental illness in relation to its size. It is a community baited by the media, suffering constant attacks on its cultural and social identity and deterred from political mobilisation by the threat of imprisonment and exile under the Prevention of Terrorism Act. The root of these problems lies in racism against the Irish, a factor yet to be acknowledged as a major problem in British society.[60]

While anti-black racism had been acknowledged as a feature of British society for some time, the first public institutional acknowledgement of anti-Irish racism was recorded in the above report. The identification of specifically Irish needs in London and the claiming of a visible Irish identity in the 1980s gained momentum with the development of analyses focusing on racism against the Irish in Britain. Anti-Irish racism, according to Hickman and Walter, involves a construction of the Irish as both inferior and alien. They argue that a myth of British homogeneity emerged in the 1950s and 1960s, which was generated by both the state and by 'race relations' activists.[61] By ignoring internal heterogeneity in Britain and the long-term presence of Irish immigrants, they suggest that the British state constructed the issues of immigrants and racism as relating only to post-war black immigrants.[62] Because 'whiteness' became an increasingly important signifier of 'insiderness' in Britain,[63] Irish immigrants found themselves in an ambivalent position in relation to discourses and policies of anti-racism. Connolly *et al.* capture the ambivalent positioning of the Irish in Britain when they suggest that 'the Irish have been both racialised and included, constructed as threatening and yet part of the British "family" because they are white'.[64]

The Prevention of Terrorism Act, which came into force in 1974, could be seen as an institutionalized instrument of surveillance and discrimination. This Act is widely used to collect and collate data on the Irish in Britain and is operated in such a way as to make the Irish, especially when moving between Britain and Ireland, 'a suspect community'.[65] The complex political nexus of Anglo-Irish relations past and present contributes to the ambivalence that marks many debates about anti-Irish racism and the positions of Irish immigrants to Britain. A London Irish Women's Centre Report in 1993 suggested that 'anti-Irish racism is a deeply embedded aspect of British society . . . [which] . . . is invisible to the main body of people in Britain'.[66] This constructed invisibility de-legitimizes activism relating to anti-Irish racism and makes reference to the particularity of the experiences of Irish people in Britain appear exaggerated.[67] Nonetheless, by the 1990s, anti-Irish racism had become a recognized discourse within the English political landscape and was legitimized to some extent by the research on discrimination against Irish people in Britain commissioned by the Commission for Racial Equality (CRE) and published by the CRE in 1997.[68]

As well as offering opportunities for Irish welfare and cultural organizations to develop and facilitating a discourse of anti-Irish racism, 'multicultural' policies can be seen as transforming an Irish immigrant or cultural community into an Irish 'ethnic minority' in Britain.[69] This shift in status and the need to demonstrate 'ethnic' group disadvantage contributed to a range of localized research projects on the welfare of the Irish in London since the mid-1980s. These projects were poorly funded and were aimed mostly at obtaining resources for disadvantaged Irish people in London. Much of this research, therefore, focused on the levels of disadvantage experienced by the Irish.[70] With the increased attention to disadvantage and service development for Irish people in this period, many Irish activists became involved in lobbying and providing for the welfare of Irish immigrants and second-generation Irish in Britain.[71] The increasing activism of the Irish in London in the 1980s produced a particular formation of Irishness based on assumptions of disadvantage, discrimination, Catholicism and nationalism. Some Irish Protestants, middle-class, gay and lesbian Irish felt misrepresented, if not actively excluded from these more visible versions of Irishness in London.[72]

Meanwhile, Irish women were just beginning to challenge the male-dominated image and practices of the Irish in London. Until the 1970s, there were no centres or organizations which addressed issues specific to Irish women. In 1972 the 'Women and Ireland' group was established to discuss and publicize events in Northern Ireland and to highlight women's activism within nationalism.[73] By the early 1980s, a network of 'Women and Ireland' groups was established extending to twelve British cities. The Irish Women's Abortion Support Group came together in 1980/81 primarily as a support group for Irish women travelling to Britain for an abortion.[74] In 1983, the London Irish Women's Centre (LIWC) was established as a central co-ordinating body for Irish women's groups.[75] The Centre was set up to counteract the erosion and marginalization of Irish women and held annual conferences in the 1980s focusing on political, social and cultural issues affecting Irish women. Existing Irish community organizations were seen as being dominated by men and the many needs of Irish women were not being met.[76] At the third London Irish Women's Conference in 1987, the Irish Lesbian Group discussed the discrimination they experienced within the Irish community epitomized by the *Irish Post*'s refusal to print the words 'Irish lesbian'. In their 1987 report, the LIWC suggested that 'many [lesbians] were forced to shed their Irish identity and assimilate into English society to find support in the English Feminist Movement'.[77] The establishment of the Centre meant that the composite identities Irish and woman, Irish and feminist, Irish and lesbian could be supported and legitimized in London.[78]

Although some groups, such as Irish feminists and lesbians, were beginning to gain a voice, other groups of immigrants experienced an even more ambivalent relationship to Irishness in London. For example, a Protestant Unionist informant in Kells's study commented on his discomfort with having his Irish accent equated in Britain with support for a united Ireland.[79] Kells notes that '[t]hose Protestants who consider themselves British first, Northern Irish second, tend to feel less desire to maintain an Irish identity and are more disposed, theoretically at least, to integrate into British society'.[80] A Northern Irish woman informant split her identity into emotional and factual elements by representing her Northern Irish identity as something she 'felt' and her Britishness as something she was, a 'fact'.[81]

Irishness in London in the 1980s, as in any other decade, was internally differentiated in relation to religion, class, generation, region of Ireland, gender, sexuality and many other factors. For all the opportunities offered by 'multiculturalism', there are also problems with this approach. A hegemonic and apparently fixed form of 'ethnic' identity emerges which is partly structured by funding criteria and definitions of 'ethnic minority' status. Discourses and policies of 'multiculturalism' tend to produce a reified Catholic and nationalist profile of the Irish in Britain, focusing more on a unified picture of disadvantage and discrimination than on the contradictory narratives that constitute Irish identity in London and elsewhere. Irish women have succeeded to some extent in challenging a predominantly masculine defined sense of Irishness in Britain. However, other Irish groups have been less successful in carving out spaces that influence emerging formations of Irishness in 'multicultural' Britain.

'Multiculturalism': legitimating Irish cultural expression

Numerous commentators have noted that new cultural forms of Irishness emerged in London in the 1980s and 1990s which rendered the Irish in Britain a very complicated and difficult group to define.[82] Ward suggests that: 'A wave of Irish pride has swept Britain in the last few years with the introduction of Irish Studies[83] in the school curriculum, the establishment of Irish newspapers in Britain, the London Irish Women's Centre and all kinds of consciousness raising groups throughout Britain'.[84] In the decade since 1985, Holohan argues that 'there has been what some would describe as a revival of Irish ethnic identity, among the older generation, their children born in Britain and the '80s wave of emigrants'.[85] On further reflection, Holohan suggests that a more accurate characterization of this phenomenon might be that Irish people are more willing to make their Irishness visible. She suggests that many of the recent emigrants and second-generation Irish people she interviewed acted 'more publicly as Irish people, than Irish people did in the past'.[86]

The terms and the aims of this increased visibility varied considerably within the Irish community in the 1980s. Although some groups were more politically focused and saw themselves as 'fighting back' against marginalization and invisibility, others were negotiating ways of 'celebrating' Irishness which might enhance their standing in British society. In different ways, both groups were attempting to bring about a re-evaluation of Irishness in Britain. For some, this was about gaining 'minority ethnic' status in order that discrimination would be addressed and those in need could have equal access to resources. For others, it was more about being able to maintain a pride in their Irish national identity while also attempting to generate a positive view of Irishness at all levels of the British establishment. The receptivity of a British public to the celebration of Irish cultural activities was facilitated both by a discourse of 'multiculturalism' that valorizes cultural diversity and by the increasing globalization of the cultural industry epitomized in the 1990s by the show *Riverdance*.

The 1980s also saw the emergence of new middle-class Irish organizations in London such as the London Irish Network (LIN) and the London Irish Society (LIS). LIN was formed in the late 1980s for Irish 'people of all ages, who are keen to . . . engage in a greater range of social activities'. The LIS held an inaugural Ball in September 1987 at the London Hilton and organized Christmas and St Patrick's Day parties to raise money for Irish charities in Britain. In the first copy of their newsletter *Ballyhoo!*, the LIS announced their commitment, not only to the less well off Irish in London, but also to their country of origin. They expressed their aim to develop 'projects which will, to coin a phrase "put something back into Ireland" '. While wanting to 'put something back into Ireland', this group of Irish emigrants also saw themselves as contributing significantly to British society: 'One of the beliefs of the society [is] that the Irish in London have something valuable to contribute to sport, culture and the arts in Britain and should not be too inward-looking in this'.[87] This implies a perceived danger in getting too absorbed in things Irish and an aspiration to value the diversity of the Irish contribution to British society. The outward thrust of the activities of the LIS is further emphasized by Collins's article in *Ballyhoo*! on future LIS events:

> The purpose of the [Sense of Ireland] Festival[88] is not to lend added weight to the paraphrase 'nothing fascinates the Irish as much as the Irish'; the activities are of such diversity that they will likely appeal as much to other nationalities as to Irish people. It is an international cultural event that happens to be focusing on Irish culture.[89]

Collins is keen to debunk the stereotype of an Irish community obsessed with itself. He appeals to a 1980s middle-class constituency of Irish immigrants to London who he perceives as wanting to avoid the ghettoization that is often associated with earlier generations of immigrants and Irish centres in London. Members of the LIS represent themselves through this newsletter as different from previous generations of Irish immigrants and challenge perceptions of Irishness in Britain as a working-class identity. They explicitly represent their presence in Britain in terms of their positive and confident contributions to British society. Their identities are also articulated in relation to an Ireland they had to leave in order to progress their careers, but which nonetheless equipped them with the skills to participate in an international economic and social context.[90]

These groups saw Irish cultural activities as resources that had to be managed in order to negotiate some form of integration into British life while also maintaining an identification with their Irish roots. This 'double consciousness' or doubling of identity arising from the immigrant negotiation of identity, both in relation to 'where they're from' and 'where they're at',[91] emerged as a strong theme in my own research with Irish women immigrants to London. In the following two sections of the chapter, I investigate this doubling of identity by drawing directly on my own research. The tone of the discussion shifts in these sections as the complexities of 'living' gendered emigrant and immigrant Irish identities are articulated in the women's accounts.

Bridging 'multiculturalism' and diaspora

My research was undertaken with Irish women who immigrated to London in the 1980s, and with Irish women who remained in the Republic of Ireland. The study focused on the relationships between emigration, national and gender identities.[92] Two themes that emerged from my analysis of the accounts of those women who immigrated to London are considered briefly below. The first theme relates to the experience of living a life in relation to two places, Ireland and London. The second theme focuses on the gendered significance of family relationships in negotiating Irish identity in migration.

As well as giving rise to a distinctive Irish minority 'ethnic'/cultural formation in London, 'multiculturalism' offered 1980s immigrants the opportunity to experience a diversity of cultures and ways of life. Most of those who took part in my research articulated a cosmopolitan sense of identity in London which related to what they described as their exposure to and experience of diverse cultures and identities. When it came to that part of their identity that they saw as Irish, Ireland was their main reference point for Irishness, and not Irish groups or activities in London. This ongoing relationship to Ireland was facilitated by the fact that they had only recently left Ireland and were able to keep in touch as a result of relatively cheap transport and communications between Ireland and England. Their sense of themselves as Irish, therefore, had a multi-located dimension that involved reference to both Ireland and England/London and everyday practices that involved bridging the gaps between these places, both culturally and emotionally.[93] This meant negotiating an Irishness in London that was increasingly being structured by discourses of 'multiculturalism' alongside a consciousness of other formations of Irishness in Ireland and elsewhere. In this sense, those taking part in my study can be seen as negotiating a diasporic sense of Irishness.

The following sections re-introduce the activity of emigration addressed in the first section of this chapter and offer some evidence for the argument that immigration is partly structured by how the act of emigration is accounted for and integrated into the immigration narrative. It may also be the case that the act of emigration is more immanent when the country of immigration is geographically proximate to the country of origin.

Bridging two lives with a hybrid Irishness

Many of the informants expressed a doubleness of identity related to the composite experience of emigrating from the Republic of Ireland and immigration to England/London. For example, Cath[94] (who had lived in London for seven years at the time of the research) described her experience in the following way: 'you could lead a completely different life over here to the one you were living at home . . . and people over there would never know the you over here . . . I've struggled against that, but I used to feel like it was two lives.' The experience of living two lives is represented as a struggle which involves Cath in building bridges between London and Ireland. Through this work of actively maintaining connections with 'home', she produces her Irishness in one multi-located life instead of two separate lives. Her account suggests, however, that a multi-located Irishness does not resolve the issue of belonging. She goes on to state: 'I wonder if I could fit in any more after seven years away . . . I would feel constricted in every way if I went home . . . your attitudes change when you come over here.' Because London is relatively close to Ireland, there is the potential to maintain connections with Ireland and thereby to re-evaluate changing relationships to Ireland and Irishness. Cath saw her Irishness as coming out of her experience of having grown up in Ireland and her continued connections with Ireland. However, her account suggests that she was beginning to question this basis for Irishness based on the obstacles to her belonging there now. It is possible that she may find ways of defining her Irishness more in relation to Irish 'ethnicity' in London if she remains there.

Some of the women described a privatizing of their Irishness in London in order, as they saw it, to succeed in the labour market there. For example, Fionnula (who had lived in London for nine years at the time of the research) suggested that: 'the easiest way to be successful with your colleagues [in London] is to be one of them . . . then after a number of years you become very Anglicised yourself . . . when you go home you don't feel Irish either . . . they all say "Oh your accent" . . . And your lifestyle is so different to theirs anyway . . .'. By 'fitting in' with the way things are done in London, Fionnula can potentially succeed career-wise in London, but her Irish identity becomes subordinated to career success. She attempts to negotiate two lives: the life she has created for herself in London, and her potential 'Irish life' in Ireland. Yet, in her case, her life in London seems to deny her the possibility of being accepted as Irish in Ireland (particularly by her family).

While Cath describes a simultaneous sense of not belonging in relation to both London and Ireland, Fionnula suggests a kind of accommodation with London, while feeling an 'outsider' in relation to Ireland. These accounts of negotiating two lives and identities between Ireland and London may be related to length of time living in London. Jenny, who had lived in London for fifteen years at the time of my interview with her, describes a sense of simultaneous belonging in relation to both Ireland and London: 'I think I fit in fairly well when I go back . . . you know everybody so well, you don't get away from it . . . if you don't live in a place your interest in it does begin to slip . . . I am quite interested in London . . . It has become more relevant for me. And the longer you are away the greater that feeling becomes.' Jenny goes on to suggest that she sees herself in terms of being 'Irish in London'. She links length of absence from Ireland with her level of affinity for London. Her affiliation with both London and Ireland offer her the possibility of the hybrid identity, London-Irish.

The hyphenated identity 'London-Irish', and relocation of Irishness in London implied by the term 'Irish in London', situates Jenny as simultaneously belonging in relation to both 'where she's from' and 'where she's at'. The sense of belonging to Irish identified groups in London and familiarity with Irishness in Ireland implied by 'London-Irish' offers a basis for belonging that does justice to her everyday experience. Jenny's identification with London means she doesn't have to identify with Englishness or even Britishness in order to belong in England or Britain. The adoption of a hybrid identity such as 'London-Irish' or 'Irish in London' disrupts the hegemony of both a territorially based Irishness and a nationally defined identity particularly with regard to her residence in England.

One of the themes emerging from these Irish women's accounts of living their Irishness in London is the considerable personal distress and emotional work involved in the experience of living two lives and overcoming this split. The adoption of a more London-based identity by Jenny suggests one means of resolving the conflicts that Cath and Fionnula articulate with regard to bridging the expectations and obligations associated with their lives in Ireland and in London. These personal accounts of immigration and settlement in London challenge 'multicultural' notions of 'ethnicity' which locate identity within the nation of destination. They complicate the simple criteria by which 'ethnicity' is defined and assumptions about how it is 'lived'. They point to the inadequacy of understanding immigrant identity with reference only to the country of destination regardless of how 'multicultural' its approach to social organization and identity. In the following section, I consider the women's accounts of their relationships to the idea of 'homeland' and how these are tied up with anticipation of return, familial contracts and obligations.

Burning bridges to 'home' and an 'Irish future' through marriage

Ireland, as noted earlier, is represented in many women's accounts as the repository of Irishness. Many felt that the only way to have what they called 'an Irish future' would be through return to Ireland to live. Most of the women taking part in my study were between the ages of 24 and 35, a point in the life-cycle that is linked with plans for return.[95] Although it might be acceptable to be away from 'home' when young and single, Malcolm notes that the idea of return seems to arise at the times of establishing a family or of retirement. Because London is close to Ireland contact can be more easily maintained and the prospect of return a recurring theme.[96] The possibility of return for some of the women taking part in my study is complicated, as they see it, by their relationships with partners/husbands and children. Their accounts differentiate between their relationship to Ireland 'for themselves' (and maybe their children) and when mediated through their relationships with husbands or partners who are not Irish. Those women with non-Irish husbands expressed a high level of responsibility for their decision to marry non-Irish men and saw this as having major implications for their hopes of returning to Ireland. The accounts below point to the ways in which the negotiation of migration and national/ethnic identity may be gendered.

The marriage contract or committed relationship significantly affects women's relationships to Ireland and their decisions to return or not. For example, Anne, who noted that she is planning to marry an English man, had the following to say: 'I would never ask him to come to Ireland, because I was the one who made the decision to come to London . . . one day I would like to go and live in Ireland . . . It would have to be up to him . . . I would never ask him. That was the decision I had to come to make . . .'. Anne sees her decision to emigrate as bringing about a series of events, including her impending marriage, which prevents her, as she sees it, from having the freedom to return to Ireland. Her desire to live in Ireland is subsumed to the will of her husband in marriage. Ireland's limited labour market is a significant factor in this reasoning because men's identities continue to be closely associated with the role of 'breadwinner'.

Doreen, who has returned from London to live in Ireland with her English husband, offers a similar account: 'I was not going to come home until John said we'll do it . . . it had to be his decision . . . He knew that I really wanted to come back, but I thought I had burnt my bridges . . . I thought I was going to live my life in England and it depressed me. The thought of children with English accents, for some peculiar reason, depressed me.' These accounts suggest that Irish women's initiative in emigrating and increasing success in the labour market in London may not reflect their experiences in other aspects of their lives. Those Irish women in intercultural marriages found that their relationships to Ireland, and therefore their sense of Irishness, was mediated and constrained by their married status. Gender and immigration come together here to complicate the negotiation of Irish identity in London.

For many of the Irish women taking part in my study, their continuing relationships to Ireland, facilitated at the end of the twentieth century by faster and relatively cheap forms of travel and communications, can produce greater expectations of negotiating identity and belonging *between* places. Although academic attention to the implications of the politics and policies implemented within the place of destination is important, it is equally important to recognize the dynamic between emigration and immigration. The rhetoric of 'multiculturalism' attempts to locate identity within a pluralist framework, but also very much *within* the country of immigration and settlement. These women's accounts suggest that emigration, immigration and settlement have to be brought together if the experiences of recent migrants (particularly of those migrating to Britain which is relatively close to Ireland) are to be analysed. Their experiences are essentially multi-located or diasporic experiences which produce particular dynamics of belonging and identity. If 'the logic of multiculturalism [is] to assume that all members of a specific community share the same relationship to the same culture',[97] the concept of 'diaspora', in contrast, allows for multi-located identities that are reproduced differently within different times and spaces. The idea of belonging *in* displacement and the multiple structures of affiliations that are seen as structuring identity in diaspora appear more in keeping with the women's accounts discussed above than 'multicultural' discourses of integration. The conclusion addresses the theme of diaspora and its relevance for addressing the issues raised in this chapter.

Conclusion

Irish immigrants to London in the 1980s encountered a 'multicultural' city, but also a city that, due to fraught Anglo-Irish relations and the IRA bombings in London, constructed the Irish in Britain as a 'suspect community'. Dominant features of Irish public culture in London of the 1980s included: a celebration of Irish culture which was gaining increasing popularity within a global culture market; activism in relation to Northern Ireland; and political lobbying for culturally sensitive welfare service provision and for the elimination of anti-Irish racism. The Irish were positioned and positioned themselves, therefore, in a range of complex ways. It is clear from the debates addressed in this chapter that emigration and immigration involve economic, political, cultural and emotional dynamics and relationships across space and time. Questions remain, however, as to how Irish immigrants in London negotiate the doubling of being Irish in relation to their country of origin and their positions as 'Irish' in London? Paul Gilroy argues that doubleness is produced in the tensions between 'roots and routes' which are central to the diasporic experience.[98] Many of the informants in my study suggested a tense negotiation between perceptions of 'roots' in Ireland, but also a sense of being deeply marked by their 'routes' from Ireland to England (often via elsewhere) and back to Ireland again (even if only imaginatively). These routes often involve career plans, marriages, children and other commitments that further complicate relationships to place and identity and which are gendered. If many of the 1980s young Irish men emigrants to London fell into stereotypical labour market niches, many 1980s young women emigrants broke new ground both in the labour market and in gaining visibility as Irish women. Yet, as the accounts quoted in this chapter suggest, Irish women in diaspora continue to struggle with traditional constructions of gender relations and gendered expectations that are not always escaped through emigration.

This chapter began by pointing to the appropriation by the state and media of the high-flying emigrant as a symbol of a progressive and developed Republic of Ireland in the 1980s. The discussion then moves from how 1980s emigration was analysed as a national phenomenon, to the positioning of the Irish as an 'ethnic' group in 'multicultural' London, and finally to Irish women's accounts of emigration and immigration. By taking this route, the chapter demonstrates that emigration and immigration at the end of the millennium cannot be easily contained within a national or 'multicultural' framework of analysis only. The chapter ends by invoking the concept of 'diaspora' as a means of holding together some of the complexity of late twentieth-century migration between Britain and Ireland. It was not until the 1990s and Mary Robinson's presidency that Irish people, in the Republic of Ireland at least, began to use the term 'diaspora' to describe a multi-located Irish people. President Robinson opened up the definition of Irishness through the notion of 'diaspora' to include the Irish from Argentina to London, as well as the Irish in Ireland. Through a discourse of Irishness as diasporic she attempted to give legitimacy to the many spaces of Irishness and the 'multiculturalism' that marks them all, whether 'at home' or abroad. This chapter offers some insights into discourses and practices that construct one small segment of the multi-generational and world-wide phenomenon that is the Irish diaspora.[99]

Notes

1. F. Ryan, 'The Land that Makes us Refugees', *The Big Issues*, 15 (1995), pp. 4–5.
2. L. Ryan, 'Irish Emigration to Britain Since World War II', in R. Kearney (ed.), *Migrations: The Irish at Home and Abroad* (Dublin, 1990). See also J. Mac Laughlin, *Historical and Recent Irish Immigration* (London, 1994).
3. L. King and I. Shuttleworth, 'The Emigration and Employment of Irish Graduates: The Export of High-Quality Labour from the Periphery of Europe', *European Urban and Regional Studies*, 2, 1 (1995), pp. 21–40. When all the Irish-born in Britain are considered, i.e. all generations of immigrants, then nearly half of these live in the south-east of England, with the single largest concentration being in the Greater London area. The second largest concentration is in the West Midlands metropolitan area, followed by Greater Manchester and Scotland. Northern Irish born (im)migrants have a geographical distribution similar to that of the 'white' population as a whole. (D. Owen, *Irish-Born People in Great Britain: Settlement Pattern and Socio-Economic circumstances*, Census Statistical Paper No. 9 (Warwick, 1991), p. 5.
4. P. Popham, 'The London Irish', *The (London) Independent Magazine*, 11 August 1990, Issue 101, pp. 21–18 – quoting an *Irish Press* article.
5. Of course the parameters of the diversity celebrated were closely policed with implications, in particular for homeless and unemployed Irish immigrants. The implementation of the Prevention of Terrorism Act (PTA) had implications for all Irish immigrants and particularly for those travelling between Britain and Ireland.
6. J. Mac Laughlin, *Ireland: The Emigrant Nursery and the World Economy* (Cork, 1994).
7. As noted earlier, London and the south-east of England were the main destinations for these emigrants to the UK.
8. M. Hickman and B. Walter, *Discrimination and the Irish Community in Britain: A Report of Research Undertaken for the Commission for Racial Equality* (London, 1997). Hereafter referred to as the 'CRE Report'.
9. CRE Report.
10. Shuttleworth notes from analysis of the 1991 census that traditional geographical patterns of emigration, with more leaving from Connacht and Munster, were reasserting themselves in the latter decades of the 1980s. While in 1981–86 the east had the highest level of out-migration, in the period 1986–91 this region had the lowest rates of emigration. Ian Shuttleworth, 'Irish Graduate Emigration: the Mobility of Qualified Manpower in the Context of Peripherality', in R. King (ed.), *Mass Migration in Europe: The Legacy and the Future* (Chichester, 1993), pp. 310–26. See also J.J. Sexton, 'Recent Changes in the Irish Population and in the Pattern of Emigration', *The Irish Banking Review* (Autumn, 1987), pp. 31–44.
11. The Central Statistics Office began doing annual breakdowns of migration based on the annual Labour Force Survey (now known as the Quarterly National Household Survey) in the late 1980s. These were then revised following collation of the 1996 census data.
12. King and Shuttleworth, 'The Emigration and Employment of Irish Graduates'.

13. CRE Report. See also Owen, *Irish-Born People in Great Britain*, who found possession of higher education qualifications to be even more of an advantage in the labour market for the Irish than the 'white' population as a whole (p. 24).
14. CRE Report, p. 41.
15. When non-health occupations were considered, thereby excluding the large numbers of Irish women in nursing, 29.7 per cent of Irish-born women (in the age category 18–29) were in other occupations within the categories 1, 2, and 3 (CRE Report). Owen's analysis of the 1991 UK census noted that Irish-born men are more likely than any other group to be self-employed, but not entrepreneurs (i.e. employing others). These findings point to the continuing significance of the construction industry (as many building workers are nominally self-employed) for Irish men in Britain. Irish-born women were less likely to be self-employed than any other group of women in Britain.
16. CRE Report, Table 4.1, p. 255.
17. The CRE Report notes that at a conservative estimate, young Irish-born men aged between 18 and 29 may be underestimated in census figures by about 15 per cent.
18. J.J. Lee, 'Dynamics of Social and Political Change in the Irish Republic', in D. Keogh and M.H. Haltzel (eds), *Northern Ireland and the Politics of Reconciliation* (New York, 1993). See also B. Walter, *Geography Working Paper No. 4 Gender and Irish Migration to Britain* (Cambridge, 1989).
19. E. Hazelkorn, *Irish Immigrants Today: A Socio-Economic Profile of Contemporary Irish Emigrants and Immigrants in the UK* (London, 1990). While the services sector was growing, the 1980s saw the longest decline in manufacturing employment in the Republic since the formation of the state. See Mac Laughlin, *Ireland: The Emigrant Nursery*, p. 30.
20. See C. Ni Laoire, 'Gender Issues in Irish Rural Outmigration', in P. Boyle and K. Halfacree (eds), *Migration and Gender in the Developed World* (London, forthcoming).
21. I. O'Carroll, *Models for Movers: Irish Women's Emigration to America* (Dublin, 1990); and 'Breaking the Silence from a Distance: Irish Women Speak of Sexual Abuse', in P. O'Sullivan (ed.), *Irish Women and Irish Migration* (Leicester, 1995).
22. See A. Maguire, 'The Accidental Immigrant', B.J. Lynch, 'A Land Beyond Tears' and C. Smyth, 'Keeping it Close. Experiencing Emigration in England', all in I. O'Carroll and E. Collins (eds), *Lesbian and Gay Visions of Ireland – Towards the Twenty-First Century* (London, 1995). See also A. Maguire, *Invented Identities: Lesbians and Gays Talk about Migration*, ed. B. Cant (London, 1997).
23. See also J. Chance, 'Gender Differences in Irish Migration and Settlement Patterns in England 1971–1997', conference paper delivered at The Scattering; Ireland and the Irish Diaspora: A Comparative Perspective, University College Cork, 14–17 September 1997. It is important to note that when all generations of Irish-born immigrants to Britain (women and men) are considered, this group is clustered more strongly in the lowest category (Social Class V) than any other birthplace/ethnic group in Britain. Neither do the Irish share the same level of upward mobility as the population as a whole (CRE Report). The report argues that there are more similarities between the positions of Irish Republic born immigrants and other non-'white' groups than with the 'white' indigenous population, suggesting that the Irish have not assimilated more easily on the grounds of 'whiteness' (CRE Report, p. 72).
24. B. Walter, 'Irishness, Gender and Place', *Environment and Planning. Society and Space*, 13 (1995), pp. 35–50.

25. See Owen, *Irish-Born People in Great Britain*.
26. See CRE Report.
27. A. Rossiter, 'Bringing the Margins into the Centre: A Review of Aspects of Irish Emigration', in S. Hutton and P. Stewart (eds), *Ireland's Histories. Aspects of State, Society and Ideology* (London, 1991), pp. 223–42.
28. Despite the emphasis on middle-class emigration as unique to the 1980s, it is important to note that this group was also well represented in previous periods of emigration. See, for example, G. Hanlon, 'Graduate Emigration: A Continuation or a Break with the Past', in P. O'Sullivan (ed.), *Patterns of Migration, Vol. 1, The Irish World Wide History Heritage Identity* (Leicester, 1992); P. Blessing, 'Irish Emigration to the United States, 1800–1920', in P.J. Drudy (ed.), *The Irish in America: Emigration, Assimilation and Impact* (Cambridge, 1985); Drudy, 'Editorial Introduction', *The Irish in America: Emigration, Assimilation and Impact*; J.A. Jackson, 'The Irish in Britain', in Drudy (ed.), *Ireland and Britain since 1922*.
29. National Economic and Social Council, *The Economic and Social Implications of Emigration* (Dublin, 1991).
30. J. Jackson, 'Review Symposium: National Economic and Social Council, The Economic and Social Implications of Emigration', *Irish Journal of Sociology*, 1 (1991), pp. 69–73.
31. G. Hanlon, 'The Emigration of Irish Accountants: Economic Restructuring and Producer Services in the Periphery', *Irish Journal of Sociology*, 1 (1991), p. 62.
32. S. Sassen, *The Global City* (Princeton, 1991). See also J. Eade (ed.), *Living in the Global City: Globalization as Local Process* (London, 1997).
33. See M. Corcoran, *Irish Illegals: Transients Between Two Societies* (Westport, Conn., 1993) for a discussion of New York as a 'global city' and the labour market experiences of Irish 'illegals' in the 1980s.
34. Hanlon, 'The Emigration of Irish Accountants'. Shuttleworth, 'Irish graduate emigration', found that 'facilitating cultural and personal factors' such as family and friendship networks were important in emigration decision-making for graduates. In his study with University College Galway graduates in London in 1989, he found that half had not sought a job prior to arriving in London. These findings suggest that career planning is not necessarily the sole stimulus for leaving and that jobs are not always acquired before leaving Ireland.
35. Hanlon, 'Graduate Emigration', p. 193.
36. Sexton, 'Recent Changes in the Irish population'.
37. D. Massey, 'Making Spaces: Or, geography is Political too', *Soundings*, 1 (1995), p. 204; See also Y. Kobayashi, 'Was it the Right Move? Social Class Comparison of Irish Stayers and Irish Migrants in Britain: Educational Perspective', paper presented at The Scattering: Ireland and the Irish Diaspora: A Comparative Perspective, University College Cork, 24–27 September 1997.
38. Massey, 'Making Spaces', p. 197.
39. Jackson, 'Review Symposium', p. 73.
40. Shuttleworth, 'Irish Graduate Emigration', p. 318.
41. See also F. O'Toole, *Black Hole, Green Card. The Disappearance of Ireland* (Dublin, 1994) and *The Ex-Isle of Erin. Images of a Global Ireland* (Dublin, 1996).
42. Owen, *Irish-born people in Great Britain*, in his analysis of the 1991 British census, found that most Northern Irish (im)migrants to Britain were in the younger age ranges up to 45, whereas those from the Republic were predominantly middle-aged. The census patterns suggest that Republic-born population in Britain is dominated by 1940s/50s immigrants, while most of those from Northern Ireland

left in the 1970s and 1980s. He also noted that those leaving Northern Ireland did so with high levels of education. See also Halpin's chapter in this book. I am not aware of any research done on the impact of 'The Troubles' on emigration from the North (with the exception of S. Pink, 'From Belfast to London: A Case Study of Identity and Ethnicity among Young Migrants from Northern Ireland', unpublished M.A. (Manchester University, 1990), referenced in M. Hickman, *The Irish Community in Britain: Myth or Reality* (London, 1996). See also M. Kells, *Ethnic Identity Amongst Young Irish Middle Class Migrants in London* (London, 1995), p. 11.

43. See J. White McAuley, 'Under an Orange Banner: Reflections on the Northern Protestant experiences of emigration', in P. O'Sullivan (ed.), *Religion and Identity* (London, 1996), pp. 43–69.

44. B. Gray, 'Unmasking Irishness: Irish Women, the Irish Nation and the Irish Diaspora', in J. Mac Laughlin (ed.), *Location and Dislocation in Contemporary Irish Society: Emigration and Irish Identities* (Cork, 1997), pp. 209–35.

45. It is important to acknowledge the emigration of significant numbers of young Irish people in the 1990s. For example, in 1995 and 1996 out-migration was respectively 33,100 and 31,200 (CSO Population and Migration Estimates, April 1997). These figures represent significant levels of emigration comparable to the middle years of the 1980s. See B. Gray, 'Steering a Course Somewhere between Hegemonic Discourses of Irishness', in R. Lentin (ed.), *The Expanding Nation: Towards a Multi-Ethnic Ireland* (Dublin, 1999).

46. J. Donald and A. Rattansi, 'Introduction', in *'Race', Culture and Difference* (London, 1992), pp.1–10.

47. Ibid.

48. An umbrella body for the Irish community in Britain. In 1999 FIS had over 100 affiliates.

49. Quoted in L. Curtis, J. O'Keefe and C. Keatinge, *Hearts and Minds: Anam agus Intinn: The Cultural Life of London's Irish Community* (London, 1987).

50. Hickman, *The Irish Community in Britain*, p. 11. Hickman notes that the 1950s generation of immigrants in particular identify with the interests, images, politics and culture represented in the *Irish Post*.

51. See The Irish Video Project, *Irish in England, Video 1* (London, 1983), in which the centrality of the Catholic Church for 1950s immigrants is emphasized.

52. This Act was passed in 1974 following the bombing of two public houses in Birmingham in which 21 people died and for which the IRA denied responsibility.

53. A. Holohan, *Working Lives: The Irish in Britain* (Middlesex, 1995).

54. There was some local protest to the re-establishment of the parade in 1996 and many Irish groups themselves were unsure about its revival following the Canary Wharf bomb. However, the parade went ahead and has gone from strength to strength since 1996.

55. The hunger strikes followed a series of events including the granting of 'special category status' (including the right to wear civilian clothes) to persons convicted of terrorist offences in 1972 and its withdrawal in 1976 in order to redefine violence as 'criminal'. Republican prisoners responded by refusing to wear prisoner clothes and wearing only a blanket. This was followed by a 'dirty protest'. When these forms of protest did not bring any concessions from the British government, the hunger strikes began in 1980. These ended at the end of 1980s but recommenced in 1981 and by the end of the strikes, which lasted seven months, ten men had died. R. Foster, 'Anglo-Irish Relations and Northern Ireland: Historical Perspectives', in Keogh and Haltzel (eds), *Northern Ireland and the Politics of*

Reconciliation, pp. 13–33, sees the hunger strikes as a turning point in relation to increased support for the IRA, north and south of the border. See D. Beresford, *Ten Men Dead: The Story of the 1981 Irish Hunger Strike* (London, 1987); P. O'Malley, *Biting at the Grave: The Irish Hunger Strikes and the Politics of Despair* (Belfast, 1990).

56. Hickman, *The Irish Community in Britain*, pp. 8–9, argues that the low public profile taken by the Irish in Britain arises from British state's active attempts to incorporate the Irish since the nineteenth century. This incorporation involved the regulation of potentially oppositional groups in the process of creating a single nation-state. The unwillingness of the Irish to assert themselves as Irish in Britain, she argues, is not just a product of the conflict in relation to Northern Ireland since 1968, but arises from the positioning of the Irish as a potential threat since the Act of Union in 1801. See also S. Fielding, *Class and Ethnicity: Irish Catholics in England, 1880–1939* (Milton Keynes, 1993).

57. Curtis *et al.*, *Hearts and Minds*.

58. Irish-identified groups proliferated in the 1980s, with one example being the 'Irish Representation in Britain Group' (IRBG), which formed in 1981 to offer an effective voice for the Irish in Britain on social and political matters. Another example is the 'Action Group for Irish Youth', which first met in April 1984 in response to the perceived increase in numbers of young Irish people arriving in London.

59. London Strategic Policy Unit, *Policy Report on the Irish Community* (London, 1984). This report was based on proceedings of the consultation conference held in 1983.

60. London Strategic Policy Unit, *Policy Report on the Irish Community*, p. 11. S. O'Doherty, drawing on figures produced by Homeless Network, suggested that Irish people made up 15 per cent of homeless people sleeping on the streets of London in the mid-1990s ('No Blacks, No Dogs, No Irish: Live Human Exports from Ireland to London', *Big Issues*, 17 (1995) pp. 6–8). While 60 of the 2,400 housing associations in Britain in the mid-1990s were run by ethnic minorities, the Irish community had only four registered associations, demonstrating, in O'Doherty's view, that the Irish were not organizing effectively to help themselves abroad.

61. M. Hickman and B. Walter, 'Deconstructing Whiteness: Irish Women in Britain', *Feminist Review*, 50 (1995), pp. 5–19.

62. Ibid.

63. See, for example, P. Gilroy, *There Ain't No Black in the Union Jack* (London, 1987).

64. C. Connolly *et al.*, 'The Irish Issue: The British Question', *Feminist Review*, 50 (1995), p. 1.

65. P. Hillyard, *Suspect Community. People's Experiences of the Prevention of Terrorism Acts in Britain* (London, 1993). See also J. O'Flynn, D. Murphy and M. Tucker, *Racial Attacks and Harassment of Irish People* (London, n.d.) and G. Pierce, 'The Guildford Four: English Justice and the Irish Community', *Race and Class*, 31, 3 (1990), pp. 81–90. The miscarriage of justice cases prevented many Irish people from reporting racist incidents for fear of unjust treatment. Action Group for Irish Youth, *Irish Unfairly Treated* (London, 1996).

66. London Irish Women's Centre, *Roots and Realities: A Profile of Irish Women in London* (London, 1993), p. 5.

67. See B. Gray, 'Locations of Irishness: Irish Women's Accounts of National Identity', unpublished Ph.D. thesis (University of Lancaster, 1998).

68. CRE Report. The CRE also supported a number of cases which have proven discrimination against Irish people on grounds of 'race'.

69. Curtis *et al.*, *Hearts and Minds*.

70. See O'Flynn *et al.*, *Racial Attacks and Harassment of Irish People*; U. Kowarzik (AGIY and FIS), *Developing a Community Response: The Service Needs of the Irish Community in Britain* (London, 1994); Camden Borough Council, *The Voice of the Irish in Camden, Conference Report* (London, 1990); Greater London Council, *Report on the Prevention of Terrorism Act in London and Report on Consultation with the Irish Community* (London, 1984); M. Maguire (for Ealing Council and Brent Irish Advisory Service), *The Irish in Ealing: An Invisible Community* (London, 1989); Action Group for Irish Youth, *Young and Irish: Meeting the Need* (London, 1988); Action Group for Irish Youth *et al.*, *The Irish Community: Discrimination and The Criminal Justice System* (London, 1997); Irish in Britain Representation Group, *Survey into the Promotion of Irish Culture within Haringey School Curriculum* (London, 1986); M.G. Marmot, A.M. Adelstein, and L. Bulusu, *Immigrant Mortality in England and Wales, 1970–78.* (London, 1984). The Irish are also highly represented amongst deaths in police custody, those being stopped by the police (two and a half times higher than white British), and in the prison population (*Irish Post*, 27 July 1996, p. 4), P. Murphy, 'The Invisible Minority: Irish Offenders and the English Criminal Justice System', *Probation Journal*, 2–7 March 1994; T. Woodhouse, G. O'Meachair, N. Clark, and M. Jones, *The Irish and Policing in Islington* (London, 1991).
71. Some 1980s immigrants became professionally employed in voluntary and statutory organizations, while others were active on a volunteer basis. These groups and activities are very different from the more 'privatized' activities of the county and diocesan associations in the 1950s. A further change in the 1990s was the shift to lobbying the Republic of Ireland government by Irish welfare activists in Britain. For example, the Irish Representation in Britain Group (IBRG) requested unsuccessfully that the Republic of Ireland Central Statistics Office (CSO) include emigrants in the 1996 census. The IBRG, Federation of Irish Societies (FIS) and Glor an Deori have and continue to lobby the government of the Republic of Ireland on issues from emigrant's welfare, to the right to vote for emigrants in Irish national elections. The Irish government in 1984 publicly acknowledged the disadvantage that some Irish emigrants experience in Britain by establishing the Dion committee – the Irish Government's Advisory Committee for the Irish community in Britain and which makes recommendations for the disbursement of Irish government funding of £750,000 per annum (at 1999 figures) for Irish welfare agencies in Britain. Since 1990 there has also been provision for grants to Irish voluntary groups in the USA and since 1996 to groups in Australia. The Report by the Minister for Social, Community and Family Affairs entitled *Strengthening Families for Life* (1998) recognized the significance of the diaspora for Irish family life by devoting Chapter 16 to 'Family Networks – the Irish Diaspora', pp. 368–78.
72. See Gray, *Locations of Irishness*; M. Kells, 'Ethnicity in the 1990. Contemporary Irish Migrants in London', in U. Kockel (ed.), *Landscape, Heritage and Identity: Case Studies in Irish Ethnography* (Liverpool 1995), pp. 223–36.
73. Rossiter, 'Bringing the Margins into the Centre', p. 239.
74. A sister group, the Irish Abortion Solidarity Campaign, was established after the X Case in 1992 with a political campaigning brief as distinct from a support role. For a discussion of the X Case and its implications for the many temporary Irish women migrants see A. Smyth (ed.), *The Abortion Papers: Ireland* (Dublin, 1992) and L. Smyth, 'Narratives of Irishness and the Problem of Abortion: The X Case 1992', *Feminist Review*, 60 (1998) pp. 61–83.
75. The Centre itself did not open until 1986.

76. London Irish Women's Centre, *Annual Report* (1987), p. 2. Solais Anois, a women's refuge specifically for Irish women escaping domestic violence, was set up in London in 1993.

77. London Irish Women's Centre, *Annual Report* (1987), p. 2. Amach Linn, an organization to advance the social and cultural welfare of Irish lesbians and gay men in London, was set up in 1995. Many of those involved in setting up these organizations had left Ireland in the 1980s.

78. Curtis *et al.*, *Hearts and Minds*. See also London Irish Women's Centre, *Roots and Realities*. Association of London Authorities, *Seminar on the Needs of Irish Women* (London, 1989); O. O'Brien (Action Group for Irish Youth), *HIV and a Migrant Community: The Irish in Britain* (London: 1997); Haringey Council, *Equal Opportunities the Irish Dimension: An Agenda for Change* (London, n.d.).

79. Kells, 'Ethnicity in the 1990s', p. 230.

80. Ibid., pp. 232–3.

81. M. Kells, ' "I'm Myself and Nobody Else": Gender and Ethnicity Among Young Middle-Class Irish Women in London', in O'Sullivan (ed.), *Irish Women and Irish Migration*, pp. 201–34.

82. Kells, *Ethnic Identity*. See also Holohan, *Working Lives* and Nuala O'Faolain, 'Back in the Shadows'.

83. Irish Studies Centres have been established within some higher education institutions in Britain since the early 1980s. Until that late 1970s there were hardly any courses with 'Irish' in the title. M. Hickman, 'The Irish Studies Scene in Britain: Perceptions and Progress', *Text and Context*, 4 (1990), pp. 18–22. By the mid-1990s there are large Irish Studies Centres within at least three different institutions of higher education in England and the British Association for Irish Studies has been established to encourage the development of Irish Studies at all levels within the education system.

84. R. Wall, *Leading Lives: Irish Women in Britain* (Dublin, 1991), p. 11.

85. Holohan, *Working Lives*, p. 8. See also J. Ambrose's novel, *Serious Time* (London, 1998), which is based on the music scene and hedonistic lifestyles of some 1980s Irish immigrants to London.

86. Holohan, *Working Lives*, p. 8.

87. G. Galligan, 'A Letter from the LIS Committee', *Ballyhoo!*, 1 (1998), p. 3.

88. This festival was sponsored, not by LIS, but by the FIS, which was established in 1974, and Riverside Studios, London.

89. P. Collins, 'Sense of Ireland', *Ballyhoo!*, 1 (1988), p. 4.

90. The first copy of *Ballyhoo!* included articles on enjoying life in London; Irish solicitors in London; the development of the new International Financial Services Centre in Dublin; Landmark Trust weekends away; photographs from the LIS Ball; developments at Bord Failte (the Irish Tourist Board) and the Bank of Ireland; the presentation of a £5,000 cheque (raised at the Ball) to the London Irish Centre; an account of the work done for less well off Irish emigrants at the Camden Irish centre; golf around London; a short story; property buying tips; and two accounts of changing careers in London. Overall the newsletter has a professional and business feel to it.

91. These phrases are taken from P. Gilroy's article: 'It ain't where you're from, it's where you're at . . . : The Dialectics of Diasporic Identification', *Third Text*, 13 (1990/1), pp. 3–16.

92. One hundred and eleven women took part in the study. All of the women were born in the Republic of Ireland, they came from urban and rural backgrounds,

different class backgrounds, some had children, some didn't, and most were between the ages of 25 and 40 years old. Women who emigrated to London and to Luton in the 1980s and their peers who remained in the Republic of Ireland took part in the study. My aim was not to do a 'representative' study with a view to generalizing my 'findings', but rather to carry out a systematic qualitative, in-depth study that might contribute to a re-mapping of the research agenda in relation to Irish national identity, emigration and the category of Irish women. The study involved focus group discussions and one-to-one interviews. This chapter draws only on the accounts of women who immigrated to London.

93. A small minority of women also defined their relationship to 'home' in economic terms and spoke about sending money back to Ireland to help support family members in Ireland.

94. Pseudonyms are used in the interests of confidentiality.

95. E. Malcolm, *Elderly Return from Britain to Ireland: A Preliminary Study* (Dublin, 1996).

96. The late 1990s has seen the development of a cross borough 'London Irish Elder's Forum' which lobbies for equal rights with Irish elders in Ireland and the development of conditions in which they can return to Ireland if they so desire.

97. N. Yuval-Davis, '[Racial] Equality and the Politics of Difference', *New Formations*, 33 (1998), p. 137.

98. P. Gilroy, *The Black Atlantic. Modernity and Double Consciousness* (London, 1993).

99. I am grateful to all of the Irish women who so generously gave of their time and their knowledge to make the research upon which some of this chapter is based possible. Thanks also to Andy Bielenberg for his helpful comments on an earlier draft of this chapter.

CHAPTER 5

Who are the Irish in Britain? Evidence from Large-scale Surveys

BRENDAN HALPIN

(Institute for Social and Economic Research, Essex)

The Irish in Britain

Britain has always been an important destination for migrants from Ireland. The Gaels of Scotland have Irish origins, and the Lleyn peninsula in Wales is named for the Leinster people who settled there.[1] Throughout the industrial revolution the Irish provided a great deal of labour and are conventionally said to have dug the canals and built the railways. In more recent time there has been a steady flow of people to (and sometimes back from) Britain in search of work or a better life. In the 1950s and early 1960s the sharp contrast between a booming Britain and a stagnant Irish economy triggered flows of an almost intolerable level, a situation which also threatened to develop in the mid-1980s. As a result of the more recent migration, there is a substantial Irish-born minority in Britain. The Labour Force Survey estimates that there are 500,000 to 550,000 people born in the Republic of Ireland living in Great Britain:[2] this is approximately 1 per cent of the British population, but perhaps 15 per cent of the Irish population. When second-generation Irish are taken into account this represents an even more significant proportion.

There are many sources of information on who these people are and what their experience has been, from anecdote and personal experience at one extreme, through journalistic and literary accounts, to tables of government-collected statistics at the other. When we go beyond the published tables and consider the raw data sources, the Labour Force Survey (LFS), already quoted, represents a very important source of information because it surveys a very large sample (of the order of 150,000 respondents) four times a year. The census is another important source, decennial and comprehensive in coverage, though the frequency of the LFS and the fact that it is available directly to researchers makes it preferable for many purposes. However, officially collected surveys tend to ask a relatively limited range of questions. In the case of the LFS these are mainly limited to education, training and the labour market. Therefore it is tempting to look to other survey sources to get richer information. But here we run into the problem of small numbers: a group that represents as little as 1 per cent of the population may provide too few sample members to carry out meaningful analysis. Any candidate survey must have a large sample. In this chapter I draw from, as well as the LFS, the British Household Panel Survey (BHPS) and the British portion of the multinational European Community Household Panel survey (ECHP). Combined, this sample runs to over 23,000 and contains 240 respondents born in the Republic of Ireland. Though the number is small, the sort of information is rich enough to warrant analysis, tentative though it may have to be.

The British Household Panel Study is a survey of approximately 5,500 households, the members of which are interviewed annually. The first wave of interviews took place in September 1991, and there are at present five waves of data in the public domain. Extensive information is collected on employment, education, family formation and fertility, health, housing, income and wealth, household consumption, political behaviour, values and attitudes, and so on. In terms of employment, continuous information is collected on every job or employment status spell since September 1990. This is supplemented by retrospective information stretching back to when the respondent first left full-time education. Thus for most respondents we have information on their complete work-life histories. By combining the Wave 1 sample with new entrants in the subsequent four waves, we can assemble a sample in excess of 12,000 individuals.

The European Community Household Panel is a multinational panel study that is developing into an important resource for Europe-wide research. However, it is not fully available yet, nor have the participant countries been collecting data for very long. Nonetheless, it is possible to use data from the first wave of the British portion, which was collected in 1994, and has over 10,000 respondents. In many respects this study collects equivalent information to the BHPS, with the exception of the retrospective work histories. In what follows we exploit this similarity by combining the two panel samples where this is appropriate.

Who are the Irish in Britain?

I will begin by presenting some important summary information on the Irish in Britain: what are their sex and age distributions, and when did they come?

Sex distribution

Table 5.1 shows the sex distribution of Irish-born residents in Great Britain. The first panel consists of LFS data (1994, second quarter) grossed up to population figures using weights based on the 1991 census. This can be considered a good estimate of the true figure in Britain, whereas the figures generated from

Table 5.1: Sex distribution (000s)

1: LFS 1994 Quarter 1 (grossed up to population)

	Non-Irish		RoI		Total	
Male	27,216	(49.1)	250	(47.4)	27,467	(49.1)
Female	28,183	(50.9)	277	(52.6)	28,460	(50.9)
Total	55,399	(99.1)	527	(0.9)	55,926	(100.0)

2: BHPS/ECHP (non-weighted)

	Non-Irish		BHPS RoI		BHPS NI		ECHP RoI		Total	
Male	11,003	(47.7)	53	(44.9)	37	(47.4)	50	(41.0)	11,143	(47.7)
Female	12,063	(52.3)	65	(55.1)	41	(52.6)	72	(59.0)	12,241	(52.3)
Total	23,066	(98.6)	118	(0.5)	78	(0.3)	122	(0.5)	23,384	(100.0)

Note: Percentages in parentheses.
Adapted from: LFS, BHPS and ECHP.

panel data (in the second panel) are too small to make such generalizations but they are nonetheless indicative of the overall pattern.

The first thing apparent is that Irish-born women are over-represented, at 52.6 per cent versus a population value of 50.9 per cent according to the LFS. Given a ratio of 50.3 : 49.7 in Ireland in 1991,[3] it seems that they are slightly more likely to emigrate to Britain (or to stay, once there) than are men. This over-representation is also apparent in the panel samples, where it is accentuated by the slight general over-representation of women (this is often the case in surveys, and normally weighting is used to compensate for it; however, since the panel data come from two different surveys they are not weighted in the summaries reported in this chapter). Interestingly the Northern Irish figures are much closer to the overall figures.[4]

Age distribution

Figure 5.1 shows smoothed frequency distributions[5] of age in 1994, for BHPS/ECHP respondents, broken down into the three categories of non-Irish, Republic of Ireland, and Northern Ireland. The curve for non-Irish residents in Great Britain shows the conventional shape (apart from the omission of children from the samples), with the peak at a relatively young age and a slow subsequent decline. By contrast, immigrants from the Irish state are predominantly old, typically aged 50–70, but with a fair proportion in their late twenties and early thirties. This reflects the high level of emigration in the 1950s and early 1960s. However, the curve for Northern Ireland is dramatically different: there is a distinct preponderance of younger people, in the 20–40 range, with a peak around 28. We can speculate about reasons: presumably the industrial strength of the North relative to the Republic in the 1950s meant it retained more of its people in that period, whereas the disorder and economic decline of more recent years is driving young people to Britain.

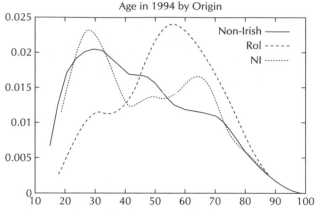

Figure 5.1: Age and origin: the age distribution for BHPS/ECHP non-Irish respondents, BHPS/ECHP respondents from the Republic and BHPS respondents from Northern Ireland. Adapted from: BHPS and ECHP.

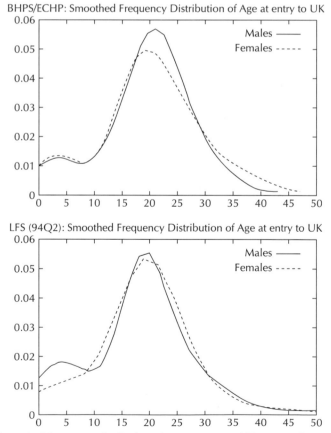

Figure 5.2: Smoothed frequency distribution of age at entry to UK, men and women. Adapted from: BHPS, ECHP and LFS.

Age at entry to Britain

The distribution of age tells us something about the current state of the Irish in Britain: by contrast, the distribution of their age at first entry to Britain will tell us something about their life experience. Figure 5.2 shows the smoothed frequency distribution of age at entry to Britain for men and women separately, with the combined BHPS/ECHP data set shown in the top panel. For both sexes the main feature is a sharp peak around or slightly after age 20, falling off to quite low proportions from about age 30. A second notable characteristic is the substantial numbers of children that come to Britain, as children of adult immigrants.

A third feature worth commenting on is the difference in the age profiles of men and women: while both sexes are most likely to come in the 15–30 age range, men are relatively more likely than women to come at ages under 30, whereas women are relatively more likely after.

When we compare these figures against LFS figures from the second quarter of 1994 (lower panel, Figure 5.2), we see the general pattern is reinforced, though the difference between adult men and women is lessened. However, we see one curious feature: there are relatively more males than females entering Britain as children (I have checked the data to ensure that this is not an artefact of the smoothing, and that it also shows up in other quarters' surveys).

Thus we see that emigration is typically, but not exclusively, a young adult's experience, with the vast bulk of first entries to Britain occurring between the ages of 15 and 30.

Age at entry and historical time: age now

By looking at age now and age at entry together we get a more general view of the historical pattern of immigration. It allows us to see *when* the immigration occurred, and to what extent the pattern of age at entry may change across cohort or historical time. The most immediate means of doing this is a scatterplot, such as those in Figure 5.3, of age against age at entry. The diagonal lines on the plots represent calendar time, exploiting the simple arithmetic relationship between age now, age at entry and year of entry. Thus by inspection of these scatterplots we can get an idea of the combined age-related and historical pattern of migration (ignoring for the moment those immigrants who have left the sample frame, through death, further migration or return to Ireland).

The lower panel, using LFS data, is perhaps better to inspect, given it is denser and therefore the patterns are clearer, though the same patterns are apparent in the BHPS/ECHP data in the top panel. The single clearest feature of the plot is the dense cloud indicating entry to Britain in the period roughly between the early 1940s and the early 1960s, by people roughly between 15 and 25 years. This was the period of mass immigration (though since those immigrating earlier in the period are less likely to be represented in the sample, this is not necessarily a true representation of the contemporary pattern of immigration). The next clearest feature is the lighter echo of this cloud in the mid-1980s/early

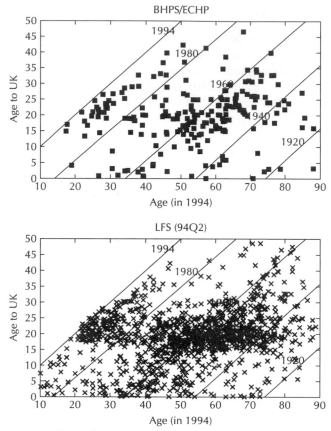

Figure 5.3: Age now and age of entry to UK.
Adapted from: BHPS, ECHP and LFS.

1990s (relatively speaking, this will overstate the level of recent migration compared with that in the 1950s, as it contains higher proportions of individuals not likely to stay long in Britain). What can also be seen is that there is a relatively sharp jump in the distribution of age at entry, around 15 to 17, and that this age rises with time, as education becomes more important.

General characteristics

In this section a number of further characteristics of the Irish in Britain are examined, namely education, religion, health, region, and current employment status.

Education

The level of education of the Irish in Britain is patterned by when they immigrated (and, potentially, who remained). If we use the Labour Force Survey to

Table 5.2: Graduates, by age group

Age range	Non-Irish	Irish-born	Total
23 to 30	1,037,538	12,650	1,050,188
	(14.6)	(24.4)	(14.7)
31 to 40	1,304,758	8,914	1,313,673
	(16.1)	(14.1)	(16.0)
Over 40	1,973,644	15,330	1,988,974
	(8.3)	(3.9)	(8.2)
Total	4,315,941	36,894	4,352,835
	(11.1)	(7.3)	(11.0)

Note: Percentages in parentheses. Figures weighted to 1991 census levels.
Adapted from: LFS 94Q2.

look at the proportions holding a degree (discarding those 22 and under who have not had sufficient time to earn one) we see that there are proportionally fewer Irish (from the Republic: the LFS does not identify those from Northern Ireland) than native graduates (7.3 per cent versus 11.1 per cent; see Table 5.2). However, if we break this down by age a different story emerges. Less than 4 per cent of the over-40 Irish-born hold degrees, compared with 8.2 per cent in the population as a whole. For those in their thirties, the proportions are much closer, but for those in the 23–30-year age range, almost one in four holds a degree, substantially exceeding the British level of 14.6 per cent.

Numerous processes lie behind these figures, most important of which are the general levels of education in the two countries, the differential likelihood of emigrating of people at different levels of education and the differential likelihood of remaining in Britain by level of education. It is probable that change in all three has contributed to the present pattern. The general level of education in Ireland may have overtaken the British level (or may always have been ahead: I do not have the historical figures but the current level of participation in third-level education for instance, is substantially higher, roughly 50 per cent versus 33 per cent); the relative chances of emigrating may have become higher for those with more education; the relative chance of remaining in Britain may be higher for those with lower education. However, the most important effect may be a shift between emigration of those who didn't have the qualifications to get work in Ireland (in the 1950s and 1960s, when the demand for relatively unskilled labour was great in Britain) and emigration of those who had the qualifications to get a job anywhere, in other words an increase in the relative chance of emigrating of those with more education.

However, it is not sufficient to look only at the high end of educational achievement: what of those with little or no qualifications, those whom the educational system has failed? LFS figures are presented in Table 5.3. For the over-40s, the Irish are over-represented, at 47 per cent versus 34 per cent, but younger Irish show a rate closer to the population rate, with the youngest even slightly under-represented. However, we do not see the reverse of the story

Table 5.3: Those with no qualifications, by age group

Age range	Non-Irish	Irish-born	Total
23 to 30	1,775,032	8,472	1,783,504
	(14.9)	(13.6)	(14.9)
31 to 40	1,458,369	14,950	1,473,320
	(18.0)	(23.6)	(18.0)
Over 40	4,999,921	113,155	5,113,076
	(34.0)	(46.6)	(34.2)
Total	8,233,323	136,578	8,369,901
	(23.7)	(37.1)	(23.9)

Note: Percentages in parentheses.
Adapted from: LFS 94Q2.

coming from degree-level: the young Irish are not under-represented among the unqualified as they are over-represented among graduates. Since the LFS does not identify those from Northern Ireland, we must look to the panel data to compare these with those from Britain and from the Republic. Figure 5.4 shows the proportions of each of these three groups achieving degree level, complete second level, incomplete second level, and less education. The top panel is for all respondents, the lower for those 35 and under. For all respondents, those from the Republic have lower levels of education than those from Britain, with particularly high levels of no-qualifications. For those 35 and under, the picture is more or less reversed, with those from the Republic showing higher rates of second level, or higher, than Britain.

However, the picture for the Northern Irish is distinctly different. Even without restricting to younger ages, they show substantially higher levels of education than those from Britain. This is partly because their age distribution is very skewed, with the 20–35 age range over-represented. Nonetheless, even when we restrict to the younger range, the Northern Irish still stand out. They show more with complete second level even than those from the Republic, and have a much higher proportion of graduates than either other group.

Over and above any general flight from Northern Ireland, one can speculate that this pattern may be deepened by the UK system of higher education, and its expectation of, and support for, the practice of leaving home in order to go to university. For Northern Irish A-Level students, this means they are presented with the whole list of UK universities to which to apply, and high numbers do choose to go to Britain. Once graduated, many remain. However, it is also likely that the level of education in Northern Ireland is higher than that in the Republic as well as that in Britain.

Health

Both the panel surveys ask about health, including an overall question on how the respondent regards his/her general health, on a five-point scale. While

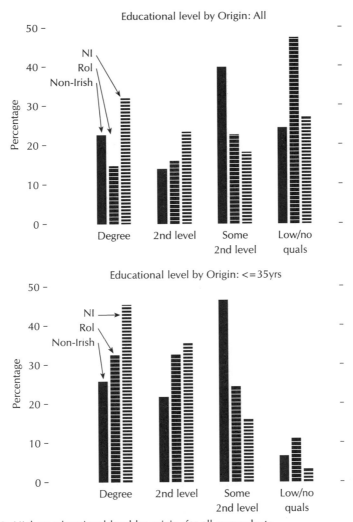

Figure 5.4: Highest educational level by origin, for all respondents and for those aged up to 35. (Information on Northern Ireland from BHPS only.) Adapted from: BHPS and ECHP.

subjective health assessment is not a particularly powerful measurement of health status, it is interesting to examine how it is distributed in the population.

Table 5.4 gives the mean value of the health score (which ranges from 1 for 'excellent' to 5 for 'very poor') by sex and origin. The Northern Irish are happiest with their health, and those from the Republic least. Men feel healthier than women, and this difference is greatest among those from Northern Ireland. However, subjective health assessment is strongly related to age, and the ethnic differences reflect the different age distributions, as examination of the figures controlling for age confirms (not shown).

Table 5.4: Health status: mean value on 5-point subjective health measure

	Mean	Std Dev
Non-Irish	2.11	0.96
Male	2.06	0.95
Female	2.17	0.96
Republic of Ireland	2.24	1.05
Male	2.14	1.02
Female	2.32	1.07
Northern Ireland	2.05	0.90
Male	1.92	0.76
Female	2.17	1.00
Total	2.12	0.96

Adapted from: BHPS and ECHP.

Table 5.5: Religion of the BHPS respondents

Religion	Republic of Ireland		Northern Ireland		Total	
None	10	(9.3)	19	(30.6)	29	(17.2)
Catholic	88	(82.2)	21	(33.9)	109	(64.5)
Protestant	8	(7.5)	21	(33.9)	29	(17.2)
Other	1	(0.9)	1	(1.6)	2	(1.2)
Total	107	(63.3)	62	(36.7)	169	(100.0)

Note: Percentages in parentheses.
Adapted from: BHPS Wave 1.

Religion

The BHPS asked respondents their religion in the first wave, and therefore we have this information for most, but not all of the BHPS Irish sample. The LFS does not ask this question routinely in Great Britain (though it has been asked in Northern Ireland), and it is not asked in the ECHP. Table 5.5 shows the breakdown: those from the Republic are 82 per cent Catholic, while those from Northern Ireland show equal proportions of Catholic and Protestant at one-third each, which is somewhat of an over-representation of Catholics with respect to the proportions in Northern Ireland. (Protestants from the Republic may also be over-represented but the numbers are too small to be reliable.)

Region

Where within Great Britain is the flow of Irish immigration directed? Table 5.6 presents figures from the 1994 second quarter LFS, weighted, showing percentages of the Irish-born and non-Irish populations by standard region. The clearest feature of the table is the high proportion of the Irish living in London and the south-east: 54 per cent of men and 56 per cent of women live there. For London the Irish are substantially over-represented. The other regions where

Table 5.6: Population distribution by region and by sex (%)

Region	Men			Women		
	Non-Irish	Irish-born	Total	Non-Irish	Irish-born	Total
Tyne & Wear	2.0	0.7	2.0	2.0	0.5	2.0
Rest of northern region	3.5	0.9	3.5	3.5	0.8	3.5
South Yorkshire	2.3	1.2	2.3	2.3	0.2	2.3
West Yorkshire	3.8	2.9	3.8	3.7	2.8	3.7
Rest of Yorks & Humberside	2.9	0.5	2.8	2.9	1.1	2.8
East Midlands	7.3	5.0	7.3	7.2	2.1	7.2
East Anglia	3.8	2.1	3.7	3.7	1.5	3.7
Inner London	4.5	18.8	4.7	4.6	13.1	4.7
Outer London	7.5	20.9	7.6	7.5	22.4	7.6
Rest of south-east	19.2	14.3	19.2	19.1	20.9	19.1
South-west	8.4	3.9	8.4	8.5	4.6	8.4
West Midlands (met county)	4.6	8.1	4.7	4.6	8.2	4.6
Rest of West Midlands	4.8	2.5	4.8	4.7	3.3	4.7
Greater Manchester	4.5	7.5	4.6	4.5	8.1	4.6
Merseyside	2.5	1.9	2.5	2.6	2.0	2.6
Rest of north-west	4.2	2.6	4.2	4.2	3.1	4.2
Wales	5.1	2.2	5.1	5.2	1.8	5.2
Strathclyde	4.0	1.6	4.0	4.1	2.0	4.1
Rest of Scotland	5.0	2.5	5.0	5.1	1.3	5.0
Total	100.0	100.0	100.0	100.0	100.0	100.0

Adapted from: LFS 94Q2, weighted.

they are over-represented are the metropolitan West Midlands (i.e. greater Birmingham) and Greater Manchester. It may be surprising that the Irish are under-represented in two formerly important destinations, Liverpool (Merseyside) and Glasgow (Strathclyde). Otherwise the pattern is for low levels in more rural regions (south-west, north, north-west, East Yorkshire, East Anglia, Wales and Scotland) and moderate levels in the other urban regions (East Midlands, West Yorkshire) apart from Tyne and Wear.

The general urban concentration is to be expected: Irish migration is usually to cities, where there is work to be found. The exceptions of Merseyside, Strathclyde and Tyne and Wear probably reflect the fact that these areas have been economically depressed for the past few decades, with traditional heavy industries in decline.

Current employment status

The LFS is clearly the preferred source for current employment information. Therefore we use it in this section to examine current employment situation and occupation. Table 5.7 shows current employment status by origin and

Table 5.7: Employment status, by origin and sex

	Men			Women		
	Non-Irish	Irish	Total	Non-Irish	Irish	Total
Employee	11,268,607	95,181	11,363,788	10,225,913	107,766	10,333,679
	(41.6)	(38.0)	(41.6)	(36.4)	(38.9)	(36.4)
Self-employed	2,391,121	35,585	2,426,705	788,060	9,292	797,352
	(8.8)	(14.2)	(8.9)	(2.8)	(3.4)	(2.8)
Unpaid family worker	48,540		48,540	89,062	369	89,430
	(0.2)		(0.2)	(0.3)	(0.1)	(0.3)
Non-employed	13,389,679	119,458	13,509,137	17,009,892	159,763	17,169,655
	(49.4)	(47.7)	(49.4)	(60.5)	(57.6)	(60.5)
Total	27,097,946	250,224	27,348,170	28,112,926	277,190	28,390,116
	(99.1)	(0.9)	(100.0)	(99.0)	(1.0)	(100.0)

Note: Percentages in parentheses.
Adapted from: LFS 94Q2, weighted.

Table 5.8: Occupations in which Irish-born males are under- or over-represented (%)

SOC Minor Group	Non-Irish	Irish
Over-represented		
11 Managers in Building etc.	2.9	4.5
17 Managers in Service industry (e.g. pubs)	4.8	6.4
19 Managers and administrators nec	0.9	1.8
22 Health professionals	0.9	1.5
29 Psychologists, clergy, social workers	0.5	1.6
50 Building crafts	4.1	8.4
57 Wood workers	2.3	3.9
62 Waiters, bar staff	1.5	2.6
64 Health and related occs.	0.5	0.8
67 Cleaners, domestics	0.5	1.2
69 Security guards etc.	0.4	0.7
73 Door to door sales	0.6	1.0
84 Engineering operatives	0.8	1.2
85 Assembly workers	0.9	1.5
89 Varied operatives incl construction	1.8	3.8
91 Industrial labourers	0.4	0.6
92 Building labourers	1.2	5.5
Under-represented		
14 Managers in transport	1.2	0.5
16 Farm managers etc.	1.4	0.3
32 Computer programmers and analysts	1.1	0.3
52 Elec/electronic trades	3.3	0.6
54 Motor trades	2.0	0.6
56 Printers etc.	0.7	0.3
59 Dental, musical instrument makers etc.	2.0	0.8
72 Sales assistants, checkout workers	0.8	0.3

Note: SOC Minor Groups where the Irish were under- or over-represented by 50 per cent or more are included.
Adapted from: LFS 94Q2, weighted.

Table 5.9: Occupations in which Irish-born females are under- or over-represented (%)

SOC Minor Group	Non-Irish	Irish
Over-represented		
12 Specialist managers	2.9	5.4
17 Managers in Service industry (e.g. pubs)	3.8	8.2
21 Engineers (qualified)	0.3	0.8
22 Health professionals	0.6	1.0
26 Architects, town planners etc.	0.1	0.7
32 Computer programmers and analysts	0.3	1.1
34 Nurses	5.3	14.2
64 Health and related occupations	5.1	7.9
95 Other sales	8.8	13.1
Under-represented		
10 Managers in large organisations	0.9	0.4
19 Other managers	0.9	0.3
23 Teaching professionals	5.6	2.3
30 Scientific technicians	0.6	0.3
38 Arts occupations	1.3	0.7
39 Associate technical and professional	0.9	0.3
40 Low level Civil Service	2.3	0.3
44 Store clerks	0.6	0.3
45 Secretaries, etc.	6.6	3.2
46 Receptionists, etc.	2.4	1.1
67 Cleaners, domestics	0.6	0.3
72 Sales assistants, checkout workers	9.2	5.2

Note: SOC Minor Groups where the Irish were under- or over-represented by
50 per cent or more are included.
Adapted from: LFS 94Q2, weighted.

sex. Irish-born men are more likely than non-Irish to be self-employed, and slightly less likely to be employees or non-employed. Irish-born women are slightly more likely to be employed or self-employed, at the expense of non-employment.

However, this is relatively uninformative and the differences are likely to be at least partly due to the different age distribution. More interesting is *where* the Irish are employed: are the stereotypes true, suggesting builders, bar workers and nurses? Tables 5.8 and 5.9 pick out occupational groups where Irish-born LFS respondents are under- or over-represented relative to the non-Irish rate, to the extent of plus-or-minus 50 per cent or more.[6] For men, it looks as if the stereotypes have a basis in fact: they are over-represented among managers in building and related industries, building crafts, woodworking crafts, construction operatives and building labourers; among service industry managers (this includes pubs), waiters and bar staff. However, some of the other popular occupations may be less expected: groups 22 and 64, health industry jobs; psychologists, clergy and social workers (of course, the stereotype of the Irish priest!); cleaners, domestics and security guards. The latter categories are probably the refuge of those with few skills who are now too old for labouring jobs. Where Irish-born men are under-represented seems largely to be locations requiring training and apprenticeship in industries not (formerly) common in Ireland.

Women present quite a different profile. One stereotype is immediately confirmed: there are lots of Irish nurses and other health workers. As their numbers in group 17, service industry managers, suggest, they are also present in the bar trade. But the other over-represented categories are interesting: specialist managers (financial, marketing, purchasing, advertising, personnel, etc.); engineers; architects and town planners; and computer professionals. These are predominantly occupations that require substantial training and educational qualifications, and perhaps the Irish educational system is better at steering women into the requisite disciplines than is the British. Under-representation is also interesting. There are particularly low numbers as secretaries, receptionists, and Civil Service clerks, which may confound some stereotypes; also low numbers of cleaners and lower-grade sales assistants. Irish women are also poorly represented among teachers, which may be due to the poor portability of teaching qualifications.

Thus we find the occupational profile of women more surprising than that of men, with women over-represented in high-skill white-collar occupations, while men seem to remain in what might be thought to be their traditional locations. However, this could be due to occupational sex segregation causing under-representation of British women in these occupations, rather than under-representation of Irish men.

Work-life histories

While the LFS is a particularly good source for information on current employment and occupation, the BHPS has the advantage of collecting complete work-life histories, with retrospective data to supplement that collected during the period of the panel. Thus for some of our panel respondents we can reconstruct their complete working lives, and relate that to their coming to Britain. For this analysis we must drop the ECHP respondents, because the ECHP does not collect retrospective information, and the BHPS respondents from Northern Ireland, as we do not know their date of coming to Britain. This gives us relatively small numbers, but the information available is quite rich, making a tentative analysis very interesting.

Employment status history

There are 58 respondents who started their work-lives in Ireland, or within twelve months of moving to Britain, for whom we have complete employment-status histories.[7] I include those who had recently moved to Britain, prior to entering the labour force, because they can be considered very like those who work for a short period before moving. Table 5.10 presents the person-months

Table 5.10: Person–months in employment statuses, before and after migration, by sex

	Men			Women		
	Before	After	Total	Before	After	Total
Self-employed		1,300	1,300	74	57	131
		(14.0)	(8.7)	(1.3)	(0.8)	(1.0)
Full-time employee	5,388	5,595	10,983	3,555	1,593	5,148
	(94.3)	(60.3)	(73.2)	(61.7)	(21.6)	(39.2)
Part-time employee	39	54	93		2,363	2,363
	(0.7)	(0.6)	(0.6)		(32.1)	(18.0)
Unemployed	146	303	449	16	53	69
	(2.6)	(3.3)	(3.0)	(0.3)	(0.7)	(0.5)
Retired		1,350	1,350		578	578
		(14.5)	(9.0)		(7.8)	(4.4)
Maternity leave				8	23	31
				(0.1)	(0.3)	(0.2)
Family care				2,076	2,648	4,724
				(36.1)	(35.9)	(36.0)
Full-time student/school	8		8			
	(0.1)		(0.1)			
Long-term sick, disabled		611	611		52	52
		(6.6)	(4.1)		(0.7)	(0.4)
Other	132	72	204	29		29
	(2.3)	(0.8)	(1.4)	(0.5)		(0.2)
Total	5,713	9,285	14,998	5,758	7,367	13,125
	(38.1)	(61.9)	(100.0)	(43.9)	(56.1)	(100.0)

Notes: Percentages in parentheses. Person–months before emigrating are likely to be over-estimates.
Adapted from: BHPS.

spent in various employment statuses, by when they took place (before or after emigrating) and by sex.

For men, the dominant state before and after is that of employee. Time spent otherwise before emigrating is negligible. For women, time before is largely divided between full-time employment and family care duties. After emigrating, men spend their time in employment, self-employment, retirement, sickness and unemployment, in that order. Women move from the simple pattern of full-time work versus home, to spend much more time in part-time work. That retirement becomes a significant category after migration highlights the fact that much of the difference is due to life-cycle: of necessity, the respondents were younger before they emigrated, and many of them have lived long lives in Britain since. But it is not simply retirement that is a life-cycle effect: so too perhaps the move into part-time work for women concomitant with having children (we can speculate also that they would not as easily have found part-time work in Ireland, given its different labour market), and also the incidence of self-employment for men, this being a status typically entered into after gaining experience and capital.

Occupational history

Given that most people went to Britain to work, it is interesting to consider what sort of jobs they held. For this again we have recourse to the BHPS, this time exploiting its occupational life history data. Due to the data collection design, this is available for fewer people, giving us 45 persons with complete histories, who began work in Ireland or within twelve months of moving to Britain.

This number is small enough to examine the individual cases, though of course they cannot be reported individually, for confidentiality reasons. Looking through the data we see many 'typical' careers: several women work (or train on the job) as nurses for two or three years in Ireland, before moving to Britain where they continue to work in nursing; several men start in low-skilled jobs of various descriptions, and continue in Britain in low-skilled jobs in construction and allied areas. On the other hand there are cases of women starting in clerical/secretarial work in Ireland, resuming in similar jobs in Britain but quickly climbing the career ladder into management; also several men start at the bottom but end up in management in construction. Information technology jobs also seem to offer opportunities for advancement for those in younger cohorts. Semi-skilled jobs in the transport industry (bus drivers and conductors, HGV drivers, railway maintenance) also recur. Women's careers tend to show interruptions, some long, and one or two do not work at all after moving to Britain (presumably on marriage). Men in low-skilled careers show a good deal of instability, with spells of unemployment and frequent changes of occupation.

We can look at the data more systematically, as in Table 5.11 which represents job spells before and after emigration, by broad occupational group and sex. The same caveat must be entered here as with the analysis of person-months of employment statuses: the pattern is strongly age-related. It should also be noted that the average spell length is probably less before than after migration, again due to the age pattern of employment. Thus, the substantial increase in management jobs, for instance, may be as much due to career advancement as to moving to another country. On the other hand, the big rise in 'plant and machine operatives', especially for men, is clearly due to the greater availability of such jobs in Britain. 'Personal and protective services' – a broad category including hairdressers, bar and hotel staff, child-minders, cleaners, soldiers and security guards – shows a rise for women but a fall for men. So also do sales occupations. This is also the case for quite a different category, associate professional and technical occupations, which also seems to offer opportunities for women after moving to Britain, but not for men.

An alternative to the somewhat uninformative occupational group classification (numbers are too small to use a finer version) is social class. While this is largely based on occupation (combined with information about managerial or proprietorial status) it represents a more orderly set of categories. Here we see a substantial rise in spells in the professional/managerial class for women, but not men: Britain seems to offer them an increase in opportunities

Table 5.11: Job spells before and after migration, by sex (SOC major groups)

SOC major group	Men			Women		
	Before	In GB	Total	Before	In GB	Total
Managers &	5	20	25		8	8
administrators	(11.6)	(17.5)	(15.9)		(7.3)	(5.6)
Professional		3	3	1	2	3
occupations		(2.6)	(1.9)	(2.9)	(1.8)	(2.1)
Associate prof. &	4	4	8	2	8	10
tech. occupations	(9.3)	(3.5)	(5.1)	(5.7)	(7.3)	(6.9)
Clerical & secretarial	1	7	8	7	25	32
occupations	(2.3)	(6.1)	(5.1)	(20.0)	(22.9)	(22.2)
Craft & related	7	20	27	3	4	7
occupations	(16.3)	(17.5)	(17.2)	(8.6)	(3.7)	(4.9)
Personal & protective	5	5	10	7	19	26
service occupations	(11.6)	(4.4)	(6.4)	(20.0)	(17.4)	(18.1)
Sales occupations	4	4	8	4	13	17
	(9.3)	(3.5)	(5.1)	(11.4)	(11.9)	(11.8)
Plant & machine	4	25	29	5	8	13
operatives	(9.3)	(21.9)	(18.5)	(14.3)	(7.3)	(9.0)
Other occupations	13	26	39	6	22	28
	(30.2)	(22.8)	(24.8)	(17.1)	(20.2)	(19.4)
Total	43	114	157	35	109	144
	(27.4)	(72.6)	(100.0)	(24.3)	(75.7)	(100.0)

Note: Percentages in parentheses.
Adapted from: BHPS.

Table 5.12: Social class spells before and after migration, by sex (SOC major groups)

Social Class	Men			Women		
	Before	In GB	Total	Before	In GB	Total
Professional and	9	28	37	3	18	21
managerial	(21.4)	(24.6)	(23.7)	(8.6)	(16.5)	(14.6)
Routine non-manual	4	2	6	13	39	52
	(9.5)	(1.8)	(3.8)	(37.1)	(35.8)	(36.1)
Small proprietors		16	16		2	2
		(14.0)	(10.3)		(1.8)	(1.4)
Skilled and	9	8	17	3	5	8
supervisory	(21.4)	(7.0)	(10.9)	(8.6)	(4.6)	(5.6)
Semi-skilled	13	58	71	15	45	60
	(31.0)	(50.9)	(45.5)	(42.9)	(41.3)	(41.7)
Agricultural labour	7	2	9	1		1
	(16.7)	(1.8)	(5.8)	(2.9)		(0.7)
Total	42	114	156	35	109	144
	(26.9)	(73.1)	(100.0)	(24.3)	(75.7)	(100.0)

Notes: Percentages in parentheses. Class is the 7-point 'EGP' version of Goldthorpe's
schema. See R. Erikson and J.H. Goldthorpe, *The Constant Flux: A Study of Class
Mobility in Industrial Societies* (Oxford, 1992).
Adapted from: BHPS.

that it doesn't offer men. The routine non-manual class (lower white-collar) is predominantly female, but doesn't show growth with migration. Self-employment (small proprietors) shows up only in Britain (the slight inconsistency with Table 5.10 is due to working with a smaller data set). Skilled and supervisory blue-collar occupations are poorly represented after migration: these tend to be occupations which require specific training from a fairly young age, less available in Ireland.[8] On the other hand, semi-skilled work features strongly, for both men and women. For men, migration leads to a growth in such work, with over 50 per cent of men's spells in Britain in low-skilled occupations (this high proportion is partly due to the inherent insecurity of such jobs: the unskilled tend to have series of shorter jobs, whereas those with more skill, and especially those in the professional/managerial class, tend to spend much longer in each job). Almost as a footnote: agricultural labour hardly features at all, with only two spells in Britain. Emigration is largely to cities, and away from the farm. The class of farm proprietors is completely absent from the table: farming is a very absorbing occupation, in that once people acquire farms they tend ⁺o stay farming all their working lives. Thus farmers don't tend to emigrate.

For men the general picture is dominated by people moving from semi-skilled work in industry and agriculture, and moving to semi-skilled work in industry, with important subgroups in professional/managerial work and self-employment. For women, the move is one from routine non-manual and semi-skilled work to the same categories, with an interesting growth in professional managerial work.

Conclusions

Large-scale surveys can tell us quite a lot about the Irish in Britain, despite their relatively low proportion in the population. Granted, surveys by their very nature leave many questions unanswered, but this is more true of the LFS than the smaller panel surveys used. On the other hand, the narrowness of the LFS goes hand in hand with its very large sample size and concomitant precision. The panel surveys compensate for their smaller sample size by bringing in more information, and this is particularly the case with the BHPS's retrospective histories.

The overall picture they give us of the Irish in Britain is that they are old, and largely the products of the 1950s emigration of the less educated and less skilled. There is nonetheless a younger wave of immigrants, which seems to have very different characteristics as far as education and occupation go. However, the simple dichotomy between low-skill 1950s emigration and high-skill 1980s emigration does not hold entirely: even among more recent migrants, the poorly educated are well represented.

The BHPS further allows us to consider the differences between emigration from the two parts of the island, and these seem to be profound. Northern Irish emigration tends to be much more recent, and the migrants are disproportionately well educated. This chapter has been exploratory and entirely descriptive. As a result it raises questions as often as it answers them: why, for instance, are Irish women over-represented in skilled white-collar occupations? Why are the Northern Irish so well educated? Is the experience of the poorly educated recent emigrant similar to, or worse than, that of the unskilled of the 1950s? These are all questions for further research, some requiring other sources of data, but it is clear that large-scale survey data is a very important resource for describing the Irish in Britain.

Notes

1. D. Ó Corráin, 'Prehistoric and Early Christian Ireland', in R.F. Foster (ed.), *Oxford History of Ireland* (Oxford, 1992), pp. 6–7.
2. Figures derived from LFS 1994, second quarter data set, and LFS 1996, first quarter data set, using 1991 census weights.
3. Central Statistics Office of Ireland, Principal Statistics (1997) web page at *http://www.cso.ie/principalstats/princstat.html
4. Information on Northern Ireland is only available for the BHPS: neither the ECHP nor the LFS ask region of birth. But even the BHPS fails to ask Northern Ireland-born respondents when they came to Great Britain.
5. Smoothing is by means of kernel density estimation, using Lisp-Stat (L. Tierney, *Lisp-Stat: An Object-Oriented Environment for Statistical Computing and Dynamic Graphics*, New York, 1990). This is a means of taking a sample and non-parametrically estimating the underlying distribution function.
6. The occupational groups are the so-called minor groups of the Standard Occupational Classification (SOC) of the UK Office of National Statistics, of which there are approximately 75.
7. See B. Halpin, *Unified BHPS Work-Life Histories: Combining Multiple Sources into a User-Friendly Format*, Technical Paper 13, ESRC Research Centre on Micro-Social Change, University of Essex (1997).
8. Alternatively, people with such qualifications may have good prospects of work in Ireland, and emigrate less.

Part Two
The Americas

CHAPTER 6

Irish Migration to North America, 1800–1920

DONALD HARMAN AKENSON

*(Department of History, Queen's University, Kingston, Ontario and
Beamish Research Professor of Migration Studies, The Institute of
Irish Studies, University of Liverpool)*

I

Wrapped within every Irish story lies another one. And if one reads much Irish
historical writing, one quickly discovers that it is often hard to distinguish the
teller from the tale. When we deal with the story of the migration of the Irish
to North America we find that the only way to get to an accurate history of
events is to pass through historiography – that is, to acquire an understanding
of how the historical story of the migrants works. This is particularly important with the Irish migrants to the United States (who make up the numerically
largest portion of North American migration), because the accepted literature
on the Irish migrants to the United States is, in its general outlines, sharply
divorced from historical reality.

Of course, that is a generalization, and like all such has to be qualified. There
are some quite wonderful books in the field of Irish-US studies, especially
local and regional studies.[1] But the overall picture is disheartening. As Patrick
O'Sullivan has observed, Irish culture has 'mystified' migration. This mysti-
fication has been particularly acute in Irish-US historiography, because of a
predilection for psychological explanations of various 'facts'. This is doubly bad,
because, as O'Sullivan points out, the historians who practise this rhetoric
are not trained in the discipline,[2] and also because the pseudo-psychological
explanations involve a presumption of certain 'facts' that are anything but factual. Thus arises a historiography with an investment in denying historical reality.

II

Denial of what? First, of the almost universally ignored fact that *the bulk of
the Irish ethnic group in the United States at present is, and probably always
has been, Protestant.* The historical literature of the last 50 years deals almost
entirely with Roman Catholics and in many cases explicitly states that the Irish
in the United States are, and were, entirely Catholic.[3]

In order to deal with this peculiar historiography, a simple matter of method and vocabulary must be underscored, namely that the migrant generation and the entire ethnic group in any country are quite different entities. The migrants are sometimes referred to as the *Irish-born* or as the *first generation*.[4] In contemporary historical accounts these persons are called 'emigrants' or 'immigrants'. (Because these two usages are confusing, they are not here employed.) All of these terms apply to a single generation.

In contrast, the ethnic group is a *multi-generational* phenomenon and in historical discussion it includes not only the migrant generation but their direct offspring and, often, subsequent generations of descendants. Exactly what the borders of any ethnic group are is a matter of great argument (for how long does a sense of ethnicity last?) and certainly cannot be decided here. The effective point is that when a historian refers to 'the Irish' in the United States (or in Great Britain, or in any new homeland) he or she should make it clear whether the reference is to the migrant generation or to the multi-generational ethnic group. Assertions that hold true for the migrant generation are frequently not true for the entire ethnic group, and too often conclusions about 'the Irish' as a multi-generational group have been drawn from data that really concern only the Irish-born. Therefore, in this chapter, 'the Irish' means the entire ethnic group. When the migrant generation is meant, that will be clearly indicated by such terms as 'Irish-born' or 'migrant generation' or 'first generation'.

The data which indicate that 'the Irish' – that is, the entire multi-generational group – in the United States are predominantly Protestant come from three independent sources. The first of these is a set of studies done in the 1970s by the National Opinion Research Center (NORC) of the University of Chicago[5] and the second in the 1980s by the Gallup polling organization.[6] These revealed that most Americans who said that their primary ethnic group was Irish were Protestants – 56 per cent in the NORC survey and 54 per cent in the Gallup study. These were sophisticated and technically expert studies, but they have been dwarfed by the material that is at present being published as a result of the National Survey of Religious Identification 1989–90, being conducted under the directorship of Professor Barry A. Kosmin by the Graduate Center of the City University of New York (CUNY). This study involves the random survey of 113,000 American households (a massive number for a random survey) and deals with religion, ethnicity, race and a number of demographic variables. The religious affiliations of persons who identified themselves as being of Irish ethnic origin are shown in Table 6.1.

Within Irish demographic studies a standard (if perhaps unintentionally sectarian) mode of expressing religious identity is a ratio of Catholics to 'non-Catholics'. In the United States in 1989–90 the Catholic/non-Catholic ratio of persons of Irish ancestry was 33/67. I think, however, that this ratio over-emphasizes the degree of Protestantism, for it is only in the Irish homeland that a person who is non-Catholic can with reasonable accuracy be assumed to be a Protestant. I would suggest that the most accurate reading would be to lump the 'undefined Christian' category with the Protestants. This would yield the following conclusion: that the ratio of Protestants to Catholics among persons

Table 6.1: Religious affiliation of Americans identifying themselves as being of Irish origin, 1989–90

Religious affiliation	%
Christian ('so stated')	3
Roman Catholic	33
Jewish	0
Protestant	51
No religion, or non-Christian other than Jewish	13
Total	100

Adapted from: Barry Kosmin *et al., Research Report: The National Survey of Religious Identification, 1989–90,* selected Tabulations (New York, CUNY Graduate Center, 1991), p. 14.

who professed a Christian religion was 54 to 33. That is to say, the Protestant proportion of Irish persons in the United States was 58.6 per cent of those professing Christianity.

The import of these studies cannot be rationally denied: they were conducted independently of each other, at an acceptable level of professional competence, and they produced similar results. One naturally asks, how far back in the history of the United States does the predominantly Protestant character of the Irish as an ethnic group hold?

For reasons that I will explain in the next section, one cannot cite any direct data in answer to that question, because the United States government never collected any information on the matter. Nevertheless, a strong logic tree exists. It works as follows. Given that the bulk of persons who lived in the United States in the second half of the twentieth century were Protestants, then this situation held throughout US history *unless* either (1) at some time in earlier US history there was a massive apostasy whereby a predominantly Catholic group of Irish persons switched to Protestantism, or (2) the Irish as a group in some period early in their history in the United States (in the colonial period, or, in any case, prior to the Great Famine) were overwhelmingly Roman Catholic and these numbers were later swamped by great hordes of migrating Irish-born Protestants.

Neither of these alternatives holds. Nowhere in the vast literature of American religious history is there any serious documentation of large-scale Irish Catholic apostasy.[7] Indeed, the success of the Catholic Church in holding the faithful (and in reindoctrinating those who had become virtually irreligious) is one of its proudest claims.

Further, virtually the entire historiography of Irish migration to the United States, and the documentation which surrounds that writing, indicate that the great flood of migration in the century after the famine was Roman Catholic in character. Even if the degree of Catholicism of the post-Famine migrants is over-emphasized (as I suspect it is), it is clear that overwhelmingly the migrants were Catholics. Therefore, condition '2' does not hold any more than does condition '1'. Hence the unavoidable conclusion is that the Irish as an ethnic group in the United States always have been mostly Protestant.

Here we enter a minefield. Some of the more politically 'progressive' attacks on racism (as, for example, the Human Rights Code of Ontario) have defined racism as appertaining not merely to skin colour but to ethnicity, religion and national origin. Anything that demeans, derogates or devalues an individual or group unjustly on any of these matters is seen as racism. And rightly so. With very rare exceptions, the history of the Irish in the United States (and, especially, almost all of the general surveys) have either been written so as to make the Irish Protestants in the United States non-existent, or have made them appear as historical anachronisms, odd groups that arrived before the 1840s and faded into inconsequence thereafter. This would be morally wrong (for racism is a moral, more than a merely intellectual, failing) even if the Protestants were merely a slim minority of the Irish ethnic group. Considering that they were the majority, one is encountering a historiographical omission of astounding proportions.[8]

A variety of ingenious methods of excusing this racism have been (and I think will continue to be) employed. The crudest of them is simply to argue that no Protestant can be 'truly' Irish. This viewpoint has a considerable resonance in Irish nationalist thought, and at present is used by extremists to justify acts of violence against Protestants within Ireland. There is little one can say in response to such a viewpoint, since it is based upon a faith equivalent to that of religious belief and so is not capable of examination in the present world. Within the United States it has its counterparts in persons who say that Jews, blacks, Buddhists or gays cannot be real Americans.

Sometimes it is suggested that the Protestants from Ireland were almost entirely Presbyterians (Ulster Scots) and that they called themselves 'Scotch-Irish' and refused to identify themselves as Irish, in the United States, so they can be ignored. There is just enough accuracy in these beliefs to be misleading. It is true that, when the Famine floods arrived, the Irish Protestants in the inland rural areas were willing to escape nativist prejudice against the Irish Catholics. But in fact the adoption of a separate sobriquet was not necessitated by American events, but rather was a function of something that happened in the homeland in the first half of the nineteenth century. Daniel O'Connell, the Great Liberator, was not merely one of the greatest persons in modern Irish history but one of the shrewdest. He understood that, to be successful, he had to unite in one crucible Irish nationalism, Irish cultural identity and Roman Catholicism. In this he succeeded. As D.G. Boyce has pointed out, by 1840 when a person in Ireland talked of 'Ireland for the Irish' everyone knew he meant the Catholics; and when someone talked about the Irish people he meant the Catholics; and when someone talked of the faith of the Irish people he meant Roman Catholicism.[9] This nominalist by-play is a standard technique of the propagandist, but no less successful for being that. The result was that the Protestants of Ireland, while thinking of themselves as being 'Irish and a bit more', when talking to a wider audience were forced to make it clear that they were not Irish in O'Connell's sense. In the United States, since the name they had

Table 6.2: Proportions of different denominations revealed by the Irish religious censuses of 1834 and 1861

Year	No. of Catholics	% of Population	No. of Anglicans	% of Population	No. of Presbyterians	% of Population
1834	6,427,712	80.9	852,064	10.7	642,356	8.1
1861	4,505,265	77.7	693,357	12.0	523,291	9.0

Note: The residual population in each year's figures consists of 'Other Protestant Dissenters (especially Methodists)', 'Jews', 'Atheists' and 'Unknown'.
Adapted from: *First Report of the Commissioners of Public Instruction, Ireland*, pp. 9–45 [45], HC 1835, XXXII, and from *Report and Tables relating to the Religious Profession, Education and Occupations of the People*, p. 28 [3204–III], HC 1863, LIX. The 1834 data were later 'corrected' by various governmental authorities, not always convincingly, yet not to such an extent as to change by more than a few tenths of a percentage point the figures taken from the primary document.

once used for themselves was now pre-empted by the Catholic migrants, they had to develop a new terminology. Among themselves they kept alive a sense of their Irish background (however else would they have been evident in the NORC, Gallup and CUNY surveys?), but to uninformed outsiders who told them that they were not Irish they merely shrugged and walked away.

For a historian who does not wish to become stained by the sectarianism that runs through so much Irish historical writing (however unconsciously), there are only two parameters for encompassing an accurate historical discussion of the Irish in the United States. The first is that any permanent resident of Ireland who migrated from Ireland to the United States – whatever his or her religious or political background – should be counted as an Irish migrant. That is methodologically simple. It includes everyone who grew up in the social system that was Ireland. And, secondly, anyone who says that his or her ethnicity is Irish should be credited with being Irish. Once those two parameters are accepted, more subtle matters can be dealt with.

In almost all the instances when Protestants have been included in the historiography of the Irish in the United States they have been mislabelled and chronologically segregated. Segregated? In the sense that it is held that there was no significant Irish Protestant migration after the Famine. This is almost certainly untrue, although it is difficult to ascertain directly. And mislabelled? This has occurred because of the assumption that the Irish Protestants were overwhelmingly Presbyterian – that is, Ulster Scots – in background. Actually there is no solid proof that the Presbyterians predominated. It is probable that the other major Protestant group – the 'Anglo-Irish', consisting of 'Anglicans', to use an anachronistic term, or, properly, adherents of the Church of Ireland – sent as many migrants. This can be inferred (although not directly proved) by examining the Irish census data. The first Irish religious census was taken in 1834 and the second in 1861. They yielded the results shown in Table 6.2.[10]

That is, although within Ireland the Anglican or Presbyterian proportions of the total Irish population rose, they experienced a considerable decrease in their absolute numbers. Moreover, if one adds to the statistical series the data

Table 6.3: Proportions of different denominations in Ireland, decennial intervals, 1871–1901

Year	No. of Catholics	% of Population	No. of Anglicans	% of Population	No. of Presbyterians	% of Population
1871	4,150,867	76.7	667,998	12.3	497,648	9.2
1881	3,960,891	76.5	639,574	12.4	470,734	9.1
1891	3,547,307	75.4	600,103	12.8	444,974	9.5
1901	3,308,661	74.2	581,089	13.0	443,276	9.9

Adapted from: Census of Ireland, 1901, Part II, *General Report*, p. 50 [Cd 1190], HC 1902, CXXIX.

Table 6.4: Source of Irish emigrants, by province, 1851–1900

Province	No.	%
Munster	1,346,889	36.8
Ulster	1,015,737	27.7
Leinster	683,209	18.7
Connaught	616,439	16.8
Total on whom information available	3,662,274	100.0

Note: The table does not include 110,668 emigrants of unspecified origin belonging mostly to the years 1851–52, before the improvement in record keeping introduced in 1853.
Adapted from: Commission on Emigration and Other Population Problems, 1948–54, *Reports* [Pr 2541] (Dublin, 1954), pp. 315–16 and 325. The figures have to be derived indirectly, as the Republic's governmental commission that produced this study apparently did not wish to highlight the high proportion of overseas emigration that came from what is now Northern Ireland.

for the remainder of the nineteenth century, the results are striking (Table 6.3). Of course, there is a myriad of possible hypotheses that would explain these trends in census data,[11] but certainly there is a *prima facie* case for social historians investigating these two: that in the second half of the nineteenth century the Irish Protestants in general emigrated in large numbers and that this Protestant emigration was not solely from among the Ulster Scots but even more from among the Anglican population (which, for convenience, if not with perfect accuracy, we may identify as the 'Anglo-Irish').

Unlike the Anglicans, who were distributed, at least patchily, around the entire country, the Presbyterians were concentrated in Ulster. Thus the data on post-Famine emigration from Ulster are illuminating, if somewhat sketchy.[12] They reveal that the historical province of Ulster (nine counties) was the second major provincial source of emigrants (Table 6.4). And, to take a mid-point in this period, 1871, the religious composition of Ulster was as shown in Table 6.5.

Granted, this does not prove that Protestants of whatever stripe migrated in large numbers, but note two facts: first, that 70.0 per cent of the emigrants from Ulster in the period 1851–1900 came from the six counties, that is, from

Table 6.5: Religious composition of Ulster in 1871

Religion	%
Catholic	47.8
Anglican	21.8
Presbyterian	25.9
Other	4.5
Total	100.0

Adapted from: W.E. Vaughan and A.J. Fitzpatrick (eds), *Irish Historical Studies, Population 1821–1971* (Dublin, 1978), p. 59.

the predominantly Protestant part of Ireland,[13] and second, that within the historical nine counties of Ulster the largest outflow in absolute terms came from the most Protestant counties, Antrim and Down.[14] No one would suggest that this proves that there was a major Protestant exodus from Ulster: a cynic might suggest that conceivably all the migrants were Catholics who were shrewd enough to leave at the first opportunity. But, cynicism aside, the hypothesis that large numbers of Ulster Scots and Anglo-Irish left Ireland in the second half of the nineteenth century seems reasonable, given the available Irish data. And one can reasonably suggest that a significant number migrated to the United States, the recipient of the largest number of Irish migrants in the nineteenth century.

The most promising way of making sense of the religious pattern of Irish migration to the United States and of the subsequent religio-ethnic history is to recall the basic distinction between migrants and the multi-generational ethnic cohort – and then to introduce the variable of *time of arrival*, which is a crucial determinate of the overall character of any ethnic group. By taking into account the differential time of arrival of the two major religious strands among Irish migrants, one can see a simple pattern. (1) At some period in the pre-Famine migration to the United States (precisely what years is in doubt) the Protestant Irish migrants (both Anglo-Irish and Ulster Scots) significantly outnumbered the Catholic migrants. (2) Nevertheless, it is almost certainly true that, over the entire history of Irish migration to the United States, more individual Catholics than Protestants arrived. The Catholics, however, in general came later. That pre-Famine (or, at least, pre-1815) migration was tilted towards Protestant groups means that a multiplier existed. To use a simple example: although a Catholic migrant from Munster in 1930 and an Ulster Protestant in 1830 were both single dots on the graph of migration flow, by 1930 the Ulster migrant had scores of descendants within the Irish-descended group, but the Munster migrant only one: him or herself. That there was a significant difference along these lines is indicated by the NORC General Social Survey, which found that in its sample 41 per cent of Irish Catholics (as of the 1970s) were fourth-generation in the United States, while 83 per cent of the Irish Protestants were.[15] (3) It is thus easy to accommodate within this framework the fact that significant Protestant migration continued after the Great Famine. It was much smaller than the Catholic migration, but far from inconsequential. And (4) it is also easy to accept within this framework the suggestion that the

Protestant migration to the United States was not an Ulster Scots migration but was broadly representative of the entire spectrum of Irish Protestantism, which included two major denominations (Presbyterian and Church of Ireland) and several minor ones. Protestant migration had a wide geographical range, and did not stem merely from Ulster. Nor indeed did origin in Ulster imply that the Protestant migrant was Presbyterian, for a considerable portion of the Ulster plantation was formed by Anglicans. Therefore (5) one can accept the corollary of Protestant variation in the homeland, namely that the Protestant Irish in the United States took many forms. Any serious non-racist history of the Irish in the United States should spend as much time upon the Baptists (especially the Southern Baptists), Methodists, Anglicans and Presbyterians as upon the history of the Catholic Church. Only when the life of William Bell Riley (the founding father of twentieth-century American fundamentalism) is as well known as, say, that of Cardinal Spellman will the historiography of the Irish in the United States have come of age.

III

Denial – again, of what? Secondly, of the awkward fact that *there is not and never has been accurate systematic demographic data on several of the most fundamental characteristics of the Irish in the United States.* Yet there are hundreds of books that generalize about the Irish as an ethnic group, and even the most careful of local and community studies usually take for granted an assumed national context that in fact is unrelated to any verifiable data base.

'Demography' is a word that scares some historians, but it need not. What it refers to is simply the counting of people. If one wishes to draw accurate generalizations concerning the Irish in the United States, what one requires is either (1) a professionally conducted random study, such as was done in the case of the NORC, Gallup and CUNY studies that were cited earlier, or (2) a direct count of all the people in a certain jurisdiction (such as a state or an entire nation). The governments of most modern nations conduct periodic 'enumerations' or 'censuses' of population. In each instance, random survey or full census, the group's most important characteristics – economic, religious, etc. – are ascertained. Each person studied by either type of demographic investigation is a dot on a great social map, and taken together these dots potentially permit a set of accurate generalizations about the Irish or whatever group one wishes to study. But without the existence of either of these two forms of basic demographic data – accurate direct censuses or reliable surveys – generalizations about any ethnic or social group are mere fancy or, worse, prejudice.

Thus it comes as an unpleasant recognition to note this fact: there exists *no* body of basic demographic data on the Irish (or any other group) as an ethnic group in the United States. None. Until 1969–70 none of the decennial censuses of the United States asked a question concerning the ethnicity of the individuals whom they were enumerating, and the census is the only potential source of such data. Granted, in the late 1920s the American Council of Learned Societies tried to rework the 1790 census data to give an indication of ethnicity at the end of the colonial period, but this effort failed miserably.[16] No further comprehensive attempt at dealing with ethnicity was made until 1969–70, when the Census Bureau asked an ethnicity question. Unhappily, the collection of the data was bungled and no firm conclusions came from it.[17] In 1980, and again in 1990, the ethnicity question was again asked, and again it was mishandled, so as to be virtually useless.[18]

Even more extraordinary is that *never* have the United States census authorities collected information on the religious affiliation of specific individuals. The Census Bureau once, in 1957, asked a religion question of a voluntary sample group, but it met with so much opposition that the attempt was never repeated.[19] This refusal to deal with religious persuasion, except by querying the various denominational authorities for their alleged total number of adherents, seems so perverse to non-American historians as to be almost pathological. But whatever the reasons for this refusal to enumerate individuals by religion,[20] it precludes the formulation by historians of any general statement based on official census information of the relationship of religion and of Irish ethnicity.

Given that there are no comprehensive data either on Irish ethnicity or upon the religious persuasion of individuals of Irish background in the United States, it follows, *mutatis mutandis*, that there are no cross-tabulations extant which relate either the ethnicity or the religious persuasion of persons of Irish background to such fundamental characteristics as their place of residence and occupation. Granted, there are several – indeed, dozens – of valuable studies of the Irish in various cities of America, but in none of them is the matter of ethnicity or of religion defined for the entire population of the town or city with which the authors deal, and for none of them is it established where in the total context of the Irish in America their study group fits. This is not the authors' fault; the census data are lacking. But, unfortunately, because of the lack of data defining the entire Irish profile, ethnically or religiously, historians have studied the sub-groups on which data come most easily to hand – Catholics in large cities – and have given the impression that the characteristics of these easily researched Irish persons were universal in America.

But, surely, there must be some pieces of comprehensive data about the Irish? There are. Beginning with the 1850 census of the United States, we know, at decennial intervals, the birthplace of everyone in the population.[21] This is useful indeed, as long as one remembers three points: first, that the data on the foreign-born in general, and on the Irish in particular, are information only on migrants, not on the bulk of the ethnic group; second, that the data on the Irish include both Catholics and Protestants, with no effort having been made to distinguish the respective proportions of each denomination; and, third, that the earliest data we have on the Irish reflect the situation *after* the extraordinary migration induced by the Great Famine had been several years in full spate. In other words, we have *no* demographic baseline which allows us to determine what the character and extent of Irish migration to the United States were before the Famine. This is especially crippling because, although it is quite clear that there was heavy Irish migration to the United States before the Famine, the US immigration statistics before 1855 are not trustworthy.

Manifestly, the material available on the number of Irish-born persons among the American population from 1850 onwards is much better than no information at all, but it is not until 1860 that one finds even rudimentary printed cross-tabulations of the data on Irish-born persons with residence in various cities, and not until the 1870 census are data on occupation and on place of birth cross-tabulated.

In 1870 the census authorities asked each individual whether or not he or she had foreign-born parents, but the information was elicited only in the form of a yes-or-no answer, not what country the parents were from. The next census, that of 1880, asked the specific origin of those natives of the United States who had foreign-born parents and cross-tabulated this material in a refreshingly useful fashion. This quasi-ethnicity item was as close as the Census Bureau ever came in the last century to dealing with ethnicity in the true sense. As one authoritative study conducted in the early 1920s lamented, 'The foreign stock can be traced back only one generation . . . Beyond this the population must, in most cases, be treated as an undifferentiated body of native stock.'[22]

There are ways out of the evidentiary black hole into which the history of the Irish in the United States threatens to disappear, but they will take time and money. Many of the original manuscript census records still exist, and these give data on specific individuals which can be linked to various other pieces of information – assessment records, vital statistics, etc. – and then retabulated to produce results that the nineteenth- and early twentieth-century authorities did not elicit. It is immaterial whether a sampling technique on these original census data is employed or a complete retabulation essayed.

The promise of this sort of restudy of census data is that, from 1850 onwards, it would be possible to determine where persons of Irish birth lived in the United States and, potentially, this could be linked to socio-economic data from other sources. From 1880 onwards it would be possible to determine the place of residence both of the Irish-born and of persons who had Irish parents, and perhaps to link this to socio-economic data.

But one must accept the limits of such a mega-cost project. For instance, the 1890 census schedules were burned in 1921,[23] and US policy about releasing personal records makes it unlikely that historians will be given full access to material even up to the First World War. And, whatever such a large project learnt, it would not be able to break through the two great barriers of Irish–US historiography, namely that in the historical records religious data simply do not exist and neither do real ethnic data.

IV

Denial? Yes, again in a third instance. Perversely, framers of the US historiography of the Irish have refused to look to the one source of information that would help them out of many of their difficulties, namely the Canadian material. This is based on the denial of the fact that *there is no history of the Irish in the United States: the history is of the Irish in North America*, and that is something very different indeed.

The necessity of dealing with North America as a unit is simply put. Until very recently (until roughly the middle of the twentieth century) the US–Canadian border was a very permeable membrane. Despite ideological differences between the two nations, individuals and families moved across the border with relative ease. It was not at all uncommon for a person to spend part of his or her working life in, say, Toronto and then move on to Buffalo, later to Minneapolis, and then on to Winnipeg. Branches of various Irish families spanned the border, half in Seattle, say, half in Vancouver. The Eastern Townships of Quebec contained many Irish families with branches in Vermont. The border between Maine and Canada was in many places a figment, and the axis of movement between the Maritimes and the 'Boston States' was a virtual highway. To segregate the Irish in Canada is to trepan the history of the Irish in North America, the largest of the New Worlds to which the Irish migrated. It is similar to someone truncating the history of Ireland by removing from the story the life histories of everyone, say, from Connacht.

Secondly, in arguing the absolute necessity of dealing with the Irish in the United States within the context of North America, one should note that there are certain sources of crucial historical data for the Irish migrants and for the Irish ethnic group that are not found any place else in North America. For instance, some Canadian provinces conducted censuses of population well before the Great Famine. These allow the historian to establish a baseline and thus permit the drawing of accurate generalizations about the nature of Famine migration, which is impossible if one is limited to US sources.

Part of the American problem is that, until 1855, US immigration statistics are much less help than one would expect. The Immigration Act of 1819, effective in 1820, required that all ships bringing migrants to the United States should prepare passenger lists or manifests giving the sex, age, occupation and the 'country to which they severally belong' of all their passengers. The data thereby collected suffered by virtue of incomplete enforcement of the law (and, thus, undercounting) and by an ambiguity in the definition of nativity: it was not made clear whether it meant the country of birth, of citizenship or of last long-term residence. These matters were corrected by the Immigration Act of 1855, but that is too late to throw light on the crucial dark ages of the Irish migration into America, the period from the end of the Napoleonic Wars to the census of 1850.[24]

But even if the pre-1850 US immigration data had been trustworthy, one would still need to adopt a wider, North American perspective. Why? Because before the mid-1840s, when changes in the navigation laws removed the price advantage of sailing to St John's, Newfoundland, St John, New Brunswick, or to Quebec city, the cheapest way to get to the United States was by way of Canada. Hence, even had they been accurate, US port-arrival data would have seriously underestimated the actual number of Irish-born persons who eventually fetched up in the States. One mid-nineteenth-century authority estimated that in the 1820s (when most migrants from the British Isles to Canada were Irish) 67,993 immigrants came to the United States through Canada and that in the 1830s the number was 199,130 (again, at a time when most migrants from the British Isles to Canada were Irish).[25] This same authority estimated

Table 6.6: Foreign-born persons arriving in the United States via Canada

Decade	No.
1815–20	12,157
1820–30	26,524
1830–40	56,364
1840–50	90,718

Adapted from: Edward Jarvis, 'Immigration', *Atlantic Monthly*, 29 (1872), p. 456, quoted in E.P. Hutchinson, 'Notes on Immigration Statistics of the United States', *American Statistical Association Journal*, 53 (1958), pp. 968–79, at p. 976.

that US immigration totals should have been increased by 50 per cent to allow for arrivals from Canada. A rather more conservative estimate was made in the early 1870s and suggested that the number of foreign-born persons coming to the United States via Canada was as shown in Table 6.6. Given that from 1825 onwards (when data become available) the Irish migrants comprised considerably more than half the migrants from the British Isles to Canada, it is highly likely that most of the persons in the above estimate were Irish-born.[26]

Were not these individuals recorded in US immigration statistics? No. Efforts at recording land-border crossings into the United States began – and then fitfully – only in 1853 and were completely abandoned during the American Civil War. The practice was reintroduced in 1865, but abandoned as being unsatisfactory and without a legal basis in 1885. The counting of migrants from Canada and Mexico to the United States did not begin again until the fiscal year 1908.[27] An indication of the data thus lost is found in a study showing that for the years 1879–85 the very incompletely recorded immigration from Canada and Mexico together totalled more than one-seventh (almost 14.6 per cent) of all recorded immigration into the United States (99.4 per cent of this Canadian and Mexican total was Canadian). And, since the Irish were a larger proportion of the immigrant population in Canada than they were in the United States,[28] one can reasonably guess that more than one-seventh of the Irish immigrant flow was entering the United States unrecorded, and that at a very late date. Early in the process, before 1845, the proportion of the flow from Canada must have been considerably higher, the Canadian flow comprising perhaps as much as one-quarter of the total Irish-born influx into the States.

Thus, if one is to make any headway in understanding the fundamental mysteries of pre-1850 Irish migration to the United States, one must think in terms of a *North American* pool of migrants from Ireland, some of whom sailed to Canada and stayed, others of whom migrated direct to the United States and settled, but others of whom arrived in the United States and moved to Canada and many more of whom disembarked in Canada and subsequently moved on to the States.

There are two statistical series which try to define the primary dimensions of this North American pool of Irish migrants. Both of these series were put together during the late 1940s and early 1950s, and they are far from being in agreement. Unfortunately, having been compiled roughly conterminously, each was published in isolation from the other, with the result that neither

Table 6.7: UK estimates of migration from Irish ports to North America, 1825–50

Year	To US	To Canada	Total
1825	4,387	6,841	11,228
1826	4,383	10,484	14,867
1827	4,014	9,134	13,148
1828	2,877	6,695	9,572
1829	4,133	7,710	11,843
1830	2,981	19,340	22,321
1825–30	22,775	60,204	82,979
1831	3,583	40,977	44,560
1832	4,172	37,068	41,240
1833	4,764	17,431	22,195
1834	4,213	28,586	32,799
1835	2,684	9,458	12,142
1836	3,654	19,388	23,042
1837	3,871	22,463	26,334
1838	1,169	2,284	3,453
1839	2,843	8,989	11,832
1840	4,087	23,935	28,022
1831–40	35,040	210,579	245,619
1841	3,893	24,089	27,982
1842	6,199	33,410	39,609
1843	1,617	10,898	12,515
1844	2,993	12,396	15,389
1845	3,708	19,947	23,655
1846	7,070	31,738	38,808
1847	24,502	71,253	95,755
1848	38,843	20,852	59,695
1849	43,673	26,568	70,241
1850	31,297	19,784	51,081
1841–50	163,795	270,935	434,730
Grand total 1825–50	221,610	541,718	763,328

Adapted from: General Register Office, *Studies on Medical and Population Subjects* 6, *External Migration: A Study of the Available Statistics, 1815–1950*, by N.H. Carrier and J.R. Jeffery (London, 1953), p. 95. For a discerning discussion of the limits of the data see p. 136.

addresses its disagreements with the other. The first appeared in 1953 and was done on behalf of the General Register Office of the United Kingdom by N.H. Carrier and J.R. Jeffery. In its approach it was comprehensive, being a complete study of all the available statistics on external migration from the British Isles from 1815 to 1950. The Irish data, which began in 1825, were one subset of the larger British Isles information base. The compilers were scrupulous in discussing the limits on the reliability of their data. In particular, however, it must be emphasized that the direct data on emigrants given in Tables 6.7

Table 6.8: Number of overseas emigrants from Ireland (32 counties), classified by destination, 1825–50

Year	US	Canada	Total
1825	4,387	7,031	11,418
1826	5,447	10,669	16,116
1827	10,372	9,229	19,601
1828	7,573	6,816	14,389
1829	9,583	7,935	17,518
1830	12,467	19,877	32,344
1825–30	49,829	61,557	111,386
1831	13,240	42,221	55,461
1832	14,675	39,184	53,859
1833			n.a.
1834			n.a.
1835	13,039	9,818	22,857
1836			n.a.
1837	21,702	23,856	45,558
1838			n.a.
1839			n.a.
1840			n.a.
1831–40	62,656	115,079	n.a.
1841	3,893	24,089	21,982
1842	6,199	33,410	39,609
1843	23,421	13,578	36,999
1844	37,269	16,485	53,754
1845	50,207	24,713	74,920
1846	68,023	37,889	105,912
1847	118,120	98,485	216,605
1848	151,003	23,543	174,546
1849	180,189	31,865	212,054
1850	184,351	25,264	209,615
1841–50	822,675	329,321	1,151,996

Adapted from: Commission on Emigration and Other Population Problems, 1948–54, *Reports* [Pr 2541] (Dublin, 1954), pp. 314–16.

and 6.8 (ultimately based on ships' muster rolls, whatever the intermediate source) dealt only with migrants from Irish ports.

But of course Irish emigration was not limited to Irish ports. Many Irish persons left for the New World from Liverpool and from Greenock and a few other British ports. Until 1853, however, precise data on Irishmen on British-originating ships are not available, so some compensation has to be allowed for. This is done in the second major emigration series, published in 1954 by the Republic of Ireland's Commission on Emigration and Other Population Problems. This body added to the Irish total two-thirds of the number of persons who sailed overseas from Liverpool in the period 1825–40, and for 1840 onwards made some considerable augmentations in the Irish estimates, but did not tell us on what they were based. (The statistics based on the sources, the reports of the Colonial Land and Emigration Commissioners, contain elements of estimation, the basis of which varied from time to time.) The resulting series purported to be a complete estimate of Irish emigration to the New World.

The main problems with the Republic's series were, first, that unnecessarily large gaps were left in the estimate for the 1830s (the data, as the UK series indicated, were available) and, second, that the procedures by which the compilers corrected the raw data for the 1840s were not recorded.

In any case, for the 1825–30 period, it is virtually certain that even the Republic's augmented estimates of migration to the New World were low, because the compilers corrected only for the probable Irish emigration from Liverpool. In fact in addition to the Liverpool route (which was used almost exclusively for the US trade from the south of Ireland) there were in many years a greater number of migrants from Greenock and Glasgow who went mostly but not exclusively to Canada. (That the Republic's commission ignored this trade from the north of Ireland is culturally diagnostic.) Second, children were undercounted, sometimes not being kept on ships' muster rolls, sometimes being counted as equal to one-third an adult, sometimes as equal to one-half. The under-enumeration varied from year to year, but in general was much greater for ships going to Canada than for ships going to the United States. Therefore the figures both for the United States and for Canada need further augmentation, but those for Canada need proportionally greater adjustment. Further, especially in the case of the Canadian trade, over-packed ships often off-loaded illegal passengers in Newfoundland or in the Maritimes before proceeding up the St Lawrence river.

This is not the place to try to resolve these problems, save to call attention to the work of William Forbes Adams, which, despite its having been done more than half a century ago, still stands as the only somewhat successful attempt at grappling directly with the fundamental problems concerning the data on the Irish migrants to North America. The field desperately requires someone with Adams's sense of proportion and scepticism concerning data and who is willing to work once again step by step through the primary sources.[29]

In arguing that one can discuss sensibly the size and nature of the Irish migration to the United States in the nineteenth century (and, most especially, in the years before the first census of the foreign-born in 1850) only by adopting a North American context, I am of course discussing only the migrants, the so-called first generation. There is more to the point than that, however. Ultimately historians of the Irish in America would like to be able to deal not only with immigrants but with the entire ethnic group. Hence it is worth noting that, in all probability, of these second- and third-generation Irish in America a significant component were the children and grand-children of migrants who had settled not in the United States but in Canada. In the absence of direct studies on this matter, the point has to be drawn inferentially from the facts that (1) the Canadian-born were a large element in the US population (for reference, comparative figures for the Irish-born are provided), and (2) persons of Irish ethnicity composed the largest non-French ethnic group in

Table 6.9: Proportion of Canadian-born in the US population, decennial intervals, 1850–1930

Year	Canadian-born			Irish-born	
	No. in US	% of US population	% of foreign-born	% of US population	% of foreign-born
1850	147,711	0.64	6.6	4.15	42.8
1860	249,970	0.79	6.0	5.12	38.9
1870	493,464	1.28	8.9	4.81	33.3
1880	717,157	1.43	10.7	3.70	27.8
1890	980,938	1.56	10.6	2.80	20.2
1900	1,179,922	1.55	11.4	2.13	15.6
1910	1,204,637	1.31	8.9	1.47	10.0
1930	1,286,389	1.05	9.1	0.75	6.5

Adapted from: Leon E. Truesdell, *The Canadian Born in the United States: An Analysis of the Statistics of the Canadian Element in the Population of the United States, 1850 to 1930* (New Haven, Conn., 1943), tables 2 and 7, pp. 10 and 19; Niles Carpenter, *Immigrants and Their Children* (Washington, D.C., 1927), p. 79; Arnold Schrier, 'Ireland and the American Emigration, 1850–1900', Ph.D. thesis (Northwestern University, 1956), p. 231. Despite the author's wide reading, Marcus Lee Hansen's posthumous volume *The Mingling of the Canadian and American Peoples* (New Haven, Conn., 1940), has very little in the way of statistical evidence.

Canada until the late 1880s or 1890s.[30] Hence, unless one wished to postulate a much lower propensity to migrate on the part of Canadians of native Irish ethnicity than for other groups, one has to infer that a significant proportion of the Irish-American ethnic cohort actually came, most recently, from Canada, and was of Canadian nativity.

Obviously, what the US census data say about the Canadian-born and what they mean in terms of the Irish in America are two different things. Although the Canadian-born were tallied as foreign-born (and thus as first-generation Americans), the fact is that they were at least second, and sometimes third or fourth, generation *North* Americans. Thus they should be plugged into any explanation of the total ethnic pattern of the Irish in the United States, not in the immigrant generation, but in the second and subsequent generations. Just as the path of the Irish migrants to the United States can be understood only as a forked one, some coming direct, others via Canada, so that of the second, third and fourth generations can be understood only if one accepts their duality of nativity, Canadian and US. Manifestly, once one recognizes these facts the permutations of immigration patterns and of ethnic mobility multiply and the accepted picture of the Irish in the United States as having stemmed from a simple, if cruelly uncomfortable, transatlantic passage to New York or Philadelphia, or Boston, disappears.

In arguing the absolute necessity of dealing with the Irish in the United States (both the migrant generation and the entire ethnic group) within the overall context of North America, I have pointed out that there are certain pre-Famine censuses of Canadian provinces that were conducted before the Famine.

Crucially, from the early 1840s onward, various Canadian enumerations enquired not only into nativity but also into religion, something that never was done in the United States. And, most important, from 1871 onwards the Dominion of Canada census authorities recorded not only each person's religion and place of birth but also his or her primary ethnicity, something that, again, has never been done in the United States.

Clearly, if one wishes to draw any valid generalizations about the Irish as an ethnic group – What, for example, was their rate of social mobility? What occupational patterns emerged? In what sort of environment did they settle? How geographically mobile were they? How upwardly mobile economically were they? And how did religion affect these matters? – one would do well to use the Canadian information. Of course the situation in, say, Ontario in 1880 was not identical to that of, say, Illinois in the same year. No two social situations are ever identical. But careful experimental design can produce reliable results that are transportable across state and provincial borders.

The fact is, the historian of the Irish in any part of the United States who does not the Canadian data know, knows not the Irish in the United States.

V

Denial? The final form of denial that characterizes the historiography of the Irish in the United States is a refusal to see that *much of the literature is based on a derogatory (and inaccurate) interpretation of the cultural background of the nineteenth-century Irish Catholic migrants*. Simply put, the general view has been (and still is) that the cultural characteristics associated with Roman Catholicism in Ireland were an impediment to the migrants' adaptation to the New World.

Potentially, being Catholic could have been a handicap to Irish migrants to the United States in two ways. One was that the existing American society treated Catholics with prejudice. Certainly this happened in the nineteenth century, on a widespread basis, and to a lesser degree in the early twentieth century. To note such an occurrence is in no way potentially misleading, nor in any way derogatory of the nineteenth-century migrants.

The second potentiality, however, can be harmful: the idea that the culture of Roman Catholicism as it was imported from Ireland in some way made the Irish migrants and their offspring backward and not fully able to cope with modernizing America. Usually this view has been put forward by persons who themselves are of Irish Catholic background, so no conscious racism is involved. And, when put forward by professional historians who are non-Catholic, the intent of these ideas has been to understand, not to defame. It is indeed possible that the Irish Catholic culture as imported from the homeland was in some ways a handicap to the migrants, a shackle that made them relatively backward as compared with other migrant groups in the United States. However, if one is articulating such a potentially derogatory conclusion about any ethnic group, even though no conscious racism is involved, one owes it to everyone concerned to operate at a high standard of proof.

Fortunately, we possess an excellent test case of that conclusion, one that saves us from the tedious necessity of having to provide portmanteau citations. This is the *ne plus ultra* of the historiography of the Irish in the United States, Kerby Miller's monumental *Emigrants and Exiles*. The volume captured both the Merle Curti Award in American Social History and the Saloutas Memorial Book Award in American Immigration History. The study is at once an encapsulation of almost the entire body of literature on the Irish in the United States (up to the time of its writing) and the most forceful and expert articulation of what US historians of the Irish believed they knew (again, at the time of its writing). The volume, therefore, is an appropriate and fair place to focus upon the historians' view of the Catholic culture of the nineteenth-century migrants, for it is the strongest statement available of the conventional wisdom.

Miller's volume is in most ways an advance over anything done by his predecessors. Not least among these are his attempts to include the Protestant migrants and their descendants in history. That in fact he leaves them on the periphery and does not include them in his main set of hypotheses is unfortunate, but at least he granted their existence as part of the Irish migrant stream, something few of his predecessors did. And, unlike almost all of his predecessors, Miller attempts to write about the Irish in North America, not merely about the Irish in the United States. This means that he understands that his assertions and theories can legitimately be examined by reference to the appropriate Canadian data as well as to whatever one finds available in the US demographic sources.

The heart of the book, on which it must be judged, concerns the years 1815–1921, the era of the great Irish diaspora. Miller writes gracefully, and it is with an apologetic philistinism that one must wrench his argument from his prose and coldly outline his logic. To begin with, he has a phenomenon that he wishes to explain. This is his observed fact that nineteenth-century Irish emigrants were predisposed to perceive or at least justify themselves not as voluntary, ambitious emigrants but as involuntary, non-responsible 'exiles' compelled to leave home by forces beyond individual control, particularly by British and landlord oppression.[31] Note that this observation involves only Irish Catholic emigrants, not Protestant ones. Miller pays considerable attention to Protestants, but his primary observation and his explanation of it concern only Roman Catholics.

To explain this primary phenomenon he introduces several causal factors. First, beginning in the late 1820s, *relatively* (italics Miller's) poor Catholics from the three southern provinces constituted a major proportion of the movement overseas.[32] Second, the increasingly Catholic stream of emigrants was a river of reluctant exiles. According to Miller, much evidence indicates that Catholics throughout Ireland, not just in remote Irish-speaking areas, were much more reluctant to leave home than were their Protestant countrymen.[33] Third, for Catholics emigration posed severe social, cultural and even psychological problems.[34]

As a link between his primary observed phenomenon and these causal factors Miller presents an intervening variable. He does not give it a name, but it can be denominated the 'Gaelic-Catholic Disability'. He says, concerning 'traditionalist rural Catholics', that, among those who emigrated, 'their outlook on life . . . was fatalistic and dependent, and their religious faith was usually neither generalized nor internalized, but instead was almost inseparable from archaic customs and landmarks rooted in particular locales now thousands of miles behind them'.[35] He postulates 'a Catholic Irish propensity to avoid individual responsibility for innovative actions such as emigration and to fall back on communally acceptable explanations embedded in archaic historic and literary traditions and reinforced by modern Irish political rhetoric'.[36] Even the Irish language is fitted into this variable: the semantic structure of the Irish language itself reflected and reinforced an Irish world view which emphasized dependence and passivity.[37] Thus, 'armed with a world view so shaped, the Irish experienced the socioeconomic changes associated with the modern commercial and industrial revolutions with certain psychological, as well as political and economic, disadvantages'.[38] Such people perceived their movement into the then modern world of nineteenth-century North America as banishment. As the century progressed, and as a higher and higher proportion of emigrants came from western districts with a strong Gaelic-Catholic culture, the pervasive sense of exile increased.

The potential importance of Miller's Gaelic-Catholic Disability in the study of Irish history is prodigious. This is because the alleged phenomenon is not just a matter that relates to the Irish in the United States. It represents a theory of the Irish Catholic culture at home. And that culture was eventually taken not only to the United States but around the world. Therefore his Gaelic-Catholic Disability is nothing less than a theory of Irish Catholic culture world-wide.

How does one examine such a world-encircling thesis? One could test for accuracy the hundreds of quotations from the collections of roughly 5,000 emigrant letters and memoirs that are found in Miller's text, but this is just short of impossible: Miller's publisher has allowed him only one endnote for each paragraph and, since there are usually multiple quotations within each paragraph as well as statements of fact, it is difficult, if not impossible, to identify the source of any given statement. Alternatively, one could collect still more emigrant letters and thus try to ascertain whether the attitudes that Miller purports to find are indeed representative. Suffice it to say that at this point no one has checked Miller's quotations for accuracy and representativeness and that the only scholar to work through material similar to his concerning North American emigrants does not find the passivity or the other characteristics that led Miller to create his Gaelic-Catholic Disability variable.[39] Nor do studies conducted of emigrant letters from non-US migrants find anything like the backwardness-inducing attitudes that Miller posits. However, I think that it would be a mistake to make too much of these contradictions, since there are technical differences in the various collections of emigrant letters that make it difficult to compare them with Miller's.[40] For the moment, one should assume the accuracy of Miller's data collection, transcription and selection of material as far as migrant attitudes are concerned.[41]

If we make that assumption, the next logical step is to ask: what are the implications of what I have called Miller's 'Gaelic-Catholic Disability variable'? If that intervening variable is accurate and apposite, not only will it explain why the Irish Catholics wrote all those mournful exile songs and sent those tear-stained letters home, it will permit us to form hypotheses about the Irish Catholics in North America that can be empirically tested. If the hypotheses are confirmed, the probability that Miller's Gaelic-Catholic Disability variable is valid will be greatly heightened. If, on the other hand, the hypotheses are disproved, the validity of Miller's argument will have been shown to be so improbable as to be worthless.

Fortunately, the elegant simplicity of Miller's model permits a series of simple and effective tests. Since his position is that the Irish Catholic culture was both singular and a liability, then if it were found that the Irish Catholics (either in the migrant generation or among their immediate descendants) and Irish Protestants (who certainly did not share the Gaelic-Catholic culture) were fundamentally similar in behaviour, it would have been proved that the Gaelic-Catholic Disability was a chimera and that this interpretation of the Irish Catholic culture should not be adopted as part of the explanation of the history of the Irish Catholics world-wide.

It seems fair to suggest that from Miller's model of Gaelic-Catholic culture, and from his contrasts, both explicit and implicit, between Irish Protestants and Irish Catholics, one would predict of nineteenth-century North America, first, that because of the communal and familial nature of their culture, as described by Miller, they would be much less successful than Irish Protestants in operating in the isolated world of nineteenth-century North American agriculture, and thus one would expect the Irish Catholics necessarily to huddle together in cities and to avoid the solitariness of rural life; second, that they would have a significantly lower occupational profile than would Irish Protestants; third, that Irish Catholics would show less rapid upward social mobility over time than would Irish Protestants.

Fortunately, there are three separate sets of studies, each of which includes wide-scale observations of the behaviour of Irish migrants or of the entire ethnic group. Each set deals with behaviour, not psychological presumptions, and each set is capable of being replicated. The first set, and the most important, is the extraordinary work of Gordon Darroch and Michael Ornstein.[42] This work is by far the most sophisticated research design yet adopted in North American ethnic historiography, and it should serve as a model for what eventually must be done with the US manuscript census data. What Darroch and Ornstein did in substance was virtually to retabulate from original manuscript sources the 1871 Dominion of Canada censuses. This was done so as to permit the framing and answering of many questions that did not occur to the nineteenth-century enumeration officials. In particular, the nineteenth-century Canadian censuses are notoriously frustrating in that they contain data on several important variables but do not provide cross-tabulations of those variables. To overcome such difficulties, Darroch and Ornstein drew from the 1871 census a random group of 10,000 male heads of household, on each of whom there were data on several dozen characteristics. They followed up this massive sampling by linking a large body of their 1871 data to other records on individuals who lived in central Canada during the third quarter of the nineteenth century. This allowed the tracing of several thousand randomly selected life patterns.

What Darroch and Ornstein's studies revealed was, first, that Irish Roman Catholics were not disabled by their cultural background from entering the most important entrepreneurial occupation of the time: farming, either on the frontier or in already settled areas. Indeed, farming was the most common Irish Catholic occupation, as it was of the Irish Protestants. The Irish Catholics were only slightly less likely to go into farming – less than 10 per cent below the national average – than were the average run of Canadians. The Irish were not ineluctably urban.

Further, Darroch and Ornstein show that, contrary to the hypothesis, Irish Catholics in Canada did not have a markedly lower economic profile than did persons of Irish Protestant ethnicity. The proportions of Irish Catholics and Irish Protestants among manufacturers, white-collar workers and artisans were virtually identical in Canada in 1871. Catholics were under-represented in the professional class – only 3 per cent of the total population, in any case – and were more likely than other groups to have labouring occupations, but *not* markedly so. Put simply, persons of Irish Catholic ethnicity did slightly less well than did persons of Irish Protestant ethnicity, but not enough to lend credence to the idea that Catholics were heavily handicapped by their cultural background. Strikingly, in rural areas it was found that the Irish Catholics had slightly greater proportions in the bourgeois occupations than did the Scots or Germans.[43]

Moreover the data show that, contrary to the hypothesis, Irish Catholics did not evince significantly less upward mobility over time than did Irish Protestants. Among Irish-born persons – that is, Irish migrants – linked by Darroch and Ornstein between 1861 and 1871 there was no dramatic difference either in occupational distribution or in occupational mobility between Irish Catholics and Irish Protestants. Irish Catholic immigrants started out somewhat over-represented in labouring occupations, but their rate of mobility out of labouring into more desirable occupations – and especially into the nation's most desired way of earning a living, farm ownership – *exceeded* that of the Irish-born Protestants.[44]

What this adds up to is a crushing disproof of the validity of Miller's main explanatory concept, the idea that the Gaelic-Catholic culture was a heavy disability for individuals dealing with the modern world of nineteenth-century North America. Admittedly, one could suggest that, somehow, the Irish Catholics who settled in Canada were more able than those who settled in the United States, but, if anything, the opposite is true. From the beginning of the Famine onwards, US regulations were more strict than Canadian regulations, and Canada, not the United States, was most apt to be the repository of the most tired, hungry and worn.

A second set of studies which permit an evaluation of the validity of interpreting the Gaelic-Catholic background as a cultural disability is my own work.

Found in five recent books that deal with New Zealand, Australia, South Africa, as well as with Canada and the United States, these studies present several million datum points, each systematically generated by the census authorities in most of the jurisdictions where the Irish settled in large numbers.[45] The student of the Irish diaspora will necessarily encounter those books directly: here suffice it to say that in no jurisdiction in which there are comprehensive and reliable data is there any indication of the Gaelic-Catholic culture being a disabling factor. More important, in those jurisdictions in which there is information upon the religious persuasion of the Irish migrants there is compelling evidence of close similarities between Irish Catholic and Irish Protestant matters of residence, occupation, family structure and economic mobility. And where multi-generational data are available there is strong positive evidence of close similarities between the Catholic portion and the Protestant portion of the Irish ethnic group. The concept of the Gaelic-Catholic culture being linked to backwardness and inability to take advantage of the various New Worlds is fully disproved.

A third set of studies conducted in the 1970s and 1980s serves as confirmation of the previous two. These are the results yielded by data collected by the National Opinion Research Center of the University of Chicago. (Because these data were generated quite late in the history of the Irish diaspora they are not as compelling as the nineteenth- and early twentieth-century data, but they are revealing nonetheless.) The NORC studies found that the Irish group in the United States was polarized between two groups: Catholics, 70 per cent of whom lived in the north-east and north-central United States, and Protestants, over half of whom lived in the American south. The Catholics of Irish ethnicity were less likely to be working-class than were the Protestants. As a group the Catholics were twice as likely to be university graduates as were Protestants of Irish ethnicity, and the Catholic Irish had family incomes significantly higher than those of the Protestant Irish.[46]

The intriguing questions that follow from this information are: when did the Irish Catholics cross the US demographic line to the side of privileged status? And when did the Irish Protestants slide below it, on their way to becoming the most disadvantaged of major groups? Andrew Greeley's estimate, based on his employment of survey data to reconstruct earlier group cohorts, is that this socio-economic watershed was crossed by the Irish Catholics during the decade of the First World War, 1910–19.[47] Irish Protestants, on their collective way downward, crossed by later, probably in the 1930s.

These data are very spiky indeed. The association for most of the present century of Irish Catholicism with relative privilege and of Irish Protestantism with relative disadvantage makes it very hard to present the Irish Catholic culture as a disabling force in US society.

Does this mean that one is rejecting the concept of a Gaelic-Catholic cultural background as part of the heritage common to many of the migrants from Ireland to the United States? Or that one is rejecting the picture whereby the wider society discriminated strongly against the Irish Catholics on the basis of their religion? No. What is rejected is the idea that their cultural background was in itself a handicap for the Irish Catholics as they coped with the New World.

VI

Denial. In this assessment of the historiography of the Irish in the United States I have used 'denial' to describe four specific behaviours practised by historians. At no time have I imputed motive to persons exhibiting those behaviours, or engaged in a 'psychological' explanation of such behaviour. The historiography of the Irish in the United States has gotten itself in deep trouble because of its predilection for pop psychology, as Patrick O'Sullivan has made clear.

The wonderful thing about behaviour is that it can be changed. Accurate scholarly work is a behaviour that is rewarding in itself. And it is the best homage that one can pay to the Irish migrants and their descendants.

Notes

1. For example, R.A. Burchell, *The San Francisco Irish, 1848–1880* (Berkeley, Ca., 1980); Dennis Clark, *Hibernia America: The Irish and Regional Cultures* (Westport, Conn., 1985); David M. Emmons, *The Butte Irish: Class and Ethnicity in an American Mining Town, 1875–1925* (Urbana, Ill., 1989).
2. Patrick O'Sullivan, 'Introduction', to Patrick O'Sullivan (ed.), *The Irish in New Communities* (London, 1992), p. 7.
3. For entry into the literature see R.A. Burchell, 'The Historiography of the American-Irish', *Immigrants and Minorities*, 1, 3 (1982), pp. 281–305; David Noel Doyle, 'The Regional Bibliography of Irish America, 1800–1930: A Review and Addendum', *Irish Historical Studies*, 23, 91 (1983), pp. 254–83; Seamus P. Metress, *The Irish-American Experience: A Guide to the Literature* (Washington, D.C., 1981).
4. This is North American usage. British Isles usage sometimes employs 'first generation' to mean the first generation born in the new homeland. Here North American usage is adopted.
5. Andrew M. Greeley, 'The American Irish: A Report from Great Ireland', *International Journal of Comparative Sociology*, 29 (1979), pp. 67–81; 'Ethnic Minorities in the United States: Demographic Perspectives', *International Journal of Group Tensions*, 7 (1977), pp. 84–97; *Ethnicity in the United States: A Preliminary Reconnaissance* (New York, 1974), pp. 35–89; 'The Success and Assimilation of Irish Protestants and Irish Catholics in the United States', *Social Science Research*, 72, 4 (1988), pp. 229–36; Fred Boal, 'Who are the "Irish Americans"?', *Fortnight*, 155 (1977), pp. 4–5.
6. George Gallup, Jr, and Jim Castelli, *The People's Religion: American Faith in the '90s* (New York, 1989), pp. 119–22.
7. The closest anyone with historical evidence has come to suggesting such an apostasy is Michael O'Brien. He was a late nineteenth- and early twentieth-century antiquarian, of prodigious devotion, and not a fool. He attacked the idea that the only colonial Irish settlers were Ulster Scots, and on that point he was certainly correct. He also believed that both Anglo-Irish and Ulster Scots were Irish, and on this one must concur (for certainly they saw themselves as Irish). What is doubtful is

O'Brien's view that many Irish Catholics abandoned their faith in colonial New England and other colonies. O'Brien cites numerous Irish names in baptismal records of Protestant churches. In future writing I shall attempt to assess in some detail O'Brien's work on the 'appostasy' issue. See Michael J. O'Brien, *Irish Settlers in America: A Consolidation of Articles from the Journal of the American-Irish Historical Society* (Baltimore, Md., 1979), *passim*.

8. When one leaves the historical literature of the 'Irish-Americans' (a code phrase for Roman Catholics of Irish background), and enters that of the so-called 'Scotch-Irish', one enters a strange underwater kingdom. The two classic books on the subject which set the framework for the continuing emphasis on the eighteenth century and upon a virtually racialist view of the differences between the Ulster Scots and the Irish Catholics are: Charles A. Hanna, *The Scotch-Irish, or, The Scot in North Britain, North Ireland, and North America* (New York, 1902) and Henry Ford Jones, *The Scotch-Irish in America* (Princeton, N.J., 1915). In a summary of his own book, written for a popular audience, James G. Leyburn states categorically that 'There was almost no further influx from northern Ireland after the Revolutionary war' ('The Scotch-Irish', *American Heritage*, 22, December 1970, p. 99.) See also James G. Leyburn, *The Scotch-Irish: A Social History* (Chapel Hill, N.C., 1962). For a revisionist view concerning the eighteenth century see David Noel Doyle, *Ireland, Irishmen, and Revolutionary America, 1760–1820* (Dublin, 1981). The substance of R.J. Dickson's *Ulster Emigration to Colonial America 1718–75* (London, 1966) is a dispassionate, thorough and convincing monograph. The author's introduction, however, repeats the assertion that there were two distinct groups of people who emigrated from Ireland to the United States: 'The hundreds of thousands of Irish emigrants to colonial America who have been overshadowed by the millions who emigrated from Ireland in the second half of the nineteenth century' (p. ix). One of the more engaging discussions of the Ulster Scot as a rural phenomenon was provided by the late Estyn Evans, Ireland's pioneering historical geographer, in 'The Scotch-Irish in the New World: An Atlantic Heritage', *Journal of the Royal Society of Antiquaries of Ireland*, 95 (1965), pp. 39–49. Rather broader recent interpretations of the same agreed phenomenon are Forrest McDonald and Grady McWhiney, 'The Antebellum Southern Herdsman: A Reinterpretation', *Journal of Southern History*, 41 (1975), pp. 147–66; Forrest McDonald, 'The Ethnic Factor in Alabama History: A Neglected Dimension', *Alabama Review*, 32 (1978), pp. 256–65; Forrest McDonald and Grady McWhiney, 'The Celtic South', *History Today*, 30 (July 1980), pp. 11–15.

9. D.G. Boyce, 'Sense and Sensibility', *Irish Literary Supplement* (fall 1990), p. 28.

10. This use of census data, admittedly quite crude, is loaded *against* suggesting that the Irish Protestants emigrated quite frequently: presumably the Catholics, being over-represented in the pauper class, more frequently starved or died of Famine-related disease than did the Protestants; therefore, much of their population loss was from those causes, not solely from emigration. Religious percentages in Ireland before 1834 are highly problematical. For a sensible, although not definitive, attempt to deal with the earlier situation see Appendix B, 'Statistics of Religious Affiliation in Ireland in the Eighteenth and Nineteenth Centuries', in S.J. Connolly, *Priests and People in Pre-Famine Ireland, 1780–1845* (Dublin, 1982), pp. 281–3.

11. For example, one might hypothesize that the drop in the Protestant population came from a lowering of family size (and thus of religious-specific fertility) while the Catholic drop in population came chiefly from emigration. Actually, however, the opposite is more likely to have happened. That is, the brunt of the Famine having

fallen on the Catholic poor, the limits on marriage that developed in the post-Famine era (described, for example, in Conrad M. Arensberg and Solon T. Kimball, *Family and Community in Ireland*, Cambridge, Mass., 1968), probably fell more severely on the Catholics. Again, I am presenting the census data in such a way as to minimize the possibility of our having to accept the idea of large-scale Protestant emigration; even so, that hypothesis emerges as one most needful of being tested.

12. As David Fitzpatrick points out in 'Irish Emigration in the later Nineteenth Century', *Irish Historical Studies*, 22 (September 1980), pp. 127–8, from 1851 to 1876 the data are wobbly but not without worth. In 1876 the method of making the count was revamped to abolish local anomalies in the collection method.

13. Derived from the same source as Table 6.4.

14. See W.E. Vaughan and A.J. Fitzpatrick (eds), *Irish Historical Statistics, Population, 1821–1971* (Royal Irish Academy, 1978), pp. 311–32.

15. Greeley, 'The Success and Assimiliation of Irish Protestants and Irish Catholics in the United States', p. 229.

16. See Donald H. Akenson, 'Why the Accepted Estimates of the Ethnicity of the American People, 1790, are Unacceptable', *William and Mary Quarterly*, 3rd series, 41 (1984), pp. 102–19.

17. The problem was that persons returning more than one ethnic origin were lumped into an 'other' category which embraced roughly half the population! See Charles A. Price, 'Methods of Estimating the Size of Groups', in Stephen Thernstrom (ed.), *Harvard Encyclopedia of American Ethnic Groups* (Cambridge, Mass., 1980), pp. 1033–4.

18. Once again, individuals were allowed to list multiple ancestries rather than a single dominant one, so that 55 per cent listed two or more in the 1980 census. Thus the data on ethnicity cannot be related to any other variable, nor, in fact, can they serve as the basis of anything but the crudest guessing about what the real ethnic composition of the country actually is.

19. Price, 'Methods of Estimating', p. 1040.

20. For a fascinating discussion of this fear of collecting religious data, and especially of the trouble which arose when it was proposed to include religion on the 1960 census, see William Petersen, 'Religious Statistics in the United States', *Journal for the Scientific Study of Religion*, 1 (1965), pp. 165–78. This article also discusses the Census Bureau's suppression (!) of the data it had collected in the 1957 voluntary-sample study.

21. A very useful version of that census was compiled by J.D.B. Debow, superintendent of the US census, *A Statistical View of the United States . . .* , (Washington, D.C., 1854).

22. Niles Carpenter, *Immigrants and their Children: A Study Based on Census Statistics Relative to the Foreign-born and the Native Whites of Foreign or Mixed Parentage* Census Monographs VII (Washington, D.C., 1927), p. 2. Although the US Census Bureau's collections of ethnic data went no further than the migrants and their offspring, it is of course possible to do extrapolations of the gross number of persons in the third generation. This was attempted by the Census Bureau for the 1920 census (see Carpenter, p. 92) and, further, amateur demographers were always willing to try to establish the total strength of the Irish ethnic group from the limited knowledge available concerning the first two generations in the United States. Michael J. O'Brien, historiographer of the American-Irish Historical Society, surveyed some of the early attempts and shrewdly, if tiredly, remarked that 'to form any reliable estimate of the numerical strength of the Irish and their

descendants in the United States, I believe, would be a hopeless task and while several have attempted to do so, I am of the opinion that all such estimates should be discarded as mere conjecture', 'The Irish in the United States', in Joseph Dunn and P.J. Lennox (eds), *The Glories of Ireland* (Washington, D.C., 1914), p. 208.

23. Burchell, 'The Historiography', p. 281. A 'public use sample' for 1900 is available.
24. E.P. Hutchinson, 'Notes on Immigration Statistics of the United States', *American Statistical Association Journal*, 53 (1958), pp. 968–79. I am here leaving aside entirely the problem involved with the counter-flow from the United States to various foreign countries. Net migration data are what one requires, but in the absence of records on alien departures from the United States there is no way of measuring net immigration before 1908. (Carpenter, *Immigrants and their Children*, p. 3.)
25. Estimate found in J.D.B. DeBow, *The Industrial Resources Statistics, etc., of the United States* (New York, 1854), Vol. 3, pp. 396, 424, cited in Hutchinson, 'Notes on Immigration Statistics', p. 975.
26. I am here avoiding the virtually insoluble question of how great was the counter-flow of British Isles-born persons who shipped to the United States and came from thence to Canada. Undoubtedly it was much less than the flow from Canada into the United States, but whether it was 2 per cent or 20.3 per cent or 30 per cent no one really knows (see Hutchinson, 'Notes on Immigration Statistics', p. 976).
27. Hutchinson, 'Notes on Immigration Statistics', pp. 974–81.
28. Computed from Hutchinson, 'Notes on Immigration Statistics', p. 981. For instance, the Irish-born constituted 4.81 per cent of the US population in 1870, while in 1871 the Irish-born constituted 6.2 per cent of the Canadian population. Compare the text above with *Seventh Census of Canada, 1931* (Ottawa, 1936), Vol. I, p. 517.
29. William Forbes Adams, *Ireland and the Irish Emigration to the New World from 1815 to the Famine* (New Haven, Conn., 1932). See especially his appendix, 'Statistics of Irish Emigration, 1815–45', on which my comments in the text are largely based. Adams's work is often paid lip service but its substance is generally ignored, largely, one conjectures, because it runs against the grain of the present consensus among historians of the Irish in the United States. That is, Adams's work implicitly affirms three points: first, that the central episode in the history of the Irish in the New World begins not with the Famine but in 1815; second, that one must deal with all of North America if one is to come to terms with the Irish in the United States; and, third, that, no matter how difficult the task, one must work with the available demographic data and in particular have an explicit understanding of the limits of that data. That, 60 years after Adams's work, I am having to argue explicitly what Adams accepted implicitly is not entirely heartening.
30. The precise date is problematical. The Irish were the largest Canadian ethnic group in 1881, but the English had surpassed them by 1901. Unfortunately, the 1891 census did not yield ethnicity data in a form comparable to that provided by the censuses of 1881 and 1901, so one must necessarily be vague. For the data see *Seventh Census of Canada, 1931*, Vol. I, p. 710.
31. Kerby A. Miller, *Emigrants and Exiles: Ireland and the Irish Exodus to North America* (New York, 1985), p. 556.
32. Ibid., p. 198.
33. Ibid., p. 238.
34. Ibid., p. 240.
35. Ibid., p. 259.
36. Ibid., p. 277.

37. Ibid., p. 119.

38. Ibid., p. 8.

39. Ruth-Ann Harris, 'America Imagined, America Realized: New Perspectives on the American Letter', unpublished paper, American conference for Irish Studies, April 1990; Ruth-Ann Harris to author, 22 May 1990.

40. See D.H. Akenson, 'Reading the Texts of Rural Immigrants: Letters from the Irish in Australia, New Zealand, and North America', *Canadian Papers in Rural History*, 7 (1990), pp. 387–406, reprinted in *Migration and New Zealand Society* (Wellington, New Zealand, 1990), pp. 1–17; David Fitzpatrick, ' "An Ocean of Consolation": Letters and Irish Immigration to Australia', in Eric Richards, Richard Reid and David Fitzpatrick (eds), *Visible Immigrants: Neglected Sources for the History of Australian Immigration* (Canberra, 1989), pp. 47–86; E.R.R. Green, 'Ulster Emigrants' Letters', in E.R.R. Green (ed.), *Essays in Scotch-Irish History* (London, 1969), pp. 87–103; Cecil J. Houston and William J. Smyth, *Irish Emigration and Canadian Settlement: Patterns, Links and Settlers* (Toronto, 1990), pp. 241–333; Patrick O'Farrell, *Letters from Irish Australia, 1825–1929* (Sydney and Belfast, 1984). The chief problem of comparability is the over-representation of Protestants in most of the studies mentioned above, in comparison with Miller's sample. This is particularly true of the Green, O'Farrell, and Houston and Smyth items.

41. The fundamental difficulty in using emigrant letters as the basis for any study of the Irish diaspora is that there are so few letters in relation to the huge population of migrants, and this is doubly true of the Catholics. The really troublesome question is why are there so very few surviving emigrant letters sent back from Irish Catholic migrants. This holds not only for the United States but for Australia, New Zealand and Canada. This despite the fact that the Irish Catholic emigrants were mostly literate and despite the fact that Irish Catholic families in the homeland have shown themselves very good at maintaining family artefacts and heirlooms – and one would have thought they would have kept letters and that they would have found their way, after 1922, into the museums and archives of newly independent Ireland. Miller has done the best collecting job yet, but even he has only 5,000 letters drawn from a migrant population of millions and (one assumes) from a flow of migrant letters home that numbered in the several millions. Such a sample size just might be large enough to produce meaningful results if it were drawn (1) with a knowledge of the context within which each letter was written or (2) if it were part of a competently designed random survey (always assuming that the message of each letter is not misrepresented by its being gutted to fit an historical argument). In fact the context of the letters Miller cites is hardly ever known, and the actual letters themselves cannot be taken as anything approaching random. Thus any conclusions that one could draw from them in all probability are not representative of the reference group (Irish migrants) to which they are believed to refer.

42. Gordon Darroch, 'Class in Nineteenth-century Central Ontario: A Reassessment of the Crisis and Demise of Small Producers During Early Industrialization, 1861–71', in Gregory S. Kealey (ed.), *Class, Gender, and Region: Essays in Canadian Historical Sociology* (St John's, Nfld., 1988), pp. 49–72; A. Gordon Darroch and Michael Ornstein, 'Ethnicity and Class: Transitions over a Decade: Ontario, 1861–71', Canadian Historical Association, Ottawa, *History Papers, 1984*, pp. 111–37; 'Ethnicity and Occupational Structure in Canada in 1871: The Vertical Mosaic in Historical Perspective', *Canadian Historical Review*, 61 (1980), pp. 305–33.

43. Darroch and Ornstein, 'Ethnicity and Occupational Structure', pp. 320–5.

44. Compare the table in Darroch and Ornstein, 'Ethnicity and Class', pp. 121–2.

45. *Occasional Papers on the Irish in South Africa*, Institute of Social and Economic Research, Rhodes University, Grahamstown, 1991; *Half the World from Home: Perspectives on the Irish in New Zealand* (Wellington, 1990); *Small Differences: Irish Catholics and Irish Protestants, 1815–1921: An International Perspective* (Kingston and Montreal, 1988, and Dublin, 1990); *Being Had: Historians, Evidence and the Irish in North America* (Toronto, 1985); *The Irish in Ontario: A Study in Rural History* (Kingston and Montreal, 1984).

46. Greeley, 'The Success and Assimilation of Irish Protestants and Irish Catholics in the United States', pp. 231–2.

47. Ibid., p. 231.

CHAPTER 7

'Scotch-Irish', 'Black Irish' and 'Real Irish': Emigrants and Identities in the Old South

KERBY A. MILLER
(Department of History, University of Missouri-Columbia)

In 1804 Thomas Addis Emmet, exiled leader of the United Irishmen, sailed from his temporary haven in Napoleonic France and disembarked in New York City. Shortly thereafter, Richard McCormick, a former comrade who had preceded him to the United States, wrote to Emmet from Georgia, urging him to settle in the 'Old South', that is, in one of the American states or territories that lay south of Pennsylvania and the Ohio river and whose socio-economic and legal systems were dominated by the institution of African-American slavery. Emmet declined his friend's invitation, despite the South's admitted attractions, refusing on principle to reside where his family would be dependent on coerced labour.[1]

Emmet's scruples were not widely shared, and other Irish political exiles managed to accommodate republican principles and American slavery.[2] Indeed, during the eighteenth century and the first few decades of the nineteenth century, there was a substantial Irish migration to and settlement in the Old South. David N. Doyle, Ireland's premier historian of the American Irish, has analysed the first US census of 1790 and concludes that approximately one-fifth of the white population of the southern states, over a quarter-million southerners, were of Irish birth or descent. The Irish-stock proportions of the populations of individual southern states ranged from 17–18 per cent in Delaware, Maryland, Virginia and North Carolina to as high as one-third in Kentucky and Tennessee, while in Georgia and South Carolina the Irish comprised slightly over one-quarter of their white inhabitants. Doyle estimates that roughly two-thirds of these early Irish-American southerners were what later generations would usually call the 'Scotch-Irish' – that is, the descendants of Scottish Presbyterians who, in the seventeenth and early eighteenth centuries, had settled in Ulster before remigrating later to North America. However, Doyle contends that this group also included many whose Irish ancestors had been Anglicans or Catholics but who had converted to Presbyterianism, either shortly before or after their migrations to the New World, and who subsequently were absorbed into what he calls the 'Ulster-American' community. Finally,

Doyle concludes that in 1790 the other one-third of the 'Irish' in the Old South represented families whose members or ancestors had been born in the south of Ireland; originally most had been Catholics, but, given the dearth of priests and chapels in eighteenth- and early nineteenth-century America, the great majority also joined Protestant congregations and eventually merged into the so-called 'Scotch-Irish' group.[3]

Yet despite the size and significance of this early Irish emigration to the Old South, by the late 1830s and 1840s most Irish-born men and women were avoiding the southern states, primarily for economic reasons that included a reluctance to compete with slave labour. And when Irish emigration peaked during and immediately after the Great Famine of 1845–52, relatively few newcomers settled in the Old South. Thus, although in 1860 there were in the entire United States about 1.6 million Irish-born inhabitants, representing roughly 6 per cent of the nation's white population, only 11 per cent of these emigrants – fewer than 200,000 – resided in the slave states, where they comprised merely 2.25 per cent of the South's white population. Moreover, nearly 70 per cent of these Irish-born southerners were concentrated in a handful of exceptionally urbanized 'border states' – in Louisiana, Delaware, Maryland, Kentucky, and Missouri – and primarily in cities such as New Orleans, Wilmington, Baltimore, Louisville and St Louis. In the long-settled and overwhelmingly rural states of the south-east, Irish emigrants were very rare; for instance, in 1860 fewer than 5,000 Irish emigrants lived in South Carolina and only about 6,600 in Georgia, comprising merely 1.7 and 1.1 per cent of their respective white populations.[4]

In 1860 the comparatively few Irish-born men and women enumerated in the Old South were predominantly Catholics, part of the immense Famine exodus that primarily flowed to and settled in the northern United States or in Canada.[5] And by 1860, of course, the overwhelming majority of the eighteenth- and very early nineteenth-century Irish-born settlers in the Old South had died, and since the 1860 census did not record parental birthplaces, the ancestral origins of their living descendants also went untallied. Very recently, however, the 1990 US census has recorded some rather curious statistics. In 1990 some 38.7 million Americans responded to a question concerning their ethnicity by listing 'Irish' as their response. Remarkably, 34 per cent of these self-described 'Irish-Americans' (approximately 13.3 million) resided in the South – more than triple the mere 11 per cent of all the Irish emigrants reported in the 1860 census as resident in the southern states. Put another way, in 1990 one-fifth of white southerners identified their ancestry as Irish, although in 1860 merely 2 per cent of white Southerners had been Irish-born. However, what is most surprising is that, although the respondents to the 1990 census questionnaire were given the option of designating 'Scotch-Irish' as their ancestry, relatively few southern whites did so. Only 2.6 million whites in the South – less than 4 per cent of all southern whites – stated their ethnicity as 'Scotch-Irish', compared with the 20 per cent of white southerners who simply claimed to be 'Irish'. For example, in 1990 21 per cent of Georgia's whites claimed 'Irish' ancestry, whereas only 4 per cent labelled themselves 'Scotch-Irish', and in South Carolina the respective figures were 20 per cent 'Irish' compared with fewer than 7 per cent 'Scotch-Irish'.[6] Thus, given the paucity of Famine emigrants in the Old South, it would appear that by 1990 a surprisingly large number of the remote descendants of the South's early Irish Protestant settlers – of those who had emigrated prior to the America Revolution or, at the latest, prior to the mid-1830s – were not only willing to identify themselves with the birthplace of ancestors who had left Ireland 200 or even 250 years earlier, but even to designate their ethnic identity as 'Irish' rather than as 'Scotch-Irish', although the overwhelming majority of their forebears had been Ulster Presbyterians.

Ultimately, of course, the question of ethnicity is not one of ancestral birthplace or religious affiliation but one of individual and collective identification, which in turn is subjective and variable, shaped by a multitude of shifting social, cultural, political and psychological circumstances.[7] To provide an extreme example, at least through the 1960s St Patrick's Day in New York City was celebrated by an association named the Loyal Yiddish Sons of Erin, whose founders were the Irish-born children of Polish and Lithuanian Jews for whom Ireland was merely a brief interlude in a multi-staged migration from Eastern Europe to America.[8] This suggests that, within certain limits, ethnicity can be a matter of individual choice – as well as an extremely complex, situational, multi-layered phenomenon. This may be especially true in the United States, at least for whites, and indeed one of the purported benefits of migration from Europe to America was that it allowed the newcomers to create identities that might differ significantly from the categories imposed by public officials, landlords, clergy, or even kinsmen in their former homelands.

Usually, however, there are 'certain limits' within which emigrants, their descendants, or even 'impartial observers' can define ethnicity or nationality, and these constraints are often political in nature: overtly so in places like Northern Ireland, where sectarian and political affiliations are commonly both synonymous and inherited; but covertly even in the United States and, during the nineteenth and early twentieth centuries, particularly among Irish emigrants and their offspring. For instance, from the 1830s on, celebrants of what the early Irish-American historian Michael O'Brien called the 'Scotch-Irish Myth' made sharp and often invidious comparisons between their Irish Protestant ancestors and the Irish Catholic emigrants of the Famine and post-Famine decades. Ignoring Ulster Presbyterian emigrants whose economic distress or political activities did not exemplify group prosperity or patriotism, they projected the frailties of their own unfortunates and misfits onto Irish Catholic emigrants, implying that the Scotch-Irish could not have been failures because, by definition, the virtues inherent in their religion and British origins guaranteed their moral, cultural, and, hence, their economic and political superiority.[9]

To be sure, as scholar James Leyburn has written, 'Scotch-Irish' is 'a useful term . . . express[ing] a historical reality', and, if employed carefully and neutrally, can reflect valid distinctions between Ulster Presbyterian emigrants of Scottish origin and Irish Anglicans, Quakers, Methodists, Baptists of

English, Scottish, Welsh, Huguenot and Palatine descent – as well as Irish Catholics (and Protestants) of Gaelic, Hiberno-Norman, or Scottish Highland backgrounds. However, although Ulster-born students at Glasgow University were commonly registered as 'Scottus Hibernicus', use of the term 'Scotch-Irish' in eighteenth-century America, either by contemporaries or by Ulster Presbyterians themselves, was apparently quite rare (Leyburn found only a handful of documented instances).[10] The label was reborn in the early nineteenth century, in the evangelical fervor of the Second Great Awakening, among middle-class Americans of Ulster Presbyterian descent who were appalled by the possibility that they or their ancestors might be identified with the increasing numbers of poor Catholic emigrants. By the late nineteenth and early twentieth centuries, the term had developed to include all Americans of Irish descent who were not currently Catholic, as the authors of county histories in states as far afield as South Dakota blithely designated as 'Scotch-Irish' the ancestors of respectable Methodist and Baptist farmers and businessmen named O'Brien, O'Sullivan, and O'Callaghan![11]

In the eighteenth and very early nineteenth centuries, however, designations such as 'Irish Protestants', 'north Irish', or, most frequently and most vaguely inclusive of all, simply 'Irish', were much more common than 'Scotch-Irish'. But what did it mean to be 'Irish' in Ireland and in America during that era? In some respects, ethnic identification among the Irish-born had both more and less significance than it does today. It had more significance because, prior to the American Revolution and the repeal of the Irish penal laws, a person's religious affiliation determined the extent of his or her civil rights and economic opportunities, to the benefit of Protestants (especially Anglicans) and to the detriment of Catholics. Yet, it also had less significance because, on local and personal levels, the boundaries of these ethno-religious communities were often much more permeable than they later became, and a remarkable degree of ethnic and religious fluidity prevailed in eighteenth-century Ireland and especially among early Irish emigrants in America. In Ireland, for example, it now appears that religious conversions, particularly from Catholicism to Protestantism, were much more common at all social levels than was later acknowledged.[12] On the other side of the Atlantic, the earliest Irish-American organizations – the St Patrick's and Hibernian associations in seaports such as Philadelphia and New York – included merchants and professionals of all denominations, expressing a tolerance that reflected shared business interests as well as Enlightenment rationalism.[13] Among poorer migrants, the relative frequency of intermarriage and conversion reflected a pragmatic understanding that ethnic and religious affiliations were not absolute but contingent on local economic and social circumstances. Early Irish emigrants appear to have been relatively nonchalant about what subsequent generations would regard as religious apostasy or ethnic treason. The result, as noted earlier, was the absorption of nearly all early Irish Catholic (and also Irish Anglican) emigrants into the Presbyterian faith of the great majority.[14]

Furthermore, on the formal political or ideological level, contemporary scholars generally acknowledge that the boundaries of eighteenth-century Irish 'nationality' were fluid and expansive, and that especially after mid-century new, secular, and inclusive definitions of 'Irishness' temporarily promised to subsume Ireland's different religious and ethnic strains. Ultimately, of course, the era of Grattan and Tone was cut short by rebellion and reaction, and both the old popular and the new political traditions of tolerance faded – rapidly in Ireland, more slowly in the United States. Ireland's future would belong to those who practised the politics of ethno-religious polarization, but among the emigrants in America the ecumenical ideals of the United Irishmen flourished through the Jeffersonian and into the Jacksonian era, as most Irish Protestant and Catholic emigrants subsumed their religious differences under the banner of a shared Irish-American republicanism.[15]

To be sure, as early as the 1820s, some Irish Protestant newcomers, often former members of the Loyal Orange Order (founded in mid-Ulster in 1795), were conspicuous in their leadership of American nativist movements, temperance associations, and street mobs that demonized and assaulted Irish Catholic emigrants. And by the 1850s, nearly all Irish-American Protestants and Catholics in the northern United States were mobilized in opposing political camps – the former in the Whig *cum* 'Know-Nothing' *cum* Republican parties, the latter in the Democratic coalition.[16] However, the old traditions of tolerance and sociability, and the new tradition of ecumenical nationalism, seem to have lingered longer in the Old South than elsewhere in the United States. For example, during the first three or four decades of the nineteenth century, the most flourishing Hibernian and Irish-American nationalist societies were situated not in Boston or New York but in southern cities, such as Charleston and Savannah, where they were usually led by Protestants of Ulster birth or descent.[17] In part, this apparent anachronism may reflect the institutional weakness of the Catholic Church in the Old South – its consequent inability either to mobilize its own flock or to frighten Irish-American Protestants away from secular alliances with their Catholic countrymen.[18] It may also reflect the general tendency of all southern whites to downplay internal differences for the sake of solidarity against the region's large and potentially rebellious black population – for slaves outnumbered whites by a ratio of 3:2 in South Carolina and by 9:1 in the coastal districts around Charleston and Savannah.[19]

It would be inaccurate to conclude that early Irish Protestant and Catholic emigrants or their descendants ever comprised a single, homogeneous, or harmonious group in the Old South, much less in the rest of eighteenth- and early nineteenth-century America. However, much evidence suggests that during this period 'Irish' ethnic identity was much more varied, flexible and inclusive than it would later become, and that the social and political issues that engaged the attention of Irish emigrants, and that caused them to define themselves, often transcended the religious divisions that later became so prominent. Keeping this argument in mind, the next section of this chapter briefly sketches the history of early Irish migration to the Old South, relying primarily on the emigrants' own letters, memoirs, and other writings, before returning at the end to employ similar sources to provide some biographical illustrations of the complexity and mutability of Irish ethnic identities in that region.

Of the one-quarter to one-third of a million Irish who emigrated to North America between 1700 and the American Revolution – most of them Ulster Presbyterians – perhaps half settled eventually in the southern colonies: *eventually* because, while a minority arrived directly from Ireland, aboard ships that disembarked at southern ports, the majority first landed at Philadelphia and then moved west and then south, often over several generations, down the Great Wagon Road into the backcountries of Maryland, Virginia, the Carolinas, and Georgia, where they mingled with the smaller streams of emigrants coming up the rivers from Charleston and Savannah. In addition, during the 50 years or so after the American Revolution perhaps as many as 100,000 Irish – again, primarily Ulster Presbyterians – migrated to the southern states. Increasingly, they disembarked at New Orleans or Mobile, rather than at Charleston or Savannah, and settled in new south-western states such as Alabama, while others landed in Philadelphia and Baltimore and moved westward via the Ohio river into Kentucky, Tennessee and Missouri.[20]

In the eighteenth century, their motives for leaving Ireland were a subject of controversy. Ulster Presbyterians, especially the clergy, usually claimed that emigration was motivated primarily by religious and political persecution. Thus, Robert Witherspoon, who in 1734 migrated from Belfast to Charleston, later recorded that his family's exodus was determined by his grandfather's resolution 'to seek relief from civil and ecclesiastical oppression' in Ireland.[21] In the nineteenth century, 'Scotch-Irish' eulogists expanded upon this theme, likening the early emigrants to the English 'pilgrims' who settled early seventeenth-century Plymouth, Massachusetts, in order to claim 'founding father' status for their ancestors.[22] However, although religious zeal coloured and justified their departures, the primary motives for early (as well as for later) Irish emigrants were economic. High rents, tithes and taxes; low wages and periodic depressions in the linen trade; poor harvests and outbreaks of livestock disease: such conditions, operating in a context of small farms and large families, contrasted unfavourably with a vision of unlimited acres, cheap homesteads, high wages, and seemingly boundless opportunities in the New World. As James Lindsey of Desertmartin, County Derry, wrote at mid-century to his cousins in Pennsylvania: 'The good bargains of the lands in your country do greatly encourage me to pluck up my spirits and make ready for the journey, for we are now oppressed with our lands set at eight shillings per acre and other improvements, cutting our land in two-acre parts and [hedging] and only two years' time for doing it all – Yea, we cannot stand more!'[23]

After the American Revolution, the failure of the 1798 Irish rebellion, and the election of the Virginian, Thomas Jefferson, as President in 1800, the new United States became doubly attractive as both an economic and political asylum. This may have been particularly true of the Old South where, as Ulsterman John Joyce reported from staunchly republican Virginia, '[t]hey are very fond of Irish emigration here, . . . it is given as a toast often at their fairs', and the people 'much applaud the Irish for their resolution and spirit of independence'.[24] Thus, writing shortly after the Revolution, Andrew Gibson, a farmer in Lisnagirr, County Tyrone, told his brother in North Carolina: 'I think you are blessed living in a land of liberty and free from the great oppression of landlords and everyone in authority which indeed poor Ireland labors under at present. . . . The gentlemen are laying on so great taxes . . . that it is hard to live here. I pay upwards of £1.10 per year and I have come to great losses these three bad seasons by overflowing of floods and some loss of cattle. . . . My wife and I are too old to undertake the danger', Gibson lamented, but 'our young folk would fondly go to America'.[25]

Letters such as those received by Andrew Gibson undoubtedly provided the primary encouragement for emigration to the Old South. However, there were other inducements as well. On several occasions prior to the Revolution, the South Carolina and Georgia governments offered land grants, tools, provisions, and religious freedom to Irish Protestants willing to settle in the southern back-country – to create a buffer against Indian attacks and to reduce the danger of slave revolts by increasing the white population. Private land speculators also encouraged Irish emigration. For example, in 1765 John Rea, an Ulster-born Indian trader, advertised in the *Belfast News-Letter* for 'industrious' emigrants from the north of Ireland to settle at Queensborough township, on his 50,000-acre land grant in the Georgia backcountry, promising the newcomers 100 acres per family, plus horses, mules, and other supplies. 'The land I have chosen', he declared, 'is good for wheat, and any kind of grain, indigo, flax, and hemp will grow to great perfection, and I do not know any place better situated for a flourishing township than this place will be. . . . People that live on the low land near the sea are subject to fever and agues, but high up in the country it is healthy [with] fine springs of good water. The winter is the finest in the world, never too cold, very little frost and no snow.' Rea candidly admitted that he would not 'advise any person to come here that lives well in Ireland, because there is not the pleasure of society [here] that there is there, [nor] the comfort of the Gospel preached, no fairs or markets to go to. But we have greater plenty of good eating and drinking, for, and I bless God for it, I keep as plentiful a table as most gentlemen in Ireland, with good punch, wine, and beer.' Rea concluded with the clinching enticement that, '[i]f any person that comes here can bring money to purchase a slave or two, they may live very easy and well'.[26]

Yet emigration to the Old South was not without hazards, as both Gibson and Rea implied. Before the Revolution, voyages from Belfast to Charleston and Savannah normally took from eight to ten weeks. By the 1830s the average voyage was merely six to eight weeks, but fear of Atlantic storms and shipboard epidemics still made many Irish men and women quail at the prospect. Also, during the era's frequent Anglo-French wars, Irish emigrants had to brave the danger of attacks by French naval vessels and privateers – and, during the French revolutionary and Napoleonic wars, of seizures by British ships and impressment into the British navy. In 1806–7, for example, John O'Raw, a young emigrant from north Antrim, experienced an unusually miserable voyage to Charleston that combined all these hazards. After his vessel nearly shipwrecked on the coast of Donegal, he wrote, '[w]e encountered the most dangerous storms and head winds for three weeks and was driven into the Bay of Biscay off the coast of France. A great many of our passengers now took the bloody flux and one child died of it. The weather continued most dreadful for six weeks, during which we were frequently carrying away our yards and rigging in dangerous storms of thunder and lightening. The captain said he never was at sea in such [a storm] before. I was for four weeks . . . almost reduced to the point of death by sickness.' After nearly two months being blown back and forth across the Atlantic, O'Raw's ship was wrecked on the coast of Bermuda. The emigrants were saved, but nearly all their possessions were lost, and most of his friends were forcibly conscripted into the British navy when they went to the island's capital – a fate which O'Raw escaped by hiding in the remote parts of the island until he and his remaining companions were able to chart another, smaller vessel to convey them to Charleston. After more violent storms that nearly sank his second ship, O'Raw finally reached South Carolina, more than five months after he had left Belfast![27]

Even after disembarking in southern ports, early Irish emigrants had to endure unaccustomed hardships. Usually landing in summer, they found the climate oppressively hot, and they were assailed by diseases, such as malaria and yellow fever, which had been virtually unknown in Ireland. Historians estimate that the great majority of the Irish indentured servants transported to the southern colonies and the West Indies during the seventeenth century died within a few years of arrival. By the eighteenth century conditions were less lethal, but yellow fever epidemics remained common. Even in the early nineteenth century southern ports such as New Orleans and Mobile had well-deserved reputations as Irish emigrant graveyards, and migrants to Charleston and Savannah still had to survive a 'seasoning' process of six months or more before they were fit to work. For example, although John O'Raw took care, soon after his arrival, to leave Charleston and the lowlands for the healthier South Carolina upcountry, he took ill for four months at Newbury and nearly died of 'fever' before he could resume his occupation of schoolmaster.[28]

Even healthy immigrants were often discouraged, at least initially, by what John Rea had described as the primitive state of southern society, especially in the eighteenth century. To be sure, in 1768 Hester Wylly from Coleraine, County Derry, found her new home in Savannah quite congenial. 'My dear Helen,' she wrote to her sister, 'I am sure it will give you pleasure to hear that this place agrees with me as well as Ireland. I have not found any difference. It's true in the heat of summer the people that is exposed to the sun is subject to what they call fever and ague, but it soon leaves them and is seldom dangerous. . . . As for the people here, they are extremely polite and sociable. We form a wrong notion of the [American] women', she concluded, 'for I assure you I never saw finer women in any part of the world, nor finer complexions in my life. They are very gay and spritely, [and] we have constant assemblys and many other amusements to make the place agreeable.'[29] Of course, as the wife of a wealthy planter and slave-owner, and as sister of the speaker of Georgia's colonial legislature, Mrs Wylly rarely socialized with the great majority of 'the people that is exposed to the sun'. More typical was the response of Robert Witherspoon, who penned quite a different account of his family's first years (in the 1730s and 1740s) on the banks of the Black river in back-country South Carolina. After travelling upriver from Charleston, he wrote, 'my mother and we children were still in expectations of coming to an agree-able place, but when we arrived and saw nothing but a wilderness, and instead of a comfortable house, no other than one of dirt, our spirits sank. . . . We had a great deal of trouble and hardships in our first settling', Witherspoon recalled, for '[w]e were also much oppressed with fear . . . , especially of being massacred by the Indians, or torn by wild beasts, or of being lost and perish-ing in the woods, of whom there were three persons [in our party] who were never found. . . . [M]any were taken sick with ague and fever, some died and some became dropsical and also died.'[30]

The initial hardships were the worst, and those who survived, and acquired legal title to farms and sufficient capital to purchase slaves, often prospered. Thanks to slave labour and a flourishing market for indigo, when Robert Wither-spoon's father died in 1768 (the same year Hester Wylly arrived in Savannah), he inherited an estate worth $25,000, including a substantial planter's house built on the 'English' or 'Virginia' model.[31] The steady expansion of market agriculture into the southern backcountry transformed many of the Irish who had settled there from subsistence farmers and cattle-drivers into planters and slave-owners, especially after 1791 when the invention of the cotton gin enabled the spread westward of short-staple cotton production. By the early nineteenth century, the Carolina and Georgia backcountries had spawned their own aristocracies of Irish-stock planters, such as the family of John C. Calhoun, the future architect of southern secession, and also by this time Irish newcomers such as John O'Raw could count on assistance from a dense network of well-established kinsmen and friends who had preceded them.[32] However, the conditions that Robert Witherspoon had described in the 1730s – and the semi-barbarous society that the probably-Irish Anglican missionary, Charles Woodmason, lamented in the Carolina backcountry in the early 1770s[33] – were replicated time and again on the retreating margins of the southern frontier.

Moreover, a large number, perhaps a majority, of early Irish settlers in the Old South did not become successful planters, even in the backcountry regions where land was relatively cheap. In the 1780s, for example, over half the adult males were landless in the 'Scotch-Irish' strongholds of Augusta and Rockbridge counties, in Virginia's upper Shenandoah valley, and during the next 50 years such men and their families migrated further west or south, on a trek which often found an economic dead-end in the Appalachian foothills, the Piney Woods of Mississippi, or the Ozark mountains of Missouri and Arkansas.[34] Even before the American Civil War of 1861–65, falling cotton prices, and the boll weevil ravaged the Southern economy, northern visitors such as Frederick Law Olmsted were appalled by the cultural and economic impoverishment and slovenliness prevailing among the Old South's 'yeoman' farmers.[35] And, belying their eulogists' claims of inherent superiority, by 1900 the 'Scotch-Irish' of the southern states were generally poorer and less educated than the Catholic Irish who had settled in the urban-industrial North during the previous century.[36]

A final, closer examination of the careers of four late eighteenth- and early nineteenth-century Irish emigrants to the Old South illustrates the initial argument concerning the variety and mutability of early Irish and Irish-American identities. The first and perhaps the most fascinating story is that of Samuel Burke, who, for several technical reasons, was not precisely an Irish *emigrant*, although culturally and linguistically he was arguably more 'Irish' than most of those who migrated from Ireland to America during this period. Burke was actually born in Charleston about 1755, but he was taken back to Cork as a mere infant, christened and raised there. In 1774, when he was about 20 years old, Burke left Ireland and returned to America, as personal servant to an Anglo-Irish official, Montford Browne, the newly appointed royal governor of the recently established British colony of West Florida. When the American Revolution broke out, both Browne and Burke were seized by the rebellious colonists and sent to prison in Hartford, Connecticut. After their release through a prisoner exchange, they went to the British military base in New York City, where Burke married a widow with a small fortune and employed his fluency in the Irish language to assist Browne and other officers in persuading Irish Catholic dockworkers to join a loyalist regiment in the British army. Burke himself enlisted in the regiment he helped recruit and, accompanied by his wife, served under the now Brigadier General Browne in the southern campaign of the Revolutionary War, during which he was wounded on several occasions. Burke hoped to settle in his native South Carolina, on property that the British confiscated from American rebels, but the British defeat dashed his hopes, and in 1782 he and his wife evacuated Charleston with the British navy. By 1785 Burke was living in London and employed in an artificial flower garden for 1s. per day, although he was scarcely able to work because of his war wounds. In great distress, he applied to the British government for compensation for his military service and lost possessions.[37]

Outside Pennsylvania and the other middle colonies, where Irish-American enthusiasm for independence was virtually unanimous, a large minority of Irish emigrants were loyalists during the American Revolution.[38] Indeed, in the Carolinas and Georgia the conflict degenerated into a vicious, bloody civil war between rival Ulster-American factions, some motivated by political ideals, others by greed and revenge.[39] For example, most of John Rea's Ulster settlers in Queensborough township, Georgia, remained faithful to their king, and in reprisal the victorious patriots confiscated their lands and obliterated the very name of their settlement. Likewise, the rebels seized the great plantations owned by Hester Wylly's kinsmen, who fled to the West Indies, although eventually they recovered part of their former possessions.[40] Thus, it is not Samuel Burke's political allegiance that is surprising. Rather, given the fact that Burke was 'Irish' in nearly every meaningful respect, what *is* mind-boggling – and what clearly perplexed the British commissioners in London who, rather grudgingly, granted him a small pension – was that Samuel Burke was what the commissioners described as 'a Black' in their official documents![41]

The second biography is that of John O'Raw, the young emigrant from near Ballymena, in County Antrim, who in 1806–7 endured the long, miserable voyage to Charleston described above. Unlike most contemporary Ulster emigrants, O'Raw was Catholic, not Presbyterian. In 1798, although merely 15 years old and despite the admonitions of his priest, O'Raw had joined his Presbyterian neighbours and fought with the United Irishmen. Clearly, in the late eighteenth century Presbyterian–Catholic relations in north Antrim were much more congenial than was later the case. Members of both denominations generally felt oppressed by an Anglican artisocracy, and the Catholic O'Raws and O'Haras socialized and intermarried with Presbyterian Moores, McCauleys and Boyds, whose kinsmen gladly assisted John O'Raw when he came to South Carolina[42]

After a short tenure as a schoolmaster in the Carolina backcountry, O'Raw decided to try his fortunes in Charleston. By 1820 he had progressed from the position of store clerk to the ownership of a moderately prosperous grocery on Meeting street and also of two slaves. In addition, he was a member of St Mary's Catholic church and also of the city's interdenominational Hibernian Society. However, although O'Raw became an American citizen and served in the Anglo-American War of 1812–15, in the late 1820s he returned to County Antrim and died there in 1841.[43] Perhaps his eventual return 'home' suggests how O'Raw resolved the tensions inherent in an 'Irish-American' identity, but even more intriguing is what O'Raw and other Irish Catholics did in 1815–19 during the so-called 'Charleston schism'. During those years, Archbishop Leonard Neale of Baltimore tried to impose an ultra-royalist French priest, a refugee from the French Revolution, on the Catholics of St Mary's. Despite the archbishop's charge that they were 'disloyal' to the Church and faced excommunication if they did not submit to his authority, O'Raw and St Mary's other Irish parishioners (most of them, like O'Raw, formerly associated with the United Irishmen) refused to accept Neale's nominee. Significantly, their objections were not to the French priest's nationality but to his outspoken animosity to the republican principles for which they and their Protestant countrymen had fought in Ireland.[44] Fifty to one hundred years later, very few Irish-American Catholics (particularly men as 'respectable' as O'Raw and his friends) would have dared defy their bishop so openly and vigorously, for by then Irish Catholics on both sides of the ocean regarded religious loyalty as paramount and integral to their conceptions of Irish identity and nationalism. However, as noted above, in the late eighteenth and early nineteenth centuries, Irish Catholics (and Protestants) often defined 'Irishness' in predominantly political – rather than religious – ways that united rather than divided them.

O'Raw tried to adapt his religion to his political principles, but the third subject is a Catholic emigrant whose ambitions and circumstances in the Old South persuaded him to abandon his faith and embrace the Protestantism of his neighbours. Andrew Leary O'Brien was born in County Cork in 1815, the son of a strong farmer who intended him to become a priest and thereby enhance the family's spiritual and social status. In 1837, after years of expensive schooling in Ireland, O'Brien's parents sent him to finish his clerical studies at Chambly seminary in Quebec. O'Brien's erotic shipboard dreams, recorded in his memoir, of beautiful and seductive blonde-haired women, probably suggested his unsuitability for a celibate life, and so perhaps he was fortunate when the Canadian Rebellion of 1837 shut down the seminary and cast him adrift. O'Brien made his way south to Pennsylvania, where he found work as a stonemason in the building of the Susquehanna canal. There, surrounded by hundreds of what he described as uncouth, illiterate, frequently drunken, and often violent Irish Catholic canal workers, O'Brien discovered for the first time that, in his words, 'I felt mean at the thought that I was an Irishman'. Despite his father's entreaties that he return to Ireland and resume his studies, O'Brien decided to escape both his current associates and, one suspects, his entire past. He took his earnings and sailed from New York to Charleston. For several years, he taught school in Barnwell district, South Carolina, where he married into a Methodist family whose church he joined after attending a camp meeting. In 1848 he moved to Cuthbert, Georgia, where in 1854 he founded what was then called Randolph – now Andrew – College. Today, very few of its faculty or graduates are aware that their college, still piously Methodist, was established by an Irish Catholic seminary student and canal worker who had concluded that acceptance and respectability in an overwhelmingly Protestant southern society were more important than the retention of his ethnic and religious heritage.[45]

The last biography is that of William Hill, who lived in Abbeville district, South Carolina, from 1822 until his death, aged 80, in 1886.[46] Hill was born in 1805 in Ballynure parish, County Antrim, into a Presbyterian family that had been implicated in the 1798 rebellion. According to family tradition, Hill disliked his stepmother and so, at the age of 17, emigrated to Charleston, bearing letters of introduction to a Major John Donald, an earlier emigrant from Ballynure who had settled in Abbeville and fought in the War of 1812. At first Hill clerked in Donald's store, but within two years he had married his employer's daughter, Anna, and commenced farming land which his father-in-law gave him as a wedding present. By the late 1820s Hill had begun concentrating on trade, selling goods in his own country store, although he always retained ownership of about 360 acres which he usually planted in wheat, oats, and Indian corn.[47] Sometime in the 1840s, he moved into Abbeville town, population 400, where he prospered as a merchant. Although Hill had no formal legal training, he gained a reputation as an honest, competent adviser in probate law and estate administration, and in 1852 he was elected to the first of eight successive terms as Abbeville district's judge of the court of ordinary. The 1860 census listed Hill as possessing $20,000 worth of real and personal property, in addition to fifteen slaves.[48] As for many southern whites, the Civil War and its immediate aftermath were disastrous for William Hill and his family. Two of his sons-in-law died of wounds or disease while serving in the Confederate army, and his own eldest son was severely wounded. As a result of the South's defeat, Hill claimed to have lost over $30,000 in slaves, in Confederate bonds and currency, and in the general depreciation of real estate, while the advent of Radical Republican rule in South Carolina deprived him of his office of probate judge.[49] Hill continued to dabble in trade until about 1871 when he retired to his farm outside Abbeville town, where he died fifteen years later.

Throughout his life, Hill wrote regularly to his brother, David, back in Ballynure, and, using his correspondence in conjunction with what is known about his career in South Carolina, we can try to reconstruct the changes in his sense of ethnic identity. One of Hill's obituaries described him as 'a most enthusiastic Irishman, never being entirely weaned of his love for his native land'.[50] Certainly, Hill's emotional identification with Ireland comes through most strongly in his *earliest* surviving correspondence. In one letter, for example, he chides his brother for not writing more often: '[t]here is little or nothing here [in South Carolina] to concern you', he admonished, but 'every nook and corner of the neighborhood of Ballynure teems with absorbing interest to me. Although it is upwards of thirty-two years since I left "the green hills of my youth", I can still luxuriate in fancy, . . . young again, strolling over the old green sod.' Repeatedly in such letters, Hill declared his longing to return to his native land, if only for a visit.[51]

There are several probable reasons for William Hill's profound homesickness for Ireland. One is the circumstance of his emigration: at a relatively young age, and impelled not so much by ambition as by a deteriorating relationship with his stepmother. Another is his romantic attachment to a woman he left behind in Ireland and to whom he referred in one of his early letters, when he remembered 'whispering words of artless love to her who was – most beautiful, most lovely, but now alas, how changed'. Hill asked his brother, '[d]o you surmise to whom I allude? – Well then, tell me of her. Although the vase is long broken, yet still the fragrance of the once sweet flower remains.'[52] By contrast, in not one of his six extant letters written before 1867 did Hill ever refer to his wife in South Carolina. Thus, although Hill's obituary referred in a formulaic manner to his 'beloved wife' and their 'happy union for nearly sixty years', it appears that his deepest affections long centred on someone back in Ballynure.[53]

Indeed, if Hill had not married so young and so soon after his migration, it is not unlikely that he might have returned to Ireland permanently, as did John O'Raw. For although Hill's first 20 years or so in South Carolina are shrouded in relative obscurity, they appear to be characterized by a lack of both material success and personal commitment to his adopted country. For example, it may be significant that Hill did not apply for American citizenship until 1834,[54] eight years after his emigration, and he took no part in public life until 1836, when he joined Abbeville's militia company for service in the Seminole War. Significantly, it was just *before* those years, in 1832–33, that John C. Calhoun and South Carolina's other political leaders precipitated the so-called Nullification crisis and first challenged the federal government's authority. During and after that episode, white South Carolinians were under intense pressure to demonstrate communal loyalty and solidarity. Since Hill's obituaries made no mention of any participation in the Nullification crusade, as they surely would have done had he been involved, it is probable that Hill was included in the one-third of Abbeville district's voters (mostly poor men, as was Hill at that time) who opposed Nullification – and so he may have hastened thereafter to conform to communal standards. Certainly, it was during the 20 years following the Nullification crisis that Hill rose in prosperity and public esteem: by acquiring the military credentials, the membership in Abbeville's Presbyterian church, and the ownership of slaves which marked his entrance into the second tier of the district's elite and that made him electable to public office. By 22 November 1860, Hill's eminence was signalled by his membership, alongside the kinsmen of the late John C. Calhoun and other wealthy planters, of the local committee that organized Abbeville's public meeting that in turn selected delegates to South Carolina's fateful secession convention.[55]

During the same decades that Hill was becoming more 'American' (which, in Abbeville, meant more 'southern'), several specific developments in both Ireland and South Carolina operated to lessen or qualify Hill's identification with his homeland. During the Nullification crisis, South Carolina's only Irish-American newspaper, the Charleston *Irishman and Southern Democrat*, was 'violently anti-nullification',[56] and the consequent association of 'Irishness' and 'disloyalty' to South Carolina in the minds of many local whites may have shaken Hill's attachment to Ireland. More certainly, in the early 1840s Daniel O'Connell, political leader of Ireland's Catholics, joined with Irish, British and Yankee abolitionists in denouncing southern slavery, urging all 'true Irishmen' in America to work for immediate emancipation. In response, Hibernian societies throughout the South either shut their doors or repudiated O'Connell's leadership.[57] Indeed, one of William Hill's own letters to his brother David, vehemently denying that 'slavery and Christianity were inconsistent', indicates the growing gap between the anti-slavery sentiments that prevailed in Ireland and his own commitments – not merely to his propertied interests, but to the safety of the white minority in a district where, between 1820 and 1850, the proportion of slaves in the local population had risen from 40 to 60 per cent.[58]

Another crucial development in the late 1840s and 1850s was the arrival in South Carolina of several thousand Irish Catholic peasants, impoverished refugees from the Great Famine. William Hill's 'Irish' identity was ecumenical in theory, shaped by the United Irishmen's republican ideals which forbade invidious distinctions between Irish Protestants and Catholics. Hill was true to that legacy: he named one of his sons Robert Emmet Hill; and in his letters he denounced England's 'oppressive' rule over Ireland, expressed his detestation of Irish Orangemen for their loyalism and anti-Catholic activities, refused to consider allowing his son to attend the Queen's College of Belfast, because of its royalist associations, and gleefully predicted that the British would lose the Crimean War.[59] However, Hill's sense of 'Irishness' had been shaped by his local, native environment, and that environment had been almost exclusively Protestant, as well as relatively genteel. In Ballynure parish, 85 per cent of the inhabitants had been Presbyterians, only 5 per cent Catholics.[60] As a result, Hill was shocked and embarrassed by what he described as the 'poverty and want, rags, squalor, and wretchedness' of the Famine Irish who came to South Carolina at mid-century and who, in his words, 'reflect discredit on the better class of their countrymen'. Although acknowledging that 'most of the [new Irish] emigrants . . . never had opportunity of polish', for the first time he was obliged to distinguish between his own people and what he called 'the *real* Irish, of papist stock'.[61] Hill's fear of guilt by association was not imaginary, for in the mid-1850s the American (or Know-Nothing) party, pledged to halt the Irish influx and curtail emigrants' political rights, briefly flourished in South Carolina. Indeed, in 1857 Hill himself was nearly defeated for re-election as probate judge by a Know-Nothing candidate who denounced him for his 'Irish' background.[62]

On one hand, white South Carolina's defeat and devastation in the Civil War, plus the partial wreck of his own fortune, rekindled Hill's nostalgia for Ireland and made him yearn to 'go back even in my old age to the dear land wherein I first drew breath'.[63] On the other hand, however, Hill's real commitment to the South – and his real estrangement from Ireland and from most of its people – was increasingly evident. For example, in his post-war letters Hill blamed the Confederacy's defeat on the 'tens of thousands' of Irish 'mercenaries' in the victorious Union army, who had helped the 'accursed' Yankees 'crush a people struggling for self-government regardless of anything but their filthy pay', and he was appalled that the Irish-American soldiers stationed in Abbeville allegedly 'mingle[d] with the Negroes with as much affinity as if of the same blood'.[64] To be sure, in 1867 Hill did visit Ireland briefly, for the first and only time since his emigration 45 years earlier. But the letter he wrote to brother David, on his return to Abbeville, was so uncharacteristically devoid of sentiment as to suggest that his visit had been deeply disappointing, memorable only for 'the cough [with] which [he] had been so much troubled' in the damp, cold Irish climate to which Hill was now unaccustomed. Significantly, it was only in this and subsequent letters that Hill first made reference to his wife of 40 years![65]

Perhaps in 1867 William Hill finally came 'home' to South Carolina, in a psychological as well as in a physical sense. Given the evolution of his own ethnic identity and nationalist sympathies – from Irish to white southern – perhaps it was no wonder that, in the early twentieth century, his grand-daughter would write in a school essay that she was not of 'Irish' but 'of Scotch-Irish descent', although neither William Hill himself nor the authors of his obituaries ever employed the term.[66] However, what may be more significant is that apparently today, according to the 1990 census and for reasons that merit analysis in another essay, many of the present descendants of the William Hills – and of the hundreds of thousands of other Ulster Protestants who settled in the Old South – once again regard themselves as inclusively, if vaguely, 'Irish'.

Notes

1. T.A. Emmet, *Memoir of Thomas Addis and Robert Emmet* (New York, 1915), Vol. I, p. 227.
2. D.A. Wilson, *United Irishmen, United States: Immigrant Radicals in the Early Republic* (Ithaca, N.Y., 1998), ch. 7.
3. D.N. Doyle, *Ireland, Irishmen and Revolutionary America, 1760–1820* (Dublin and Cork, 1981), pp. 51–76.

4. United States Census Office, *Population of the United States in 1860; Compiled from the Official Returns of the Eighth Census* (Washington, D.C., 1864).
5. K.A. Miller, *Emigrants and Exiles: Ireland and the Irish Exodus to North America* (New York, 1985), ch. 7.
6. Bureau of the Census, *1990 Census of Population. Social and Economic Characteristics. United States*, Vols CP-2-1 through CP-2-52 (Washington, D.C., 1993). The 2.6 million southern whites who claimed 'Scotch-Irish' ancestry in 1990 represented 47 per cent of all American whites who did so.
7. The scholarly literature on ethnicity is voluminous. On Irish-American Catholic ethnicity, see K.A. Miller, 'Class, Culture and Immigrant Group Identity in the United States: The Case of Irish-American Ethnicity', in V. Yans-McLaughlin (ed.), *Immigration Reconsidered: History, Sociology and Politics* (New York, 1990), pp. 96–129.
8. Memoir of Emmanuel Steen, River Edge, N.J. (copy supplied by Mr Steen and in the author's possession).
9. M.J. O'Brien, 'The "Scotch-Irish" Myth', *Journal of the American Irish Historical Society*, 24 (1925), pp. 142–53. Invidious comparisons between Irish Catholic and 'Scotch-Irish' emigrants can be found in the historical and popular literature on the latter from the early nineteenth to the early twentieth centuries; e.g. in Rev. E.L. Parker, *The History of Londonderry* [New Hampshire] (Boston, 1851); *The Scotch-Irish in America: Proceedings of the Scotch-Irish Congresses*, 10 vols (Cincinnati, Ohio, 1889–1901); and M. Glasgow, *The Scotch-Irish in Northern Ireland and in the American Colonies* (New York, 1936).
10. J.G. Leyburn, *The Scotch-Irish: A Social History* (Chapel Hill, N.C., 1962), pp. 327–34.
11. For example, *Memorial and Biographical Record of Turner, Lincoln, Union and Clay Counties* [South Dakota] (Chicago, 1897).
12. Doyle, *Ireland, Irishmen*, chs 1–2; T.P. Power, 'Converts', in Power and K. Whelan (eds), *Endurance and Emergence: Catholics in Ireland in the Eighteenth Century* (Blackrock, Co. Dublin, 1990), pp. 101–28; and the relevant chapters of D. Bowen, *History and the Shaping of Irish Protestantism* (New York, 1995); and R. Blaney, *Presbyterianism and the Irish Language* (Belfast, 1996).
13. J.M. Campbell, *A History of the Friendly Sons of St. Patrick and of the Hibernian Society* (Philadelphia, 1982); R.C. Murphy and L.J. Mannion, *The Society of the Friendly Sons of St. Partick . . . in New York* (New York, 1962).
14. Doyle, *Ireland, Irishmen*, chs 3–4.
15. On Ireland: J. Leerssen, *Mere Irish and Fíor Ghael: Studies in the Idea of Irish Nationality, its Development and Literary Expression prior to the Nineteenth Century* (Cork, 1997), chs 7–8; and K. Whelan, *The Tree of Liberty: Radicalism, Catholicism and the Construction of Irish Identity, 1760–1830* (Cork, 1996), chs 3–4. On Irish-America: Doyle, *Ireland, Irishmen*, ch. 7; and Miller, *Emigrants and Exiles*, chs 5–6.
16. Miller, *Emigrants and Exiles*, chs 6–7.
17. M.F. Funchion, *Irish-American Voluntary Organizations* (Westport, Conn., 1983), pp. 117, 141–5, 239.
18. J.P. Dolan, *The American Catholic Experience: A History from Colonial Times to the Present* (Garden City, N.Y., 1985), ch. 4; R.M. Miller and J.K. Wakelyn (eds), *Catholics in the Old South* (Macon, Ga., 1983).
19. United States Census Office, *Population of the United States in 1860*.

20. For the contours of eighteenth- and early nineteenth-century Irish (especially 'Scotch-Irish') emigration and settlement, as described in this and the following paragraphs, see: Doyle, *Ireland, Irishmen*; and Miller, *Emigrants and Exiles*, chs 4–6.
21. Robert Witherspoon, Memoir, copy in Mary S. Witherspoon, Genealogy of the Witherspoon Family (1894), ms. (South Caroliniana Library, University of South Carolina, Columbia, S.C.; hereafter cited as SCL-USC). This and subsequent quotations from Irish emigrants' letters, memoirs, and other documents have been modernized in spelling, punctuation, and capitalization.
22. R.S. Wallace, 'The Scotch-Irish of Provincial New Hampshire', unpublished Ph.D. thesis (University of New Hampshire, 1984), ch. 1.
23. David Lindsey, 19 March 1758 (T.2269, Public Record Office of Northern Ireland, Belfast; hereafter cited as PRONI).
24. John Joyce, 24 March 1785, in 'Virginia in 1785', *Virginia Magazine of History and Biography*, 23 (1915), pp. 407–14.
25. Andrew Gibson, 22 September 1789 (T.3610, PRONI).
26. John Rae, 15 May 1765, in *Belfast News-Letter*, 3 September 1765 (Ulster Linen Hall Library, Belfast).
27. John O'Raw, 1 April 1809 (D.3613/1/2, PRONI).
28. Ibid.
29. Hester Wylly, 14 December 1768 (D.955/11, PRONI).
30. Witherspoon, Memoir.
31. W.W. Boddie, *History of Williamsburg* (Columbia, S.C., 1923); J.B. Witherspoon, *The History and Genealogy of the Witherspoon Family* (Fort Worth, Tex., 1979).
32. R.N. Klein, *Unification of a Slave State: The Rise of the Planter Class in the South Carolina Backcountry, 1760–1808* (Chapel Hill, N.C., 1990).
33. R.J. Hooker (ed.), *The Carolina Backcountry on the Eve of the Revolution: The Journal and Other Writings of Charles Woodmason, Anglican Itinerant* (Chapel Hill, N.C., 1953).
34. R.D. Mitchell, *Commercialization and Frontier: Perspectives on the Early Shenandoah Valley* (Charlottesville, Va., 1977). Also see R.L. Gerlach, 'Scotch-Irish Landscapes in the Ozarks', in H.T. Blethen and C.W. Wood, Jr (eds), *Ulster and North America: Transatlantic Perspectives on the Scotch-Irish* (Tuscaloosa, Ala., 1997), pp. 146–66.
35. F.L. Olmsted, *The Cotton Kingdom*, ed. A.M. Schlesinger (New York, 1953). Also see G. McWhiney, *Cracker Culture: Celtic Ways in the Old South* (Tuscaloosa, Ala., 1988).
36. D.N. Doyle, *Irish-Americans, Native Rights and National Empires: The Structure, Divisions and Attitudes of the Catholic Minority in the Decade of Expansion, 1890–1901* (New York, 1976), pp. 48–9, 59–63.
37. Samuel Burke petition and testimony, in American Loyalists: Transcripts of the Manuscript Books and Papers of the Commission of Inquiry into the Losses and Services of the American Loyalists (New York Public Library) 41, pp. 539–46 (microfilm edn, London Examinations, reel 13).
38. W. Brown, *The King's Friends: The Composition and Motives of the American Loyalist Claims* (Providence, R.I., 1965).
39. Klein, *Unification of a Slave State*; J.J. Nadelhaft, *The Disorders of War: The Revolution in South Carolina* (Orono, Maine, 1981); and R.S. Lambert, *South Carolina Loyalists in the American Revolution* (Columbia, S.C., 1987).

40. E.R.R. Green, 'Queensborough Township: Scotch-Irish Emigration and the Expansion of Georgia, 1763–1776', *William and Mary Quarterly*, 3rd series, 17 (1960), pp. 183–99; Wylly Correspondence (D.955, PRONI).
41. Samuel Burke petition and testimony.
42. John O'Raw, 1 April 1809; biographical data from Brian Moore O'Hara, Ballylesson, Ballymena, County Antrim.
43. Traces of O'Raw can be found in: J.W. Hagy (ed.), *People and Professions of Charleston, 1782–1802* (Baltimore, 1992); B.H. Halcomb (comp.), *South Carolina Naturalizations, 1783–1850* (Baltimore, 1985); K. Scott (comp.), *British Aliens in the United States during the War of 1812* (Baltimore, 1979); A.H. Mitchell, *History of the Hibernian Society of Charleston, S.C., 1799–1981* (Barnwell, S.C., 1982); *Charleston Directory and Stranger's Guide* (Charleston, S.C., 1816–25; titles vary slightly); and 1820 US census, unpublished ms. schedules, Charleston, South Carolina (microfilm), p. 36A. Information from Brian Moore O'Hara on O'Raw's return to and death in County Antrim.
44. For opposing views of the 'Charleston schism', see P. Carey, *People, Priests and Prelates: Ecclesiastical Democracy and the Tensions of Trusteeism* (Notre Dame, In., 1987); and P. Guilday, *The Life and Times of John England, First Bishop of Charleston* (New York, 1927). O'Raw's role on the side of the Charleston 'schismatics' was confirmed by his signature on petitions from the rebellious trustees to Archbishop Neale; for this information, I am grateful to Rev. Paul K. Thomas, archivist of the Archdiocese of Baltimore, Md.
45. A. McD. Suarez, *The Journal of Andrew Leary O'Brien* (Athens, Ga., 1946).
46. Unless otherwise cited, biographical data on William Hill in this and the following paragraphs are derived from information either contained in his obituaries in *The Abbeville Medium*, 21 January 1886, and especially *The Abbeville Press and Banner*, 20 January 1886, or communicated by Dr and Mrs William G. Hill of Abbeville, S.C., whose assistance I gratefully acknowledge.
47. United States Agricultural Censuses, 1850, 1860, 1880: Abbeville District, South Carolina (mss. in the South Carolina Department of Archives and History, Columbia, S.C.).
48. 1860 US Census, unpublished ms. schedules, Abbeville Court House, South Carolina (microfilm), p. 21.
49. William Hill, 8 September 1865 (William Hill Correspondence, SCL-USC).
50. *Abbeville Press and Banner*, 20 January 1886.
51. William Hill, 24 January 1855 (William Hill Correspondence, SCL-USC; and T. 1830/3, PRONI). Also, see Hill's letters of 14 July 1847 (SCL-USC, and T.1830/1, PRONI), and of 21 January 1858 (SCL-USC).
52. William Hill, 24 January 1855.
53. *Abbeville Press and Banner*, 20 January 1886.
54. Halcomb, *South Carolina Naturalizations*.
55. On the Nullification and Secession crises, and antebellum South Carolina politics generally, see L.K. Ford, *Origins of Southern Radicalism: The South Carolina Upcountry, 1800–1860* (New York, 1988), and 'Republics and Democracy: The Parameters of Political Citizenship in Antebellum South Carolina', in D.R. Chesnutt and C.N. Wilson (eds), *The Meaning of South Carolina History* (Columbia, S.C., 1991), pp. 121–45; W.W. Freehling, *Prelude to Civil War: The Nullification Controversy in South Carolina* (New York, 1965); and S.A. Channing, *Crisis of Fear: Secession in South Carolina* (New York, 1970).

Information on Hill's organization of Abbeville's secession meeting from Dr and Mrs William G. Hill, Abbeville, S.C.

56. Freehling, *Prelude to Civil War*, pp. 181–2.
57. G. Osofsky, 'Abolitionists, Irish Immigrants, and the Dilemmas of Romantic Nationalism', *American Historical Review*, 80 (October 1975), pp. 889–912.
58. William Hill, 24 January 1855; demographic data from Ford, *Origins of Southern Radicalism*, p. 45.
59. William Hill, 24 January 1855; William Hill, 7 March 1872 (copy of letter, courtesy of Dr and Mrs William G. Hill, Abbeville, S.C.).
60. In 1766 Ballynure parish contained 383 Protestant and 8 Catholic families (T.808/15,264, PRONI). According to the 1831 Irish religious census, 3,380 of Ballynure's 3,549 inhabitants were Protestants, of whom 3,004 were Presbyterians (Report of the Commissioners of Public Instruction, Ireland, *British Parliamentary Papers* 33 [1835]). On society in early nineteenth-century Ballynure, see A. Day and P. McWilliams (eds), *Ordnance Survey Memoirs of Ireland, Vol. 32, Parishes of County Antrim XII, 1832–3, 1835–40: Ballynure and District* (Belfast, 1995), pp. 31–73.
61. William Hill, 7 July 1859 (William Hill Correspondence, SCL-USC).
62. William Hill, 21 January 1858.
63. William Hill, 8 September 1865.
64. Ibid.
65. William Hill, 15 August 1867 (William Hill Correspondence, SCL-USC).
66. Mary Hill, 'Who I am' (undated school essay, copy courtesy of Dr and Mrs William G. Hill, Abbeville, S.C.).

CHAPTER 8

Searching for Missing Friends in the Boston Pilot Newspaper, 1831–1863

RUTH-ANN M. HARRIS

(Department of History and Irish Studies, Boston College)

The Boston *Pilot* was an immensely popular newspaper, distributed widely throughout the world of Irish immigrants. Week after week, the paper carried names and locations of new distributors showing the paper expanding across the United States and into Canada. By the late 1840s it was distributed overseas in Ireland, Scotland and England, reaching Australia by the early 1850s. In the 1850s County Wexford emigrant Andrew Hendricks subscribed to the *Pilot* in Fort Smith, a frontier town only fourteen miles from Indian territory in the state of Arkansas. In a family memoir, his grand-daughter, Bessie Hendricks, recalled that he would read the news 'from the Boston Pilot paper [which] carried news of Ireland. When the paper arrived many of the families met in [the] home and grandfather would read the news to them.'[1]

The column 'Missing Friends' ran in the Boston newspaper from 1831 to 1916, after which it was suspended shortly after the weekly paper was purchased by the Archdiocese of Boston. Six volumes, containing approximately 7,000 advertisements per volume (1831–70), have been published. Volume 7 will include the years 1871–76/77, and the remainder will fit in one volume.[2] The ads reflect the varied fortunes of Irish emigrants, from a trickling out in increasing numbers in the 1830s to the flood of the Famine decade (1845–55). After 1855 the frequency of ads dwindled as the Irish became a more established population and were either less likely to lose contact with relatives or developed better ways of locating each other. Phrases that appear frequently after 1855 are 'last heard from . . .', 'last seen in . . .', suggesting that ads were being used to keep in touch rather than the outright loss of contact so common in the earlier years.

Analysis of the information in the ads is derived from a computerized database containing a possible 50 items of information for each transcribed advertisement. The database permits information to be cross-referenced and analysed systematically. While each volume is limited to the ads appearing in a particular period, the database is fully cumulative, so that the present analysis is based on 30,286 (1831 to July 1863) distinct persons sought.[3]

Lacking other evidence, such as systematic counts of the numbers of persons arriving in America, the thousands of persons sought through the 'Missing Friends' column of the *Pilot* newspaper constitute a sample of persons emigrating from Ireland, before, during and after the Famine.

Although the various United States censuses record the number of immigrants arriving from Ireland, and the British censuses also indicate numbers of persons whose birthplace was Ireland, there are no systematic records to identify the places in Ireland from which they came. Ship passenger lists indicate port of embarkation, but not place of origin. There are Irish census data showing population at the level of parish, barony and county, thus making it possible for measures of net changes of population to be calculated for these regions, but there is no way to distinguish from these figures what factors caused population changes. Population change could have resulted from a number of factors: changes in fertility and mortality behaviour (which is clearly important for explaining the huge declines following the Famine); movement within Ireland (internal migration); temporary or permanent movement to England and Scotland; or finally emigration to North America, Australia, and other distant destinations. But if historians are to be able to analyse emigration as a response to various factors *arising within Ireland*, they need geographically disaggregated data. The dynamics of population movement included some persons remaining in a place, some engaging in recurrent seasonal migration, some moving elsewhere within Ireland, and some emigrating permanently in response to changing opportunities, misfortunes or disasters.

With this in mind, the *Pilot* data could be a unique source of identification of the local origins of emigrants to North America. But obviously the 30,286 persons on whom we have presently collected data are still only a tiny sample of the estimated more than 1.58 million Irish immigrants recorded as coming to the United States between 1820 and 1863.[4] In addition to this there are a sizeable additional number of persons who came to and stayed in Canada, persons who are also well represented in the *Pilot* advertisements. In order to be advertised for, a person had to have become missing, to have friends or relatives who were willing to pay for the chance of locating the lost one, and they had to know of and be able to use the facilities of this Boston newspaper.

First then, it must be asked how representative was this sample of persons who were in some way lost? There is considerable variation in the data used to identify the *Pilot* emigrants. Table 8.1 reports the presence of information about significant variables, based on the total number of 30,286 persons sought. High rates appear for reported county of origin, while somewhat lower rates appear for reported ports of entry and occupations.

What the *Pilot* data reveal about patterns of emigration from Ireland

1847 was the most calamitous of the Famine years, when what had once been emigration based on choice became flight; and that is borne out by the evidence appearing here which shows an increase in the reported year of departure

Table 8.1: Significant variables reported

	No. of valid cases reported	% of totals
County of origin	26,893	88.8
Relationship of seeker to sought	24,936	82.3
Geographic locations after Ireland	25,097	82.9
Year of departure or arrival	15,744	52.0
Port of departure	3,347	11.1
Port of entry	7,106	23.5
Occupation in Ireland	1,365	4.5
Occupation in America	2,243	7.4

or arrival from 511 persons in 1845 to 1,916 persons in 1847. Following that, the numbers fall in 1848 to 1,231, remaining at about that level until 1851, after which they drop fairly sharply (e.g. 999 persons in 1852, falling to 258 by 1855).[5]

Prior to 1840, the propensity to emigrate was highest in the provinces of Ulster and Leinster, which is consistent with a growing body of evidence asserting that those leaving were the relatively skilled, many of whom were the non-inheriting sons and non-dowered daughters of farming families consolidating their economic position.[6] In a study of males emigrating to Newfoundland from the 1760s through the 1870s, John Mannion concluded that the majority of those leaving south-eastern Ireland were the sons of comfortable Catholic farmers whose family strategy was to encourage non-inheriting sons to emigrate to keep the family farm intact.[7] This is also consistent with *Pilot* evidence from County Cork, where emigrants tended to be persons with higher skills from parishes with advantages such as schooling and improved communication systems such as roads.[8] The discovery that it was those with greater resources who emigrated in the earlier period is hardly surprising, given the fact that it took substantial assets to finance transatlantic migration. Emigrants had to be able to support themselves for a period of time until employment was found, as is apparent from their letters. Immigrants describe their early months or years in America as a constant search for work and betterment.

By the second third of the nineteenth century, patterns of seasonal migration developed in the poorer parts of western Ireland in which regular work in England or Scotland was combined with subsistence based on a potato diet.[9] Given the optimal manner in which this system functioned, permanent transatlantic migration would remain for a while both less attractive and less feasible for the majority of the population.

The *Pilot* data show changing patterns of emigration from Ireland over the period. While the relative importance of those leaving Ulster and Leinster fell during the Famine years, the proportions of persons from the province of Connacht rose. This pattern is consistent with Fitzpatrick's analysis of cohort depletion, much of which was a result of emigration.[10] Since the observed patterns of emigration among provinces over time are consistent with other analyses, our belief that the *Pilot* data provide a reasonable picture of Irish migration patterns is reinforced. The shift in emigration streams shows that the earliest 'emptying out' was located in the provinces of Ulster and Leinster; with the onset of the Great Famine, the proportions of persons leaving Munster and Connacht rose.

Comparing the *Pilot* data, by province, against three other counts – the ten-year count of emigration between 1851 and 1861, and census counts for 1841 and 1851 – is useful.[11] It suggests that the *Pilot* emigrants from the provinces of Munster and Connacht are probably over-represented relative to the 'true' migration flows, while Ulster and Leinster are under-represented.

In the censuses the reported sex ratios were roughly 50 per cent female, while in the *Pilot* data females are consistently under-represented, accounting for between 22 and 24 per cent of the persons sought for each province. While this disparity means that the *Pilot* data cannot be used to estimate the true proportion of females, there is little variation by province (or county), so that valid inferences can be drawn about changing patterns over time. Interestingly enough, it appears that there was very little variation in the sex composition of emigrants, by county or over time. This contrasts with the data on seasonal migration to England where males dominated the flow, while in longer-term migration to England and North America sex ratios were about equal.

Why were women under-represented in the *Pilot* data?[12] The most plausible explanation is that women were on the whole less likely to get lost. In the early years of emigration (eighteenth and early nineteenth century) most women left in family groups. Later, when the female emigration stream was dominated by single females, women not only tended to have more stable employment in domestic industry but there was a high demand for their services. The best jobs for males in North American were on canals and railways – jobs that were highly geographically mobile. So men were prone to getting lost. Advertisements were relatively expensive (three dollars for three insertions) and in a culture that put less value on women than on men, it is hardly surprising that fewer women were sought. It is also true that the majority of searches were for economic reasons – that is, to find your brother, cousin or uncle who would 'put you onto a job', and women's unequal earning capacity may have affected the decision to spend the money to locate them. Overall women were more rooted to one place than were men, although the evidence from female letter-writers would suggest that women were quite willing to leave for better opportunities. Yet it is probable that when women did move the distances were considerably less – making them less likely to go missing.[13]

In propensities to migrate ('Missing Friends' per 100,000 residents), prior to 1840 Ulster had the lowest level (13); Connacht and Leinster both had roughly 23; whereas Munster had 36. In response to the Famine in 1846–50, the increases in emigration rates varied substantially among the provinces. Ulster was almost unaffected (rising from 13 to 18), Leinster rose to 45, Connacht to 82 and Munster to 100. Thus the counties with the highest rates of out-migration during the Famine years [Kerry (146), Clare (120), Limerick (110), Roscommon (98), and Cork and Mayo (92)] were not the counties with the highest rates in the pre-Famine period. Indeed, only Cork among the counties that had the highest rates prior to 1840 (Leitrim, Kildare, Longford, Queens, Westmeath, Cork, Limerick, Waterford and Cavan, all of which had rates in excess of 30) remained among the high out-migration counties during the Famine years. This may be in part because counties that had 'emptied out' early had less population pressures and were less vulnerable, while others – such as Longford, Kilkenny and Kildare – may not have been as hard hit by the Famine.[14]

What the *Pilot* data reveal about the Irish in America

After arrival in America, where did Irish immigrants go? These data allow us to document the wide distribution of Irish throughout the United States. This is contrary to the commonly accepted view that the Irish refused to leave the port cities of the eastern seaboard. Indeed, there appears to have been little reluctance for males to follow job opportunity wherever it might take them, even when it meant leaving wives and children to fend for themselves.

When *Pilot* migrants were compared with the Irish in the 1860 American census, they were over-represented in the north-eastern states,[15] which is not surprising given the Boston location of the paper. This was also true of the New York City and New York State region as a whole. Some 18 per cent of *Pilot* immigrants were in Massachusetts whereas in the census 12 per cent of the Irish-born in the United States were located there. The remainder of New England accounted for 9 per cent of *Pilot* immigrants while the proportion was 7 per cent in the census. In New York State, both the *Pilot* and the census were 31 per cent of the population.

In the 1860 census *Pilot* migrants were under-represented in the Mid-Atlantic region (in the *Pilot* they were 12 per cent versus 19 per cent in the census).[16] This appears to be mostly due to a low proportion of *Pilot* migrants in the state of Pennsylvania (8 per cent versus 13 per cent) relative to all Irish in that state. Two explanations come to mind: first, that a majority of the Pennsylvania Irish were Protestant and thus somewhat less likely to be aware of and resort to this newspaper, and secondly, that the Pennsylvania Irish appear to have developed more stable communities by the 1840s and 1850s because they were long established in the region – and thus had less need to locate the essentially floating population represented by those advertised for in the Boston *Pilot*.

The *Pilot* also is slightly under-represented in the Midwest (19 per cent versus 22 per cent in the census), and the West (0.5 per cent versus 2.4 per cent in the census), while somewhat over-represented in the South (5 per cent versus 3 per cent in the census) and the Mississippi Gulf (6 per cent versus 3 per cent in the census).

Some of the most significant findings relate to *Pilot* immigrants in the Mississippi and Gulf States[17] and the watershed regions of the Mississippi and Ohio rivers. When ports of entry and destinations are linked, the two regions appear to be a unit. In addition there were Irish settlements in the two states of Illinois and Ohio, where about two-thirds of the Irish-born were clustered along the rivers. The remainder appear to have arrived in those states by way of the Great Lakes route.

Pilot migrants in the Midwestern states are under-represented relative to the census.[18] When it is possible for our analysis to follow migrants beyond their first destination in the United States we expect to find greater representation of the *Pilot* migrants in these states.[19] It is clear that *Pilot* migrants are under-represented in the western part of the country.[20] However there were 492 *Pilot* 'Missing Friends' sought in California, individuals undoubtedly drawn there by the Gold Rush.

The findings in the distribution of *Pilot* migrants in North America by their Irish province of origin shows that the four provinces were fairly evenly represented across North America, with a few more Ulster persons located in Canada and more persons from the province of Munster located in New England.[21]

Some persons were reported as migrating first to other locales prior to reaching North America. Their numbers were small and undoubtedly under-represented the actual number of persons who may have travelled to other countries before migrating to North America. The foreign locations which were reported as a first destination after leaving Ireland included 54 persons who were reported as having gone to Australia, 2 to India, 672 who lived elsewhere in Ireland prior to migrating, 71 to Scotland, 38 to Wales, 2 to South Africa, 8 to Europe (France and Italy); and 20 to South America (which includes destinations in the West Indies).

Relationships of persons seeking to those sought

As has been reported, 22 per cent of all persons sought were females, and this varied only slightly across the four provinces. However when we look at the seekers by gender we see that females were 38 per cent of those seeking. The importance of sibling relationships is apparent in that 63 per cent all persons sought were siblings, and of these 42 per cent were brothers. The percentages varied only slightly across the four provinces.

Given the nature of this 'floating population' of Irish persons, it is surprising that only 5.23 per cent of the ads were placed by wives seeking husbands. A number of these were like the very first ad, placed on 1 October 1831 – presumably by immigration officials – seeking a Patrick M'Dermott, native of County Kildare, who was not there to meet his wife and four children when they arrived in Boston. A stonemason, he was last known to be in the Boston suburb of Roxbury. If not located, the immigration laws mandated that the family return to Ireland. Parenthetically, in most ads in which mothers sought young sons who had accompanied fathers in their search for work, the mothers were concerned to locate the sons but did not mention their missing husbands. Other relationships reported were those of cousins (5.2 per cent), fathers (5.1 per cent) and brothers-in-law (3.7 per cent).[22]

Mothers were almost as likely as wives (5.09 per cent of all ads) to seek missing male family members. Their language is worth noting because they were prone to use words such as 'abandoned', 'desperate', 'in want', and 'destitute', while wives were less likely to use such language. While some of the mothers instituting searches may have been in North America, many were, I believe, in

Ireland, using a contact person in America to locate their missing children.[23] The search can be explained by the family survival strategy whereby Irish children were expected to repay familial obligations. Donegal-born Patrick MacGill worked in the potato fields of Scotland before emigrating to Fall River, Massachusetts, and spoke for many when he said that he was 'born and bred merely to support my parents'. The belief that he would never have a day's luck in his life if he didn't give them every penny he earned was deeply ingrained in him.[24]

Ports of departure and entry

By mid-century there were significant changes in both the cost of the journey to America and the kind of individual choosing to become an emigrant. We know that family emigration dominated prior to the Famine, while following that period young single persons became the typical emigrant. Among explanations for these changes is that a reduction of the total cost of emigration enabled less-prosperous persons to leave Ireland and that there was a greater possibility of assisted emigration, either from government sources or from landlords. Another important factor was a reduction in the cost of the journey after steamships were introduced. The fare from Liverpool to New York at about mid-century was about a month's income for a skilled worker, and two or more month's income for an unskilled worker. Furthermore, the emigrant had to have saved enough to live on until he or she located employment following a hazardous and uncomfortable journey of up to three months by sailing ship. All would change when steamships became common on the North Atlantic route because they reduced the length of the journey and thus the cost. The transformation is illustrated by the fact that in 1856 135,000 immigrants arrived at New York in sailing vessels and only 5,000 in steamships. Four years later, 74,000 came by sail and 34,000 by steam, and by the end of the next decade nearly all immigrants were travelling by steamship.[25] Regular departure timetables reduced the amount of time an emigrant had to spend in port where emigrants often fell victim to abuse and expense during long weeks spent awaiting the departure of the ship. The creation of shipping lines specializing in the emigrant trade was a tremendous improvement also. Prior to this ships brought lumber and grain to Europe and returned with emigrants forced to endure the passage in hastily constructed bunks. The *Queen of the West* was a three-decked packet ship, built in New York in 1843 and designed with the emigrant trade in mind.[26] One of the *Pilot* immigrants, Edward Reelin, from Moher in the parish of Lavey in County Cavan, arrived in this ship in 1845 and worked in the Pennsylvania coal mines before moving to Virginia when his brother, Peter, sought him through an ad in the *Pilot* ten years later.[27]

Another great improvement which would transform both travelling and those who chose to travel was the growth of the railway system. Now the immigrant could reach his or her destination with some degree of certainty. These changes, by reducing the hazards of emigration, also changed the nature of emigration itself, in many cases making it much less likely to be an irrevocable decision.

Thus, what we are observing in the following section that analyses the *Pilot* data reflects many of these changes.[28]

Undoubtedly many of these changes also account for the great shift in the immigrant traffic from Irish ports to Liverpool to New York instead of the Canadian ports. Connections between the two were strengthened when entrepreneurs realized that the emigrant trade could be very profitable if the traffic was systematically organized. The immigrant trade between New York and Liverpool was helped, also, by the business falling into the hands of closely related houses in the two cities. One of these was the Grimshaw–Thompson combination, whose Liverpool operation had originally been in the slave trade from the West African coast.[29] On the basis of their past experience in the slave trade, this and other houses were well prepared for the emigrant trade dependent on compressing the maximum number of human beings into the minimum space.

Mary Ann Smyth boarded the *Ocean Monarch* in Liverpool with 395 other passengers, most of them emigrants. The ship caught fire when it was just a few miles off the north coast of Wales. About 180 passengers were saved, while the rest were missing and presumed dead. Mary Ann was one of the survivors, later arriving in New York aboard the *Sea King* in 1848. Harnden & Co. sought her in a 'Missing Friends' advertisement.[30] In covering the story, the *Pilot* stated that Harnden and Co. gave each survivor £50.[31] When her name appeared on the survivor list the company had the responsibility to locate her and complete their contract by transporting her to Boston or whatever was her final destination. In this case, as with so many other 'Missing Friends', we are left with a mystery.

A port of departure was reported for 11 per cent of *Pilot* emigrants while a port of arrival was reported for 23.5 per cent, or approximately one-quarter of the total number of persons. The data show that prior to 1840 the two leading ports were Dublin and Cork. In Ulster the leading ports were Derry, Belfast, Drogheda, Dundalk and Warrenpoint; and the other Munster ports were Bantry, Baltimore, Berehaven, Kilrush, Kinsale, Limerick, Tralee, Valentia, Waterford and Youghal. All of these were important prior to 1840, but then diminished steadily in importance. The cities of Limerick and Galway were important during the Famine years, after which the numbers leaving from those ports dropped considerably. For example, 148 *Pilot* emigrants left from Limerick in the years between 1846 and 1850, while only 42 were reported to have left from there in the succeeding seven years.

London and the other English, Welsh and Scottish ports assumed greater proportional importance in the years after 1850. Departures from Scottish ports were proportionally equal prior to the Famine and after the Famine, but declined in importance during the Famine.

What is remarkable about ports of departure are shifts over time, so that the smaller Irish ports which dominated the emigration routes earlier (with destinations to Canada and the relatively less important American ports) diminished in importance over time. After 1851, more than 50 per cent of all *Pilot* emigrants were leaving by way of Liverpool with New York as the main destination. What was less expected is the significance of New Orleans as a port of entry. We need to learn more about characteristics of this immigration stream. We do know that 44 per cent of *Pilot* immigrants who entered through the port of New Orleans were from the province of Munster, 27 per cent from Connacht, 20 per cent from Leinster, while only 8 per cent were from Ulster.

Most of those leaving from the city of Cork prior to 1860 went, in order of importance, to Quebec City, New York and Boston in equal proportions, and then to the Canadian Maritime ports (which included Newfoundland). During the same period, most emigrants leaving from Dublin arrived by way of Quebec, while the port of New York was next in importance. The most important tie was the Liverpool–New York connection, while the most important single port of entry was Quebec.

Occupations of immigrants

Information was collected in the advertisements on the occupations of the person sought, either in Ireland or in America. There were 1,365 persons reported as having an occupation in Ireland and 2,243 with a reported occupation in America. Of this total of 3,608 reported occupations, only 130 were reported with an occupation both in Ireland and in America. Furthermore, in those 130 cases, the occupational category was the same in both places for 89 persons. Thus there are only 41 cases where different occupations were given.

Looking at the regional picture of occupations we find, as expected, that persons from Leinster and Ulster had the highest skill levels. When the information on occupations is broken down by time period, we can see a decline in skill levels over time. Those with the highest skill levels arrived before 1840.

What is somewhat surprising today is that age and occupation were relatively unimportant for identifying missing family members.[32] In the case of 'Missing Friends' this may be partly explained by the fact that 48 per cent of all ads sought more than one person and in these ads occupation was less likely to be reported.[33] Another explanation lies in the nature of the job market in America. Then, as now, recent immigrants could not be sure of finding employment in whatever occupation they had had in Ireland. Persons trained as blacksmiths in Ireland were frequently to be found working on the railroad in America.

What may be an under-reporting of occupation leads to a significant problem of interpretation. Of those persons with an occupation reported, some 70 per cent were listed as having skilled occupations. The question arises as to what proportion of those remaining were unskilled? It seems fairly clear that listing an occupation was a distinguishing feature only for fairly well-defined occupations. For the vast majority of persons, their skills were probably undifferentiated. However, it is probably not justified to conclude that the remainder was unskilled. On the other hand, it is also probably wrong to conclude that the listed occupations are drawn from a random sample of migrants.

One more piece of data is worth looking at – the proportion of persons having a reported occupation by province and by period, showing that the proportion of migrants with occupations listed is directly consistent with other data. For example, Leinster and Ulster report a higher proportion of persons with an occupation, and these proportions declined steadily over the period covered by this analysis.

While the consensus of most scholars of Irish emigration has been that the great majority of Irish immigrants arrived in America 'without marketable skills', data on the occupations of the 'Missing Friends' immigrants suggest a more complex story. [34] Indeed it supports the argument that emigrants were not selected from the very poorest and that a significant proportion of the Irish in America were not as badly off as is generally assumed.

Some 500 persons were artisans, including 207 blacksmiths, 157 shoemakers, 47 bakers and 33 coopers. The next most important category was the building trades with 153 carpenters, 139 stonemasons and 66 bricklayers and masons. In America, 413 persons were reported as railroad or canal workers.

Some 29 persons sought had been in the British army, while 8 had been policemen in Ireland, and 187 men became soldiers in America, including 29 veterans of the War of 1812. The Mexican War must account for many persons prior to the Civil War. The outbreak of the American Civil War was a major upheaval for the immigrant community and is reflected in the *Pilot* searches: 57 soldiers placed searches for relatives and friends from whom they had been separated.

In contrast to the usual belief that the Irish did not enter farming in great numbers, it is interesting to note that 130 persons in this sample owned farms in America, while 54 were working as farm labourers.

The term contractor, of which 53 were sought here, is an interesting one for persons who were work gang leaders. In Ireland seasonal workers often migrated to England or Scotland, led by a 'gaffer' (a work crew leader), who negotiated terms for the workers, often serving as their banker, and in general easing the way for those who were unfamiliar with the English language. There is little direct evidence but it seems plausible that Irish gaffers became labour contractors in America. Certainly there was a body of experience in such an occupation in Ireland that could be tapped by the ambitious immigrant. Two contractors sought through *Pilot* ads may have worked in this capacity before leaving Ireland. John Cull sought his brother, railroad contractor Denis Cull or McCulla, in May 1854. Originating in the parish of Kilronan, County Roscommon, Denis had worked for the Arigna Ironworks before leaving Ireland in 1849 and was known to have been in the American state of Alabama.[35]

In one case an ad was used to warn of a dishonest contractor. Six men combined to warn other labourers of a certain A.J. Belnap who had robbed and cheated them. In this case the language of the text is worth noting:

Absconded, from La Salle, Illinois, a person named A.J. Belnap, who had a contract of 3 miles of the Central Rail Road, 19 miles from La Salle, and 4 from the Junction. It was a sub contract from Phillips, Cropsey & Williams. He robbed the poor laboring men of their hard-earned wages, after working under the rays of a burning sun for six weeks. He left this place in order to rob some other poor creatures as he has us; but we hope that all honest men will be on their guard against such notorious rogues. This A.J. Bellnap [*sic*] is a native of Newburgh, Orange Co., N.Y., and in appearance 50 or 60 years of age; about 5 ft 9 inches high, gray hair, and a hoarseness in his voice. A few of the poor fellows who were robbed are now at the Junction of the Central Railroad. The following are the names: Patrick Shea, Mathew Murphy, Thoms O'Neal, James O'Neal, Thos. Murphy, Francis McGowan.[36]

Were the searches ever successful?

A familiar theme in the story of Irish emigration is that of a family member leaving with the intention of establishing a foothold in America, and subsequently bringing out relatives. Such was the case with County Longford emigrant Miles Tiernen, from Killoe, who arrived in 1847, lived three years in New York City, before buying property after moving to Cincinnati, Ohio, in 1856. Shortly after sending for his family in Ireland, he learned their boat was shipwrecked. In June 1863 he sought them in a *Pilot* ad.[37] A month later a daughter, Bridget, replied, informing him she was in Poughkeepsie, New York.[38] Later ads suggest that Bridget joined her father in Cincinnati. Four months later he sought another daughter, Mary, only nine years old when the family left in 1851.[39] A son died on board ship, and Mary was taken to the hospital and not united with Bridget before the ship arrived in New York. Unsuccessful in locating her, he placed another, this time offering a reward of $20 for information.[40] He also sought another relative, a Mary Tiernen and her daughters, whose brother was the Rev. Patt McKirnen of Drumhuney, parish of Cloone, County Leitrim.[41] There are ads for 47 other persons from this parish, telling us more of characteristics of emigration from the small (129 acres) parish. Killoe emptied out early because sixteen of the seventeen reported dates of departure were prior to 1851 – seven prior to 1840. New York was the port of arrival for all for whom a port was reported. Occupations were reported for five of the 47 persons: two millwrights, two farmers and a domestic servant. Seven of those sought had variations in spelling of the Tiernen name (Kiernan, Kernan, Kearnan, Kernin). There is no further information on Miles Tiernen's search for family members, but family dispersal, separation and attempts at reunification in America are such familiar themes in the lives of Irish immigrants that this family's story is unusual only in its documentation.

Other evidence in the *Pilot* bears out that advertisements were effective in locating people.[42] On 18 February 1854, Ellen Hanaford Buckley wrote from Ireland in response to an advertisement placed by one of her brothers on 19 November of the previous year. Reading that her brother Thomas sought the whereabouts of his father and three brothers from a 'Pinegrove, Schuylkill Co, Pa' address, she described the *Pilot* as a 'truly valuable, widely circulated, and ably-conducted journal' and sought information about the meaning of the location 'Pa', as she was unfamiliar with it and wished to contact her family.[43] Her enquiry tells us that the advertisements were being read in Ireland.

Another successful search was reported by a J. Hannigan, living in Hermann, Missouri, in a notice published on 15 April 1854.[44] He heaped praise and 'unfeigned thanks' that his ad had located friends lost to him for more than 20 years. In another case, a Jeremiah Marnena, from the parish of Imly, in County Tipperary, used an ad to let his friends and relatives know that he could now be located in Grass Valley, Nevada County, California.[45]

County Cork as a microcosm of Ireland

What follows is an examination of data compiled from *Pilot* ads of emigrants from County Cork, taken from the advertisements from 1831 to 1855.[46] Nineteenth-century Cork was almost a microcosm of Ireland itself.[47] It was the largest and most populous of the 32 counties, containing 10 per cent of the population.[48] Furthermore, like Ireland as a whole, neither the land nor the people of Cork were homogeneous. The eastern districts were relatively prosperous, resembling to a great extent the eastern counties of Ulster and Leinster. The middle districts of Cork resembled the central part of Ireland; while the western districts resembled the poorer counties of the west of Ireland, from County Donegal in the north to County Kerry in the south.[49]

According also to the 1841 census, 65 per cent of all Cork holdings were less than fifteen acres. Evidence from the Devon Commission Report,[50] based on the reports of the Poor Law Commissioner, show discrepancies between census figures for holdings from one to five acres and the poor-law returns, showing only about half as large a percentage of holdings in this category as indicated in the census.[51] Dangerous subdivision of holdings may not have been as severe in Cork as elsewhere, where the dominant role of dairying may have tended to obstruct the progress of division within the agricultural economy and the slower rate of population growth slowed the process of land division. According to James Donnelly, there was a slower rate of population growth in Cork than elsewhere in Ireland, suggesting that permanent emigration was already reducing the population prior to the Famine, a conclusion that would seem to be borne out by the evidence from the *Pilot* data.[52]

Prior to 1850 Cork was the county of origin for almost 20 per cent of all persons sought through the 'Missing Friends' column and had by far the highest propensity to emigrate (36 per cent). While during the decade from 1845 to 1855 this proportion fell to 16 per cent, the numbers of persons from that county still remain significantly high. S.H. Cousens estimated that a total of 95,000 emigrants left Cork between 1841 and 1851, a number which is 10–12 per cent of its 1841 population.[53]

While it is customary to think of migrants from Ireland as rurally based, a considerable number of the 'Missing Friends' emigrants in the years covered by this study (1831–63) were reported as natives of the city of Cork – approximately 415. Many of these may have been industrial workers and artisans from declining trades and industries, notably textiles.[54] County Cork lost more population than any other county in Ireland between 1851 and 1891 (from

649,000 to less than 439,000) and this would contribute further to the decline of the region's industrial base.[55]

Several sources of data exist that describe particular characteristics and conditions of the geographic subdivisions of County Cork, although all are subject to criticism and concern about their reliability. Of particular concern for the pre-1845 period are the population censuses of 1821, 1831 and 1841, and the Poor Inquiry of 1835, all of which report data by parish.[56]

The distribution of *Pilot* data by parish shows that 110 of the 253 parishes of County Cork had at least one 'Missing Friend' identified, with one parish having 72 such respondents for a total of 2,996 individuals.[57] There was a high correlation between the number of 'Missing Friends' and population levels, suggesting that populous parishes generated larger numbers of 'Missing Friends'. Also, the various elements of the 1835 Inquiry clustered consistently with parishes reporting temporary migration also being characterized as having significant levels, with England being an important destination. There was also a strong negative relationship between loss of population (or slower growth of population) between 1821 and 1831 and the number of 'Missing Friends'.

It is possible that the Cork parishes that grew less rapidly were probably already experiencing congestion, thereby causing the standard of living to decline further. Under such conditions of stress three alternatives were open to people. One was to combine dwindling subsistence production with temporary migration – to England in particular, although there is some evidence of migration to nearby parishes and counties. Another alternative was to move to other parishes in Ireland – which shows up in high growth parishes as destinations of such movement.[58] Finally, there was the option of permanent emigration to North America.

If temporary and permanent migration were alternative responses to the same circumstances, we might expect low population growth parishes to generate more of both temporary and permanent migrants. There is likely to be a positive correlation between the numbers of temporary and permanent migrants, although the relationship is likely to be weak since the numbers will partly offset each other. Such a relationship is more likely to be positive for the period where both are being measured contemporaneously (the 1835 Inquiry report and the 'Missing Friends' sample). This was borne out by statistical analysis.[59]

Attempting to discover the conditions that might have prevailed to explain why people left some parishes and not others, a sample was taken of eleven parishes in which there were 75 or more seasonal migrants and more than six 'Missing Friends'.[60] Samuel Lewis's *Topographical Index* indicates that four of the parishes were in the western division of the county where almost 75 per cent of landholdings were valued at less than £15; seven were in the middle division; while none were in the more prosperous eastern division of the county where only 55 per cent of holdings were valued at less than £15. Clearly it would be necessary to look at a larger cross-section of parishes as well as more sources before drawing firm conclusions, but the parishes did have two characteristics in common. Each was located along a road system or what may be termed a communication route – often what was called a post road connecting towns.[61] And almost all of the selected parishes were reported as being relatively well provided with schools. And so it would appear that two factors that functioned to facilitate and encourage emigration from Cork were education and proximity to communication routes. Like Ulster and Leinster, the economy of Cork was more commercially oriented.

Conclusions

A number of conclusions can be drawn from the data here about the nature of Irish migration to America. In Ireland, we see shifts in the regions from which emigrants came. The earliest emigrants came from the provinces of Ulster and Leinster, and here in the *Pilot* data we can see this depicted in the diminished proportions of persons from those regions over time for which searches appear in the column. The province of Munster has always been a significant element of this data set because of the preponderance of persons sought from County Cork. Approximately 20 per cent of all persons prior to 1848 were reported to come from Cork, while the next Munster county in order of importance was Tipperary with only 7 per cent of persons sought. It must be kept in mind that Cork was a very large county and with a commensurately large population, so that when the *Pilot* emigrants are measured against the population figures for that county and measured also against other counties, the numbers leaving Cork seem less dramatic, and while still high are matched almost exactly by persons leaving from County Waterford prior to 1840. Nevertheless it must be kept in mind that the counties of origin from which large numbers of persons left changed greatly during the Famine years. We see the proportions of persons leaving Cork decline while those leaving from Kerry, Clare and Limerick rise. Following 1850, levels drop again in all counties except that of Kerry where they continue to rise. Thus County Kerry best exemplifies that post-Famine phenomenon of what has been called 'a haemorrhage of emigration' – a region emptying out.

From 1846 to 1850 proportionately more persons from the province of Munster continued to emigrate, but there was already an apparent shift to the province of Connacht. Then, from 1851 to 1857 we see that Counties Kerry and Clare remain high in proportions of persons leaving, but we also see the stream of persons from Galway, Mayo and Roscommon under way. In Leinster, only in Counties Kilkenny and Kildare do we see significant numbers of persons still leaving; and in Ulster, only County Cavan emigrants continue to leave in significant numbers, and even these proportions are significantly less than in the counties of high migration of the other three provinces.

In North America overall we see the growing importance of the Liverpool–New York nexus for those arriving in the United States and the declining importance of the Canadian ports which had accounted for 65 per cent of all arrivals prior to 1850. Much of this can be explained in terms of the changed nature of ocean shipping. Perhaps the most surprising evidence coming from the analysis of this period is the growing importance, not only of the port of New Orleans, but of the whole Mississippi–Ohio rivers watershed region as a place of settlement for thousands of Irish immigrants. The persistent notion that the Irish were reluctant to leave the cities of the eastern seaboard needs to be modified in the light of this new evidence.

There are also significant changes in the distribution of skill levels of the immigrants who arrived during and after the Famine. Those who arrived in the early decades were more skilled than those arriving later, so that we see a decline of skill levels among the persons who arrived during and after the Famine.

Questions have been raised about the degree to which the *Pilot* data is a representative sample of the Irish who came to North America. On the Irish side, analysis of the data by parish of the Cork emigrants would tend to demonstrate that what appears here is a good sample of Irish immigrants. In America, the large numbers of persons arriving at ports other than Boston and then distributing themselves all over the country tends to emphasize the national and even international nature of the evidence derived from the advertisements.

We can also see good evidence of patterns of chain migration and the clustering of migrant streams – that is, that there would be a spill of persons from one parish while in an adjacent parish there would be no 'Missing Friends' sought. In some cases more than a hundred persons left a small parish while there was no one from a nearby parish, and while this may speak to a kind of selectivity as to who knew of the *Pilot* and used it for searches, it does suggest that certain parishes emptied out while others did not.

The seekers and sought represented here were part of a transnational community of individuals from the same area in Ireland. Bound first by attachment to townland, then to parish and in some cases to barony, they saw themselves as emigrants from Kenmare or Carrickmacross or Omagh. It would take the experience of being in America to create a national Irish identity.

Notes

1. Memories of Bessie Hendricks written down by Mary Sheehan appear in *A Farewell to Famine*, by J. Rees (Arklow, Wicklow, 1994), p. 105.
2. The senior editor for Vols I–IV is R.A.M. Harris. B.E. O'Keeffe is editor for the subsequent volumes.
3. The database is maintained on a PC-486, under Windows 95 in a .dbf format, accessed using Alpha5 (trademark Alpha Software Co.) as the principal program. This will enable scholars and genealogists to access the data when it is fully available. For copies of the ads until 1860 and analysis of the responses, see the individual volumes of R.A.M. Harris (ed.), *The Search for Missing Friends, Immigrant Advertisements Placed in the Boston Pilot* (1989, 1991, 1993, 1995) Vols I–IV (Boston: New England Historic Genealogical Society). Ads for the years 1847–48, as well as all ads in which persons were reported to have departed or arrived in those years, are accessible on website: (http://dpls.dacc.wisc.edu/friends/index.html).
4. W.E. Vaughan and A.J. Fitzpatrick (eds), *Irish Historical Statistics* (Dublin, 1978), pp. 260–1.
5. It should be kept in mind here that this figure refers only to the number of persons reported as departing or arriving during that year.
6. Sons and daughters were compensated for their loss of property or dowry with paid passages and sums to establish them in the New World.

7. See J. Mannion, 'The Regional and Social Origins of Irish Emigrants to Newfoundland, 1780–1830', paper delivered at the Social Science History Association Conference, New Orleans, Louisiana, November 1991.
8. See R.A.M. Harris, 'Transatlantic Migration from County Cork to North America: An Anthropogeographic Study of Pre-Famine Ireland, 1831–1855', paper delivered at the Social Science History Association Conference, New Orleans, Louisiana, November 1991.
9. See R.A.M. Harris, *The Nearest Place That Wasn't Ireland: Early Nineteenth Century Irish Labor Migration* (Des Moines, Iowa, 1994).
10. See D. Fitzpatrick, *Irish Emigration, 1801–1921, Studies in Irish Economic and Social History 1* (Dublin, 1984), p. 12.
11. 1841 was the first year in which the British government collected systematic data on the county of origin for persons leaving Ireland.
12. Some 38 per cent of seekers were women.
13. Another immigrant, Mary Harlon of County Louth, described newspapers as full of ads offering good jobs in domestic service in her letter to Vere Foster who had sponsored her emigration. For more on this, see the introduction to Vol. IV of *Missing Friends*.
14. This is consistent with the findings of A. Bourke. See '*The Visitation of God'? The Potato and the Great Irish Famine* (Dublin, 1993).
15. The states of Massachusetts, Connecticut, Maine, New Hampshire, Vermont, and Rhode Island.
16. The states of New Jersey, Delaware, Pennsylvania, Maryland, and the District of Columbia.
17. The states of Louisiana, Arkansas, Mississippi, Tennessee, and Alabama.
18. The states of Michigan, Missouri, Ohio, Illinois, Wisconsin, Minnesota, Iowa, and Indiana.
19. Note that the 'Location after Ireland' data reported here represents only the *first* geographic location the individual being sought was reported to have been. Many persons were reported as being in three, four, five or more places, information that will be in a form in which it can be analysed in the future.
20. The states of California, Oregon, Arizona, Texas, New Mexico, and Kansas.
21. The Canadian regions are comprised of Upper Canada (now the province of Ontario), Lower Canada (now the province of Quebec), and the Canadian Maritime provinces of New Brunswick, Nova Scotia and Prince Edward Island, which includes the island of Newfoundland.
22. This analysis is based on 22,087 persons sought through 1856. See Table 12, 'Relationship of Seeker to Sought' in Vol. III of *Missing Friends*, p. xvi.
23. The common use of contact persons in the ads makes it difficult to ascertain a location for seekers.
24. P. MacGill, *Children of the Dead End* (London, 1982), p. 48.
25. R. Greenhalgh Albion (with the collaboration of Jennie Barnes Pope), *The Rise of New York Port, 1815–1860* (Boston, 1939, 1967, 1984), p. 349.
26. Albion, *Rise of New York Port*, p. 342.
27. See Vol. III of *Missing Friends*, p. 324.
28. For a substantive discussion of changes in European emigration during this period, see D. Baines, *Emigration From Europe, 1815–1930, Studies in Economic History and Social History* (London, 1991). Note particularly Chapter 6, 'Did Emigration Change in Character?', pp. 43–9.
29. Albion, *Rise of New York Port*, p. 341.

30. The *Pilot* of 16 September 1848 listed names of passengers believed to have been saved from the burning ship, among them is a Mary Smith, presumably an incorrect spelling for the Mary Ann Smyth sought in the 'Missing Friends' advertisement.

31. See the Boston *Pilot*, 9 December 1848. In 1854 the Harnden Company was the dominant express business in America according to Richard Robinson, *United States Business History, 1602–1988* (New York, 1990), p. 66. For the account from which the *Pilot* got its information about the survivors, see the *Illustrated London Times*, 2 September 1848. Bridget Knightly, associate editor for Vol. III, conducted the research on Harnden & Co.

32. Reported occupations are somewhat unreliable overall since many persons had more than one, do many tasks, or had multiple sources of income. In contemporary third-world countries, people tend to report the occupation that they followed most recently.

33. As of 3 November 1992, of a total of 22,706 persons sought, 10,269 of these were in advertisements seeking more than one individual.

34. See Fitzpatrick, *Irish Emigration*, pp. 8–9.

35. Ad of 6 May 1854, Vol. III of *Missing Friends*, p. 88. Note the transformation of the spelling of the brother's names. The original name must have been McCullough which had first been transformed into McCulla by Denis and then into Cull. John was now spelling his surname only as 'Cull'.

36. Ad of 12 November 1853, Vol. II of *Missing Friends*, p. 500.

37. Ad of 27 June 1863, Vol. V of *Missing Friends*, p. 207.

38. Ad of 25 July 1863, Vol. V of *Missing Friends*, p. 214.

39. Ad of 21 November 1863, Vol. V of *Missing Friends*, p. 251.

40. Ad of 16 April 1864, Vol. V of *Missing Friends*, p. 322.

41. There is no townland of Drumhuney in Cloone, but it may be the townland of Drumhirk. Cloone adjoins the Longford parish of Killoe. There are a number of variations of spelling of the McKiernan name in the five ads.

42. The ads cost $3 for three insertions. A labourer in Boston made approximately $6 a week in 1850, while females in non-domestic paid employment were paid about $3 a week.

43. Ad of 18 February 1854, Vol. III of *Missing Friends*, p. 29.

44. Ad of 15 April 1854, Vol. III of *Missing Friends*, p. 74.

45. Ad of 1 July 1854, Vol. II of *Missing Friends*, p. 120.

46. See Harris, 'Transatlantic Migration'.

47. To quote from the historical geographer, T.W. Freeman: 'The county [Cork] has therefore some claim to be regarded as a microcosm of the entire country'. T.W. Freeman, *Pre-famine Ireland: A Study in Historical Geography* (Manchester, 1957), pp. 203, 226, 229, 236.

48. There were 850,000 inhabitants in the census of 1841.

49. The 1841 census also shows that while 65 per cent of all families in Ireland were dependent upon farming for livelihood, in County Cork more than 70 per cent of families were totally dependent on farming, accounting for a total of 98,000 families out of 133,000 employed in agriculture.

50. *Devon Commission Digest*, Vol. I, pp. 393–6.

51. Bourke has argued that in the 1841 census farm size was expressed in terms of the larger Irish acre (1.62 statue acres) and waste land was ignored in computing size of holdings. P.M.A. Bourke, 'The Extent of the Potato Crop in Ireland at the Time of the Famine', *Statistical Society of Ireland Journal*, 20, 3 (1959), pp. 20–6. Also, 'The Agricultural Statistics of the 1841 Census of Ireland: A Critical Review', *Economic History Review*, 2nd series, 18, 2 (August 1965), pp. 377–81.

52. J.S. Donnelly, Jr., *The Land and the People of Nineteenth Century Cork, the Rural Economy and the Land Question* (Boston, 1975), p. 121. From *2nd Annual Report of the Commissioners for Administering the Laws for Relief of the Poor in Ireland*, pp. 171–4; *Third Annual Report of the Commissioners for Administering the Laws for Relief of the Poor in Ireland* [1243], HC 1850, xxvii, 449, pp. 82–4; *Fourth Annual Report of the Commissioners for Administering the Laws for Relief of the Poor in Ireland*: with appendices [1381], HC 1851, xxvi, 547, pp. 161–5.

53. S.H. Cousens, 'The Regional Pattern of Emigration During the Great Famine, 1846–1851' *Transactions and Papers of the Institute of British Geographers*, 28 (1960), p. 121. He notes also that there was a high proportion of landless labourers in Cork, which is consistent with a story of persons supplementing inadequate incomes by the returns from seasonal migration.

54. For the economic history of County Cork, see A. Bielenberg, *Cork's Industrial Revolution, 1780–1880, Development or Decline?* (Cork, 1991) and Donnelly, *Land and the People*.

55. Bielenberg, *Cork's Industrial Revolution*, pp. 122–4.

56. The 1835 Inquiry was undertaken by asking standardized questions of 'knowledgeable informants' – clergymen, magistrates and the like – in a sample of parishes within each barony of the country. Among the questions included in this valuable survey were those relating to whether seasonal migration was an important practice, how many persons were engaged in such migration, and whether persons from that parish migrated to England. Geographer and folklorist Dr Anne O'Dowd has used this source in an innovative fashion in her book, and I acknowledge her work as stimulating me to utilize the 1835 Poor Inquiry data in this analysis. A. O'Dowd, *Spalpeens and Tattie Hokers, History and Folklore of the Irish Migratory Agricultural Worker in Ireland and Britain* (Dublin, 1991).

57. As most persons placing advertisements were unfamiliar with the spelling, as well as the correct names, of the townlands and parishes from whence they came, it is hardly surprising to find many incorrect names reported. In order to prepare the data for analysis it was necessary to correct the parish and townland information, as much as was possible.

58. Migrants themselves often testified to the fact that the hostility which they encountered in nearby parishes and counties caused them to prefer migration to England, or as in the case of the northern counties of Ireland, to Scotland.

59. See Harris, 'Transatlantic Migration'.

60. Lewis's Topographic Index reported on conditions in the parishes indicated. See S. Lewis, *A Topographical Dictionary of Ireland*, 2 vols (London, 1839).

61. Communication routes were ascertained by superimposing a map of communication routes from the Drummond Report over the mapped data by parish. Ó Gráda has drawn attention to what he terms the 'pre-famine revolution in communications' which saw 'the blossoming of a comprehensive network of road passenger transport, which by 1845 had established a regular service between all towns of any size for about 1s.5d. per mile'. See Ó Gráda, *Ireland Before and After the Famine, Explorations in Economic History, 1800–1925* (Manchester, 1988), pp. 30–1. 'The work of Richard Griffith in the south-west brought daily coach services to the Tralee – Cork and Killarney – Cork routes, and reduced the journey time on the latter by two-thirds'. S.O. Luing, 'Richard Griffith and the Roads to Kerry', *Journal of the Kerry Historical and Archaeological Society*, 8 (1975), pp. 89–113, and 9 (1976), pp. 92–124.

CHAPTER 9

Immigrants on the Land: A Comparative Study of Irish Rural Settlement in Nineteenth-Century Minnesota and New South Wales

MALCOLM CAMPBELL

(Department of History, Auckland)

Introduction

On 16 September 1882 William Geraghty, an Irish settler in Murray County, Minnesota, wrote to John Sweetman, Managing Director of the Irish-American Colonization Company, declaring his intention to give up life on the land:

> To ask to continue living in such a way I could not do, so I have decided to turn all I have into cash, pay my debts here and with the exception of my team to hand the balance to you . . . I am not going to any situation I now know of – my intention is to go to Saint Paul and I have every hope of getting lucrative employment there.[1]

The same month another settler, Robert Antrim, informed Sweetman that: 'I have concluded that it is impossible for me to make it in this country. You will find yourself repaid for anything I received from you by the improvements I put on the land.'[2] Despite Geraghty's promise to make good all his debts, and Antrim's assertion that he had effectively discharged his obligations, the colonization company fared poorly in the subsequent months. In May 1883 it reported a loss of £5,104 for the previous year, the financial statement noting that 'there was undoubtedly cause for vexation on the part of the directors and shareholders because of the failure of the colonists to meet the interest payments due for them last year, and the instalment of the principal, as well as the accrued interest which became due the present year'.[3]

These examples of farming failure and the renunciation of life on the land are consistent with much Irish-American historical writing, which emphasizes the inability of the immigrant Irish to adjust to rural life. Rather than take to the land, most historians argue, the Irish adjusted poorly to the demands of industrial America and so remained cast in a subordinate role in American cities.[4] As Donald Akenson has pointed out, several standard explanations recur in the literature to explain this phenomenon. The immigrants, it has often been argued, lacked sufficient capital to move westward from the cities on the eastern seaboard; they did not possess the skills appropriate for the extensive farming patterns of the New World; they felt a psychological aversion to life on the land as a result of the scarring effects of the Great Famine; and they possessed a gregariousness of character which discouraged movement away from the familiar and socially congenial world of the city.[5]

This chapter compares Irish rural settlement in the American state of Minnesota and the south-west region of the Australian state of New South Wales in order to scrutinize and assess the validity of these propositions. These locations share a number of features that suggest their potential for comparison. In the mid-nineteenth century both Minnesota and south-west New South Wales experienced rapid increases in their European populations as the frontier gave way to more established settlement. In both regions, the Irish-born were prominent among the early arrivals who sought to take advantage of the opportunities available in the still unrefined settings. In 1850, 68 per cent of the British Isles born population in the Minnesota territory was of Irish birth, while in south-west New South Wales approximately one in three of the settler population were Irish-born, others children of Irish descent.[6] Parallels continued in the second half of the nineteenth century too: settlement extended and became more intense, towns developed to service farming communities, and as the population in each location increased, a significant Irish presence remained a feature of both regions.

However, during the last quarter of the century significant differences also emerged between the two. In south-west New South Wales the large Irish-born population gradually diminished in significance, though the presence of second- and third-generation Irish ensured the region maintained its reputation as a location of intensive Irish settlement. In Minnesota, while the proportion of Irish-born in the population declined, the organization of Irish settlement underwent significant changes. Colonization schemes, especially those organized by Bishop John Ireland and the Irish-American Colonization Company, achieved prominence, and increasingly these ventures departed from the processes which had underpinned the successful establishment of Irish settlers in the state. These colonization schemes undermined old configurations and, for the most part, proved unsuccessful in promoting viable Irish rural communities. Yet, in the historical literature, it is this less auspicious second phase of settlement which has achieved the most prominence, and has reinforced stereotypical assertions about the Irish incapacity for rural life.

Cross-cultural comparison of the experiences of immigrant groups is rare, and has for the most part been conducted at a national level. This chapter seeks to move beyond the constraints imposed by a national-oriented approach. Although comparison at a local or regional level is unusual, such *mezzo* level analysis is potentially invaluable.[7] It provides an opportunity to compare in much finer detail than is possible in a transnational study the experiences of an emigrant group in different destinations. It also lends itself to a more focused and precise assessment of the relative influences of cultural heritage and local conditions in shaping immigrant experiences. The comparison that follows points to the necessity for a renewed appraisal of Irish rural settlement throughout the diaspora.

Minnesota

In 1850 the Irish-born, though few in number, constituted 4.5 per cent of the total population of the infant Minnesota territory, and 13.2 per cent of the total foreign-born (see Table 9.1). By 1860, however, the Irish presence was far more pronounced, amounting to 7.5 per cent of the total population and nearly 22 per cent of the foreign-born in the state. Indeed, as Morton Winsberg has demonstrated, the Irish were over-represented in Minnesota compared to their share of the total United States population throughout the period from 1850 until 1870. However, although such figures are indicative of a strong Irish presence, the census data provides little assistance in identifying the broader multi-generational Irish ethnic group. For example, the largest foreign group in Minnesota in the 1850 census was those born in the then British North America, some 23 per cent of the territory's total population, a significant proportion of whom were likely to be Irish-born or the children of Irish immigrants. Obscured, too, are those second-generation Irish born elsewhere in the United States who chose Minnesota.

Given the quality of United States census data, information on the regional origins of the Irish who settled in mid-nineteenth century Minnesota is sparse. However, some suggestive material is available. A study of a sample of Irish settlers in Scott County for the period 1853–70 found Cork and Kerry each contributing one-fifth of the total, with significant contributions from Clare, Galway, Sligo and Mayo. There were also concentrations of Scotch-Irish settlers at Eden Prairie in Hennepin County and Long Prairie in Todd County – in the former the immigrants were drawn mainly from counties Tyrone, Monaghan and Cavan.[8] Overall, the patchy evidence that is available points to considerable diversity in the immigrant base, but in the absence of further

Table 9.1: Irish population of Minnesota, 1850–90

Year	Total population	Total foreign-born	Total Irish-born	Irish-born in total population (%)	Location quotient
1850	6,077	2,048	271	4.46	1.08
1860	172,023	58,728	12,831	7.46	1.45
1870	439,706	160,697	21,746	4.95	1.02
1880	780,773	267,676	25,942	3.32	0.89
1890	1,301,826	467,356	28,011	2.15	0.71

Adapted from: United States Census Office, Seventh–Eleventh Censuses, 1850–90. Location quotients are derived from Morton Winsberg, 'Irish Settlement in the United States, 1850–1980', *Eire-Ireland*, 20, 1 (Spring 1985), pp. 7–14.

research firm conclusions are difficult to draw. David Fitzpatrick has argued for the presence of variations in the social composition of the different Irish emigrant streams – the United States drawing from the surplus subsistence rural population, whereas Australia drew more heavily upon semi-skilled farm workers. This is partially born out here: Sligo and Mayo, though contributors to Minnesota's Irish population, were the least significant counties to contribute to Irish assisted immigration to Australia; on the other hand, the presence of a strong Clare contingent in this American rural sample mirrors that county's importance as a major contributor to those entering Australia. In sum, although it appears variable streams did exist, it is difficult to see this as an adequate explanation of the widely differing interpretations of Irish life experience in the New World. As Fitzpatrick has observed, 'the structure of the host societies was a far more important factor'.[9]

Initially, the open land and infant economy of Minnesota held considerable attraction for Irish settlers in the United States. Michael Callaghan, a native of County Cork, arrived in America in 1845 and initially worked in a salt mine in Syracuse, New York. However, in 1849 he moved westward in search of a better climate for his ailing wife's health. Three years later he wrote to his brother in the east advising him to follow in his footsteps, and alerting him to the favourable conditions he would encounter:

> This country is not tried much farming yet but what I see is the finest I ever see in America so far as potatoes and vegetables . . . if you do come this fall you are better buy your flour, sugar and coffee and such things in Galena and a cow and a sow pig – they are very Dear here and if you have money enough get a yoke of cattle they will cost you about eighty dollars here . . . I think the best route for you is to Chicago and Galena . . . I think you will like this country well enough . . . people say it will be a good place for there is a good many railroads started there. It is a good place for James Coughlan for there is plenty of whiskey.[10]

For some settlers, the declining availability and increasing cost of land elsewhere encouraged consideration of Minnesota as a possible destination. Mary Jane Anderson, born in 1827 into an Anglican family in Baileborough, County Cavan, emigrated to the United States with her husband Robert in 1850. After short periods in New Orleans and St Louis, the couple moved on to Galena, Illinois, where Robert had two sisters and a brother. Mary Jane recalled the circumstances of Robert's introduction to Minnesota:

> In the spring of 1853 John Mitchell, [Robert's] uncle, came down from Minnesota to buy cattle. He was one of four families that had settled about twenty-five miles from St. Paul. By this time all the homesteads in Illinois had been taken up, and it was expensive to buy, so he persuaded [Robert] to go up and look at Minnesota, which he did that Fall. He found 160 acres which looked desirable, and left money to start a log cabin, as some improvements were necessary to hold it.[11]

In both of these cases, family connections encouraged a staged migration to the new farmlands of Minnesota.

There were, however, more elaborate settlement schemes, even in the early years. The best known of these was the Shieldsville settlement, initiated by Tyrone-born James Shields. Shields emigrated to the United States in 1822 at age 16, and worked in a variety of occupations before his election to the Illinois legislature in 1835. He was subsequently commissioned as a general in the Mexican–American war and then, after a term in the United States senate, selected land in Minnesota as reward for his career of government service. According to one account:

> He was so favourably impressed with the country that he decided to go east and organise a colony of Irish Americans to settle on the soil of Rice and Le Sueur Counties, of whose fertility he had learned while Commissioner of Federal Lands in Washington. He selected as a suitable site for a Catholic colony the district of Rice County now known as Shieldsville. After staying long enough to lay out a prospective village he went back to St. Paul returning the same year with a number of Irishmen . . . Many of this group settled in Erin township and became identified with the early growth of that locality. That same year through the columns of the catholic press, he invited to Minnesota Irish Catholics both in the eastern states and those who had not yet left Ireland.[12]

The response to Shield's appeal was enthusiastic, and Shieldsville soon spawned the neighbouring township of Erin, where, according to one account, 'there were none but the descendants of the emerald isle to be recorded in the pages of its early history'. However, relations between the settlers and Shields soon deteriorated amidst accusations of fraud.[13]

Several important characteristics of the Irish settlement of mid-nineteenth-century Minnesota stand out. First, the immigrants invariably entered the region in a staged process. As Ann Regan has observed, a common pattern of transit 'included arrival in New York or Canada, and one or two subsequent moves over a period of years to Pennsylvania, Ohio, Illinois, Indiana or Wisconsin, then to Minnesota'.[14] Sometimes American-born children accompanied their parents into the west. For example, Michael J. Boyle was born in 1856 in Allegheny City, Pennsylvania, and settled with his parents in Minnesota as a young child acutely conscious of his Irish heritage. On St Patrick's Day 1876, at age 20, he attended High Mass 'in honour of Ireland's patron saint and mine'.[15] In many other cases this movement took more than one generation, and the second-generation Irish ventured along these migratory paths alone. Other Irish settlers in Minnesota came via much more circuitous routes. Francis Logan, born in Ireland in 1825, lived first in New Hampshire, then ventured to Illinois and California, before settling down in Tyrone township, a 'well settled part of [Le Sueur] county [that] has many scores of valuable, well cared for farms'. Around him were other townships, Derrynane and Kilkenny, and organizations such as the Catholic Order of Foresters and the Ancient Order of Hibernians, all testimony to the strength of the Irish presence. These, indeed, were examples of immigrants and their descendants on the move in search of opportunity and advancement.[16]

Second, many of these Irish immigrants entered farming communities in which they appear to have had – at least initially – strong familial or communal ties.

This was aided by the pattern of distribution of the Irish within Minnesota, who exhibited a particular attachment to the south-eastern counties of the state. In 1870 72.5 per cent of Minnesota's Irish-born population lived in the 20 counties of the south-east.[17] Within this concentrated area the Irish took to the land with enthusiasm. Ann Regan has reported that '[m]ore than half (58 per cent) of Minnesota's Irish listed as employed in 1870 were farm workers and owners . . . for the next 40 years the percentage of Irish working on Minnesota farms remained slightly higher than the average for all groups in the state (which fluctuated between 45 per cent and 57 per cent), and most of these Irish were listed as farm owners rather than farm labourers'.[18]

That the Irish clustered in particular farming localities is demonstrated by the wide variations in the Irish percentage of the population in different Minnesota counties. (Appendix 1 shows the distribution of the Irish across Minnesota's counties in 1870.) The strength of the Irish presence at this local level served to ease the settlers' entry into unfamiliar surroundings. Moreover, confident in their new environment, the Minnesota Irish seem to have been subjected to less sectarian or national conflict than their compatriots further east. This was a theme emphasized by Bishop John Ireland, who, when celebrating the 50th anniversary of the Catholic Church in the north-west, remarked that 'there are few places where religious freedom has so reigned as in Minnesota and its two neighbouring states'.[19]

Third, Irish settlement in Minnesota initially outstripped the advance of the Catholic Church, and Irish clergy in particular. An advocate of western settlement by the Irish, Philip Bagenal, later portrayed the model scheme of Irish rural placement to be one where:

> The first person to enter the colony is the priest, selected with a special view to his knowledge of country life, who is to be the pastor of the flock. He is on the ground to receive the first family, who find at once in him a friend and help. The church is the first building put up . . . no public house is allowed to be opened . . . the temperance society is the first organisation formed and total abstinence is inculcated as one of the first axioms of prairie life.[20]

The reality of early Irish movement to the west was far from this. The initial Catholic clerical presence was French and the Church under-resourced – in 1849 there were only two priests stationed in what was to become the diocese of St Paul. This was to change quickly under the leadership of Bishop Cretin, and in less than a decade the Church could boast the establishment of 29 churches and five convents, and the presence of 20 priests – an achievement Bishop John Ireland later compared to the coming of St Patrick to Ireland.[21] The crucial point, however, is that Irish settlers in mid-nineteenth-century Minnesota could not and did not make settlement choices on the basis of the strength of religious infrastructure or the comforting presence of a parish community – these came later. Immigrants' settlement was motivated by the availability of land and work and the need to seize the best chance while opportunities in the region were at a premium. Religious matters could be attended to when economic security was secured.[22]

New South Wales

Irish settlement in south-west New South Wales also exhibited these important characteristics, though the immigrants' presence in this Australian region
originated in very different circumstances. Here the system of convict transportation, which brought about the forced migration of approximately 40,000
Irish men and women to eastern Australia before 1853, was crucial. As
several studies have demonstrated, the initial impetus for Irish settlement in
the south-west came from land grants awarded to emancipated convicts by
the colony's Governor, Lachlan Macquarie, in the late 1810s and early 1820s.
Encouraged by the Irish ex-convict surveyor James Meehan, his compatriots
actively sought landholdings to the south-west of Sydney.[23] From this starting
point, settlement spread rapidly in the 1830s and 1840s, forging a south-
western axis which became the key line of Irish settlement in the colony. This
was the direction to which large numbers of Irish convicts gravitated when their
period of servitude was completed; assisted immigrants followed, attracted to
a region of relatively heavy Irish settlement. The Scottish immigrant David Waugh
captured the tenor of this movement when he wrote that:

> when a convict is out of his time, if industrious, he will serve a year or two, and
> buy twenty cows, which he will get for £1 a head up with us – though not the
> very prime ones; he then goes to Burrowa Plains, 50 miles from us, or some
> open spot, he then builds a hut with an axe in a week, – encloses two or three
> acres, and breaks it up with the hoe for wheat, – makes butter and cheese far
> more than pay his expenses, and there he lives with everything in plenty.[24]

By the 1830s this pattern was clearly visible to friends and foes of Irish settlement alike. The English Benedictine bishop, John Bede Polding, appealed
to the Protestant Irish Governor, Richard Bourke, for the provision of additional resources to the Roman Catholic Church, and stressed the particular
shortage of clergy in the south-western areas of the settlement, all these
'chiefly Catholic [and] unprovided with Roman Catholic chaplains'. An
alarmed Judge W.W. Burton, in his book *The State of Religion and Education
in New South Wales*, cited Polding's appeal as evidence of unchecked Irish concentration in the south-west and expressed considerable alarm at the strength
of Irish Catholics 'in disseminating their doctrines and establishing churches'.[25]

By mid-century, the Irish presence in New South Wales was strong, the Irish-
born accounting for a fifth of the total population, as shown in Table 9.2.
However, those figures disguise the full intensity of the Irish presence on the
south-western rural frontier of the society. Table 9.3 provides figures for the
Irish-born in the major counties of the region in 1851.

The regional origins of the Irish immigrants in nineteenth-century Australia
have been the subject of examination, especially by David Fitzpatrick. Focusing on the period from 1841, he has demonstrated the strength of migration
from the south midlands counties – Clare, Limerick, Tipperary, King's County
and Kilkenny – and areas of south Ulster. All were represented in south-west
New South Wales, with clusters of Tipperary and Limerick-born settlers

Table 9.2: Irish population of New South Wales, 1846–1891

Year	Total population	Total Irish-born	Irish-born in colonial population (%)
1846	151,587	37,762	24.9
1851	187,243	38,659	20.6
1861	350,860	54,979	15.7
1871	503,981	62,943	12.5
1881	751,468	69,192	9.2
1891	1,123,954	75,051	6.7

Adapted from: New South Wales Census, 1846, 1851; James Jupp and Barry York, *Birthplaces of the Australian People, Colonial and Commonwealth Census, 1828–1991*, Centre for Immigration and Multicultural Studies, Australian National University (Canberra, 1995).

Table 9.3: Irish population of south-west New South Wales, 1851

County	Total population	Total Irish-born	Irish-born in total population (%)	Location quotient
Argyle	5,465	1,312	24.0	1.163
Georgiana	1,525	302	19.8	0.959
King	2,505	660	26.3	1.276
Murray	3,886	918	23.6	1.144
Lachlan district	2,892	847	29.3	1.419

Adapted from: New South Wales Census, 1851.

attracting particular comment from contemporary observers.[26] However, given the overwhelmingly greater scale of the American migration, and the fact that in any case 'Australia's Irish were drawn to some extent from all counties and from scattered localities within counties', it seems more than place of birth is required to explain the Australian Irish rural departure from America's often emphasized urban focus.[27]

Comparisons

As in the case of Minnesota, several crucial features stand out in the process of Irish settlement in south-west New South Wales. First, the migration was a staged one, where the Irish gained substantial opportunity to adjust to the conditions of New World farming. The period of convict servitude, in particular, was influential for many early arrivals in the region. They had served as labourers on farms, and had gained familiarity with the conditions of the land – some, indeed, had served as overseers or farm managers for their masters. In addition, this period of servitude enabled the convict workers to acquire a sum of capital sufficient to sustain their first endeavours when they moved to the rural margins of the society. In 1830, at the end of his fourteen-year sentence, Tipperary-born Edward Ryan listed his assets as 50 head of breeding cattle, a team of oxen, 200 bushels of wheat, £250 in cash, and sundry agricultural implements. Ryan's wealth at this time, like his later land acquisitions, was exceptional. However, many Irish convicts completed their period of servitude with a tidy sum of capital which would finance their attempts to settle on the land.[28] The convict period provided other Irish with the opportunity to participate in expeditions into the inland, this travel revealing favourable locations for settlement which might then be followed up when the opportunity became available.

This pattern of staged adjustment was repeated among subsequent free arrivals too. Large numbers of immigrants – assisted and full-fare-paying – entered this rural region only gradually, advised by those in place before them about opportunities available and strategies for settlement. When James Gormly arrived in the colony from County Roscommon in 1840, his parents were advised by acquaintances, including the colony's Attorney-General, John Hubert Plunkett, not to venture inland with young children but to settle in the southern coastal districts. Then, having adjusted to the rhythms of life in their new society, they ventured inland to search for farmland. Others went in search of paid employment in order to accumulate a sum which would enable them or their children to take to the land.[29]

Second, the concentrated Irish presence ensured that settlers entered into a region in which strong networks of family and kinship existed, and where those connections ensured the maintenance of a remarkably confident and assertive rural immigrant community. There exists ample documentation of the strong patterns of migration which bound the Clonoulty district of County Tipperary to Boorowa. However, there were many other examples too, some well-known, others now scarcely visible in the surviving written sources. Catholic Irish settlers gathered around John Dwyer, the son of the Wicklow chieftain Michael Dwyer, near Lake George; T.A. Murray's Yarralumla station had a strong Catholic population closely tied to Limerick. A knot of Irish settlers, also with roots in County Limerick, gathered near Tumut. In 1850 Thomas and Anne Quilty wrote from there to their daughter Ellen in Shanagolden, confidently asserting the prosperity and security of the rural region in which they lived:

> if ye exert yourselves ye will get a passage out here as well as other people, and we shall do all we can to make you comfortable here, in fact it is our fond wish that you be here with us, your brothers and sisters who are all doing very well. You cannot want for anything here you have got too many friends before you to secure you from that. We live in the immediate neighbourhood with your three married sisters and brother Tom.[30]

Partly by virtue of their strong numerical presence, Irish settlers – Catholic and Protestant – actively sought to minimize religious tension in their new homeland and to ensure generally harmonious community relations: there was here no repeat of the fierce nativism of the American east.

Third, as in Minnesota, early Irish rural settlement in south-west New South Wales was remarkably unaffected by the influence of the Roman Catholic Church. The English Benedictine hierarchy of the fledgling Australian Church seems to have in no way discouraged Catholic settlement on the land, nor did the immigrants allow the absence of priests and churches to inhibit their economic judgements – these seem to have been remarkably pragmatic and generally sound. Irish-born clergy did come later, and embarked on an impressive campaign of church-building and the encouragement of devotions, but lay responsiveness to clerical demands seems always to have been circumscribed by their own assessments of their secular and immediate material interests.[31]

At mid-century, then, strong similarities may be observed in the Irish settlement of these two rural regions. In both cases the immigrants who ventured inland, armed with considerable knowledge of their prospective new homes and usually possessing sufficient capital, made pragmatic assessments of the opportunities available. They showed a determination to seize the opportunity presented by large amounts of affordable land; on the available evidence they seem to have farmed no less successfully or persistently than settlers of other nationalities; and they viewed acquisition of the land as a positive thing – a source of pride and security.[32] Samuel Shumack, who left Ireland with his parents in 1856 and settled near Canberra, expressed what were surely the feelings of many Irish in south-west New South Wales when he wrote:

> in 1861 Robertson's Act became the law of the land and proved a blessing to thousands, and father and I took up 100 acres in February 1865 under the Free Selection Act at Weetangerra. We called our selection Springvale. We now had an object in life – to secure a permanent home . . . In February 1865 I built a bark gunyah [hut] on my selection, in which I took up residence until I could build a permanent home.[33]

Finally, there seems to be little evidence at all among early Irish settlers in either region that the relative isolation of their new environments was a deterrent to their lives on the land. Of course, it might be argued that evidence of a need for attachment to gregarious neighbours and parish communities should not be sought amongst those who took to the land, but is most visible among those who actually remained in urban areas. However, the very point that such numbers of Irish did in fact settle in rural locations in both the United States and Australia is sufficient to rebut the commonly made assertion that the Irish, a group supposedly possessing shared cultural characteristics, found country life uncongenial. In the Australian case, of course, the convict system imposed constraints on the freedom of movement of Irish prisoners, but the persistence of so many Irish in the region in the decades after the termination of transportation suggests at the very least a fair level of satisfaction with the economic opportunities and social life available to settlers.

If, at mid-century, settlement in both regions exhibited several similar characteristics, the latter decades of the century saw a significant change in the pattern of entry of the Irish-born into Minnesota. Increasingly, schemes of group migration came to dominate Irish settlement on the land. Inspired by the writings of advocates such as Thomas D'Arcy McGee and Philip Bagenal, who forcefully argued that the salvation of the Irish lay in America's western lands, various schemes were initiated to assist poor and destitute Irish to take advantage of 'the homes and fortunes, still to be made, by honest labour in America'.[34] Several schemes operated in the period from the mid-1870s to the 1880s, though it is possible here to refer to them only briefly. Best known, perhaps, are the settlements initiated by Bishop John Ireland, a long-time advocate of Irish movement to the west, who from 1875 acted as an agent for railway companies and sold land on favourable terms to Catholic settlers. Bishop Ireland's schemes especially targeted Irish already resident in cities on the eastern seaboard of the United States, and some of the Irish settled there responded with very great enthusiasm to the opportunity for rural settlement. Annie King Lacore recorded the enthusiasm with which her parents, Patrick, a native of Cavan, who arrived in the United States in 1872, and Mary, who emigrated from Roscommon in 1873, heard of the colonization scheme while at Mass in Pleasantville, New York:

> the pastor asked the attention of the congregation to an announcement which he had been asked by his chancery office to make. Seems there was a young Bishop in a place way out west, John Ireland by name, of St. Paul in the Minnesota, who had thought up a plan for peopling parts of his state with any immigrant Irish Catholics who would be interested in farming. The plan offered 160 acres of rich prairie land, together with a 4 room house, built on land of their choice, and a public school would be made available for their children through a deal with the State, and also a church would be built for members of the Colony, and all this at a cost of $5 per acre.

For this couple the opportunity 'loomed large', and they 'realised a dream . . . their own home on [160 acres of] land' in the village of Adrian, in Nobles County.[35] Yet, despite examples such as this one, Ireland's programme is best remembered for the unfortunate experience of 'the Connemaras', a group of 309 settlers transplanted directly from Galway to Graceville, in Big Stone County. These immigrants quickly showed themselves unable or unwilling to adjust to life in Minnesota, an associate of Ireland's writing that 'they would ruin the prospects of any colony into which they would find entrance'.[36]

The other major sponsor of settlement in Minnesota was the Irish-American Colonization Company Ltd, which released its prospectus in April 1881. The company, whose Managing Director was John Sweetman, sought to raise £150,000 for the purpose of facilitating Irish settlement on the land:

> In the western States of America vast tracts of magnificent tillage land are still unoccupied, affording a most favourable opening for capital and labour combined. These lands will not, however, long remain unsettled, owing to the large immigration from the Eastern states of America, and from Germany, Norway and Sweden. Great numbers of able bodied men are now emigrating from Ireland, who, for want of capital, cannot settle on these lands. This company has been formed for the purpose of supplying such want of capital. It will purchase land in suitable localities and place settlers on it, providing them with houses, farm implements, and other suitable necessaries which the Directors may consider they require for a fair start.[37]

Despite the optimism of its early years, the colonization company was later judged by Sweetman to have failed in its aim of assisting Irish immigrants to settle on the land in America, though some clusters of Catholic settlement did remain in the Minnesota countryside subsequent to the abandonment of the colonization scheme.[38]

The generally unsatisfactory results of these settlement schemes have done much to contribute to the deeply entrenched notion that the American Irish were unsuited to life on the land. The departure of men like William Geraghty, whose experience was cited at the beginning of this chapter, has seemed confirmation of long-standing tenets in the literature. However, given the strong Irish presence in Minnesota's earlier decades, and equally clear evidence of the Irish propensity for rural life in south-west New South Wales, the question arises as to why these later projects fared so poorly?

Three principal explanations for the impermanence of these later Irish settlers stand out. First, the colonization schemes tended to subvert the gradual processes by which the Irish had initially settled both rural regions discussed in this chapter. Staged movement, assisted by family and kin, was replaced by rapid transplantation to a new environment. The planning, skills, knowledge, and economic judgements which underpinned the arrival of early settlers were replaced by inexperience and reliance upon the judgements of others. The schemes encouraged the movement inland to many who were ill-prepared and ill-equipped for their new lives. Additionally, the schemes tended to depart from the successful pattern of Irish settlement which had evolved in both south-west New South Wales and Minnesota from mid-century. Whereas earlier Irish arrivals in both locations had tended to concentrate in distinctive local clusters, the new organized settlements were for the most part located in counties which lacked established Irish populations. Murray County, site of the Irish-American Colonization Company's Avoca settlement, had only one Irish settler in 1870; neighbouring Nobles County (site of the Adrian settlement) boasted no Irish settlers at all in 1870. In short, the schemes may have transplanted groups of Irish settlers, but they positioned them in locations their compatriots had previously tended to avoid.

Second, the settlement schemes encouraged the under-capitalized, or those unduly dependent on the capital of others, to move onto the land. The pastor of the Sweetman colony in Murray County, Rev. Martin Mahony, was a frequent correspondent to newspapers such as the *Boston Pilot*. While fulsome in his praise of Minnesota's climate (where winter consisted of only four or five cold snaps, and the winter weather was so pleasant that carpenters often worked out all day with the temperature-10–12°), Mahony's letters repeatedly emphasized that a man should bring at least $500 with him to fund his family's establishment on the land, preferably more.[39] However, in their enthusiasm to encourage expansion and provide salvation for destitute immigrants, the promoters of the schemes sometimes waived the requirement for a sound capital base, or bore the risk themselves – often with dire consequences to their own finances. Hence, where earlier Irish settlers on the land in both Australia and Minnesota moved onto the land only when they acquired sufficient capital, and then risked their own savings, in later Minnesota the stakes were much lower and the commitment to the land correspondingly reduced.

Finally, the schemes to settle Irish on the land occurred at a time when fundamental changes were occurring in the structures of both societies – where the Irish, like others in these New World societies, were increasingly part of an urban drift. By 1891 33 per cent of the Australian population were city-dwellers: no other society had massed its urban population in so few cities. While for many observers this was undesirable – an encouragement to an unhealthy lifestyle, crime, poor public health and detrimental to happiness – some observers took a rather different view. The American sociologist Adna Weber saw the pattern of development as a sign that Australia was 'the newest product of civilisation'; it was the model which the rest of the world would follow as industrialism became predominant.[40] David Doyle has argued that in the United States, too, the Irish were at the forefront of the urban movement.[41] For some immigrants this trend encouraged the abandonment of life on the land in favour of greater opportunities in America's cities. James Middleton, born in Ireland in 1833, arrived in the United States in the 1840s and took up land in Washington County, Minnesota. A diligent farmer and family man, Middleton was prominent in his local community before being elected to the state legislature in 1876. However, soon after he was on the move, taking up real estate sales in St Paul. Middleton's departure from the land was not a sign of a lack of farming ability – his diary testifies to his industriousness – but a sign of greater economic opportunities elsewhere, of pragmatic choices made in America's urban frontier. Just as Middleton seized the chance in St Paul, it is little wonder that later arrivals like William Geraghty forsook the opportunity for life on the land offered by the colonization company to try his luck in the state capital.[42]

Conclusion

This chapter set out to compare Irish settlement in two New World rural regions and, through the process of comparison, to evaluate the validity of American explanations for the failure of Irish immigrants to settle on the land. In the process, several points have become clear. First, on the basis of existing evidence, the Irish origin of the immigrants seems in itself an inadequate basis for explaining differential patterns of settlement across the regions, or for explaining variations in Irish performance in the United States. More surprising, perhaps, is the extent of similarity in aspects of Irish rural settlement in the two regions under review at mid-century. Successful Irish settlers in both locations seem to have followed similar strategies in their process of adaptation to life on the land, and the patterns of their local concentration seem also to bear resemblance. In both societies Irish settlers took advantage of the favourable economic opportunities that arose from their time of arrival in frontier communities and as a result of their pragmatic desire to acquire readily available land, they fared well in farming. By virtue of their strong presence in the regions they enjoyed generally harmonious and supportive relationships with their fellow settlers, a condition which made for stability and prosperity. The Irish in Minnesota and south-west New South Wales in the mid-nineteenth century were not worlds apart.

However, Minnesota's late nineteenth-century experience of group settlement schemes marked a significant departure from the earlier experiences of both regions. While these schemes certainly drew publicity for Minnesota as a point of destination for the Irish, their limited success tended to contribute to American perceptions of the Irish as a group ill-suited to the land. But, as this chapter has argued, the inadequacies and failures of those schemes should be explained in terms of their conceptualization, operation and timing, rather than by attributing responsibility to characteristics allegedly peculiar to the Irish. When viewed in such an international comparative context, the contrasts within Minnesota's experiences suggests the need for the abandonment of stereotypical assertions about what the Irish did not do (or could not do) on the land. To achieve a more balanced assessment, greater emphasis should be placed on the specific experiences of the rural Irish in different parts of the United States.

Appendix: Irish population per county, Minnesota, 1870

County	Total population	Total Irish-born	Irish-born in population (%)
Aitkin	178		0.00
Anoka	2,868	191	6.66
Becker	185	1	0.54
Beltrami	73		0.00
Benton	1,075	83	7.72
Big Stone	19		0.00
Blue Earth	12,148	523	4.31
Brown	3,311	83	2.51
Carlton	118	25	21.19
Carver	5,668	256	4.52
Cass	363	1	0.28
Chippewa	698		0.00
Chisago	2,164	106	4.90
Clay	49	1	2.04
Cottonwood	318	7	2.20
Crow King	166	4	2.41
Dakota	10,767	1,699	15.78
Dodge	6,515	153	2.35
Douglas	2,316	68	2.94
Faribault	7,422	191	2.57
Fillmore	15,178	969	6.38
Freeborn	6,518	391	6.00
Goodhue	12,164	506	4.16
Grant	148	1	0.68
Hennepin	21,338	1,896	8.89
Houston	8,176	1,053	12.88

County	Total population	Total Irish-born	Irish-born in population (%)
Isanti	865	14	1.62
Itasca	92	1	1.09
Jackson	1,192	20	1.68
Kanabec	85		0.00
Kandiyohi	668	35	5.24
Lac qui Parle	108	5	4.63
Lake	114		0.00
Le Sueur	7,710	930	12.06
Martin	3,340	86	2.57
McLeod	3,757	110	2.93
Meeker	3,737	326	8.72
Mille Lac	918	37	4.03
Monongalia	1,463	50	3.42
Morrison	1,113	48	4.31
Mower	7,238	416	5.75
Murray	185	1	0.54
Nicollet	4,281	249	5.82
Nobles	108	1	0.93
Olmstead	15,364	1,128	7.34
Otter Trail	888	3	0.34
Pembina	47		0.00
Pine	324	91	28.09
Pope	1,310	68	5.19
Ramsey	13,246	2,276	17.18
Redwood	1,147	32	2.79
Renville	1,808	146	8.08
Rice	11,349	1,167	10.28
Rock	120	5	4.17
Scott	6,625	969	14.63
Sherburne	1,524	72	4.72
Sibley	3,662	608	16.60
Stearns	8,989	238	2.65
Steele	6,088	310	5.09
Stevens	71		0.00
St Louis	1,708	408	23.89
Todd	1,499	22	1.47
Traverse	13		0.00
Wabashaw	11,321	965	8.52
Wadena	6		0.00
Waseca	5,380	619	11.51
Washington	6,440	602	9.35
Watonkan	1,424	59	4.14
Wilkin	103	11	10.68
Winona	15,168	983	6.48
Wright	6468	424	6.56

Adapted from: US Census Office, Ninth Census, 1870, pp. 419–20.

Notes

A version of this chapter appeared in *New Hibernia Review*, 2, 1 (Spring 1998). I am grateful to the editor for permisssion to reproduce material contained in that article. Research for this chapter was assisted by a grant from the Auckland University Research Committee. I am grateful to Dave Roediger and Jean Allman for their kind hospitality while I was in St Paul, and to Barry Reay who commented on a draft of this chapter.

1. Letter, William Geraghty to John Sweetman, 16 September 1882. Irish American Colonisation Company Papers, Minnesota Historical Society, 1500 Mississippi Street, St Paul Minnesota 55101 (hereafter MHS), BB2 I68, Box 1, F 4.
2. Robert Antrim to John Sweetman, 7 September 1882, Irish American Colonisation Company Papers, MHS, BB2 I68, Box 1, F 4.
3. Irish American Colonisation Company, Secretary's Fourth Annual Report, May 1883, Irish American Colonisation Company Papers, MHS, BB2 I68, Box 1, F 4, p. 3.
4. See generally Kerby Miller, *Emigrants and Exiles: Ireland and the Irish Exodus to North America* (New York, 1985) and the ambivalent approach in Lawrence McCaffrey, *Textures of Irish America* (Syracuse, 1992).
5. Donald Akenson, 'The Historiography of the Irish Americans', in *Being Had. Historians, The Evidence and the Irish in North America* (Port Credit, Ontario, 1985), pp. 37–75. For expression of these views see, for example, Oliver MacDonagh, 'The Irish Famine Emigration to the United States', *Perspectives in American History*, 10 (1976), p. 435; Lawrence McCaffrey, 'A Profile of Irish America', in David Doyle and Owen D. Edwards (eds), *America and Ireland 1776–1976. The American Identity and the Irish Connection* (Westport, Conn., 1980), p. 81. On the urban/rural issue, see David Doyle, 'The Irish as Urban Pioneers in the United States, 1850–70', *Journal of American Ethnic History*, 10, 1–2 (1990–91), pp. 36–59 and his 'The Remaking of Irish-America, 1845–80', in W. Vaughan (ed.), *A New History of Ireland, Vol. 6, Ireland Under the Union II 1870–1921* (Oxford, 1996), pp. 735–63.
6. US Census Bureau [J.D.B. DeBow], *Seventh Census 1850: Statistical View, Compendium* (Washington, D.C., 1854), pp. 116–18; Malcolm Campbell, *The Kingdom of the Ryans: The Irish in Southwest New South Wales 1816–90* (Sydney, 1997), ch. 3; on the pattern of Irish immigration to Australia generally see David Fitzpatrick, *Oceans of Consolation: Personal Accounts of Irish Migration to Australia* (Ithaca, N.Y., 1994), pp. 6–19.
7. For advocacy of comparison at this level see Nancy L. Green, 'The Comparative Method and Poststructural Structuralism: New Perspectives for Migration Studies', *Journal of American Ethnic History*, 13, 4 (1994), p. 13. See also Marc Bloch, 'A Contribution Towards a Comparative History of European Societies', in *Land and Work in Mediaeval Europe. Papers of Marc Bloch* (London, 1967), pp. 44–81. As Alan O'Day has pointed out, comparison in studies of the Irish diaspora remains a rarity: 'Revising the Diaspora', in D. George Boyce and Alan O'Day (eds), *The Making of Modern Irish History: Revisionism and the Revisionist Controversy* (London, 1996), p. 196. Examples include David Doyle, 'The Irish in the United States and Australia: Some Comparisons, 1800–1939', *Irish Economic and Social History*, 16 (1989), pp. 73–94; Donald Akenson, *Small Differences: Irish Catholics and Irish Protestants, 1815–1922. An International Perspective* (Kingston, Ontario, 1988); Malcolm Campbell, 'The Other Immigrants: Comparing the Irish in Australia and the United States', *Journal of American Ethnic*

History, 14, 3 (1995), pp. 3–22 and 'Irish Nationalism and Immigrant Assimilation: Comparing the United States and Australia', *Australasian Journal of American Studies*, 15, 2 (December 1996), pp. 24–43.

8. Ann Regan, 'The Irish', in June Drenning Holmquist (ed.), *They Chose Minnesota: A Survey of the State's Ethnic Groups* (St Paul, Minn., 1981), p. 132; Sarah P. Rubenstein, 'The British, English, Scots, Welsh and British Canadians', in Holmquist (ed.), *They Chose Minnesota*, p. 118.

9. David Fitzpatrick, *Irish Emigration, 1801–1921* (Dublin, 1984), pp. 9–13; *Oceans of Consolation*, 14–16; 'Emigration 1801–70', in W.E. Vaughan (ed.), *A New History of Ireland, Vol. 5, Ireland Under the Union 1801–70* (Oxford, 1989), pp. 562–622.

10. Michael Callaghan, St Paul, Minnesota, to his brother, 28 September 1852, Callaghan Papers, MHS, Manuscript A–C156.

11. Mary Jane Hill Anderson, *Autobiography of Mary Jane Hill Anderson, Wife of Robert Anderson, 1827–1934* (Minneapolis, Minn., 1934), pp. 3–17. Galena became an area of strong Irish concentration partly as a result of lead mining, from which some Irish accumulated capital and moved onto the land. See Mary Josephine Read, 'A Population Study of the Driftless Hill Land during the Pioneer Period, 1832–60', Ph.D. dissertation (University of Wisconsin, 1941); Grace McDonald, *History of the Irish in Wisconsin in the Nineteenth Century* (New York, 1976), ch. 2.

12. Sister Mary Gilbert Kelly, *Catholic Immigrant Colonisation Projects in the United States, 1815–60* (New York, 1939), pp. 198ff; Henry A. Castle, 'General James Shields', *Minnesota Historical Society Collections*, 15 (1915), pp. 711–30; 'Address by John Ireland at the Unveiling of a Statue of Shields', *Minnesota Historical Society Collections*, 15 (1915), pp. 731–40; William W. Folwell, *A History of Minnesota* (St Paul, Minn., 1961), Vol. 2, pp. 6–8; F. Curtiss-Wedge, *History of Rice and Le Sueur Counties, Minnesota* (Chicago, 1910), Vol. 1, pp. 169–70; Patricia Johnston, *Minnesota's Irish* (Afton, Minn., 1984), pp. 26ff.

13. See Dennis Clark, *Hibernia America. The Irish and Regional Cultures* (New York, 1986), p. 120; Kelly, *Catholic Immigrant Colonisation Projects*, p. 200.

14. Regan, 'The Irish', p. 132. Staged migration was also a feature of the profile of Irish rural settlers in neighbouring Wisconsin: see McDonald, *History of the Irish in Wisconsin*, p. 11.

15. Michael J. Boyle, Diary, Entry for 17 March 1876, Boyle Papers, MHS, P 1435.

16. William G. Gresham, *History of Nicollet and Le Sueur Counties Minnesota. Their Peoples, Industries and Institutions* (Indianapolis, 1916), pp. 407, 439, 528.

17. United States Census Office [Francis A. Walker], *A Compendium of the Ninth Census, 1870* (Washington, 1872), p. 420.

18. Regan, 'The Irish', pp. 132–3. On the strength of Minnesota as a centre of Irish farming see also Philip H. Bagenal, *The American Irish and Their Influence on Irish Politics* (Boston, 1882), pp. 75–6 where, after visiting Bishop John Ireland, the author notes 'in no other state is there relatively such a large number of Irish farmers as in Iowa and Minnesota'. Regan's analysis differs from that of David Doyle, 'The Irish as Urban Pioneers', table 4, p. 49 which shows 47.89 per cent of Minnesota's Irish-born population residing in counties he classifies as rural.

19. John Ireland, 'Fifty Years of Catholicity in the Northwest. Sermon Preached by Most Rev. John Ireland on the Fiftieth Anniversary of the Arrival of St Paul's First Bishop, 2 July 1901'. Irish American Colonisation Company Papers, MHS, BB2 168, Box 3, F 4. See also Annie King Lacore, 'Reminiscences', MHS P1337, p. 9.

20. Bagenal, *American Irish*, p. 79.

21. Ireland, 'Fifty Years of Catholicity', pp. 3ff.

22. A similar situation existed in neighbouring Wisconsin. See McDonald, *History of the Irish in Wisconsin*, p. 202.

23. See Campbell, *Kingdom of the Ryans*, ch. 2; James Waldersee, *Catholic Society in New South Wales 1788–1860* (Sydney, 1974); Patrick O'Farrell, *The Irish in Australia*, revised edition (Sydney, 1993), pp. 33–6.

24. David Waugh, *Three Years Practical Experience of a Settler in New South Wales* (Edinburgh, 1838), p. 25. An extract from a letter dated 30 October 1834.

25. William W. Burton, *The State of Religion and Education in New South Wales* (London, 1840), p. 278. Peter Cunningham, *Two Years in New South Wales* (London, 1827), Vol. 1, p. 109.

26. Fitzpatrick, *Oceans of Consolation*, pp. 15–16; on Irish localities in south-west New South Wales see Campbell, *Kingdom of the Ryans*, pp. 62–90, and Richard Reid, 'Aspects of Irish Assisted Emigration to New South Wales 1848–1870', Ph.D. thesis (Australian National University, 1992), especially chs 4–5.

27. Fitzpatrick, *Oceans of Consolation*, p. 16.

28. Colonial Secretary, Letters re Land, Entry for Edward Ryan, Archives Office of New South Wales. For an account of Ryan's life see Campbell, *Kingdom of the Ryans*. See also Patrick O'Farrell, *Vanished Kingdoms: Irish in Australia and New Zealand* (Sydney, 1990), ch. 1.

29. Gormly's experience, and those of others, are discussed in Campbell, *Kingdom of the Ryans*, pp. 80–2. See also David Fitzpatrick's commentary on the Fife family letters: *Oceans of Consolation*, pp. 426ff.

30. Thomas and Anne Quilty to Ellen Quilty, Shanagolden, County Limerick, 15 October 1850, Monteagle Papers. See also Reid, 'Irish Assisted Emigration', ch. 5; Errol Lea-Scarlett, *Queanbeyan District and People* (Queanbeyan, NSW, 1968), p. 230; see also Gwendoline Wilson, *Murray of Yarralumla* (Melbourne, 1968).

31. Campbell, *Kingdom of the Ryans*, ch. 6.

32. On Irish persistence on the land, see the analysis of Irish occupational distribution in Kieren D. Flanagan, 'Emigration, Assimilation and Occupational Categories of Irish Americans in Minnesota', M.A. thesis (University of Minnesota, 1969), table 18, pp. 226–7.

33. Samuel Shumack, *An Autobiography or Tales and Legends of the Canberra Pioneers* (Canberra, 1977), p. 45.

34. Thomas D'Arcy McGee, *A History of Irish Settlers in North America from the Earliest Period to the Census of 1850*, 2nd edition (Boston, 1852), pp. 179–86; Bagenal, *American Irish*, chs 7–8. Australia had its own attempts at group settlement, the best known of which was initiated by Bishop James Quinn in the northern state of Queensland. See Patrick O'Farrell, *The Catholic Church and Community: An Australian History* (Sydney, 1985), pp. 129–36; Fitzpatrick, 'Irish Emigration 1801–70', p. 599. I intend to examine further this scheme in future work.

35. Lacore, 'Reminiscences', p. 3.

36. James P. Shannon, 'Bishop Ireland's Connemara Experiment', *Minnesota History*, 35 (5 March 1957), p. 208 quoting William Onahan. The literature on John Ireland's settlement schemes is extensive: see Shannon, *Catholic Colonisation on the Western Frontier* (New York, 1976); Marvin O'Connell, *John Ireland and the American Catholic Church* (St Paul, Minn., 1988), especially ch. 7; Bagenal, *American Irish*, ch. 7; Howard Egan, 'Irish Immigration to Minnesota', *Mid-America*, 12 (1930), pp. 133–66.

37. Prospectus of the Irish-American Colonisation Company Ltd, Irish American Colonisation Company Papers, MHS, BB2 I68, Box 1, F 3.
38. John Sweetman, 'The Sweetman Catholic Colony of Currie, Minnesota: A Memoir', *Acta et Dicta*, 1, 3 (1911), pp. 41–65. The scheme is also discussed in Alice E. Smith, 'The Sweetman Irish Colony', *Minnesota History*, 9 (1928), pp. 331–46. Sweetman outlined some details of the operation of his scheme: Sweetman, *Recent Experiences in the Emigration of Irish Families* (Dublin, 1883).
39. Martin Mahony, *Sweetman Catholic Colony in Murray County, Minnesota: Letters from the Pastor and Others* (Currie, Minn., 1885), pp. 5, 11.
40. Adna Weber, *The Growth of Cities in the Nineteenth Century: A Study in Statistics* (Ithaca, N.Y., 1967), pp. 1, 138–50.
41. Doyle, 'Irish as Urban Pioneers', *passim*.
42. James Middleton Papers, MHS P1070. On farming activities, see his diary, especially Vol. 1, 1869.

CHAPTER 10

Irish Emigration to Argentina: A Different Model

PATRICK MCKENNA

(Local historian, Co. Maynooth)

Introduction

Irish emigration to Argentina is one of the better places for a student to begin Irish migration studies, for a number of reasons. The numbers who emigrated there from Ireland are very small in the overall context of Irish emigration; this allows the researcher a broad view of the emigration while still maintaining contact with individual emigrant experiences. The migration is comparatively well documented; this affords the student a comprehensive set of records to work from and due to the relatively small numbers the records are of manageable size. Finally, the period of Irish emigration to Argentina covers the entire span of New World settlement and consequently picks up the waves of Irish emigration between 1500 and the start of the First World War, whereas Irish emigration to the English-speaking New World only began towards the end of the eighteenth century.

The first Irish to set foot on Argentine soil were two cabin boys from Galway, William and John ———. They sailed with Magellan on his voyage to circumnavigate the world in 1520.[1] The first recorded Irish to settle in Argentina were members of an expedition to conquer and claim the Rio de la Plata for Spain. Led by Pedro Mendoza, they sailed from Cadiz, arriving in the River Plate in February 1536.[2] Among those first emigrants were two brothers called John and Thomas Farel,[3] natives of San Lucas de Barrameda, Spain.[4] Other Irish names which appeared in Magellan's expedition were Colman,[5] Lucas,[6] Galvan[7] (a very common Argentine name)[8] and Martin.[9] The name 'Martin' occurs frequently throughout Europe as well as Ireland and Spain and it is therefore impossible to be certain which, if any, Martins were Irish. Other Irish names appear among sixteenth-century conquerors, such as Juan Fays (probably Hays) and also the first Irish woman, Isabel Farrel (possibly a relative of John and Thomas Farel), the wife of a Captain Hernando de Sosa, a colonist in Corrientes.[10] A point to note here is that assuming that Isabel is related to John and Thomas Farel, in addition to travelling under her husband's protection she also had the protection of male relatives, possibly her brothers. This point will be developed further later when looking at female emigration to

Argentina in the nineteenth century. Mendoza's expedition brought with them cattle, sheep, horses and pigs. These must have been among the first of these species to reach the American continent. The animals thrived in the Pampas and became part of the foundation stock of the 'native' Argentine horses, cattle and sheep.

A small group (which included at least one of the Farels together with Isabel Farrel and her husband) began exploring the river systems feeding the River Plate. The following year, in 1537, they founded the settlement of Asuncion de Paraguay on the east bank of the Parana river about 2000 km north of Buenos Aires. The Farels decided to stay in that region and in 1588 Rafeal Farel, a son, exercised his right as one of the original settlers to acquire 'lands and Indians' near Asuncion in Corrientes Province[11] just one year after the province was founded.[12]

During the next 400 years Irish emigration to Argentina continues to fit comfortably into the broad parameters of the Irish emigration taking place throughout that period. The anti-Catholic laws in force in Ireland during much of that time denied Catholics of good families an education or career opportunities in the civil and military administration at home until Catholic Emancipation was enacted in 1829. Because of Ireland's good relationship with Catholic Europe throughout the period prior to 1829, young Irish men went there to be educated and many remained to follow a career in the military and public service of those countries. Some rose to very high positions in the armies and civil administrations throughout Catholic Europe.[13] Spain and France were the preferred destinations for those elite emigrants.[14] Some of the elite emigrants, or their European-born children, re-emigrated to the New World colonies in the service of their adopted land. Because Argentina (the land of Silver) did not possess the precious metals the early conquerors believed it contained, it was largely forgotten by the Spanish until the New Enlightenment. Consequently little or no recorded Irish emigration appears to have taken place to Argentina between Mendoza's expedition and the ascent of the Bourbons to the Spanish throne in the eighteenth century.

Eighteenth-century Irish immigration

The creation of the Viceroyalty of the Rio de la Plata, which was the result of the reforms known as 'The New Enlightenment' introduced by Charles III in 1776, necessitated a surge of emigration from Spain, of civil and military personnel to govern the new Viceroyalty. A number of those officials were born in Ireland. Michael O'Gorman, for example, was born in Ennis in 1749, educated in France, and completed his studies in Spain where he graduated in medicine.[15] He left Spain for Buenos Aires in 1777, travelling under a Royal Order placing him in charge of the Sanitary Commission. He later founded the faculty of medicine in Buenos Aires and remained professor of medicine there until his death. Another Irishman to arrive in Argentina under the Spanish flag towards the end of the eighteenth century was Thomand O'Brien from Wicklow, who held the rank of Captain, later rising to the rank of General in the army of the new republic.

The New Enlightenment

Under the 'New Enlightenment' commercial agricultural production became the measure used to determine a nation's economic wealth. This change greatly added to the value of the herds of cattle and horses roaming the pampas. It is not surprising therefore that merchants began arriving in the port soon afterwards to get ownership of, and to trade in, these suddenly valuable resources. In addition to the civil and military administration, Irish names were appearing among the most powerful merchants and landowners around Buenos Aires port at that time. The Lynchs, O'Gormans, Dogans, Cullens,[16] O'Ryans and Butlers were all established *portenos*[17] at the beginning of the nineteenth century.[18] Incidentally the 'O'Gormon' who arrived in Buenos Aires about 1792 was Thomas O'Gorman, a brother of the Portomedico Patrick O'Gormon. Thomas was an officer in the French army serving in the French colony of Mauritius prior to becoming an influential Buenos Aires merchant. This illustrates the ability, even then, of Irish emigrants to use family connections on a global basis to maximize their economic opportunities.

These merchants soon married into the important local Creole families and some even became members of the town council (*cabildo*). It was the function of the *cabildo* to allocate ownership of the various herds of wild horses and cattle roaming the pampas within the jurisdiction of the *cabildo*. This group needed labourers and shepherds to develop their *estancias* (cattle farms) and slaughterhouses to European standards. The slaughterhouses were required to process cattle, which up until then had been slaughtered on the plain solely for their hides; the rest of the carcass was abandoned to rot where it lay. This necessitated the importation of labour skilled in up-to-date methods of butchering and preserving meat, as well as unskilled labourers, to work in the slaughterhouses.

Possibly because of the large Irish trade in beef and leather between Galway and Spain, the new Viceroyalty looked to Ireland for the technology and skill to complement the 22,500 African and Brazilian slaves brought in to provide the unskilled element of the labour force. One hundred Irish skilled workers, comprising salters, butchers and tanners, were brought to Buenos Aires in 1785 and more were recruited over the next 20 years.[19] The new skills introduced by these Irish tradesmen laid the foundation of the Argentine beef industry.[20] Very little is known, as yet, of those Irish immigrants or their origins. They appear to have been unmarried and being Catholic they assimilated immediately into the local community of co-religionists.

By the mid-1790s the success of the new industries growing up around Buenos Aires led to the development of a considerable trade with Europe via independently owned merchant ships (free traders).

The Free Traders were merchants trading from neutral ports who were allowed to trade in the port of Buenos Aires. The Free Traders who quickly replaced the merchants as the main traders in the port were typically of a lower social class than the merchants. They were very often shipmasters turned owners. John Dillon from Dublin is one such example. Arriving with his family in

Montevideo, he set about making his fortune by importing goods legally into Montevideo and then smuggling them across the river to Buenos Aires in a fleet of small river boats which he soon acquired. Within a few years Dillon became established as one of the leading Irish merchant families in Buenos Aires. There he expanded his business to include meat-processing and started the first brewery in the country.

In the city, guilds were forming and a substantial artisan class was growing up around the port. Influential elements in Spain soon came to suffer from the increased competition created by this new production and the increase in trade by outside shipping. These elements hoped to restore the old Spanish monopolies and avoid the competition from this new and vigorous colony. They realized that by allowing 'Free Traders' to operate in Buenos Aires they would quickly undermine the growing strength of the local established elites.

Faced with such stiff competition in the port from the Free Traders, those *portena* merchants who could turned their attention to developing their *estancias* into commercial enterprises which were better fitted to the new opportunities of the nineteenth century: beef and wool production. Patricio Lynch was a substantial landholder by 1810 and Patrick Cullen from the Canary Islands was granted lands in Santa Fe to the north of Buenos Aires.

The origins of sheep farming

While these *portena* merchants and the Creoles were willing to improve their cattle herds, they were unwilling to go into wool production. Sheep farming was a low status enterprise associated with the gaucho class. As there was an almost unlimited supply of fertile land beyond the *estancias* which was still inhabited by hostile native tribes, the *estancieros* welcomed settlement in those areas by immigrants. Sheep farmers, therefore, could provide a buffer between the indigenous population and the Creole-owned *estancias* as well as supplying those goods which the *estancieros* were unwilling to become directly involved in themselves. In fact the *estancieros* promoted such settlement to the extent that they were willing to finance the stock purchase necessary to graze the new 'camps'[21] while allowing the settler to earn equity in the stock by contributing his labour.

The system they operated was as follows. An *estanciero* would provide a flock of about two thousand sheep, while the immigrant was responsible for looking after the sheep, including the provision of grazing. At the end of the contract the shepherd and the owner would divide the flock, the owner getting back his 2,000 sheep plus the agreed percentage of the increase (usually 50 per cent) as well as his share of the price for the wool clip for the contract period. The typical length of contract, in the beginning, was about four or five years, by which time the flock, under good management, would have grown to 10,000 in number. The shepherd would then own up to 4,000 sheep. He would then divide his flock into, for example, two flocks of 2,000 and hire shepherds on a similar type of contract to that he had worked.[22] In this way one migrant brought out first his brothers and later his cousins and neighbours, and so a highly regional specific chain migration began.

The merchants and the members of the *cabildo* of Buenos Aires knew the calibre of the Irish immigrants not only from the butchers, salters and tanners they recruited and from the odd merchant sailor left behind in the port, but also because of direct British military contact with that part of the world. On 2 November 1762 a Captain John McNamara sailed up the River Plate and attacked Colonia del Sacramento across the river from Buenos Aires in what is now Uruguay. All but 60 of this expedition perished in the battle. The survivors waded ashore and some at least were exiled 800 km into the interior to Cordoba. The most important military contact, however, was the British invasion of 1806–7. This involved a number of Irish regiments, many of whose members came from around the military barracks of Mullingar and Athlone. A number of these soldiers either deserted or were captured by the defenders of Buenos Aires. Some of these ex-soldiers who remained in Buenos Aires, according to local tradition, settled in the city among the free Negroes in the area of San Telmo along the river bank.[23] Those soldiers are believed to have worked deepening the port and using the stone which came in the ships as ballast for building along the docks. Others opted to work on the Creole *estancias* around the city and appeared to have played an important role in bringing out more members of their families from Ireland, thus establishing emigration to Buenos Aires as an option for those from around Mullingar and Athlone at least. An example of this is Thomas Murray from Streamstown, County Westmeath.[24] Thomas remained following the 1806–7 invasion and obtained work on a local Creole *estancia*. His knowledge of 'modern' farming soon ensured his rise to manager or 'mayordomo' of the *estancia*. Such was his service to the family in maintaining their estates for them when they had to flee the country during the Rosas dictatorship that when the family returned the *estanciero* purchased a large *estancia* for the Murray family in Santa Fe, just north of Buenos Aires Province. The Murrays are still one of the principal landowning families in southern Santa Fe today.

Following the failed British invasion and Spain's feeble attempt to defend the colony, Argentines realized that independence was theirs for the taking. Thomand O'Brien from Wicklow fought the Spanish on land while at sea William Brown from Foxford in Mayo who founded the Argentine navy saved the fledgling republic on more than one occasion. O'Brien on land and Brown at sea were aided by a number of the Irish troops left behind after the 1806–7 invasions. The important contribution of the Irish to Argentine independence, particularly as there is no record of them ever looking for personal gain in land or high office for their services afterwards, resulted in a great respect as well as admiration and affection for Irishmen among all levels of Argentine society. This patriotism to their adopted country contributed greatly to the acceptability of the Irish as immigrants throughout the nineteenth century.[25] Another important reason why Irish immigrants were in such demand was because following independence in 1810 Spain tried to blockade Buenos Aires and forbade Spanish emigration to there. The effect of this was to deny the new Argentine state Basque immigrants, the other major ethnic group believed by them to be capable of independent sheep farming. Scottish immigrants were also in demand but came out in much smaller numbers and tended to bring out capital with them and therefore were independent from the start.[26] The Irish had to sell their labour for a period in order to build up capital. While both groups played a similar role in land settlement and sheep production, the Irish also provided labour to the *estancieros* and to the meat-processing plants to a far greater degree than the Scots and in that role were more valuable as well as being more numerous.

Following Argentine independence there was renewed interest in Buenos Aires by the British. A further wave of British merchants and capital arrived in the port. Among those arriving then were two brothers from Athlone, John and Thomas Armstrong, along with the banker Patrick Browne from Wexford and Peter Sheridan from Cavan. Browne represented the Liverpool bank of Dixon and Montgomery while the Armstrongs worked for the local merchant house of Armstrong & Co. Despite all of this interest in Buenos Aires it was obvious that the lack of a suitable labour force was the single greatest impediment to the success of all of them. Labourers willing to settle the land, produce sheep and wool, and provide the labour to process these products in the slaughterhouses were essential for the economic success of the region. European immigration of necessity became a priority for all concerned, the government as well as the merchants and *portenos*. Already familiar with the ex-soldiers together with the butchers and tanners brought out at the end of the eighteenth century, the merchants and *estancieros* were very anxious to recruit labour of similar calibre and were therefore eager to employ immigrants, especially Catholics, from an already proven source.

The Irish emigrants in the government and merchant classes appear to have formed a coalition to promote Irish immigration and designed a very specific settlement model for the Irish immigrants. The groups within the coalition were made up of the Irish elite, the portenos and the 'English' merchants such as Peter Sheridan from Cavan and Patrick Browne from Wexford who were Catholic and Thomas and John Armstrong, sons of a British army colonel from Athlone, who were Protestant.

In addition to Europe the US was also becoming interested in the potential of Argentina as a source of raw material at that time. The US Congress went so far as to commission a report on the opportunities for the US in Argentina at that time.[27] The publication of this report in the US persuaded a number of Irish to emigrate from there to Buenos Aires city during the 1820s and commence business as cobblers, coach builders, coopers, tailors and hoteliers. These individuals, who became known as the Yankee Irish, appear to have come from all parts of Ireland and do not appear to have been responsible for the rural emigration from Ireland.[28] They were, however, part of the general artisan class in Buenos Aires city then and they appear to have become just as successful as anyone else. The reason why the Irish did not continue to urbanize in Buenos Aires lies in what appears to have been a deliberate policy by the Irish elite and the Catholic Church to prevent Irish urbanization.

Pre-selection of Irish immigrants

By the mid-1820s the economic production in Buenos Aires was becoming seriously restricted by the shortage of suitable labour. In order to meet some of this demand the Irish elites in Argentina sent General Thomand O'Brien back to Ireland in 1828 to select only the type of emigrant that would suit their purposes. He made it a condition that the immigrants would be accompanied by their own chaplain and physician to be 'solely at their disposition and for their use'.[29] Part of O'Brien's remit was to recruit only 'moral and industrious' emigrants.[30] A local committee appears to have been formed among the Irish interests in Buenos Aires to promote Irish immigration to there at that time.

The visits by O'Brien and Armstrong were followed up by letters from prominent members of the Irish community to the Archbishop of Dublin with the object of influencing him to put the Irish church behind emigration to Argentina rather than to the United States. Dr Oughagan[31] wrote to the archbishop on 28 June 1828[32] that 'North America is not a country proper for Irish settlers – These, their identity, their ancient faith, and the peculiar cast of their national character, in the mixture of many nations, is totally confounded and lost for ever.' In promoting Argentina he wrote, 'Thanks to Providence a very different destiny awaits them here'. Dr Oughagan went on to state that 'this country, fertile and vast beyond limits, . . . will welcome [the Irish] with special preference and instead of being the *drudges* for the rest of mankind, may set themselves down in societies in various parts of these boundless plains . . . '. In a further letter to the archbishop dated 22 February 1829,[33] the Irish chaplain Fr. Moran wrote from Buenos Aires, 'This My Lord is the country for the Irish farmer to emigrate to. The most productive soil in the world, the best horses & oxen. And a people, who will show themselves more friendly to Irishmen than to any other nation. They are partial to us.' From the beginning, the Irish groups in Argentina were intent on encouraging the formation of an Irish rural community based on livestock farming. There was no mention whatever of the quite prosperous Irish artisan community in the city. The fact that there was a need for an urban labour force, at least equal to the need for a rural one, to man the new industries springing up or the opportunities that existed for tradesmen and small merchants in the city appear to have been ignored by the sponsors of Irish immigration. From the beginning the Irish were encouraged to form rural communities well away from the city, where with the aid of the Irish chaplaincy they remained a little piece of Ireland in the New World for over a century.

Recruiting working-class Irish labour

The fact that the Irish elites appear to have been deliberately ignoring the needs of the British merchants to recruit immigrants who would be willing to remain permanently in the city as labourers may well have been why Thomas Armstrong decided to return to Ireland at the same time as O'Brien. The only region in Ireland to supply truly working-class emigrants to Argentina to meet that demand in significant numbers was the Ballymahon–Ballymore–Mullingar area which straddles the Westmeath–Longford border. The Armstrong family were the local landlords and were (and still are) highly respected in that locality.

Farmer's sons, such as Nicholas Cunningham, emigrated to Argentina from that area also, but the majority appear to have been from a labouring background. As early as 1842 Brabazon[34] records in his journal that many of the emigrants from the Ballymore area were of a different type from the rest of the emigrant community when he wrote that some of the Westmeath and Longford people were 'respectable' and that 'the Wexford people were all respectable people' but 'Ballymore people were such divils as ever filled the Jail of Mullingar'.

Emigrant numbers

There is no definitive record of the total number of Irish who emigrated to Argentina. A reasonable estimate based on current information is that around 40,000 to 45,000 Irish emigrated there during the nineteenth century.[35] Of this number a reasonable estimate for Irish emigration between 1800 and 1861 would be somewhere in the region of 12,000 to 18,000.[36] The great bulk of those would have emigrated after about 1835.

Earliest estimates of the size of Irish population resident in Buenos Aires in 1824 is 'a little less than 500'. This figure was stated by the British Consul, Woodbine Parish, and was based on his own reckoning of the British population living in the River Plate in that year.[37] In 1832 the Irish Chaplaincy estimated that the Irish community had grown to about 1,500.[38] This figure may include the emigrants' Argentine-born children. McCann estimates a figure of 3,500 Irish in the country 'prior to the Anglo-French intervention' in 1842.[39] By 1853 the total 'Irish' colony in Buenos Aires was estimated by Fr. Fahy in a letter to Archbishop Murray of Dublin as being 30,000.[40] As this figure did include the Argentine-born children of the emigrants, the actual number of Irish emigrants would have grown to about 10,000 by 1853. This may be an overestimate by Fr. Fahy, to increase pressure on the Archbishop of Dublin to provide extra priests for the Irish community.

The general consensus is that the Irish community, including Argentine-born children, had grown to 30,000 during the period, depending on the sources, at some point between 1853 and 1861.[41] The total Irish community in the country was to remain near this level for most of the rest of the century. Out-migration of Irish, principally to the United States, roughly balanced in-migration, from Ireland, certainly from 1869.[42] Of the 40,000 or so Irish who emigrated to Argentina, about 4,000 were to form the nucleus of the present Hiberno-Argentine community.[43] The rest left no permanent trace of ever having been in Argentina. Some would have assimilated into the wider immigrant community and lost all contact with their Irish compatriots. Others would have out-migrated again, some returning to Ireland after a few years in the Argentine.[44] Others, probably the great majority, would have re-emigrated to the United States, Canada and Australia.[45]

The role of the Irish Church in the community

By the late 1830s the Irish had spread across the camp. Some were already becoming financially successful and, like the butchers, tanners and soldiers before them, were assimilating into the local community, especially around Chascomus, the first region settled by the Irish. It was essential, therefore, if the Irish immigrants were to be kept a separate ethnic group, that the plans for creating a distinctly Irish community were implemented quickly. Realizing the danger, Archbishop Murray of Dublin approached his friend the Bishop of Ossary to persuade the Dominican Prior of Black Abbey in Kilkenny, Fr. Anthony Fahy, to go to Argentina and take on the work of forming a community that reflected the values espoused by those interested in promoting Irish immigration. Fr. Fahy, having previously had experience of Irish communities in both urban and rural (largely Protestant) Ohio in the USA, held identical views to both Archbishop Murray and the Irish elites in Argentina as to the desirability of keeping Irish immigrants both rural and separate as the only means of preserving their 'true' Catholic Irish identity.

Upon arriving in Argentina Fr. Fahy moved into the home of a family friend from Ireland, Thomas Armstrong. He lived rent-free in his own apartment in Armstrong's home for the rest of his life, the two remaining inseparable, lifelong friends. Armstrong had assimilated into the Creole community in typically Irish merchant fashion. He married Justa Villanueva, the daughter of the Alcalde (chief officer under Spanish rule) of Buenos Aires of 1807. Being such a powerful business figure and because of his wife's connections, Thomas Armstrong was also a very influential if unseen force in the political life of the country. He was the business counsellor and close friend of 'almost every Argentine governmental administration from the Directorship of Rodriguez to the Presidency of Avellaneda',[46] acting as 'honest broker' (*amigable componedor*) between the British and Argentine governments in their commercial affairs for over 40 years.[47] Given that Argentina was dependent on British capital, which was antipathetic to the Catholic Church, it was a master stroke of Fr. Fahy and the good fortune of the Irish community that he was able to recruit to his cause an Irish Protestant merchant, who so well understood the Irish Catholic culture and who was in such sympathy with it.

Upon his arrival Fr. Fahy immediately set about organizing the Irish community to conform to the model already agreed. From that point until their deaths in the early 1870s they were the undisputed leaders of the Irish community and were in every way the human centre of the Irish settlement model. They were the ones who developed the social and religious structure that would not impede in any way the complete economic integration of the Irish into the wider economy while building a separate and very distinct ethnic Irish community in the country. Fr. Fahy maintained contact with the Irish while Thomas Armstrong remained in the background from the immigrant's perspective; he dealt with the merchant community and the government.

The Irish settlement model

The most effective way to explain the Irish settlement model as implemented by Fr. Fahy and Thomas Armstrong is to illustrate how they as individuals came to control and organize the Irish community between 1843 and 1870. Fr. Fahy began his work by creating a separate church organization for his scattered congregation. He made the Irish priests visibly different from Argentine priests by wearing civilian clothes instead of clerical garb, citing the unsuitability of clerical dress for the huge distances he had to travel to minister to his congregation. He was seen as the English priest, 'Padre Ingleses', there solely to serve the Irish immigrant community. Yet the cornerstone of their success was due to his, and Thomas Armstrong's, ability to understand and mesh the cultures of the Argentines and the Irish for the benefit of the Irish and business communities. The most important example of this ability to blend Irish and local custom when building their settlement model was the land and capital ownership structure which they developed.

The background to the settlement plan

Because of the huge distances involved in travelling, it could take often two or three weeks journeying through open country without roads or bridges to make a round trip to Buenos Aires. During this time a traveller's family and property were without his protection. This isolation meant the majority of the Irish were only able to travel to the city, possibly, once every one or two years. Fr. Fahy soon became their agent, conducting business in the city on their behalf, following one of his twice yearly visits to all of the emigrants. Because he was trusted as a priest, and for convenience, the Irish allowed him to transact their business in the city in his own name. Having the immigrant's business transacted as though it were Fr. Fahy's had several advantages for both the individual immigrant as well as the wider Irish community. There was always a tradition (though never a law) in Argentina that the Church, and by extension the priest, was never taxed on property transactions done on his own behalf. This tax was quite large, as the only means the government had to raise revenue was import, export and stamp duties on all written contracts. Tax was due by both sides to a contract, i.e. both buyer and seller. If the buyer or seller was Fr. Fahy, such taxes on his side were avoided.

Apart from the considerable savings made by an immigrant not paying tax, this also ensured that his estate after his death was passed on to his heirs quickly, untaxed and without legal fees. In addition, because Fr. Fahy 'owned' the immigrant's property the immigrant could not be easily cheated out of it by unscrupulous conmen or by gambling etc., of which there was plenty in the camp at that time. Under all of those conditions it was perfectly logical for an immigrant, who was himself poorly educated and unsure of the customs in a strange country, to entrust all his financial and legal affairs to the one man best equipped to deal with that side of his business, especially as there is no record of Fr. Fahy ever charging for this service. That left the immigrant free to concentrate on the side of the business he knew best, finding good pastures and raising his sheep while at the same time avoiding all the costs, in time and aggravation as well as cash, normally incurred when transacting business at that time in Argentina.

The benefits of common ownership to the individual

The practice of the great majority of immigrants holding all of their assets in common, in Fr. Fahy's name, had advantages for the whole Irish community. He was considered by the merchants and those in the city to be the wealthiest man, by far, in Argentina. The emigrants soon came to believe this also. Therefore when land or sheep came to be bought and sold among the Irish, the price was fixed between the emigrants themselves, and as they all banked with Fr. Fahy, he was informed of the position during his next visit to that part of the country. Cash rarely changed hands. If an emigrant did not have the cash to close the transaction, he 'borrowed' the difference from Fr. Fahy and agreed the repayments with him. The seller left the cash with Fr. Fahy certain that it was secure. All of this capital (plus the cash from the sale of sheep and wool to the merchants, by the Irish) was held in the Banco Provincia, Thomas Armstrong's bank. Armstrong therefore had a growing surplus available for investment in expanding the industries which were required to process the rapidly expanding Irish production. The effect of this tax-free and fee-free status was that the Irish had a considerable economic advantage over all other communities in the country when it came to acquiring and holding property. As this was an unintended benefit from the point of view of the Argentine government, it was a remarkable achievement for Fr. Fahy that he was able to carry it off for almost 30 years, ending it only when forced to by the newly established Irish families.

The Irish communication network

Fr. Fahy's immense local knowledge of the Irish community also ensured that the Church was the medium of all communication affecting the Irish throughout the province. With his constant travelling through the countryside he became aware almost immediately of the quality and potential of new areas of land as they were opened up. He was thus able to direct his congregation to suitable new fertile areas where they could quickly expand their business, more often than not providing the 'loans' to finance this expansion. He knew who was looking for labourers, so when the next boat of emigrants arrived he was able to direct them immediately to jobs in the country. By doing this he was removing the temptations of city life from the new immigrant's experience as well as earning their gratitude for finding them work and the gratitude of the employers for finding them labour. This had the double effect of strengthening the rural communities and preventing the growth of a viable Irish community in the city. By such efforts on their behalf Fr. Fahy soon gained the complete confidence of the Irish community throughout the province in all matters affecting their lives both spiritual and temporal.

The expansion of The Irish Church

As the Irish community grew and spread over an ever greater area, more priests were required to minister to them. The education of twelve priests was paid for by the Irish community, to the Archbishop of Dublin, who oversaw their education in All Hallows in Dublin. Fr. Fahy was insistent that they were especially well-educated and paid extra to All Hallows for this.

The first task of each new Irish community was to build a local church. The existing Argentine churches were never used by the Irish community except on very rare occasions such as weddings or funerals of important Irish immigrants. They continued to hear the 'Irish Mass' on a centrally located (usually) Irish *estancia* until they had the funds to build their own church. The church building also contained a library stocked with books in English. Local Irish newspapers such as the *Wexford People* and the *Westmeath Examiner* were also subscribed to by the libraries. Each little Irish church therefore became the local 'social centre' for emigrants for a 50 or 60 km radius, where they would meet to hear Mass, read the local papers from Ireland, play cards, pass around letters from home and from their brothers and sisters in the UK, the United States and Australia or Canada and discuss current happenings with their neighbours, and write letters in reply knowing the priest would ensure their postage. The libraries closed the circle within the overall model to the extent that the Irish community in rural areas of Buenos Aires province were an enclave, isolated by language from the wider community and insulated as much as possible from the real world of Argentina by the very structure of their society. They were able to continue to speak English, socialize exclusively among themselves, and with the libraries supplying local Irish papers remain psychologically back in Ireland.

The Irish community in Argentina by virtue of reading Irish newspapers and family letters was almost certainly better informed about conditions in the English-speaking world of Ireland, England, the US, Canada and Australia than they were about conditions in much of their adopted land. Provided there was a reasonable sex balance and the community remained fairly concentrated in particular districts, there was no incentive whatever to assimilate into the wider community. Consequently it is not surprising that if an emigrant wished to relocate he chose an Irish community outside Argentina rather than face the challenge of striking out alone in a country he really knew very little about.

In addition to the Church-run libraries which catered for the intellectual needs of the Irish immigrants, there was a complete welfare system run by Irish Mercy Nuns, but under Fr. Fahy's all-seeing eye, to take care of members unable to look after themselves, such as widows and orphans, together with an education system which was the model for other emigrant communities. Because Fr. Fahy was banker to the Irish community he knew exactly how much each member of the community could afford to contribute to those charities. And the emigrant was in a very weak position to refuse, considering his respect for, and his personal obligations to, Fr. Fahy.[48]

Thomas Armstrong's role

The fact that Thomas Armstrong was banker to Fr. Fahy enabled him to become one of the leading business figures in Buenos Aires. He was a co-founder of the Buenos Aires Stock Exchange and a director of the Banco Provincia, which he made, in effect, the central bank of Argentina.[49] He was also the director and substantial investor in the major railway company and served on the boards of most of the major stock companies in the city. His connections with the Creole community were also beyond reproach.

When one looks at who benefited most from the settlement model operated by the Irish in Argentina one sees that a very high proportion of Irish shepherds, who arrived during Fr. Fahy's and Thomas Armstrong's time, became *estancieros*. By about 1880 the Southern Cross estimated that the Irish owned abut 1.5 millon acres of land and about 5 million sheep. Some 20 million sheep were owned by the 28,000 Irish, comprising 5,000 families, at the end of the decade.[50] They were without doubt the most financially successful group of Irish emigrants in the world at that time, and certainly the most successful ethnic group, by a wide margin, in Argentina. Thomas Armstrong became one of the most influential men in Argentina and made a huge personal fortune for himself, as did a great number of his merchant colleagues, and Fr. Fahy built an Irish Church and an Irish community modelled on the values of nineteenth-century Gaelic Catholic Ireland which is still functioning in Argentina over a century after his death.

This system worked perfectly until the late 1860s when Fr. Fahy's advancing years and failing health meant that he was no longer able to pursue the overall welfare of the immigrants with the same energy as he had previously. He, or Thomas Armstrong, never groomed a successor to take over from them when they were no longer able to look after the community.

After his death in 1871 there was no one of stature in the community to take over from him, though many fought each other for the opportunity. Prior to his death he had handed over clear title to the assets he had held in trust to the owners. Thomas Armstrong made up the undisclosed shortfall out of his own funds. Thomas Armstrong was dead within three years.

Those two deaths ended an era in Irish emigration to Argentina. The capital previously held in common was now held individually. Each *estanciero* made his own arrangements with individual merchants. A new emigrant had no Fr. Fahy to turn to, to borrow the funds to purchase land. If he had the money he had to cope with the local bureaucracy and pay his taxes, like everyone else. He no longer had the advice, based on the knowledge of the entire community, on where to settle or purchase land. In short the old settlement model which was so hugely successful was being quietly abandoned, and was being replaced by a version of the English model, in that individual effort alone from that point on was the arbiter of success. However, the new immigrant was not given the means to establish himself as he would have had he been in a true British colony.

The Irish community changed radically after the deaths of those two men. Though Fr. Fahy is still revered almost as a saint by the Irish in Argentina today, the Protestant Thomas Armstrong has been written out of the Irish settlement history. The expansion of the Irish community ceased with their deaths. Rather than building on their success and continuing their work of settling the Argentine Pampas with prosperous Irish farms, those who followed and who claimed to be working in their name, through a combination of lack of vision among some and sheer self-interest among others, set themselves a different agenda. Theirs was one of consolidating the existing position rather than continuing with the work of expanding the Irish community. Just as all, including Argentina, had benefited from the work of Fr. Fahy and Thomas Armstrong, all, with the exception of a very few very rich Irish families, were to lose out heavily, in the long term, by this change of direction in community settlement.

Conclusion

Throughout its 400-year history, Irish emigration to Argentina was typical of Irish migration to other regions taking place at the same time. Up until the late eighteenth century only an educated elite arrived there to take up positions in the service of a colonial power not available to them at home because of their religion. When the great grassland regions of the world began to be opened up by British trade, the Irish settled in significant numbers in the Buenos Aires Pampas just as they did in North America, southern Africa, Australia and New Zealand.

The important difference with the settlement in Argentina was that it was outside direct British control and was not obliged to follow the handed down British settlement pattern where each immigrant was granted a specific parcel of land in a designated area. Under this model the immigrant was tied to a specific dot on the map and he succeeded or failed largely as a result of his own efforts in clearing a wilderness and replicating the European model of farming, that of a mixed agriculture on a small plot of land. So the rugged individualist with the 'Protestant work ethic' tended to prosper best under those conditions. By contrast, the settlement model designed specifically for and largely by the Irish in Argentina was based on pooling the knowledge and capital of the whole community and filling a single niche within the wider community, that of producing sheep and wool for the European market. The role of the individual in this model was to use his expertise in animal husbandry and to make best use of the communal capital and pool of knowledge in expanding his own capital. He used these resources to move to the most fertile land available at the time and working his way via partnerships and borrowing unused community assets via Fr. Fahy he developed into owning substantial capital of his own. If at any point, because his surplus capital was held in cash by Fr. Fahy, the immigrant was not making full use of his assets, they could be lent to another more enterprising member of the Irish community. The immigrant's capital was initially held in sheep and only later was part of this asset converted into land and cattle. The weakness of this model proved to be the complete dependence on one or two exceptional people at the very centre who could be trusted by the entire community with its life savings and who were honest enough and had sufficient vision to operate the model for the wider benefit rather their own immediate short-term gain.

While this model lasted for just one generation in just one country, it did make those who operated within it arguably the most successful Irish immigrant community anywhere in the world within their own lifetimes..It also showed, despite its undoubted limitations, that the British model of colonial settlement was not the only settlement model that could work. Where a community worked together they were arguably even more successful than the rugged individualist. Furthermore there are more models for land settlement by European societies than the 'Protestant work ethic' of the British settlement model.

Notes

1. Peter Boyd-Bownan, *Indice Geobiografico de 40,000 Probladores espanoles de America in el Siglo XVI* (Bogota, 1964), p. 267.
2. David Rock, *Argentina 1516–1987* (London, 1986), p. 10.
3. R. de Lafuente Machain, *Conquistadores del Rio de la Plata* (Buenos Aires, 1937), p. 192.
4. Thomas Murray, *History of the Irish in Argentina* (New York, 1919), p. 7.
5. De Lafuente Machain, *Conquistadores*, p. 129.
6. Ibid., p. 346.
7. Ibid., p. 220.
8. Edward Maclysaght, *The Surnames of Ireland* (Dublin, 1980), p. 118. States that Galvan originated in County Clare and spread to surrounding counties. This would place it in the area of Ireland in greatest contact with Spain.
9. De Lafuente Machain, *Conquistadores*, pp. 361–8.
10. Ibid., p. 193.
11. Murray, *History of the Irish in Argentina*, p. 7.
12. David Rock, *Argentina 1516–1987* (London, 1987), ch. 1 gives fuller account of the founding of Buenos Aires and Asuncion de Paraguay.
13. By way of a random example, born within 5 km of Summerhill, County Meath, where this chapter is written, were O'Higgins who became the Viceroy of Peru, and deLacy who became Marshall of the armies of Peter the Great of Russia. Taffe, the Chancellor of Austria, was born about 25 km away. The gaelic name for Summerhill is Cnoc Linsig or Lynch's Hill. When Lynch lost his lands at Summerhill during the Cromwellian wars, members of his family fled to France. Possibly with help from their Galway cousins they became wealthy merchants in Bordeaux. They also founded the famous Lynch Bodega there that the family still run. They also converted to Protestantism in the vain hope of recovering their lands in Summerhill. Incidentally a descendant of the Wellsley who acquired some of Lynch's lands at Summerhill became the famous Duke of Wellington and Prime Minister of Britain. Almost every part of Ireland has similar examples of local heroes. O'Leary of Peruvian fame and Lord Kitchener both came from close by each other in County Kerry.
14. After 1829, which coincided with the decline of imperial Spain, the British offered similar opportunities to the Irish in India.
15. Eduardo Coghlan, *Los Irlandeses en la Argentina su Actuacion y Descendencia* (Buenos Aires, 1987), p. 418.

16. The Cullens have been (and still are) one of the leading merchant families of the Canary Islands since early in the seventeenth century. One of the sons of this family, Patrick (note not Patricio), founded the Cullen merchant house in Buenos Aires and a little later one in Santa Fe where the Cullens settled to become one of the leading landowning and political families in the country. Patrick was eventually executed by Rosas on account of his political activities.

    I am grateful to Sr. Domingo Cullen, Senior Minister in the Argentine Embassy, London, who is a direct descendant of Patrick Cullen, for giving me much of the background to the Cullen family of Argentina.

17. The term *porteno* or 'man from the port' has changed radically in meaning over the past two centuries. Today it is almost a term of abuse in Buenos Aires, but in the context of that time it meant exactly the same as 'working in the city' means in modern-day London.

18. Murray, *History of the Irish in Argentina,* p. 37.

19. Andrew Graham-Yooll, *The Forgotten Colony* (London, 1981), p. 32.

20. W.H. Koebel, *Argentina Past and Present* (London, 1910), p. 134.

21. 'Camp' is an Irish-Argentine term derived from the Spanish word '*campo*' meaning 'countryside'. It is used in exactly the same way among the Irish in Argentina as the word 'prairie' is used in North America or 'outback' in Australia.

22. The Irish sheep-owners drove much harder bargains with the new immigrants than the Creole *estanciero*. By mid-century the share was one-fifth and by 1870 'shares' had virtually disappeared. The shepherds were hired on a waged basis from then on. This was a significant factor in ending Irish immigration to Argentina.

23. The only written source that I could find for this statement was in the general tourist literature for the district. It is however widely accepted among the citizens of Buenos Aires.

24. I am grateful to Sr. Elena Murray of Santa Fe for providing me with this information while she was visiting Dublin in 1996.

25. This writer in common with all other Irish people of his acquaintance who have visited Argentina can personally confirm the exceptional welcome Argentines still reserve for Irish visitors 190 years later.

26. The Welsh emigration to Chubut, Patagonia, is quite different in concept; it was a 'colonization', i.e. a group of people left Wales to settle in a specific predetermined spot on the map. This model is similar broadly to the Canadian model. Settlement by the Irish in Buenos Aires was more akin to the US pattern of Irish settlement where the emigrant migrated to a port and once there used personal contact to arrange a means of personal support, i.e. a job. The job dictated where the person settled and as their circumstances improved they relocated to further maximize their own earning ability, eventually finally settling often far away from the original point of entry. The end result may well be the same in that large numbers of Irish still chose to settle close by each other in specific areas but the area settled in this case was decided by the individual long after arrival rather than before the emigrant left their home port.

27. *Report of Theodoric Bland Esq. on South America* [A] Buenos Ayres 1918, United States Serial Set House Document No. 48, 15th Congress, 2nd Session.

28. Ironically I found none from either the Westmeath/Longford area or Wexford.

29. Murray, *History of the Irish in Argentria*, p. 266.

30. Ibid., p. 53. Murray places the term 'moral and industrious' in quotation marks, which indicates that he is quoting directly from an unnamed source, very probably the original document.

31. Murray and Ussher spell Oughagan's name 'Oughan'. I am using the spelling Oughagan himself used when writing to the Archbishop of Dublin. It may well be that Oughagan used different spellings of his names at different times just as Fr. Fahy spelled his name 'Fahey' on occasion.

32. The original letter is in the archive of the Archbishop of Dublin, All Hallows College, Drumcondra, Dublin. A photocopy is in my possession.

33. All letters to the Archbishop of Dublin quoted in this chapter can be seen in the archive of the Archbishop of Dublin. Photocopies of all quoted correspondence are in my possession.

34. John Brabazon was an emigrant from Westmeath who kept a journal of his early experiences in Argentina. The manuscript, or at least part of it, found its way to Eduardo Coghlan who gave a photocopy of it to the Irish embassy in Buenos Aires. Brabazon, a Protestant, came from a large farming background near Mullingar. His family in Mullingar died out in the late 1980s and the original home is now the property of a great-grand-nephew Mr Greg Potterton who was completely unaware of the family connection with Argentina.

35. For a more thorough analysis of the numbers of Irish who emigrated to Argentina during the nineteenth century as well as the sources see Patrick McKenna *Nineteenth Century Irish Emigration to and Settlement in Argentina*, unpublished M.A. thesis (St Patrick's College Maynooth, County Kildare, 1994).

36. This figure is based on an assumption of low out-migration between 1853 and 1861. As this was the period when Irish emigrants could make vast fortunes with surprising ease, it is unlikely that many left. If Fr. Fahy's figures for 1853 are correct, out-migration had to equal in-migration during this period, making the top estimate of 18,000 the more likely figure.

37. Murray *History of the Irish*, p. 56.

38. James, Ussher, *Fr. Fahy* (Buenos Aires, 1950), p. 54.

39. William McCann, *Two Thousand Miles' Ride Through The Argentine Provinces* (New York, 1853, Reprinted 1971), p. 196. He gives Fr. Fahy as the source for this figure, which he states 'includes all ages and sexes' though he points out that 75 per cent are single men. Assuming that women and children were about equal in number, roughly 3,200 of the total were born in Ireland. As 1842 was the year Fr. Fahy arrived in Argentina this figure was probably given to him by another, unstated source.

40 This letter still exists in the archive of the Archbishop of Dublin.

41. All the literature is agreed on this: Murray, Latham, Mulhall, McCann, Fr. Fahy etc. It does appear, however, that they may all be using the same source, i.e. official estimates, probably British, prior to 1861. While there appears to be no reason to question this estimate, I have been unable to prove or disprove its accuracy. The post-1861 data is more satisfactory in that it does lend itself to a reasonable amount of cross-checking.

42. A comparison of the age data in the census of 1869 and 1895 confirms this.

43. Coghlan, *Los Irlandeses en la Argentina* is probably the most comprehensive genealogy of any Irish community anywhere in the world. It lists just under 4,000 entries.

44. Anecdotal evidence in both sending areas of Longford/Westmeath and Wexford would suggest a much higher return migration from Argentina than from English-speaking destinations. The folk memory is very much of several family members emigrating and the grandparent(s) returning after a few years with sufficient capital to purchase the, often present, family farm. William Bulfin would also suggest this in *Rambles in Eireann* (1907, Republished London, 1981).

45. There is no reason to suppose that the Irish were any less prone to re-emigration than other European communities, especially as the Irish would have such well established communities in the US and Canada. Brabazon in his diary mentions out-migration casually as though it was not considered that unusual. Members of his own family left Argentina to take part in the California gold rush of 1849 and never returned. Others left for British colonies, principally Australia, during times of civil strife. Furthermore private diaries of Irish in both North and South America indicate that internal migration between Irish communities in the Americas was very high and re-emigration to another Irish community was considered the norm. The fact that the Irish in Argentina were at the other end of the world seems to have been completely overcome by the fact that there was considerable trade between the US and Buenos Aires and sea travel was a relatively easy matter compared to overland movement in those pre-railway, pre-road days.

46. Murray, *History of the Irish in Argentina*, p. 394.

47. Coghlan, *Las Irlandeses en La Argentina*. p. 12.

48. The one weak link in Fr. Fahy's system was the health service he provided. The Irish appear to have opted in the main to be treated in the 'British Hospital' (which still exists under that name and is still one of the leading hospitals in Argentina) rather than the 'Irish Hospital' which closed shortly after Fr. Fahy's death.

49. The Banco Provincia failed in the late 1870s about five years after Armstrong's death. By that time most of the Irish community appear to have withdrawn their assets from it and were therefore largely unaffected by its failure. As it falls outside this work I don't know to what extent the Irish contributed to its failure by withdrawing their assets. The current Banco Provincia in Argentina has very little connection to Armstrong's bank other than the name. The Banco Nacional would be its real successor as it was formed out of the ashes of Armstrong's Banco Provincia. I am grateful to the Argentine Ambassador to Ireland Sr. Juan M. Figurerro for supplying me with much of the information for this note.

50. Mulhall, M.J. and E.T. *Handbook of the River Plate* (Buenos Aires, 1872).

Part Three
The Empire

CHAPTER 11

Irish Emigration to the British Empire, 1700–1914

ANDY BIELENBERG

(Department of History, University College, Cork)

Introduction

Despite a growing and diverse volume of published material on Irish emigration and settlement throughout the British Empire, the only comprehensive survey of the topic is a series of chapters in Akenson's book *The Irish Diaspora*.[1] Akenson broadly challenges the exceptionalist view that the Irish were significantly different from other European peoples, placing Irish emigration and settlement in the wider context of European expansionism. He detects a general resistance among Irish historians in the past to assimilate the historical reality of Irish participation and 'collaboration' in the expansion of the largest empire in human history, the Second British Empire (which begins with American Independence and ends with the establishment of the British Commonwealth). Morgan refers to this involvement in empire-building as 'an unwelcome heritage'; he points out that the Irish 'far from empathising with indigenous peoples overseas, whatever their experience at home, were as brutal as any other white colonisers'.[2] In the pursuit of self or family interest and advancement, wealth, land and a range of other objectives, the Irish proactively engaged in British colonial expansion in the New World, effectively replicating the process of colonization which had occurred in Ireland. In many cases, they took land previously used by indigenous inhabitants whose cultures they contributed to displacing, while others became wealthy through employing large numbers of black slaves. In short, Akenson argues the Irish were not always passive victims of British imperialism; they behaved in a colonial context very much like other white Europeans.[3]

Furthermore, he challenges Miller's view that Irish Catholic migrants left behind in Ireland a fatalistic, dependent and archaic culture, which initially inhibited their economic progress in the New World. Census data to study the Irish multi-generational ethnic group in some of the British settlement colonies is superior to that for the USA and Britain, the main destinations of the Irish diaspora. The British Empire has therefore been Akenson's happiest hunting ground, with the Irish who settled in various colonial contexts providing the laboratories to test the theory of exiled Irish Catholic disability.[4]

Akenson asserts that Ireland's greatest boon to the British Empire 'was through the massive number of everyday settlers that it provided'.[5] This assessment, if it is correct, identifies Irish migration and settlement within the empire as a key facet of British imperialism. With that issue very much in view, this chapter surveys the major episodes of Irish migration and settlement to various parts of the British Empire roughly between 1700 and 1914. Finally, the conclusion compares and contrasts Irish colonial migrants in this period with those who emigrated to the USA and Britain, which provides the basis for an assessment of some of Akenson's conclusions on Irish emigration and settlement within the British Empire.

I

As the connection between the Caribbean, the eastern seaboard of America and Europe deepened during the First British Empire, the demands of the colonization process drew increasingly on Irish resources. The growth of the Atlantic economy drew Ireland further into the colonial orbit, not just in terms of the growth of a transatlantic trading relationship, but most crucially through the impact the Irish had on the supply of labour and settlers to the New World. It has been estimated that the net migration from Ireland to British North America and the West Indies was roughly 165,000 between 1630 and 1775.[6] A majority were indentured servants, which is hardly surprising given that 50–60 per cent of the labour flow from Britain to its colonies in this period were servants.[7]

As the major source of tropical agricultural products for the markets of western Europe and North America, the West Indian economy created a demand for capital and labour. A number of Irish merchant families built up trading networks and plantations in the Caribbean, which also became an important destination for Irish migrants in the seventeenth and early eighteenth centuries.[8] By the mid-seventeenth century the Irish already accounted for roughly half the entire population of the English West Indies.[9] Over the remainder of the seventeenth and early eighteenth centuries about 40,000 Irish moved to the West Indies, where they comprised the largest stream of white immigrants.[10]

If the Irish were well represented among the lower-class white population, they were also reasonably represented in the colonial gentry on a number of the islands.[11] With the expansion of the colonial economy between 1630 and 1800, a number of Irish Catholic and Protestant families established profitable slave plantations on the islands, providing much work for Irish overseers, artisans, merchants and indentured servants. According to Akenson, most Irish households on Montserrat owned slaves by the 1730s and they no longer did field labour; the demand for Irish unskilled labour had declined with a resulting drop in migration. The Irish presence on this island was strongly linked to the implementation and maintenance of the slave economy, and the trade connected with it. Irish links with the island were largely terminated by the full abolition of slavery in 1838.[12] This considerably reduced Irish connections with the British West Indies.

Already by the first half of the eighteenth century, the thirteen American colonies became the preferred destination for Irish migrants. Fogeleman estimates that they accounted for about half (109,000) the total migrants from the British Isles entering the thirteen American colonies between 1700 and 1775, making them the most constant and frequently the largest group of European migrants to colonial America.[13] The emigrants to the New World, while not the poorest, were largely drawn from lower ranks of Irish society. They included labourers, artisans, small farmers and cottier weavers. Those arriving with some capital had significant advantages. John Rae, who settled in Georgia, wrote back to a relative in Belfast 'if any person that comes here can bring money and purchase a slave or two, they may live very easy and well'.[14] Cullen suggests roughly one-tenth of those migrating from Ireland came from high-status families. These included some Scotch-Irish pioneer families in the backcountry ascendancy, like the Calhouns who acquired thousands of acres and many slaves, and the Polks who could count three future presidents among their descendants and relations by marriage.[15]

Irish immigrant merchants played an important role in American commercial expansion in the colonial period, bridging the connections and emigrant routes between Ireland and the New World. They were also involved in the West Indian–American trade, with crews partially drawn from the lower-class Irish and Irish Creole populations of the Caribbean.[16]

The rising demand for a range of commodities in Europe from North America and the West Indies during the eighteenth century intensified trading links. The American colonies and the West Indies provided significant demand for Irish linen and provisions, while the American middle colonies supplied the flaxseed which was largely destined for Ulster's staple industry. This, combined with the provisioning of transatlantic shipping, directly linked a number of Irish ports to the main migrant routes to the colonies.[17]

In the initial period of heavy emigration after 1715, New England was a popular destination, but when land became increasingly unobtainable, the main flow shifted in the 1720s to Philadelphia and Newcastle in Delaware. The middle colonies (notably Pennsylvania) became the main focus; there was religious toleration and good land to be had, and it was here that the system of indentured labour was strongest. By the eve of the Revolution the Irish had also moved into Maryland, Virginia and the Carolinas.[18] The Irish in America numbered 350,000–450,000 by the Revolution. By 1790, they accounted for over 26 per cent of the white population in Georgia, almost 26 per cent in South Carolina, and almost 24 per cent in Pennsylvania. In New York, New Jersey, Delaware, Maryland, Virginia and North Carolina they accounted for anything between 12 and 18 per cent of the white population. However, crucially there were few women in this phase of migration from Ireland; Doyle points out that Irishmen therefore did not marry Irish women, partially explaining why a more strongly visible Irish American presence did not emerge from the colonial period.[19]

The majority of Ulster immigrants in the colonial period were backcountry farmers pioneering the region from western Maryland and central Pennsylvania to the Carolinas. Recent research indicates that the settlement behaviour of the Protestant Irish in colonial America was similar to that of their German, English and Scots co-religionists whose colonial ethos they largely shared. As a dominant pioneering group, their pattern of settlement and land use (a corn and woodlands-pasture culture based around family farms) altered the landscape. Inevitably this brought them into conflict with the native American Indian population, whose subsistence base was increasingly undermined.[20] If the detail of this conflict is somewhat muted in the historiography, the outcome is very clear.

With the dramatic growth in trade and output, the demand for labour in the American colonies rose in the 1760s and 1770s, increasing the migrant flow. The cost of passage had halved since the 1730s and the term of indenture had been reduced. A growing Irish presence in the colonies increased the propensity of friends and relatives in Ireland to follow the lure of cheap land and employment opportunities on the frontier. Downturns in the Irish linen industry also contributed; the normal Ulster outflow of up to 5,000 per annum had by the first half of the 1770s increased to over 10,000. A greater number of these migrants were paying their own passage, reflecting the fact that a greater proportion of the new arrivals had more resources and skills at their disposal. The *Belfast Newsletter* reported in 1773 that in the past it had been 'chiefly the very meanest of the People that went off, mostly in the Station of Indented Servants'; most of those now going were 'people employed in the Linen Manufacture, or Farmers, and of some Property'.[21]

It seems probable that the Irish were the largest ethnic group from the British Isles migrating to the West Indies between the 1630s and the early eighteenth century. They were also the largest European ethnic group moving into the American colonies between 1700 and 1775. Ireland was among the most important regions in Europe providing settlers for the New World, thus contributing significantly to European imperial expansion during the First British Empire. This validates James's contention that 'any study of the British Empire before the American Revolution that neglects close attention to Ireland is bound to be incomplete'. The Catholic component among Irish migrants in the American colonies, at 25–30 per cent between 1700 and 1780, also appears to be somewhat higher than was generally supposed, most being indentured servants.[22] The Catholic Irish component migrating to the West Indies in the seventeenth century was probably higher.

Though Ireland had been thoroughly colonized during the First British Empire, it seems very clear that Irish migrants and settlers played a critical role in the last stages of that phase of British imperial expansion, in both the West Indies and colonial America. Ironically, they also played an important role in achieving American independence, which drew the history of the First Empire to a close.

II

The small and largely Protestant Irish presence in British North America (which later became Canada) increased in the decades after American independence.

Catholics at this point were only to be found in greater numbers in the New-foundland cod fishery which had traditionally been an important destination for Irish seasonal migrants from the south-east of Ireland.[23]

The growth of the timber trade set up a much larger wave of migration from Ireland to British North America from the end of the Napoleonic War, by redu-cing fares on the return leg westwards. From then until 1845, half a million Irish moved to British North America. In the 70 years after the Famine, a further one-third of a million left. The cataclysmic impact of the Famine swelled Irish depar-tures to Canada to 25,000 in 1846, rising to an unprecedented 90,000 in 1847; death during the crossing was much heavier in these years, and many died slowly on arrival. The Canadians reacted against this deathly pauper tide with port taxes in 1847, which stemmed the flow of poorer Irish migrants to Canada, simultaneously increasing their entry to the USA.[24] Despite this disincentive, the flow continued; the numbers living in Canada who were born in Ireland rose from 122,000 in 1841 to 286,000 in 1861, by which time they accounted for 10.6 per cent of the Irish-born living in North America and Great Britain.[25]

Ulster and some of the counties in north Connacht and north Leinster dom-inated Canadian settlement between 1815 and 1845. If Belfast, Derry and Sligo dominated the outflow, Dublin, Cork and Limerick also made a contribution. However, with the exception of a brief period during and after the Famine (when Munster dominated), Ulster continued to provide the bulk of migrants to British North America. In absolute terms the Protestant Irish settlers accounted for 60 per cent of the Canadian Irish ethnic group by 1871, but settlement was regionally highly varied.[26] In New Brunswick, for example, the Irish in 1871 accounted for 35.2 per cent of the population; just over half were Protestant, and they dominated Irish settlement in the south-western part of the province, while Catholics dominated the northern and eastern parts. The Irish were well represented in some of the cities. In St John, (the main port of entry for New Brunswick), they accounted for 54.1 per cent of the population and 43 per cent in Toronto.[27]

Darroch and Ornstein have demonstrated that farming was by far the most significant occupation among the Canadian Irish in 1871, as it was for the entire population. However, Irish Catholics were under-represented in farming and over-represented in rural labouring when compared to Irish Protestants in every province. While there was no marked under-representation in bourgeois and artisanal occupations among the Catholic Irish ethnic group in Canada, they were over-represented in semi-skilled and labouring occupations. In urban areas they deviated far from the Canadian norm in one important respect: a much higher percentage were employed as labourers (30.2 per cent as opposed to 15.6 per cent of the Canadian urban population). The picture that emerges is that the urban Catholic Irish were marked by lower social status than all other ethnic groups, while in rural areas they compared much more favourably with Canadian norms.[28] This important distinction will be taken up in the conclusion.

Between 1815 and the mid-1860s, emigrants from Ireland to British North America exceeded those from England, Scotland and Wales combined in most years. Well before the Great Famine they were the single most important group of migrants, and Ontario was the area of heaviest settlement. The Irish in Ontario in 1871 were not a city people; over three-quarters lived in rural areas. Farming was the most common occupation for both Catholics (48.1 per cent being farmers) and Protestants (59.4 per cent being farmers). Irish Catholics and Protestants adjusted well to commercial farming in a new setting. Akenson concludes from the Ontario data that Irish Catholic migrants in that region were 'much quicker, more technologically adaptive, more economically alert, and much less circumscribed by putative cultural limits inherited from the Old Country than is usually believed'. However, greater differences emerged in the city, where a minority of each group lived and Catholics were more highly represented within the urban working classes.[29]

By 1855, an intense phase of Irish migration to Canada had largely reached its conclusion. The bulk of this movement comprised members of the small farming class, neither rich nor poor, but the flow included a small but influential group of colonial administrators, larger landowners, professionals and clergy, in addition to poorer elements of Irish society who became part of Canada's urban proletariat. By the 1870s, the Irish had played an important role in the first wave of pioneering in central and eastern Canada; the Irish ethnic group of 850,000 accounted for roughly a quarter of the Canadian population, making them the second largest group after the French. They were to be much less significant in the second wave of migration, which extended westwards. By 1901, there were only 20,000 people claiming Irish descent in British Columbia, a far cry from the large volume in central and eastern Canada.[30]

The majority of emigrants from Ireland to Canada were not assisted by the state. The high cost of the first experimental schemes in 1823 and 1825 (when over 2,500 emigrants were moved to Upper Canada) did little to increase enthusiasm for state assistance in the pre-Famine period. From the end of the Famine the Board of Guardians were allowed to borrow on foot of the rates to assist pauper migration to Canada. A few Crown estates were cleared with state assistance, which also contributed to relieving congestion in the west of Ireland, notably in the 1880s. However, the overall influence of state assistance was far less important in British North America than for the Irish destined for the antipodes.[31]

III

Irish migration to Australia was initially largely involuntary since most of the emigrants were convicts. From the arrival of the first convict ship in Botany Bay in 1788 to 1853 when transportation to the eastern colonies ceased, almost 40,000 were transported directly. A further 8,000 of Irish birth were transported from Britain in this period. By the 1830s, the Irish born (90 per cent of whom were convicts) accounted for about a quarter of the colony's population. If some emancipists did exceptionally well, modest success was probably collectively more typical, with a number participating as pioneers in the opening years of the squatting age in the 1840s and 1850s.[32]

Although Irish women convicts formed a smaller absolute number of those transported, they formed a larger share of the female component of the convict population than their male compatriots. At least half of the transported women of Botany Bay had been born in Ireland, and most later settled in New South Wales as family or working women.[33] It seems probable that this over-representation was mirrored within the total white female population of New South Wales down to the 1840s, especially since the Irish also accounted for 48 per cent of assisted migrants between 1829 and 1851, at a time when few paid their own passage.[34]

Irishmen were also well represented among the gaolers, guards and governors working in the colony's penal settlements, and among the regiments stationed in New South Wales.[35] The Anglo-Irish had a disproportionate influence on shaping the administrative, political, legal, educational and cultural institutions of pre-gold rush Australia.[36]

The Irish ethnic group accounted for more than half of the white population of Australia in 1840 according to Duncan. However, Irish migration to the antipodes was largely a post-Famine phenomena.[37] The discovery of gold initiated a major new phase of migration to Australia in the 1850s, contributing to its economic development over the following decades, which further increased immigration.[38] With 227,000 Irish-born persons living in Australia by 1891, they accounted for 7.8 per cent of the Irish-born population living in North America, Great Britain and Australia.[39] Between the 1840s and 1914 about a third of a million Irish moved to Australia. Only the eastern provinces of Canada drew more heavily on Irish settlers. The Irish could be found right across the social spectrum, but they remained over-represented in unskilled occupations.[40] If settlement was predominantly rural initially, towards the end of the nineteenth century the Irish representation in the cities was becoming significant. By the 1880s over half the population of the Victoria Irish were living in metropolitan Melbourne.[41]

Chain migration, combined with state assistance and remittances, dominated Irish movement to Australia between the 1840s and 1880s, when Clare, Tipperary, Limerick and Kilkenny were the major source of emigrants, with a secondary concentration around Fermanagh, Cavan and Tyrone. After the 1880s, in the absence of state assistance, the focus shifted from west Munster and west Ulster to the rich grazing lands of Leinster and the more industrialized counties of east Ulster.[42]

Political and civil parity were substantially established in the Australian colonies by the mid-nineteenth century.[43] The revolutionary and republican traditions of Irish nationalism were not strong in a colony where the British connection remained crucial to the economic and political well-being of the white population. The Irish of Catholic origin largely supported Home Rule for Ireland within the empire.[44] An upwardly mobile Australian Irish population was disposed in Farrell's view towards greater Anglicization, not less. Economic opportunity and social mobility provided a strong motive for assimilation and imperial loyalty in Australia.[45] The same probably held for New Zealand, since it had the highest per capita income in the world by the eve of the First World War, which increased its appeal to potential Irish migrants.[46]

The period from the early 1870s to the beginning of the First World War was the most important phase of Irish migration to New Zealand. There was a significant Irish presence in a few regions prior to this; in 1851 they accounted for one-third of the population of Auckland. The New Zealand gold rushes of the 1860s accelerated entry and regional concentration. More significantly, the severe economic downturn in Ireland in the later 1870s coincided with prosperity in New Zealand; these factors, combined with government assistance down to 1885, made it an attractive destination. The Irish-born hit a high point in 1886, when they accounted for 51,408 (or 8.9 per cent) of the population. At this point the multi-generational Irish ethnic group had reached about 109,000 according to Akenson's estimates, rising to over 195,000 by 1916.[47]

Protestants formed a significant minority of the Irish ethnic group of between roughly 22 and 25 per cent between the 1860s and the 1930s. The bulk of Irish migrants to New Zealand came from Ulster and Munster, with the latter dominating down to the 1880s and the former being preponderant from 1891. The New Zealand demographic data enabled Akenson to unearth material relating to residential patterns and occupation among the multi-generational Irish ethnic group. Using Catholics as a surrogate for the entire Irish Catholic multi-generational group, Akenson shows that by 1921 they were not untypical of the general population in occupational terms, the largest male group (22 per cent) being primary producers (mostly farmers); Catholic women were little different from the rest of the population. In terms of settlement pattern a comparison in 1916 of the regional distribution of New Zealand Catholics, the Irish-born and the entire population did not reveal any significant variation. An examination of the urban/rural ratio of these same groups in 1921 also yielded little variation. Akenson concludes therefore that neither Irishness nor Catholicity were impediments to success in New Zealand.[48]

The main incidence of Irish migration to the settlement colonies was over by the end of the nineteenth century. After this, Irish migrants only accounted for a twentieth of the total flow to Canada and Australia, the most important colonial destinations of the Irish diaspora.[49]

IV

The Irish influence in Africa and Asia was more transient than in the major settlement colonies, with South Africa probably attracting the largest number of permanent Irish settlers. However, with a first-generation Irish population of only 18,000 in 1904, it was not a major destination of Irish emigrants. Soldiers probably swelled this figure after the Boer War, when 28,000 Irish fought against the Boers. The Irish multi-generational ethnic group in 1891 was only about 3.7 per cent of the white population in South Africa, compared to 18.7 per cent in New Zealand and 25.7 per cent in Australia. Their influence on South African society was therefore less significant and somewhat untypical. According to McCracken, South Africa 'offered little to the destitute in the way of employment or cultural support networks and because it was expensive to get to, the region attracted those Irish with marketable skills'. Protestant representation was significantly higher than in Australia and New Zealand, and two-thirds of the Irish population in 1911 were male, which was much higher than in North America or Australia where the ratio was fairly even. Apart from temporary military personnel, the police and public service attracted many Irish, including top-ranking officials. The Irish were also to be found in the gold and diamond mines, as navvies, engineers and managers, and on the railways and in retailing. Irish representation, however, quickly faded after South Africa gained dominion status. The Irish presence elsewhere in Africa was more limited. There were 794 Irish, or 3.4 per cent, in the small white population in Rhodesia in 1911. By the 1920s, Irish migration to South Africa was insignificant.[50]

As the largest non-settlement dependency within the British Empire, India provided significant employment opportunities for Irishmen (and a very small number of women), most notably for soldiers. From the beginning, Protestant Irish officers were well represented in the East India Company army; 19.5 per cent of the officers between 1758 and 1834 were from Ireland; it was more open than the British home army to officers of lower social status. Rank and file recruitment also increased from the Seven Years War (1756–63) when the ban on Catholic recruits was ignored. In 1778, for example, about 500 (or 30 per cent) of the new recruits sent to India were from Ireland, rising to 52.3 per cent of all recruits between 1816 and 1824. Ireland's role as a recruiting ground for the regular British army also became more significant from the 1790s both in the ranks and among officers. By the 1850s, the Irish accounted for about 16,000 (or over 40 per cent) of the soldiers of the combined regular and company armies serving in India. The Irish accounted for about 21 per cent of the British-born population of India in 1871. In that year the Indian census recorded 16,000 Irish-born people living in India, falling to about 12,000 by 1911, reflecting a gradual decline in Irish representation in the ranks of the British army.[51]

The Irish also worked as doctors, engineers, lawyers, journalists, policemen, or for the state in railways, telegraphs or as public servants in the Indian administration. Irish representation in the Indian Civil Service increased from the mid-1850s, when recruitment took place through competitive examination; it peaked at 15 per cent in the mid-1880s, employing around 1,000 Irish in total. The Irish, like most Europeans, largely remained aloof and secluded from Indian society, living among other Europeans. This and their small numbers, particularly when the army is excluded, meant they had a limited impact on Indian society.[52]

With limited Irish settlement, the Irish influence in Africa and Asia was much less significant than in the settlement colonies. However, the Irish were at the forefront of Catholic missionary activity in the first half of the twentieth century, notably in Africa and the Far East. The development of this large Catholic spiritual empire was perhaps the most enduring Irish impact in Africa and Asia in the twentieth century.[53]

Table 11.1: A rough estimate of emigration from Ireland, 1815–1910

	No. of emigrants	%
To the USA	4,765,000	61.7
To Great Britain	1,468,000	19.0
To British North America	1,057,000	13.7
To Australasia	361,000	4.7
To Africa	35,000	0.5
Other overseas	34,000	0.4
Total	7,720,000	100.0

Adapted from: D. Akenson, *The Irish Diaspora: A Primer* (Belfast, 1996), p. 56.[54]

Conclusion

Between 1500 and 1800, the Irish formed part of the European migrant stream of between two and three million people who moved to the New World. At the outset of white colonization it is estimated that there were perhaps 10 million native American Indians in North America, who were subjected to land robbery, disease, extermination and social and economic destruction at the hands of white Europeans (including the Irish), which considerably reduced the native American population to 2 or 3 million.[55] In addition, about six million Africans were forced to migrate to the New World between 1500 and 1800, facilitating the foundation and growth of plantation colonies in the Caribbean and in the southern part of North America.[56] Irish settlement in the Caribbean and colonial North America from the seventeenth century down to 1775 was intimately linked with this process of European imperial expansion. This had a major influence on the type of social and economic relationships that Irish settlers formed with those of European, African or native American extraction. The interests of slaves of African origin and the native American population were utterly subordinated to those of European ethnic origins. The collective Irish settlement experience needs to be located in the context of these social realities. Few will dispute that Ireland was thoroughly colonized during the First British Empire, a process which left many victims. In the New World, the main victims of British imperialism were not Irish, although undoubtedly there were Irish casualties, such as transported convicts. The main victims were native Americans whose land was seized and culture displaced, and Africans whose liberty was lost and whose labour was barbarously exploited. Those of European extraction, including the Irish, were net beneficiaries from these circumstances.

The British colonies were less significant for Irish emigration after the United States had asserted its independence from the empire. However, the Second British Empire became an important destination for Irish emigrants in the century after 1815 (see Table 11.1). This crude estimate suggests Irish emigration to the British Empire in this period was roughly comparable with the numbers moving to Great Britain.

Did migrants from Ireland to the British Empire differ from the far larger numbers who emigrated to the USA and Britain? The limited comparative evidence suggests that from the 1860s, in small measures, they did. In 1867 labourers accounted for over 85 per cent of US-bound male migrants and just over 66 per cent of those going to Canada. In the same year, just under 80 per cent of male migrants to Australia and New Zealand combined were labourers.[57] With some variation, the skills threshold of those going to the major settlement colonies was higher than those going to the USA over the next half century. Confirmation of this skills bias in favour of the colonies is provided by Akenson's comparison of the occupational distribution of Irish male migrants in 1912–13. This reveals those collectively engaged in commerce, finance, professions or skilled trades accounted for 48.7 per cent of those going to South Africa, 17.3 per cent of those going to Canada, 16.1 per cent of those going to Australia and New Zealand, and only 8.3 per cent of those going to the USA. Labourers, in contrast, accounted for 2.2 per cent of those going to South Africa, 14.1 per cent of those going to Australia and New Zealand, 44.5 per cent of those going to Canada and 48.2 per cent of those going to the USA.[58]

Fitzpatrick's broad comparison of the geographical origins of the Irish diaspora suggests Irish colonial migrants tended to come from more economically developed counties. Although the USA accounted for the majority of migrants from most Irish counties between 1876 and 1914, US-bound migrants were more likely to come from less economically developed counties in the west of Ireland. Canadian migrants were more likely to come from Ulster, which also had strong links with New Zealand. Australia and New Zealand also had strong links with the south-western and north midland counties. Following the decline of state-assisted emigration in the 1890s, migration to the antipodes became focused on the more economically developed counties of Ulster and the eastern seaboard.[59]

In the initial stages of settlement in the New World, those coming from more economically developed counties presumably had some advantages over their compatriots from the poorer counties of the western seaboard, who were over-represented among US-bound migrants. Lack of literacy (and at least some degree of education), for example, would have excluded Irish emigrants from certain jobs. Some 72 per cent of the Connacht population older than four years in 1841 could neither read nor write, compared to 40 per cent in Ulster, 44 per cent in Leinster and 61 per cent in Munster. Though the significance of illiteracy was steadily eroded over the remainder of the nineteenth century by the national system of education,[60] these regional differences in the mid-nineteenth century when emigration peaked should not be dismissed lightly in terms of how this impacted on emigrant prospects in the New World. Even as late as 1871, Ireland compared badly with the rest of the United Kingdom with much higher levels of illiteracy.[61] Skill thresholds amongst Irish US-bound emigrants were relatively lower than their English counterparts. During the nineteenth and early twentieth centuries, the number of Irish immigrants to the US who claimed a professional or skilled occupation was never higher than 25 per cent; English emigrants in this group ranged between 40 and 60 per cent during this period.[62] Between the 1860s and the eve of the First World War, Irish imperial migrants had slight advantages over their US-bound compatriots, in terms of social status, skill thresholds and literacy. The bulk of Irish migrants during this period (who were unassisted) chose the cheaper routes to USA, or Britain. Fitzpatrick contends that: 'the minority which chose the colonies prospered precisely because these remained inaccessible to the majority'.[63]

The more rural and dispersed pattern of settlement of Irish migrants to the British colonies widens the contrast with the higher proportions bound for the cities of the USA and Britain. The poor data in these two major destinations precludes any comparison of the Irish multi-generational ethnic group with other ethnic groups in occupational terms. However, Darroch and Ornstein's sample of the 1871 Canadian census data facilitates an occupational comparison between the Irish and other ethnic groups in both rural and urban contexts, distinguishing between Irish Catholics and Protestants. The latter group compared favourably across the board. Irish Catholics who settled in rural contexts compared reasonably well with other groups in terms of their occupational profile, with farming being the largest single occupation.[64]

While Akenson has drawn attention to the much larger numbers of Irish Catholics who settled successfully in rural contexts, he understates the circumstances of the urban Catholic Irish multi-generational ethnic group, who compared much less favourably. The latter deviated far from the Canadian norm, with a much higher percentage employed as labourers (30.2 per cent as opposed to 15.6 per cent of the Canadian urban population). This Canadian sample implies that while Irish Catholics compared reasonably well in comparison to other ethnic groups in rural contexts, this was not the case in urban contexts, where they were significantly over-represented at the lower end of the social spectrum.[65] It seems probable that the greater proportion of Irish migrants settling in the cities of the USA and Britain would reveal a similar over-representation at the lower end of the spectrum in occupational terms. Agriculture was less significant for nineteenth-century Irish settlers in the USA and Britain than in the British colonies. By 1890, only 2 per cent of Irish-born immigrants in the USA worked in agriculture.[66]

However, Akenson's evidence has placed a significant dent in the argument that Catholic Irish social origin inhibited economic advancement on the agricultural frontiers of the New World, and within the British Empire in general. His evidence from the British Empire suggests that Irish Catholic social origin was not an important factor in inhibiting social advancement during the nineteenth century. Class origin, regional origin and skill thresholds on departure from Ireland were probably far more important than religion in determining what potential opportunities could be exploited on arrival in the New World in the short term. Communications with communities already established in specific locations in the New World was another critical variable in determining opportunity.

If religion did play a role in inhibiting social and economic advancement this was determined by attitudes in the country of reception rather than the country of origin. Akenson notes that in the USA, anti-Catholic discrimination was much worse than anywhere else in the world, including Canada where the Quebec Act of 1774 (confirmed in 1791) gave Catholics full civil rights.[67] With regard to Australia, Fitzpatrick concludes that for the Irish, disadvantage and exclusion 'was less pronounced than in most countries of settlement'.[68] MacDonagh suggests that the better position the Irish enjoyed in Australian society relative to the US and Britain was that they were a founding people. With 20–30 per cent of the Australian population until the early twentieth century it was easier for the Irish to participate fully in the opportunities on offer, in contrast to GB or the USA, where the Catholic Irish entered 'firmly stratified' societies, and the Irish accounted for a much smaller proportion of the total population.[69]

Perhaps the most important result of Akenson's statistical research on the Irish diaspora in a British colonial context is his finding that neither Irishness nor Catholicity were handicaps for the economic and social advancement of migrants. Their occupational profile and settlement patterns did not differ greatly from other British ethnic groups in New Zealand, Australia, Canada and South Africa, with many successfully establishing themselves on the agricultural frontiers of the empire. In so doing, they participated in the displacement of the aboriginal cultures of the New World.[70] In New Zealand, for example, where there were only about 2,000 whites by 1840, the Irish multi-generational ethnic group alone expanded to over 212,000 by 1921. The Maori population in contrast, which was estimated to have been about 200,000 by the end of the eighteenth century, stood at just over 50,000 in 1906, by which time the number was recovering slightly. In Australia, the Aboriginal population fell from about 300,000 at the beginning of British colonization to about 77,481 in 1921.[71]

Farrell, however, contends that in Australia: 'in contrast to Protestant paternalist or exploitative whites, Irish Catholics treated the Aborigines as human beings, as equals, an equality extending to marriage, as distinct from the sexual exploitation common in white relations with Aborigines: the Shamrock/ Aboriginal names prominent among contemporary Aboriginal activists testifies to that relationship'.[72] However, the suggested difference between Protestants and Catholics has yet to be substantiated by strong empirical evidence. Emigrant letters are a valuable source for Irish migration studies which could be used to gain greater insights in this sphere.[73]

With regard to slavery, Akenson's case study of Montserrat finds no evidence that Irish Catholic slave-owners treated their slaves better than Protestants. Indeed, the historical evidence indicated that substantial Irish Catholic plantation-owners if anything were slower to abandon slavery than Protestants in the decades leading up to full abolition in 1838. This provides a sharp antidote to those who assume (without evidence) that Irish Catholics were exceptional and essentially different from other white Europeans. On the other hand, Akenson's contention that hundreds of thousands of slaves were owned by people of Irish extraction between the seventeenth and nineteenth centuries in the West Indies and North America also requires some degree of substantiation.[74]

Akenson identifies Irish colonial migrants as the perfect 'prefabricated collaborators', isolating four types: 'soldiers, administrators (including police), clergy (of all faiths) and ordinary settlers'.[75] If this concept has some use with regard to the position of soldiers and administrators, it is too passive to be of any use in describing the behaviour of clerics. The creation of a large Catholic spiritual empire within the British Empire is the best example of this proactive pursuit of an agenda, which was certainly not part of England's colonial strategy. Far from being collaborationist, Irish engagement in the spread of Catholicism needs to be located in the wider context of European expansionism. In religious matters, Catholic communities of Irish extraction living in the colonies in the second half of the nineteenth century frequently took their marching orders from Rome and Dublin, not London. In this period the Irish, for example, took control of the Australian Catholic Church, dominating episcopal appointments into the twentieth century. They fought for and retained a separate education system, enabling the Catholic Irish multi-generational group in Australia to retain a distinctive identity.[76] This was a pattern which with local modification was replicated in other parts of the colonies with a strong Irish Catholic presence, such as New Zealand and the Atlantic region in British North America.[77] The growth of these Catholic communities of Irish extraction and a Catholic education system in the settlement colonies and the 'non-Christian' missions in Africa and Asia do not fit simply into a 'prefabricated collaborator' model. Even if those of Irish extraction were largely loyal to the empire in political terms, Catholicism facilitated the retention and creation of a world-view which did not necessarily replicate Anglophile values in a colonial setting.

If Catholicism enabled those of Irish Catholic extraction to retain a different identity, in contrast the Protestant churches in Canada, according to Houston and Smyth, acted 'as forums for ethnic fusion', interlinking Protestant settlers of Irish, Scots, English and American backgrounds.[78] The Orange Order provided another avenue of social and political association for Protestants of Irish extraction. By 1835 the order had 1,500 lodges around Ireland, 259 in England and 154 in British North America. Lodges were also subsequently established in Australia, New Zealand, India and further afield, so that by 1877 already there were 5,000 across the British Empire.[79] The transfer of the Orange Order throughout the empire during the nineteenth century contributed to deepening colonial sentiments and loyalty in the face of the perceived threat of republicanism and Catholicism. The garrison mentality of Protestant Ireland found a new frontier throughout the empire. Houston and Smyth see the order as a bulwark of colonial Protestantism and Britishness. It was not merely an ethnic cultural retention from Ireland; it played an important role in extending the 'colonial frame of mind' through a network of lodges which had an important social and political dimension for both immigrants and their offspring. By the high watermark of the Canadian Orange Order at the end of the First World War, there were 2,000 lodges in Canada.[80]

Ireland was effectively a junior partner in that vast exploitative enterprise known as the British Empire, according to Kennedy, with the Irish gentry and middle classes participating willingly in its administration. However, he points out that Protestant Ireland was far more enthusiastic in the pursuit of imperial objectives than Catholic Ireland.[81] Bartlett, however, argues that Irish Catholics were also by and large 'enthusiastic imperialists', taking full advantage of the imperial opportunities opened up by the Union, which were not available in Ireland. He suggests that the empire was greatly admired and highly prized in Ireland, the bond of empire in the nineteenth century being 'at all times stronger than that of the Union'.[82]

Irish emigration and settlement between 1700 and 1914 throughout the British Empire needs to be placed in the wider context of Ireland's colonial and imperial relationship with Great Britain. Fitzpatrick notes that: 'both in form and in practise, the government of Ireland was a bizarre blend of "metropolitan" and "colonial" elements. Ireland could therefore be pictured either as a partner in Britain's empire or as her colony.' Ireland during the Union, for example, sent representatives to the House of Commons in London, unlike other colonies. On the other hand, the police force was armed and the army was used to enforce law and order more frequently (notably from 1916 onwards), which had more colonial than British parallels.[83] This blend of colonial and metropolitan elements characterizes other features of the relationship Ireland had with Great Britain. This survey concludes that between 1700 and 1914 Irish emigrants and settlers throughout the British Empire, along with Irish soldiers and administrators, played a critical role in the colonization process. This group were part of the metropolitan core of empire, and, like other Europeans in the New World during this phase of European expansionism, they took their chances.

The First World War and the rise of Sinn Féin completely altered nationalist Ireland's psychological and political relationship with the British Empire. The coercive measures adopted by the British state in Ireland from 1916 helped Sinn Féin to re-assert traditional nationalist interpretations of British imperialism, which were quite at odds with the Redmondite stance, which had reconciled imperialism with Irish nationalism.[84] However, the main beneficiaries of the imperial relationship in an Irish context now lived far from Ireland, some still providing a platform for a dwindling stream of Irish emigrants to follow them to the countries of the British Commonwealth in the following decades.

Notes

1. D. Akenson, *The Irish Diaspora: A Primer* (Belfast, 1996). For a more general work on the Irish and the empire (excluding emigration) see K. Jeffery (ed.), *'An Irish Empire?': Aspects of Ireland and the British Empire* (Manchester, 1996).
2. D. Akenson (1997) *If the Irish Ran the World: Montserrat, 1630–1730* (Liverpool, 1997), pp. 173–5. Akenson, *Irish Diaspora*, pp. 59–151. H. Morgan, 'An Unwelcome Heritage: Ireland's Role in British Empire Building', *History of European Ideas*, 19 (1994), p. 619.
3. Akenson (1997) pp. 173–5.

4. K. Miller, *Emigrants and Exiles* (New York, 1985). D. Akenson, 'Data: What is known about the Irish in North America', in R. O'Driscoll and L. Reynolds (eds), *The Untold Story: The Irish in Canada* (Toronto, 1988). D. Akenson, *The Irish in Ontario* (Montreal, 1984). D. Akenson, *Half the World from Home: Perspectives on the Irish in New Zealand 1860–1950* (Wellington, 1990). Akenson, *Irish Diaspora*. D. Akenson, *If the Irish Ran the World*.

5. Akenson, *Irish Diaspora*, p. 148.

6. T. Bartlett, 'This Famous Island set in a Virginian Sea: Ireland and the British Empire', in P. Marshall (ed.), *The Oxford History of the British Empire: The Eighteenth Century* (Oxford, 1998), pp. 256–7.

7. H. Gemery, 'Markets for Migrants: English Indentured Servitude and Emigration in the Seventeenth and Eighteenth Centuries', in P. Emmer (ed.), *Colonialism and Migration: Indentured Labour Before and After Slavery* (Dordrecht, 1986), p. 33. H. Beckles, 'A Riotous and Unruly Lot: Irish Indentured Servants and Freemen in the English West Indies 1644–1713', *William and Mary Quarterly*, 47, 4 (1990) pp. 503–22.

8. L. Cullen, 'Merchant Communities, the Navigation Acts and Irish and Scottish Responses', in L. Cullen and T. Smout (eds), *Comparative Aspects of Scottish and Irish History 1600–1900* (Edinburgh, 1977). L. Cullen, 'Galway Merchants and the Outside World 1650–1800', in O'Cearbhaill (ed.), *Galway Town and Gown 1484–1984* (Dublin, 1984).

9. C. and R. Bridenbaugh, *No Peace Beyond the Line: The English in the Caribbean* (New York, 1972), p. 17. As early as 1643, one report estimated there were 20,000 Irish on St Christopher. If this is an exaggeration it at least indicates a significant number. In the early 1660s it was estimated that half the 4,000 men on Barbados were Irish, and in 1677–87 it was estimated that 30 per cent of the 11,000 white settlers on the Leeward Islands were Irish. R. McDowell, 'Ireland in the Eighteenth Century British Empire', *Historical Studies*, 9 (1974), p. 51.

10. Bartlett, 'This Famous Island', p. 256. L. Cullen, 'The Irish Diaspora of the Seventeenth and Eighteenth Centuries', in N. Canny (ed.), *Europeans on the Move: Studies on European Migration 1500–1800* (Oxford, 1994), pp. 113–14. Morgan, 'An Unwelcome Heritage', p. 619 suggests that about 50,000 Irish moved to the West Indies in the early modern period.

11. R. Sheridan, 'The Rise of a Colonial Gentry: A Case Study of Antigua 1730–1775', *Economic History Review*, 12, 3 (1961) pp. 342–57. D. Doyle, *Ireland, Irishmen and Revolutionary America, 1760–1820* (Dublin, 1981), p. 70.

12. Akenson, *If the Irish Ran the World*, pp. 26, 119, 155, 165, 170–7. Also see C. Fenning, 'The Mission of St. Croix in the West Indies: 1750–1769', *Archivum Hibernicum*, 25 (1962), pp. 75–122.

13. A. Fogeleman, 'Migration to the Thirteen British North American Colonies 1700–1775: New Estimates', *Journal of Interdisciplinary History*, 22, 4 (1992), pp. 691–707. This estimate and that of Cullen, 'Irish Diaspora', are more conservative than earlier estimates reviewed by Fogeleman. Also see D. Fisher, *Albion's Seed* (Oxford, 1989), pp. 608–9. W. Smyth, 'Irish Emigration 1700–1920', in P. Emmer and M. Morner (eds), *European Expansion and Migration* (Oxford, 1992), p. 51 who argues that 100,000 had left Ireland for the thirteen American colonies in the seventeenth century and 250,000–400,000 more left between 1700 and 1776. The considerable range of the estimates has done little to dispel uncertainty.

14. J. Horn, 'British Diaspora: Emigration from Britain, 1680–1815', in Marshall (ed.), *The Oxford History of the British Empire*, p. 52.

15. Cullen, 'Irish Diaspora', p. 135. Fischer, *Albion's Seed*, pp. 642–6.
16. Doyle, *Ireland*, pp. 22–49.
17. W. Smyth, 'The Western Isle of Ireland and the Eastern Seaboard of America', *Irish Geography*, 2 (1978), p. 17. Bartlett, 'This Famous Island', p. 256.
18. R. Dickson, *Ulster Emigration to Colonial America 1718–1775* (London, 1966), pp. 221–7. Also see W. Dunaway, *The Scotch-Irish of Colonial Pennsylvania* (London, 1962).
19. Doyle, *Ireland*, pp. 52–74.
20. Fischer, *Albion's Seed*, p. 639. See chapter entitled 'The Indian Wars' in H. Ford, *The Scotch-Irish in America* (London, 1915), pp. 291–324. Smyth, 'Irish Emigration', p. 66. E. Evans, 'The Scotch Irish: Their Cultural Adaption and Heritage in the American Old West', in R. Green (ed.), *Essays in Scotch Irish History* (London, 1969), pp. 73–8.
21. Cullen, 'Irish Diaspora', pp. 146–9. Doyle, *Ireland*, p. 53. Horn, 'British Diaspora', p. 47. *Belfast Newsletter*, 6 April 1773.
22. Horn, 'British Diaspora', pp. 32, 48. F. James, *Ireland in the Empire* (Cambridge, 1973), pp. 300, 312.
23. Smyth, 'Irish Emigration', p. 67. C. Byrne, 'The Waterford Colony in Newfoundland 1700–1850' in W. Nolan and T. Power (eds), *Waterford History and Society* (Dublin, 1992). J. Manion, 'A Transatlantic Merchant Fishery: Richard Welsh of New Ross and the Sweetmans of Newbawn in Newfoundland 1734–1862', in K. Whelan and W. Nolan (eds), *Wexford: History and Society* (Dublin, 1987), pp. 373–421.
24. C. Houston and W. Smyth, *Irish Emigration and Canadian Settlement* (Toronto, 1990), pp. 3–31. Smyth, 'Irish Emigration', p. 52. D. Fitzpatrick, *Irish Emigration 1801–1921* (Dundalk, 1984), p. 25. O. MacDonagh, 'Irish Emigration to the United States of America and the British Colonies During the Famine', in D. Edwards and D. Williams (eds), *The Great Famine* (Dublin, 1956), pp. 319–52.
25. Commission on Emigration (Dublin Stationary Office, 1954), p. 126.
26. C. Houston and W. Smyth, 'Irish Emigrants to Canada: Whence they Came', in O'Driscoll and Reynolds (eds), *Untold Story*, pp. 27–35. Houston and Smyth, *Irish Emigration*, pp. 3–31, 40–73, 226. Smyth, 'Irish Emigration', p. 52.
27. P. Toner, 'Another "New Ireland" Lost: The Irish in New Brunswick', in O'Driscoll and Reynolds (eds), *Untold Story*, pp. 231–5. Smyth and Houston, *Irish Emigration*, p. 210.
28. G. Darroch and M. Ornstein, 'Ethnicity and Occupational Structure in Canada in 1871: The Vertical Mosaic in Historical Perspective', *Canadian Historical Review*, 61 (1980), pp. 303–33.
29. Akenson, *Irish in Ontario*, pp. 4–15, 47, 338, 347, 352–3. W. Smyth and C. Houston, *The Sash Canada Wore* (Toronto, 1980), p. 186.
30. Smyth and Houston, *Irish Emigration*, pp. 122–339. Akenson, *Irish in Ontario*, pp. 48–9.
31. A. Brunger, 'Geographical Propinquity Among Pre-Famine Catholic Irish Settlers in Upper Canada', *Journal of Historical Geography*, 8 (1982), pp. 265–82. G. Moran, 'State Aided Emigration from Ireland to Canada in the 1880s', *Canadian Journal of Irish Studies*, 20 (1994), pp. 1–19. Fitzpatrick, *Irish Emigration*, pp. 18–19.
32. P. O'Farrell, 'The Irish in Australia and New Zealand 1791–1870', in W. Vaughan (ed.), *A New History of Ireland* (Oxford, 1989), pp. 661–72. Irish convicts accounted for about an eighth of the Irish who moved to Australia in the nineteenth

century. D. Fitzpatrick, 'Irish Emigration to Nineteenth Century Australia', in C. Kiernan (ed.), *Australia and Ireland 1788–1988* (Dublin, 1986), p. 141.

33. P. Robinson, *The Women of Botany Bay* (Macquarie, 1988), pp. 85–122.
34. Fitzpatrick, 'Irish Emigration', p. 144. M. O'Brien, 'Cork Women for Australia: Assisted Emigration 1830–1840', *Journal of Cork Historical and Archaeological Society*, 93 (1988), pp. 21–9.
35. J. Harrison, 'Governors, Gaolers and Guards: Irish Soldiers at Moreton Bay 1824–42', in R. Pelan, N. Quirke and M. Finnane (eds), *Irish Australian Studies* (Sydney, 1994), pp. 300–9.
36. G. Forth, 'The Anglo-Irish in Early Australia: Old World Origins and Colonial Experiences', in P. Bull, C. MacConville and N. McLachlan (eds), *Irish-Australian Studies* (Melbourne, 1990), pp. 51–62.
37. P. O'Farrell, *The Irish in Australia* (New South Wales, 1987), pp. 59, 63.
38. G. Bolton, 'The Gold Discovery 1851–1880', in Kiernan (ed.), *Australia and Ireland*.
39. Commission on Emigration (Dublin Stationery Office, 1954), p. 125.
40. D. Fitzpatrick, *Oceans of Consolation: Personal Accounts of Irish Migration to Australia* (Cork, 1994), pp. 6–19.
41. O'Farrell, *Irish in Australia*, p. 154.
42. Fitzpatrick, 'Irish Emigration', pp. 138–44.
43. O. MacDonagh, 'The Irish in Victoria 1851–91', in T. Williams (ed.), *Historical Studies* viii (Dublin, 1969), p. 67.
44. P. O'Farrell, 'The Irish in Australia and New Zealand 1870–1990', in W. Vaughan (ed.), *A New History of Ireland*, Vol. VI (Oxford, 1996), pp. 703–24.
45. O'Farrell, *Irish in Australia*, p. 15. B. Reece, 'Writing about the Irish in Australia', in J. O'Brien and P. Travers (eds), *The Irish Emigrant Experience in Australia* (Dublin, 1991), pp. 233–40.
46. A. Maddison, *Monitoring the World Economy 1820–1992* (Paris, 1995), pp. 194–9. For per capita income comparison of Ireland and the settlement colonies at the beginning of the twentieth century see A. Bielenberg and P. O'Mahony, 'An Expenditure Estimate of Irish National Income in 1907', *Economic and Social Review*, 29 (1998), p. 118.
47. Akenson, *Half the World from Home*, pp. 1–62. R. Davis, *Irish Issues in New Zealand Politics 1868–1922* (Dunedin, 1974), pp. 2–3.
48. Akenson, *Half the World from Home*, pp. 24–85. Akenson, *Irish Diaspora*, pp. 59–90.
49. D. Fitzpatrick, 'Emigration 1871–1921', in Vaughan (ed.), *New History*, p. 607.
50. D. McCracken, 'Irish Settlement and Identity in South Africa before 1910', *Irish Historical Studies*, 28, 110 (1992), pp. 134–49. D. Lowry, 'The Irish in Rhodesia: Wild Land-Tame, Sacred and Profane', *Southern African-Irish Studies*, 2 (1992), pp. 242–60.
51. T. Bartlett, 'The Irish Soldier in India, 1750–1947', in M. and D. Holmes (eds), *Ireland and India* (Dublin, 1997), pp. 12–26. A. Gilbert, 'Recruitment and Reform in the East India Company Army, 1760–1800', *Journal of British Studies*, 15 (1975), p. 100. P. Razzell, 'Social Origins of Officers in the Indian and British Home Army 1758–1962', *British Journal of Sociology*, 14 (1963), pp. 248–60. R. McDowell 'Ireland in the Eighteenth Century British Empire' in J. Barry (ed.), *Historical Studies* (Belfast, 1974), pp. 49–63.
52. P. Marshall, 'British Immigration into India in the Nineteenth Century', in Emmer and Morner (eds), *European Expansion and Migration*, pp. 179–196. S. Cook, 'The

Irish Raj: Social Origins and Careers of Irishmen in the Indian Civil Service, 1855–1914', *Journal of Social History*, 20 (1987), pp. 507–29.

53. E. Hogan, *The Irish Missionary Movement* (Dublin, 1992), pp. 2–138. Also see S. Gilley, 'The Roman Catholic Church and the Nineteenth-Century Irish Diaspora' *Journal of Ecclesiastical History*, 35 (1984), pp. 188–207. P. Corish, *History of Irish Catholicism: The Missions, Africa and the Orient* (Dublin, 1967–71).

54. The USA 1815–24 taken from W. Adams, *Ireland and Irish Emigration to the New World from 1815 to the Famine* (New Haven, 1932), pp. 426, 418. 1819 taken to be an average of 1818 and 1820. Canada 1815–24 taken from Adams, pp. 421–2, 426. 1819 to 1824 include only New Brunswick and Quebec. Allowing 32,709 for the USA and 75,364 for Canada 1815–24, and 8,000 for Australasia 1815–30, and 12,000 for 'Other Overseas' 1815–40. Africa taken from C. Houston and W. Smyth, 'The Irish Diaspora: Emigration to the New World 1720–1920', in B. Graham and L. Proudfoot (eds), *An Historical Geography of Ireland* (London, 1993), p. 360, with 5,000 added for 1901–10 (2,936 recorded Irish emigrants to South Africa alone for 1901–10 in I. Ferenczi and W. Willcox, *International Migrations* (New York, 1969), Vol. 1, p. 731). This adds to a total for all Irish overseas emigration (excluding GB) of 6,252,000. C. Ó Gráda, 'A Note on Nineteenth Century Irish Emigration Statistics', *Population Studies*, 29 (1975), pp. 143–9 estimates that emigration to Great Britain from Ireland was about 1,000,000 between 1850 and 1911, when all remaining emigrants numbered 4,258,403. Akenson, *Irish Diaspora*, p. 56. Assuming same ratio held for above estimate of 6,252,000 for 1815–1910, which is divided by 4.258 to give rough estimate of Irish emigration to Great Britain of 1,468,000 for same period, as an alternative to using poor official returns noted by O'Grada above.

55. A. Grenfell Price, *White Settlers and Native Peoples* (Melbourne, 1950), pp. 5–22.

56. P. Emmer, 'European Expansion and Migration: The European Colonial Past and Intercontinental Migration: An Overview', in Emmer and Morner (eds), *European Expansion and Migration*, p. 3.

57. D. Fitzpatrick, 'Irish Emigration in the Later Nineteenth Century', *Irish Historical Studies*, 22 (1980), p. 131. Akenson, *Irish Diaspora*, p. 107.

58. Akenson, *Irish Diaspora*, p. 124.

59. Fitzpatrick 'Irish Emigration in the Later Nineteenth Century', pp. 128–9, 131–3, 137–8, 142–3.

60. D. Akenson, *The Irish Education Experiment* (London, 1970), pp. 376–7.

61. Ibid., p. 377.

62. T.W. Guinnane, *The Vanishing Irish: Households, Migration and the Rural Economy in Ireland 1850–1914* (Princeton, 1997), p. 107.

63. Fitzpatrick, *Irish Emigration*, pp. 13, 32, 36. Fitzpatrick, 'Emigration 1871–1921', pp. 606–45.

64. Daroch and Ornstein, 'Ethnicity', p. 324.

65. Ibid.

66. A. O'Day, 'Revising the Diaspora', in G. Boyce and A. O'Day, *The Making of Modern Irish History* (London, 1996), p. 192.

67. Akenson, *Irish Diaspora*, pp. 241, 264.

68. Fitzpatrick, *Oceans of Consolation*, pp. 6–19.

69. O. MacDonagh, 'Emigration from Ireland to Australia: An Overview', in Kiernan (ed.), *Australia and Ireland*, pp. 121–37.

70. Akenson, *Irish Diaspora*, pp. 59–151.

71. Grenfell Price, *White Settlers*, p. 197. New Zealand Irish population from Akenson, *Half the World from Home*, p. 62.
72. O'Farrell, *Irish in Australia*, p. 72. In New Zealand too there is a folklore that Irish Catholics got along better with the Maori and intermarried with them more than other white settlers. Akenson, *Half the World from Home*, p. 201.
73. Fitzpatrick, *Oceans of Consolation*. Houston and Smyth, *Irish Emigration*. For a good example see P. O'Farrell, *Letters from Irish Australia 1825–1929* (Belfast, 1984), pp. 62–82.
74. Akenson, *If the Irish Ran the World*, p. 174.
75. Akenson, *Irish Diaspora*, p. 143.
76. O'Farrell, 'Irish in Australia 1791–1870'. O'Farrell, *Irish in Australia*, pp. 117, 252, 272. P. O'Farrell, *The Catholic Church in Australia* (London, 1959).
77. Akenson, *Half the World from Home*, p. 160, 189, Houston and Smyth, *Irish Emigration*, pp. 169–80.
78. Houston and Smyth, *Irish Emigration*, p. 169.
79. C. Houston and W. Smyth, 'The Orange Order and the Expansion of the Frontier in Ontario, 1830–1900', *Journal of Historical Geography*, 4, 3 (1978), pp. 251–64. Houston and Smyth, *The Sash Canada Wore*, p. 183.
80. Ibid.
81. L. Kennedy, *Colonialism, Religion and Nationalism in Ireland* (Belfast, 1996), p. 176.
82. Bartlett, 'This Famous Island', pp. 273–4.
83. D. Fitzpatrick, *The Two Irelands 1912–1939* (Oxford, 1998), p. 6.
84. T. Hennessey, *Dividing Ireland: World War I and Partition* (London, 1998).

CHAPTER 12

The Irish and India: Imperialism, Nationalism and Internationalism

MICHAEL HOLMES
(Centre for Peace Studies, Dublin)

Introduction

Consideration of Irish emigrant communities has usually concentrated on those which have become resident in their new homes, be it in Britain, the United States or Australia. However, Irish migration also included more transitory, though no less significant, presences in a number of countries. This chapter examines one example of this: the Irish in India. The first part of this chapter explores how the Irish came to India. This was of course connected with British colonial rule in both countries, which provided the main avenues for Irish contact with India from the outset. In particular, this chapter focuses on the three main pathways to India: military service, colonial administration, and missionary groups. Each of these is examined in turn, looking at the size and scope of Irish involvement, identifying the reasons why Irish people moved to India in such numbers, and also addressing the question of their impact in India.

Independence, first in Ireland in 1922, then in India 25 years later, brought about a dramatic shift in relations between the two countries, which is examined in the second half of this chapter. The nationalist politics which swept through the two countries in the first half of the twentieth century initially created new links between them. However, those links did not last, and the chapter goes on to examine the decline of the Irish community in India and assess the impact of this on contemporary Indian–Irish relations. This chapter reveals two paradoxes to be found in the relationship of Irish people with India. The first is a historical one, between imperialism and nationalism. On the one hand, Irish people participated in imperialism, and were instrumental in establishing and maintaining British rule in India. On the other, they also have a significant anti-colonialist reputation arising from the achievements of Irish nationalism and independence. The second is a contemporary one, between nationalism and internationalism. On the one hand, Irish nationalist rhetoric advocated close ties with and support for nationalists in other countries, especially India. On the other, the substance of post-independence ties with India reveals that Ireland's international relations have failed to live up to those ideals.

The Irish and the Raj: Irish soldiers in India

European involvement with Indian affairs stretches back to 1510, when the Portuguese occupied Goa. During the sixteenth century, British traders vied with European rivals, and the British East India Company was granted its charter in 1600. The Company gradually saw off the challenge of its rivals, culminating in the defeat of the French in 1784, and by 1820 had effectively extended its rule throughout India. The Great Indian Mutiny of 1857 spelt the end for the East India Company, with the British crown taking direct responsibility in India in the following year.

Occupations, rivalries, defeats and mutinies all bear testimony to the importance of the military dimension in the history of British India, and Irishmen played a very significant part in these events. The East India Company was first allowed to raise a small number of troops in Ireland in the 1680s, but the numbers recruited were initially very low.[1] It wasn't until the Seven Years War of 1756–63 that Irish recruitment began to take off. Between 1757 and 1763, almost 17 per cent of recruits were from Ireland – 825 out of a total of 4,911.[2] Between 1778 and 1793, almost 1,500 Irish soldiers were recruited.[3] In the early nineteenth century, as official reservations about enlisting Irish soldiers ended and demand increased, Irish recruitment rose dramatically. Cadell comments that 'it would be safe to say that at the time of the Indian Mutiny considerably more than half the Company's white soldiers were Irish'.[4]

Why did so many Irishmen find themselves in British military service in India? Partly it was due to a desire to escape conditions at home in Ireland. A military career was seen as a very attractive and adventurous life offering prospects for upward mobility.[5] It is clearly evident that large numbers of Irish served amongst the rank and file in India. It is also the case that Irishmen were disproportionately common among officer ranks. By the 1750s, it was apparent that 'Irishmen were already very heavily represented among the company's ensigns'.[6] And although the numbers of Irish among the rank and file declined in the second half of the nineteenth century, the numbers at officer level remained high to the end of the century, with estimates suggesting that around 30 per cent of officers in India were of Irish extraction.[7] Irish officers were not considered to be quite as acceptable as their English counterparts. But at the same time, Indian regiments were not the most sought-after commands, which meant that Irish officers found it easier to acquire commissions in Indian regiments. Indeed, 'from 1885 to 1914, the Irish came close to monopolising the post of Commander in Chief in India'.[8]

The Irish made a considerable impact in India, at both officer level and among other ranks. Some served with great distinction. One indication of this is that of the 22 Victoria Crosses awarded in the wake of the Indian Mutiny, thirteen went to men with Irish names.[9] The fierce reputation of John Nicholson, son of a Dublin doctor, gave rise to a small sect of 'Nikalsaini' devotees, though the sect collapsed after his death during the mutiny.[10] Another two men of Irish extraction, Frederick Roberts and Claude Auchinleck, served as Commanders-in-Chief in India, and were considered to be 'the two greatest

"Indian" field-marshalls'.[11] However, India was also a very tough posting, and 'serving in India took a deadly toll on European soldiers'.[12] For every success story, there were the graves of those less fortunate, killed in action or succumbing to tropical diseases.

However, the perception of Irish soldiers amongst the native Indian population was somewhat harsher. The use of a separate name for them, the 'Rishti', to distinguish them from the English or 'Angrese', 'was more a warning to the natives than a gesture towards Irish sensitivities'.[13] During the Indian Mutiny, Nicholson earned a gruesome reputation in the Punjab for mass executions in which mutineers were blown away from the mouths of cannons.[14] Even outside of such emergencies, Irish soldiers were noted for their contempt for and brutal treatment of the Indian population. The Irish regiment with one of the worst records was the Connaught Rangers, who 'used their boots and fists to such purpose that they were more respected and feared than any other British unit in India'.[15]

Ironically, it was to be the Connaught Rangers who provided a very different postscript to Irish participation with the British military in India. In June 1920, the Connaught Ranger company stationed at Solon mutinied. The causes of the mutiny are open to some debate. Certainly, a harsh training regime, poor officers and an unusually hot summer played their part. But news of unrest filtering through from Ireland was the signal motivation. As part of their actions, the mutineers unfurled an Irish tricolour, wore Sinn Féin ribbons and demanded the withdrawal of British troops from Ireland.[16] The situation might have been defused were it not for the deaths of two soldiers when the mutineers attempted to seize a munitions store. The outcome was that 61 Connaught Rangers were court martialled and convicted of mutiny. Fourteen were sentenced to death, though in all cases save one that was commuted to imprisonment. However, Private James Daly of Mullingar was shot by firing squad in November 1920, the last British soldier to be executed.

It is clear that Irish soldiers played an integral part in maintaining British rule in India. The numbers of Irish in the British army in India declined throughout the second half of the nineteenth century. Bartlett estimates that in the early 1870s, roughly a quarter of the troops stationed in India were Irish – around 16,000 in all. By the start of the twentieth century, the proportion had slipped below 10 per cent, to about 7,000 soldiers.[17] But for a long period, Irish soldiers had been found in disproportionate numbers, at both officer and rank-and-file level. It is also clear that Irish soldiers were just as prepared as their English, Welsh and Scottish counterparts to maintain British rule through brutal means. Indeed, this survey has suggested that the Irish were if anything even more given to violence against the native population. The mutineers of the Connaught Rangers 'made no attempt to make common cause with the Indians who surrounded them', and if anything sought to avoid any suggestion that there was a connection.[18] Thus, the legacy of the largest Irish community in India is not one which sits comfortably with the present-day notion of Ireland's sympathy for and affinity with other colonized countries.

The Irish and the Raj: the administration of British India

A second channel through which an Irish presence in India was created was through the administration of British India. Again, 'the Irish were pivotal' in the Indian Civil Service (ICS),[19] although the numbers were not quite so dramatic as in the case of the military. Indeed, in the first half of the nineteenth century, when the proportion of Irishmen in the British army in India was at its peak, only about 5 per cent of the recruits for the Indian Civil Service came from Ireland.

However, the decision to reform admission requirements for the ICS in 1855 had a profound effect on recruitment in Ireland. The reforms brought in a system of open, competitive exams rather than patronage, and the effect was that 'the Irish were formally invited to participate as partners in governing India'.[20] There was a sudden explosion in Irish recruitment. Between 1855 and 1863, 24 per cent of all ICS recruits came from Ireland. This tailed off, settling back between 5 and 10 per cent from the late 1860s onwards, but Akenson suggests that this was at least partly due to 'English horror at having so many Irish university graduates in the Indian service [which] led to the entry process being rigged against the Irish'.[21] Such reservations were less apparent in other British services in India. Between 1855 and 1909, the numbers of Irish recruits in the Indian Medical Service never fell below 10 per cent, and reached a peak of 38 per cent in the 1870s.[22]

The sudden boom in recruitment for the ICS in Ireland from 1855 also had profound effects within parts of the Irish educational system. According to Cook, some schools and colleges were 'conscious of their potential role as nurseries for future Indian civil servants', and tailored their curriculum to that end.[23] Likewise, Irish universities were heavily committed to the ICS entrance exam.[24] Trinity College Dublin set up courses in Sanskrit, Arabic and zoology, all of which were subjects required for the exam, and held the right to train ICS recruits up to 1937. Queen's College Belfast had a similar language programme, while its sister college in Cork offered courses in Indian history, Indian geography, Hindu law and Muslim law.

The prejudicial attitudes which limited the numbers of Irish in the ICS did not survive once the recruits had made their way to India. It was apparent that they came from very similar backgrounds to their British colleagues. Clearly, all had received a high degree of education. About 80 per cent were from middle-class backgrounds, and about the same proportion were Protestant, although the numbers of Irish recruits from lower-middle-class and Catholic backgrounds increased later on.[25] Furthermore, they behaved like their British counterparts. The vast majority of Irish in the ICS were just as susceptible to advancing the notion of racial superiority as their British colleagues. Even for those from Catholic, nationalist backgrounds, the 'balancing act of justifying Irish equality (with the British) and superiority over the Indians' was not too difficult to achieve, and apart from a handful of 'maverick' administrators they had nothing to do with Indian nationalism.[26]

Some Irishmen rose to positions of great prominence in the administration of British India, illustrating the 'close Irish involvement in the administration of the Raj'.[27] An early example was Laurence Sulivan, who had worked for the East India Company in Bombay in the 1730s and 1740s. On his return to London in 1752, he became Chairman of the Company, and 'for over [a] quarter of a century Sulivan was to be the Company's most influential servant'.[28] Sulivan also helped advance the career of George Macartney, an Ulsterman who served as Governor of Madras, whose efforts to clean up corruption 'set a new standard of honest government'.[29] In the 1880s, two successive viceroys, Lords Dufferin and Lansdowne, had significant ties to Ireland.[30] Dubliner Whitley Stokes, a noted Celtic scholar, was also an important Anglo-Indian jurist in the latter half of the nineteenth century, who regarded his revision of the civil and criminal codes in British India as 'the greatest undertaking of his life'.[31]

Generally, the Irishmen in the ICS advanced and enforced British rule with enthusiasm. Macartney was instrumental in undermining the rule of local Indian princes, replacing them with direct British control. One of the most controversial Irish administrators in British India was Sir Michael O'Dwyer of Tipperary, who was Governor of the Punjab at the time of the notorious Amritsar massacre in 1919. He had already earned a reputation for harsh, uncompromising rule, and when soldiers under the command of Brigadier-General Reginald Dyer (the son of an Irish brewer, who had been educated in County Cork) opened fire on an unarmed crowd in Amritsar, killing at least 379 and injuring well over a thousand, O'Dwyer immediately declared his full support for Dyer. 'The damage done to Indian goodwill was immeasurable', and in 1940 O'Dwyer was assassinated by a Sikh in London.[32] Once again, what emerges clearly is the extent to which Irish people were on the side of empire.

The Irish and the Raj: the role of missionaries

The third main route by which an Irish presence was established in India was through missionary activities. Initially, the East India Company had excluded missionaries from any Christian church from India. But by the late 1820s, Protestant missions had been allowed to work there, and during the course of the 1830s Catholic missionaries followed in turn. Christianity had become part of the imperial package, and 'by accident, but with remorseless effectiveness, the missionaries aided the spread of empire'.[33]

The Church Missionary Society of Ireland (CMSI) was founded in 1814, and was one of the first Protestant mission societies active in India. Similarly, in 1838 the Irish Presbyterian Church took the decision to establish a mission to Gujarat,[34] sending in all about 300 men and women. The Maynooth Mission to India was set up in 1837 and paved the way for Catholic congregations. These included the Presentation Sisters in 1840, the Loreto Sisters in 1841, and the Christian Brothers in 1848 (though it was not until later in the century that the latter's presence in India grew to significant proportions). Despite a precipitate decline in the number of Irish missionaries in India since independence, in 1996 there were still 20 different Catholic orders in India which had Irish missionaries, as well as the Presbyterian and Methodist churches.[35]

Again, Irish missionaries played very prominent roles in British India and achieved notable personal advancement. The first five Catholic bishops of Madras were Irish,[36] and similarly the Dublin University Mission to Chota Nagpur in Hazaribagh, near Calcutta, provided five bishops for the Church of India.[37] But the more significant impact of Irish missionaries in India was probably provided by the ranks of ordinary missionary workers who served there.

Missionaries undertook four main functions in India. First of all, they became involved in education, setting up schools and colleges. Initially, there was an emphasis on providing education for the children of expatriates, and it was clear that 'the initial responsibilities of most Irish missionaries in India were closely bound up with the spiritual needs of Irish soldiers in the British Army'.[38] Second, they established orphanages, and again the military dimension is evident here. In many cases, the orphanages were set up to cater for the children of soldiers who had been killed in action.[39] Although these orphanages were a logical extension of the educational work, they also drew the missionaries into some social care tasks as well.

The third function of the missionaries was in medical work. To begin with, it was mostly the Protestant missionary societies which developed this aspect of work, with some focused almost exclusively on medical activities, such as the Leprosy Mission. Catholic missions had more hurdles to deal with, because church law prohibited certain types of medical activity, especially relating to women's health, maternity and childcare.[40] However, in the 1920s, Irish Catholic missionary orders had begun to take on nursing and general medical work, contributing to a gradual relaxation in the stance of the hierarchy in Rome. The medical work undertaken by the missionaries ranged from trying to provide general health care to dealing with occasional emergencies and disasters. For example, the Irish auxiliary of the Hibernian Church Mission Society raised £1,700 to contribute to a special Indian Famine Fund in 1897.[41]

Finally, the fourth function undertaken by the missionaries was that of religious training, and many orders began by setting up a seminary or a novitiate. To begin with, these institutions recruited almost entirely from among the expatriate community, but by the end of the nineteenth century they had begun to take in Indians. The existence of these institutions made it easier for missionaries to expand their presence in India, as they were no longer so dependent on flows of recruitment from Europe, and 'most orders record expansion throughout the length and breadth of India after their arrival'.[42]

It is difficult to establish how many Irish missionaries there were in India. They came through a variety of sources. In the early years, many Protestant missionaries came out under the auspices of British missionary societies. On the Catholic side, a number of Irish missionaries were recruited by French and Belgian missionary orders, who specifically wanted to have English-speaking Catholics to send to places like India. From the latter half of the nineteenth century onwards, indigenous Irish missionary groups became more common as well. However, it is clear that India was not as important a missionary destination as some other parts of the globe. Between 1840 and 1896, a total of 1,407 missionary priests were trained in All Hallows College in Dublin, and the vast bulk of these went to serve in the United States and in Australia. Just 53 made it to either India or South Africa.[43] The same author notes that 'the great missionary impulse of the twentieth century, spearheaded by Irish diocesan priests, found its outlet in Africa and China, and not in India where the needs were equally urgent'.[44]

One criticism that can be voiced of the missionary presence is that it represented an imposition of alien values and beliefs. Duggan has illustrated the damage done to indigenous societies and cultures by Irish missionaries in an African context, and while this is not wholly applicable to India, it does raise important questions about the value of the missionary presence.[45] In a specifically Indian context, it is clear that they tended to cater for the elite in British India, setting up schools and colleges which were the preserve of the British establishment and, occcasionally, the wealthier echelons of Indian society. However, a number also sought to address the educational needs of the marginalized elements in Indian society. This included setting up local-language schools in some instances.[46] These practices became much more pronounced after independence. The exodus of expatriates after 1947 meant that the schools and hospitals could devote themselves to a much greater degree to the needs of the local population. However, it is also true that some Irish-founded schools remain elite institutions which 'clearly cater for the ruling classes of contemporary Indian society'.[47]

The Irish and the Raj: the paradox of imperialism and nationalism

So far, this chapter has demonstrated the very important role played by Irish people in establishing and maintaining British rule in India. The old adage about the British Empire was that 'the Irish fought for it, the Scottish and Welsh ran it, but the English kept the profits'.[48] Certainly, it is true that the Irish were a hugely significant presence in the British army in India. As Bartlett argues, 'the archetypal Irishman on the sub-continent was neither missionary nor merchant, neither doctor nor administrator, but soldier'.[49] However, the preceding sections have also shown an Irish presence in other areas. MacDonnell remarks that the end of the nineteenth century could be characterized as 'a time when Ireland had temporarily relieved England of the task of governing India'.[50] Missionaries added further substance to the Irish presence in India, where 'their actions effectively aided empire'.[51] Perhaps the only group not present were traders.[52]

The first half of this chapter has also shown that the Irish were by no means reluctant to engage in the exercise of colonial rule. Despite some anti-Irish prejudice, which for a time restricted their numbers, 'in India, distinctions among Englishmen, Scotsmen and Irishmen were obscured by the more visible and critical differences between the British community of colonisers and the vast Indian population below'.[53] Indeed, Irish soldiers in particular had something of a reputation for being even more racist towards the native population than their British colleagues. Although Irish people were critical of British rule in their own country, few of them considered British rule in India to be equally unjust, and 'far from empathising with indigenous peoples overseas, the Irish, whatever their experience at home, were as brutal as any other white colonisers'.[54]

There is thus clear evidence of what has been termed 'an unwelcome heritage' for Ireland.[55] Although it was itself under British rule, in some ways it can be considered a privileged colony, whose citizens could share in some of the benefits of empire. However, Ireland's collaboration with British imperialism has not damaged the country's image. Instead, Ireland enjoys a reputation as a country which struggled against colonialism, both at home and abroad. The key to resolving this paradox lies in an examination of nationalism and the movement towards independence in Ireland.

Nationalism and independence

To begin with, nationalism helped to forge new links between the two countries, and these were very important for overturning some of the perceptions about the Irish in India. The spread of nationalist ideas in the latter half of the nineteenth century brought a new element into Indian–Irish relations. First of all, it encouraged nationalists to make comparisons with the circumstances of people in other parts of the British Empire, from which they could develop a shared analysis of the problems of colonization. Secondly, the awareness of shared experiences meant that nationalists could draw inspiration and lessons from each other.

A number of Indian nationalist leaders have noted how they were inspired by events in Ireland, and sought to apply those lessons in their own country. V.V. Giri, later to become President of India, was in Ireland studying for the Bar during the 1916 Rising, and described those experiences as playing a vital formative role in his own nationalist beliefs.[56] Another Indian nationalist leader who was particularly conscious of Irish parallels was Subhas Chandra Bose, described by one paper as 'India's De Valera', who claimed that in his native Bengal there was hardly 'an educated family where books about the Irish heroes are not read and, if I may say so, devoured'.[57] Bose 'frequently referred to the example of Ireland in trying to place India's struggle in the context of world history and the experience of other countries'.[58]

Jawaharlal Nehru was another who noted the close parallels that existed between the two countries. He first visited Ireland in 1906, where he 'was impressed by the Sinn Féin movement'.[59] In the 1920s, his father, Motilal Nehru, headed a committee which attempted to draft a constitution for an independent India, and the committee drew in particular on the constitution of the Irish Free State.[60] Jawaharlal Nehru's book, *Glimpses of World History* (1962), devotes considerable attention to Ireland's liberation struggle. He visited Ireland on two further occasions after becoming Prime Minister of India at independence, in 1949 and 1956, and maintained good relations with Eamon de Valera.

However, these ties were not reciprocated to the same degree. For the most part, Irish nationalist leaders showed only mild interest in Indian affairs. An early exception was Edmund Burke, who drew attention to the similarities between the two countries and 'warned in each case that if people were not treated fairly they would reject British rule'.[61] At the end of the nineteenth century, Frank Hugh O'Donnell, an MP of the Irish Party, was active in the India Reform Society and argued that his party were the 'natural representatives and spokesmen of the unrepresented nationalities of the Empire'.[62] O'Donnell even sought to have an Irish seat in the House of Commons given to an Indian nationalist.

Very few Irish people were directly involved in the Indian struggle for independence. Those that were drawn into it included two remarkable women. Margaret (or Gretta) Cousins had been active in the Irish Suffragette Movement before moving to India. There, she helped found the Indian Women's Association and the All-India Women's Conference.[63] Annie Besant had moved to India in 1893, where she helped found the Home Rule League, which adopted 'a policy of Irish obstruction'.[64] She became the first woman president of the Indian National Congress (INC), and a later leader of the INC went so far as to say that 'had there been no Annie Besant, there would have been no Mahatma Gandhi'.[65]

Ireland's experiences under British rule and the path it took towards independence were seen as having many resonances with the Indian experience. The Irish Famine of the late 1840s found a special echo in India, which had similarly suffered a number of serious famines. Indeed, British authorities in India tried to apply some of the responses that had been adopted in Ireland. And in both countries, the experience of famine contributed to a strengthening of the desire for independence, a point captured in Kelleher's comparison of the famine literature of both countries.[66] There are also parallels in the way that the nationalist movements in both countries were developed into mass movements, and in the response by the British authorities, with Mahatma Gandhi and Subhas Chandra Bose making comparisons between violent incidents in India in the 1930s and the infamous 'Black-and-Tans' irregular police force deployed in Ireland prior to independence.[67] And some of the incidents in the path to Irish independence struck a particularly strong chord in India, for example the sacrifice and passive resistance typefied by the hunger strike of Terence MacSwiney.[68]

The achievement of independence created further similarities of experience, none more so than the fact that both Ireland and India had to undergo the traumatic experience of partition in order to gain that independence.[69] In both cases, partition was a response to a political-religious divide. In Ireland, the unionist-dominated north-eastern corner of the island remained part of the United Kingdom as Northern Ireland, a division which remains a source of conflict on the island. In India, where the Moslem leader Jinnah was acutely conscious of the parallels with Ireland,[70] the Moslem-majority areas in the north-west and in the east were given separate independence as Pakistan.[71] The partition of India generated serious intercommunal violence and population transfers, and of course there have been three Indo-Pakistani wars since independence, with the status of Kashmir a particular bone of contention.

Post-independence: internationalism

By the middle of the twentieth century, there were two main frameworks within which an Indian–Irish relationship had developed. There was the historical imperial relationship between them which had left the legacy of an Irish community in India, and those ties had been bolstered by the links established through nationalism and independence. It seemed reasonable to assume that the two countries would maintain good ties after independence. First of all, having shared similar experiences on their way to independence, they now faced very similar problems of transition into a post-independence environment. In addition, both countries professed to wanting to build their new states on the basis of internationalist principles of mutual support and friendly relations. Finally, there was the Irish community in India. However, as this section will show, those ties never developed. Instead, the post-independence relationship is characterized by a decline in the links between the two countries.

First of all, although Ireland and India faced very similar problems in the post-independence world, they adopted quite different solutions to them, which reduced their sense of affinity. One such area was the question of relations with the former colonial master, Britain. There was of course a forum available to deal with this – the British Commonwealth. Ironically, just as India was gaining its independence and was gauging how to fit in to the Commonwealth, Ireland was pulling out of the organization. In 1948, the Inter-Party government led by John A. Costello announced that Ireland would leave the Commonwealth and become a republic. However, within a year, India had negotiated continued Commonwealth status alongside becoming a republic. Undoubtedly, Indian negotiators had paid very close attention to Ireland's arguments, and equally Britain was more prepared to accommodate Indian interests after losing one country from the organization already. But the absence of Ireland from the Commonwealth table has deprived the two countries of a forum in which they could have met on a regular basis.[72]

Another area where Ireland and India shared an outlook but ended up taking different paths was in relation to their international policies. Ireland had been neutral during the Second World War, and retained that stance in the postwar world. Similarly, India chose non-alignment, with Nehru becoming one of the leading members of the Non-Aligned Movement (NAM). Indeed, Nehru cited the example of Irish neutrality as one of the motivations for India's policy. However, despite these parallels, the relationship never developed further.[73] As Keatinge notes, Ireland never sought to develop closer links with the NAM, either as a full member or even as an observer.[74] Instead, by the 1970s Ireland was firmly established as part of the western bloc of nations, albeit as one with a slight leaning towards the developing world

Secondly, although both countries professed the desire to build good relations, this too failed to develop adequately. The nationalist links did at least lead to a symbolic exchange between the two countries. Formal diplomatic ties were established soon after Indian independence, with India opening an embassy in Dublin in 1951 and Ireland following suit in New Delhi in 1964, and there have also been a succession of formal state visits, with Indian Presidents Radhakrishnan and Reddy visiting Ireland in 1962 and 1982, and Irish Presidents Hillery and Robinson reciprocating in 1978 and 1993. The historical ties arising from the shared colonial experiences were cited by one Irish ambassador as 'one of the original reasons for [the] establishment of [an] embassy'.[75] But by the time of Mary Robinson's state visit to India, even polite diplomatic exchanges acknowledged that 'our general images of each other have perhaps remained a little hazy and a little romanticised'.[76]

One indication of the failure to build upon existing contacts is the trade relationship. Trade between the two countries declined steadily from the time of Indian independence. In the 1950s, over 2 per cent of Irish imports came from India, but by the late 1980s and early 1990s that had declined to less than 0.2 per cent. This reflected the declining importance of India as a source of Irish tea imports, particularly as the Kenyan tea market grew in significance. The proportion of Irish exports to India has always been minuscule, and has accounted for less than 0.1 per cent of all Irish exports virtually every year since 1950. What trade relations there were between the two countries were also subject to occasional disputes. In the 1980s, Irish trade unions complained at the damage being done by cheap clothing and footwear being imported from India. India in turn has protested at the restrictions placed on it by the European Union.[77]

Perhaps the nadir of post-independence Irish–Indian relations was the débâcle over Ireland's Bilateral Aid Programme (BAP) in the 1970s. In 1973, the Irish government set up its first programme of development assistance, and India was one of five priority countries chosen. But 'the Irish appear to have entered on the aid programme to India with more enthusiasm than intelligence'.[78] An initial aid project was established in 1974, but budgetary cutbacks in Ireland meant that no projects were funded until late in 1976, and in 1978 India was dropped as a priority country. Subsequently, India has received only small amounts of aid from Ireland. Partly this is because few Irish non-governmental organizations work there: 'Irish NGO's have never been quite as active in India as they have elsewhere'.[79] In addition, government funding has been limited, with the Irish embassy admitting that 'the sums are small' , though they add 'it is wonderful to see what quite a small grant can achieve'.[80]

The failed attempt to categorize India as a priority country epitomizes the lack of understanding that has developed between the two countries. The initiative suffered from a lack of planning. 'The decision to classify India as a priority country appears to have been taken without consultation', either with the relevant Indian authorities or even with the Irish embassy in Delhi.[81] Second, the initiative betrays a lack of sensitivity on the part of the Irish. Although it does face considerable problems, India is also a country of great wealth and advancement, with for example its own nuclear and space technology programmes. To have a small and not all that well developed country like Ireland announcing it would 'help' it was not the most diplomatic way to proceed.[82] Finally, the attempt to make India a priority country failed because Irish aid became much more focused on Africa. Both Irish NGOs and government development assistance have prioritized Africa.

The Irish community in India has declined precipitately during the twentieth century. Irish independence in 1922 dealt the initial blow, as it created a host of new opportunities within Ireland and persuaded many who might otherwise have thought of a career in the Indian Civil Service or in the British army to stay at home instead. When India gained its independence, that situation was compounded by the exodus of expatriates from the country. The British army was of course withdrawn, and almost all European personnel with the ICS left as well.

That left the missionary community as the one remaining pillar of the Irish presence in India. However, it too has declined hugely over the last 50 years. At independence, India adopted a policy of 'Indianization', which meant that there would be deliberate efforts to replace expatriate personnel by Indians in all sectors, including schools and hospitals. The consequences of this were felt most severely among the Irish missionary community. Although Irish missionaries already in India were allowed to remain, it became extremely difficult for new personnel coming out from Ireland to receive residential visas which would allow them to work in India. Instead, the emphasis switched to training Indian teachers, doctors and nurses to take over the tasks. By 1996, just 138 Irish missionaries remained, and many of those have have retired from active work.[83]

The paradox of nationalism and internationalism

Thus, despite constant assertions of friendship it must be concluded that the relationship between Ireland and India has declined over the course of the twentieth century. To begin with, the prospects for close ties appeared to be very good. The new nationalist links that emerged at the start of the century promised to add a new dimension to the existing Irish presence in India. Nationalism offered the prospect of a more equal and sympathetic relationship between the two countries, which would in time allow them to view the historical legacy of Irish soldiers, administrators and missionaries in a benevolent light. And as each country developed its independence, there was the prospect that nationalist links would evolve into internationalist ties. But this never occurred.

Why should nationalism have proved such a poor basis for relations? First of all, it was based on a very thin layer of elite contacts. There were very few substantive links to keep the relationship ticking over once the elites lost interest in each other. In addition, there is an inherent isolationist dimension to nationalism. This is noticeable in the way that both India and Ireland embarked upon economic strategies of self-sufficiency after independence, erecting protectionist barriers and attempting autarkic development programmes.[84] Whatever the economic value of these policies, this certainly did not help the development of closer ties between the two countries.

Nationalism also proved ill-suited to developing a more internationalist relationship because of the rather unreal expectations it engendered. These were particularly evident on the Irish side. For a time, the Irish government had vague ideas of leading the decolonized world, but they were rapidly disabused of these notions. For example, when Ireland joined the United Nations peacekeeping operation in the Congo, 'with her anti-colonial record and her neutral status he [Sean Lemass] thought Ireland well fitted to attract support from and possibly to lead the new nations'.[85] However, it soon became clear that the newly emerging nations, including India, were not crying out for guidance from Ireland, and in time Ireland also became increasingly tied into European regional relations.

The Irish community in India today is minuscule by comparison with former days. In 1997, the Irish embassy in India estimated that there were about 200 or 300 Irish citizens resident in India, most of them businessmen, missionaries or NGO workers,[86] a far cry from the time when thousands of Irish could be found there. While it would be unrealistic to expect a significant Irish community to become re-established in India, it would benefit Ireland both domestically and internationally if it were to rebuild the close relationship it once had with India.

First of all, as Ireland developed rapidly in the 1990s and became a more attractive location for foreign migrants, the spectre of racism and anti-immigrant policies raised its head. There is a sizeable Indian community in Ireland, both north and south, and while in general 'the Indian community integrated well with the local population',[87] MacGréil's studies of racial attitudes and discrimination in Ireland suggest there is some cause for concern.[88] The Irish have already shown themselves capable of racism by the behaviour of many soldiers and administrators during the British Raj. It is to be hoped that the country can learn from that past and avoid repeating those mistakes. Second, Ireland has become increasingly focused on its relations with the European Union. While that in itself is no bad thing, and indeed India has embarked upon similar paths towards Asian cooperation, it has meant that Ireland's broader international relations have tended to be ignored. This chapter has shown that there is a remarkable historical relationship between Ireland and India, from the colonial period through to the independence movements in both countries. While the contemporary relationship has not been as strong, it is important for modern Irish society to remember that the Irish diaspora includes links with India and for the country to continue to develop a spirit of international cooperation.

Notes

1. At this time there were probably more Irish soldiers serving in the French army in India than with the British. At the battle of Wandewash in 1760, the French forces were led by Count Lally-Tollendal, from Galway, and the British by Eyre Coote, born in Limerick. J.A. MacCauley, 'Lally-Tollendal in India, 1758–1761', in *Irish Sword* Vol. 5 (1961–62), pp. 81–7.

2. The analysis by Joel Mokyr and Cormac Ó Gráda, 'The Height of Irishmen and Englishmen in the 1770s: Some Evidence from the East India Company Archives', *Eighteenth-Century Ireland*, 4 (1989), p. 90, illustrates that Irish personnel were on average slightly taller than their British counterparts, and were felt to be better suited to survive the rigours of service in India.
3. Thomas Bartlett, 'The Irish Soldier in India, 1750–1947', in Michael Holmes and Denis Holmes (eds), *Ireland and India: Connections, Comparisons, Contrasts* (Dublin, 1997), p. 15.
4. Sir Patrick Cadell, 'Irish Soldiers in India', *Irish Sword*, 1 (1953), p. 79.
5. One interesting though rather atypical case is that of George Thomas, the so-called 'Rajah from Tipperary'. After deserting from the British navy, he stayed on in India and fought for local rulers. He briefly established his own fiefdom in the Punjab. Maurice Hennessy, *The Rajah from Tipperary* (London, 1971).
6. Bartlett, 'The Irish Soldier in India', p. 17.
7. Edward Spiers 'Army organisation and society in the nineteenth century', in Thomas Bartlett and Keith Jeffery (eds), *A Military History of Ireland* (Cambridge 1996), pp. 335–57.
8. Bartlett, 'The Irish Soldier in India', p. 21.
9. Hiram Morgan, 'An Unwelcome Heritage: Ireland's Role in British Empire-Building', *History of European Ideas*, 19, 4–6 (1994), p. 620.
10. Narinder Kapur, *The Irish Raj: Illustrated Stories About Irish in India and Indians in Ireland* (Antrim, 1997), p. 19.
11. T.G. Fraser, 'Ireland and India', in Keith Jeffery (ed.), *'An Irish Empire'? Aspects of Ireland and the British Empire* (Manchester, 1996), p. 78.
12. Bartlett, 'The Irish Soldier in India', p. 15.
13. Ibid., p. 22.
14. Anthony Bishop, 'John Nicholson in the Indian Mutiny', *Irish Sword*, 8 (1967–68), pp. 277–87.
15. Frank Richards *Old Soldier Sahib*, London 1928.
16. Bartlett, 'The Irish Soldier in India', p. 24.
17. Ibid., p. 20.
18. Ibid., p. 25.
19. Donald H. Akenson, *The Irish Diaspora: A Primer* (Toronto and Belfast, 1996), p. 145.
20. Scott B. Cook, 'The Irish Raj: Social Origins and Careers of Irishmen in the Indian Civil Service, 1855–1914', *Journal of Social History*, 20, 3 (1987), p. 521.
21. Akenson, *Irish Diaspora*, p. 145. Two other reasons that can be cited for the drop in Irish recruitment are the growth in middle-class job opportunities in Ireland at this time, and the increasingly unfavourable reputation of 'competition wallahs'. Cook, 'Irish Raj', p. 512.
22. Cook, 'Irish Raj', p. 525, fn. 27.
23. Ibid., p. 511.
24. Kieran Flanagan, 'The Rise and Fall of the "Celtic Ineligible": Competitive Examinations for the Irish and Indian Civil Services in Relation to the Educational and Occupational Structure of Ireland, 1853–1921', D.Phil dissertation (University of Sussex, 1977), p. 292.
25. Cook, 'Irish Raj', pp. 515–17.
26. Ibid., p. 522.
27. Fraser, 'Ireland and India', p. 88.
28. Ibid., p. 80.

29. Ibid., p. 81.
30. Cook, 'Irish Raj', p. 520.
31. R.I. Best, *Whitley Stokes (1830–1909): A Memorial Discourse* (Dublin, 1951), p. 9.
32. Fraser, 'Ireland and India', pp. 88–9.
33. Akenson, *Irish Diaspora*, p. 147.
34. Kapur, *The Irish Raj*, pp. 9–14.
35. IMU, *Survey of Personnel* (Dublin, 1996), pp. 18, 35.
36. Anne Maher, 'Missionary Links: Past, Present and Future', in Holmes and Holmes (eds), *Ireland and India*, p. 49, fn. 4.
37. Alan Acheson, *A History of the Church of Ireland, 1691–1996* (Dublin, 1997), p. 221.
38. Maher, 'Missionary Links', p. 33.
39. Perhaps the most famous (albeit fictional) Indian orphan of all is the son of an Irish soldier – the Rudyard Kipling character Kim, or 'Kimball O'Hara'.
40. Edmund M. Hogan, *The Irish Missionary Movement: A Historical Survey, 1830–1980* (Dublin, 1990), pp. 106–7.
41. Acheson, *History of the Church of Ireland*, pp. 222–3.
42. Maher, 'Missionary Links', p. 35.
43. Hogan, *Irish Missionary Movement*, p. 20.
44. Ibid., pp. 30–1.
45. Carolyn Duggan, 'Black Skins, White Souls: Some African Literary Responses to the Irish Mission', paper presented to the conference on 'The Irish Diaspora', University College Cork, November 1997.
46. Maher, 'Missionary Links', p. 34.
47. Ibid., p. 48.
48. Hennessy, *Rajah from Tipperary*, p. 13.
49. Bartlett, 'The Irish Soldier in India', p. 12.
50. Quoted in Cook, 'Irish Raj', p. 520.
51. Akenson, *Irish Diaspora*, p. 146.
52. Morgan, 'An Unwelcome Heritage', pp. 621–2.
53. Cook, 'Irish Raj', p. 514.
54. Morgan, 'An Unwelcome Heritage', p. 619.
55. Ibid., p. 619.
56. Sarmila Bose and Eilís Ward, ' "Ireland's Cause is India's Cause": Elite Links and Nationalist Politics', in Holmes and Holmes (eds), *Ireland and India*, p. 57.
57. Quoted in ibid., p. 62.
58. Ibid., p. 60.
59. S. Gopal, *Jawaharlal Nehru: A Biography, Vol. 1 (1889–1947)* (London, 1975), p. 22.
60. Kapur, *The Irish Raj*, p. 38. Brian Girvin, 'Political Independence and Democratic Consolidation', in Holmes and Holmes (eds), *Ireland and India*, pp. 313–14 explores further similarities between the Indian constitution adopted in 1949 and the Irish constitution adopted in 1937, though he emphasizes that there are as many differences as points of comparison.
61. Girvin, 'Political Independence', p. 121.
62. Keith Jeffery, 'Introduction', in Jeffery (ed.), *'An Irish Empire'?*, p. 8.
63. Bernadette Whelan, 'Women and the Struggle for Independence', in Holmes and Holmes (eds), *Ireland and India*, p. 86.
64. Tara Chand, *History of the Freedom Movement in India* (Delhi, 1967), p. 449.

65. Quoted in Kapur, *The Irish Raj*, p. 23.
66. Margaret Kelleher, 'Literary Connections: Cultural Revival, Political Independence and the Present', in Holmes and Holmes (eds), *Ireland and India*, pp. 107–12.
67. Bose and Ward, ' "Ireland's Cause is India's Cause" ', p. 61.
68. Ibid., p. 55.
69. T.G. Fraser, *Partition in Ireland, India and the Palestine* (London, 1984) and Nicholas Mansergh, 'The Prelude to Partition: Concepts and Aims in Ireland and India', in Mansergh, *Nationalism and Independence: Selected Irish Papers* (Cork, 1997).
70. See Kapur, *The Irish Raj*, p. 34.
71. In 1972 East Pakistan was to gain its own independence as Bangladesh.
72. Nicholas Rees, 'International Affairs: Principles and Practice', in Holmes and Holmes (eds), *Ireland and India*, pp. 211–13.
73. Ibid., pp. 213–16.
74. Patrick Keatinge *The Formulation of Irish Foreign Policy* (Dublin, 1973).
75. Michael Holmes, Nicholas Rees and Bernadette Whelan, *The Poor Relation: Irish Foreign Policy and the Third World* (Dublin, 1993), p. 75.
76. See Michael Holmes, 'A Friend of India? Ireland and the Diplomatic Relationship', in Holmes and Holmes (eds), *Ireland and India*, p. 243.
77. Ibid., pp. 240–3.
78. Holmes, Rees and Whelan, *The Poor Relation*, p. 89.
79. Holmes, 'A Friend of India?', p. 237.
80. Ibid., p. 236.
81. Holmes, Rees and Whelan, *The Poor Relation*, p. 88.
82. Holmes, 'A Friend of India?', pp. 234–5.
83. Maher, 'Missionary Links', pp. 42–3.
84. Sharit Bhowmik and Sophia Carey, 'Trade Unions, the Economy and the State After Independence', in Holmes and Holmes (eds), *Ireland and India*, pp. 150–4.
85. Nina Heathcote, 'Ireland and the United Nations Operation in the Congo', *International Relations*, 3, 11 (1971), p. 881. See also Holmes, Rees and Whelan, *The Poor Relation*, pp. 154–8.
86. Holmes, 'A Friend of India?', p. 233.
87. Narinder Kapur, 'The Settlement of Indians in Ireland', in Holmes and Holmes (eds), *Ireland and India*, p. 177.
88. Ibid., pp. 179–80.

CHAPTER 13

Odd Man Out:
The South African Experience

DONAL P. MCCRACKEN

(History Department, Durban-Westville)

There was a time during the apartheid era when the historian of the Irish dia-spora in South Africa was inundated with requests from white South Africans wanting to prove their Irish ancestry. An Irish passport was a prized posses-sion. The bizarre thing about most of these entreaties was that the petitioners knew little of Ireland and cared nothing for it. In the USA such third genera-tion might have been 'Irish'; in South Africa they were biltong-eating South African.

It was ironic. Their grandfathers – and it was usually a male link with the emerald isle – had been ideal emigrants. They themselves had maintained an affection for the Erin's green shores, but they had seen to it that their children had become South Africans. In a land tortured by race-speak, many Irish for-got their own ethnicity and their religious bigotry. In South Africa 'Irishness' was – and still is – essentially a first-generation phenomenon, a characteristic observed by Thomas O'Culleanain in February 1921:

> There are hundreds of young South Africans, men and women, Irish on both sides for two generations, who are in no sense Irish. Their parents and grand-parents might [as] well have come from Yorkshire or Devon. They have Irish names and Irish blood, but they are English of English. In no other country has there been such a complete loss of nationality.[1]

We few, we happy few, we band of brothers . . .

Professor Akenson has observed that the 'great value of the South African case is that it defines one end of the range of possible patterns that Irish emigra-tion could take'.[2] That is largely true, but there is one major problem facing the historian of the Irish diaspora in southern Africa. Statistical informa-tion concerning South Africa in the nineteenth century is fragmented and deceptive. One point needs to be kept firmly in mind: the white population of nineteenth-century South Africa was small and their immigrant segment tiny in the jigsaw of political units and subunits with black, Afrikaner and British vying for hegemony. Despite the mineral revolution, South Africa remained poor,

Table 13.1: Number of first-generation Irish in South Africa

Date	Total	Cape	Natal	Transvaal	OFS/ORC
1875	?	3,759	?	?	?
1891	?	4,184	1,060	?	?
1904	17,899	8,605	2,229	5,362	1,703
1911	14,572	5,260	1,775	6,531	976
1918	11,822				
1921	12,289				
1926	12,336				
1936	10,622				
1946	8,903				
1951	9,620				
1985	11,259				

Note:
Transvaal = Transvaal + Swaziland
Orange Free State = pre 1900 and post 1911
Orange River Colony = 1900–10

restless and unattractive to the potential emigrant and the Afrikaner republics of the Transvaal and Orange Free State shunned English-speaking immigrants.

Half-hearted emigration schemes to the British colonies of the Cape and of Natal brought in occasional trickles of English-speaking settlers. In 1875 there were 28,200 immigrants at the Cape of whom 13 per cent were first-generation Irish. By 1891 this immigrant population had grown to 49,800 but the proportion of immigrants who were Irish was down to 8 per cent. In terms of the entire white population the Irish constituted a mere 1.1 per cent in 1891.[3] To the north-east, in the colony of Natal, the small number of whites at that time – only 47,000 – meant that the thousand or so Irish there made up 2.3 per cent of the white population.[4]

The meagre Irish component of the meagre white population in these two British colonies clearly indicates that the 'huddled masses yearning to breathe free' went elsewhere. The precise numbers of first-generation Irish in South Africa are illustrated in Table 13.1. In none of these regions does the Irish component exceed 2.3 per cent of the white population.[5] It has been estimated that the multiplier between first and previous generations of immigrants to the Cape was 3.375, thus making the total of Irish and colonial Irish in 1891 about 14,000 persons. This represents 3.7 per cent of the white population then, but 10.9 per cent of all people of British Isles origin. This 3.7 per cent compares with 18.7 per cent in New Zealand and 25.7 per cent in Australia at that time.[6] In 1911 the Irish were the fifth largest immigrant group in South Africa, behind the English, Scots, Russians and Germans but, interestingly, ahead of the Dutch.

Early Irish settlers

The British occupied the Cape from 1795 to 1803 and returned permanently in 1806. The occasional practice of granting 'colonial passes' of residence in the Cape to soldiers being discharged meant that a number of Irish ex-soldiers lived in the Cape during the early days of the British regime. Irish deserters were also quite common, some fleeing the colony to live beyond the eastern frontier in the land occupied by the Xhosa.[7]

The first concerted attempt by the British government to Anglicize the Cape and one of the earliest state-financed emigration schemes to involve Irish emigrants came in 1820 with the arrival of some 4,000 'English' settlers; 8 per cent (350) of these came from the counties of Wicklow and Cork. For the Irish the scheme was a disaster. They were sent 125 miles north of Cape Town to the semi-desert area around Clanwilliam in the north-western Cape. The Reverend Francis McCleland writing to the Bishop of Waterford mournfully observed, 'The poorest curacy in Ireland would be preferable to our present situation'. When George Thompson visited Clanwilliam a few years later he was horrified that such a large number of people should have been set down in a place

> which is barely sufficient for the competent subsistence of two boor's families. There did not appear to me to be above forty acres of land fit for cultivation in the whole place. The foundation of a house begun by the eccentric and speculative Mr Parker, the original head of the Irish emigrants, was a melancholy memorial of the entire failure and dispersion of this party.

It was William Parker, the more vocal of the leaders of the two main Irish parties, who firmly believed that sectarianism lay behind the shabby treatment of the Irish. In a vilifying pamphlet entitled *Jesuits unmasked*, this fervent Irish Protestant lambasted the Colonial Secretary at the Cape, Lieutenant Colonel Bird, who happened to be a Catholic.[8]

After an abortive attempt to establish a fishing port at 'New Cork', beside Saldanha Bay, the Irish were moved in July 1820 to the Albany district of the Eastern Cape. Six families remained behind and for many decades an Irish community existed in remote Namaqualand. While Irish farms with such names as Home Rule, Kildare, Dromore and The Dargle were scattered across the Cape and Natal, Namaqualand and the areas around the Assegai and Ncazala rivers, south-west of Grahamstown in the Eastern Cape, remained the only Irish rural communities. And these Irish farmers in Africa were no landed elite. In the mid-1820s one traveller between Grahamstown and the Kowie river mouth noted:

> On my way I called at Captain Butler's, an Irish settler, abounding in hospitality, but at that time, poor fellow! but ill supplied with the means of exercising this liberal disposition, so general among his countrymen. We dined upon a little cheese and butter-milk; but it was his best, and given with cordiality. A short time before, his only daughter, a child about three years old, had died of the bite of a serpent, which she had trod upon while playing in the garden. Poor Mrs Butler appeared very disconsolate, and her mind in a morbid, disordered state, in consequence of this distressing event.[9]

Another equally disastrous attempt at Irish immigration to the Cape occurred in 1823, when an Irish speculator, John Ingram, shipped out on the *Barossa* 352 destitute people from Cork. But news of the treatment of the 1820 settlers had already reached Ireland and Ingram had great difficulty in finding suitable emigrants to sign indentures prior to sailing. A later commission of inquiry reported:

> From an influence which Mr Ingram attributes to the Catholic Priests in the County Cork, but which from the evidence of some people we think is with more justice to be imputed to certain Reports of the failure of the former Emigration that were then circulated in Ireland, a great majority of those who had promised to embark subsequently declined to go, and several who had signed Indentures embarked in the ship *Barossa* and remained on board for some time, but suddenly renounced their engagements and all intention of proceeding to the Cape.

Described as 'generally very illiterate, and some of them are indifferent Characters' and 'much given to drunkenness', these 1823 immigrants merely served to confirm the authorities' reservations about Irish settlers. The 1820 Irish settlers were said to have created problems even when on board ship out at sea: 'Great disturbance with the Irish people, sharpening both sides of their knives'. Conversely, the Irish immigrants complained of their treatment and wrote home

> to their friends in Ireland giving a bad account of the Colony . . . The Account [in Cork] was that the Colony was in a state of starvation and that the former emigrants only wished the government to send them to Van Diemen's Land, or some other place out of the Colony.[10]

These complaints were not made without cause. Ingram treated his fellow Irish more like slaves than indentured servants. He was not beyond having the law administer the lash on those who dared venture beyond the confines of the harsh agreements he had got them to sign once out to sea. And as for the accommodation provided, this was condemned as 'neither in a proper or tenantable state'. Some of these unfortunate souls worked directly for Ingram, others as 'mechanics and labourers' in Cape Town. Many were employed in the erection of public buildings in the Worcester area and in making the road over the Franschhoek pass.

Between 1846 and 1851 about 1,400 Irish were brought in under an emigration scheme. In 1851, amid a storm of scandal concerning improprieties on board their emigrant ship, 46 girls arrived in Table Bay. The captain, crew and surgeon had mixed quite freely with the girls and only the behaviour of the ship's steward warranted the usual end-of-voyage gratuity. Lady Duff-Gordon was later to write of these *Gentoo* girls:

> Miss Coutts and the Bishop . . . emptied a shipload of young ladies from a 'Reformatory' into the streets of Cape Town and what in London is called a 'pretty horse-breaker' is here known as one of 'Miss Coutts' young ladies'.

In 1857, 163 Irish women and 10 Irish males, including three infant boys, were taken to the Eastern Cape on board the 583-ton *Lady Kennaway*. The average age of the Irish on board was 22 years old. The idea was that the girls would marry German veteran mercenaries of the Crimean War. Only a few, however, did marry soldiers, though most of them did settle in the Eastern Cape.[11] By 1859 Lady Duff Gordon could remark, 'every ragged Irish girl is in place somewhere'.

Between 1857 and 1862 about 5,000 Irish were shipped out to South Africa under another scheme. But by then the colonial antipathy to unskilled Irish settlers, mainly on the grounds of drunkenness, was very great and in 1860 the Cape's immigration agent in London was instructed not to seek out Irish emigrants. Of the period 1857–67 one historian has written:

Not all Irish settlers were difficult but as a group they caused more trouble than any other settlers. They refused offers of employment in outlying districts where there were no Catholic churches and stubbornly insisted on remaining in Cape Town or Port Elizabeth. Their overall lack of training of any sort caused dissatisfaction and they frequently professed to trades of which they were totally ignorant. The Fort Beaufort Immigration Board was particularly unhappy with their Irish settlers and in 1860 refused to take more. In a letter received on 17.1.1861 Field [immigration agent in London] promised to limit Irish immigration in future but applications from Irish settlers already at the Cape [to bring out friends and relatives] continued to flow in.

This local hostility did not stop the flow of Irish-assisted emigrants but it did reduce it, so that by the turn of the century the total of assisted Irish passages granted over the previous 80 years stood at around 15,000, or about 30 per cent of assisted settlers.[12] This small figure was despite efforts to promote Irish immigration, from as early as May 1840, by the Cape's celebrated Irish Attorney-General, William Porter, and those of the magistrate of Ladysmith in Natal, Dr T.T. Kelly, to do the same in 1855 and again in 1857. Kelly's dream was to flood Natal with 'hardy and industrious peasant farmers of Ulster'.[13]

These statistics do not include the Irish who came in government or military service and who stayed on, nor do they include those who came at their own expense. Between 1844 and 1910 about 60,000 Irish emigrants left parts of the British Isles for the Cape or Natal, the peak years being 1848–50 (9,280 immigrants), 1858–64 (17,084), 1872–67 (20,965) and 1897–1905 (11,563).[14]

The abortive scheme of 1849–50 to establish a convict settlement at the Cape would have boosted considerably both the numbers of the white population at the Cape and the Irish component of it. In September 1849 a prison hulk named the *Neptune* with 288 ticket-of-leave men on board arrived in Table Bay: most of the prisoners were Young Irelanders. John Mitchel, himself incarcerated in the ship, might praise the Cape for rejecting the scheme 'in defence of their honour', but its failure and the departure of the *Neptune* in February 1850 for Tasmania finally closed the door for mass Irish convict emigration to South Africa.[15]

There were also some Irish who moved on to Australia from South Africa on a voluntary basis, especially after gold was discovered in Australia in 1850. Names and numbers are hard to come by, but we do know that eleven ships which sailed from the Cape to Australia and/or New Zealand between April 1863 and April 1865 had 137 Irish on board.[16] One suspects that from the 1860s up to the discovery of gold in the Transvaal in the 1880s such onward Irish migration was not uncommon.

By 1876 the *Cape Town Daily News* was concluding:

> We are afraid we could not induce the Irish labouring classes to come to this colony in anything like sufficient numbers. They know nothing of it beyond having a dim idea that it is associated with Kaffir wars; but they know all about America and Australia, or think they do, having heard them talked about from their infancy by those who had friends there – and away they pour across the Atlantic, sometimes to a glutted labour market, where they find themselves worse off than at home. There is much in a name.[17]

That was it in a nutshell: by the 1870s Irish emigration patterns were fixed, family and cultural ties and support networks were well developed in the Americas and in the antipodes. While Irish chain emigration existed to some extent in the South African retail trade and in Port Elizabeth in the 1850s, this was not the norm.

In 1850 the potential Irish emigrant with money for a fare could get to North America for £4, steaming-time being eleven days to New York. The Cape cost at least £12 steerage passage and was 30 days with steam and a good two to three months with sail. It is true that Australia was two months by steamer and possibly as much as four months under sail, but the fare of £15 was not excessively more than to the Cape. It is true that land could be cheaper in South Africa than in South Australia, but there was no getting around South Africa's bad reputation. Take two examples from a contemporary emigration tract:

> The Eastern Province [of the Cape] was the scene of the late Caffre war, and is the *habitat* of the lion, river horse, panther, elephant, wolf, baboon, porcupine, quaqqa, antelope, ostrich, and the most deadly snakes. It produces the tropical fruits in perfection, a sure sign of a nearly torrid climate.

> It has been for some time observed that the 'Irish difficulty' has been lately show-ing a tendency to solve itself by the emigration of the inhabitants of whole dis-tricts to America . . . In other colonies emigrants are absorbed into an existing civilized population. At Natal they only land to have to cope with strangers, the wilderness and savages. Emigration will not do there. Nothing but wholesale colonization, upon well matured, and orderly contrived plan will answer.[18]

The truth was that there was neither the need nor the desire on the part of the Famine Irish to venture to 'darkest Africa'. It is not, therefore, a surprise that Dublin Castle was wont to use South Africa as a dumping ground for such exposed informers as Alfred Aylward, the Fenian, and James Carey, the Invincible.[19]

Tolerant of others?

This reluctance of the Irish to come to Africa had a profound effect on the nature of what Irish community there was in colonial and republican South Africa. The obvious consequence was that the Irish were numerically few and proportionately a minority of a minority: a section of the English-speaking white population which barely had its own group identity in the early decades of the nineteenth century. Hamilton Ross (1774–1853), with his fleet of merchant ships, carriages and slaves, might proclaim his origins by employing an Irish piper at his country estate, but most Irish in this early period blended into colonial society.[20] What is noteworthy is that the Irish were assimilated not only into English society, but also on occasion into black and Afrikaner culture: the existence of people of mixed blood with names such as Ogle, Fynn and MacBride, and of Afrikaner stock with names like O'Reilly, O'Grady and most notably O'Neil, is testimony to that phenomenon. An anonymous anti-slave pamphlet, dated 1828, recorded the following extraordinary allegation:

> In one instance, which came under the observation of the writer, in one of the most genteel families in Cape Town, an Irishman is kept, for no other apparent purpose but that of improving the stock of slaves. The children of this man are the fairest and handsomest slave children I have seen in South Africa.[21]

Be this as it may, cross-cultural alliances were made by some Irish men in the early nineteenth century. That this process came to an abrupt halt in the 1840s can be ascribed to the expansion of the influence of the Catholic Church in the Cape under its first bishop, a Wexford Dominican named Patrick Raymond Griffith. As well as imposing discipline on what had been a fairly lax flock, he actively discouraged cohabitation between white and black. In his diary for 30 August 1838 Bishop Griffith records his visit to Fort Beaufort in the Eastern Cape: 'I was instantly visited by an Irish Papist named McMahon from near Lim-k, who told me a sad story of his own State and that of the other only two Catholics in this Town, all three living with Black Women. MacMahon promises change . . .'.[22] For the scholar a dearth of South African Irish letters or diaries in the nineteenth century has meant that little is known about how these people who crossed racial or cultural divides responded to an increasingly racially stratified society. One can only imagine their sad plight.

Marriage with Calvinists was equally intolerable to the Catholic Church authorities in South Africa. Yet strangely, even when penal legislation operated against Catholics in the Transvaal republic, almost to a man, Irish Catholics living there supported the republican cause long before it became fashionable in Irish nationalist circles to be overtly pro-Boer. No evidence exists for the thesis that Irish Catholics were intimidated against emigrating to South Africa because a majority of the white population was Calvinist.[23]

As the nineteenth century progressed, other factors militated against further assimilation and a South African Irish identity emerged. With the obvious failure of assisted emigration schemes, financial restrictions prohibited an influx of any poor Catholic Irish who might have desired to risk diverging from the norm. This meant that, as in the case of Ontario, an anomaly existed: as will be seen, only those capable of artisan or professional work (the skilled and semi-skilled) and the adventurous or foolhardy dared to venture to Africa. By the nature of Irish society this meant that the better-off Protestants began to look on South Africa as a viable destination for themselves or, more likely, for their sons. One Ulster immigrant wrote of the 1880s: 'Quite a few young men and women left Armagh for South Africa during my boyhood. They were mostly young business people like myself and when my turn came, I wrote to South Africa with a view to making this my home.' Once there the young Ulster Protestant could alleviate his homesickness with the consolation – real or imaginary – that the Afrikaners

> are just like our people. They are religious, their Sunday is like ours. They are fond of jokes and stories. They are generous, but their hospitality surpasses anything you can think of. I spend most of my weekends at farms and feel just as much at home as in Armagh. I see a tremendous similarity of character to our own Ulster people.[24]

Precise figures of the Irish Catholic/Protestant breakdown do not exist, but in the Cape Mounted Police at the turn of the century the religious background of Irish recruits was 60 per cent Protestant to 40 per cent Catholic. Of the Protestants, the Church of Ireland constituted 65 per cent. This would seem to be a fairly accurate picture of the overall religious affiliation of Irish people in late nineteenth-century South Africa.[25]

It is true that the outward trappings of an Irish sectarian divide existed in the Cape, but the fervour of their respective devotees was ameliorated by the intimacy of colonial society and by common dangers far more immediate than the threat of Rome or the Orange menace. In 1900 *The Gael* noted, 'Irish blood is a sure recommendation to the friendship of all Cape Irishmen'.[26] On the Protestant side an Orange warrant from the Grand Lodge of England had been issued for the Cape as early as 1824, though the first lodge was formed in Cape Town only in 1852. By 1907 at least nineteen lodges had existed at one time or another in South Africa; of these six were in the Transvaal, including several 'Dutch' lodges. Those in the Cape seem to have been connected with the military; in the Transvaal an unholy alliance of mining and retailing concerns, coupled with Boer fundamentalists, seems to have dominated Orangeism. In 1905, after the second Anglo-Boer war, the Loyal Orange Institution of British South Africa was formed. By 1909 it had 26 lodges, two-thirds of which were in the Transvaal.[27]

Conversely, from the 1880s the Irish National Foresters (INF) had at least five lodges in South Africa, the most notable being the Sarsfield lodge in Cape Town and the Wolfe Tone lodge in Johannesburg.[28] Until the highveld section was hijacked by John MacBride and Arthur Griffith in the late 1890s, the INF's political stance was of a moderate Home Rule variety. In September 1899 the republican *Standard and Diggers' News* reported the statement that: 'The Barberton Irishmen heartily sympathise with the Transvaal and decline to believe that the Durban Irishmen will join the cry of the capitalists'.[29]

In Natal the United Irish Association had as its patrons the Governor and the Prime Minister, both Irishmen. Only when the third Home Rule bill crisis arose in the second decade of the twentieth century did serious Irish sectarian tensions arise in South Africa. Before then non-sectarian Irish societies flourished, the first apparently being formed in Cape Town in 1829,[30] and the annual St Patrick's Day society dinners in many South African towns were the occasion of much celebrating, an interchange of telegrams of greeting between Irish societies and lengthy, and at times dramatic coverage in the local press.[31] One such account in early Johannesburg ended with the baton-wielding police entering by the doors and the special government guests exiting by the windows.

The emergence of an Irish identity was promoted by such Irish quasi-religio-political organizations and by the network of Irish social and benefit societies. But it was also the consequence of a range of other factors, such as the growth of an organized Catholic Church, including a famous Irish-dominated Christian Brothers' school in Kimberley. Not that the Christian Brothers were averse to taking Irish Protestant boys: in 1898 the Kimberley school had 114 pupils, of whom 52 were Protestant. There were 35 boys we know were Irish, four of whom were Protestant. Most of the Irish boys' parents worked on the diamond mines in one capacity or another, the Irish Protestant parents having somewhat better positions. Two Catholic parents were farmers in Basutoland (Lesotho).

Irish clergy were to be found in many areas, but they were especially prominent in the Eastern Cape where there was a long succession of Irish Catholic bishops. The impact of such Irish ecclesiastics cannot be underestimated, yet in the South Africa context 'Irishness' and 'Catholicism' do not strike the historian as being one and the same. Writing in 1915 Elliot O'Donnell recognized this phenomenon:

> The religious element among the South African Irish is not so pronounced as in America and elsewhere, there being a marked and growing tendency towards indifference, which may be, partly at all events, accounted for by the fact that the majority of the Irish immigrants are Anglo-Irish and not Celts.[32]

The troublemakers

On a different level nineteenth-century South Africa witnessed the periodical emergence of notorious Irishmen who, while not holding a monopoly on trouble-making, did draw attention to the fact that there were Irish in the region. In 1808 two Irish ne'er-do-wells instigated a slave revolt in the Zwartland of the Western Cape and then deserted, leaving their ragtag slave army to the mercy of the dragoons.[33] In the 1880s a gang of Irish bandits, ex-navvies, in an 'Irish Brigade' and under a 'Captain Moonlight', terrorized the Eastern Transvaal and parts of Portuguese Mozambique.[34] At the beginning of the decade as the first Anglo-Boer war loomed, the 'ubiquitous' Alfred Aylward, editor of the *Natal Witness* in Pietermaritzburg, was actively promoting the Boer cause in direct opposition to the loyalties of his readers. It was said of Pietermaritzburg at that time that there was 'mud in the streets and mud in the press'.

Aylward had already caused much trouble for the British authorities on the diamond fields in the 1870s, when he had been one of the instigators of the abortive 'Black flag rebellion'. His remarkably detached book *The Transvaal of Today: War, Witchcraft, Sport and Spoils in South Africa* was published in 1878 but his apogee came when with the Boer forces at the battle of Majuba in 1881 he placed the brain of Dubliner General George Colley back into its skull. In 1899, ten years after Aylward's death in America, Griffith resurrected back in Ireland the legend of 'Joubert's Fenian'.[35] Griffith, like Aylward, had taken a similarly dismissive view of his readers' political leanings when editing the *Middelburg Courant* in the 1890s before the second Anglo-Boer war.[36]

Farm and ghetto

Perhaps of more significance in creating in the public mind the concept of an Irish identity in South Africa was the concentration of the Irish in specific places. While Irish agricultural labourers could be found in the Western Cape in the early nineteenth century, the Irish who ventured to South Africa in the colonial period were predominantly urbanized: in 1891 at the Cape 85 per cent of the Irish lived in towns. Indeed there was not a white settlement in the Cape with a population over 2,000 which did not have at least one Irish person living there.[37] This is reinforced by the number of South African settlements with such Irish-related names as Donnybrook and Belfast. (It might also be said that there was not a gaol in the colony without at least one Irishman: the Breakwater Jail in Cape Town had no shortage of inmates with Irish names.)

During the British occupation of the Transvaal (1877–81), a harebrained scheme was devised to sell 6,000-acre Transvaal farms to potential immigrants in Ireland. It was backed by a Dublin-published guide to the former republic. Though by this time the leaders of Afrikaner and Irish nationalism had already made tentative overtures to each other, which were soon to involve the land league, nothing came of the scheme.[38] A contributing factor to this failure was the propensity of the South African Irish to urban living. This was in part a reluctance of some to return to the agricultural existence from which they were escaping, but also it seems that large numbers of Irish emigrants to the region came from the provinces of Ulster and Leinster, where as well as being more Anglicized, economic development was more advanced than elsewhere. For example, the only Irish county in the south and west to rival Dublin and Antrim for recruitment to the Cape Mounted Police was Cork. The pattern for the Irish in the Natal Mounted Police is similar, with Ulster and Leinster consituting 68 per cent of the recruitment and counties Dublin, Antrim and Cork providing the highest number of recruits.[39]

Irish ghetto areas existed in at least two Cape settlements, though they were small areas and it is doubtful whether they were exclusively Irish. In the 1890s at Newlands, then outside Cape Town, an impoverished Irish community lived in Irish Town, centred on Kildare Street. They gained a livelihood from working in the nearby Ohlsson's brewery. In the twentieth century the community disappeared, as did the name, and the single-storey cottages were occupied by people of mixed race.[40] Earlier, part of Zonnebloem in central Cape Town had a high rate of Irish residency. Perhaps here lived the Irish cabbies whose brogues dominated the streets of Cape Town in the mid-century; it is likely that they were employed by the Hibernia Omnibus Company.[41] Along the coast at Port Elizabeth another Irish Town existed: situated between Main Street and the harbour, it was regarded as a rough area. In 1909, at the end of the colonial era, the Kynoch Explosive Company of Arklow opened a factory just south of Durban at Umbogintwini. Initially it was run by workers whom the company brought out from Ireland. Of the four Irish settlements only the remnants of this one survive into the late twentieth century.[42]

In the mining regions of Griqualand West, around Kimberley, and on the gold-rich Rand of the Transvaal Republic, communities of poor Irish miners existed. In the Transvaal, Johannesburg, Barberton, Pilgrim's Rest and possibly Lydenburg had Irish diggers. In Johannesburg there appears to have been a concentration of Irish *uitlanders* in wards 3 and 4. In 1896 there were 807 Irish people living within three miles of Market Square in Johannesburg and a further 190 in outlying suburbs, making a total of almost 1,000 Irish people in the town, two-thirds of whom were male. This was about 4 per cent of the town's *uitlander* population and about the same as the Australian element in the mining settlement.[43]

Irish people were prominent in many South African towns, but because they were not impoverished they were residentially scattered. Considering the size of the total Irish population of the subcontinent, it is remarkable how many prominent Irish citizens there were. Cape Town had the Irish Attorney-General William Porter; the politician and commander of the Cape Town Irish Rifles, the Chevalier T.J. O'Reilly; the hotelier James Cavanagh and a host of other Irish dignitaries. Kimberley had businessmen such as Moses Cornwall, John Orr and R.H. Henderson, this last eventually becoming a cabinet minister under General Hertzog. East London had the shipping and forwarding agent John Gately. In Bloemfontein there was the 'Irish Pioneer', W.D. Savage; and in Pretoria there was the all-powerful colonial Irishman, Solomon Gillingham, whose baker's shop had a back room where the *Freeman's Journal* could be read.[44] These men were also the patrons of Irish societies and their prominence in public life generally tended to exaggerate the perception of the size and influence of the Irish community.

South Africa got the cream?

The impact of this Irish community on South Africa seemed far out of proportion to its numerical strength. Was this the product of a superior class of Irish immigrant?[45] The breakdown of 'Irish colonial gentry' listed by Burke's might suggest not (see Table 13.2).

On the other hand, we know South Africa offered little to the destitute in the way of employment or cultural support networks, and it was expensive to get there. The region predominantly attracted those Irish with marketable skills.

Table 13.2: South African-Irishmen listed in Burke's *Colonial Gentry*

Region	No. Irish gentry listed
Australian colonies	49
Canada	16
New Zealand	7
Cape of Good Hope	2
Fiji	1
Jamaica	1
New Guinea	1
Natal	0
Total	76

Table 13.3: Former occupations of Irish members of the Cape Mounted Police and the Natal Mounted Police

Former occupation	Cape Mounted Police (%)	Natal Mounted Police (%)
Military, naval and police	44	15
Artisan	31	53
Farmer	15	16
Unskilled	6	4
Middle-class profession (teacher, engineer, etc.)	4	12
Total	100	100

Only 6 per cent of Irish recruits to the Cape Mounted Police could be termed unskilled. The former occupations of the Irish intake to this force and to the Natal Mounted Police illustrates this point (see Table 13.3).

South Africa may well have got the cream of Irish emigrants, but it also got those who were drawn to specific professions and trades, once again creating an impression of dominance. Excluding the military and the six Irish regiments who were stationed at the Cape or Natal in the nineteenth century and who were, as elsewhere in the empire, birds of passage, public service attracted a high proportion of Irish officials.[46] A third of the Cape's Governors were Irish – and noticeably so. When Sir Lowry Cole arrived at the Cape as Governor in September 1828, onlookers grumbled of yet another Irishman sent to rule over them.[47]

There were also many Irishmen in the Cape and Natal judiciaries. Both the colony's legislative assemblies had prominent Irish members, with Sir Thomas Upington, 'the Afrikaner from Cork' holding the Cape premiership from 1884 to 1886; and in Natal over the second Anglo-Boer war period Colonel, later Sir, Albert Hime from Kilcoole, County Wicklow, was Prime Minister from 1899 to 1903.[48] Wherever there was a sizeable English-speaking community, notable Irish doctors, dentists, architects and even botanists could be found. At least 30 newspapers were at one time edited by Irishmen. These ranged from the *Cape Times* (Frederick St Leger) and the *Star* (William Monypenny) to the *Natal Witness* (Alfred Aylward) and the *Middelburg Courant* (Arthur Griffith).[49]

John O'Mahoney, writing in the *Natal Mercury* in 1882, observed that, 'in all our Colonies – or anywhere out of Ireland – the Irish are much like all other people'.[50] Once out of the ghetto that is, of course, true in that the influences of Anglicization were marked, yet collaboration with colonial regimes, or perhaps more accurate, assimilation into white society, became more pronounced when, as in South Africa, the immigrant Irish population had a high preponderance of Protestants and held a position of status in colonial society. But even with powerful influences of assimilation at work, in four trades the Irish constituted a sufficient number either to dominate or to be a tangible influence in the occupation. These occupations included: diamond mining in Griqualand West and to a lesser extent gold mining in the Transvaal; police work, about a quarter of the Cape Mounted Police and the Natal Mounted Police appearing to have been Irish; the railways, as navvies, engineers and management personnel; and lastly retailing.

The retailing profession in South Africa was dominated by Ulster Protestants. John and Joseph Orr, R.H. Henderson and W.M. Cuthbert and others played a significant part developing haberdashery and shoe chain-stores, not only in South Africa but later also in Rhodesia and Portuguese East Africa. These firms gave preference to Irish applicants for employment and Cuthbert's shoe and boot stores actively recruited apprentices direct from Ireland.[51] In the republican Transvaal the Irish gained a foothold in retailing, though the Ulster dominance was less. Arthur Griffith, whose experience as a young Irish immigrant in the republic was the only one he was to have of a foreign country, observed that on boards over shops in Pretoria in 1897 could be seen such Irish names as Burke, Geraghty and O'Brien.[52]

All four of these occupations actively encouraged if not insisted upon the recruitment of young single men. The preponderance of Irish males to Irish females is a strikingly South African phenomenon. In Johannesburg in 1896 two-thirds of the Irish population were male. This ratio existed in the total South African Irish population as late as 1911, in marked contrast to Irish communities in North America and Australia where parity between the sexes was often close. The consequences of this male imbalance were both obvious and subtle. Irish lads who married non-Irish girls were more easily assimilated into the general community. On the other hand, single young Irish immigrants were also free to move around and a fair number appear to have sailed on to Australia, moved up to Rhodesia or indeed returned to Ireland after a number of years.[53] In his biography of Griffith, Padraic Colum stated: 'Going to South Africa was not the same as emigrating, it was more like going for a long sojourn'.[54]

This feeling that one could return to Ireland when one pleased had a psychological impact. Sentimentality among South African Irish immigrants for Erin's green fields never reached the level of unwholesome melancholy experienced among sections of the American Irish. This is in part because the South African Irish were not destitute, but it is also symptomatic of the unfettered freedom of movement of the young male Irish emigrant to South Africa. Such a man came to South Africa because he wanted to come and not because he had to come. In contemporary mythology Africa, the 'dark continent', was portrayed in Europe as a place of danger, excitement and adventure. This appealed to the educated, skilled or semi-skilled youth of Victorian Ireland. Once in Africa, and unrestrained by marriage, opportunities existed for high adventure. For some this might take the form of big game hunting or of pioneering nature conservation. Alternatively, life in the Natal or Cape police forces, the Frontier Armed and Mounted Police or the British South African Police meant days in the saddle on patrol in the veld, often shooting for the pot and on occasion breaking up African faction fights or acting as scouts for regular troops operating against black or Boer forces.

For the devoted young Irish nationalist South Africa offered another attraction. It was the only place in the English-speaking world where a white nationalist people were effectively standing up to the British Empire. As already indicated, in the Cape and Natal Irish nationalism tended to be of the Home Rule variety. This dominance was consolidated by the extraordinary link which existed between South African arch-imperialist and capitalist Cecil John Rhodes and Parnell, which continued after Parnell's death through John Redmond. Not only did Rhodes supply moderate Irish nationalism with huge sums of cash, but two of his South African Irish associates, James Rochfort Maguire and John Morrogh, obtained Irish seats in Westminster as Parnellite MPs.[55]

This unholy alliance of high imperialism and fervent nationalism was initiated by a recuperative visit to the Cape in 1887 by the eccentric, newly elected nationalist MP for South Donegal, J.G. Swift MacNeill. His chance shipboard meeting with Rhodes initiated contact between the mining magnate and Parnell. The trip also opened Irish nationalist eyes to the fact that quasi-political Irish nationalist societies existed in South Africa.

'The Irish, now that you are here, will insist on Home Rule meetings which I will "Chairman".' This was Rhodes's prediction as the RMS *Garth Castle* neared Table Bay. He also observed: 'The ship will not have anchored for 10 minutes in Table Bay before you will be surrounded by Irishmen clamouring for speeches'. On both counts Rhodes proved correct, and Swift MacNeill spoke at Home Rule meetings in Kimberley, Port Elizabeth and Cape Town. It was about this time that a statue to Robert Emmet was erected in front of the Dutch Reformed Church in Uitenhage. Swift MacNeill returned to the Cape in 1891, but noted how the Parnellite débâcle had dampened Irish ardour.[56] None the less South Africa was now recognized by Irish nationalist leaders as a region of Irish settlement. In 1894, the same year that Parnell's former private secretary, O'Hea, settled in Durban, John Redmond visited the Cape, possibly to negotiate further financial support from Cecil Rhodes, then the Cape's Premier. Redmond was fêted and received by the Governor, Sir Henry Loch, as well as by fellow Irishman Sir Thomas Upington.[57]

Exiles and revolutionaries

But for the young advanced Irish nationalist in South Africa in the 1890s the excitement was on the Rand. Advanced nationalists in Ireland became increasingly mesmerized by the Boer cause as the decade progressed. Slowly but surely Irish pro-Boer sentiment permeated through Irish nationalist society, especially after the Jameson raid. Between 1896 and 1899 a steady stream of young Irish activists slipped into the Transvaal republic via Lourenco Marques. When John Whelan of the Irish National Association suddenly gave up a lucrative appointment in Ireland to emigrate to the Transvaal, Assistant Commissioner John Mallon of the Dublin Metropolitan Police commented on it to the under-secretary:

> his departure for South Africa at this time is very suspicious. He is the fifth such I.N.A. man who has gone to South Africa within a recent very short period. McBride – Gill – Briscoe – two members of the Independent staff and now Whelan.[58]

The pattern of earlier Irish emigration was soon repeated and the small Rand Irish community gradually gained prominence. At the time of the Jameson raid an 'Irish Brigade' was formed in Johannesburg, though its members seem to have been uncertain as to which side to support.[59] Two months later the anti-Parnellite and Healyite MP for Birr, King's County, B.C. Molloy, addressed an enthusiastic crowd at the St Patrick's Day dinner in Johannesburg. In September one of the Irish Brigade leaders, H.G. Hasken, along with Moses Cornwall from Kimberley, attended the Irish race convention in Dublin. At this was read a solution which called for unity among Irish nationalists.[60]

But the new Irish arrivals on the Rand were not interested in associating with parliamentarians. John MacBride, supported for some 21 months (January 1897 to *c*. October 1898) by Arthur Griffith, united the Irish *uitlander* population in the Fenian tradition and in support of the Boer republic.[61] With Gillingham acting as the *éminence grise*, the Irish alienated themselves from *uitlander* society – even to the extent of breaking up at least one *uitlander* meeting – and endeared themselves to the Kruger regime. The Wolfe Tone branch of the INF in Johannesburg and the John Daly branch in Pretoria were overtly Irish republican, as was the Johannesburg-based Amnesty Association. The climax came with a large march through the centre of Johannesburg by the Irish and several Boer leaders to commemorate the '98 rising. Indeed the '98 celebrations in Johannesburg were more successful than they were in Dublin. For the first time dissension was caused in the South African Irish community, dividing it along contemporary South African political lines, with Irish unionists and home rulers supporting Britain and advanced nationalists on the Rand advancing the surrogate of Afrikaner nationalism. The *Standard and Diggers' News* reported from Grahamstown in the Eastern Cape: 'A meeting of local Irishmen is to be called shortly for the purpose of repudiating the actions of Irishmen at the Rand in forming a corps, and also to express strong and unswerving loyalty to Britain'.[62]

When the second Anglo-Boer war broke out on 11 October 1899, an Irish Transvaal Brigade had already been formed by 'Colonel' John Blake, an Irish American adventurer, and the now 'Major' John MacBride.[63] The activities of this commando, and of a second and rival Irish Transvaal Brigade formed by Arthur Lynch in 1900, have been exaggerated, but their significance, both for the Irish in South Africa and for Irish nationalism, has not.[64] Blake claimed that he took command of 300 men, a sizeable proportion of the Irish male population in Johannesburg. Though a handful of recruits joined the commando from Ireland, it was to all intents and purposes a South African Irish unit.[65]

Thanks to the daredevil activities of MacBride and his associates, and telling propaganda whipped up in Dublin by Arthur Griffith, who had only recently returned from Africa, the stirring prospect was presented of a population the size of the city of Dublin taking on and beating the British in battle. The fact that some 28,000 Irishmen fought against the Boers in Irish regiments of the British army was glossed over or conveniently forgotten.[66]

The ghost of Erin

The immediate effect of the eventual defeat of the Boers and the British annexation of what became the Transvaal Colony and the Orange River Colony was that most of South Africa's Irish advanced nationalists left the country. The sanctum of Boer republicanism had for the moment been destroyed. But for every Irishman who fled across the Komatipoort border post, many more came into South Africa. The army of Roberts and Kitchener showed many a world they would never have dreamt of entering.[67] Some Irish troops returned to Ireland only to make their way back to South Africa. Other Irish people, stirred by the fanatical espousal of pro-Boerism in Ireland and fascinated by tales of this distant land, ventured south to the subcontinent. Between 1902 and the onset in 1905–6 of postwar depression, 6,000 Irish immigrants arrived in the region. As in the past these new Irish immigrants tended to be skilled or semi-skilled and thus were unaffected by the 1903 Prohibited Immigrants Act in the Cape, which prescribed an entrance qualification to the colony of £5, rising to £20 in 1904, as well as the ability to write a European language.[68]

During the twentieth century, South Africa gained dominion status and the British administrations and garrisons, with their high percentage of Irish officials, disappeared from the Cape and Natal. For those ordinary Irish people in South Africa getting or keeping a job could at times now be difficult. In November 1921 Gerald Little in Johannesburg wrote home to his father: 'This Smuts is a nationalist at heart. All the men who have been fired in the P.O. and Railways are home born men.'[69]

Ireland and South Africa drifted apart. The traumatic events in Ireland between 1916 and 1923 dwarfed any lingering impact of the Boer war, and soon it and the Irish links with Africa had become merely a folk memory. And yet while the leaders of the Union of South Africa and of the new Irish Free State maintained occasional contact – with their 'fellowship of disaffection' within the British Empire[70] – Irish emigration to South Africa became a mere trickle, averaging 187 per annum between 1926 and 1939.[71]

In the early 1920s the members of the Irish Republican Association of South Africa managed to maintain a thriving and politically very active organization, allying themselves firmly, but unofficially, with General Hertzog and his Nationalists against General Smuts. The organization had its own fortnightly periodical, *The Republic*. This was edited by Ben Farrington from Cork, the future South African communist intellectual. This outburst of Irish consciousness was short lived: Farrington and some of the IRA(SA) supported the Treaty, while others bitterly opposed it.

To complicate matters, some Irish got involved in the 'white soviet', the 1922 Rand Revolt. When the Durban Light Infantry swept into the trenches of the insurgents in the Johannesburg white working-class suburb of Fordsburg, they captured a large Irish flag.[72] By the end of 1922 Irish political activity in South Africa was a thing of the past. The IRA(SA) and its journal had ceased to exist. While an occasional Irish person might make good – one even became a cabinet minister – 'Irishness' now tended only to emerge for the annual St Patrick's Day dinner or ball, when an Irish rugby test team arrived, or when an Irish celebrity visited, such as Bernard Shaw, John McCormick, Gerry Adams or Mary Robinson.[73] Erin had become a ghost in Africa.

Notes

1. *The Republic*, 12 Februrry 1921. This chapter is a revision of the article, 'Irish Settlement and Identity in South Africa before 1910', *Irish Historical Studies*, 28, 110 (November 1992), pp. 134–49.
2. See D.H. Akenson, *The Irish Diaspora: A Primer* (Toronto and Belfast, 1993), 'South Africa: A Small Elite Band', pp. 123–39.
3. *Results of a census of the Colony of the Cape of Good Hope . . . 5 April 1891* (Cape Town, 1892), pp. xii and xvii. Though the British had ruled the Cape continuously for 85 years, in 1891 the English-speaking element constituted only a third of the white population.
4. *Blue Book of the Colony of Natal, 1890–91*, T4.
5. For sources for Table 13.1 see British Colonial, Union and Republic of South Africa census reports (1875, 1891, 1904, 1911, 1918, 1921, 1926, 1946, 1951 and 1985). See also Donald H. Akenson, *Occasional papers on the Irish in South Africa*, (Grahamstown, 1991). For surveys of the Irish in South Africa in the nineteenth and twentieth centuries see, 'The Irish in Southern Africa, 1795–1910', *Southern African-Irish Studies*, 2 (hereafter SAIS), (1992) and 'Ireland and South Africa in Modern Times', *SAIS*, 3 (1996).
6. Donald H. Akenson, *Occasional Papers on the Irish in South Africa* (Grahamstown, 1991), pp. 42 and 66.
7. See Peter Philip, 'Discharged Soldiers and Sailors who were Granted Permission to Remain at the Cape: 1815–1824', *Supplementa ad Familia* (South Africa), 14, 3 (1989), 20pp. See also Philip, *British Residents at the Cape, 1795–1819* (Cape Town, 1981), p. 246.
8. For the Irish 1820 settlers, see G.B. Dickason, *Irish Settlers to the Cape: A History of the Clanwilliam 1820 Settlers from Cork Harbour* (Cape Town, 1973);

M.D. Nash, *The Settler Handbook, A New List of the 1820 Settlers* (Cape Town, 1987).

9. George Thompson, *Travels and Adventures on Southern Africa* (London, 1827), p. 17.

10. George Theal, *Records of the Cape Colony* (Cape Town, 1897–1905), vol. xxi, (1825), p. 452. For details of the Ingram settler party see also George Theal, *History of South Africa from 1795 to 1872* (London, *c.* 1915), vol. ii, p. 462, and *Records*, 1824, vol. xviii, pp. 186–8, 199 and 256; 1824, vol. xxi, pp. 262 and 435; and 1826, vol. xxvi, pp. 316, 363 and 421.

11. K.P.T. Tankard, 'The Lady Kennaway Girls', *SAIS*, 2 (1992), pp. 278–86.

12. Esme Bull, 'Aided Irish Immigration to the Cape, 1823–1900', *SAIS*, 2 (1992), pp. 269–77.

13. *The Porter Speeches* (Cape Town, 1886), pp. xli–xliv; and South African Archives, Pietermaritzburg, Ladysmith magistrate letterbook, 1854–1962, 1/LDS, 3/1/1/4, T.T. Kelly to Colonial Secretary (Natal), 14 October 1857. See also, J.L. McCracken, *New Light at the Cape of Good Hope: William Porter, the Father of South African Liberalism*, (Belfast, 1993).

14. Akenson, *Occasional Papers*, pp. 54 and 56, and D.P. McCracken, 'The Land the Famine Irish Forgot', in E. Margaret Crawford (ed.), *The Hungry Stream: Essays on Emigration and Famine* (Belfast, 1997), pp. 41–7.

15. Ralph Kilpin, *The Romance of a Colonial Parliament* (London, 1930), pp. 69–70; *Transport of Convicts to Cape*, HC 1849, xliii (217), pp. 49–52; and *Reception of convicts at Cape*, HC 1850, xxxviii [1138].

16. Esme Bull, *Aided Immigration from Britain to South Africa, 1857–1867* (Pretoria, 1991), pp. 727–61.

17. *Cape Town Daily News*, 2 February 1876.

18. Sidney Smith, *The Settler's New Home; or Whether to Go, and Whither* (London, 1850), pp. 1–7.

19. Ken Smith, *Alfred Aylward: The Tireless Agitator* (Johannesburg, 1983). See also J.L. McCracken, 'The Death of the Informer James Carey', *SAIS*, 3 (1996), pp. 190–9.

20. *Dictionary of South African Biography* (Cape Town and Johannesburg, 1972), vol. ii, p. 606.

21. *Remarks on the demoralising influence of slavery by a resident of the Cape of Good Hope* (London, 1828), pp. 7–8.

22. J.B. Brain (ed.), *The Cape Diary of Bishop Patrick Raymond Griffith for the Years 1837 to 1839* (South African Catholic Bishops Conference, Mariannhill, 1988), p. 160.

23. For the Irish contribution to the Catholic Church in South Africa, see J.B. Brain, 'The Roman Catholic Church', *SAIS*, 2 (1992), pp. 120–31; and F.B. Doyle, 'South Africa', in Patrick J. Corish (ed.), *A History of Irish Catholicism* (Dublin, 1971).

24. R.H. Henderson, *An Ulsterman in Africa* (Cape Town, 1944; 2nd edn, 1945), pp. 16 and 23.

25. D.P. McCracken, 'The Irish in South Africa: The Police, a Case Study', *Familia: Ulster Genealogical Review*, 2, 7 (1991), pp. 40–6. The papers of the Cape Mounted Police are housed in 161 boxes in the South African Archives, Cape Town, reference CMP.

26. M.C. Seton, 'Irishmen in South Africa', *The Gael* (January 1900), p. 21.

27. John Brown, 'Orangeism in South Africa', *SAIS*, 2 (1992), pp. 110–19. When South Africa became a republic in 1961, surviving Orangemen in the country burnt most of the Orange records.

28. Little is known of the Irish National Foresters in South Africa. Reference to the organization occasionally appeared in the *Argus Annual and South African Directory*.

29. *Standard and Diggers' News*, 28 September 1899.

30. *South African Commercial Advertiser*, 6 June 1829.

31. See T.K. Daniel, 'Faith and Stepfatherland: Irish South African Networks in Cape Colony and Natal, and the Home Rule Movement in Ireland', *SAIS*, 2 (1992), pp. 73–90. For two boisterous Irish functions, see the dramatic accounts which appeared in the *Standard and Transvaal Mining Chronicle* (Supplement), 19 March 1899, and in the *Transvaal Mining Argus*, 18 March 1888.

32. Elliot O'Donnell, *The Irish Abroad* (London, 1915), p. 334, and K. Nolan to D.P. McCracken, 28 August 1993.

33. Theal, *History of South Africa from 1795 to 1872*, vol. i, p. 222; and *Records*, vol. vi, pp. 392–5 and 408–44.

34. T.V. Bulpin, *Storm over the Transvaal* (Cape Town, 1955), pp. 42–5; and Barry Ronan, *Forty South African Years* (London, 1919), pp. 110–23.

35. See the *United Irishman*, 26 August; 2, 9 and 16 September 1899.

36. Patricia McCracken, 'The Quest for the *Middelburg Courant*', *SAIS*, 3 (1996), pp. 282–9.

37. *Census of the . . . Cape . . . 1891*, p. xxiv.

38. Charles J. Becker, *Guide to the Transvaal* (Dublin, 1878). This guide was published by J. Dollard of Dame Street. H.W. Donnelly of 30 College Green, Dublin, acted for the Transvaal Land Agency in Great Britain and Ireland. The financial institution used by the agency was the Hibernian Bank. On clandestine links at this time between advanced Irish nationalism and the Transvaal republic, see Sir Robert Anderson, *Side Lights on the Home Rule Movement* (London, 1906), pp. 113n. and 159–60; *Hansard*, cclvii, 21 January 1881, cols 1152–3; Henri Le Caron, *Twenty-Five Years in the Secret Service* (London, 1893), pp. 169–70; and F.H. O'Donnell, *The History of the Irish Parliamentary Party, 1870–1892* (New York, 1910), vol. i, p. 220.

39. The surviving papers of the Natal Mounted Police are contained in sixteen volumes of manuscript material in the Natal Archival Depot.

40. C. Pama, *Wagon road to Wynberg* (Cape Town, 1979), pp. 7 and 66.

41. B.J. van de Sandt, *Cape of Good Hope Almanac and Annual Register* (1847), p. 472, and (1848), p. 448.

42. *Wicklow People*, 7 November 1908; and H. Murphy, *The Kynoch Era in Arklow, 1895–1918* (pamphlet, n.d.).

43. *Rapport van den census directeur: Census, 15 July 1896* (Johannesburg, 1896), pp. 54–5.

44. For an attack on Solomon Gillingham, see *The Great Transvaal Irish Conspiracy* (anonymous pamphlet, *c.* 1899).

45. Details for Table 13.2 extracted from Sir Bernard Burke and Ashworth Burke, *A Genealogical and Heraldic History of the Colonial Gentry*, 2 vols (London, 1891 and 1895). The entries for the Cape were two colonial Irishmen: the celebrated Charles Orpen and Walter Piers, the retiring resident magistrate of remote Peddie in the Eastern Cape.

46. Details for Table 13.3 extracted from enrolment papers of the Cape Mounted Police (Western Cape Archives) and Natal Mounted Police (Kwazulu-Natal Archives). For Irish involvement in the British army in South Africa see S. Monick, *Shamrock and Springbok: The Irish Impact on South African Military History* (Johannesburg, 1989), pp. 198–315.

47. For details of Irish governors, see J.L. McCracken, 'Irishmen in Government in South Africa', *SAIS*, 2 (1992), pp. 25–38; and Hymen W.J. Picard, *Lords of Stalplein, Biographical Miniatures of the British Governors of the Cape of Good Hope* (Cape Town, 1974).

48. J.L. McCracken, 'Irishmen in South African Colonial Parliaments', *SAIS*, 1 (1991), pp. 73–82.

49. For example, see Eileen McCracken, 'Of Veld and Flora: Irish Botanists in South Africa', *SAIS*, 2 (1992), pp. 179–90; and P.A. McCracken, 'Shaping the Times: Irish Journalists', *SAIS*, 2 (1992), pp. 140–62.

50. *Natal Mercury*, 25 January 1882.

51. N.D. Southey, 'Irish Retailers in South Africa', *SAIS*, 2 (1992), pp. 163–78.

52. Padraic Colum, *Arthur Griffith* (Dublin, 1959), p. 33.

53. For the Rhodesian Irish, see D.W. Lowry, 'The Irish in Rhodesia', *SAIS*, 2 (1992), pp. 242–60; and Col. A.S. Hickman, 'The Mashonaland Irish', *Rhodesiana*, 5 (1960), pp. 1–6.

54. Colum, *Arthur Griffith*, p. 32.

55. Donal P. McCracken, *The Irish Pro-Boers, 1877–1902* (Johannesburg, 1989), pp. 22–34; and D.P. McCracken, 'Parnell and the South African Connection', in Donal McCartney (ed.), *Parnell: The Politics of Power* (Dublin, 1991), pp. 125–36.

56. J.G. Swift MacNeill, *What I Have Seen and Heard* (London, 1925), pp. 263 and 269.

57. National Library of Ireland, Redmond papers, Mss. 15235/1–2, papers relating to the visit of John Redmond in Cape Town in 1894. For O'Hea, see *Men of the Times* (Johannesburg, 1905), pp. 282–3.

58. National Archives of Ireland, State Paper Office, Dublin, Crime Branch Special papers, S/13020, 14 January 1897. It was Mallon who had despatched Aylward and Carey to South Africa.

59. *Shan Van Vocht*, 1, 1 (7 February 1896); and the *Star*, 4 January 1896.

60. Trinity College, Dublin, Dillon papers, 685/a/3; *Proceedings of the Irish Race Convention* (Dublin, 1896), p. 8; and *Freeman's Journal*, 24 October 1899.

61. Patricia McCracken, 'Arthur Griffith's South African Sabbatical', *SAIS*, 3 (1996), pp. 227–62.

62. *Standard and Diggers' News*, 10 October 1899.

63. D.P. McCracken, *MacBride's Brigade: Irish Commandoes in the Anglo-Boer War* (forthcoming) and D.P. McCracken, 'The Irish Literary Movement, Irish Doggerel and the Boer War', *Etudes Irlandaises*, New Series, 22 (1995), pp. 97–115.

64. Both brigade leaders later wrote highly dramatic accounts of their time in South Africa. Neither account is particularly reliable. See J.Y.F. Blake, *A West Pointer with the Boers* (Boston, 1903); and Arthur Lynch, *My Life Story* (London, 1924).

65. Later in the war Blake's commando was joined by a 40-strong Chicago Irish-American 'ambulance' corps under Captain Patrick O'Connor. See Michael Davitt, *The Boer Fight for Freedom* (London and New York, 1902), pp. 325–27.

66. McCracken, *The Irish Pro-Boers*, pp. 123–7. See also G.A. Chadwick, *The Role of the Fifth (Irish) Brigade in the Battles of Colenso and Tugela Heights* (pamphlet, Durban, 1990). There were in the region of 4,000 casualties in the Irish regiments serving in the campagne.

67. It was not only soldiers who came to South Africa from Ireland during the Boer war. For the role of the Royal Irish Constabulary hospital corps in the conflict, see

The Royal Irish Constabulary Magazine, 1, 9 (July 1912); 2, 1 (Nov. 1912); 2, 2 (Dec. 1912); 2, 4 (Feb. 1913); 2, 5 (Mar. 1913); and 2, 6 (Apr. 1913).

68. D.P. McCracken, 'Fenians and Dutch Carpet-Baggers: Irish and Afrikaner Nationalisms, 1877–1930', *Eire-Ireland*, 29, 3 (Fall 1994), pp. 109–25.

69. National Library of Ireland, Ms. 15,507(3).

70. Donal Lowry, 'Irish-South African relations and British Commonwealth, *c.* 1902–1961', *SAIS*, 3 (1996), pp. 89–135.

71. Akenson, *Occasional Papers*, p. 61.

72. D.P. McCracken, 'The Irish Republican Association of South Africa, 1920–2', *SAIS*, 3 (1996), pp. 46–66.

73. D.P. McCracken, 'Irish Identity in Twentieth-Century South Africa', *SAIS*, 3 (1996), pp. 7–45.

CHAPTER 14

'The Desired Haven'?
Impressions of New Zealand in
Letters to and from Ireland,
1840–1925

ANGELA MCCARTHY

(Department of Modern History, Trinity College, Dublin)

The history of the Irish in New Zealand has received minimal attention in Irish diaspora studies, although recent research is rectifying this situation.[1] In fact, prior to Donald Harman Akenson's *Half the World from Home* (1990), the only investigation of the Irish in New Zealand was Richard Davis's *Irish Issues in New Zealand Politics* which appeared sixteen years earlier.[2] While the relatively minor size of the Irish migrant stream to New Zealand compared to other destinations is one possible reason for the dearth of studies, Irish migrants did form a significant proportion of the colony's nineteenth-century population. In 1867, at their peak, the Irish constituted 12.8 per cent of the population, while their proportion of foreign-born settlers peaked in 1881 and 1886 at 18.5 per cent.[3]

Most migrants arrived between 1871 and 1885, lured by a range of financial subsidies and incentives, particularly assisted and nominated immigrant schemes. These inducements contributed to the chain migration process and, consequently, certain areas were predominant in the supply of migrants. For instance, Akenson's analysis of the Irish Registrar-General's figures indicate that the majority of Irish sailing direct to New Zealand from Ireland in 1876–90 originated from Munster (45.63 per cent) and Ulster (35.83 per cent).[4] The dominance of these two provinces also emerges from studies of Irish migration to Otago and Southland, and Canterbury.[5] Most Irish migrants to New Zealand were Catholic. However, substantial Ulster migration, particularly from the dominant Protestant counties of Down and Antrim, ensured that a significant minority of the colony's Irish population, estimated at one-quarter,[6] were Protestant.

New Zealand's Irish population, half the world from home, maintained contact with family and friends through the exchange of letters. The surviving correspondence, however, has not received the in-depth analysis accorded to letters relating to the Irish in Australia and America.[7] Although Donald

Akenson and Trevor Parkhill conducted exploratory essays of Irish New Zealand letters, their discussions largely relied on Ulster Protestant emigrant accounts held at the Public Record Office of Northern Ireland (PRONI).[8] While my research utilizes PRONI's material, it also incorporates privately held letters that originate from Ireland as well as New Zealand. This approach adopts the framework of David Fitzpatrick's *Oceans of Consolation*, which examined fourteen sequences containing 111 letters exchanged between Australia and Ireland.

While recognizing that the surviving letters do not represent the experiences of all letter writers or all migrants, personal correspondence does provide an intimate glimpse of the migration process and life progress of writers and recipients. This chapter, exploring Irish impressions of New Zealand, is an introduction to several collections of Irish–New Zealand correspondence which convey the diverse nature of the migrant experience.

Prior to arrival in the colony, images of New Zealand mesmerized the migrant's mind. Such perceptions, invariably shaped by emigrant letters, returned migrants, emigration agents, and newspaper reports, also influenced the intending migrant's friends and family. 'It is reported that that place is a wicked place and little or no clergey or publick worship', declared Elizabeth McCleland from Dunronan, County Londonderry, to her daughter Ann in 1840.[9] Elizabeth's impression was probably influenced by her local minister, the Reverend Campbell, who had an old schoolfriend in the fledgling colony, also a clergyman.

The publication of persuasive propaganda to the contrary ensured that these early representations of New Zealand as an uncivilized colony were short-lived. In fact, James Belich claims that migrants to New Zealand were 'prised out of their British contexts by powerful myths and prophecies' that promoted New Zealand as an earthly and British paradise in the Pacific.[10] Whether or not aspirations for an antipodean Arcadia spurred Irish migrants to New Zealand, the utopian ideal was echoed by some Irish correspondents in their letters home. 'I have travelled over about fifteen thousand miles of water and at last got to the desired haven', sighed Bessie Macready, an Ulster migrant who reached Port Lyttelton in 1878.[11]

Despite proclamations of paradise in the Pacific, various forms of financial assistance played a more significant role in encouraging Irish emigration to New Zealand. Free land grants also attracted settlers, while the quest for gold lured migrants such as James and Hamilton McIlrath, natives of Killinchy, County Down. The brothers, in their early twenties, migrated from Belfast to Liverpool in December 1860 and from there voyaged for 94 days on the *Donald McKay* to Australia with people 'from all parts of the known world. Whole families young and old of every creed contry and clime.'[12] After less than a year in Australia, knowledge of newly discovered goldfields in New Zealand propelled James across the Tasman Sea. Hamilton and another Down migrant, William James Alexander, followed in December 1861.

The McIlraths, like Bessie Macready, settled in Canterbury and James, like Bessie, praised the colony in utopian overtones when he announced: 'I am far enough from Church But I sincerly Believe New Zealand is as near Heaven as any contry'. If New Zealand was considered a heaven or haven it had, James confessed, minimal religious facilities. 'I have not been to Church Mass or Meeting but twice since I left Home and that was in Australia. There is not a House of worship within 25 miles of me.'[13] James probably emphasized his absence from all forms of divine worship, including Anglican, Catholic and Presbyterian services, in order to reassure his family in Ireland who may have suspected he had defected to another faith had he merely announced his non-attendance at a Unitarian meeting.

As the settlement expanded, James could later inform his family, 'I am as sound a Unitarian as when I left Killinchy altho I never heard a unitarian sermon since. We have a very eloquent little Presbeterian here but I must confess that I cannot believe all he says.'[14] James was not alone in reassuring his parents that emigration had not threatened his beliefs, although, in order to participate in colonial religious practices, adaptability was frequently necessary, as James's brother, Hamilton, indicated: 'I gave an acre of land for a presbitarain Church about a hundred yards from my house, whitch will improve the lack of it a bit. By the bye there is no uniterians here leastways no churchs or clergyman so when I do go I go to the presbiterian.'[15]

Meagre facilities for formal worship, brought about by limited church finances and a dispersed population, contributed to movement between denominations. Facilities gradually improved, but while there was general religious tolerance among adherents of the major creeds, some denominations encountered disapproval. As James McIlrath confided to his family, 'Now this Southbridge is a Nice little Town with one English Church and one Scotch or Presbeterian but by the way there is no Uniterian. (Hush) it is a thing never mentioned here.'[16] In similar terms, Hamilton informed, 'I still hold the same views but people from here would call you a heritic if you mentioned such a thing'.[17]

Although Catholic writers, in their letters to Ireland, were less inclined to discuss aspects of their faith in depth, they did display, like their Protestant counterparts, interest in their religious personnel. Sometimes the migrant requested information about their local parish priest in Ireland, while on other occasions, such as Patrick Quinn's account of Father McGrath's visit to Dargaville,[18] migrants mentioned their interaction with clergy in New Zealand:

> Wee had a roman Catholick Priest here a month or 6 weeks befor Christmas the rev Father Maggrah. He is on a mission. He is from Deerry in the North of Ireland. He was talking to mee and asked mee my name. I told him Patrick Quinn and he asked mee where I came from. I told him I came from Newry and he told mee that he was there. I went to Confession to him.[19]

Patrick and his brother William, like the McIlraths, lived in relatively close proximity to each other, but, unlike the McIlraths, the elderly Quinns communicated infrequently with each other. They had, as Donald Akenson expressed, 'come half way around the globe, only to be worlds apart'.[20] While William possessed substantial assets in Auckland, Patrick dug for gum at Dargaville.

The supplementary income Patrick derived from digging for gum was, how-ever, less vital for his survival than the pension: 'I am at the Gum Digging and I dont avarage 2 shillings a week. It is no good. If there is one man making Wagges there is 20 barrely making tucker and onley for the pension I wood bee verry badley of[f].'[21]

Other migrants fared somewhat better. David McCullough, a 23-year-old native of Ballycreely, Moneyreagh, County Down, arrived in Dunedin in 1875 and initially toiled as a labourer before gaining employment with the Albion Brewing and Malting Company. 'I like the country its customs and its people', David enthused. 'I have never regretted coming out as I have been in constant employment since I came.'[22] Eventually, David joined a goldmining cooperat-ive and he described his goldmining exploits in subsequent letters home.

Like David, several migrants pursued various employment options in search of a livelihood. Men laboured, dug, mined and farmed, but competition was intense. James O'Neill, a Limerick-born Catholic based at Auckland, complained that 'there is not a ship that comes but brings 1 or 2 wheelers or body makers'.[23] Other trades, O'Neill noted, possessed better prospects. Coachsmiths, in par-ticular, could command at least £3 a week for eight hours work a day.

Wages and work hours featured more than 40 years later in 1905 when Catherine Sullivan wrote from Foxton, Manawatu, to her brother-in-law at Ballingarry, County Limerick: 'Dear Tom this is a good country for working men as some men have from ten to twelve shillings per day. It is not like at home. The worst men here won't come to work for less than 7/- per day; and only work from 8 to 5 pm.'[24] That same year, however, Hugh Rea's letter from Clinton, Otago, to his brother-in-law at Scribb, Seaforde, County Down, indic-ated the instability of colonial employment: 'The wages in this country is good but in a great manny cases you cannot get Steady Employment so that when you calculate your earnings for the year it comes to be a verry Small avrage'.[25]

Females also migrated in search of employment, while others sought mar-riage partners. Irrespective of their motive for migration, women's work was described in letters sent home. Bessie Macready, for instance, settled with her aunts, but she felt it was 'not a place to progress rapidly. In fact it was a losing game with me.' Bessie therefore accepted sole charge of a shop in Lyttelton which, though weary and dull, she endured in the belief that 'I was gaining something and that enabled me to bear up in prospect of a happier future'.[26]

Thirty-two years after Catherine Sullivan sailed to New Zealand from Limerick with her husband John and their children, she indicated that she milked four cows, while her daughter Bridget milked 35 and 'Nellie milks 83 cows besides all the dry cattle'. This female contribution to the domestic economy took on greater significance for widows such as Ellen Piezzi and Agnes Lambert who were left with young families. Ellen ran a West Coast hotel where for-tunes depended to a large extent on the profitability of the goldfields, always uncertain: 'I had agreat many losses this year pepel gone true the cort turning onsolvent. I lost afine cow £15 pounds Wurt [worth] in ahole in the bush. I canot get any of my old acounts in. The pleas [place] is so poor the bisnes Was Never quarter so bad before.'[27] Likewise, Agnes Lambert complained from

Auckland in 1890: 'I am not doing very well at present as I am Doing nothing now as Bisonus is very Bad and I have lost a Deal of money'.[28]

Almost 20 years earlier, adverse financial conditions prevented Agnes from encouraging female family members to New Zealand: 'I would like to see some of my sisters out here But if they are doing any way well at home they had Better stay there for this is not much of a place unless you have plenty of money'.[29] This verdict was reiterated by David Bell, an Antrim migrant based at Duntroon in Otago, whose impressions of the colony during the 1880s were influenced by the downturn in the colony's economy. Ample meat and higher wages in New Zealand counted for little when David recalled the comforts of home:

> It is not what is represented to the people at home, and then the will stand up and tell you about the Poverty that the people at home have to suffer. I tell you, people at home may eat less mutton and pies, and earn less wages than the do here but if the only thought it they have a lot more comfort than is to be found in this country unless you have plenty of money. If it was not that I think it will do me good I would not be long in it and even so you need not be surprised if you see me home in about this time next year.[30]

Several writers catalogued food prices to portray the cost of living in New Zealand. Bessie Macready, however, provided a more general observation, noting that coals and clothing were expensive in the colony but that other items were cheaper and superior: 'We have got good & cheap butchers meat good flour our baker's bread is equal if not better than the best home bread & as cheap . . . butter very nice & cheaper than home but to counteract these we have house rent very dear'.[31] The prohibitive cost of accommodation also concerned James O'Neill in Auckland: 'House rent is awful dear. If the place in Brunswick St was here they would be at least £4,000 [£40.00] a year got out of it. Most every week there is a ship from England with emigrants. It is a bad place for some of them.'

The high cost of living caused financial hardship and migrants sometimes sought assistance from kin in Ireland, though not all requests met with success, as is evident in the letters Edward Lysaght received from Cappamore, County Limerick. 'So you would prefer taking £150 sooner than come home', Edward's brother William mused. 'I think you would act foolishly in taking the money. Anyway we could not send it at present.'[32] Edward's father also spurned his migrant son's requests for money, citing 'heavy losses'[33] for his inability to assist.

Despite financial constraints, Edward Lysaght resolved to remain in the colony resisting all efforts to lure him back to Limerick permanently. This determination is also evident in Hamilton McIlrath's letter sent from Canterbury in 1886 during a period of depression in the colony:

> There is a great cry of hard times here as elsewhere. It is pretty hard to make much money at present but still I can hold my own pretty confortable. Sheep that sold last year for 18/- are fetching at present about eight or nine shillings

but after all I dont think their is any better country than N. Zealand. A few years ago people here were doing too well and speculated too much on Land and other ways and got haeily into debt and now the reaction has set in they feel as woeful as a drunken man when he is getting sober again.[34]

Although the McIlraths obtained land at an early stage in the province's settlement, later migrants begrudged the inability to purchase land, an impediment that was particularly acute in Canterbury and Otago where a wealthy minority monopolized land ownership:

taking everything in particular the country is very dull and will continue to be so untill the get some sort of agitation such as was at home and make the big sheep farmers break up their big lots of land or Stations as the call them here. All the good available land in this district is taken up in big blocks of from 2 & 3 thousand acres up to as much as one hundred thousand acres . . . if it was Broken up in farms from 200 up to 500 acres It would form one of the best places in the world for a farmer to speculate upon, for it is splendid land almost all the farming land having limestone bottom . . .

David Bell's remarks echoed the widespread concerns circulating the colony that large tracts of land in private hands would lead to exorbitant rents and evictions, problems that had plagued Ireland. Interestingly, David's solution to the situation in New Zealand was based on his recollections of the Land War in Ireland.

Commentators in Ireland also made comparisons and recommendations based on previous events. For instance, William Lysaght perceived parallels between Irish and Maori experiences and advised his brother Edward accordingly:

So the Maori war is again closing [on] Auckland. I cannot say I regret it as I wish the Maories every success. Take care join no party to fight against them. They are the same as Irish men fighting for their own Land. Twas a regal Humbug the way their land were confiscated. Again I say to you do not fight again them – help them if you wish. I have it on good authority that they are assisted by many Irishmen.[35]

Correspondents in New Zealand also confirmed that some settlers supported the Maori. As James O'Neill observed from Auckland in 1863: 'Their is some white men deserters in amongst them these many years drilling them'. Possibly those Irish renegades who supported the Maori possessed Fenian sympathies.[36] However, not all Irish correspondents, such as Lysaght, supported Fenian initiatives. Richard Flanagan, a civil servant in London, remarked in a letter to his brother, Michael, in New Zealand: 'I see by the news that those misguided people, the Fenians, are not without sympathisers in your part of the world. I hope you will have sense enough to hold aloof from mixing up in any way with people who have anything to do with them.'[37]

Some commentators have suggested that 'because they share a history of oppression and land loss, and have both been the butt of racist jokes, the Maori and the Irish in New Zealand have long identified with one another'.[38] There is, however, minimal evidence of such empathy in the Irish letters sent from New Zealand. Instead, Irish Catholic involvement against the Maori is confirmed: 'The people got a great start one Sunday and we all at mass. They alarm bells rung out (and they was Maories seen the evening before about 15 miles away in their canoes). The Priest stopt mass and all the men got up and left chapels and churches.'

Most disruptions occurred in the North Island and settlers in the South, such as the McIlraths, did not experience first-hand activity. 'There is great talk of the Mowrie war but we have nothing of it here', James reassured in 1863.[39] Although the conflict posed no immediate danger, the McIlraths were aware of events, as Hamilton made clear:

> The Moris In the North Island has Been very troublesom lately. The more the are civilized the *the* worse the get, Burning Houses and killing the setlers But I think the will be forecd to give over soon. The Goverment gave grants of land to all the young men that would volenter and has raised a force of about three thousand Men Besides 2 thousands from England.[40]

James O'Neill wrote home from Auckland around the same time and correctly judged that many recruits would not remain on their land:[41] 'They are promised 50 acres of the Waikato land when the war is over but they must live 3 years on it before they get a title to it and 100 out of the lot wont do that'.

Not all discussions of the Maori, in letters to Ireland, related to hostile events. Hamilton McIlrath colourfully remarked: 'I expect Mother would like to see one of them with there face tattooed and all the Devices you could imagine painted on them and A Boars tusk strung to there ear'.[42] Such comments added to the impressions about the Maori gathered from newspapers, hearsay, and assumptions.

While the Maori population may have been a vivid contrast for Irish migrants, other aspects of colonial life also generated comment, particularly the climate. 'We like this place very much only we have had A very severe winter. It was every bit as cold as home. The snow does not lie as long but we have far more rain. The sun rises in the east and goes left about instead of right as at home which I thought rather curious at first.'[43] Hamilton McIlrath may have found the southern hemisphere initially disorientating but Bessie Macready considered it pleasing. She celebrated the colony's climate for its favourable contribution to her well-being: 'We have here nine months of splendid summer weather most of it a great deal warmer than the warmest summer day you experience at home & I believe my health has been greatly benefitted by the change'.[44] While farming initiatives relied on a conducive climate, the letters indicate that other occupations were just as susceptible to the weather's vagaries. As Ellen Piezzi noted from her West Coast hotel: 'The Weder is very dry just A Now and this is very bad for the digers canot doo Nothing When the have Now [*no*] Water'.[45]

Writers not only reported their impressions of life in the colony but also that of their acquaintances. For instance, David McCullough indicated that his friend, Alex Young, 'says he never was in better health or more contented in his life. He says he would not go home now at all.'[46] Michael Flanagan, a migrant from County Louth, revealed that his brother, Patrick, was also 'one of the very few upon whom the climate or the hardships to be endured in this vagabond life seems to have no effect'. Michael, on the other hand, bemoaned the 'dreary monotony of a life in this climate'.[47]

The weather and its contribution to health, favourable or otherwise, was not the only feature compared and contrasted with Irish conditions. Farming was a particular preoccupation, especially among migrants involved in farming or writing to farmers back in Ireland. The ability to purchase land without encumbrances was enthusiastically noted by Hamilton McIlrath: 'We intend to buy some land and let it lie. It will be valuable some day. You can get as much land as you like here free of everything for ever for £2 an acre.'[48] Subsequent letters in the McIlrath series focused on the novelty of encountering contrasting conditions and learning new skills: 'You people at home would think it strange to begin on land where there was not a fence whatever nor one sod turned since it was land and this is land of the richest quality'.[49]

Bessie Macready also noted that there was 'not much land lost by fences here'.[50] Exposed to colonial farming methods by acquaintances, Bessie relayed this information to her cousin who had obviously questioned her. Although Bessie considered farming 'not quite in my line', she indicated that 'it is principally done by machinery here. The farms are very large as a rule and the land very productive.' The Canterbury farm of Bessie's acquaintance consisted of:

> one field or paddock as they are called here containing fifty acres. This would not be considered a bad farm in Ireland. It grows a great quantity of wheat and very fine wheat it is that is grown in New Zealand . . .
>
> You would like to know something about the cattle. Well we have very fine fat cows quite as nice as the home ones. You see they were all brought from home at first. Then our sheep are quite as woolly and quite as nice to eat. I believe they are better. They get such nice grazing.[51]

Further comparisons between New Zealand and Ireland appear in Catherine Sullivan's letter: 'They don't churn the cream out here like we did at home. They take it to the factory.' The flax also differed: 'Dear Tom the flax here is not like the flax at home. One blade would tie the strongest horse. It is about 6ft long more or less.' Of course, conditions varied throughout New Zealand. James O'Neill, based at Auckland, advised that 'There is not much tillage about here. The land is bad.'

Developing land was costly in terms of money and time. Traditional skills were either adapted or abandoned in the new environment, while new techniques were frequently adopted. As Hamilton McIlrath mentioned: 'We do not go to the trouble of draining and manureing just ploughs and harrows and rolls and leaves it there untill fit for cuting. No weeding [*erased*: of] or thistle pulling here. Thrashes the grain in the paddocks and burns the straw. Makes no manure except what the horses makes.'[52]

Advances in mechanization continued throughout the late nineteenth century and by 1906 Hamilton revealed the colony's utilization of machinery:

People here have far more up to date implements to work the land than at home. We have from a one furrow to a four furrow plough, disc harrows and cultivator, grain and manure drill and two reapers and binders and one man works from four to six horses in a teem. But they dont work near so long hours here as at home. Only eight hours a day and a half holiday a week. We never house the cattle here so there is no trouble with manure.[53]

Despite drawing attention to the disparities of colonial life, migrants also stressed similarities, probably to allay the fears of concerned friends and family in Ireland. As such, interaction with acquaintances from home developed great significance. 'Do not suppose for a moment that we are in a wild, uncivilised place', James McIlrath reassured. 'No only for the look of the contry when we go to a cattle show or any other gathering one almost forgets but that he is in Ireland. I was at one of Thursday last and there was any amount of people we all know ... not one of which has cause to regret leaving Home.'[54]

It was not surprising that James and Hamilton frequently encountered companions from their native land as just over half of Canterbury's Irish population originated from Ulster, with County Down providing 16.6 per cent.[55] Some comrades were more recognizable than others: 'C*u*osin Rob[t] is liveing close by us. He is farming on his own hook and getting on very well. There is a great many from home about here.'[56] The lists of names in the McIlrath letters indicate a community migration based not solely on kin but also locality. 'You would be surprised to find how many of the Killinchy people was there', James reflected after attending Leeston's inaugural horse racing event in 1864. 'Sometimes I forget where we were. The only thing that is the great difference is the want of Ladies. The are very scarce.'[57]

This absence of females also concerned the colonial government, who set about encouraging female emigration to New Zealand. Despite the influx of females from 1870 onwards, James wrote home in 1875 enquiring of his parents if they knew of 'any young Woeman or girl that would like to come here willing to milk & so. There is no rough work here like at home. I would pay all expences from she left home and make this a home for Her too. I would give from twenty to £25 per year.'[58]

By early 1876, Maggie Auld was working for James. Despite the litany of names contained in the McIlrath letters, Maggie Auld's emigration is the only mention of encouragement and assistance being offered to a potential emigrant. Yet this does not mean that other friends and family were not encouraged or assisted. Mary Patterson, sister of James's wife, Agnes Matthews, and her family arrived in New Zealand in 1876 as assisted immigrants, possibly aided by James and Agnes. For James, his local network must have extended as a result of his marriage in 1869 to Agnes, born near Comber, five miles from Killinchy.

Although Irish migrants frequently found themselves among friends and family in the colony, several reflected on the idea of returning to Ireland. 'Twelve years is now past and gone since last we parted', James McIlrath nostalgically reminisced in 1872. 'I thought to have seen you all before this but time here seems to roll on much faster than at Home . . . .'.[59]

It is possible that when the McIlraths emigrated in 1860, they did not consider their relocation permanent. Yet, although James wrote of coming home and mentioned others who did return, by 1873 he was wary of what reverse migration would entail:

> I would be far more afraid of rueing coming Home to Ireland than I was of leaving which I never once done. I doubt a good many I wont say all that goes Home would wish to be back again but if I thought I could do anything well at Home I might come before many years. I know the time is past I said I would and meant it too but what did I then know.[60]

David McCullough's first letter home from London, *en route* to the antipodes, suggests that he also migrated with the intention that he would one day go home. He reassured his aunt with the words, 'I can not turn back now but I hope soon to return'.[61] As time went by, David used his continued involvement in digging for gold, as part of a cooperative, as an excuse to remain in the colony when his parents requested that he to return to Ireland: 'Dear Father & Mother you are both asking me to come home. It would be very akward at the present time to get away. We are still holding on the cascade claim. We have got a good bit of money sunk in it now but I will try and be home in the inside of Twelve Months.'[62] David never did return.

Agnes Lambert, however, came very close to venturing back to Antrim, as her last letter to a niece revealed: 'I would love to go back to Ireland now but of course it is impossible. I was leaving for Ireland some years ago – had my passage booked and luggage aboard but at the last minute had my things taken off and came ashore but now I wish I had gone after all.'[63]

Most Irish settlers in New Zealand never returned to Ireland but continued, like James McIlrath, to consider their native country as home. As James summarized more than 30 years after his emigration: 'It is refreshing to get news from Home. I still call it Home yet although I have lived longer here than in old Ireland but I believe if we were to live here for a Century we would still call the place of our Birth Home.'[64]

This chapter's exploration of Irish impressions of New Zealand does not represent the perceptions of all Irish migrants or of all Irish letter writers. It does, however, highlight the diverse opinions and range of information conveyed by Irish correspondents. Both Catholic and Protestant letter writers discussed issues such as employment, wages, prices, agricultural conditions, community networks and religion. Their correspondence indicates that impressions of the colony varied according to personal circumstances and fluctuating economic conditions. Many challenges were encountered and adjustments often resulted, such as Protestants altering their denomination to suit local provision. However, most correspondents viewed contrasting colonial conditions favourably and their unfamiliar surroundings were made less disturbing due to wide kin and neighbourhood networks. Although contemplation of reverse migration suggests that home was always Ireland, during periods of contentment and prosperity New Zealand was 'the desired haven'.

Notes

1. See Lyndon Fraser, *To Tara Via Holyhead: Irish Catholic Immigrants in Nineteenth-Century Christchurch* (Auckland, 1997) and Seán G. Brosnahan, 'The Battle of the Borough and the Saige O Timaru: Sectarian Riot in Colonial Canterbury', *New Zealand Journal of History*, 28 (April 1994), pp. 41–59.

2. Donald Harman Akenson, *Half the World from Home: Perspectives on the Irish in New Zealand 1860–1950* (Wellington, 1990); Richard P. Davis, *Irish Issues in New Zealand Politics 1868–1922* (Dunedin, 1974).

3. America's Irish population peaked at 5.12 per cent in 1860. See Donald Harman Akenson, 'Immigration and Ethnicity in New Zealand and the USA – the Irish Example', in Jock Phillips (ed.), *New Worlds? The Comparative History of New Zealand and the United States* (Wellington, 1989), pp. 29, 42.

4. More than 70 per cent of migrants sailing direct to New Zealand from Ireland in 1876–90 were from Clare, Antrim, Kerry, Limerick, Tipperary, Cork, Londonderry, Tyrone, Down and Galway. See Table 22, pp. 70–1 in Akenson, *Half the World from Home*.

5. Munster supplied 40.04 per cent and Ulster 40.46 per cent of assisted Irish migrants to Otago and Southland in 1872–88. See Seán Brosnahan, 'The Greening of Otago: Irish [Catholic] Immigration to Otago and Southland 1840–88', unpublished paper delivered at the New Zealand Historical Association Conference, February 1993, p. 8 and Fig. 7. More than half (53.2 per cent) of Canterbury's Irish population originated from Ulster with Munster supplying 20.8 per cent. See Table 1:50, p. 222 in Keith Anthony Pickens, 'Canterbury 1851–1881: Demography and Mobility. A Comparative Study', unpublished Ph.D. thesis (Washington University, 1976).

6. Akenson, *Half the World from Home*, p. 69.

7. The main works are David Fitzpatrick, *Oceans of Consolation: Personal Accounts of Irish Migration to Australia* (Cork, 1994), Kerby A. Miller, *Emigrants and Exiles: Ireland and the Irish Exodus to North America* (New York, 1985) and Patrick O'Farrell, *Letters from Irish Australia, 1825–1929* (Sydney, 1984). Personal correspondence, particularly that preserved by his parents, is also at the heart of Patrick O'Farrell's *Vanished Kingdoms. Irish in Australia and New Zealand. A Personal Excursion* (Sydney, 1990).

8. D.H. Akenson, 'Reading the Texts of Rural Immigrants: Letters from the Irish in Australia, New Zealand and North America', *Canadian Papers in Rural History*, 7 (1990), pp. 387–406; Trevor Parkhill ' "Prospects of this New Colony": Letters of Ulster Emigrants to New Zealand 1840–1900', *Familia*, 2, 5 (Belfast, 1989), pp. 38–42.

9. Elizabeth McCleland (Londonderry) to her daughter Ann McCleland (Wellington), 1 October 1840, Public Record Office of Northern Ireland (PRONI), T3034/1. Extracts from the McCleland letters and other collections held at PRONI are reproduced by permission of the Deputy Keeper of the Records, PRONI.

10. James Belich, *Making Peoples: A History of the New Zealanders From Polynesian Settlement to the End of the Nineteenth Century* (Auckland, 1996), p. 279.

11. Bessie Macready (Canterbury) to her cousins (Down), 27 March 1878, PRONI D1757/2/4.

12. James McIlrath (Liverpool) to his family (Down), 7 December 1860. The letters of James and Hamilton McIlrath form the largest collection of emigrant letters from New Zealand, so far known to exist. I am grateful to Jenny Langford for supplying

copies of the original letters. Transcripts of the McIlrath letters are held at the Alexander Turnbull Library, Wellington, New Zealand, MS-Papers-5061.

13. James McIlrath (Canterbury) to his family (Down), 8 September 1862.

14. James McIlrath (Canterbury) to his family (Down), 31 January 1875.

15. Hamilton McIlrath (Canterbury) to his brother (Down), 13 July 1873.

16. James McIlrath (Canterbury) to his family (Down), 27 June 1873.

17. Hamilton McIlrath (Canterbury) to his brother (Down), 15 July 1878.

18. The town of Dargaville took its name from Joseph McMullen Dargaville, born in Fermoy, County Cork, in 1831.

19. Patrick Quinn (Dargaville) to his brother John (Belfast), 29 January 1906, PRONI T1552/11.

20. Akenson, 'Reading the Texts', p. 397.

21. Patrick Quinn (Dargaville) to his brother John (Belfast), 9 October 1900, PRONI T1552/9. The Old Age Pensions Act was introduced in 1898 and restricted to those who were already, or close to being, destitute.

22. David McCullough (Otago) to his family (Down), 21 December 1875. Provided by Sandra Gilpin.

23. James O'Neill (Auckland) to his brother Thomas (Limerick), 30 November 1863. Provided by the author.

24. Catherine Sullivan (Manawatu) to her brother-in-law Tom Sullivan (Limerick), 7 March 1905. Provided by Catherine Habes.

25. Hugh Rea (Otago) to his brother-in-law William McCance (Down), 6 November 1905, PRONI D965/1.

26. Bessie Macready (Canterbury) to her cousins M and Jane (Down), 14 July 1881, PRONI D1757/2/6.

27. Ellen Piezzi (Westland) to her brother-in-law Victer Piezzi (California), *c.* 1878. Provided by Teresa O'Connor.

28. Agnes Lambert (Auckland) to her sister Susan Jenkinson (Antrim), 30 August 1890. Provided by Beverley Baird.

29. Agnes Lambert (Auckland) to her sister Susan Jenkinson (Antrim), 16 January 1871.

30. David Bell (Otago) to his brother John (Antrim), November 1884. Provided by Tom Bell.

31. Bessie Macready (Canterbury) to her cousin William (Down), 14 July 1881, PRONI D1757/2/5.

32. William Lysaght (Limerick) to his brother Edward (Auckland), 19 December 1869. Provided by Reg Brown.

33. Edmund Lysaght (Limerick) to his son Edward (Auckland), 7 June 1871.

34. Hamilton McIlrath (Canterbury) to his brother William (Down), 2 May 1886.

35. William Lysaght (Limerick) to his brother Edward (Auckland), 19 December 1869.

36. See Belich *Making Peoples*, p. 243.

37. Richard Flanagan (London) to his brothers Michael and Patrick Flanagan (West Coast), 1 June 1868. Provided by Donald Murphy.

38. Anna Rogers, *A Lucky Landing: The Story of the Irish in New Zealand* (Auckland, 1996), p. 92.

39. James McIlrath (Canterbury) to his family (Down), 1 December 1863.

40. Hamilton McIlrath (Canterbury) to his brother (Down), 5 December 1863.

41. Some 80 per cent of soldiers who received land grants in the mid-1860s had departed by 1871. Belich, *Making Peoples*, p. 386.

42. Hamilton McIlrath (Canterbury) to his brother (Down), 5 December 1863.

43. Hamilton McIlrath (Canterbury) to his family (Down), 12 August 1862.

44. Bessie Macready (Canterbury) to her cousins M & Jane (Down), 14 July 1881, PRONI D1757/2/6.
45. Ellen Piezzi (West Coast) to her brother-in-law Victer Piezzi (California), *c.* 1878.
46. David McCullough (Otago) to his family (Down), 21 December 1875.
47. Michael Flanagan (West Coast) to his brother Richard (London), 10 August 1867.
48. Hamilton McIlrath (Canterbury) to his family (Down), 12 August 1862.
49. James McIlrath (Canterbury) to his family (Down), 1 December 1863.
50. Bessie Macready (Canterbury) to her cousin William (Down), 14 July 1881, PRONI D1757/2/5.
51. Ibid.
52. Hamilton McIlrath (Canterbury) to his brother William (Down), 15 February 1874.
53. Hamilton McIlrath (Canterbury) to his brother William (Down), 22 October 1906.
54. James McIlrath (Canterbury) to his family (Down), 21 December 1872.
55. Pickens, 'Canterbury', Table 1:50, p. 222.
56. Hamilton McIlrath (Canterbury) to his parents (Down), 9 June 1867. Robert McIlrath, born in 1840, was the son of James and Anne McIlrath.
57. James McIlrath (Canterbury) to his family (Down), 12 March 1864.
58. James McIlrath (Canterbury) to his family (Down), 26 August 1875.
59. James McIlrath (Canterbury) to his family (Down), 21 December 1872.
60. James McIlrath (Canterbury) to his family, (Down), 27 June 1873.
61. David McCullough (London) to his aunt (Down), 12 January 1875.
62. David McCullough (West Coast) to his parents (Down), 2 July 1899.
63. Agnes Lambert (Wanganui) to her niece Alice (Antrim), *c.* 1925.
64. James McIlrath (Canterbury) to his brother William (Down), 24 February 1891.

Part Four
General Studies

CHAPTER 15

A Quantification of Irish Migration with Particular Emphasis on the 1980s and 1990s

DAMIEN COURTNEY

(Department of Social and General Studies,
Cork Institute of Technology)

Introduction

This chapter focuses on the quantitative dimension of Irish migration[1] and is set in a demographic context. It is difficult to understand fully the causes and consequences, the personal and cultural circumstances, the social, economic and political realities of migration without particular reference to the numbers involved, their countries of origin or destination, their sex, age, marital status and other demographic characteristics.

Migration is the most difficult component of population change to define, record and analyse. It is generally defined in terms of the area to be studied. It can be either internal or external, and inward or outward.[2] We are concerned here essentially with Irish external migration, which has traditionally centred on emigration, with immigration only becoming significant since the 1970s. In Ireland migration has consistently had a much greater influence on population change than natural increase (the numbers of births less deaths). This chapter illustrates the extent and variety of the statistics available for a quantification of Irish migration, demonstrating their development and potential use.

The highest levels of migration from Ireland were recorded in the nineteenth century. This is well illustrated by the number of Irish-born persons living abroad. The highest level was in 1881 which was equivalent to 60 per cent of the Irish-born who lived in Ireland at the time, in 1911 it was 50 per cent, whereas by 1931 it had fallen to 30 per cent.[3] Table 15.1 provides details of the population on the island of Ireland and the distribution of Irish-born persons living in the United States of America (USA), Canada, Australia and Great Britain (GB) between 1841 and 1991. We see that for the countries indicated Irish-born persons living there increased until 1871 (1851 for Canada) and declined thereafter, especially during the twentieth century.

A quantification of Irish migration is essential for our understanding of this complex subject. This chapter is an attempt to document the availability of

Table 15.1: Population of Ireland (both parts) and geographical distribution of Irish-born persons, 1841–1991 (000s)

Country	1841	1851	1871	1901	1991
Population in Ireland	8,178	6,552	5,412	4,459	5,104
Irish born people living in:					
United States	NA	962	1,856	1,615	187*
Canada	122	227	223	102	42#
Australia	NA	70	214	184	77
Great Britain	415	727	775	632	837
Total for countries listed	—	1,986	3,068	2,533	1,143

Notes:
* The figure for the United States relates to 1990. It involves an estimate for those born in Northern Ireland (on the basis of 1980 census data).
# The 1991 population total for Canada involves an estimate for those born in Northern Ireland.
NA not available.
Adapted from: Economic and Social Research Institute, Compilation of Irish Born Persons Living Abroad (unpublished).

recent Irish migration statistics with particular reference to official published data. The significance of Irish external migration is well documented. The principal means of migration data collection and related publications by the Irish Central Statistics Office (CSO) are the five-yearly Census of Population, the annual Labour Force Survey recently replaced by the Quarterly National Household Survey, and the Vital Statistics. Gross migration flows, emigration and immigration estimates since the late 1980s are now available in a CSO Statistical Release.

It is significant that even in 1991 there was an estimated 1.143 million Irish-born persons living in GB, Canada, Australia and the USA when the population in the Republic of Ireland (Ireland) was just three times greater at 3.526 million. Since 1961 the population of Ireland has grown steadily and significantly except for a small decline during the 1986–91 intercensal period. Higher emigration among males in recent years has contributed to a situation where there are now more females in the population. The age groups 15–24 years especially and 25–34 years have been most affected by emigration. During the 1980s more than three out of every four migrants from Ireland to GB were aged between 15 and 44 years. Since 1981 emigration has been greater each year than immigration, except for the year ending in April 1992 and those since April 1995. Emigration was highest at 70,600 during April 1988–89.

Recent data suggest a considerable number of Irish-born (return) immigrants. The number of one-year immigrants was much higher for 1990–91 than 1980–81, of whom more than a half came from England and Wales. The country of previous residence for three-quarters of them was the United Kingdom (UK).[4] It is the most important country of origin and destination for Irish migration. Among families who migrated from GB to Ireland especially before 1981, many of the parents were born in Ireland, unlike their children. Two in every five immigrants were aged 25–44 years. The 1996 census indicated that four out of every five immigrants in Ireland arrived since 1971. Immigration from the UK is particularly important for the years preceding 1981, especially during the 1970s. Immigration from other European Union (EU)[5] countries increased steadily throughout the 1980s and 1990s. Within Ireland the predominant direction of migration since the mid-1980s was from south to north whilst the number of applicants for refugee status has increased dramatically in recent years, especially since 1994.

It is difficult to undertake population projections for Ireland and especially to make assumptions about Irish migration. Projections make use of the most recent relevant data available and need to be updated regularly in order to enhance their accuracy. They are necessary for good planning and development. A quantification of Irish migration is an essential element in this process, too.

Sources of migration statistics

In Ireland the CSO has statutory powers and resources to collect, compile, analyse and publish population and migration statistics. This is achieved mainly through the Census of Population, the Labour Force Survey, now the Quarterly National Household Survey, and the Vital Statistics, along with reliance on a number of other measures. Unfortunately, in Ireland there does not exist a population register, which in some of the Scandinavian and Benelux countries, for example, facilitates the continuous observation of biographical details of individuals from the cradle to the grave, though used confidentially in aggregate form. Population registers provide better migration statistics than is otherwise possible, as they centralize a variety of sources, providing an exact measure of the size and structure of a population for analysis at any given time.

In Ireland the greatest source of migration statistics is the Census of Population. It consists of gathering demographic, social, economic and administrative data at a given time relating to all persons and households in a country. It provides information about a population's structure such as its sex, age, conjugal condition, place of birth, education, principal economic status, occupation, industry, housing and household composition, language, religion, fertility and migration. Most of the Irish census years with their populations are indicated in Table 15.2. Censuses are now held every five years. It is the single largest statistical enquiry conducted by the CSO and is the principal source of demographic and migration statistics in Ireland. By the end of 1998 results from the 1996 census had been published in a Preliminary Report, a new and innovative volume on Principal Demographic Results, nine other volumes and detailed County and County Borough Reports. Volume 1 on Population Classified by Area provides up-to-date data on the Irish population and migration during the 1990s. Volume 2 which relates to Ages and Marital Status is of particular demographic value, whilst Volume 4 on Migration and Birthplace provides an invaluable source on Irish migration. The increasing availability of small area population statistics (SAPS) and unpublished cross-tabulated census data is of great value for a wide range of research.

The detailed information provided by the census reports is, as we have seen, available only at intervals usually of five years. During intercensal periods

Table 15.2: Population and average annual rates (per 1,000) of population change in the Republic of Ireland*, 1871–1996

Intercensal period	Population# (000s)	Marriage rate‡	Birth rate	Death rate	Rate of natural increase	Net migration rate	Rate of change
1871–81	3,870	4.5	26.2	18.1	8.0	−12.7	−4.6
1881–91	3,469	4.0	22.8	17.4	5.3	−16.3	−10.9
1891–01	3,222	4.5	22.1	17.6	4.5	−11.9	−7.4
1901–11	3,140	4.8	22.4	16.8	5.6	−8.2	−2.6
1911–26	2,972	5.0	21.1	16.0	5.2	−8.8	−3.7
1926–36	2,968	4.6	19.6	14.2	5.5	−5.6	−0.1
1936–46	2,955	5.4	20.3	14.5	5.9	−6.3	−0.4
1946–51	2,961	5.5	22.2	13.6	8.6	−8.2	+0.4
1951–56	2,898	5.4	21.3	12.2	9.2	−13.4	−4.3
1956–61	2,818	5.4	21.2	11.9	9.2	−14.8	−5.6
1961–66	2,884	5.7	21.9	11.7	10.3	−5.7	+4.6
1966–71	2,978	6.5	21.3	11.2	10.1	−3.7	+6.4
1971–79	3,368	6.8	21.6	10.5	11.1	+4.3	+15.4
1979–81	3,443	6.3	21.5	9.7	11.8	−0.7	+11.0
1981–86	3,541	5.5	19.1	9.4	9.7	−4.1	+5.6
1986–91	3,526	5.1	15.7	9.0	6.8	−7.6	−0.8
1991–96	3,626	4.6	14.0	8.8	5.2	+0.2	+5.3

Notes:

* Population and average annual rates for that part of Ireland which became the Irish Free State in 1921 and the Republic of Ireland in 1949.

Population at end of intercensal period (April); population (000s) in 1841: 6,529; 1851: 5,112; 1861: 4,402; 1871: 4,053.

‡ The marriage rates 1871–1926 are averaged around end of year rather than April, e.g. 1871–80.

Adapted from: CSO, Censuses of Population and Reports on Vital Statistics.

supplementary data are published on population movement through Vital Statistics in the form of quarterly and annual reports. Recent quarterly reports provide a series of births, marriages and deaths and their rates per 1,000 population for each quarter since 1970. The Fourth Quarterly Report includes a separate Yearly Summary. The Annual Report, which is much more comprehensive, is published some years later.

Sample surveys are of increasing importance as a source of demographic and migration statistics. They are cheap relative to the other principal data collection methods. They have been used in developing countries which lack sophisticated national statistical organizations like the CSO. In other situations they are available in conjunction with the census, more regularly, and probe deeper into particular subjects, thus enhancing the quality of responses. A survey may also serve to reduce the length of a census questionnaire for the other respondents excluded from the sample. It is unlikely, however, that sample surveys will ever fully replace the widely used means of demographic data outlined above which provide extensive details about each individual in a country.

The annual Labour Force Survey has been replaced by a Quarterly National Household Survey and the first results, for September to November 1997, were published in May 1998. The former is a major source of employment, demographic and, since 1987, migration statistics. Its special value is the comparative dimension afforded by this harmonized survey undertaken simultaneously in each member state of the EU. The 1996 Irish Labour Force Survey sample consisted of 45,900 private households and some non-private ones comprising 144,674 persons, i.e. about 4 per cent of the total population. Information for the Quarterly National Household Survey is collected continuously, with 3,000 households surveyed each week to give a total of 39,000 households in each quarter.

CSO estimates of net migration are used in conjunction with the natural increase (births less deaths) to determine intercensal annual population estimates. Difficulties brought about by the underestimation of the 1979 population, when compared subsequently with the census results, has compelled the CSO to consider and develop other methodological means of measuring migration. The publication of details of net passenger movements has been discontinued given their unreliability as a measure of net migration, especially during the 1970s, when there was unprecedented net immigration to Ireland. They are now published as part of the *Economic Series* under four headings: passenger movement by sea and by air; outward and inward. It is still possible, of course, to aggregate the data to provide one overall estimate of net passenger movements which, of necessity, includes short-term travellers such as business people and tourists. Greater details are available on tourism and travel derived from estimates based on two sample surveys of passengers, the Country of Residence Survey and the Passenger Card Inquiry, and used in conjunction with passenger movement figures. At present an Electoral Register is compiled by the local authorities. The CSO should be given responsibility for it and allocated additional resources to provide a comprehensive list of questions which would yield additional information on gross migration flows including those under 18 years of age and the reasons why people migrate.

The CSO is making continuous efforts to improve the accuracy of its estimates by also having recourse to the following data: child benefit in respect of children under 16 years of age; children enrolled at first and second level schools; the aggregate register of electors of all persons 18 years of age and over; labour force and quarterly national household survey estimates of gross migration flows; the number of immigrant visas issued to Irish persons by the USA, Canada and Australia; and in the context of the UK new registrants from Ireland with the National Health Services and the National Insurance Scheme.[6] In addition, data are now available from the administrative records of the Irish Government Department (Ministry) of Social, Community and Family Affairs to identify returned migrants amongst new registrants on the Live Register of the Unemployed.

Questions about usual residence at the time of the census and one year previously introduced in 1971 have been very useful in providing continuity of data about internal migration and 'one year immigrants' since then. This is of particular value given that compulsory population registration in Ireland is confined to births, deaths and marriages.

The most welcome and significant methodological development in making migration statistics available was the introduction of a relevant question in the Labour Force Survey and its subsequent redesign in 1988. This has yielded estimated gross migration flows since 1987. A *Statistical Release, April 1997* provides the first complete revised series for an intercensal period on annual population and migration estimates 1992–97. The *Statistical Release, April 1998* contains annual estimates of the population for 1993–98 by sex and by five-year age group, along with an estimated number of emigrants and immigrants classified by sex, by broad age group, by country of destination and origin and estimated immigration classified by sex and nationality. For 1998 the population is also estimated according to marital status and provided for each regional authority area. The new Quarterly National Household Survey really offers an exciting prospect not just for population, household and labour force statistics but also for information on migration flows and their characteristics.

Irish migration statistics are also available in respect of residence abroad as provided in censuses and other statistical publications of statistical offices in countries elsewhere. Visas are also a valuable source of information. The relevance of the census and other existing data depends on the nature of the relationships between Ireland and the other countries. Detailed analysis of migration between Ireland and GB has been commissioned by Eurostat, the Statistical Office of the EU, and is currently in progress.[7] Published and unpublished data are available which should form the basis for other comparable studies.

Irish migration and population change

Demographic change may be explained by means of the following population components equation:

$$P_1 = P_0 + (B - D) + (I - E)$$

where P_0 and P_1 represent a population at the beginning and end, respectively, of a specified interval, usually a year, where persons enter the population through births (B) and immigration (I) and leave it through deaths (D) and emigration (E). Table 15.2 provides rates for the different components of population change expressed per 1,000 of the mean population.

Historically, there was reliance on the use of indirect methods to measure Irish net migration.[8] The most used one is a variation of the above equation as follows:

$$(I - E) = P_1 - P_0 - (B - D)$$

Table 15.2 provides details of demographic change in what is now the Republic of Ireland, since the 1841 census and the introduction in 1864 of the compulsory registration of births, deaths and marriages.

In Ireland, the late eighteenth and early nineteenth centuries were times of rampant population growth. When the population for all of the island peaked in 1841 at 8.174 million it was a little more than half of the number of persons

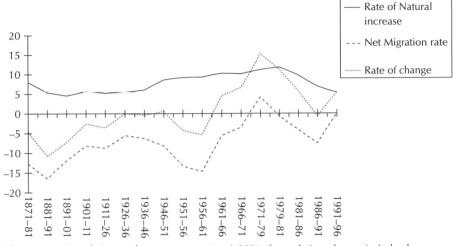

Figure 15.1: Population and average rates (per 1,000) of population change in Ireland, 1871–1996.
Adapted from: CSO, Censuses of Population and Reports on Vital Statistics.

in England and Wales then. The population in what is now the Republic of Ireland fell from 6.529 million in 1841 to 5.112 million and 4.402 million in 1851 and 1861, respectively. Table 15.2 indicates that by the time of the first post-independence census in 1926 it was 2.972 million, just over 45 per cent of what it was in 1841. In spite of exceptionally high mortality during the 1840s due to the Famine, this population decline was due essentially to emigration. Even later net emigration amounted to 202,703 between 1871 and 1926. The population continued to decline until it reached its lowest level in modern times at 2.818 million in 1961. Since then it has increased for each intercensal period, except 1986–91. The 1998 estimated population of 3.705 million is higher than at any time for over a century.

It is evident from Table 15.2 and especially Figure 15.1 the impact which net migration has had on Irish population change. They show annual averages in each intercensal period between 1871 and 1996 for population change, natural increase and net migration. In most countries population change is largely determined by natural increase yet in spite of its generally high level in Ireland it has consistently been less important than migration. From 1926 to 1951 there was population stability due to the losses from net emigration being offset by natural increase. The significant increase in net emigration during the 1950s resulted as we have seen in 1961 in the lowest population recorded since independence. The unprecedented net immigration of the 1970s combined with an increase in natural increase gave rise to growth levels which were four times higher than the European Community (now the EU) average. During the 1980s fertility decline combined with the return and gradual increase in net emigration resulted in a fall in the rate of population increase, and subsequent decline. Since 1991, however, there was substantial growth due to renewed net immigration and in spite of a further decrease in fertility.

Table 15.3: Average annual change in population, natural increase and net migration by sex, 1871–1996

Intercensal period	Decrease in population (+ increase)		Natural increase		Net emigration (+ net immigration)			Females per 1,000 male migrants
	Males	Females	Males	Females	Males	Females	Total	
1871–81	8,003	10,314	16,955	14,900	24,958	25,214	50,172	1,010
1881–91	18,384	21,749	10,873	8,727	29,257	30,476	59,733	1,042
1891–01	11,852	12,836	8,463	6,491	20,315	19,327	39,642	951
1901–11	2,058	6,156	9,706	8,234	11,764	14,390	26,154	1,223
1911–26	5,508	5,672	8,426	7,396	13,934	13,068	27,002	938
1926–36	+1,357	1,714	8,612	7,706	7,255	9,420	16,675	1,298
1936–46	2,558	+1,227	8,700	8,680	11,258	7,453	18,711	662
1946–51	+2,390	1,271	12,699	12,804	10,309	14,075	24,384	1,365
1951–56	8,734	3,732	12,923	13,964	21,657	17,696	39,353	817
1956–61	9,276	6,709	12,639	13,777	21,915	20,486	42,401	935
1961–66	+6,496	+6,636	14,019	15,234	7,523	8,598	16,121	1,143
1966–71	+9,345	+9,504	14,295	15,335	4,950	5,831	10,781	1,178
1971–79	+24,689	+24,057	17,030	18,099	+7,659	+5,958	+13,617	778
1979–81	+18,041	+19,553	19,647	20,470	1,606	917	2,523	571
1981–86	+8,067	+11,380	16,350	17,474	8,283	6,094	14,377	736
1986–91	3,254	+270	11,610	12,239	14,865	11,969	26,834	805
1991–96	+9,363	+10,711	9,051	9,375	+311	+1,336	+1,647	4,296

Adapted from: *Report of the Commission on Emigration and Other Population Problems*, Table 13 and CSO, Censuses of Population.

Table 15.3 provides for each intercensal period from 1871 to 1996 details of the average annual change in population, natural increase and net migration for males and females. Natural increase was consistently higher among males until the 1940s, after which it was lower than for females. Since the 1946–51 intercensal period the greater female longevity more than compensated for the relatively higher number of male births. The annual level of net emigration fluctuated extensively during different periods. It was highest during the nineteenth century and again in the 1950s and late 1980s. Net emigration was higher among males during the 1950s and since 1979, whilst it was lower in-between. During the last intercensal period, 1991–96, there was much higher immigration among females than males. This pattern of net migration by sex is reflected in overall population change, although there are a number of periods when the population of one sex increased and the other decreased, e.g. in the early decades of the new state and in the late 1980s. In general, there was a greater decrease in the female population until the 1950s, except for 1936–46. During the 1960s and 1970s the overall increase in population was shared fairly evenly between the sexes. Since then the gap widened again with the female population undergoing a higher increase than the male one. During the late 1980s, whilst the female population continued to increase a little there was a significant decline among males, reflecting their higher level of net emigration.

Migration by sex and age group

Greater details of the components of natural increase, i.e. births and deaths, and the related estimate of net migration for males and females for the five-year period 1991–96 are given in Table 15.4. The difference between the 249,428 births and 157,297 deaths provides a natural increase of 92,131. When compared with the actual increase in population of 100,368 we derive an estimate of net immigration (higher immigration than emigration) of 8,237 as follows:

$$(3,626,087 - 3,525,719) - (249,428 - 157,297) = 100,368 - 92,131$$

Table 15.4: Ireland, estimated net migration, 1991–1996

	Persons	Males	Females
Population in 1996	3,626,087	1,800,232	1,825,855
Population in 1991	3,525,719	1,753,418	1,772,301
Population increase	100,368	46,814	53,554
Births	249,428	128,628	120,800
Deaths	157,297	83,371	73,926
Natural increase (births–deaths)	92,131	45,257	46,874
Estimated net migration	8,237	1,557	6,680

Notes: The data for births and deaths relate to registration in the five-year period ended 31 March 1996. The figures for the first quarter of 1996 are provisional. Adapted from: CSO, Census 96, Population Classified by Area, Table 2; Vital Statistics, First Quarter 1997, Tables 2, 3.

Table 15.5: Ireland, the effect on selected age groups of net migration during intercensal periods, 1951–1996

Age group (Years)	1951–56	1956–61	1961–66	1966–71	1971–81*	1981–86	1986–91	1991–96
				(000s)				
Males								
0–14	−11.7	−2.2	+4.8	+5.6	+24.4	−3.3	−4.5	+10.3
15–24	−44.7	−59.3	−39.7	−31.2	−4.9	−26.7	−40.2	−26.1
25–34	−32.8	−26.8	−3.0	−4.3	−1.3	−12.1	−28.1	+1.4
35–44	−12.4	−6.8	+2.3	+3.1	+22.7	−1.5	−4.3	+6.1
45–54	−6.1	−6.6	−1.1	−0.6	+7.6	−1.4	−1.9	+3.0
55–64	−1.9	−7.7	−1.6	−1.4	+0.4	−0.2	+1.0	+3.4
65+	+5.7	+2.5	+1.3	+4.0	+9.0	+3.9	+3.9	+3.5
Total males	−103.9	−106.9	−37.2	−24.8	+58.1	−41.4	−74.0	+1.6
Females								
0–14	−7.6	−5.0	+5.0	+6.1	+23.0	−3.0	−3.6	+9.8
15–24	−43.9	−56.0	−36.9	−29.2	−5.3	−21.8	−37.6	−22.8
25–34	−19.3	−21.7	−2.9	−4.6	+0.2	−7.0	−19.6	+7.6
35–44	−7.6	−9.1	−1.1	+0.2	+16.9	−0.1	−1.8	+5.9
45–54	−5.4	−9.3	−4.0	−2.4	+2.6	−1.2	−1.3	+1.6
55–64	−1.2	−4.5	−2.6	−2.4	−0.8	−0.1	+1.1	+2.1
65+	+0.6	+3.8	+0.5	+3.3	+9.2	+2.6	+3.3	+2.4
Total females	−84.6	−101.9	−41.9	−28.9	+45.8	−30.5	−59.6	+6.7

Note:

* Ten-year period.

Adapted from: CSO, Census of Population of Ireland, 1971, Ages and Conjugal Conditions, Table XI; Census 96, Principal Demographic Results, Table K.

It is estimated there was net immigration of 1,557 males and 6,680 females between 1991 and 1996.

A refinement of the residual method of estimating migration provides information on the effect of migration on age groups. This is achieved through cohort analysis by applying survival ratios to groups of cohorts and comparing the actual population to the 'expected/projected' ones from one census to the next. This has been done in Table 15.5 for selected age groups from 1951 to 1996. For both males and females aged 15–24 years the impact of net emigration has been greatest. This age group experienced a net loss of persons during each intercensal period even during the 1970s and more recently in the 1990s when the effect on the overall population was positive, i.e. when there was net immigration. Net emigration among this age group has been higher for males in each period except during the 1970s when it was a little lower than for females. The same was true for the 25–34 year age group except in the late 1960s when net emigration was slightly less among males than females. In general, this age group too experienced high levels of net emigration except in the early 1990s, and among females during the 1970s. The size and direction of migration among those aged 35–44 years is greatly influenced by overall migration and includes many returning migrants to Ireland. Their children are included in the 0–14 years age group where since 1961 there has been net immigration, except during the 1980s. Finally, the net immigration among those aged 65 years and over is associated with persons moving to Ireland, in many cases returning, for their retirement.

Usually resident population by place of birth, by country of residence one year before the census and by duration

Another traditional measure of migration which is census-based is concerned with the usually resident population by *place of birth*. This approach too has some drawbacks. It takes account of a maximum of just one migration if the place of residence differs from that of birth. As the frequency of migration is likely to increase with age, the efficacy of this method decreases for persons at older ages. Nevertheless, it provides an indication of long-term migration and it is useful for internal migration analysis and immigration. Recent censuses reveal increasing mobility within Ireland. The current economic buoyancy and related high levels of immigration are evident from information about the usually resident population born outside Ireland. A question on place of birth was asked at almost every census in recent years: in 1971, 1981, 1986, 1991 and 1996. It was not ascertained at the limited 1979 census.

The same pattern exists for two questions first asked in 1971 concerning *usual residence now* and *usual residence one year ago*. They provide details about 'one year migrants', both internal and external. The addition of this information has been one of the two most significant developments in the quantification of modern Irish migration based on official statistics. The other relates to a question about emigration in the annual Labour Force Survey, now the Quarterly National Household Survey. The questions on usual residence at the

Table 15.6: Persons usually resident in Ireland, in 1971, 1981, 1991 and 1996, classified by other places of birth

Birthplace	1971	1981	1986	1991	1996
Northern Ireland	26,183	40,557	36,538	35,986	39,567
England and Wales	75,189	133,831	128,668	126,487	139,330
Scotland	8,849	12,577	12,586	11,378	11,751
Belgium	240	490	497	600	740
France	701	1,997	2,460	4,512	3,593
Germany	2,066	3,482	3,853	5,792	6,343
Italy	1,022	1,350	1,314	1,507	1,844
Netherlands	712	1,710	1,888	1,985	2,490
Spain	NP	NP	1,113	1,801	2,104
Other European Countries	NP	NP	NP	NP	5,723
USA	11,145	16,591	15,350	14,533	15,619
Rest of World	11,189	19,800	19,733	24,144	22,520
Total	137,296	232,385	224,000	228,725	251,624

Note: NP = Not Published.
Adapted from: CSO, Census of Population of Ireland, 1971, 1981, Birth places; Census 86, 91, Birth places; Census 96, Principal Demographic Results.

time of the census and one year previously focus on the most recent period in persons' lives and indicates at least one migration and its place of origin. It is unlikely that multiple migrations in such a short period are critical. The relevance of these data is that for external migration it provides details of one-year migrants into Ireland from elsewhere by sex, age, marital status and other characteristics. When analysed with official estimates of net emigration, and as we shall see later with Labour Force Survey statistics on emigration, it is possible to derive series on gross migration, immigration and emigration.

The addition in the 1986, 1991 and 1996 censuses of a question addressed to persons who lived outside of Ireland *for a period of one year or more* furnishes an account of the year of taking up residence in Ireland and the country of last previous residence. Taken together, the latter along with census questions about place of birth, usual residence at the time of the census and one year previously facilitate a greater knowledge and understanding of Irish immigration and its origin.

Although place of birth data suggest increasing mobility within Ireland, especially since the 1980s, the 1996 census indicates that 93 per cent of the population emunerated were born in Ireland. Table 15.6 shows that persons usually resident in Ireland and born elsewhere increased significantly from 137,926 in 1971 to 251,624 in 1996. The 1981–86 intercensal period was an exception during which it declined from 232,385 to 224,000. Since 1971 those born in England and Wales have represented the highest number of persons born outside of Ireland. They have ranged from between 55 per cent and 58 per cent of the total. In 1996 there were 139,330 of them. Similarly, the numbers born in Northern Ireland increased during the 1970s and early 1990s and declined throughout the 1980s. They are the second largest such group in this period and numbered 39,567 in 1996. The number of persons born in all of the other European countries included in the table shows a steady and spectacular increase, apart from the Italian-born where the increase was lower and the number actually fell a little between 1981 and 1986. Outside of those born in the UK (Northern Ireland, Scotland, England and Wales) there were 6,343 German and 3,593 French born persons usually resident in Ireland in 1996. Those born in the USA increased from 11,145 in 1971 to 15,619 in 1996, having peaked in 1981 at 16,591 and fallen to 14,533 in 1991.

There was a higher proportion of children, adolescents and retired persons among the Irish-born population usually resident in Ireland in 1996 compared with those born elsewhere. The opposite was true for persons aged 25–44 years. In 1991 more immigrants, albeit a small number, were recorded as born in Ireland than elsewhere. The proportion of Irish-born persons increased with age except for those aged 65 years and over where it is a little lower than for the 45–64 years age group. Most immigration has occurred since 1971. The 1991 census reveals that three in every four immigrants did so. By 1996 this was true for four out of every five such persons.

Irish emigration and immigration during the 1980s and 1990s

By far the most significant recent development in the quantification of Irish migration has been the CSO *Statistical Release on Annual Population and Migration Estimates*. This provides population estimates classified by sex, age group, marital status and regional authority area. Estimates of the number of emigrants are given by sex, age group and country of destination/origin, whilst immigrants are also estimated by nationality. This valuable publication exploits a number of traditional and innovative methods of population data collection in Ireland. It uses Census, Vital Statistics, Labour Force and now Household Survey data together with the relatively new, continuous Country of Residence Inquiry of Passengers and a number of different unpublished series referred to already such as information on visas, education, health and social security. The genesis of this series goes back to the publication of the 1979 census results which indicated that the actual population was about 100,000 greater than the anticipated one derived from the intercensal measure of natural increase and estimated net migration. Apart from the unusually long, by Irish standards, intercensal period of eight years, the unprecedented surplus in modern times of immigration over emigration by comparison with the traditional pattern of net emigration exposed the inadequacy of CSO dependence on traditional ways of intercensal population and migration estimation. There followed a period of review, experimentation and the establishment of a number of different series of data derived from government departments and embassies in Ireland and from ministries, statistical offices and other state agencies elsewhere.

By the late 1980s, however, the old scourge of emigration was well and truly part of the Irish landscape again and there was a lot of political and social

Table 15.7: Ireland, estimated annual population, change, natural increase, net migration, one-year immigrants and gross emigration (000s), 1981–1998

Year	Population		Mid-April	Change in population		Natural increase		Net migration			One-year immigrants		Gross emigration		
	(1)	(4)		(1)	(4)	(1)	(4)	(1)	(3)	(4)	(2)+(3)	(4)	(2)	(3)	(4)
1981	3,443		1981–82	37		38		−1							
1982	3,480		1982–83	24		38		−14			15.6		−29.6		
1983	3,504		1983–84	25		34		−9			15.4		−24.4		
1984	3,529		1984–85	11		31		−20			13.6		−33.6	(−20.2)	
1985	3,540		1985–86	1		29		−28			13.3		−41.3	(−24.3)	
1986	3,541		1986–87	2		29		−27			17.0		−44.0	(−35.3)	
1987	3,543	3,546.5	1987–88	−5	−15.8	26	26.1	−32	−37.3	−23.0	19.1	17.2	−51.1	−56.4	−40.2
1988	3,538	3,530.7	1988–89	−23	−21.2	23	22.7	−46		−41.9		19.2			−61.1
1989	3,515	3,509.5	1989–90		−3.7		19.2			−43.9		26.7			−70.6
1990		3,505.8	1990–91		19.9		21.9			−22.9		33.3			−56.3
1991		3,525.7	1991–92		28.9		21.5			−2.0		33.3			−35.3
1992		3,554.6	1992–93		19.5		19.9			7.4		40.7			−33.4
1993		3,574.1	1993–94		11.8		16.5			−0.4		34.7			−35.1
1994		3,585.9	1994–95		15.4		17.3			−4.7		30.1			−34.8
1995		3,601.3	1995–96		24.8		16.8			−1.9		31.2			−33.1
1996		3,626.1	1996–97		34.5		19.5			8.0		39.2			−31.2
1997*		3,660.6	1997–98		44.3		21.4			15.0		44.0			−29.0
1998*		3,704.9								22.8		44.0			−21.2

Note:
* Preliminary.
Adapted from:
(1) CSO, Vital Statistics, First Quarter 1997, Tables 2, 3 and unpublished series on Population and Net Migration.
(2) Damien Courtney, 'Recent Trends in Emigration from Ireland', paper presented at the annual conference of the Development Studies Association, Belfast, 1989, Table 3.
(3) Donal Garvey and Maurice McGuire, *Structure of Gross Migration Flows* (Dublin, 1989), Tables 1 and 6.
(4) CSO, Annual Population and Migration Estimates 1987–97, Tables 1, 2.
      CSO, Annual Population and Migration Estimates 1998, Tables 1, 5, 6.

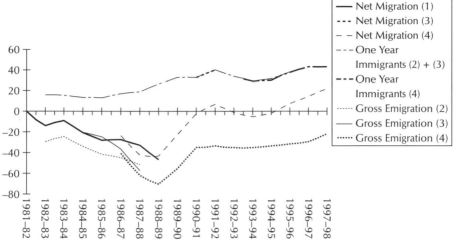

Figure 15.2: Ireland, net migration, one-year immigrants and gross emigration (000s), 1991–1998.
Adapted from:
(1) CSO, Vital Statistics, First Quarter 1997, Tables 2, 3 and unpublished series on Population and Net Migration.
(2) Damien Courtney, 'Recent Trends in Emigration from Ireland', paper presented at the annual conference of the Development Studies Association, Belfast, 1989, Table 3.
(3) Donal Garvey and Maurice McGuire, *Structure of Gross Migration Flows* (Dublin, 1989), Tables 1 and 6.
(4) CSO, Releases on Population and Migration Estimates 1987–1997, Tables 1, 2.
(5) CSO Annual Population and Migration Estimates 1998, Tables 1, 5, 6.

interest in the topic. I was one of a small number of persons undertaking research in this area and my quest for knowledge gradually focused on the inadequacy of existing estimates of net migration by comparison with the efficacy, for example, of tracking animal movements at the time between Ireland and elsewhere. To adapt Chubb's (1963) journal paper title of 'politicians persecuting civil servants',[9] I was certainly one academic 'persecuting' CSO statisticians for data to derive estimates of gross emigration flows. One of the results of my perseverance was the estimates of annual gross emigration for 1982–83 through to and including 1987–88 which I presented in September 1989[10] and are reproduced in Table 15.7 and Figure 15.2. The twelve-month period dates from April to the following April. Up to then commentators referred exclusively to net emigration, which of course consistently underestimated the intrinsic emigration level. My estimation, which was derived essentially from official data on net emigration and unpublished statistics based on questions about usual residence at the time of the Labour Force Survey and one year previously, provoked very mixed reactions ranging from the legitimate concerns of lobby activists on behalf of emigrants to the defensiveness of some politicians. At the time the 1988–89 estimate of net emigration of 46,000 was widely quoted and used in public discourse on the subject. My suggestion that the actual emigration level might be as high as 65,000 in that year, an under-estimate as it transpired, was used as a 'political football' in Dáil Éireann and elsewhere. My estimate of gross emigration for the period 1982–88 was 224,000 and 51,000 for 1987–88, when net emigration was 130,000 and 32,000, respectively. It is a measure of the growing maturity of the body politic that long before the return of surplus immigration the debate about and the alloca-tion of blame for emigration became more refined, less acrimonious and was aimed at policy-driven solutions.

In the circumstances of the time it was extremely courageous for Garvey and McGuire, two CSO statisticians, to present in November 1989 a further elaboration of gross migration flows and in exceptional detail for 1984–85 through to and including 1987–88.[11] Some of their results are also displayed in Table 15.7. They concluded by cautioning that their estimates would have to be carefully monitored over a number of years before a final view could be taken on their real value. I enthused publicly at the related seminar in the Economic and Social Research Institute (ESRI) about the significance and poten-tial of this development; others present were more cautious in their comments. Garvey and McGuire's estimate of gross emigration differed and was more accurate than mine as it was derived from the refinement and toning down of a Labour Force Survey question about emigration. A question asked in 1985, 1986 and 1987 which referred specifically to persons emigrating did not pro-duce satisfactory results. Its replacement in 1988 and in subsequent Labour Force Surveys by a softer one referring to persons living abroad has yielded an outcome of much greater accuracy. Garvey and McGuire provided extra-ordinary and unprecedented details about the structure of gross migration flows which are not reproduced here. They outlined the way in which annual net migration estimates were compiled and the sources used. Their gross immigration flows were given by age and sex distribution, country of origin, nationality, regional data, family and socio-economic group characteristics, principal eco-nomic status and educational level completed. Internal migration data was ana-lysed by sex and age, position in the family unit, principal economic status and inter-regional migration. The most exciting information related to gross emig-ration flows. They included classification by sex and age, destination, origin and month of departure, household characteristics and regional balance. They suggested that the appropriate time for a definitive position on this matter would be 1997 when such estimates could be verified and cross-referenced by data from the complete 1991–96 intercensal period. Such data have been revised based on the 1996 Census of Population and appear in the Population and Migration Estimates (April 1997).

The reality, however, is that the CSO is limited in what it can do and must concentrate on its core activities. I hope that this chapter provides some insight into some of the possibilities that may arise from access to its demographic, labour market and social statistics. In the circumstances the publication in May 1994 of the CSO's first *Statistical Release on Annual Population and Migration Estimates* was very welcome. By early 1999 there have been five re-leases. This equally exciting and innovative development has furnished for the first time annual population and migration estimates classified by sex and five-year age group from 1987 to 1998. Estimated 'out-migration' and 'in-migration' was used in the early releases whereas 'emigrants' and 'immigrants' classified by sex, age group and country of destination/origin have been adopted in the April 1997 and 1998 releases. These data constitute the fourth source in Table 15.7, which provides estimated annual population, change, natural increase, net migration, one-year immigrants and gross emigration for the period extending from 1981 to 1998. Where more than one estimate appears for some of the data it is due to official revisions which have taken place for intercensal periods following the publication of definitive census statistics.

Such official revisions are, therefore, more likely to represent the intrinsic situation in preference to earlier estimations. It is noteworthy that immigration constitutes an important component of Irish population movement even during times of high emigration levels. Having fallen somewhat between 1984 and 1986 it has experienced since then a steady and considerable increase except between 1992 and 1994. Gross emigration estimates differ somewhat for 1986–88 when emigration reached very high levels. The official figures suggest that it peaked at 70,600 in 1988–89 and amounted to a total of approximately 481,300 from 1986–87 to 1997–98, i.e. an average annual level of a little over 40,000. Immigration averaged about 32,800 per annum for the same period. The overall situation is that whilst natural increase has undergone a significant decline since 1981, it still remains high by European levels. Nevertheless, the major determinant of Irish demographic change is the migration balance. Between 1981 and 1995 there was a higher level of emigration in each year than immigration except for 1991–92. Between 1995 and 1998 there were, however, approximately 127,200 immigrants compared with approximately 81,400 emigrants. Between 1961 and 1998, the total population has risen by almost 887,000 or 31.5 per cent, which included an increase of about 261,900 since 1981.

Tables 15.8 and 15.9 provide an amalgam of the five statistical releases for the period between 1987 and 1998. Table 15.8 presents estimates of gross emigration and immigration by sex and age group. It confirms what we have already learned from the earlier census data that the age groups most affected by emigration are those from 15 to 24 years and to a lesser extent the age group 25–44 years. Immigration is more widely distributed across all age groups, with those aged 25–44 years most affected. Immigration is consistently higher for females than males aged 15–24 years. The high number of children (0–14 years) suggests the immigration of many families. The number of older immigrants is also important. During this period there were in general more male emigrants. This was also true for immigrants between 1988 and 1993. There was a higher number of female immigrants for the years before then and since. Table 15.9 confirms the pre-eminence of the UK as the country of destination for Irish emigrants and of origin for Irish immigrants. After the UK there is not any clear preference among Irish emigrants. On the other hand, immigrants came in order of magnitude from the UK, the rest of the world, the rest of the EU, and the USA. This is especially true for males.

Table 15.8: Ireland, estimated gross emigration and immigration classified by age group and sex, 1987–1998

Sex/Year ending April	Emigration						Immigration						Net migration
	0–14	15–24	25–44	45–64	65 and over	Total	0–14	15–24	25–44	45–64	65 and over	Total	
Persons													
1987	2.8	24.0	11.8	1.7	0.0	40.2	3.1	5.1	6.1	1.8	1.1	17.2	−23.0
1988	8.3	31.2	18.3	3.2	0.0	61.1	3.0	5.4	7.2	2.2	1.4	19.2	−41.9
1989	7.8	37.0	21.9	3.8	0.0	70.6	4.4	7.7	10.6	2.2	1.8	26.7	−43.9
1990	6.7	30.8	16.9	1.9	0.0	56.3	5.2	10.1	14.0	2.7	1.4	33.3	−22.9
1991	4.6	19.9	10.5	0.4	0.0	35.3	5.2	9.3	14.6	2.5	1.7	33.3	−2.0
1992	0.7	22.5	8.8	1.2	0.2	33.4	6.2	12.5	16.5	4.1	1.4	40.7	7.4
1993	1.1	23.6	9.1	1.2	0.2	35.1	5.6	10.3	14.5	3.6	0.8	34.7	−0.4
1994	1.4	24.6	8.2	0.6	0.0	34.8	4.4	9.7	12.1	3.1	0.9	30.1	−4.7
1995	1.2	22.6	8.5	0.8	0.0	33.1	5.3	8.0	14.6	2.6	0.7	31.2	−1.9
1996	0.9	21.4	8.1	0.7	0.0	31.2	6.6	10.9	16.9	3.6	1.2	39.2	8.0
1997*	0.7	17.9	9.6	0.9	0.1	29.0	6.4	13.8	18.2	4.4	1.3	44.0	15.0
1998*	1.4	11.8	7.0	1.0	0.0	21.2	7.2	12.0	19.1	4.2	1.6	44.0	22.8
Males													
1987	1.4	12.3	6.9	1.0	0.0	21.6	1.3	1.9	3.4	1.0	0.5	8.1	−13.5
1988	4.3	17.0	11.0	1.6	0.0	34.0	1.5	2.4	4.0	1.1	0.9	10.0	−24.0
1989	4.1	19.2	13.7	2.2	0.0	39.2	2.3	3.7	5.8	0.8	1.0	13.6	−25.7
1990	3.6	14.3	9.7	1.0	0.0	28.6	2.7	4.7	8.0	1.5	0.8	17.8	−10.8
1991	2.3	9.5	5.8	0.1	0.0	17.6	2.7	4.5	8.0	1.4	0.9	17.6	−0.1

1992	0.3	10.8	5.8	0.5	0.0	17.3	3.4	6.0	9.3	2.4	0.8	21.8	4.4
1993	0.6	10.9	5.7	0.4	0.1	17.6	2.9	4.2	7.8	2.0	0.5	17.4	-0.2
1994	0.6	11.6	5.3	0.0	0.0	17.6	2.4	4.0	6.3	1.6	0.4	14.8	-2.7
1995	0.6	11.8	5.5	0.3	0.0	18.2	2.6	3.2	7.5	1.3	0.2	14.7	-3.4
1996	0.4	9.8	5.1	0.0	0.0	15.3	3.1	4.2	8.7	2.2	0.6	18.8	3.5
1997*	0.4	8.2	5.5	0.5	0.1	14.7	2.9	5.9	9.6	2.4	0.8	21.6	6.9
1998*	0.6	5.6	3.9	0.7	0.0	10.8	3.3	4.9	10.7	2.1	0.9	21.8	11.0
Females													
1987	1.3	11.7	4.9	0.7	0.0	18.6	1.8	3.2	2.7	0.8	0.6	9.1	-9.5
1988	4.0	14.3	7.3	1.6	0.0	27.1	1.5	3.0	3.2	1.0	0.5	9.2	-17.9
1989	3.7	17.8	8.2	1.5	0.0	31.3	2.1	4.0	4.7	1.4	0.9	13.1	-18.2
1990	3.1	16.5	7.2	0.9	0.0	27.7	2.5	5.4	5.9	1.2	0.5	15.6	-12.1
1991	2.3	10.4	4.7	0.3	0.0	17.7	2.6	4.8	6.5	1.1	0.8	15.8	-1.9
1992	0.4	11.7	3.0	0.7	0.2	16.0	2.8	6.5	7.2	1.7	0.6	18.9	2.9
1993	0.5	12.7	3.4	0.8	0.1	17.5	2.6	6.0	6.6	1.6	0.4	17.3	-0.2
1994	0.7	13.0	2.9	0.6	0.0	17.3	2.0	5.7	5.8	1.4	0.4	15.3	-2.0
1995	0.6	10.8	2.9	0.5	0.0	14.9	2.7	4.8	7.1	1.3	0.5	16.5	1.6
1996	0.6	11.7	3.0	0.7	0.0	15.9	3.6	6.7	8.1	1.3	0.6	20.4	4.4
1997*	0.3	9.6	4.1	0.3	0.0	14.3	3.5	7.8	8.6	2.0	0.5	22.4	8.0
1998*	0.8	6.2	3.2	0.3	0.0	10.4	3.9	7.0	8.5	2.1	0.7	22.2	11.8

Note:
* Preliminary.
Adapted from: CSO, Annual Population and Migration Estimates, 1987–93, 1991–96; Population and Migration Estimates April 1998, Table 6.

Table 15.9: Ireland, estimated gross emigration and immigration classified by country of destination, origin and sex, 1987–1998

Sex/Year ending April	Emigration					Immigration					Net migration
	UK	Rest of EU	USA	Rest of World	Total	UK	Rest of EU	USA	Rest of World	Total	
Persons											
1987	21.8	3.1	9.9	5.4	40.2	8.1	2.2	3.0	4.0	17.2	−23.0
1988	40.2	2.8	7.9	10.2	61.1	9.9	2.6	3.4	3.4	19.2	−41.9
1989	48.4	3.9	8.2	10.0	70.6	14.2	3.6	3.1	5.8	26.7	−43.9
1990	35.8	5.1	7.7	7.6	56.3	17.6	5.0	3.9	6.9	33.3	−22.9
1991	23.0	3.1	4.8	4.4	35.3	18.7	4.2	4.3	6.1	33.3	−2.0
1992	16.9	7.5	3.5	5.5	33.4	22.7	6.5	4.6	6.9	40.7	7.4
1993	16.4	7.3	5.6	5.8	35.1	17.5	6.6	5.0	5.7	34.7	−0.4
1994	14.8	5.5	9.6	4.9	34.8	15.2	5.8	4.3	4.8	30.1	−4.7
1995	13.3	5.1	8.2	6.6	33.1	15.6	6.3	3.8	5.5	31.2	−1.9
1996	14.1	5.1	5.2	6.8	31.2	17.6	7.2	6.4	8.0	39.2	8.0
1997*	12.9	4.1	4.1	7.9	29.0	20.0	8.1	6.6	9.3	44.0	15.0
1998*	8.5	4.3	4.3	4.1	21.2	21.1	8.7	4.9	9.3	44.0	22.8
Males											
1987	13.1	1.2	4.8	2.6	21.6	4.1	1.0	1.2	1.8	8.1	−13.5
1988	23.5	1.5	3.8	5.3	34.0	5.4	1.2	1.7	1.6	10.0	−24.0
1989	28.5	1.7	4.3	4.7	39.2	7.4	1.4	1.6	3.2	13.6	−25.7
1990	18.7	2.2	4.1	3.6	28.6	9.9	2.2	2.0	3.6	17.8	−10.8
1991	12.2	1.4	2.3	1.8	17.6	10.6	1.9	2.2	2.9	17.6	−0.1

Year											
1992	9.4	3.5	2.0	2.4	17.3	13.0	3.4	2.1	3.4	21.8	4.4
1993	8.2	3.4	3.1	3.0	17.6	9.0	2.9	2.5	3.1	17.4	-0.2
1994	7.7	2.6	5.0	2.2	17.6	7.8	2.7	2.1	2.2	14.8	-2.7
1995	7.8	2.5	4.6	3.2	18.2	7.3	2.6	1.8	3.1	14.7	-3.4
1996	6.7	2.2	2.7	3.6	15.3	8.4	3.2	2.8	4.3	18.8	3.5
1997*	6.4	1.9	2.5	3.8	14.7	10.2	3.9	2.7	4.8	21.6	6.9
1998*	4.5	1.8	2.7	1.9	10.8	11.0	3.4	2.6	4.8	21.8	11.0
Females											
1987	8.7	1.9	5.2	2.8	18.6	4.0	1.2	1.7	2.2	9.1	-9.5
1988	16.7	1.3	4.2	5.0	27.1	4.5	1.4	1.7	1.7	9.2	-17.9
1989	19.9	2.2	3.9	5.3	31.3	6.7	2.2	1.4	2.7	13.1	-18.2
1990	17.1	2.9	3.6	4.0	27.7	7.7	2.7	1.9	3.3	15.6	-12.1
1991	10.8	1.7	2.5	2.7	17.7	8.1	2.3	2.1	3.2	15.8	-1.9
1992	7.5	4.0	1.5	3.1	16.0	9.7	3.2	2.5	3.5	18.9	2.9
1993	8.2	3.9	2.5	2.9	17.5	8.4	3.8	2.5	2.6	17.3	-0.2
1994	7.1	2.9	4.6	2.7	17.3	7.4	3.1	2.2	2.6	15.3	-2.0
1995	5.4	2.6	3.6	3.4	14.9	8.2	3.7	2.1	2.5	16.5	1.6
1996	7.4	2.8	2.5	3.2	15.9	9.2	3.9	3.6	3.7	20.4	4.4
1997*	6.4	2.2	1.6	4.1	14.3	9.8	4.2	3.9	4.5	22.4	8.0
1998*	4.0	2.6	1.6	2.2	10.4	10.1	5.3	2.3	4.5	22.2	11.8

Note:
* Preliminary.
Adapted from: CSO, Annual Population and Migration Estimates, 1987–93, 1991–96; Population and Migration Estimates April 1998, Table 5.

An earlier study focused on the particularity of migration between Ireland and the UK during the 1970s and set it in its historical context of the nineteenth and twentieth centuries.[12] In addition to an analysis of the return of former emigrants to Ireland, it considered the feasibility of gross migration flows and presented data on marital and economic status. Net migration of Irish-born persons between 1971 and 1981 using statistics from the censuses of Great Britain are particularly interesting. In spite of a decline in migration from Ireland to GB during the 1970s, reference is made to the importance which this migration had on the GB population and the earlier establishment of many large Irish communities there, especially in London and Birmingham.

The UK National Health Service Central Register enables us to identify individuals born in Ireland who registered for the first time with a Family Health Service Authority in England and Wales using one-year inflows from Ireland to GB between 1980 and 1991. In that period there was a total of 90,954 male and 92,509 female one-year inflows. In fact, the pattern among men and women is very similar, increasing rapidly from 1985, reaching a peak in 1988 and thereafter declining somewhat. More than three out of every four persons, male and female, were aged between 15 and 44 years. By contrast, there were more males aged 25–44 years than females. There were proportionately almost twice as many females aged 15–24 years as 25–44 years of age. The number of children (under 15 years of age) at about 15 per cent was almost identical between boys and girls. By 1991 the proportion fell to 11.1 per cent for boys and 12.6 per cent for girls. The proportion aged 25–44 years increased from the twelve-year average for 1980–91 to that for 1991, from 41 per cent to 44.2 per cent for males and from 27.8 per cent to 30.1 per cent for females.

All of the previous tables with the exception of Tables 15.1 and 15.7 have been derived directly from official CSO statistics, mostly census material. Table 15.10 is taken from a forthcoming joint study by the CSO and the Office for National Statistics (ONS) in the UK. It is one of a number of multinational studies designed to improve migration statistics. It was funded and will be published by Eurostat. This study, which is an analysis of migration between GB and Ireland from 1981 to 1991, undertakes a very sophisticated process of demographic accounting and reconciling of Irish and British data sources. It does this from two different perspectives, one using migration stocks and flows in GB and the other in Ireland.

Table 15.10 is a product of 'demographic accounting' and indicates net migration from Ireland to GB using data from the UK National Health Service Central Register and the Irish Labour Force Survey. It employs a correction factor to estimate migrants born in GB, Ireland and elsewhere. During the 1980s there were slightly more male migrants than females and the direction of the movement was primarily from Ireland to GB. Male migrants were older than females. The age group with the highest number of males was from 25 to 34 years compared to females who were younger, from 20 to 29 years of age. In contrast with this the balance of migrants for older persons, males over 60 years of age and females aged 55 years and over, was from GB to Ireland. Estimating gross emigration for 1986–91 from Ireland to GB of British-born

Table 15.10: Net inward migration* from Ireland to Great Britain, 1981–1991

Age group (Years)	Males	Females
0(1)– 4#	1,197	1,175
5– 9	4,348	4,280
10–14	3,226	3,353
15–19	3,085	5,669
20–24	9,728	16,143
25–29	18,457	21,772
30–34	12,892	9,769
35–39	6,744	3,353
40–44	4,072	1,342
45–49	3,144	952
50–54	1,746	465
55–59	607	−86
60–64	−108	−538
65–69	−496	−713
70+	−451	277
Total	68,191	67,213

Notes:
* Includes migrants born in all countries.
# Migration of persons under 1 year of age derived from the GB National Health Service Central Register but not the Irish Labour Force Survey.
Adapted from: CSO (Ireland) and ONS (UK) (forthcoming), *An Analysis of Migration Between the United Kingdom and Ireland in the Period 1981 to 1991*, Table 7.

persons leads the Irish CSO and the British ONS to conclude that an understatement of about 39 per cent in the immigration of children under 5 years of age may be replicated for other age groups and for the earlier period 1981–86. They are satisfied that the Irish Labour Force Survey is a much more reliable measure of migration than the UK one, which is hindered by its relatively small sample size. This is hardly surprising given the greater significance of migration for Ireland and its smaller size, compared with the UK. The Irish Labour Force Survey compares well with the census and its greater accuracy for estimating migration flows than the International Passenger Survey vindicates the CSO in the compilation of its *Statistical Release on Annual Population and Migration Estimates* which depends on it.

More conventional census data provides a focus on migration from GB to Ireland classified by age group. The greatest proportion of migrants were aged 25–44 years, though the proportion of persons born outside of Ireland both in 1981 and in 1986 was highest for children. This confirms the movement of families from GB to Ireland especially before 1981 where many of the parents were born in Ireland unlike their children. Retired migrants too were predominantly born in Ireland, though the differential had fallen dramatically by 1991.

The migration of persons aged 15 years and over was fairly evenly balanced between the sexes during the 1980s. Such migration was three times greater in 1991 than in 1981, having fallen even lower in 1986. The number of males at work was consistently higher, as was the number of females who were 'inactive' (in terms of paid employment). There were more males unemployed than females. The number of immigrants to Ireland who were born in GB declined between 1981 and 1991. This was especially true for those under 15 years of age, which reflects the fall in the number of immigrant families after the 1970s. Migrants over 25 years of age increased for all ages during this period.

The Northern Ireland Statistics and Research Agency within the Department of Finance and Personnel has produced a migration series for recent years between Northern Ireland and other parts of the UK and elsewhere including the Republic of Ireland. Since 1986–87 it shows a negative balance overall for migration between Northern Ireland and elsewhere. Within this island migration was predominantly from south to north from the 1980s until 1995–96 when as during the 1970s it was in the opposite direction, from north to south. Such estimated gross flows are small compared with Northern Ireland's migration to and from the rest of the UK. They were highest in 1995–96, the most recent data available, with 4,510 migrants from north to south and 3,332 from south to north when there was a cease-fire and peace.

The Higher Education Authority (HEA) has for many years undertaken a series of annual surveys of the recipients of awards in higher education and their subsequent activities. *The First Destination of Award Recipients in Higher Education*, based on recipients of educational awards in 1982 from the universities and the Dublin Institute of Technology, was first published in June 1983. The National Council for Educational Awards established a separate survey during 1979 of recipients of their awards for students from the National Institutes for Higher Education, now the University of Limerick and Dublin City University, and the Regional Technical Colleges, now the other Institutes of Technology. Nowadays, they are included in the composite report along with data from the Colleges of Education and the Royal College of Surgeons in Ireland. Detailed information on recipients of certificates, diplomas and degrees classified by broad disciplines is provided for first destinations. They are differentiated between Ireland and Overseas in respect of research work or further academic study, teacher training, other vocational and professional training, and those who have gained employment. Further categories exist for those not available for employment or study and those seeking employment.

The overall number of graduates who emigrated increased from 1,342 in 1986 to 2,039 in 1989, fell back to 1,271 in 1992 and rose again to just less than 2,000 each year between 1994 and 1996. Table 15.11 details the number of graduates from Ireland in employment overseas by region. More than three out of every four emigrant graduates in those years between 1991 and 1995 and in 1997 have gone to countries either in the EU or in North America. This was a little less than 70 per cent in 1996. But 1992 was exceptional in that fewer went to GB and to North America and more to other EU countries than in any of the other years except for 1996 when the latter increased significantly. In 1997 about 31.5 per cent went to GB, 36 per cent to other EU countries and less than 8 per cent to North America. The fact that the

Table 15.11: Graduates from Ireland in employment overseas by region, 1991–1997

Region	1991	1992	1993	1994	1995	1996	1997
Great Britain	495	308	458	609	583	542	504
Other EU	316	431	316	311	387	324	580
Other Europe	23	31	48	36	34	39	21
North America	134	116	295	347	266	219	125
Australia and New Zealand	11	5	31	40	81	115	95
Middle and Far East	124	103	116	98	125	118	133
Other	22	23	76	260	121	195	144
Total	1,125	1,017	1,340	1,701	1,597	1,552	1,602

Adapted from: Higher Education Authority, *First Destination of Award Recipients in Higher Education* (various years), Table Q.

Table 15.12: Percentage of leavers from second-level schools who emigrated, 1991–1997

	Male	Female	Total
1991–92	3.2	5.5	4.4
1992–93	3.1	5.9	4.5
1993–94	3.7	5.5	4.6
1994–95	0.6	2.1	1.4
1995–96	1.8	3.8	2.8
1996–97	2.0	4.2	3.1

Adapted from: Department of Enterprise, Trade and Employment, Department of Education and the Economic and Social Research Institute, *The Economic Status of School Leavers: Results of School Leavers' Surveys* for 1992–94, 1993–95, 1994–96 and 1995–97, Appendix B, Table 1.

numbers emigrating to Middle and Far Eastern countries has been greater than to the historically significant destinations of Australia and New Zealand probably reflects more employment opportunities for Irish graduates there.

For many years there also exists an annual survey of the career paths of second-level school-leavers. Results from the 1993 and subsequent surveys carried out by the Economic and Social Research Institute (ESRI) on behalf of the Department of Enterprise, Trade and Employment and the Department of Education and Science were published in annual reports on the *Results of the School Leavers' Surveys* for 1992–94 through to 1995–97. The estimated number of such emigrants was 2,944 in 1992, 2,916 in 1993, 3,105 in 1994, 945 in 1995, 1,918 in 1996 and 2,136 in 1997 (Table 15.12). The proportion is consistently higher among females, e.g. 4.2 per cent in 1997 compared with 2.0 per cent for males. By contrast, the proportion of unemployed males seeking their first job in Ireland is higher than for females. Both the HEA and ESRI surveys are likely to underestimate the overall level of emigration due to non-responses. Nevertheless, they are useful in providing an indication of trends.

Conclusions

We have considered Irish migration flows in both directions. Most attention has rightly centred on the many facets of Irish emigration. Recent population developments, however, have resulted in a growing interest in Irish immigration, including that of returned emigrant families. A quantification of Irish migration is essential for our understanding of this complex subject. Migration has always formed a part of this island's heritage and culture. It has impacted on so many Irish individuals and families, in times past and present, in Ireland and in every corner of the world.

The most influential study of Irish migration was undertaken by the Commission on Emigration and Other Population Problems, between 1948 and 1954.[13] The *Report* (1955) provides a very comprehensive account of Irish demography and especially migration, emigration and immigration up to and including the early 1950s. It contains chapters on population and migration structures and change, economic, social and policy developments. Its contribution to quantification comes in 99 separate tables. In particular, it was responsible for the 1951 Census of Population which established the practice ever since of holding a census in Ireland every five years, except for 1979. In more recent times the National Economic and Social Council commissioned a study of *The Economic and Social Implications of Emigration*.[14] It is a worthy successor to the Commission's report and also furnishes many other more recent quantitative characteristics of Irish migration.

This chapter documents the availability of recent Irish migration statistics with particular reference to official published data. It does not undertake a detailed analysis. The significance of Irish external migration is well documented. Its particular demographic importance is the consistently greater influence which it has, relative to natural increase, as a determinant of population change. The principal means of migration data collection and publication by the CSO are the five-yearly Census of Population and the annual Labour Force Survey which was replaced in 1997 by a Quarterly National Household Survey. A number of other publications exist of which the most important is the recent *Statistical Release on Annual Population and Migration Estimates*. Other demographic publications include the quarterly and annual *Reports on Vital Statistics*.

The population components equation provides estimates of net migration and depends on the census and Vital Statistics. Survivorship ratios are applied to census data to determine the effect on selected age groups of net migration during intercensal periods. Census questions have resulted in enhanced migration statistics through a progression from place of birth, usual residence one year before the census and the date of migration for persons who spent more than one year abroad. Information from the annual Labour Force Survey which has provided a series on gross migration flows, emigration and immigration, since the late 1980s is now available in a *Statistical Release*. Access to data from the United Kingdom Office for National Statistics available from the National Health Service Central Register facilitates a system of demographic accounting of migration between the two countries. Likewise, migration flows between Northern Ireland and the Republic of Ireland have been estimated by the Northern Ireland Statistics and Research Agency. Emigration also forms part of surveys undertaken about the destination of school-leavers and graduates. Finally, information about asylum-seekers and those granted refugee status is available in the context of recent legislation in that sphere.

It is significant that even in 1991 there was an estimated 1.143 million Irish-born persons living in Great Britain, Canada, Australia and the United States when the population in the Republic of Ireland was just three times greater at 3.526 million. Since 1961 the population of Ireland has grown steadily and significantly, except for a small decline during the 1986–91 intercensal period. Higher emigration among males in recent years has contributed to a situation where there are now more females in the population. Between 1911 and 1986 there was a higher number of males. The age groups 15–24 years especially and 25–34 years have been most affected by emigration. More males than females of those ages migrate. An important increase in the number of persons usually resident in Ireland and born elsewhere occurred since 1971. The highest numbers relate to those born in England, Wales and Northern Ireland. They peaked in 1981. Place of birth and usual residence one year prior to the census date indicated relatively higher female than male immigration from France and Spain. Persons born in England and Wales, Italy and Scotland constituted the highest proportion of those aged 25–44 years. The number of one-year immigrants was much higher for 1990–91 than 1980–81, of whom more than a half came from England and Wales. Data for 1991 suggest a considerable number of Irish-born (return) immigrants. The country of previous residence for three-quarters of them was the UK. This was lowest among other European countries. Unlike other countries of previous residence in 1991 the Irish-born were fewer among the small but increasing number of immigrants from European Union countries other than the UK. Two in every five immigrants were aged 25–44 years. The 1996 census indicated that four out of every five immigrants in Ireland arrived since 1971. Immigration from the UK was particularly important for the years preceding 1981, especially during the 1970s. By contrast, immigration from other EU countries increased steadily throughout the 1980s and 1990s.

The CSO *Statistical Release on Annual Population and Migration Estimates* represents the culmination of a lot of innovative effort, breaking new ground by establishing a series of published net migration, immigration and emigration flows. Since 1981 emigration has been greater each year than immigration, except for the years ending in April 1992 and since April 1995. Emigration was highest at 70,600 in 1988–89. The ages most affected by it are those between 15 and 24 years, and to a lesser extent those from 25 to 44 years. Age is of less significance among immigrants. During that period emigration was higher among males and between 1988 and 1993 for immigrants too. These data confirm the UK as the most important country of origin and destination for Irish migration. Among families who migrated from GB to Ireland especially before 1981 many of the parents were born in Ireland unlike their children. During the 1980s more than three out of every four migrants from Ireland to

Table 15.13: Applications of asylum-seekers and decisions* on refugee status in Ireland, 1994–1999

	1994	1995	1996	1997	1998	1999‡
No. of applications	362	424	1,179	3,883	4,626	468
Total no. of cases on hand	0	6	214	2,317	3,859	459
Granted refugee status	4	15	36	213	168	49
Refused refugee status	27	43	32	304	1,202	377

Notes:

* It should be noted that the decisions taken in each year do not necessarily relate to applications made in those years. In addition to the decisions taken, a significant number of applications were withdrawn for various reasons in the years in question.

‡ 28 February.

Adapted from: Parliamentary Debates, Dáil Éireann, *Official Report* (unrevised), Vol. 486, No. 6, 10 February 1998, updated by the Department of Justice, Equality and Law Reform (March 1999).

GB were aged between 15 and 44 years. Whilst the number of males and females were fairly similar, females tended to be a little younger. Within the island of Ireland the predominant direction of migration since the mid-1980s was from south to north except for 1995–96 when more persons migrated from Northern Ireland. Finally, the number of applicants for refugee status has increased dramatically, especially since 1994.

Ireland has for many decades been a popular destination for retired immigrants, Irish and foreign-born, the former mainly from the UK and the latter from other European countries. An unprecedented and unusual combination of relatively poor personal economic and welfare circumstances combined with internecine warfare has resulted in the arrival of an increasing number of non-indigenous immigrants including new age travellers, gypsies and asylum-seekers. Some sections of new legislation, the Refugee Act 1996, have now come into effect. Table 15.13 is taken from the updated answer to a parliamentary question to the Minister for Justice, Equality and Law Reform on 10 February 1998 about decisions on applications for refugee status in Ireland.[15] The number of applications for asylum increased from 362 in 1994 to 3,883 in 1997 and 4,626 in 1998. There were an additional 468 during January and February 1999. The total number of applications from January 1994 until the end of February 1999 was 10,942. In that period there were 485 granted refugee status, 213 of which were in 1997, and 1,985 refused refugee status, including 1,202 in 1998. At the end of February 1999 there were 6,855 asylum-seekers awaiting a final determination of their applications.

Until the early 1990s the number of asylum-seekers in Ireland was less than 50 a year. The significant increase since 1994 and the implementation of the Refugee Act have changed the role operated by the United Nations High Commissioner for Refugees (UNHCR) from 1985 until then. Individual assessment by the UNHCR, which was possible when the numbers were smaller, has been replaced by appropriately trained Irish government officials. The more wide-ranging and general role played by the UNHCR representative now resident in Ireland is designed to guarantee protection to those in fear of persecution in their countries of origin. It has been policy for some time not to reveal the nationality and other demographic characteristics of asylum-seekers or refugees for reasons of confidentiality as the number of applicants of some nationalities is small and identification could have serious implications for family members in their own countries.

The fact that some asylum-seekers are migrants who have come principally in search of employment rather than from persecution and violence has resulted in refused status and contributed to slowing down the process of dealing with *bona fide* refugees. Sustained economic development and growth, however, is making Ireland an increasingly attractive destination for migrants and is likely to lead to greater heterogeneity than in the past. For a country which has created the Irish diaspora the future is likely to challenge its people and its values to provide a welcome to the many foreigners coming to Ireland in need of the same basic requirements which the Irish sought elsewhere, and some continue to do, albeit on a much smaller scale, on the eve of the new millennium.

We have seen that by comparison with the components of natural movement of population, i.e. fertility and mortality, the least elaborate demographic methodologies exist for migration.[16] This is compounded in Ireland because of its volatility, the absence of border controls and the openness of its economy and labour market. Consequently, it is difficult to undertake population projections for Ireland and especially to make assumptions about Irish migration. Accurate data in this sphere are becoming increasingly necessary for good planning and development. In this regard, the introduction of a population register in Ireland comparable to our Scandinavian and Benelux neighbours would significantly improve the data available for potential analysis.

Notes

I wish to acknowledge the time and expertise given to me by Aidan Punch and Joe Treacy of the Central Statistics Office, Ireland. I am also grateful to the former, to Jacquie Hyvart of the Northern Ireland Statistics and Research Agency and to Jerry Sexton, a Research Professor at the Economic and Social Research Institute, Dublin, for providing me with some unpublished statistics. I particularly value the support and encouragement of Mary, my wife, and our three young sons. Finally, my gratitude goes to Chris Lynch for her word-processing skills and to Barry O'Sullivan for his graphics.

1. In this chapter the terms Ireland and Irish refer exclusively to the Republic of Ireland and its people.
2. Damien Courtney, 'Demographic Structure and Change in the Republic of Ireland and Northern Ireland', in P. Clancy, S. Drudy, K. Lynch and L. O'Dowd (eds), *Irish Society: Sociological Perspectives* (Dublin, 1995).
3. Commission on Emigration and Other Population Problems, *Reports 1948–1954* (Dublin, 1955).
4. Great Britain consists of England, Scotland and Wales, whereas the United Kingdom comprises Great Britain and Northern Ireland.

5. In 1999 there are fifteen member states of the European Union. They are the Republic of Ireland, the United Kingdom, Austria, Belgium, Denmark, Finland, France, Germany, Greece, Italy, Luxembourg, The Netherlands, Portugal, Spain and Sweden.

6. Aidan Punch, 'Measuring Population Structure and Change in the Republic of Ireland', paper presented at the conference 'Statistical Sources for Local and Regional Development in Ireland' (Belfast, 1992).

7. Central Statistics Office and UK Office for National Statistics, 'An Analysis of Migration Between the United Kingdom and Ireland in the Period 1981 to 1991', *Indicators of Migration Between Ireland and Great Britain*, Part 3 (Luxemburg, forthcoming).

8. Damien Courtney, 'Some Indirect Measures of Migration in Ireland, 1946–1961', unpublished thesis (Université Catholique de Louvain, 1973).

9. Basil Chubb, 'Going About Persecuting Civil Servants: The Role of the Irish Parliamentary Representative', *Political Studies*, 2, 3 (1963).

10. Damien Courtney, 'Recent Trends in Emigration from Ireland', paper presented at the annual conference of the Development Studies Association (Belfast, 1989).

11. Donal Garvey and Maurice McGuire, *Structure of Gross Migration Flows* (Labour Force Survey Estimates), CSO (Dublin, 1989).

12. Donal Garvey, 'The History of Migration Flows in the Republic of Ireland', *Population Trends*, 39 (1985).

13. Commission on Emigration and Other Population Problems, *Reports 1948–1954* (Dublin, 1955).

14. J.J. Sexton, B.M. Walsh, D.F. Hannan and D. McMahon, *The Economic and Social Implications of Emigration*, National Economic and Social Council, Report No. 90 (Dublin, 1991).

15. Parliamentary Debates, Dáil Éireann, *Official Report* (unrevised), Vol. 486, No. 6, 10 February 1998 (Dublin, 1999).

16. Damien Courtney, 'Irish Emigration in the 1980s', *Proceedings of the Seminar on Demographic Problem Areas in Europe* (Strasbourg, 1986).

CHAPTER 16

Changing Attitudes to 'New Wave' Emigration? Structuralism versus Voluntarism in the Study of Irish Emigration

JIM MAC LAUGHLIN

(Department of Geography, University College, Cork)

Introduction

Emigration has long been considered an intrinsic, even a 'defining' feature of Irish society. Yet it still attracts considerably less attention from critical social theorists than it does from Irish novelists, poets, artists and, more recently, 'pop' psychologists and philosophers. What makes this theoretical neglect of emigration all the more surprising is the fact that attitudes to Irish emigration, both inside and outside the country, have long been refracted through social class, not just cultural and artistic lenses. Historically speaking at least, popular attitudes towards emigration have shaped, and have been shaped by, prevailing political orthodoxies concerning Ireland's right to self-determination on the one hand, and its rightful contribution to the international labour market on the other. This was particularly the case in the first half of the nineteenth century. This was a period when Malthusianists, on both sides of the Irish Sea, regarded emigration as a historical inevitability, a necessary social evil which facilitated the transition from tradition to modernity in Ireland by dispatching the country's 'surplus' sons and daughters to Britain, the United States and other core areas of the world economy. By the late nineteenth century neo-Malthusianists on opposite sides of the religious divide in colonial and nation-building Ireland often condoned emigration, so long as it affected only the socially subordinate or poorer elements of Catholic society. The more radical of these openly advocated state-sponsored emigration as a solution to unemployment and landlessness among the Irish poor. By the close of the century many among the Catholic hierarchy also believed that the disadvantaged in nation-building Ireland had far better social prospects outside Ireland than they could ever have within it. In so doing they contributed to an early sanitization of Irish emigration, suggesting that all those who literally left the country fared well outside it. This set in motion a long train of thought, still evident today, which suggested that

Irish emigration could be explained away in simple economic or geographical terms. At its most extreme this was a line of argument which insisted that emigration was 'caused' by revolutions in transportation which literally drew Ireland closer to Britain and the United States, where, it was argued, the 'troublesome Irish' properly belonged.[1]

Nationalists were among the first to attack this naturalization and sanitization of Irish emigration. They Anglicized the causes of Irish emigration and nationalized its solutions. They suggested that involuntary emigration, especially from rural Ireland, was nothing short of a racially inspired bourgeois exercise in social engineering which sought to remove the Irish from Ireland to make room for 'graziers and their bullocks'.[2] Although cultural nationalists never fully worked out their solutions to involuntary emigration, they were nothing if not forceful in their insistence that emigration was a state-sponsored exercise for removing the Irish 'overseas' when they were most needed to build a strong Irish nation at home. Like Marx they feared that it was Ireland's destiny to become nothing less than 'an English sheepwalk and cattle pasture', a country from which people were 'banished by sheep and ox'.[3]

In attributing emigration to 'rancherism', especially to landlordism and English 'misrule', nationalists carefully avoided the origins of modern Irish emigration in the economic and class structure of nation-building Catholic Ireland. They traced it instead to the Anglicization of the Irish economy and the modernization of post-Famine Irish society. With the emergence of such a highly articulate organic intelligentsia, subjectively and objectively related to the dominant sectors of the Irish tenantry, confident rationalist, and nationalist, conclusions were embodied across a wide spectrum of Victorian social sciences in late nineteenth-century Ireland. Rudimentary though they were, these historicist critiques of emigration and underdevelopment in Ireland also problematized a whole range of other social issues whose solutions were predicated upon the operation of *laissez-faire* principles in rural Catholic Ireland. Thus nationalists attacked as erroneous the widespread assumption that 'rancherism' was necessarily more productive than the 'petit culture' which they advocated as a solution to the social and economic problems of rural Ireland.[4]

Even before this, however, 'political arithmetic' – i.e. the collection of population statistics in Ireland – was deeply committed to the containment of the 'lower orders', or their outright banishment from Irish society. This was because from a very early stage in its evolution, modern demography, operating in the guise of a 'disinterested' version of 'political arithmetic', clearly served the class interests of hegemonic sectors in Irish society. In Britain population statistics and political demography were first associated with the writings of Thomas Hobbes and Adam Smith. These disciplines reached their fullest expression in Ireland in the writings of William Petty in the 1690s. Students of demography in Ireland after Petty did not so much collect information about the size of populations, they debated the causes and consequences of population growth, especially among the 'lower orders'.[5] They regularly expressed great concern about changes in the social class composition, especially the racial and ethnic 'mix', of national and colonial populations. As a result the category

'population' was transformed from a 'natural' entity into an ideological construct.[6] Indeed, for eighteenth-century colonial administrators in particular,
as for Irish nation-builders in the nineteenth century, the very term could
sometimes lose all links with actual people. In both periods it increasingly
now referred to the reproductive capacities of rural and urban communities,
especially the poor, who were seen as threats to the social and political fabric
of 'civilized' societies. When the racial or social 'mix' of national societies reached
dangerous proportions, as it appeared to do when the rural poor vastly outnumbered 'respectable elements', the Irish petty bourgeoisie, perhaps even more
so than the Anglo-Irish ascendancy, defended emigration as a strategy for their
own social and political survival, and for the survival of the propertyless poor.

Cultural nationalists defended emigration from urban areas especially, not
least from the slums of Dublin, Limerick and Cork. They regarded the inner
city areas of these cities as sources of moral debasement and threats to the social
and cultural integrity of the Irish nation-state.[7] That nation, they insisted, was
not only to be built by, but also for, the sturdy sons and virtuous daughters
of the country's substantial Catholic farmers. Thus slums were considered legitimate targets for emigration because they were said to be 'infested' by an 'alien'
people responsible for their own moral and social degradation. For that very
reason they had to be 'cleared', either through emigration or through slum clear-
ances. The latter, as often as not, were little more than urban exercises in mass
eviction. Nationalist discourse in this Ireland not only constructed the slums
of Dublin as 'different' from the rest of the Irish nation. They also stressed the
socio-cultural differences between Dublin slum-dwellers and the Catholic Irish
in the countryside. They did this in such a way as to suggest that the former
could be excluded from nation-building Ireland because they were culturally,
even biologically, inferior to the 'respectable' elements in Catholic nation-
building Ireland. What needs stressing here is that there was little disagreement
indeed in nation-building circles over the ontological and cultural differences
between slum-dwellers on the one hand and the 'respectable' rural Irish on
the other. Neither was there much doubt about the necessity for policing the
borders separating the latter from the former. It was not just that nationalist
Ireland created 'representations' of itself that excluded slum-dwellers and the
rural poor, considering these as legitimate targets of emigration. It constructed
these representations in order better to master and control the rural and urban
poor, and to justify their continued expulsion from nation-building Ireland.
The dominating element in this genre of bourgeois discourse bestowed order
and orderliness on property-owners and the respectable working class. Because
they associated poverty with anarchy, filth and an unruly republicanism, these
same sectors could turn a blind eye on the emigration of the Irish poor. Indeed
they used narrative techniques and historical reasoning to accentuate the
essentialism of their own Irishness, and to separate out the respectable Irish
from the physical and moral decay of the propertyless poor in town as well as
in the countryside.

All this points to a marked overlapping between two sets of attitudes towards
emigration in nation-building Ireland, namely those which linked nationalism

with social progress, and those which stressed the need for emigrants to be drawn chiefly from the ranks of the rural and urban poor. Both these sets of attitudes go back to the circumstances in which the Irish nation-state was conceived as a cradle for Catholic bourgeois respectability, not as a haven for 'men of no property'.[8] The latter, particularly those in inner city areas, were considered threats to hegemonic notions of respectability, industry and work in Catholic nation-building Ireland. Their very gregariousness rendered them social vagabonds which in turn made them the bane of a settled Irish modernity. When they were not spurring political leaders and property-owners into what Zygmunt Bauman terms an 'ordering and legislating frenzy', they were silently, and in their hundreds of thousands, taking to emigrant trails out of Ireland.[9]

Emigration among these groups also contributed to the social disintegration and senilization of communities throughout urban and rural Ireland well into the twentieth century. It clearly also linked the peripheralization of rural and urban Ireland to core-formation at home and abroad. Far from being peripheral to the process of capitalist production, Ireland occupied a central position in the international circuits of the world economy from at least the eighteenth century onwards. Revolutions in transportation, especially when they affected the costs of travel, clearly facilitated but by no means 'caused' the growing diaspora of the Irish overseas. They also forced isolated pockets of rural and urban Ireland into the world economy, thereby transforming them into 'emigrants nurseries'. Ireland then, as now, was integrated into global society through the annihilation of spatial barriers to the circulation of capital and labour.[10] In the nineteenth century this contributed to a heightened commodification and internationalization of Irish labour, something which continues to this day. Then, as now, this also caused new values to be placed on Irish rural and working-class communities because they were major suppliers of skilled, unskilled and highly adaptable workers destined for the international, not just the national, labour market.

More recently still, Irish attitudes to emigration have been 'de-nationalized', this time by Irish academics and political commentators who tend to explain emigration away either as an historical and locational inevitability, or as a socially progressive attribute of Irish youth enterprise culture.[11] Certainly revisionism since the 1960s has exorcized the 'blame Britain' ethos from interpretations of Irish emigration. However, it has also influenced political perceptions of a whole range of other Irish social issues. Thus problems like involuntary emigration, urban poverty, unemployment, and urban and rural decay have been so sanitized and 'individualized' that they hardly appear as social problems any longer, let alone as national problems. Indeed, nothing better indicates the narrowing of nationalism to a focus on constitutional issues, including its 'devaluation' as a philosophy informing Irish social and economic policy, than the growing acceptance of emigration as at once 'natural' and 'traditional'. This appeared all the more justified in the 1960s and 1970s when a sharp downturn in emigration, brought about by a new industrialization of Irish society, was widely interpreted as the passing of traditional and the birth of modern Ireland.[12] It seemed to some then at least that the Irish had reached 'the end of emigration history'. To the extent that emigration was still discussed in this 'new Ireland', it was a cultural tradition so deeply embedded in Irish rural life that it was considered inevitable and natural that Irish young adults should leave home to find opportunities abroad.

The roots of this sanitization and voluntarization of 'new wave' emigration are traceable to revisionist accounts that transformed interpretations of the rural exodus from Ireland from the 1960s onwards. Under the influence of modernization theory, economic historians and economists in particular portrayed emigration as an inevitable response to the progressive and persistent modernization of Irish society since the late nineteenth century.[13] Emphasizing the inevitability of emigration, they also de-politicized its causes and consequences. Reflecting the neo-classical framework within which they couched their arguments, economists, demographers and economic historians in particular portrayed emigration as a simple 'labour transfer mechanism'. Adopting a cost-benefit analysis, they assumed that the market provided all relevant information upon which decisions to emigrate were based. In so doing they posited the decision to emigrate at the level of the individual emigrant. They largely avoided any structural or social class analysis of the causes and consequences of Irish emigration. In these accounts historical and contemporary emigration was simply assumed to be 'caused' by market forces. The market signalled differences in income between Ireland and overseas labour markets, indicated job opportunities abroad, channelled emigrants to overseas fields of opportunity, and ultimately determined the length of time emigrants would remain in any particular location.

This mode of theorizing, which is increasingly popular in the Celtic Tiger society of today's Ireland, continues to reduce emigration to economic causes. It also subjects emigrants to the compelling logic of an 'iron law' of labour transfer. In conceptualizing the 'new wave' emigrant as a geographically mobile *homo economicus* logically moving between one labour market and another, it ignores the socio-economic and political functions of 'new wave' emigration. It also characterizes as free choices decisions which are in fact structured in the context of an evolving world economy. Such decisions, moreover, are often as not structured within the places which emigrants seek to leave, just as they are influenced by the destinations where they choose to 'settle'.

Quantitative and behavioural revolutions in social sciences in Ireland in the 1960s and 1970s have also caused Irish geographers and sociologists to offer detailed empirical descriptions of the socio-geographical spread of Irish emigration. However, they avoided any structural analysis of its local, national and international causes and consequences. Thus emigration is increasingly now explained away in terms of Ireland's peripheral location, or attributed to the social psychological attributes of young Irish adults anxious to till foreign fields of opportunity.[14] Contrary to core–periphery theorists, however, locational factors alone did not, and still do not, 'cause' Irish emigration. As in other European peripheries, improvements in transportation and reductions in travel costs were as much consequences as causes of emigration from Ireland. This means that, although it is intrinsically geographical, emigration should not, and cannot, be explained away by recourse to simple spatial terms like 'core' and 'periphery'. We need to look at it instead in terms of the intersections between local and global forces operating in specific regional, socio-historical contexts. Far from being 'caused' by the 'adventurous spirit' of individualistic and upwardly mobile young adults, Irish emigration has always been a social response to structuring processes operating at the level of the national and the global economy. In attributing emigration to locational attributes alone, we risk reifying places by suggesting that 'peripheries' generate emigrants while 'cores' attract them. This is not only a myopic image which suggests that it is simply a strategy for controlling numbers. It treats places in a highly abstract manner and fails to address fundamental features in the social structure and productive capacities of the communities which emigrants leave behind, and those where they literally 'settle'.[15]

'Emigration' as 'migration': the devaluation of 'nation' as 'home' in contemporary Irish society

It could be argued that Irish attitudes to emigration have altered significantly since the nineteenth century. Thus emigration since the 1980s has been sanitized and 'naturalized', this time by Irish political leaders and by the corporate sector. In other regards, however, contemporary attitudes towards 'new wave' Irish emigration still mirror those of neo-Malthusianists in the late nineteenth century. Thus it could be argued that we have been witnessing the slow rebirth of a modern variant of seventeenth-century 'political arithmetic' in the Celtic Tiger economy of modern Ireland. In an early statement on government attitudes towards 'new wave' emigration in the opening years of the 1980s, an Taoiseach, Mr Charles J. Haughey, welcomed the phenomenon, suggesting that these new emigrants were 'climbing social ladders' in the 'benign taxfields' of western Europe and the United States.[16] The country's Minister for Foreign Affairs subsequently argued that 'we could not all live in such a small island'. He further stated that: 'We regard emigrants as part of our global generation of Irish people. We should be proud of them. The more they hone their skills and talents in another environment, the more they develop a work ethic in a country like Germany or the U.S., the better it can be applied in Ireland when they return'.[17] In the 1980s another senior Irish education planner working with the World Bank insisted: 'If we are true EEC members and we believe in European integration, we should see the increasing manpower shortage in Europe as a fortuitous opportunity for our young people facing unemployment to think of "mobility" and "migration" as natural solutions'.[18]

Perhaps nothing better indicates the 'devaluation' of nation as 'home' than this widespread acceptance of emigration as something entirely natural and traditional to modern Irish youth. Revisionism has clearly influenced these popular perceptions of 'new wave' emigration. It has certainly contributed to its 'sanitization' and 'voluntarization'. While one dominant tendency in Irish enterprise culture views 'new wave' emigrants as a people set apart from their predecessors and their peers by their spirit of adventure and enterprising spirit, another portrays emigration as an indispensable element in Irish youth enterprise culture. Both sets of attitudes suggest that emigrants now are upwardly mobile individuals, not a victimized social group. Current defenders of emigration have also implied that most recent emigration is now simply migration. This transformation of 'emigration' into 'migration' bears testament to the devaluation of nation as home in contemporary Ireland. Conventional wisdom suggests that the majority of those leaving Ireland since the 1980s have been qualifying themselves out of local labour markets and qualifying themselves into overseas labour markets, particularly in Europe. The qualitative dimensions of the recent exodus have been so overemphasized, not least within the corporate sector, that it has encouraged an official view of 'new wave' emigration almost exclusively as a 'brain drain'. This has been supported by reference to Higher Education Authority reports indicating that large numbers of Irish graduates have been emigrating since the early 1980s.[19] The latter are drawn from the most articulate in Irish society, and this, together with availability of data on graduate emigration, may explain why they have such a high profile in sanitized and popular accounts of recent Irish emigration.

In popular perceptions also the proximity of Ireland to Britain and the United States, and the opening up of new linkages between Ireland and mainland Europe, have once again been used as explanatory factors in the recent upsurge of 'new wave' emigration. Thus conventional wisdom in Ireland today attributes emigration to locational factors, to the peripherality of the Irish economy, to the proximity of Ireland to Britain, the United States, and Europe, and to the social psychological attributes and educational achievements of Irish young adults. Indeed there is every danger that the unopposed development of these locational and behavioural explanations of Irish emigration may result in its causes being traced solely to Ireland's peripheral location, or to the 'enterprising spirit' of Irish young adults.

The intellectual origins of such explanations are traceable to anthropological and behavioural accounts that emerged in the post-independence era.[20] The latter certainly succeeded in removing the study of emigration from the nationalist camp and did much to counteract the overt determinism in economic reductionist and structuralist accounts. However, voluntarism replaced structuralism in this literature, and most writers failed to develop a place-centred structural model of emigration capable of accommodating their behavioural findings. They instead passed from a critique of the obvious flaws in nineteenth-century nationalist accounts to behavioural explanations of modern Irish emigration. Voluntarism and 'locationalism' tend to be mixed in equal proportions in this literature. Hannan, who pioneered behavioural approaches to Irish migration in the 1970s, suggested that 'the openness' of modern Irish communities and 'the great improvements in the means of transportation and communications' explain migration.[21] He also attributed migration to the frustration with rural life experienced by young adults, and their inability to meet social and economic aspirations locally.

Given the volume of recent emigration it is surprising how it has been 'sanitized' in the official mind. In the apt description of one journalist writing in the mid-1980s: 'the exodus of young people in the past decade has so depopulated parts of western Ireland that parish priests in rural Mayo and Galway can't put together a dance'.[22] Another journalist may only have been slightly exaggerating when he stated that 'for those in their twenties, Christmas has become the only time of the year when one half of their generation meets the other'.[23]

Emigration since the 1980s: 'nothing but the same old story'?

In order to establish the social characteristics and destinations of recent emigrants, the author of this chapter conducted surveys in a number of urban and rural settings in the west and south of Ireland.[24] I shall briefly analyse the results of this project in this section. The survey was conducted between February and June of 1989. It targeted almost 6,900 families with a total population of almost 17,000 young adults aged 16 years or older and collected data on just under 2,200 emigrants. Post-intermediate students in secondary schools acted as surrogates for their parents in this survey. The questionnaire adopted here was simply designed to gather basic data on the social characteristics and destinations of family members who had emigrated in the 1980s. The results of this survey suggested that 'new wave' emigration in the 1980s still functioned as a survival strategy which permitted families to 'dispose' of 'surplus' sons and daughters overseas. However, it also revealed that emigration not only affected young adults, many of whom emigrated while still teenagers; it clearly also affected the structure of the families and local communities in Ireland.[25] Thus one-fifth of the families in the survey had at least one member living abroad. Some 13 per cent of these 'emigrant families' had three or more members living abroad. A further 6 per cent had four or more members who were emigrants. This suggests that the popular portrayal of emigration as 'a blight on Irish society' is neither socially or geographically accurate. The findings of this survey also suggested that emigration in the 1980s was more deeply embedded in small farming and working-class families than in suburban middle-class families. However, it did confirm that the field of emigration had by then penetrated middle-class suburbs in Ireland. The 'embeddedness' of emigration in rural families was particularly noticeable in areas in the northwest of the country where one in four families had at least one member living abroad. 'Emigrant families', i.e. families with one or more member living abroad, were one-quarter of all families in the Kerry survey. This meant that large numbers of families throughout Ireland today could be classified as 'transnational households' simply because they have so many family members living at home and abroad. Although less common in highly developed economies like West Germany and France in the 1980s, this is also a feature of family life in other 'emigrant nurseries' in countries as far apart as Ecuador and Algeria.[26] The results of this survey suggested that towns and villages throughout Ireland were being transformed into 'dormitory towns'. Contrary to King and

Shuttleworth, the urban bias in this 'new wave' emigration was not simply a reflection of urbanization of the Irish population.[27] It was also due to the deterioration of urban labour markets and the lack of opportunities in many Irish towns and cities in the 1980s.[28] Indeed this was a period which witnessed the reopening of emigrant trails from urban Ireland that were only temporarily closed during the 'boom' years of the 1960s and 1970s.

Despite the high volume of emigration in recent years, the tendency today is to treat emigrants as enterprising individuals, rather then seeing them as at once social class victims and benefactors of restructuring processes operating at the level of Irish society and at the level of the global economy. The exodus was estimated at approximately 72,000 between 1981 and 1986. By 1986 net emigration had reached 28,000 or just under 8 per 1,000 of the total population.[29] Courtney estimates that almost a quarter of a million people left the country between 1982 and 1988. The three years up to April 1989 were the period of heaviest out-migration. Record levels of over 50,000 per year were leaving the country at this time. The exodus has been estimated at approximately 14,400 per annum in the first half of the 1980s, rising to over 50,000 in 1987–88. These figures exclude the very large number of illegal Irish immigrants in the United States in the late 1980s. The Irish Emigration Reform Movement estimated Irish 'illegals' in the United States alone at approximately 135,000 in the late 1980s. Upwards of 20,000 of these were living in Boston alone. Estimates of the number of 'illegal Irish' in New York city in the late 1980s varied from a low of 40,000 to a high of over 100,000.[30]

Given the volume of recent Irish emigration it is difficult to understand how the gentrified image of the modern Irish emigrant managed to survive throughout the 1980s and 1990s. Moreover, those who stressed the preparedness of young adults for emigration during this period may have been overestimating the voluntary nature of much recent emigration. Certainly the age structure of emigrants in this survey seriously challenged the official 'sanitized' image of recent emigration. If age is as an indicator of the 'preparedness' of young adults for emigration, the findings of this survey suggested that very many young adults were emigrating while still in their teenage years. This was particularly the case in disadvantaged rural and urban areas with high levels of unemployment. Young adults in these areas were also taking to the emigrant trail out of Ireland before completing secondary schooling. Indeed 40 per cent of emigrants in this survey who went to Britain left Ireland before they were 20 years old. Those leaving larger urban centres were probably leaving older than their rural counterparts and this may have been particularly true of young male emigrants. Thus 40 per cent of urban emigrants to Britain in this survey were 22 years or older when they left the country. The corresponding figure for rural emigrants was just over 30 per cent. For many Irish young adults growing up in the 1980s the teenage years may have been years of considerable stress to which emigration contributes. Stress induced through competitive examinations at school was often succeeded by the stressful experiences of either choosing or having to emigrate. While those who emigrated to mainland Europe and the United States were generally older than those who moved to

Britain, it was nevertheless found that one-quarter of emigrants to the US, and almost one-third of those who went to mainland Europe, were under 20 when they left home.[31]

Although the findings of this survey offered strong support for a qualitative dimension to recent emigration, they also warned against any exaggeration of the 'yuppification' of the recent exodus. The majority of emigrants from rural areas and small towns were not the well-qualified from middle-class families. Just under 50 per cent of emigrants had a leaving certificate, and as many as 23 per cent had an intermediate certificate in secondary education. While emigrants with university degrees have certainly added a strong qualitative dimension to recent Irish emigration, they are hardly significant enough to talk of the 'gentrification' of recent Irish emigration. Nevertheless they have attracted more attention than diploma holders from regional technical colleges and those with only leaving certificates in secondary education. In emigrant blackspots in Donegal and Kerry, those with third-level qualifications probably accounted for less than one-fifth of total emigrants and the majority of these were not university graduates but graduates from regional colleges. The results of this survey also found that 'new wave' emigrants were inventing new traditions in Irish emigration by frequently returning 'home' on holidays, at least in their initial years away from home. 'New wave' emigrants certainly returned home more often than their predecessors. This at least sets them apart from many of their predecessors. The majority of young emigrants in the 1980s returned home at least once a year. Many of them entered relatively unchartered territory for modern Irish emigrants in moving to mainland Europe, the Middle East and Japan. However, Britain still was the most popular destination of Irish emigrants in the 1980s. Some 70 per cent of all emigrants went there, the majority of them going to London. The United States and Canada accounted for just under 20 per cent of emigrants and the European Community accounted for less than 6 per cent. This suggests that many young adults in Ireland in the 1980s and early 1990s were looking on London, not Dublin, as 'their' capital. They may also have seen it in much the same light as their peers from the north of England and Scotland still see this metropolis – a field of opportunity for those capable of adapting to labour markets, and an easy place from which to return home on a frequent basis. Young emigrants have been returning home on holidays so frequently since the 1980s that we may be witnessing a new form of 'seasonal migration' in Ireland. Emigrants with professional qualifications undoubtedly constituted an 'emigrant aristocracy' in this survey, although not all of them were in professional occupations. They were certainly higher on the social ladder, and more widely scattered across the occupational field, than poorly qualified emigrants from working-class and poor farming backgrounds. The pinnacle of the male emigrant aristocracy in the 1980s was occupied by engineers, dentists, doctors, accountants and other professionals. Indeed this group accounted for 16 per cent of male emigrants in the survey. The professions accounted for significantly more male than female emigrants. Below this emigrant aristocracy the majority of male and female emigrants tended to lead humbler lives in the traditional job ghettoes of the

Irish emigrant. Yet popular perceptions are poor foundations for providing an understanding of recent Irish emigration. The time-honoured image of the Irish emigrant is that of the Irish navvy or a male worker in the construction industry.[32] This was radically displaced in the 1980s and earlier when more and more young women were represented on the emigrant trails out of Ireland. As Meenan has shown, women outnumbered men on emigrant trails out of Ireland for at least three decades between 1891 and 1961.[33] They also left for quite different reasons than males. In the past at least, the exodus of large numbers of young women created serious sex imbalances that may have contributed to socially induced psychological disorders in rural communities.[34] Females accounted for 47 per cent of emigrants in surveys carried out by this author in the late 1980s.[35] Until recently they were also among the most neglected sector in modern Irish emigration. The feminization of Irish emigration since the 1980s is hardly surprising, especially given the marked feminization of the traditional overseas labour markets that attracted Irish emigrants in the past. The feminization of overseas labour markets in the 1980s and 1990s was certainly a factor in attracting large numbers of young women workers from all over Ireland. Irish women and young girls in the past were strongly represented in domestic service and factory work abroad, while many who emigrated during and after the Second World War entered middle-class positions thrown up by the welfare state. Today young Irish women are scattered across a wide range of occupations, from the 'neo-domestic' service sector (e.g. cleaning workers, 'au pairs' and waitresses) to lower-middle-class occupations and professional employment. Some 38 per cent of recent female emigrants in this survey left the country before they were 20 years old. One-tenth had only primary or intermediate education. Some 30 per cent of those who went to Britain had a third-level qualification and almost two-thirds had a leaving certificate in secondary education (the corresponding figure for males with leaving certificates was 37 per cent); 43 per cent of the 317 female emigrants in this survey who went to destinations other that Britain had a third-level qualification. Many of these belonged to the female emigrant aristocracy. At first glimpse it may appear that these emigrants were better placed than their male counterparts, given their strong representation in lower-middle-class jobs like secretarial work, nursing, teaching and banking. These occupations accounted for just under 50 per cent of all female emigrants in the survey. However, when wage levels in these occupations are compared to those in construction and related industries, it could be argued that, financially at least, male emigrants were better off than females. This does not mean that they fare better than the latter in terms of job security, work conditions and holiday allowances. Despite the 'gentrified' image of the successful 'career emigrant', this survey found that most young Irish women were still holding jobs in the traditional job ghettoes of Irish women workers.

Conclusion

This chapter suggests that a combination of structuralism and behaviouralism offers a number of advantages over conventional explanations of Irish emigration, not least those couched either in the logic of behaviouralism or in the logic of modernization theory. Firstly, they avoid the pitfalls of exceptionalism and cultural reductionism in behavioural accounts which overemphasize the peculiarities of Irish emigration. Secondly, they enable us to see Irish emigration for what it has always been – a social process linking core-formation at home and abroad with emigration and with processes of peripheralization operating within Ireland. Thirdly, they show that, far from being untouched by the forces of industrialization, Ireland and the Irish occupied central positions in the international division of labour from a very early stage in the construction of a world economy. Emigrants from Ireland still fulfil important functions in the postmodern societies of global society today.

This chapter also suggests that far from being caused by the adventurous spirit of emigrants, Irish emigration has been a rational response to restructuring processes operating at the level of the Irish nation-state and at the level of global society. Finally, except for short periods when emigration was halted by war, or when it was reversed through short-term upswings in the Irish economy, Ireland has continued to function as an important emigrant nursery for the world economy. Indeed, the Irish have helped to establish the core areas of the world economy and they also maintained them by filling labour gaps and literally regenerating the labour forces of the core areas of the world economy.

The history of Irish emigration, like the history of class formation and state formation in Ireland, testifies to the radical openness of Irish society since at least the nineteenth century. It also stresses the links between a geography of closure and a politics of exclusion which allowed the Irish nation-state, including today's Celtic Tiger economy, literally to take shape by shedding, or excluding, very large numbers of young adults from the nation-building project.[36] The links between emigration and nation-building in Ireland have a long history which stretches down to the present day. The Anglicization and commercialization of Ireland which linked the country to Britain and to the world economy have an even longer history. Society, politics, culture and landscapes in Ireland have been responding to the globalizing force of a dynamic British and global capitalism from at least the sixteenth century onwards. Nevertheless, the globalization, and more recently, the Americanization and Europeanization of Irish society accelerated tremendously between the 1960s and the 1980s. These years witnessed an exacerbation of the power of globalizing forces operating in Irish society and in the Celtic Tiger economy. They also witnessed the substitution of a nationalism of 'mutual exclusiveness' for a new image of Ireland as a country invaded by a uniformity of social standards and cultural forms emanating from outside the country. As I have stressed here, however, this is by no means a new development. Like their nineteenth-century predecessors, many young adults in Ireland in recent decades have probably regarded this country as 'unreal', even 'unrecognizable'. Unlike many of their peers in unemployment blackspots in the United States, Britain, Spain, Italy and Holland, for example, they have long regarded emigration as a natural response to the slow pace of political change, and to economic restructuring within Ireland. That is why writers like Fintan O'Toole can quite legitimately argue that emigration is the great guarantor of continuity in contemporary Irish society. It has become 'the badge of our identity' in a postmodern world where other more familiar cultural markers – the Irish language, dreams of economic self-sufficiency, Irish Catholicism – have melted away in the wake of a radical globalization, modernization and secularization of Irish society since the 1980s.[37]

Certainly recent changes in the political and territorial organization of Irish society have been so far-reaching that they constitute an equally radical discontinuity with more traditional views of Ireland as a self-governing and identifiable territorial community. In our anxiety to become 'modern' or 'European', John Waters has suggested, 'we have denied ourselves the ability to survive at all'. Aptly quoting Milan Kundera, he concludes that we have now 'become the allies of our own gravediggers'.[38] The deterioration of national politics and the emergence of a culture of dependency have not only affected attitudes towards 'new wave' Irish emigration. They may also have affected patterns of emigration, as more and more Irish young adults think in terms of Europe and the world outside Ireland when considering solutions to the lack of work and opportunities at home. That is why perceptions of Europe as an 'untilled field' of opportunity are still are so deeply embedded in Irish youth enterprise culture.

Notes

1. George Dangerfield, *The Damnable Question: A Study in Anglo-Irish Relations* (London, 1979).
2. Gerard R.C. Keep, 'Official Opinion on Irish Immigration in the Later Nineteenth Century', *Irish Ecclesiastical Record*, 81 (1954), pp. 412–21, at p. 419.
3. K. Marx and F. Engels, *On Colonialism* (London, 1959), p. 288.
4. Clive Dewey, 'Celtic Agrarian Legislation and the Celtic Revival', *Past and Present*, 22, 3 (1978), pp. 30–69, at pp. 32–5.
5. Jim Mac Laughlin, 'Nation-Building, Social Closure and Anti-Traveller Racism in Ireland', *Sociology*, 33, 1 (1999), pp. 129–51.
6. B. Duden, 'Population', in W. Sachs (ed.), *The Development Dictionary* (London, 1992), pp. 72–6.
7. P. Prunty, *Dublin Slums, 1800–1925: A Study in Historical Geography* (Dublin, 1999).
8. D. Lloyd, *Anomalous States* (Dublin, 1993).
9. Z. Bauman, *Life in Fragments* (London, 1995).
10. Marx and Engels. *On Colonialism*.
11. Raymond Crotty, *Irish Agricultural Production* (Cork, 1966); Louis Cullen (ed.), *The Formation of the Irish Economy* (Cork, 1969); F.S.L. Lyons, *Ireland Since the Famine* (London, 1971).
12. Garett Fitzgerald, *Towards a New Ireland* (London, 1966); David Lerner, *The Passing of Traditional Society* (Glencoe, 1962).
13. Crotty, *Irish Agricultural Production*; Louis Cullen (ed.), *An Economic History of Ireland Since 1660* (London, 1973); Joseph Lee, *The Modernisation of Irish Society* (Dublin, 1973): Lyons, *Ireland Since the Famine*.

14. Damian Hannan, *Rural Exodus: A Study of the Forces Influencing the Large-Scale Migration of Irish Youth* (London, 1976); James A. Walsh, *To Go or Not to Go: The Migration Intentions of Leaving Certificate Students* (Dublin, 1984).
15. Hassan Hakimian, *Labour Transfer and Economic Development: Theoretical Perspectives and Case Studies from Iran* (New York, 1990).
16. Charles J. Haughey on 'Today Tonight', RTE, 19 November 1988.
17. Quoted in Tom Whelan, 'The New Emigrants', *Newsweek*, 10 October 1987.
18. Robert Foster, 'Young Emigrants Still Looking West', *Irish Times*, 14 April 1987.
19. R. Breen. B.J. Whelan and J. Costigan, *Department of Labour Summary Report, School Leavers 1980–85* (Dublin, 1986); J.J. Sexton, 'Recent Changes in Irish Population and in the Pattern of Emigration', *Irish Banking Review*, 3 (1987), pp. 31–44.
20. Hannan, *Rural Exodus*; Walsh, *To Go or Not to Go*.
21. Hannan, *Rural Exodus*.
22. D. de Breadun, 'Three Hundred Have Gone From Lettermore in a Year', *Irish Times*, 3 February 1986.
23. Mark T. Brennock, 'A Time of Bitter-sweet Reunions for Young Emigrants', *Irish Times*, 21 December 1988.
24. Jim Mac Laughlin, *Ireland: The Emigrant Nursery and the World Economy* (Cork, 1994) and 'The Devaluation of Nation as "Home" and the De-politicisation of Recent Irish Emigration', in Jim Mac Laughlin (ed.), *Location and Dislocation in Contemporary Irish Society: Emigration and Irish Identities* (Cork, 1997), pp. 179–208.
25. F.H. Aalen and H. Brody, *Gola: Life and Last Days of an Island Community* (Cork, 1969); H. Brody, *Inniskillane: Change and Decline in the West of Ireland* (London, 1973).
26. Elizabeth M. Thomas-Hope, 'Caribbean Skilled International Migration and the Transnational Household', *Geoforum*, 19, 4 (1988), pp. 423–32.
27. Russell King and Ian Shuttleworth, 'Ireland's New Wave Emigration in the 1980s', *Irish Geography*, 21 (1988), pp. 104–8.
28. Sexton, 'Recent Changes'.
29. Mac Laughlin, *Ireland: The Emigrant Nursery*; Jim Mac Laughlin, 'Emigration and the Peripheralization of Ireland in the Global Economy', *Review Journal of the Fernand Braudel Center*, 17, 2 (1994), pp. 243–73.
30. A. Cronin, 'The Law That Keeps the Huddled Masses Out', *Irish Times*, 15 January 1988.
31. Mac Laughlin, 'The Devaluation of Nation as "Home"'.
32. D. Mac Amhlaigh, *The Irish Navvy* (London, 1979).
33. P. Meenan, *The Irish Economy Since 1922* (Liverpool, 1970).
34. N. Scheper-Hughes, *Saints, Scholars and Schizophrenics* (Berkeley CA, 1979).
35. Jim Mac Laughlin, 'Social Characteristics and Destinations of Recent Emigrants from the West of Ireland' *Geoforum*, 20, 3 (1991), pp. 1–13.
36. Jim Mac Laughlin, 'Ireland in the Global Economy: An End to a Distinct Nation?', in Ethel Crowley and Jim Mac Laughlin (eds), *Under the Belly of the Tiger: Class, Race, Identity and Culture in the Global Ireland* (Dublin, 1997); Jim Mac Laughlin, 'The Evolution of Modern Demography and the Debate on Sustainable Development', *Antipode: A Radical Journal of Geography*, 31, 3 (1999), pp. 324–33.
37. Fintan O'Toole, 'Permanence and Tradition are Illusions in a Makeshift Society', *Irish Times*, 19 January 1994.
38. J. Water, *Every Day Like Sunday?* (Dublin, 1995).

CHAPTER 17

Placing Postwar Irish Migration to Britain in a Comparative European Perspective, 1945–1981[1]

ENDA DELANEY

(School of Modern History, Queen's University, Belfast)

Introduction

All too frequently large-scale migration and the concomitant process of rural depopulation is viewed as a uniquely Irish experience.[2] However, mass migration was a phenomenon which affected most European states in the postwar period either as sending or receiving societies.[3] The Irish Republic was clearly divergent from the general European trends in terms of the *rate* of migration, particularly in the late 1950s, but it will be demonstrated that many of the features associated with postwar Irish migration to Britain are to be found in other European migratory flows, especially those from southern European countries to the industrialized western European states of Germany, France and the Netherlands. The analysis for the most part will be concerned with the period from the end of the Second World War in 1945 until 1981, although some comment on more recent trends will be incorporated where appropriate. Comparative studies of Irish society in general are rare, apart from the notable exception of Mjøset's long-range review of Irish economic performance, and a number of analyses which employ comparative reference points such as Girvin's assessment of Irish economic and social policy, Lee's writings on the economic performance of the independent Irish state and Kennedy's *ballon d'essai* which places the Irish historical experience within a wider comparative European context.[4] The comparative European case studies selected for consideration in this discussion are Greece, Portugal, Spain and Italy, all southern European countries which are traditionally associated with high rates of migration in the postwar period.[5] Other obvious similarities include location on the periphery of Europe and, with the exception of Greece, a Roman Catholic religious ethos. Recent work by Pcillon on the appropriate case countries to compare with the Irish Republic is of particular value since he draws attention to the differences between the Irish Republic and other semi-peripheral

European states such as Portugal and Greece in terms of socio-political structure and state intervention in social and economic life.[6] Whilst acknowledging
these intrinsic contrasts between the Irish Republic and our other case countries, and indeed the differences within this grouping of southern European
countries, it is clear that in a comparative European context these countries
are the most appropriate reference points for this analysis.

In the first instance, the patterns of migration are examined in order to
provide a statistical backdrop for this discussion. Migration was a regional
phenomenon in all of the case countries, a feature which is frequently over-
looked within the context of Irish migration studies. The regional incidence of
migration will be considered, focusing on the range of factors which explain
high rates of migration from particular regions. The role of the state in facilitating, encouraging or hindering migration is a crucial consideration and state
policy *vis-à-vis* migration is outlined for the five states presently under consideration. Finally, large-scale return migration, which was a central feature
of European migration flows during the 1970s, is also analysed, specifically
in relation to the effects of this return movement. The overall objective is to
demonstrate the value of assessing the Irish experience within the broader framework of European migration patterns during the postwar period. The purpose,
therefore, is not to present definitive research findings as this would involve
an extended discussion, but rather to sketch out the form that such an analysis
might take.

Patterns of migration

In the postwar period until 1981 well over 500,000 people migrated from the
Irish Republic.[7] Unfortunately the Irish state did not publish annual emigration statistics for a number of reasons, not least being the difficulties stemming
from the absence of frontier controls with the United Kingdom. We have, therefore, to rely on estimates of *net* migration (emigration less immigration) in
intercensal periods (see Table 17.1). It has been estimated that one in three of
the Irish population aged under 30 years in 1946 had left the country by 1971,
although many subsequently returned.[8] Somewhere in the region of 10 million

Table 17.1: Average annual Irish net migration, 1946–1981

Period	Total	Males	Females
1946–51	−24,384	−10,309	−14,075
1951–56	−39,353	−21,657	−17,696
1956–61	−42,401	−21,915	−20,486
1961–66	−16,121	−7,523	−8,598
1966–71	−10,781	−4,950	−5,831
1971–79	+13,617	+7,659	+5,958
1979–81	−2,523	−1,606	−917

Adapted from: Census of Population, 1981, I: Population of District Electoral
Divisions, Table J, p. xxi.

Table 17.2: Annual emigration, 1945–1959 (000s)

Year	Greece	Italy	Portugal	Spain
1945	—	—	5.9	3.5
1946	1.6	110.3	8.3	7.5
1947	4.9	254.1	12.8	15.2
1948	4.8	308.5	12.3	20.9
1949	4.3	254.5	17.3	44.8
1950	4.6	200.3	21.9	59.1
1951	14.2	293.1	33.7	61.3
1952	6.6	277.5	47.0	63.0
1953	8.8	224.7	39.7	50.7
1954	18.7	250.9	41.0	59.3
1955	29.8	320.1	29.8	67.6
1956	35.3	344.8	27.0	57.0
1957	30.4	341.7	35.4	62.5
1958	24.5	255.5	34.0	54.5
1959	23.7	268.5	33.5	34.6

Source: B.R. Mitchell, *International Historical Statistics: Europe, 1750–1988*, 3rd edn (London, 1992), pp. 128–35. Used with permission of Macmillan Press Ltd.

migrant workers travelled to western Europe from the Mediterranean basin for employment between the end of the Second World War and the mid-1970s.[9] Inevitably cross-country comparisons of the level of migration are fraught with problems owing to the varying quality and coverage of the data available. Estimates of the volume of migration in terms of the sheer numbers leaving each of the southern European case countries are presented in Tables 17.2 and 17.3. As with all migration statistics these should be interpreted with some degree of caution, since it is commonly acknowledged that these data understate the true extent of migration, especially since no account is taken of clandestine migration.[10] Still the most cursory inspection of these sets of data indicates that across the five case countries, the 1950s and 1960s were decades of large-scale migration. The parallels between the Irish Republic and Italy are particularly striking since the Italian flow of migrants, like the Irish flow, gathered pace in the immediate postwar period.[11] Indeed in the late 1940s and early 1950s, Italy was the main source of migrant labour for neighbouring countries such as France and Switzerland.[12] In the case of other southern European countries, however, peaks in migration were registered somewhat later, in the 1960s and early 1970s, prior to the onset of the oil crisis of 1973–74. For example, the peaks in migration from Greece occurred in 1962–66 and 1969–70 when approximately 100,000 people left the country annually.[13]

Another way of viewing the Irish experience in a comparative context is to compare the estimates of the average annual rate of net migration per 1,000 of the population for each country. As can be seen from Table 17.4, from 1960 onwards Portugal fared worst of the five case countries, followed by Greece and then the Irish Republic. The timing of peaks in migration depends on a number of factors, not least being the economic climate in both the sending

Table 17.3: Annual emigration, 1960–1980 (000s)

Year	Greece	Italy	Portugal	Spain
1960	47.7	383.9	33.7	30.5
1961	58.8	387.1	34.8	43.0
1962	84.0	365.6	38.2	62.3
1963	100.0	277.6	54.0	83.7
1964	105.5	258.5	86.3	102.1
1965	117.2	282.6	117.0	74.5
1966	86.9	296.5	132.8	56.8
1967	42.7	229.3	106.3	25.9
1968	50.9	215.7	104.2	66.7
1969	91.5	182.2	153.5	100.8
1970	92.7	151.9	173.3	97.7
1971	61.8	167.7	151.2	113.7
1972	43.4	141.9	105.0	104.1
1973	27.5	123.3	120.0	96.1
1974	24.5	112.0	70.3	50.7
1975	20.3	92.7	44.9	20.6
1976	20.4	97.2	33.2	12.1
1977	18.4	87.7	28.8	11.3
1978	14.5	85.6	30.3	12.0
1979	11.0	88.9	20.6	13.1
1980	—	83.0	18.0	14.1

Source: Russell King, 'Population Mobility: Emigration, Return Migration and Internal Migration', in Allan Williams (ed.), *Southern Europe Transformed: Political and Economic Change in Greece, Italy, Portugal and Spain* (London, 1984), p. 148.

and receiving countries: the impact of the recession in West Germany in 1966–67 on the migrant flow from southern Europe is a good example of this. The halt called to the recruitment of migrant workers by the main sources of demand, West Germany and France, after the first oil crisis in 1973 is also reflected in these estimates. That the political situation could also influence migration is illustrated by the return flow to Portugal in the wake of the revolution in 1974 (see Table 17.4). But the effects of economic prosperity are also evident in these migration estimates. For example, it has been demonstrated that return migration to the Irish Republic in the 1970s was not primarily as a result of the recession in Britain but rather the relative prosperity in Ireland.[14]

Broadly speaking the following patterns in terms of the destination of migrants from these five countries may be highlighted. The vast majority of Irish migrants in the postwar period until 1981 travelled to Britain.[15] Thereafter whilst Britain remained the principal destination, Irish migrants also departed for the United States, one of the main receiving countries during the nineteenth century, and continental European countries.[16] The reasons why so many Irish migrants crossed the Irish Sea include the restrictions on immigration imposed by the American authorities from the 1920s onwards, geographical proximity and the fact that unlike many other immigrant groups, Irish migrants had unrestricted access to the British labour market. In addition, a point which is

Table 17.4: Annual rates of net migration per 1,000 of average population, 1960–1981

Year	Greece	Irish Republic	Italy	Portugal	Spain
1960	–3.7	–14.8	–1.9	–25.3	–4.7
1961	–2.8	–7.0	–2.8	–2.4	–2.4
1962	–5.7	–3.5	1.6	–6.1	–1.9
1963	–6.6	–4.9	–1.6	–6.5	–2.0
1964	–5.6	–6.6	–1.6	–10.3	–3.0
1965	–4.7	–7.5	–1.7	–14.1	–2.2
1966	–0.6	–4.5	–2.0	–14.6	–1.8
1967	–3.3	–5.7	–1.8	–10.0	–1.9
1968	–4.4	–5.1	–2.0	–10.0	–1.2
1969	–7.6	–2.6	–2.3	–14.7	–0.5
1970	–5.3	–1.2	–2.2	—	–0.8
1971	–1.8	+2.0	–3.1	–14.1	+0.6
1972	–0.1	+4.6	+0.2	–8.4	–2.0
1973	–4.8	+5.2	+0.2	–9.7	–1.9
1974	–2.1	+5.9	+0.2	+19.9	–0.7
1975	+6.5	+5.4	+0.2	+38.2	+0.4
1976	+6.1	+3.7	+0.2	+1.1	+1.5
1977	+6.7	+2.2	+0.1	+2.1	+1.9
1978	+7.0	+4.1	+0.1	+3.2	+1.1
1979	+4.3	–0.2	—	+3.8	–0.9
1980	+5.2	–0.2	–0.1	+4.3	+3.0
1981	+0.7	+0.3	–0.5	+1.7	—

Adapted from: NESC, *The Economic and Social Implications of Emigration*, NESC report no. 90 (Dublin, 1991), Pl. 7840, p. 63.

frequently neglected is that postwar Irish migration, unlike the pre-Second World War movement to the United States, was rarely viewed as a permanent move, either by the migrants themselves or by those who stayed behind. Many Irish migrants left with the intention of staying in Britain for a couple of years before eventually returning, although a significant proportion never returned. Return migration from Britain was not altogether unusual even in the immediate post-war period. The Commission on Emigration and Other Population Problems appointed by the Irish government in 1948 noted that 'in many cases, the out-going traveller was not, in any sense, a permanent emigrant and frequently came and went like a seasonal migrant'.[17]

Similarly, whereas the majority of southern European migrants had travelled across the Atlantic prior to the Second World War, in the postwar period it was other European countries which became the destinations for most migrants, especially during the 1960s. For example, even though a continuous, if considerably reduced, flow of Portuguese migrants continued to leave for Brazil, Canada and the United States in the 1960s, the majority travelled to France, with smaller numbers leaving for West Germany and other countries.[18] The destinations of Italian migrants were somewhat more diverse, with Switzerland, France and Belgium being the main receiving countries in the immediate postwar period, while in the early 1960s West Germany became an increasingly important destination for Italian migrants.[19] In addition, the long-established pattern of transatlantic migration of Italians continued, although this flow declined in significance relative to the movement within Europe.[20] Between 1945 and 1974 nearly one in six of the Greek population left the country; roughly a quarter of these migrants later returned.[21] Collection of official data on Greek migration only began in 1955 and in the first five years for which information is available, non-European destinations – notably Australia, Canada and the United States – were the main receiving countries.[22] In the 1960s and early 1970s West Germany received the majority of Greek migrants: in the period between 1955 and 1973, 53 per cent of all Greek migrants travelled to West Germany.[23] Finally, Spanish migration, which had historically been directed towards South America prior to the Second World War, continued to be transatlantic in orientation until the mid-1950s, with over 40,000 migrants leaving Spain annually for Argentina, Brazil and Venezuela.[24] By the late 1950s, owing to the economic recession in Latin America and more selective migration policies on the part of the receiving countries, this flow was only 20 per cent of that enumerated in the early 1950s. In the early 1960s, the patterns of Spanish migration altered dramatically when France and, to a lesser extent, West Germany and Switzerland became the principal destinations for Spanish migrants, with over 700,000 Spaniards migrating to France between 1956 and 1971.[25]

A number of general patterns can therefore be identified. Firstly, in terms of volume, Irish and Italian migration peaked in the late 1940s and 1950s and thereafter declined. The main sending societies in the following decade were Portugal, Spain and Greece. The timing of migration peaks was dependent both on the economic climate in the sending country and the demand for labour in the receiving country. For example, the high level of migration from the Irish Republic in the late 1940s and throughout the 1950s reflects the crises in the Irish economy at this time and the availability of unskilled employment in Britain. Second, in terms of the rate of migration, the countries which had the highest rates over the complete period were Portugal, Greece and the Irish Republic. Lastly, migration in the postwar period was for the most part a European rather than a transatlantic movement for all five case countries. It is clearly evident that these migrant flows were from the peripheral or semi-peripheral fringes of Europe to the advanced capitalist economies of West Germany, the Netherlands, France and the United Kingdom. Clearly this is a movement of population out of the underdeveloped agricultural economy into the advanced capitalist one, albeit across national boundaries.

Migration and regions

It is a truism of migration studies that migration affects particular regions. The regional incidence of migration is more often than not concealed in 'national' estimates which provide little indication of the impact of migration on local communities. As Baines has argued, 'the big problem is to explain the incidence of emigration'.[26] It is only with detailed micro-studies of migration using techniques such as the construction of life histories that we can begin to analyse and explain this phenomenon. Scholars concerned with European migration are increasingly analysing this movement of population on the basis of detailed local studies over a substantial period of time.[27] These studies highlight the benefits of investigating the reasons for migration at a regional level. Before turning to the southern European regional migration patterns, it would be instructive to examine the situation in relation to postwar Irish migration.

Data on net migration flows from each Irish county – which include movement within the Irish Republic – are available from the censuses of population from 1926 onwards. The average annual rates of net migration per 1,000 of the population for each Irish province and county for the period between 1946 and 1981 are presented in Table 17.5. It should be noted that these data refer to total net migration, including internal migration. But the available evidence suggests that the level of internal migration was quite low: for every five migrants who left provincial Ireland between 1946 and 1971, four travelled to destinations outside of the Irish state, although the level of internal migration increased greatly in the 1970s.[28] What does this evidence tell us about regional patterns of migration? In the first place, counties in the north-west such as Leitrim, Mayo, Roscommon and Donegal had high rates of net migration across virtually the entire period. Other counties which experienced higher than average rates of net migration include Longford, Clare and Kerry. A further observation is that even with the overall decrease in the levels of migration during the 1960s, some 'migration-prone' areas such as Leitrim, Mayo and Roscommon retained high rates of net migration. A caveat should be added here in that rates of net migration of course do not necessarily reflect volume since the total population of some of these counties was low. For example, even though the average annual rate of net migration per 1,000 for Dublin in the period 1951–56 may not appear unduly high (–9.7), yet in terms of volume, net migration from this county constituted over one-sixth of total movement from the Irish state during these five years.[29] The picture changes somewhat from 1971 onwards, with significant inflows being recorded for most counties in the 1970s and the return of large-scale migration in the 1980s.[30]

A number of valuable studies of postwar rural Ireland facilitate an analysis of the reasons why people left a particular area or region. Perhaps the best-known study is the Limerick Rural Survey, 1958–64, completed under the auspices of the rural development organization, Muintir na Tíre.[31] Hannan's research on the migration intentions of young people in Cavan in the mid-1960s and Jackson's detailed examination of the town of Skibbereen in west Cork in the same period are also particularly revealing on the regional incidence of migration.[32] In addition, An Foras Talúntais (the Agricultural Institute) completed a number of 'resource' surveys in the late 1960s and early 1970s dealing with areas such as Leitrim, west Cork and west Donegal.[33] The plethora of 'findings' from these studies would be difficult to summarize here, but these studies illustrate the reasons and explanations for migration on a regional level, emphasizing that the absence of non-agricultural employment was a key determinant in the regional incidence of migration.[34] In areas of the west, north-west

Table 17.5: Average annual rate of net migration per 1,000 from each Irish county and province, 1946–1981

Province or county	1946–51	1951–56	1956–61	1961–66	1966–71	1971–81
Total	−8.2	−13.4	−14.8	−5.7	−3.7	+3.2
Leinster	−2.1	−11.4	−13.1	−1.5	−1.7	+4.2
Munster	−11.7	−12.8	−14.2	−6.4	−3.5	+2.3
Connacht	−15.1	−17.4	−18.3	−13.6	−10.0	+1.8
Ulster (part of)	−14.6	−19.6	−20.7	−14.2	−6.6	+2.8
LEINSTER						
Carlow	−9.3	−12.9	−16.1	−12.2	−8.9	+1.3
Dublin	+5.5	−9.7	−10.1	+4.8	−0.7	+2.4
Kildare	−8.8	−15.5	−18.4	−8.4	+0.9	+17.3
Kilkenny	−13.1	−11.1	−15.6	−10.9	−4.2	+4.7
Laois	−12.2	−13.6	−17.2	−12.6	−6.4	+2.7
Longford	−16.8	−16.6	−20.8	−16.8	−11.3	+2.1
Louth	−3.3	−10.2	−17.1	−6.8	+0.9	+2.1
Meath	−8.6	−8.2	−14.7	−4.1	+1.3	+14.3
Offaly	−13.3	−12.3	−13.2	−11.7	−11.6	−0.5
Westmeath	−11.9	−13.3	−15.9	−12.3	−9.1	+2.6
Wexford	−12.3	−14.3	−17.4	−9.5	−4.0	+1.4
Wicklow	−2.1	−18.8	−17.2	−4.2	+7.5	+12.6
MUNSTER						
Clare	−15.9	−15.9	−14.9	−6.3	−1.9	+6.9
Cork	−7.9	−10.0	−11.2	−3.9	−1.9	+2.7
Kerry	−17.7	−14.0	−15.2	−11.2	−4.7	+1.7
Limerick	−12.7	−15.8	−17.0	−5.0	−6.5	+1.4
Tipperary N.R.	−12.6	−14.0	−16.1	−8.3	−6.5	−2.1
Tipperary S.R.	−13.5	−15.5	−18.6	−13.0	−8.2	+0.4
Waterford	−9.6	−10.6	−14.8	−5.0	+1.6	+2.6
CONNACHT						
Galway	−15.3	−15.2	−16.2	−10.6	−6.7	+3.9
Leitrim	−18.7	−23.1	−22.7	−19.1	−14.7	−3.0
Mayo	−15.3	−19.1	−20.3	−17.1	−14.0	−0.4
Roscommon	−15.9	−16.1	−17.9	−11.7	−10.9	+0.4
Sligo	−10.8	−17.1	−16.6	−12.7	−6.8	+4.1
ULSTER (part of)						
Cavan	−15.8	−18.2	−21.3	−13.8	−9.1	−3.9
Donegal	−14.6	−20.2	−17.9	−15.0	−6.3	+6.3
Monaghan	−13.2	−19.7	−26.5	−12.9	−4.4	+2.0

Adapted from: Census of Population, 1956, I: Population, Area and Valuation, Table XIII, p. xxii; Census of Population, 1971, I: Population of District Electoral Divisions, Table XII, p. xxiii; Census of Population, 1981, I: Population of District Electoral Divisions, Table L, p. xxiii.

and the midlands, few opportunities existed for manufacturing or industrial employment since such factories were located in the larger urban centres. Employment in agriculture was not an attractive option and it is noteworthy that agriculture as a way of life was rejected by many migrants, accelerating the decline of the Irish agricultural labour force in the postwar period.[35] The local 'resource' surveys which deal with areas which had high levels of migration, such as west Cork, Leitrim and west Donegal, indicate that in the poorer regions of western Ireland livelihoods other than farming were perceived to present better opportunities, the rejection of the family holding by the prospective heir being the most extreme example of this phenomenon.[36]

Detailed local studies also facilitate an examination of the relationship between migration and education. What is particularly interesting about Hannan's study of the migration intentions of young persons in Cavan in the mid-1960s is the fact that educational attainment was positively correlated with migration, with the most migratory grouping being those with secondary education.[37] Those who attended vocational school or only received primary education were more content to stay at home in the local community. To realize occupational and income aspirations, young people with a higher level of educational achievement believed that they had to leave the local area. This was also found to be the case in the Drogheda Manpower Survey, completed in 1967: 80 per cent of boys completing the Leaving Certificate intended to leave the area, with one-quarter of this grouping planning to go to Britain.[38] For females, 66 per cent taking the Leaving Certificate intended to leave the area, with half of them planning to leave the country: of this grouping 50 per cent intended to travel to Britain.[39] Finally, the role of migrants from the local area, and more especially siblings, already living in Britain was a crucial determinant both in the provision of information about employment opportunities and wages in Britain, and in facilitating migration in the short-term on a practical level by offering accommodation to migrants on arrival.[40] For example, 43 per cent of migrants who were interviewed for the Skibbereen social survey in the mid–1960s reported that they came to stay in the first instance with relatives and friends living in Britain, and 28 per cent secured their first job as a result of efforts on their behalf by relatives and friends.[41] The role of kin and friendship networks in the process of migration should be underlined as recent scholarship stresses the importance of networks since each wave of migrants was able to draw upon the links with friends and relatives already living in the host society, thereby reducing the costs and disruption of migration in terms of securing accommodation and employment.[42] These networks also ensured the existence of channels of communication which, it may be argued, resulted in the construction and maintenance of distinctive ethnic identities in host countries.[43]

Migration from southern European countries in the postwar period was also a regional phenomenon. King's summary of the variations in southern European migration patterns reviews the main factors associated with regions which experienced high levels of migration such as northern Portugal, southern Italy, northern Greece and western Spain. King concluded that

> rural economies with relatively stagnant agricultural bases (as in Portugal, Greece and parts of Spain) or experiencing a decline in the demand for labour as a result of modernisation (latterly in Italy) offer relatively poor job prospects

> and little opportunity to accumulate wealth . . . For many, if not most, there was
> no way to break the vicious circle of poverty by remaining within rural areas.[44]

In Portugal the central and northern provinces experienced rates of migration which were double the national average during the 1960s.[45] Detailed local studies of the reasons for and impact of Portuguese migration, both in historical and contemporary contexts, illustrate the significance of the decline in the agricultural economy and the lack of local employment opportunities in explaining this movement of population.[46] The principal sending areas in Spain were the western provinces, with parts of Andalusia and certain areas in the north such as Galicia also experiencing high migration rates.[47] In Portugal and Spain, migration affected underdeveloped regions which offered few opportunities for non-agricultural employment.

Greek migrants for the most part came from the north of the country, areas with poor land and little by way of economic development.[48] The regional distribution of Greek migrants reflects the country's uneven economic development in the postwar period with few industries being located in these undeveloped regions.[49] Data on the regional origins of Greek migrants indicate that three regions in northern Greece (Epirus, Macedonia and Thrace) supplied the lion's share of migrants.[50] Likewise, in Italy the regions most affected by migration – both internal and international – were those which displayed a similar range of problems, especially a surplus rural population. As Salt and Clout have remarked:

> during the postwar period southern Italy and the Islands especially, have in
> varying degree suffered from poverty, unemployment, and underemployment.
> These problems have initiated a process of rural decongestion that, as in other
> Mediterranean countries, has been partially translated into foreign migration.[51]

But migration rates were also high in areas of northern Italy, such as the region of Veneto, a poor agricultural area.[52] In contrast with the other three countries discussed, there is an abundance of regional and local studies of Italian migration which facilitates a detailed examination of the factors more generally associated with migration.[53]

It can be seen, therefore, that across the five case countries migration was a regional phenomenon. The characteristics of areas with a high incidence of migration are found to be broadly similar: an underdeveloped agricultural economy resulting in a surplus of labour; a dearth of non-agricultural employment opportunities; and lastly a tradition of migration from particular regions. Even this necessarily brief overview of the regional patterns in migration underlines the basic point that in order to explain the incidence of migration this movement of population should be viewed within its regional context. This is particularly the case in relation to postwar Ireland and there is a need for long-range studies of migration from a region, county or a parish which will begin the process of unravelling the complex set of reasons which explain why people left a local area (and equally interestingly why others stayed), what exact role relatives and friends played in the migration process, where did migrants travel to, and when, if at all, did they return.

The role of the state

In a valuable review of developments in global migration theory, Zolberg has observed that state policy in terms of frontier control will determine to a significant degree the patterns of international migration, although clandestine migration can still occur.[54] In general terms, this analysis is not only true of contemporary migration patterns but also of historical ones. Over the course of the twentieth century, and more especially in the postwar period, state policy has shaped the history of international migration. In theory, a state can prohibit its citizens from leaving the country, and similarly state policy in the form of the restriction of immigration determines who is allowed to enter a receiving country and the duration of the stay. The overarching role of the state in determining migration is a particularly important factor when analysing migration flows and therefore this issue will presently be examined in relation to our five case countries.

An investigation of Irish government policy drawing on hitherto neglected and still unpublished official records clearly demonstrates that only on specific occasions were Irish governments concerned with migration.[55] In the war years, the authorities on both sides of the Irish Sea closely monitored and regulated migration for a variety of reasons including the supply of labour, security considerations and concerns about Irish neutrality.[56] The postwar years were marked by increasing uneasiness on the part of the Irish government with regard to the level of migration to Britain, coupled with anxiety in relation to the welfare of Irish migrants living in Britain. A restriction on the migration of Irish females under the age of 21 years was considered by the Fianna Fáil administration in 1947 and again by the inter-party government in 1948, but owing to the practical difficulties involved, opposition from certain quarters and, of course, the perception that Irish citizens were being preventing from leaving the country, no ban on migration was introduced.[57] In general terms, the Irish state neither encouraged nor hindered migration but rather aimed at creating the economic conditions whereby people would not have to leave the country in search of employment. Clearly the large-scale migration of Irish citizens also reduced the level of unemployment (and underemployment) and the consequent threat to the social order, be it a perceived or real one. This aspiration is still a central element of the policy of the Irish state with regard to migration. Two statements of official policy separated by some 36 years illustrate this point clearly. The first is an official document on the policy of the Irish government, prepared in October 1960; the second is taken from the white paper on Irish foreign policy published in 1996, and indicates that an aspiration to reduce migration is still an element of Irish government policy.

> So far as the formulation of policy is concerned, Irish emigration to Britain is not distinguished from Irish emigration to other countries. Emigration is regarded as a serious problem and is not encouraged, although there are no official restrictions imposed. The objective aimed at by the policy of the Irish government is to remove the economic need for emigration by promoting increased economic activity at home.[58]

> The reduction or ending of involuntary emigration has long been a policy objective of Irish governments. The only effective solution is the creation of job opportunities in Ireland through the promotion of economic growth and this will remain at the top of government priorities.[59]

In theory, it was believed that the level of migration from the Irish Republic could be reduced by the creation of employment opportunities. In practice, the shortcomings of this element of Irish economic policy were crudely illustrated by the haemorrhage from postwar Ireland which only lessened in the 1960s when innovative economic planning initiatives began to bear fruit in the form of industrial and manufacturing employment, a development which was greatly aided by the international economic climate.

On the other side of the Irish Sea, for consecutive postwar British governments Irish labour acted as a useful supplement to the domestic labour supply, especially during the acute labour shortage in the immediate aftermath of the end of the war in 1945. Historical and practical concerns ensured that Irish citizens could freely enter Britain even after the Irish Republic left the Commonwealth in 1949. The body of immigration legislation introduced during the 1960s and in 1971 was not applied to citizens of the Irish Republic, who were instead viewed as having a 'special' status in Britain.[60] Unlike migrants recruited from southern Europe under the '*gastarbeiter*' or 'guestworker' system for employment in other European countries, Irish migrants in Britain enjoyed full voting and welfare rights and were free to stay in Britain without restriction on the length of stay.[61] What is particularly revealing is that when British immigration legislation was framed in the 1960s, a clear and telling distinction was made between Irish migrants and immigrants from the New Commonwealth, the former being regarded as more 'desirable'. The origins of this policy have been the subject of recent investigation, and skin colour and other prejudices played a part in the formulation of this subtle but important distinction, although the practical difficulties in enforcing a restriction on Irish immigration – given the land border with Northern Ireland – were also important considerations.[62]

In sharp contrast with the Irish situation, the southern European states played a pivotal role in determining the volume and direction of migration flows from their jurisdictions.[63] A network of bilateral agreements between the industrialized western European countries and their southern European counterparts with 'labour for export' provided the 'basic links for flows of information about employment and living conditions'.[64] For example, recruitment agreements for the supply of workers were signed by Greece with France in 1954, with Belgium in 1957 and lastly with West Germany under the 'guestworker' system in 1960.[65] Similarly, in the 1960s Spain signed treaties with a number of countries including Belgium (1956), France (1961), Austria (1962) and West Germany (1966), which subsequently provided the institutional framework for controlling and assisting migration to other European countries.[66] A bilateral agreement was concluded between Italy and West Germany in 1955.[67] However, the attitude of the Portuguese state was somewhat different in character.

Under the Salazar regime, 'in accordance with the interests of the political régime it was important neither to alert the public to the negative implications of emigration nor to publicise the higher standards of living enjoyed by other European countries'.[68] Nevertheless, these ideological considerations did not prevent labour recruitment agreements being concluded with the Netherlands and France in 1963, West Germany in 1964 and again with Luxemburg in 1970.[69]

Why were southern European countries willing to facilitate the migration of large numbers of their citizens to northern European countries in this manner? Of course, the removal of this 'surplus' population alleviated unemployment and the consequent potential threat to the social order. Second, remittances from migrants were a valuable source of foreign currency and provided income for the families of migrants in the sending countries.[70] It was also presumed at least initially that migration had a positive impact on the economy of the southern European sending countries in that unemployment levels would be reduced, much needed foreign currency acquired and the migrants would eventually return with useful skills. However, the available evidence indicates that the 'benefits' of migration for sending countries were in fact illusory. It would be difficult to summarize the various strands of this overarching debate on the effects of migration on the sending country here, but increasingly the consensus – insofar as one exists – appears to support the view that few benefits were accrued by southern European countries by large-scale migration to western Europe.[71]

The differences described in state policy between the Irish Republic and the other four countries may be explained by reference to ideological and historical concerns. From the establishment of the Irish state in 1922 until the late 1950s, the Irish state was essentially minimalist in terms of the extent and level of intervention in social and economic life.[72] The Irish Roman Catholic Church fiercely resisted any state intervention as a result of the perceived links with socialist regimes, social welfare and medical care being obvious examples of the ideological battlegrounds.[73] When state restrictions on Irish migration to Britain were mooted in the late 1940s, objections to this drastic course of action from the political and administrative elite centred on the possible infringements on personal liberty.[74] Opposition from prominent Catholic figures also focused on the issue of personal liberty.[75] But historical concerns were also of significance. Any Irish government which openly concluded a bilateral labour agreement with their British counterparts would have incurred the wrath of Irish nationalists since the elimination of 'emigration' was an element in the Irish nationalist rhetoric which was expounded in the pre-independence period. It was argued that with the end of British rule, the necessity for people to migrate would dissipate. When the Irish government did arrive at an informal labour agreement in 1941 during the Second World War, a key element was that the Irish authorities were not openly seen to be involved in the migration of Irish citizens to Britain since such an action would have been unpalatable for many Irish nationalists and in addition a breach of the stated position of neutrality.[76]

Apart from the reduction in unemployment and the resultant drain on limited exchequer resources, it is difficult to assess the 'costs' and 'benefits' of postwar Irish migration. The Commission on Emigration and Other Population Problems, which was instituted in 1948, devoted some attention to this issue but concluded that there was little direct evidence upon which to base firm conclusions.[77] A major report on Irish migration which was published in 1991 is similarly inconclusive on this matter, although the continuance of a 'brain drain' or migration of skilled Irish graduates was highlighted.[78] Whether large-scale migration inhibited Irish economic development is also a vexed issue. The most recent assessment of this issue by Ó Gráda and Walsh argues that the economic climate was affected by the population decline resulting from large-scale migration since it created an environment which was 'discouraging of initiative and investment'.[79] In addition, they point to the effects of migration on the age structure of the population since the majority of those who left were young people.[80] But there is a dearth of research on the 'costs' and 'benefits' of postwar Irish migration which precludes a thorough and precise analysis of this complex issue, and for the present the effects of migration on the Irish Republic during the postwar period remain very much a matter for informed speculation.

Return migration

As already stated, Irish migration to Britain was rarely regarded by migrants as a permanent or lifelong move: for example, the Skibbereen social survey indicated that over two-thirds of the sample of migrants from the area living in Britain expressed a desire to return to Ireland when interviewed in the mid-1960s.[81] Invariably, migrants living abroad do express a desire to return permanently, although whether this aspiration is ever realized is quite another matter.[82] However, in the past 30 years or so, with the expansion of inexpensive travel facilities across the Irish Sea, the distinction between permanent return migration and frequent travel back and forth becomes somewhat blurred. Throughout the period under consideration, estimates of Irish net migration clearly do not take account of the fact that a substantial number of people may have left the country and subsequently returned between the time the two enumerations were taken. Therefore, the scale of return migration across intercensal periods is not readily quantifiable owing to the absence of frontier controls.[83] However, what is clear is that migration to Britain was not an irrevocable step, unlike migration to the United States prior to the Second World War, which was almost inevitably on a permanent basis. Garvey's examination of net migration data by age and country of birth indicates that between 1961 and 1971 a trend developed whereby migrants returned from Britain with their families, a conclusion borne out by the finding that there was a net gain of roughly 32,000 children aged under 15 years who had been born in Britain.[84] Throughout the 1970s the flow of migrants to the Irish Republic was greater than the movement out of the state resulting in a net inflow of 104,000 persons between 1971 and 1981, an unprecedented development in modern

Irish demographic history.[85] Migrants who had left the country in the 1940s and 1950s but subsequently decided to return home with their children accounted for a substantial proportion of this inflow, as is evidenced by the return of a large number of married persons and children who were born in Britain.[86]

Why did these migrants return to Ireland during the late 1960s and throughout the 1970s? Without doubt the relative prosperity experienced in the Irish Republic at this time was one determining factor as an outward export-oriented approach was adopted as a key element in Irish planning, which, together with buoyant economic conditions internationally, resulted in a much improved economic climate.[87] In the 1970s and 1980s a number of scholars examined this movement of people back to the Irish Republic.[88] A study of return migration to the regions of Carrick-on-Shannon in County Leitrim and Boyle in County Roscommon, based on fieldwork conducted in 1975, found that return migrants were living in roughly a quarter of the sample households, although considering the high rates of migration from this area, this is not altogether surprising.[89] The highest rate of return migration was amongst migrants who had travelled to Britain, as might be expected. When asked for their principal motive for returning to this area a range of answers were given. It appears that males had a tendency to underline economic motives whereas females returned because they found it difficult to adjust to life elsewhere or to marry. For females, marriage was one of the principal motives which in effect involved the termination of their career as paid workers since 'the chances to find an occupation after return were non-existent' in the area.[90] However, these 'reasons' should be viewed with some caution as returnees may have rationalized their decision to return at a later date.

Gmelch's anthropological work on return migration is particularly valuable. Drawing on data collected by interviews in the 1970s and 1980s, he found that the 'pull factors, or attractions of the homeland' were cited by over 55 per cent of a sample of 606 return migrants in areas of western Ireland as reasons for their return home.[91] The desire to live near friends and relatives was an equally significant factor with 41 per cent citing this reason, whereas employment or occupational 'pull' factors were of less significance.[92] A particularly interesting observation relates to the primacy of economic factors in the original decision to migrate, yet strangely it seemed to be of little consequence for return migrants.

> Overall, economic factors were found to be less important in return decisions than were other categories. This contrasts sharply with the overriding importance of economic concerns in out-migration: 71 per cent of the respondents cited either lack of employment or desire for a better job as the primary reason for migrating. For migrants to return to their homelands while there is still higher unemployment than in the host societies attests to the importance of the non-economic motives in Irish return migration.[93]

This would certainly appear to cast doubt on the explanations which view return migration as a response to improved economic conditions, although whether this finding would apply to other areas of the Irish Republic is debatable. The availability of better social welfare provisions at home – in itself an economic factor – is also worthy of consideration here, especially during the recession in Britain in the 1970s.

In terms of the readjustment of return migrants, the data collected by Gmelch are most revealing. Over half (51 per cent) of the sample stated that during their first year back in Ireland they were not satisfied with life, and 'would have been happier had they stayed abroad'.[94] The reasons for their dissatisfaction were the lethargic pace of life in rural Ireland, the perceived 'narrow-minded' attitudes of the local people and the problems in re-establishing former relationships with friends and relatives. However, as time passed, returned migrants became more satisfied with their situation: of those who had been back more than five years, only 17 per cent expressed dissatisfaction, although this does not include an estimated 5–10 per cent who had emigrated again.[95] As Gmelch astutely observes, it was the size of the communities to which migrants returned that created many of the problems in readjustment.

> To a large extent, the problems return emigrants experience can be attributed to differences in the scale of the communities they have returned to. Nearly three-quarters of the sample had left large cities in Britain and America and returned to small villages and towns in western Ireland. Their complaints that neighbours seem narrow-minded and provincial would probably be the same had they moved to rural areas within North America or Britain. In other words, many of the complaints about life in small communities in rural Ireland are true of small communities elsewhere.[96]

This is somewhat ironic as one of the principal problems identified with Irish migration to Britain throughout the postwar period was that young people from rural Ireland had difficulty adapting to life in a large urban centre such as London or Birmingham. On their return after perhaps a few years in Britain, it appears they found it difficult to readjust to life in rural and small-town Ireland. It is a significant deficiency in the published work relating to Irish return migration that, as yet, a study of migrants returning to an urban area rather than a rural community has not been undertaken; such a study would serve as a useful counterpoise to Gmelch's work on rural Ireland.[97] Census data indicate that many migrants who returned to the Irish Republic in the 1960s and 1970s settled in large urban centres such as Dublin and Cork, reflecting the more attractive employment opportunities available in these areas.[98] Quite apart from the fact that many migrants who originally left rural Ireland returned to live in cities and larger towns, there are also the migrants originally from urban areas who left for Britain and subsequently came back. The occupational profile of the return flow is also of interest and the 1971 and 1981 censuses shed some light on this feature of the return flow, even if these data only refer to migrants who arrived in the previous year. For males, the categories of 'producers, makers and repairs', 'professional and technical workers' and 'labourers' were heavily represented; in the case of females in 1971, and again in 1981, professionals, mostly nurses, accounted for a substantial proportion of the inward flow.[99] Even this snapshot of the profile of the return flow in the 1960s and 1970s underlines the diversity of occupations represented, particularly in terms of skilled and non-skilled workers.

It is clear that the evidence presented in relation to return migration indicates that in the late 1960s and throughout the 1970s an increasing number of families and individuals came back to live in the Irish Republic. Broadly speaking, unlike the original decision to migrate to Britain, return migration was not it seems for primarily economic motives but rather for familial, social or other personal reasons. The readjustment of return migrants was a gradual process. Furthermore, it may be noted that the increasing level of return migration was also a factor in changing attitudes towards this issue. When migrants returned, they underlined the sheer transitory nature of postwar Irish migration. This no doubt had a significant effect on views towards migration since for many people it involved only a relatively brief sojourn abroad. More complex questions which concern scholars examining other European return migration flows such as the relationship between return migration and socio-cultural change, the contribution return migrants made to political life, the impact the returnees had on economic development and the different experience of migrants who had been abroad for a long period of time in the United States compared with those who were in Britain for a relatively short stay, remain areas for further research.

Return migration is a central feature of modern European demographic history since many migrants who travelled across the Atlantic in the nineteenth and early twentieth centuries subsequently came back to their home country.[100] In the postwar period, the first significant movement of migrant workers back to their home country occurred as a result of the recession in 1967 in West Germany which particularly affected Turkish migrant workers.[101] The return flow from northern Europe to southern Europe was a central feature of migration patterns during the 1970s. In 1973, with the impact of the first oil crisis on the western European countries, the recruitment of migrant workers was halted and consequently return migration to southern Europe became of increasing significance. Böhning has estimated that between 1.5 and 2 million migrant workers from southern Europe returned home from western Europe in the period between 1974 and 1979, a movement of population which he characterizes as the 'export of unemployment' by the principal receiving countries.[102] A number of factors explain this movement, including the level of unemployment in the receiving societies, the non-renewal of contracts of migrant workers and the policy of some governments, most notably the French and German governments, to encourage return migration. Financial incentives were provided including a 'return' or 'departure' bonus.[103]

The scale and impact of this return flow is perhaps best illustrated by examining the numbers involved on a national level. Between 1968 and 1977, 238,000 Greek migrants returned to their native country, roughly two-thirds of whom had been working in western Europe.[104] Over the complete postwar period until 1981, it has been estimated that over 1 million migrants returned to Greece, including migrants to western Europe, refugees from the Greek civil war (1946–49) and settlers in Turkey and Egypt.[105] Similarly, Portugal experienced large-scale return migration in the 1970s when the recession in northern Europe combined with the 1974 revolution in Portugal and the effects of decolonization in Africa resulted in a massive influx of return migrants which increased the population by 10 per cent.[106] Italy had a long tradition of return migration from the Americas in particular.[107] Between 1946 and 1984 roughly 5 million migrants came back to Italy from other European countries (83 per cent) and the Americas.[108] Lastly, Spain was also a country of mass return migration in the 1970s. Return migration to Spain reached its peak in 1975 and estimates indicate that over 750,000 migrants returned during this decade.[109]

This movement of population should not be viewed as exclusively an exodus brought about solely by the inhospitable conditions in the receiving countries in the 1970s. As was the case with Irish migrants, most southern European migrants viewed their stay in northern Europe as little more than a temporary expedient in order to improve their economic well-being. This is perhaps best captured in the Portuguese phrase, *emigrar para voltar* (emigration to return).[110] Migrants from the poorer areas in northern Portugal travelled to France in order to earn money and return with savings, thereby bypassing the limited avenues for social mobility within their local community.[111] As Brettell has cogently argued, 'in emigration, Portuguese migrants are looking outside their own social system for a way to gain prestige and social mobility within that system'.[112] Other research has illustrated that for Portuguese return migrants 'the purpose of migration was the "project", that is to save up enough money to be able to return "successfully" '.[113] Surveys of migrant intentions from across southern Europe support the contention that migration was a means to an end, rather than an end in itself. For example, roughly three-quarters of male Greek migrants living in West Germany who were interviewed in 1968 and 1974 stated that they did not intend to remain abroad for longer than five years.[114] Therefore, migration and return are part of the same process, although clearly a distinction must be made between the *intention* to return and the actual return.

The range of reasons proffered by migrants suggest that the decision to return home was not motivated solely by either contracting economic opportunities in the receiving country or the availability of employment in the home country but rather for a combination of family, personal or employment reasons. A survey conducted in April 1969 of 80,000 Italian households which either contained a migrant or returned migrant highlights the importance of non-economic factors in the minds of many returned migrants.[115] Family reasons, illness and other diverse explanations were found to be equally important in the decision to return at the end of the contract abroad or having found employment in Italy.[116] A caveat should be added here: the conclusions drawn from surveys of this type – and this applies equally to the Irish surveys – are very sensitive to the point in time when the interviews were conducted. For example, a survey of return migrants completed in the midst of an economic recession will provide quite different results from another survey undertaken during a period of prosperity in either the sending or receiving countries. Later studies of Italian return migration highlight the significance of family reasons in the decision to return home, although, as was the case in relation to the Irish Republic, males tended to attach more importance to economic reasons whereas females cited family reasons.[117] Interviews with return migrants in Bari, south-east Italy, in the early 1980s also underlined the importance of family reasons and 'general feelings of discomfort and nostalgia for the home country'.[118] Surveys of Greek returned migrants also emphasize the role of family responsibilities such as the need to look after parents or a preference to have children educated within the Greek rather than the German system.[119]

What impact did this return movement have on the home countries and within particular regions? In the first instance, it should be noted that return migrants did not necessarily return to the community from which they migrated originally but opted to settle in urban areas, reflecting both the more attractive employment opportunities available in cities and the desire to live in a more cosmopolitan environment, no doubt influenced by their experience abroad. For example, in Greece a number of studies have demonstrated that the majority of return migrants settled in urban areas even though originally most migrants left from rural areas.[120] Notwithstanding this trend, most microstudies of the impact on return migration have concentrated on return to rural areas and set out to examine the link between return migration and local economic and social development.[121] Generally speaking return migrants did not greatly influence economic development, although factors such as the length of time abroad, consumption patterns on return and the structure of the local economy were equally as important as the attitudes of the migrants themselves. It is difficult to generalize on this complex matter, although it appears that return migration to a region does not necessarily contribute to long-term economic development, as was first suggested in the 1960s.[122] Finally, on the question of the reintegration of returned migrants, as in the Irish context, it is difficult to make definitive statements about this matter. Presumably on an initial basis, returned migrants to southern Europe may have found it difficult to readjust to life. One study of returnees to a Spanish village in Granada in the mid-1970s found that return migrants complained about attitudes towards punctuality and cleanliness.[123] But as the author notes, return migrants do not necessarily act as agents of social change, since during their time abroad they developed and maintained an idealized vision of their home community, and 'contrary to popular social science belief, migration can function as preserver of the *status quo* as well as [a] stimulus to change'.[124]

Conclusion

Clearly there is much to be gained from viewing Irish migration in the postwar period within the broader framework of European migration patterns and trends. It has been demonstrated that many of the features associated with the Irish migrant flow to Britain can be compared with the flow from southern European countries such as Italy, Spain, Portugal and Greece to the western European industrialized states of France, West Germany and the Netherlands. One area which is worthy of further investigation across all five case countries is the impact of migration on particular regions since a key issue for the field in general is to explain the regional incidence of migration. Similarities in terms of the timing, rate and regional incidence of migration exist, but a number of differences are also evident such as the timing in the occurrence of peaks of migration. In relation to the role of the state, a sharp contrast emerges between the Irish Republic and the other sending countries. The Irish state did not encourage migration in the postwar period either officially through the medium of a labour recruitment agreement with the British authorities or unofficially by directly assisting migrants wishing to travel to Britain. This of course had much to do with the political climate in which 'emigration' was condemned as an 'evil' and the official policy aim of the Irish state which was to provide employment opportunities for all Irish citizens thereby obviating the need for citizens to travel abroad. Lastly, return migration, which is a feature of European migration patterns in the 1960s and 1970s, is as yet remarkably under-researched in the Irish context. There is a need for a more detailed study of the reasons underlying the decision to return and the long-term readjustment of Irish return migrants. Only with detailed studies of return migration firmly grounded in historical evidence can we begin the process of understanding and explaining the complexities involved in this movement of population. Other areas which merit further attention include the relationship between gender and migration, not alone for the Irish Republic but across the five countries. An understanding and evaluation of the role of kin and other networks is a subject which, as has been briefly illustrated here, is an integral element in any assessment of the migrant process. But the study of migration does not end as soon as the migrant leaves the sending country. Another key difference is that Irish migrants did not face any language barrier in Britain and were granted the same voting and social security rights as a British citizen, whereas Greek, Portuguese, Spanish or Italian migrants were 'guestworkers' who enjoyed relatively few privileges in the receiving society.

What emerges most strikingly from this comparative analysis is the fact that the Irish Republic was far from unique in experiencing large-scale migration and rural depopulation throughout the postwar period. Many countries on the periphery of western Europe – in terms of geographical location and the level of economic development – were unable to provide enough suitable employment opportunities to obviate the need for people to migrate, although as in the Irish case a substantial proportion of these migrants subsequently returned. In general terms, the study of Irish migration for both the historical and contemporary periods is greatly enhanced by a familiarity with wider European or global patterns, thereby facilitating an assessment of the distinctiveness or otherwise of the Irish experience.

Notes

1. I should like to thank Professor Liam Kennedy, Professor Russell King, Dr Donald MacRaild and Dr Michel Peillon for their very useful comments on earlier drafts of this chapter.

2. For a pioneering interpretation of Irish demographic history which employs comparative analysis, see T.W. Guinnane, *The Vanishing Irish: Households, Migration, and the Rural Economy in Ireland, 1850–1914* (Princeton, N.J., 1997). It should be noted that the focus in this essay is on the Irish Republic and not Northern Ireland.

3. Useful overviews of postwar European migration patterns can be found in Sarah Collinson, *Europe and International Migration* (London, 1993), chs 4 and 5; Russell King, 'European International Migration, 1945–90: A Statistical and Geographical Overview', in Russell King (ed.), *Mass Migration in Europe: The Legacy and the Future* (London, 1993), pp. 19–39; John Salt, 'International Labour Supply: The Geographical Pattern of Demand', in John Salt and Hugh Clout (eds), *Migration in Postwar Europe: Geographical Essays* (Oxford, 1976), pp. 52–125.

4. NESC, *The Irish Economy in a Comparative Institutional Perspective*, NESC report no. 93 (Dublin, 1992), Pl. 8967; Brian Girvin, *Between Two Worlds: Politics and Economy in Independent Ireland* (Dublin, 1989); J.J. Lee, *Ireland, 1912–1985: Politics and Society* (Cambridge, 1989); Liam Kennedy, 'Out of History: Ireland, that "Most Distressful Country"', in *Colonialism, Religion and Nationalism in Ireland* (Belfast, 1996), pp. 182–223. Another study which adopts a less explicitly comparative approach is Richard Breen, Damian F. Hannan, David B. Rottman and C.T. Whelan, *Understanding Contemporary Ireland: State, Class and Development in the Republic of Ireland* (Dublin, 1990).

5. This list could be extended to include Cyprus, Malta and Finland. However, for the purposes of the present discussion we shall confine our analysis to the five named countries.

6. Michel Peillon, 'Placing Ireland in Comparative Perspective', *Economic and Social Review*, 25 (1994), pp. 179–95; idem, 'State and Society in the Republic of Ireland: A Comparative Study', *Administration*, 35 (1987), pp. 190–212. See also for an assessment of an appropriate comparative framework for both the Irish Republic and Northern Ireland, Liam O'Dowd, 'The States of Ireland: Some Reflections on Research', *Irish Journal of Sociology*, 1 (1991), pp. 96–106.

7. Donal Garvey, 'The History of Migration Flows in the Republic of Ireland', *Population Trends*, 39 (1985), p. 24, Table 4.

8. Ibid., p. 25.

9. King, 'European International Migration, 1945–90', p. 43. A valuable guide to the literature on southern European migration can be found in Russell King, 'Emigration', in John Loughlin (ed.), *Southern European Studies Guide* (London, 1993), pp. 152–72.

10. For lucid explanations of the problems associated with migration statistics for southern European countries, see Russell King, 'Population Mobility: Emigration, Return Migration and Internal Migration', in Allan Williams (ed.), *Southern Europe Transformed: Political and Economic Change in Greece, Italy, Portugal and Spain* (London, 1984), pp. 147–8 and Massimo Livi-Bacci, 'The Countries of Emigration', in idem (ed.), *The Demographic and Social Patterns of Emigration from Southern European Countries* (Florence, 1972), pp. 9–14.

11. For a review of the migrant flows from Ireland and Italy in the immediate post-war period, see the data contained in a valuable publication on international migration between 1945 and 1957 issued by the International Labour Office, *International Migration, 1945–57* (Geneva, 1959).

12. Salt, 'International Labour Supply', p. 88.

13. Rossetos Fakiolas and Russell King, 'Emigration, Return, Immigration: A Review and Evaluation of Greece's Postwar Experience of International Migration', *International Journal of Population Geography*, 2 (1996), p. 172.

14. F.X. Kirwin and A.G. Nairn, 'Migrant Employment and the Recession – the Case of the Irish in Britain', *International Migration Review*, 17 (1983), pp. 672–81.

15. Enda Delaney, 'Irish Migration to Britain, 1921–71: Patterns, Trends and Contingent Factors', unpublished Ph.D. thesis (Queen's University of Belfast, 1997), pp. 269–70; NESC, *The Economic and Social Implications of Emigration* NESC report no. 90 (Dublin, 1991), Pl. 7840, pp. 60–1.

16. Cormac Ó Gráda and B.M. Walsh, 'The Economic Effects of Emigration: Ireland', in Beth J. Asch (ed.), *Emigration and its Effects on the Sending Country* (Santa Monica, Ca., 1994), p. 104; NESC, *The Economic and Social Implications of Emigration*, p. 61.

17. Commission on Emigration and Other Population Problems, *Reports 1948–54*, (Dublin, 1955), Pr. 2541, p. 128.

18. M.B. Rocha Trindade, 'Portugal', in R.E. Krane (ed.), *International Labor Migration in Europe* (New York, 1979), p. 167.

19. King, 'Population Mobility: Emigration, Return Migration and Internal Migration', p. 149.

20. Salt, 'International Labour Supply', p. 141.

21. Fakiolas and King, 'Emigration, Return, Immigration', p. 172.

22. T.P. Lianos, 'Flows of Greek Out-migration and Return Migration', *International Migration*, 13 (1976), p. 119.

23. Ibid., p. 120.

24. Salustiano del Campo, 'Spain', in Krane (ed.), *International Labor Migration in Europe*, p. 157.

25. Ibid., p. 159.

26. Dudley Baines, *Emigration from Europe, 1815–1930* (London, 1991), p. 74.

27. For an excellent example, see Caroline Brettell, *Men who Migrate, Women who Wait: Population and History in a Portuguese Parish* (Princeton, N.J., 1987).

28. J.G. Hughes and B.M. Walsh, *Internal Migration Flows in Ireland and their Determinants*, ESRI paper no. 98 (Dublin, 1980), p. 75.

29. *Census of Population of Ireland, 1956, I: Population, Area and Valuation . . .* , p. xxii.

30. NESC, *The Economic and Social Implications of Emigration*, pp. 75–82.

31. Jeremiah Newman (ed.), *The Limerick Rural Survey, 1958–64* (Tipperary, 1964).

32. Damian Hannan, *Rural Exodus: A Study of the Forces Influencing the Large-Scale Migration of Irish Youth* (London, 1970); J.A. Jackson, *Report on the Skibbereen Social Survey* (Dublin, 1967).

33. An Foras Talúntais, *County Leitrim Resource Survey* (Dublin, 1975); idem, *West Donegal Resource Survey* (Dublin, 1969); idem, *West Cork Resource Survey* (Dublin, 1963).

34. See Enda Delaney, *Demography, State and Society: Irish Migration to Britain, 1921–71* (Liverpool, forthcoming), chs 6 and 7.

35. B.M. Walsh, 'Economic and Demographic Adjustment of the Irish Agricultural Labour Force', *Irish Journal of Agricultural Economics and Rural Sociology*, 3 (1971), p. 116.

36. Delaney, 'Irish Migration to Britain', p. 403.

37. Hannan, *Rural Exodus*, pp. 167–8.

38. C.K. Ward, *Manpower in a Developing Community: A Pilot Survey of Drogheda* (Dublin, 1967), para. 20.24.

39. Ibid., para. 20.35.

40. Delaney, 'Irish Migration to Britain', pp. 291–2, 384–5.

41. Jackson, *Report on the Skibbereen Social Survey*, p. 41.

42. Douglas S. Massey, Joaquín Arango, Graeme Hugo, Ali Kouaouci, Adela Pellegrino and J. Edward Taylor, 'Theories of International Migration: A Review and Appraisal', *Population and Development Review*, 19 (1993), pp. 448–50. On migrant networks, see Monica Boyd, 'Family and Personal Networks in International Migration: Recent Developments and New Agendas', *International Migration Review*, 23 (1989), pp. 638–70.

43. Douglas T. Gurak and Fe Caces, 'Migration Networks and the Shaping of Migration Systems', in Mary Kritz, Lin Lean Lim and Hania Zlotnik (eds), *International Migration Systems: A Global Approach* (Oxford, 1992), pp. 153–5.

44. King, 'Population Mobility: Emigration, Return Migration and Internal Migration', p. 152.

45. Livi-Bacci, 'The Countries of Emigration', p. 60.

46. Brettell, *Men who Migrate, Women who Wait*; Eugene Mendosa, 'Benefits of Migration as a Personal Strategy in Nazaré, Portugal', *International Migration Review*, 16 (1982), pp. 635–45.

47. Livi-Bacci, 'The Countries of Emigration', p. 60.

48. Ibid., p. 61.

49. Demetrios Papademetriou, 'Illusions and Reality in International Migration: Migration and Development in Post World War II Greece', *International Migration*, 23 (1985), pp. 214–16.

50. Fakiolas and King, 'Emigration, Return, Immigration', pp. 173–4.

51. Salt, 'International Labour Supply', p. 141.

52. Livi Bacci, 'The Countries of Emigration', p. 60; Carminda Cavaco, 'A Place in the Sun: Return Migration and Rural Change in Portugal', in Russell King (ed.), *Mass Migrations in Europe: The Legacy and the Future* (London, 1993), pp. 179–81.

53. See, for example, Samuel Baily, 'The Village Outward Approach to the Study of Social Networks: A Case Study of the Agnonesi Diaspora Abroad, 1885–1989', *Studi Emigrazione*, 29 (1992), pp. 43–68; William A. Douglass, *Emigration in a South Italian Town* (New Brunswick, N.J., 1984).

54. A.R. Zolberg, 'The Next Waves: Migration Theory for a Changing World', *International Migration Review*, 23 (1989), pp. 403–29.

55. See Enda Delaney, 'State, Politics and Demography: The Case of Irish Emigration, 1921–71', *Irish Political Studies*, 13 (1998), pp. 25–49.

56. See the chapter (3) by Tracey Connolly in this volume.

57. Delaney, 'State, Politics and Demography', pp. 38–40.

58. National Archives of Ireland, DT S 16325 B, Emigration to Britain: brief statement of the policy of the government of Ireland, 7 Oct. 1960.

59. Department of Foreign Affairs, *Challenges and Opportunities Abroad: White Paper on Foreign Policy* (Dublin, 1996), Pn. 2133, p. 289.

60. Colin Holmes, *John Bull's Island: Immigration and British Society, 1871–1971* (London, 1988), pp. 251–3.

61. J.A. Jackson, 'The Irish in Britain', in P.J. Drudy (ed.), *Ireland and Britain since 1922* (Cambridge, 1986), p. 133.

62. Kathleen Paul, 'A Case of Mistaken Identity: the Irish in Postwar Britain', *International Labour and Working-Class History*, 49 (1996), pp. 116–42; idem, *Whitewashing Britain: Race and Citizenship in Postwar Britain* (Ithaca, N.Y., 1997). See also Ian R.G. Spencer, *British Immigration Policy since 1939* (London, 1997), chs 2–4.

63. For a brief overview of the migration policies of a number of west European states, see Sarah Collinson, *Europe and International Migration* (London, 1993), pp. 43–63 and Anthony Fielding, 'Migration, Institutions and Politics: The Evolution of European Migration Policies', in King (ed.), *Mass Migration in Europe*, pp. 40–62.

64. Salt, 'International Labour Supply', p. 99.

65. Demetrious Papademetriou, 'Greece', in Krane (ed.), *International Labor Migration in Europe*, p. 188. For an assessment of Greek migration policy and the standpoints adopted by various interested parties, see T.P. Lianos, 'Greece', in Daniel Kubat (ed.), *The Politics of Migration Policies* (New York, 1979), pp. 211–16.

66. Del Campo, 'Spain', p. 158.

67. Salt, 'International Labour Supply', p. 88.

68. Amadeu Ferreira de Paiva, 'Portuguese Migration Studies', *International Migration Review*, 17 (1983), p. 139.

69. Collinson, *Europe and International Migration*, p. 48; Salt, 'International Labour Supply', p. 100.

70. Salt, 'International Labour Supply', p. 136.

71. Important contributions to this debate include W.R. Böhning, 'Some Throughts on Emigration from the Mediterranean Basin', *International Labour Review*, 111 (1975), pp. 251–77 and Russell King, 'Southern Europe: Dependency or Development', *Geography*, 67 (1982), pp. 221–34. For an assessment of the wider issue, see Bimal Ghosh, 'Economic Migration and the Sending Countries', in Julien van den Broeck (ed.), *The Economics of Labour Migration* (Cheltenham, 1996), pp. 77–113.

72. Breen *et al.*, *Understanding Contemporary Ireland*, pp. 22–31.

73. Adrian Kelly, 'Social Welfare in Independent Ireland, 1922–52', Ph.D. thesis (National University of Ireland, Maynooth, 1996), ch. 2; Ruth Barrington, *Health, Medicine and Politics in Ireland, 1900–1970* (Dublin, 1987); for an assessment of the position of the Irish Roman Catholic Church on migration, see Enda Delaney, 'The Churches and Irish Migration to Britain, 1921–60', *Archivium Hibernicum*, 52 (1998), pp. 98–114.

74. Delaney, 'State, Politics and Demography', pp. 38–40.

75. Ibid.

76. Ibid., pp. 31–5.

77. Commission on Emigration, *Reports*, pp. 139–43.

78. NESC, *The Economic and Social Implications of Emigration*, pp. 217–47.

79. Ó Gráda and Walsh, 'The Economic Effects of Emigration', p. 140.

80. Ibid.

81. Jackson, *Report on the Skibbereen Social Survey*, p. 39.

82. For an excellent comparative example of this 'myth of return', see Muhammad Anwar, *The Myth of Return: Pakistanis in Britain* (London, 1979).

83. The 1971 census was the first census to record the place of residence one year previously of each person within a household (Hughes and Walsh, *Internal Migration Flows in Ireland and their Determinants*, p. 13).

84. Garvey, 'The History of Migration Flows in the Republic of Ireland', p. 25.

85. Ibid., p. 26.
86. NESC, *The Economic and Social Implications of Emigration*, p. 88; Garvey, 'The History of Migration Flows in the Republic of Ireland', p. 26.
87. For more details, see Kieran A. Kennedy, Thomas Giblin and Deirdre McHugh, *The Economic Development of Ireland in the Twentieth Century* (London, 1988), pp. 75–94; Liam Kennedy, *The Modern Industrialisation of Ireland* (Dublin, 1991), pp. 21–31.
88. For a brief assessment of the published work on Irish return migration, see Fiona McGrath, 'The Economic, Social and Cultural Impacts of Return Migration to Achill Island', in Russell King (ed.), *Contemporary Irish Migration* (Dublin, 1991), p. 55; Elizabeth Malcolm, *Elderly Return Migration from Britain to Ireland: A Preliminary Study* (Dublin, 1996).
89. Dick Foeken, 'Return Migration to a Marginal Rural Area in N.W. Ireland', *Tijdschrift voor Economische en Sociale Geografie*, 71 (1980), p. 116.
90. Ibid., p. 119.
91. George Gmelch, 'Return Migration to Rural Ireland', in Hans Christian Buechler and Judith-Maria Buechler (eds), *Migrants in Europe: The Role of Family, Labor, and Politics* (New York, 1987), p. 270.
92. Ibid.
93. Ibid., p. 271.
94. George Gmelch, 'The Readjustment of Returned Migrants in the West of Ireland', in Russell King (ed.), *Return Migration and Regional Economic Problems* (London, 1986), p. 186.
95. Ibid., p. 163.
96. Gmelch, 'Return Migration to Rural Ireland', p. 277.
97. It should be noted that Gmelch actually discusses this point (ibid., p. 280).
98. J.A. Walsh, 'Immigration to the Republic of Ireland, 1946–71', *Irish Geography*, 12 (1979), pp. 109–10.
99. Ibid., p. 108; Garvey, 'The History of Migration Flows in the Republic of Ireland', pp. 27–8.
100. J.D. Gould, 'European Inter-Continental Emigration. The Road Home: Return Migration from the U.S.A.', *Journal of European Economic History*, 9 (1980), pp. 41–112; Mark Wyman, *Round-trip to America: The Immigrants Return to Europe, 1880–1930* (Ithaca, N.Y., 1993).
101. Russell King, 'Return Migration: A Review of Some Case Studies from Southern Europe', *Mediterranean Studies*, 1 (1979), pp. 11–12.
102. W.R. Böhning, 'International Migration in Western Europe: Reflections on the Past Five Years', *International Labour Review*, 118 (1979), pp. 401–2.
103. Han Entzinger, 'Return Migration in Western Europe', *International Migration*, 23 (1985), pp. 268–9; Christian Dustmann, 'Return Migration: The European Experience', *Economic Policy*, 22 (1996), pp. 219–23.
104. Ross Fakiolas, 'Return Migration to Greece and its Structural and Socio-Political Effects', in Daniel Kubat (ed.), *The Politics of Return: International Return Migration in Europe* (Rome, 1984), p. 37.
105. Ibid.
106. Jim Lewis and Allan Williams, 'Portugal: The Decade of Return', *Geography*, 70 (1985), pp. 178–82.
107. Russell King, *Il ritorno in patria: Return Migration to Italy in Historical Perspective* (Durham, 1988), pp. 15–41; Dino Cinel, *The National Integration of Italian Return Migration, 1870–1929* (Cambridge, 1991).

108. King, *Il ritorno in patria*, p. 43.
109. King, 'Population Mobility: Emigration, Return Migration and Internal Migration', p. 158.
110. Caroline Brettell, 'Emigrar para voltar: A Portuguese Ideology of Return Migration', *Papers in Anthropology*, 20 (1979), p. 3.
111. Ibid., pp. 6–13.
112. Ibid., p. 6.
113. Ema Serra-Santana, 'Return of Portuguese: Economic Goals or Retention of One's Identity', in Kubat (ed.), *The Politics of Return*, p. 55.
114. Quoted in Elizabeth McLean Petras and Maria Kousis, 'Returning Migrant Characteristics and Labour Market Demand in Greece', *International Migration Review*, 20 (1986), p. 588 n.2.
115. Livi-Bacci, 'The Countries of Emigration', pp. 109–11.
116. Ibid.
117. King, *Il ritorno in patria*, pp. 81–6.
118. Russell King, Alan Strachan and Jill Mortimer, 'The Urban Dimension of European Return Migration: The Case of Bari, Southern Italy', *Urban Studies*, 22 (1985), pp. 227–8.
119. Fakiolas and King, 'Emigration, Return and Immigration', p. 174.
120. McLean Petras and Kousis, 'Returning Migrant Characteristics and Labour Market Demand in Greece', pp. 588–9; Fakiolas and King, 'Emigration, Return and Immigration', p. 175.
121. See Richard Black, 'Migration, Return and Agricultural Development in the Serra do Alvão, Northern Portugal', *Economic Development and Cultural Change*, 41 (1993), pp. 563–85; Russell King, Jill Mortimer, Alan Strachan and Anna Trono, 'Return Migration and Rural Economic Change: A South Italian Case Study', in Ray Hudson and Jim Lewis (eds), *Uneven Development in Southern Europe: Studies of Accumulation, Class, Migration and the State* (London, 1985), pp. 101–22; King (ed.), *Return Migration and Regional Economic Problems* contains a number of relevent analyses; Manuela Reis and Joaquim Gil Nave, 'Emigrating Peasants and Returning Emigrants: Emigration with Return in a Portuguese Village', *Sociologia Ruralis*, 26 (1986), pp. 20–35; R.E. Rhoades, 'From Caves to Main Street: Return Migration and Transformation of a Spanish Village', *Papers in Anthropology*, 20 (1979), pp. 57–74; idem, 'Intra-European Return Migration and Rural Development: Lessons from the Spanish Case', *Human Organization*, 37 (1978), pp. 136–47.
122. King, 'Population Mobility: Emigration, Return Migration and Internal Migration', p. 161.
123. Rhoades, 'Intra-European Return Migration and Rural Development', p. 143.
124. Ibid.

Index

Page numbers in *italics* refer to notes.